The Apprentice C++ Programmer:
A Touch of Class

The Apprentice C++ Programmer: A Touch of Class

P. A. Lee and C. Phillips

PWS Publishing Company

INTFRNATIONAL THOMSON COMPUTER PRESS
I(T)P An International Thomson Publishing Company

London • Bonn • Johannesburg • Madrid • Meboume • Mexico City • New York • Paris • Singapore
Tokyo • Toronto • Albany, NY • Belmont, CA • Boston, MA • Cincinnati, OH • Detroit, MI

The Apprentice C++ Programmer

I(T)P A division of International Thomson Publishing Inc.
The ITP logo is a trademark under licence

For more information, contact:

International Thomson Computer Press
Berkshire House
168–173 High Holborn
London WC1V 7AA
UK

http://www.itcpmedia.com

PWS Publishing Company
20 Park Plaza
Boston
Massachusetts 02116-4324

http://www.pws.com

British Library Cataloguing-in-Publication Data
A catalogue record for this book is available from the British Library

Library of Congress Cataloging-in-Publication Data
A catalog record for this book is available from the Library of Congress

97 98 99 00 – 10 9 8 7 6 5 4 3 2
Editor: David Dietz, PWS
Typeset by Florencetype Ltd, Stoodleigh, Devon
Printed in the United States of America by R. R. Donnelley & Sons Company, Inc./Crawfordsville

ISBN (ITP edition) 1–85032–160–4
ISBN (PWS edition) 0–53495–339–5

Contents

Preface

Is this book for you?

Your initial reaction on picking up this book may well have been

"What, yet another book on C++? Why should I look at this one?"

If, however, you're looking for a fresh approach to C++ that:

- introduces object-oriented design and programming;
- assumes no prior knowledge of *any* programming language, nor of any mathematics beyond high-school level;
- emphasizes the importance of top-down design and object-oriented programming from the outset;
- integrates software engineering concerns;
- adopts an informal and gentle style that relies heavily on the presentation of examples of new topics based on real-world analogies before diving into a more formal description;

then read on, because this book is just what you've been searching for.

Unlike many other books on C++, you are *not* expected to know a fair amount of C and/or accept a bottom-up approach to C++ programming. If that's what you're looking for, then read no further; this book's not for you.

The target audience for this book is first-year undergraduates, or any others requiring an introduction to programming and object-oriented techniques. As such, this book closely follows the CS1 syllabus. The book is especially suitable for those who have never been exposed to programming before, as well as those who have some experience in other programming languages. Additionally, we expect the material to be useful for those who have programming experience but require a gentle introduction to object-oriented techniques and C++.

Instructors contemplating adopting this book are encouraged to take a look at the supplementary materials available, particularly the Instructor's Manual, details of which are given later in this Preface.

AIMS AND OBJECTIVES

Our objective for people who follow this book, or courses based on it, is that they become *Apprentice C++ Programmers*. The parallel with a traditional engineering apprenticeship is apt. An apprentice programmer is someone who knows the basics of the programming trade, has a "toolbag" of useful paradigms and algorithms, and understands the tools of their trade. The apprentice programmer must also be able to apply programming skills to the problem in hand, and hence needs to acquire essential software engineering skills so that they can design, implement and maintain solutions to complex problems. Much more experience is needed to turn the apprentice into a practicing programmer, of course, but that's outside the scope of this book.

In summary, having completed an apprenticeship by following this book you will know:

- how to design and implement software systems in C++;
- the importance of object-oriented design and implementation;
- the importance of good software engineering practices.

You will also understand the relationship between these issues.

APPROACH

The fundamental approach in this book is the use of **Types** and **Objects**, and the use of these concepts pervades the whole process, from initial problem comprehension and solving, through to solution design and implementation. However, it's not feasible, nor desirable, in an apprenticeship to cover the whole spectrum of object-oriented analysis and design, especially that used in large (multi-member) software projects. Instead, we concentrate on the fundamentals: getting you to understand the concepts of objects and types, and how these can be used in algorithms to solve problems.

We don't believe that an introductory programming text (or course) can, or indeed should, cover all of the complexity inherent in object-oriented programming. Concepts like objects and types are hard enough to grasp without worrying about polymorphism, multiple inheritance and the like. So, we introduce simple objects and types based on what used to be called Abstract Data Types (ADTs). Since we extend the idea of ADTs using the fundamental concepts of objects and types (encapsulation, information hiding, separation of interface and implementation), we introduce the terminology **Programmer Defined Types** (PDTs). The PDT concept is a useful stepping stone to full object-oriented techniques, which we leave to a more advanced text.

While the focus of the book is on teaching how to program, issues concerning "software engineering in-the-small" are also addressed and integrated into the explanations concerning programming. Many chapters contain sections addressing software engineering issues, so you can build up an appreciation of the engineering points at the same time as learning the programming language constructs.

Graphical notations are used extensively to support comprehension of the software engineering process:

- to represent the interface required by a user of a type;
- to represent the top-down design of algorithms, and the flow of control in a program (structured flowcharts);
- to show C++ syntax rules (syntax diagrams).

Projects and examples are used extensively throughout to provide exemplification of the programming and software engineering concepts. Rather than develop program components from scratch, the initial emphasis is on reuse of previously-developed components wherever possible, such as PDTs and functions, provided on an accompanying disk. Once you are familiar with using components, you'll be happier with implementing your own components.

The programming language C++ is used as the vehicle for introducing programming concepts because C++ has very good support for introducing new types. However, this book is *not* intended to be a thorough C++ reference text. No attempt is made to introduce the complete C++ syntax or semantics. Indeed, in many situations we introduce syntax to represent simplified C++ constructs that are only a sub-set of the full-blown language. There are several aspects of C++ that we positively discourage use of (particularly error-prone features of C++ inherited from C), and hence these are not mentioned at all. We introduce several new C++ types to provide better abstractions than those provided in the base language (for example, for arrays and character strings). A C or C++ hacker will probably be very disappointed in, or critical of, our usage of C++. We would regard this as highly satisfactory!

While we use C++ as the primary programming vehicle, concepts are introduced in three stages:

1. The concept in general, real-world terms.
2. The concept in general programming language terms.
3. The concept in C++ terms.

Our experience with teaching programming languages has been that those who have never programmed before have difficulty relating to programming concepts; hence the need for motivation in terms of real-world equivalents which you can relate to directly.

Additional features in the book include:

- a statement of objectives at the beginning of each chapter;
- a detailed summary at the end of each chapter indicating the skills learned;
- highlighted **lessons** throughout that summarize the key issues;
- highlighted **style rules** that promote the generation of well-engineered programs;
- numerous examples illustrating the new topics being introduced;
- end-of-section exercises with worked solutions providing a ready test of your understanding of the material covered;
- end-of-chapter exercises providing a more intensive examination.

OVERVIEW

The book is organized into three parts:

Part 1 **Concepts For Apprentice Programmers** covers the basic concepts of software engineering, problem solving and program design in an object-oriented style, and computers and their programming languages.

Part 2 **Learning To Use Your C++ Toolbag** introduces the programming language C++ and basic object-oriented features.

Part 3 **Practicing Your Trade** provides worked-through software projects.

Part 1

Part 1 sets the scene by giving an overview of software systems. This overview is more extensive than that traditionally found in an introductory programming text, for two important reasons. First, we assume no prior knowledge of computers or programming. Second, we wouldn't expect a software engineer immediately to sit down in front of a computer and start typing when presented with a new problem. Instead, we'd expect them to analyze and understand the problem first to gain a clear idea of the required outcome. Similarly, we regard an understanding of what an apprenticeship in C++ programming involves as being essential before embarking on the apprenticeship itself. There's an apt analogy with constructing a building. Yes, you need to know about bricks and mortar, but you need a clear view of what the outcome is before you set about designing and building that palace or mud hut. So Part 1 concentrates on problem design and solving using types, permitting the design of object-oriented software, even though no details of a programming language have yet been presented.

Chapter 1 presents basic background concepts for people who don't really know what a computer or a program is, and tries to demystify the idea of a program as being something that only computer science specialists can understand. Chapter 2 introduces the basic ideas of problem solving for object-oriented software implementation – basic top-down ideas to start with, followed by simple object-oriented analysis techniques for producing designs for types and algorithms. By the end of Chapter 2 you should be able to produce a design for a solution to a problem, even though you won't yet know any C++ details. Chapter 3 introduces the fundamental features of a programming language, to provide background for the detailed C++ explanations that follow in Part 2.

Part 2

PDTs are used throughout Part 2 to provide a useful and interesting set of types from which interesting programs can be constructed very quickly. In the early chapters the emphasis is on *using* PDTs by means of their defined public interface without having to address the complexity of their implementation. For instance, a PDT representing a CD player is used extensively – we provide an implementation of this PDT that simulates the CD player's behavior graphically on a computer screen. You can write programs controlling an instance of a CD player and learn about declarations, repetition statements, and so on, with the graphical representation acting as a useful debugging aid. Later chapters address the issues of actually identifying, designing and implementing PDTs.

Chapters 4 through 15 introduce the C++ language details, with each chapter devoted to a single concept. The early emphasis is on changing existing programs so that interesting programming can be started early, rather than having to cover loads of syntax details before a first program can be run. We want to encourage you to concentrate on the programming details without spending a lot of time being confused by what the problem is you are trying to solve.

Part 3

Part 3 brings all the earlier issues of design, implementation and software engineering together in the form of worked-through large-scale software projects. Starting with an initial problem specification, the design and implementation phases are covered in detail. The final products are programs that illustrate almost all the features of C++ covered in the context of smaller problems in earlier chapters.

Chapter 16 puts into practice all the material covered in earlier chapters by tackling two major projects. Here the emphasis echoes that of Part 1, returning to those ideas of object-oriented analysis techniques for producing designs. Having reached this point you will be completely familiar with those programming details of Part 2, and hence able to complete the picture of the design and implementation of software products.

STUDENTS' READING PLAN

One of the key issues we address is the need to think carefully about the problem to be solved before attempting a solution. Too often the words "Write a program to . . ." are viewed as an instruction to go straight to a computer and start typing in some code. The result is a hacked piece of code that more often than not, bears little relationship with a well-engineered software product. Thus, while you may have a strong urge to dive straight into the C++ programming details of Chapter 4 onwards, we strongly recommend that you first cover the material in Chapters 1–3, taking a few weeks, during which time familiarity can be gained with a computing environment, so that you are at ease with this before getting thrown into the C++ details. Our experience is that those who have never programmed before are wary of these funny things called computers, and appreciate the background that the material of Part 1 gives them. The work involved in learning about the computer system, its interface, the editor interface, and the compilation system, as well as (possibly) a word-processing package, an e-mail tool, the World Wide Web, and so on, places you on a steep learning curve, when in fact the programming language details are complex enough to grasp by themselves!

Chapters 1 and 3 can be covered as quickly as necessary, depending on your experience. Whatever your background, you should take some time over Chapter 2, which addresses the issue of constructing a design before any implementation is started and shows the basic problem-solving strategies that a software engineer can adopt. The design emphasis is on identifying types and objects, and trying to make you comfortable with the fundamental issues of types and objects (and their manipulation) before the C++ syntax is reached. The basic ideas of control-flow and sequencing are also introduced, without which it is difficult to understand programming at all. You then only need to concentrate on the C++ syntax details in Chapter 4 onwards, and the underlying concepts will be understood.

Having taken your time with Part 1, you'll be ready for the C++ programming details of Parts 2 and 3. Your progression thereon will for the most part be linear. However, Chapter 5 is largely reference material that can be skimmed on a first reading and returned to as programming themes in later chapters are developed.

PEDAGOGICAL DEVICES

Within the text we use various pedagogical devices. These devices, or text styles, allow us to differentiate the following things. First, sometimes we want to exemplify some concept that has just been described – a real-world analogy or an example to help you to understand that concept, and this is illustrated as follows.

EXAMPLE:

This is an example of the "Example" style device.

Sometimes we use the same device to introduce a fragment of C++ code that is illustrating a point that has just been made.

EXAMPLE:

```
// This is a valid C++ comment.
```

When we've been making an important point that you should take special care to note, we highlight such points in the following **lesson** style:

Lesson: This is an important lesson to learn.

For many C++ features we indicate some important style rules that should be followed when writing a program using that particular feature. In the text we highlight the important good and bad style points as follows.

✔ *This is a good style, that should be adopted.*
✗ *Whereas this bullet introduces a bad style that should be avoided.*

At other points in a chapter we wish to pose a problem for which a solution is to be developed during the chapter. The problem will often turn into a worked example with some or all of the following sections: problem, design, implementation, and output. We indicate these sections as follows.

PROBLEM:

Think about how to make a problem statement stand out in the text, so that it can be referred back to subsequently.

DESIGN:

Sometimes the design is explained in words, and often there is a design diagram.

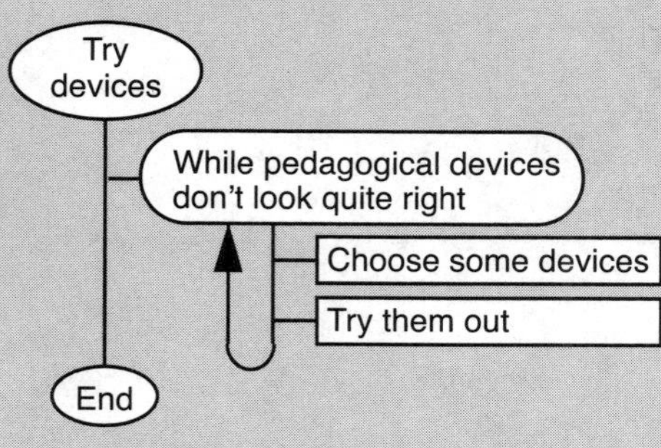

IMPLEMENTATION:

```
Book thisBook;

// C++ code fragments
for (int chapter = 1; chapter <= 16; chapter += 1)
{
  thisBook.read(chapter);
}
```

OUTPUT:

This section shows examples of output produced. It may be textual output only, and hence shown in `courier font`. Sometimes screen shots are shown captured from an Apple Macintosh computer. The fact that they're from a Macintosh isn't important, and a particular system may differ in some of the details shown on the screen. All we want to do here is establish the link between a program and the output produced.

The other pedagogical devices we use in the text are icons in the margin. These icons are used to highlight different features.

For example, what do you think the icon on the left represents?

This icon is used to represent "stop-and-think". This is a point in the text where we want to pose a question whose answer is based on some material just presented. As here, the answer is given in the paragraph immediately following the paragraph labelled with the icon. But you should try to answer the question before reading on. It wouldn't be honest to do otherwise, would it? :-)

If you're asking "What are those funny characters on the end of that last paragraph?" then you've not seen a *smiley* before. (Turn the page clockwise by 90 degrees.) Smileys originated for computer-based text messages, to indicate when something was being stated humorously or not to be taken too seriously, and we've used them in this book for the same purpose.

We additionally use the following three icons:

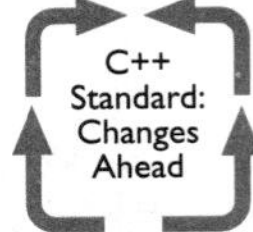

The first icon is indicating an area in the C++ programming language that may change when a new standard version of C++ is agreed upon.

The floppy disk icon is indicating that a program being discussed is available in electronic form, and the words on the icon give the names of the appropriate directories or folders. As different computer systems have different conventions for naming their computer files, it may be necessary to search around on a given system to find the actual files (assuming they've been installed).

Finally, the skull-and-crossbones icon is used when there's a C++ feature that should be used with extreme care.

SUPPLEMENTARY MATERIALS

The complete teaching package for the *Apprentice C++ Programmer* consists of four main elements:

- this book itself, written to introduce programming in C++ in a system-independent format;
- a PC-compatible disk containing example programs and implementations of the PDTs employed in the book. We also provide implementations for three major platforms: Borland on the PC, Symantec on the Apple Macintosh, and cfront and g++ on UNIX. All software is available from our WWW server;
- a separately-available system-independent Lab Manual that can form the basis for practical classes, or can provide students with additional tutorial and practical exercises to try out newly-acquired skills. System-specific issues (such as descriptions of how to use the Symantec compiler on an Apple Macintosh, or Borland on a PC) are dealt with in documents available from our WWW server;
- an electronic Instructor's Pack containing all necessary material for the succesful delivery of a course based on this book, including a Manual that explains the background to the book material, and an extensive

set of slides in a variety of formats. WWW access is password-protected. Please contact ITP at:

```
http://www.thomson.com:9966/itcp/WebExtra/apprentice.html
```

The Newcastle WWW address for on-line materials is:

```
http://www.cs.ncl.ac.uk/publications/books/apprentice/
```

ACKNOWLEDGMENTS

It is a pleasure to acknowledge the help of many of our colleagues at Newcastle in the development of this text and its supporting material. Martin McLauchlan is largely responsible for producing the Lab Manual. Robert Stroud produced many of the basic classes that we make extensive use of, and has provided much useful feedback on the overall material. Lindsay Marshall was able to bail us out on some of the more obscure features of C++. Nigel Hall, Gerry Tomlinson, Jim Wight and Chris Ritson have undertaken sterling work in producing the support for the graphics on Macintosh, Unix and PC platforms. Thanks too to the hundreds of past and current students at Newcastle who have class-tested the material, and to all those not explicitly mentioned above who have provided support in the delivery of those classes.

The production of a book of this nature is a major task. The authors put the material together, but there is much work that goes on behind the scenes by the publishing staff before a manuscript comes to the market. Our Commissioning Editor, Samantha Whittaker, is worthy of special praise, not least for having to put up with authors who never failed to get in a dig at every opportunity. Thanks Sam, it's been a real pleasure working with you. We should also mention Mike Sugarman, John Normansell and Penny Grose for their encouragement and help throughout the development of this project.

Last, but by no means least, to our families. Only other authors know the burden they've had to bear! We solemnly promise not to get involved with any other book writing – well, not for a few weeks, at least :-)!

SOME FINAL OBSERVATIONS

Learning can be, and should be, a fun and enjoyable experience. Learning to become an apprentice software engineer is no different, so we hope students will enjoy the CD player simulation, drawing pretty patterns on a canvas, discovering what the software inside a supermarket checkout register might look like, and maybe even some of our jokes. :-) Most of all, we hope students will be sufficiently encouraged by this apprenticeship to want to expand their knowledge of object-oriented programming in C++ still further.

Pete Lee, Chris Phillips
Department of Computing Science,
University of Newcastle upon Tyne,
UK
August 1996

`P.A.Lee@newcastle.ac.uk`
`http://www.cs.ncl.ac.uk/people/p.a.lee/`

`Chris.Phillips@newcastle.ac.uk`
`http://www.cs.ncl.ac.uk/people/chris.phillips/`

Part I

Concepts for apprentice programmers

1 Introduction to programming and software engineering

2 Problem solving using objects and types

3 Overview of programming language features

1 Introduction to programming and software engineering

OBJECTIVE

To set the context for the book by:

- giving an overview of the software construction process;
- introducing software engineering;
- covering the salient features of an apprenticeship;
- providing some background material on computer hardware, computer programs, and the programming language C++.

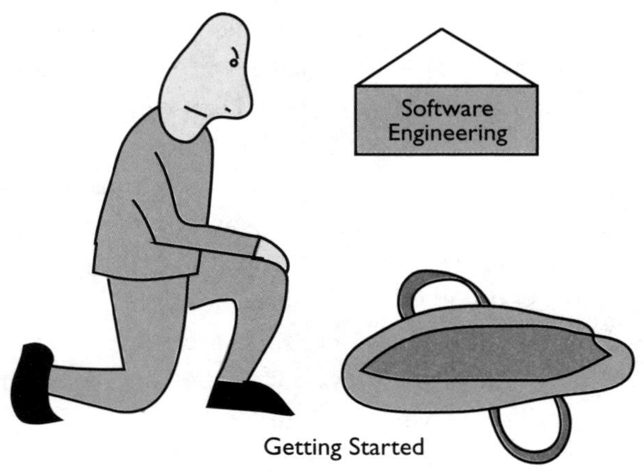

1.0 ABOUT THIS BOOK

So, you'd like to learn how to write programs in C++ (at least, we hope that's why you are reading this book). One of our objectives is to teach you about the fundamentals of constructing object-oriented software systems using the programming language C++. But ask yourself the following question: do you think that *constructing software systems* is the same as *writing programs*?

If you are not sure of the answer to this question, consider the following analogy. If someone has just acquired the skills of using building materials (bricks, cement, wood, nails) together with the associated tools (trowel, hammer, screwdriver), does this mean that they can design and construct skyscrapers? Probably not. Just as the building materials and tools are only part of the discipline of civil engineering, so writing programs is only part of constructing software systems, a discipline called software engineering.

The term **programming** and the associated job title Programmer were in common use in the software industry until quite recently. However, the term **software engineering** and the job title Software Engineer are now much more prevalent. This change in terms is not just for pedantic reasons. It reflects the rapid development of what is, after all, a relatively new engineering discipline. We now recognize that there is much more to constructing software systems than just writing programs in some programming language.

Computer systems impact our everyday lives in a much more pervasive manner than ever before. However, without their software, computers only make useful boat anchors; in other words, they aren't much use. (Some would claim that this statement is also true for some computers even with their software systems :-) The importance of software systems working correctly cannot be ignored. Just think how many systems depend on software. Banks, airline reservation, chemical process control, telephones, and fly-by-wire aircraft are obvious examples of systems in which the software's reliability is paramount. But even household appliances like TVs, CD players, videos, and washing machines are now becoming computer controlled. These appliances may not seem to have the reliability requirements of the other systems mentioned, but a company that manufactured an appliance that was unreliable due to its software would soon suffer in the marketplace.

Software systems such as those mentioned above are incredibly complicated. Indeed, it's often stated that software systems are the most complex artifacts created by humans. Until you've been involved in a team constructing a large software system it's very difficult to comprehend this statement. After all, a software system just requires writing some lines of code in a programming language, doesn't it? Unfortunately not; constructing large reliable software systems is a daunting engineering task (which isn't usually undertaken by people who are just learning how to program!).

Writing programs is a vital part of the skills of a software engineer and is what this book is primarily about. Nevertheless it's only a part of the discipline. Just as it's difficult to be an effective civil engineer without an appreciation of the basic materials and tools of the trade, so a software engineer must know how to write programs. We want to teach you how to write programs, but to do this with the larger software engineering picture in mind. If what you want to learn is how to hack programs together in C++ and how to put together obscure programs using the myriad of features in C++, then you either need to understand why this may not be the best approach to programming (and you're looking at a good book to help you with this) or you need to find another book (though our publishers will not thank us for saying this).

This book aims to be an introduction to programming with a software engineering perspective, not vice versa. It's not a book on software engineering *per se*, which is a sufficiently complex topic in its own right to be worthy of several books. Here we concentrate on technical issues arising from considering software engineering in-the-small. The *Further Reading* section at the end of the chapter provides some references to texts on the topic of software engineering in-the-large if you wish to find out more.

Disciplines involved in software construction

We traditionally talk about there being three main disciplines:

1. Art, which involves human creativity.
2. Science, where results are obtained by experiment and observation to establish rules and general principles.
3. Engineering, where known rules and guidelines are used to produce a quantifiably good end product.

As its name might suggest, software engineering principally should be an engineering discipline. However, software construction still involves significant skills in all three disciplines.

Artistic skills are needed for creativity in the design of a software system, as well as for the presentation of the documentation describing the software system. In today's graphically-oriented computer systems, artistic skills for designing the layout and information shown on computer screens are increasingly important.

Scientific skills are needed as we are still learning rules and principles for constructing software systems; indeed, recently-established principles like object-orientation form a key part of this book.

Engineering skills are an obvious requirement for software engineering. We need to move software construction away from being an expensive application of just art and science, to being more of an engineering discipline where the software system can be produced quickly, effectively and cheaply!

The inability of the software industry to keep up with the demand for the production of software systems, together with its inability to produce software systems of the required standards of quality, has naturally led to increasing emphasis being placed on the engineering aspects of software construction. This is why we have adopted the approach of introducing programming with a software engineering viewpoint in mind.

While the remainder of the book will introduce programming in general, and the C++ programming language in particular, it's worth spending a little time examining software engineering itself, to provide a view of the overall picture into which this book fits. An appreciation of this material will help you understand some of the emphases we make in later chapters.

1.1 WHAT IS SOFTWARE ENGINEERING?

Figures 1.1 and 1.2 give overviews of the life cycle of a software system, what software engineering accomplishes, and the processes that go on inside.

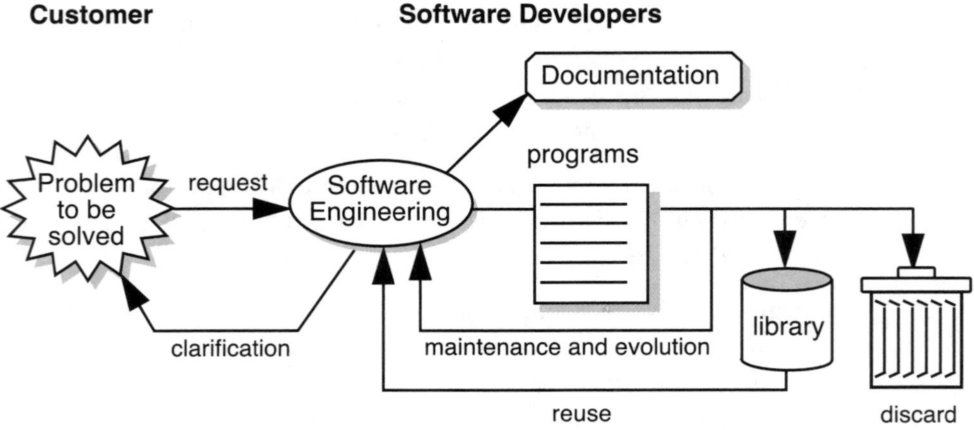

Figure 1.1 Software system life cycle

The original request for a software system comes from some form of "customer," perhaps a company in the real world willing to pay real money for the system, or in the education world in the form of an instructor (who is unlikely to pay you any money!) setting problems to test your newly-acquired programming skills. Software engineering encompasses the processes that produce the programs that satisfy this request, for delivery to the customer.

Part of the output from, and subsequent input to, the software engineering processes should also be in the form of **reusable software components**, shown in Figure 1.1 as the library. This issue of reuse of components is becoming one of the key features of software engineering. We can no longer afford the time or expense to reinvent the wheel every time a new software system is designed and implemented, a practice that has unfortunately been a feature of software engineering in the past.

If you want to produce reusable software components, it's important to adopt engineering approaches that not only encourage a component approach to designing and building software, but also facilitate the subsequent reuse of those components in new systems. It's no good having a toolbag full of components if you can't easily find out what's in there, nor how to use the ones that you find. This is where **object-orientation** comes into the software engineering picture. Designing and implementing reusable software components, in the form of **types** that can be used to create objects for your programs to manipulate in well-behaved ways, is a key element of the object-oriented approach to engineering software systems adopted in this book, as you'll see later. But for the moment, let's return to discussing the overall software engineering process.

Programs are only a part of the deliverables needed to satisfy a customer. It's also necessary to produce documentation such as:

- a **user manual**, describing how to use the system;
- a **maintenance manual**, capturing design and implementation decisions which will aid subsequent maintenance activities (fixing any faults in the software) and evolution activities (requests from the customer for additions or changes).

What goes on inside the box labeled Software Engineering in Figure 1.1? Figure 1.2 captures the main stages typically found in a large software project that involves a team of software engineers working together on a solution to a customer's problem.

Generally speaking, constructing a software system consists of design, implementation and testing stages. The starting position is the specification of the problem for which a software solution is required. **Problem-solving techniques**

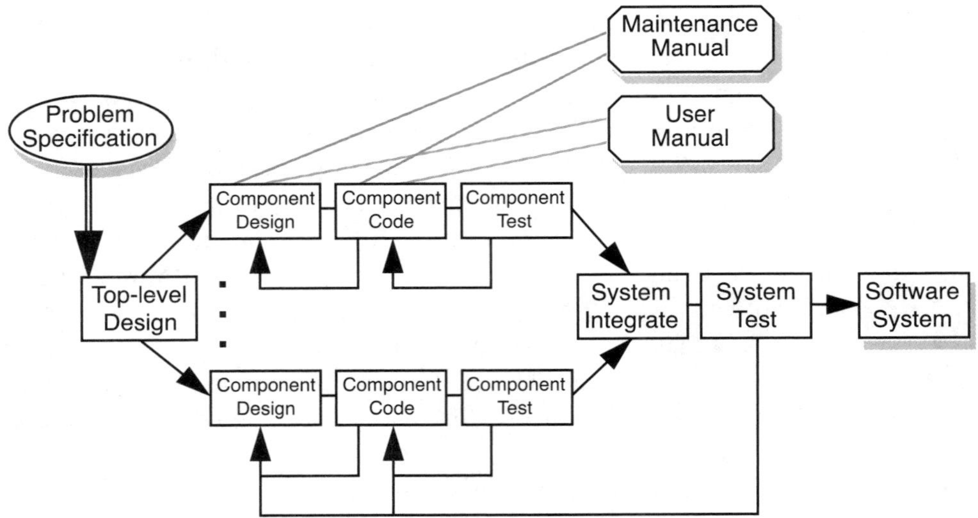

Figure 1.2 What goes on in software engineering

are applied at the design stage to move from the specification towards a computer-oriented design that identifies a solution to the problem. In a large software system, a top-level design is produced first. This is then broken down into smaller pieces, or components, each of which can be handled in parallel by one or more members of the software engineering team. At this stage, these software engineers apply what we call **software engineering in-the-small**. Each component itself generally involves some problem solving to evolve the design, followed by the implementation (code) stage which is where the software is written, and ending up with the testing stage.

What are these software components? Well, that's one of the things you're going to learn about; in particular, you'll learn how to identify *types* that are reusable components from which object-oriented systems can be constructed. As you go through this book you'll be adding types to your toolbag.

Once all of the components for the system have been individually built and tested, the whole system can be assembled and tested to see whether the parts work together. When the system testing phase is complete the final program is ready for use (or at least, for the customer to try out).

The feedback lines shown in Figure 1.2 are a very important part of the process, since the complexity of software systems means that we rarely get them right the first time. It's often necessary to go back to a previous stage to fix things; for instance, testing may reveal unexpected program behavior that has to be corrected by returning to the implementation stage. Returning to rework part of a design or a software component produced earlier can be expensive in time and effort, and thus should be minimized as much as possible. There are two lessons here that need to be highlighted:

Lesson: It's vital to get the design of a system right before embarking on its implementation.

Lesson: Implementation and testing of the software can proceed together rather than waiting until all of the software has been written before the testing starts.

These are two aspects we'll be emphasizing in this book. Getting a good design at the start is a key aspect of software engineering. A good design and a fully-tested implementation are especially important when you produce software components for reuse.

The software production process outlined in Figure 1.2 has some similarities with, but also some important differences to, the production processes in other engineering disciplines.

EXAMPLE

An automobile is assembled from a collection of components, each of which is assembled individually. However, the production of each automobile doesn't involve a new design stage for each of the individual components. A component is designed once only, and then its production simply follows this design; that is, it just has the implementation stage.

The software equivalent of this production process is the production of identical copies of a program that has already been designed and implemented, by copying it onto a storage device such as a floppy disk.

However, the replication of a program is not what software engineering is all about. The software production process is generally concerned with the design and implementation of a new piece of software, for which new components may have to be designed and implemented. Ideally, reuse comes in here. It not only avoids the cost of designing and implementing components, but also allows you to make use of software that has already been tested and, ideally, had most of its faults removed. The engineering of the very first (prototype) version of a new vehicle, where each of the component parts of the new vehicle has to be designed, is a closer analogy to the software engineering process than the production process identified above.

It's also obvious that in assembling an automobile, it's vital that the constituent parts fit together properly. It would be a bit embarrassing to find out that the engine doesn't fit into the engine compartment. Part of the responsibility of the automobile designer is to ensure that the right components are identified and that these components will indeed fit together properly. This is true also in software construction. Designing the interfaces of software components is an important part of a software engineer's responsibility.

EXERCISES FOR SECTION 1.1

1 Take a look at Figure 1.1. Why do you think the concept of a library is useful in software engineering?

2 You're going to use some components to build something. For example, the components could be Lego bricks for building a model house, or pieces of a jigsaw. If you had a library of such components, how do you think you'd want to use that library? In other words, what might you want to know about the components kept in the library?

3 Can you think of some reasons why, from a cost point of view, it's important to get the design right before embarking on the implementation stage?

1.2 A PROGRAMMING APPRENTICESHIP

How do you become a fully-fledged software engineer? Buying this book was a good first step! Recommending that your friends buy it would be nice, but that's more for the training of a sales assistant than a software engineer. What training does an engineer undertake? Some ideas can be found by examining the approach to training taken in other engineering disciplines.

Typically, most engineers start their training as **apprentices**, and during their apprenticeship period they learn:

1. The basic tools of their trade.
2. How, when and where to use these tools.
3. Features of the basic materials, particularly their strengths and weaknesses.
4. How to construct something to a given design or blueprint.
5. How to design small components, usually under the supervision of a more experienced engineer.

Apprenticeships take some time to complete. As experience is gained, larger engineering projects can be undertaken, although you would not expect someone just completing their engineering apprenticeship to go out and design a nuclear reactor.

Learning software engineering has some parallels with this traditional engineering apprenticeship approach. Indeed, the primary objective of this book is to be a programming apprenticeship aimed at producing apprentice software engineers. What might you expect an apprentice software engineer to be able to do? Well certainly such a person shouldn't be expected to design and implement the software controlling a nuclear reactor! However, if you follow this book we expect by the end that you will:

1. Know the basics of software engineering in-the-small.
2. Be able to design and implement small software components, applying an object-oriented methodology.
3. Be familiar with the programming language C++ and its use for implementing object-oriented software systems.

Clearly, these are basic things that apprentice software engineers should have in their "toolbag."

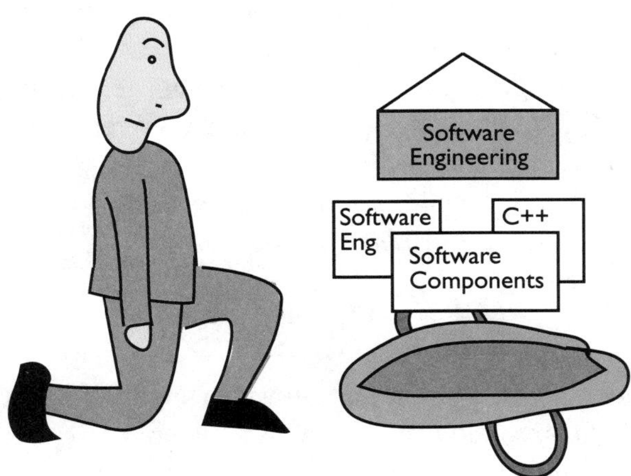

While our objective is to introduce the C++ programming language, we aim to do this in a manner that will permit you to pick up and use other programming languages relatively easily. By the end of the book you should be familiar with object-oriented technology so that programming in an object-oriented language other than C++ should be straightforward. Even if you have to program in a language which doesn't have object-oriented features, we would expect you to be able to emulate some of those features in that language, and hence obtain many of the advantages that object-orientation gives the software engineering process.

1.3 WHAT IS A PROGRAM?

So far we've been using the term "program" (or "software system") without having explained what a program is. A program is a way of solving some problem. It consists of a set of directives or instructions that state how to go about achieving some desired result. Thus, a program must provide a precise list of instructions stating what is to be done, and the order in which things must be done, such that someone or some machine can follow these instructions and achieve the end result.

You've probably been reading the last few sentences thinking "computer program" every time you came across the word "program." However, there's no reason to limit programs to things obeyed by computers, even though this is the common usage. Any list of instructions that has to be followed can be called a program.

The following two sub-sections show the style we frequently adopt throughout the book when introducing a new concept. We first explain the concept in *general terms*, using analogies with everyday things that you are likely to be familiar with. We also explain the concept in *programming language terms*, without reference to any particular programming language (particularly in Chapter 3). Finally, in Part 2 the concept is introduced in C++ terms, to provide the details of how you can use the concept in a C++ program. If you've written computer programs before, it's worthwhile skimming these sections to pick up new terminology and ideas about object-oriented systems.

Programs: in general terms

Consider the two programs shown in Figure 1.3. Neither of these programs is meant for execution by a computer (computers aren't that smart yet), yet both exhibit many of the features found in computer programs. If you can understand

Sirloin Steak with Mushrooms

Serves 4

Ingredients

4 Sirloin Steaks
1oz (30g) Butter
1 tsp (5ml) Olive Oil
8oz (225g) Mushrooms, sliced
1/2 cup (125ml) Cream

Method

1 Brush the steaks with oil, season and place on a wire rack.
2 Melt the butter and toss the mushrooms in it. Place the mushrooms in the center of a roasting pan and put the rack with the steaks on top.
3 Pour the cream into an ovenproof bowl, and place this on the bottom of the oven.
4 Grill the steaks, at 375°F according to taste, about 20 minutes for rare, 25 minutes for medium, 30 minutes for well done.
5 Stir the cooked mushrooms into the cream, season and pour over the steaks.

5 Engine - Removal

1 Remove the bonnet as described in Chapter 11
2 Disconnect the battery negative lead
3 Remove the air cleaner as described in Chapter 3.
4 Remove the radiator as described in Chapter 2.
5 Loosen the clip and disconnect the top hose from the thermostat housing
6 Place a suitable container beneath the engine then unscrew the sump drain plug and drain the oil. When completed, clean the drain plug and washer and tighten it into the sump
...
25 Raise the engine and gearbox assembly from the engine compartment.

Figure 1.3 A recipe program and a car repair program.

one or both of these non-computer programs, you can understand the basics of computer programs. Of course, you understand the language in which these programs are written, and you don't yet know the programming language C++ in which you'll be expressing computer programs. But for the moment, let's examine these two non-computer programs.

Several important points can be identified in each of the programs in Figure 1.3, and the aspects relevant to computer programming are highlighted in bold in the following descriptions, even though we don't explain these aspects here. You may wish to refer back to the analogies shown in the paragraphs below when we introduce the programming aspects in later chapters.

Consider the recipe program. It starts by identifying a set of ingredients (**objects**) that the method (**program**) is to manipulate. Each object is a different **type** of thing, and the type identifies some **operations that you can do with the object**; for example, you can pour the cream but not the steaks. Some objects have **values** specified for them (for example, ½ cup of cream), although these values do not appear specifically in the method which instead refers to the object by its **name** (for example, pour **the cream**).

The method itself specifies a set of steps that the computer must follow (in this case the computer is the chef) to turn the set of ingredients into the end result. Implicit in the execution of these steps is that the chef starts with step 1, continues with step 2, and so on until the final step is reached. In computing terms, this sequence of steps is often termed **an algorithm**. The steps must be executed in the correct order. In the recipe the order is obvious, as the sequence is straightforward and identified by the notation of the number sequence against the steps. In computer programs the sequence of steps is usually much more complex. You'll need to understand the sequencing rules for the programming language constructs you use. We'll introduce a **design notation** that allows you to express an algorithm clearly and to capture precisely the sequencing of the steps in that algorithm, to simplify the translation from the design into a computer program in C++.

The car repair program has similar characteristics to the recipe program, although the objects aren't clearly delineated at the start. For this program the mechanic is the computer, but again the steps must be followed in the right sequence. Step 1 describes an effect that the mechanic has to achieve (Remove the bonnet). You may be wondering why the mechanic has to take off a lady's hat – the bonnet on a car is the same as the hood. Therein lies a problem with an imprecise description, or rather the lack of a common interpretation of a program written in English. A mechanic might be tolerant of such problems. A computer program wouldn't be – this would be an illegal operation on an American type of car, while "remove the hood" would be an illegal operation on a British car. The moral for computer programming is that you have to know the precise details of what is legal and illegal for the objects to be manipulated by a program.

The repair program demonstrates some interesting sequencing of steps that the recipe does not. Step 1 describes an effect that has to be achieved without specifying clearly in the program how to achieve the action. "Remove the bonnet" is an abstraction of the more detailed set of steps that are described (by more repair programs) elsewhere in the manual. The mechanic is expected to go to Chapter 11 (no, not the chapter on Function Definitions in this book!) and follow the **function** or **procedure** described there, and on reaching the end of that procedure return to the engine removal program ready to proceed with the next step. Such abstractions occur several times in this program. Each chapter is like a separate component that has been used in assembling the complete system (the repair manual). The separate programs in each of these components could be independently designed, implemented and tested, just like we were discussing earlier for software engineering.

You might like to try reading each of the programs in Figure 1.3 literally and imagining what misinterpretations might be possible if a robot was attempting to follow them. The point is that English can be used in an ambiguous manner, and the correct interpretation of the program relies on intelligence in its human reader to gloss over such problems. A computer is not so forgiving, and computer programs have to be precise. The programs you write in a programming language have an exact meaning to a computer, even if the meaning isn't what you wanted!

Programs: in programming language terms

A computer program is also a list of instructions, or **statements**, to solve a particular problem, written in a programming language such as C++. In effect, the computer executes the statements in the program following the ordering defined in the program, and hence following the algorithm expressed by that program.

For example, say you need a program to solve the following problem:

PROBLEM

Calculate the sum of the first 100 positive numbers (that is, the numbers 1, 2, 3, . . ., 99, 100).

The principal part of a C++ program for solving this problem is given below (The line numbers down the side are for convenience, and are not part of the C++ fragment.) Don't worry for the moment about the C++ details or some of the terms used below; just take our word that this is indeed a C++ fragment that solves the specified problem.

A computer will execute the statements in the following sequence: first, statements 1 and 2 are executed in that order (these actually declare two variables for the program to use, and initialize one of the variables to 0); there's nothing on line 3, so then statement 4 is executed – this is a loop statement which tells the computer to execute statement 6 one hundred times, with the variable `nextNumber` being set consecutively to the values 1, 2, ..., 100. Statement 6 adds the current value in `nextNumber` to the running total being held in `sum`. The braces { and } on lines 5 and 7 respectively are being used here to indicate the start and finish of the loop, and do nothing when executed.

IMPLEMENTATION

```
1.  int nextNumber;
2.  int sum = 0;
3.
4.  for (nextNumber = 1; nextNumber <= 100; nextNumber += 1)
5.  {
6.    sum = sum + nextNumber;
7.  }
```

So, a computer program is just a sequence of steps, expressed in a precise manner in a programming language – C++ in our case. As you'll see in Chapter 3, learning a programming language has some similarities with learning a foreign language. You have to learn some new words and what those words mean (their **semantics**); for example, you'll be learning what `for` actually means in C++. You have to learn how to construct valid sentences (**statements**) in that language, following **syntax rules** for the language. Unfortunately that's not all there is to learning how to program. You also have to learn about **problem solving** – how to move from an English problem statement, via a design, to a set of C++ program statements. Chapter 2 covers this material. You also need to note the importance of the software engineering in-the-small issues identified earlier.

Finally, you also have to learn how to use a computer to run your programs. Do you have to know how computers work to be able to write programs? Fortunately, no you don't. Indeed, one of the reasons for the development of so-called high-level programming languages (like C++) has been to remove the need for programmers to know about the complexities of the underlying machinery. Nevertheless, it's useful to provide a little exposure of some of the things that go on which are normally hidden by the programming language, if only so that you can understand some of the steps involved in going from a program written in C++ to a version of the program that a computer can run. But first, there are some aspects of computer machinery that you *do* have to know about (otherwise you won't be able to use the computer at all).

EXERCISES FOR SECTION 1.3

1 Identify some non-computer programs that you've come across recently. In those programs, can you identify the things (objects) that are manipulated and the algorithm specifying the manipulation?

2 How precise are the programs you identified in Exercise 1? Can you think of any interesting ways in which they could be misinterpreted?

3 Write (in English) a set of instructions (a "program") describing how to perform a task, such as:

(a) how to interpret your college timetable. That is, how to identify when and where your computing lectures are held
(b) how to operate a TV
(c) determine whether two people are permitted to be married to each other
(d) change gear in a manual-shift automobile

What defines the sequence in which the instructions in each program should be executed?

Give your "program" to a colleague and ask them to see if they can find any problems in interpreting what you've written (apart from reading your handwriting, that is). Expand on any of the instructions where necessary to clarify what is required.

For (b) and (d) above, you could compare your resulting "program" with those of the appropriate manufacturer (via the device's user manual), and decide which set of instructions is clearer (and more complete).

4 A person's *body mass index* is defined as their weight in kilograms divided by the square of their height in meters. Write a program (a set of instructions) that specifies how to perform this calculation using your pocket calculator. Then get a colleague to act like a dumb machine and interpret the program exactly as you've written it. They must not use any prior knowledge they have about the calculator and they must not do anything other than follow your instructions. Are there faults in your program? If there are, why did they occur?

1.4 BACKGROUND

To obtain the full advantage of this book, you'll have to use a computer to implement C++ programs. We'll teach you C++, but much of your learning will come from practical experience. There are many different types of computer and many different C++ programming systems available – we cannot possibly describe all such systems here. You'll need to learn the details of your particular system from the appropriate manuals. However, you're likely to use a computer which has most of the features shown in Figure 1.4.

You'll need to use the keyboard to type C++ programs into the system, and you're likely to use a mouse when editing these programs and for controlling what the computer is doing. Results of your typing will be displayed on the monitor (or screen). Your C++ programs are likely to require some input data, either typed by you at the keyboard or read from a file on disk, and will produce some output, for example, drawing some graphics on the monitor. We'll be describing C++ features which support these actions.

The rest of this section provides material which isn't essential but is useful background material for programming. Don't worry if you don't really

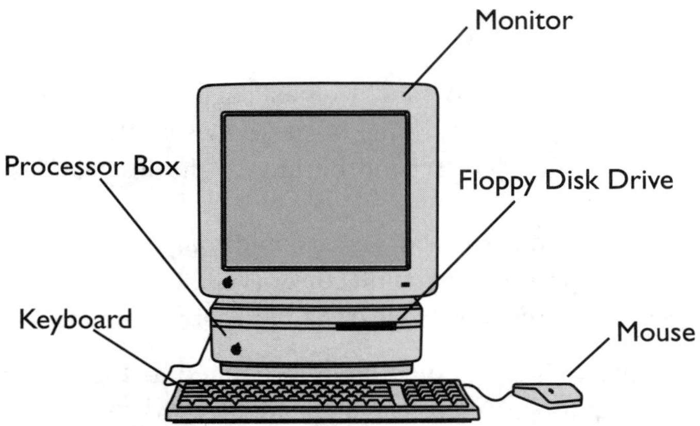

Figure 1.4 A personal computer system

understand it. If you know a bit about how computers work, you may wish to skip to the next section.

What's inside a computer: hardware

If you look through any computer magazine, you will be bamboozled with advertisements for this or that system with the XYZ whizzbang 634/99 processor running at 399 MHz, with a 70 MHz interlaced screen, SCSI interfaces and gobsabytes of this at 30 nanoseconds and megagobsabytes of that. Impressive stuff, eh?

Such technical detail is of interest to some people, but fortunately it isn't necessary to understand it all to be able to write programs. However, it's interesting to identify the main components that can be found in a computer system. A representation of these components is given in Figure 1.5.

You've already seen the monitor, keyboard and mouse in Figure 1.4; the other components are what's inside the processor box. Basically there are three main components:

1. The Central Processing Unit (usually referred to by its acronym CPU).
2. The Random Access Memory (RAM).
3. The secondary storage – hard disks internal to the processor box that cannot be seen, and perhaps a floppy disk and CD-ROM (Compact Disc – Read Only Memory) drive, generally visible by the slot into which you can place a floppy disk or CD.

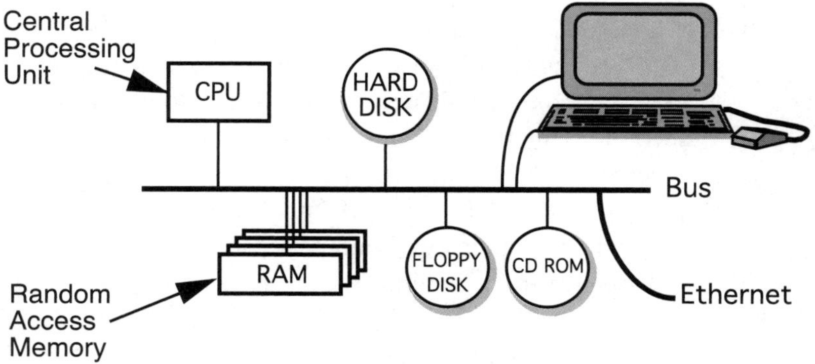

Figure 1.5 Hardware components of a computer

These components are connected together, and to the monitor and keyboard, by a bus – not the Greyhound variety, but a fancy name for a set of wires. There's often a connection to some form of external network (such as an Ethernet) that permits one computer to communicate with others. You probably won't have this network connection on a personal computer at home. Of course, you may have other things attached to your computer, like a printer or a joystick.

While secondary storage and RAM are both forms of memory in a computer, they differ in three main ways. First, the information on a disk generally cannot be accessed directly by a program; the information on a disk has to be read before the program can operate on it. In contrast, each unit of information in RAM can be accessed individually (hence the "random access" part of the name, where the term "random" indicates that you can select any unit at random, and not that you will get the value of a random unit!).

The second difference is that secondary storage units retain their state even when the electricity is turned off, whereas RAM does not. Thus any information you wish a computer to retain from one session to the next must be stored on disk. So, you use disks to store your C++ programs, typically in files in the system's file store, and the procedures for doing this will be specific to the computer system you are using. Of course, you may want your program to read information from, and write results to, files in secondary storage, and that's permitted. We'll cover the C++ provisions for reading and writing files in Chapter 15.

The third difference between secondary storage and RAM is the speed of access to data. With disks the speed of access is primarily a function of the speed of rotation of the disk. Hard disks rotate at what might appear to be a fast speed (for example, 3000 rpm), and in general the time for reading from or writing to a hard disk is measured in tens of milliseconds (a millisecond is a thousandth of a second). Isn't this fast enough? Well, not really. CPU speeds are often measured as a small number of nanoseconds (a nanosecond is a billionth of a second); thus there is a severe mismatch between the CPU's speed and that of accessing a hard disk. In other words, the CPU would run at one millionth of its top speed if all of its information was stored only on the hard disk. Floppy disks are much slower again and provide an even worse mismatch.

In contrast to secondary storage access times, RAM is built from electronic components (just like the CPU) and can effectively provide information at the speed of the CPU without degrading the CPU's rate of instruction execution. (We have to admit the picture is a little more complex than this, but this abstraction is sufficiently accurate for our purposes.) It's as if the CPU was using a Ferrari to get the information it needs; the Ferrari can get to the RAM and back quickly via the highway (the bus). However, getting information from secondary storage requires the use of a ferryboat that leaves from the pier at the end of the highway. The Ferrari can get to the boat quickly, but is then constrained by the time it takes the ferry to take the Ferrari to the information and bring it back.

Both RAM and secondary storage store information in **binary representation**, that is, as a sequence of 0s and 1s, since these values can be easily represented by the electronic components of the RAM (being ON or OFF), by magnetic devices (using two directions of a magnetized surface), and by the absence or presence of an optical dot on a CD-ROM's surface. When computer memories are being discussed, it's normal to talk about **bytes** as the unit of capacity, where a byte consists of 8 bits. (The term **bit** is used as a shorthand for **b**inary dig**it**.) We talk about there being megabytes (Mbytes – millions of bytes) of RAM in a system, with hard disks being able to store up to gigabytes (Gbytes – millions of millions of bytes) of information. Floppy disks are typically limited to 1 to 2 Mbytes, but they do fit nicely into your pocket!

So what do we use this RAM for? Battering a problem into submission? Read on . . .

How a computer executes programs

Informally, we talk about a computer **running** or **executing** a program. You'll become familiar with using these terms to describe the process by which the computer follows the instructions specified by your program. Strictly speaking, however, there are some inaccuracies here: a computer neither has legs nor does it kill a program.

Your programs will be written in C++. However, a computer can't actually execute your program in that form. "How does it run my programs then?" you may ask – a good question. We can expose a little more detail of how computers work to help in answering this question.

A computer is an automaton, which can be defined as a machine that acts by routine without intelligence. In other words, a computer follows whatever instructions it's given, with the proviso that any instruction must be a member of the set of instructions that the CPU is able to recognize. This built-in set of instructions is the language that a computer "understands" and differs from one type of CPU to another. Instructions to be executed by the CPU are stored in RAM and are specified by sequences of binary digits; we use the term **machine-code** to refer to instructions of this form. The instructions are typically low-level and general-purpose like "add two numbers in memory together," or "move the contents of a memory location somewhere else," or "test this memory location to see if it's zero."

You could program in machine-code, but it's very, very tedious and easy to make errrors. A more readable version of the binary codes can be provided by a so-called **assembly language**, but this is also a very low-level language. Writing programs in assembly language is still very time-consuming and error prone. Some measure of the difference between a low-level assembler and a high-level language like C++ is apparent from the fact that, typically, a 10-line C++ program will be equivalent to a 200-instruction assembly language program or 200 machine-code instructions. Given that some software systems comprise millions of lines of high-level code you can perhaps appreciate one of the advantages of programming in a high-level language.

So, to answer the question "How does a computer run my C++ program?" the short answer is that it doesn't. Instead a C++ program has to be transformed to a machine-code version that the CPU can execute. We describe this transformation in Section 1.5, but here let's continue exploring some of the background of computers by outlining how they execute machine-code. This execution is modeled by Figure 1.6.

The graphical notation used in Figure 1.6 is introduced fully in Chapter 2, since we'll be using this notation to express the design of software systems. Here we hope it's intuitively obvious that once the computer has been switched on (Power on), it will For ever loop around repeatedly obeying Fetch the next instruction from RAM, and then Execute that instruction. This loop never ends (except when the power is turned off), although some computers have a "Halt" instruction that also terminates the loop. Typically a CPU has the potential to execute tens or hundreds of **m**illions of machine-code **i**nstructions **p**er **s**econd (MIPS).

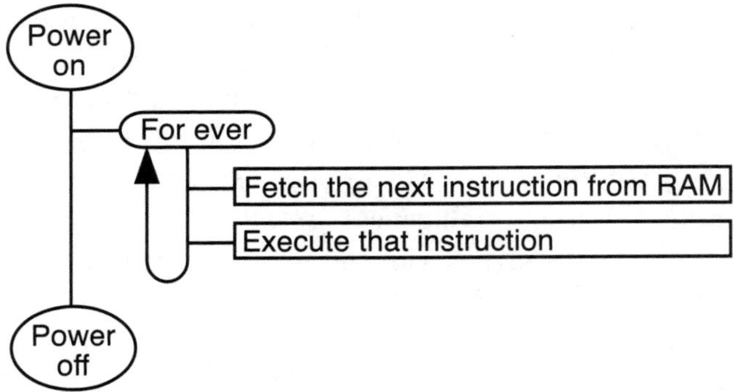

Figure 1.6 The execution cycle of a CPU

We haven't specified the exact form of a computer's machine-code because you don't need to know this information to be able to write C++ programs. Furthermore, different CPUs (for example, from different manufacturers) tend to use different forms of low-level instruction. However, a high-level programming language provides an *abstraction* that removes the need to know the exact details of the underlying CPU on which your programs will run.

We've outlined the disadvantages of having to program at the computer's machine-code level, thus illustrating some of the advantages provided by high-level programming languages. Can you think of another software engineering advantage that comes from programming in a high-level language? The answer is given in Section 1.5 (but there's a hint in the previous paragraph).

Memory model

We often talk about computers "remembering" things in their memory, but the link between computer memory and human memory is tenuous at best as they work in quite different ways. Yet the notion that values can be retained in a computer's memory is fundamental to the object-oriented programming paradigm.

You recall that information is stored in the computer's memory as a sequence of 0s and 1s. But just as you don't want to write programs in machine-code, so you don't want (or need) to express the data your programs are going to manipulate in binary representation. Imagine trying to read this book if it were written in Morse code (a language that uses a binary representation to represent characters):

. . . – – – . . .[1]

[1] The Morse code for SOS – an international distress call Save Our Souls, or is it Save Our Software?

You're going to express information in a human-readable form in your programs, and this form has to be translated into the binary representation by the C++ compiler – a process (described in Section 1.5) that you don't have to worry about how it actually works. Here we'll just look briefly at what's going on in memory at the hardware level.

Recall that we generally speak about bytes of memory. A byte contains 8 bits; each bit can be a 0 or a 1, so a byte can hold 2^8 or 256 different values. Of course, a single byte isn't an appropriate size for each piece of information you may wish to manipulate in your program. Different types of information require different numbers of bytes: for instance, to represent a number in the range

$$-32{,}768 \rightarrow 32{,}767$$

actually requires 16 bits (or 2 bytes) for the binary representation. Will you have to worry about how many bits or bytes the information in your program needs? Again, the high-level programming language answer is "no," although you will need to think about the types of information that you need to manipulate, for example, does a problem require a number larger than the maximum value available?

You'll be regarding the information in your programs as objects that are an abstraction appropriate to the problem domain you're thinking about – numbers, characters, strings of characters representing someone's name, graphical objects, bank account objects, etc. The C++ system will transform these high-level abstractions into low-level 0s and 1s as appropriate, leading to an actual memory usage something like that shown in Figure 1.7.

Of course, the 0s and 1s shown in this figure are themselves just an abstract view of the actual means by which information is stored, which is represented by different voltage levels or amounts of electrical charge, which are of course themselves abstractions of the behavior of sets of atoms, and so on. Do you have to become an electronic engineer (or an atomic physicist) in order to use a computer's memory? The software industry would be in trouble if this were the case! The point is you don't need to care about how the memory is implemented – just as long as it works! You can choose to view an abstraction of the memory in the form you want. Again, this is the power of abstraction: the ability to avoid the complexity of some implementation details (for example, memory is actually a large number of atoms) and instead concentrate on abstract behavior (numbers, letters, names, etc.).

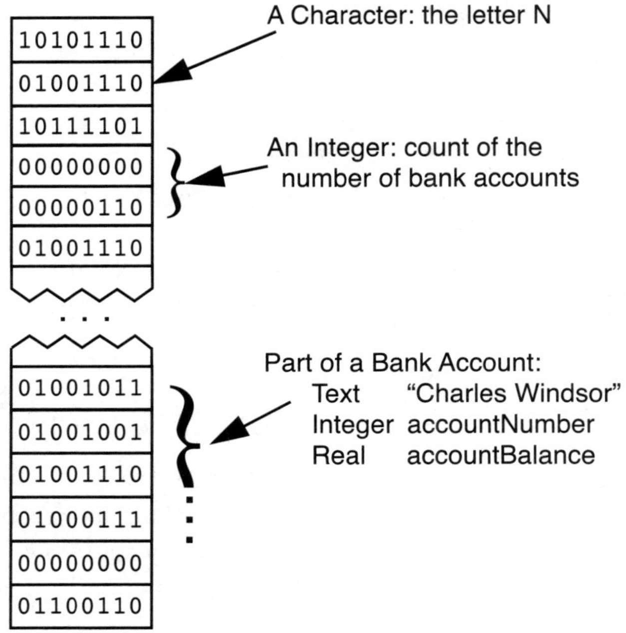

Figure 1.7 RAM usage

How do you know where in RAM your objects are? How do you know which section of RAM on your machine you can use? Do you have to worry about placing information in RAM when writing in C++? Fortunately, the answer to all of these worries is "no"; the C++ system looks after such things for you most of the time. What do you think the answer would be for programs written in assembly language? Here's a hint – it's the opposite of the C++ answer, so you can see yet another advantage of having to use a high-level language!

We hope you're beginning to understand some of the potential advantages of programming in a high-level language over having to program in assembly language (or machine-code). Real software engineers rarely use assembly language or machine-code.

What's inside a computer: operating system

If you want to write a program to read things typed at a keyboard, or to draw characters or graphics on a monitor, then the devices attached to a computer need to be controlled. The control of devices (including the disks) is quite complex. Thus, most systems run an **operating system** to make the computer system easier to use. UNIX, MS-DOS, Windows95, and MacOS are some of the names of operating systems you may encounter.

The role of an operating system is to make the parts of the computer easier to use. For example, the low-level disk control is "hidden" by an operating system and by a file system that organizes the on-disk data for you, allowing you to store information in files, to give names to files, to place files in folders or directories, and so on. The operating system provides users with a set of abstractions, the detailed implementations of which need be of no concern to you. You may wish to use some of these operating system abstractions in your programs, for instance, to read information from a file. The details of how this is achieved using C++ will be described in Chapter 15.

Note that an operating system is just a computer program, often written in a high-level programming language. It's the program that the computer executes when it's switched on – a process called "booting," after the saying "pulling yourself up by the bootstraps" – and it runs all of the time after that, until the computer is switched off. Well, it doesn't quite run all of the time; when the computer is running your programs, the operating system is suspended, but you don't need to be concerned with this.

EXERCISES FOR SECTION 1.4

1 Find out how much RAM and hard disk space is available on the computer system you'll be using. What is the name of the operating system?

2 Compare the execution cycle represented by Figure 1.6 with how the following work.

(a) an automatic bank teller machine;
(b) a supermarket checkout register.

What form do the instructions of these systems take?

1.5 How does a C++ program become executable?

If you've read the previous section you'll know that the phrase "the computer executes the statements in your C++ program" isn't quite the whole picture. The instructions actually executed can't be the statements written in the high-level programming language. A C++ program has to be translated into the machine-code instructions that the computer can execute before that program can be run. An analogy can be made with having to follow a recipe written in a foreign language that you do not understand; you require a translation into English before you are able to execute the recipe program.

The programs you write in C++ will be stored in one or more files on the computer as a sequence of printable characters; we refer to these programs as the **source files** or **source programs**. The programming statements in the source files have to be translated into an executable program containing instructions in the low-level machine-code of a particular CPU. This translation process is called **compiling and linking**.

Compiling and linking

Figure 1.8 outlines the main stages in the compiling and linking process. The first stage involves the **compiler** which reads the source file containing the C++ statements. (In the early stages, you'll only have a single source file, although later you'll construct multiple source files.) The compiler translates these statements into an intermediate form, called **object code**, which essentially is the translation of your C++ statements into machine-code. In some compilation

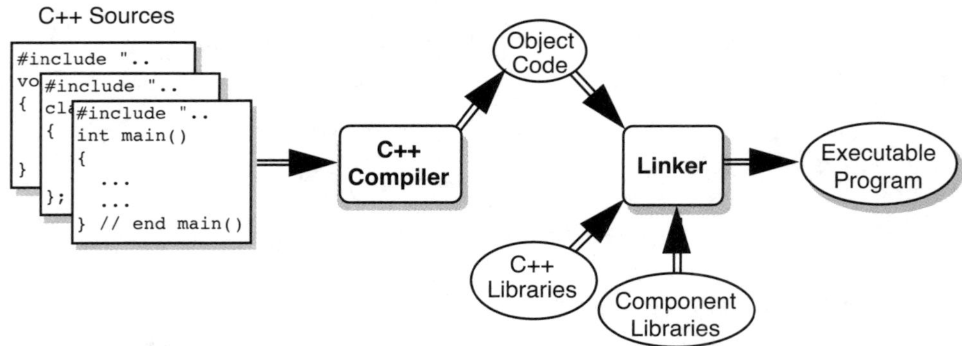

Figure 1.8 Compiling and linking process

systems this intermediate form is stored in a file called the **object file**. However, this intermediate form is likely to be incomplete, since most programs make use of other software components (that is, software reuse). Thus the **linker** is responsible for combining existing (previously compiled) libraries with the intermediate form, in order to build the **executable** version of the program. In some systems the executable version of the program is stored in a file called, strangely enough, the **executable file**. This file contains the program in the form that can be executed on the computer.

While the computer doesn't execute the source-code version of the program directly, we'll continue to use the phrase "running/executing your C++ program" even though this is not strictly accurate. Some C++ compilation systems provide the abstraction of "running" the source-code version of your program; you type the program and then issue a "Run" command. Nevertheless, the compiler and linker will be doing their work behind the scenes.

If you're a little confused about what has just been explained, don't worry. The exact details of what's going on aren't important, and many C++ compilation systems hide many of the gruesome details from you. However, you need to know about the existence of the compiler and its translation task, since you'll undoubtedly make mistakes in some of your C++ programs. Yes, you'll make mistakes, and if you haven't followed the language rules the compiler will produce error messages. We'll return to the compilation process and the errors that a compiler may report in Part 2.

Following successful compilation and linking, a C++ program is represented by a set of instructions specific to the computer system on which the program is intended to run. This means that an executable file will not be executable by a computer that's different in some way from that for which it was compiled. For example, a program compiled for an Apple Macintosh will not run on a PC. This may at first sight seem like a bit of a restriction. However, things aren't that bad since high-level programming languages like C++ are becoming standardized and are not computer-specific. All that it takes to run a C++ program on a different computer is a C++ compilation system for that computer. The C++ source file can usually remain unchanged.

This is another very important point from a software engineering perspective, namely that programs should be **portable** so they are not restricted to a single type of computer – with portability your chances of software reuse are increased. In contrast, programs written directly in machine-code or assembly language are not at all portable. These points provide an answer to the question posed earlier in Section 1.4 (which asked you to identify a benefit of programming in high-level languages).

EXERCISE FOR SECTION 1.5

1 For the C++ system on your computer, determine

(a) whether it has a help facility;
(b) if there are any user manuals on-line that you can look at using the computer;
(c) where any printed manuals are located.

1.6 WHY C++?

The evolution of software technology over the years has been accompanied by the development of a number of programming languages. In the 1970s software technology had moved forward such that a new programming language was needed, and the Pascal programming language was designed specifically for the requirements of teaching. The need for a change has also arisen in the 1990s. This need has come about because of the recognition that *object-oriented* programming languages offer significant advantages over the previous generations of languages.

It's beyond the scope of this book to compare and contrast the differences between programming languages. Let's just note that object-oriented languages offer support for a richer form of abstraction than older languages. The new abstraction mechanisms supported by object-oriented languages embody what experience has led us to believe is the best way to design and construct software systems. In other words, we believe this is the way to go!

Where does C++ fit into this picture? C++ was designed by Bjarne Stroustrup as an evolution of the popular C programming language. The C language had basically the same limited abstraction mechanisms as Pascal, and Stroustrup extended the language to add object-oriented abstraction features. C++ is the most widely used object-oriented language today, and while it's not state-of-the-art as far as programming languages are concerned, it's becoming state-of-the-industry. In other words, C++ is becoming widely used for what we might term "industrial-strength" software. It's used for writing real-world software applications; for example, for controlling the operation of telephone exchanges.

Unlike Pascal, C++ was not designed to support the teaching of programming. It's not an especially large language, but it contains many complex features and numerous pitfalls for the unwary apprentice software engineer. These problems, together with the fact that the language was derived from, and is backwards

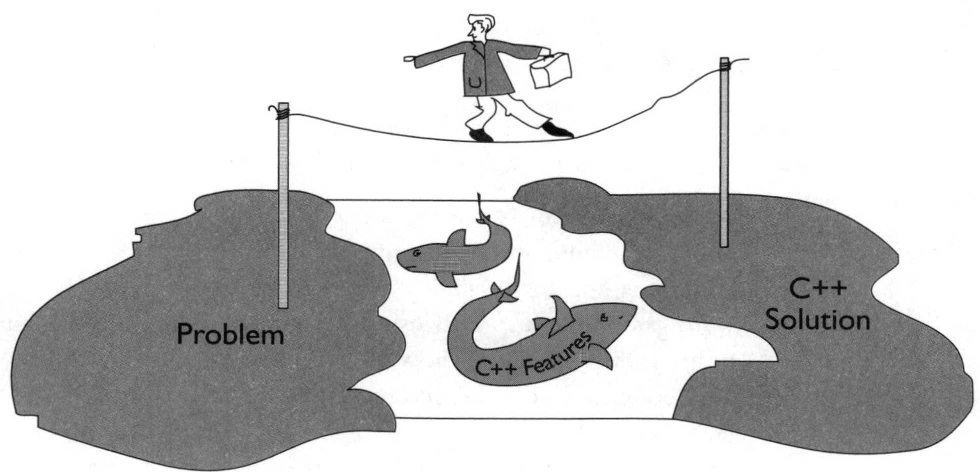

compatible with, a non-object-oriented language, do not provide the ideal teaching environment. Nevertheless, the industrial acceptance of the language, together with its wide availability, make C++ an attractive language to use for teaching programming.

We won't cover every bell and whistle in the C++ language in this book – there's just too much for the apprentice in the full language. You'll learn the majority of the important features and by the end you should be able to put together (that is, engineer) sophisticated C++ programs. In other people's programs you may come across some C++ features that we've not covered in this book. We deliberately omit some features because they cause more trouble than they're worth – just beware of those sharks ...

EXERCISES FOR SECTION 1.6

1 Visit the "computer programming" section of your local library and see how many different programming languages you can identify from the titles of books. Look at the published dates of these books to see if you can get an idea of when a particular language first appeared and whether the language in question still seems to be of current interest.

2 Using the library, find out what you can about Niklaus Wirth's contributions to the development of programming languages.

SUMMARY

In this chapter you've learned some background material so you have an idea of the context in which this book is set. You should realize that:

- **writing programs** is not the same as engineering software systems;
- **software engineering** encompasses several phases: design, writing programs and testing;
- **a programming apprenticeship** involves learning the basic tools of your trade (e.g. C++), how to use those tools, and how to design and construct software components (particularly object-oriented components);
- **programs** occur in everyday life as well as in the context of computers; if you understand the recipe as a program, you've made a solid start.

You've also covered some background information so you know a little about the following:

- **computers** – their main internal components such as the CPU and RAM;
- **executing a program** – the step-by-step execution of instructions;
- **memory** – used to store values;
- **compiling and linking** – the processes by which a C++ source program is transformed into the form of instructions that the computer can execute.

What's next?

Details of the C++ programming language start to be presented in Part II. Why not in the next chapter, you may ask. The answer is that there is some very important information we think you should read first in Chapter 2, which is concerned with how you go about solving a problem for eventual implementation in an object-oriented language like C++. If you've never written programs before you should also read the background material on programming languages presented in Chapter 3. You'll then be well prepared for the C++ details!

END-OF-CHAPTER EXERCISES

1 A magazine has asked you to write one of the following for publication in the magazine: (a) a new recipe; (b) instructions on how to build a new piece of furniture. Think about how you'd go about this task, drawing parallels to the processes that occur during software engineering as described in Section 1.1. What would a software engineer call the new recipe or the building instructions?

You're just about to embark on a new career as either a chef or a car mechanic. What, fed up with C++ already? :-) Consider the apprenticeships for these professions and identify the aspects of training that might occur in them, relating to the issues identified in Section 1.2.

2 The ACM Journal *Software Engineering Notes* regularly publishes examples of risks to the public caused by computer systems. (There's also an on-line version in the news group `comp.sys.risks`.) Look through some of these examples and identify some risks (or disasters) that have been caused by software problems.

3 You'll need to become familiar with the computer system you'll be using for the practical exercises. You'll gradually be introduced to the tools you need to know, but this exercise is concerned with general familiarization with the system. The following is stated in general, system-independent terms, and assumes you'll be using a modern workstation, PC or Macintosh-like system.

(a) **System familiarization**: You need to understand the basic user interface of your system and how to control it. You need to understand what windows on the screen are, how you control windows (hide them, display them, change their size, close them), what various icons mean, what menus are and how they work, what the mouse is used for and how the mouse button or buttons are used, and how you start up different applications.

(b) **The file system**: You'll be using the file system to save your personal files. When creating files on a computer, it's important that you organize your file space so that it doesn't become overly cluttered with lots of different types of files being stored in the same place. If you don't do this, it becomes increasingly difficult to find those files that are relevant to the task in hand, and much time can be wasted looking for that important file. Computer file systems are normally organized on a hierarchical basis, using the concept of a directory (or folder) to organize the file space, by keeping those files that are related together and by placing those files that are not relevant somewhere else. You should learn:

- the difference between a directory (folder) and a file;
- how to create directories (folders) and sub-directories (folders within folders), and hence what a hierarchical organization means;
- how to create, move and copy files around in these directories;
- the difference between moving a file and copying a file.

(c) **The editor**. When writing (and fixing) C++ programs on your computer system you'll need to make use of an **editor**. This is a piece of software that permits you to create files, type information into files, and to change the contents of files. The editor may be a part of your C++ compilation system, or it may be a separate application. Find out how to:

- move around a file with the editor, scrolling through the file, seeing its contents a window-full at a time, and positioning the cursor where you want to change the text;
- find a particular word or line in the file;
- delete single letters, whole words, whole lines;
- move sections of text from one place to another – a technique called **cut-and-paste**;
- inset new lines, words;
- save the changes you've made;
- "get out" or **exit** from the editor when you've finished using it.

(d) Learning about **printing**: Take the file you've just edited and print out a copy.

4 A Turtle is a device that can move around on a piece of paper according to instructions it's given. It contains a pen that can be in either the UP or DOWN position. When the turtle moves and the pen is in the DOWN position, a line is drawn. The turtle can only move in straight lines for a specified number of units in its current direction. The direction of the turtle can be changed in a clockwise (RIGHT) or counter-clockwise (LEFT) direction by specifying the number of degrees to turn. The turtle can also be sent to its "home", the bottom left-hand corner of the paper, with its direction set to be straight up the paper.

To achieve these actions, the turtle understands the following commands:

PENUP	lift the pen up;
PENDOWN	place the pen down;
FORWARD(*n*)	move *n* units in the current direction;

RIGHT(*n*)	change direction by *n* degrees clockwise;
LEFT(*n*)	change direction by *n* degrees counterclockwise;
INITIALIZE	move the turtle to "home."

Write "turtle" programs (i.e. a set of turtle instructions) to instruct the turtle to draw some shapes, such as a rectangle, a square, a diamond, a triangle, etc. Give your programs to a colleague and ask them to pretend to be the turtle and to interpret your program. (Don't tell them in advance what shape your program produces.) Did they draw what you expected? Repeat this experiment with a program you've written to draw a more unusual shape – something like a square with a side missing. Did your colleague uncover any errors in your programs?

5 Write three "turtle" programs that draw the following parts of a familiar game: (a) a tic-tac-toe (noughts and crosses) board; (b) a triangle shape for one player; and (c) a cross shape for the other player.

FURTHER READING

Blissmer, R.H. (1995) *Introducing Computers: Concepts, Systems and Applications*, John Wiley & Sons Inc. New York.

An introductory text if you're interested in how computers work.

Ralston, A. and Reilly, E.D. (eds) (1995) *Encyclopedia of Computer Science (3rd Edition)*, 1993, International Thomson Computer Press, Boston.

A bit of light bedtime reading in this book (over 1600 pages :-), but useful for looking up computer terminology.

Sommerville, I. (1992) *Software Engineering*, Addison-Wesley, 1992, Wokingham, England.

You'll see from the size of this book (and for many of the other books with similar titles) that there's a lot of material to cover to address software engineering. But it's worth a quick look through just to set the context for learning to program.

Stroustrup, B. (1991) *The C++ Programming Language*, Addison-Wesley, Reading, Massachussetts.

Not a book for the apprentice programmer, nor for a gentle introduction to C++. It does describe the whole language, at least for the version of C++ that preceded the international standardization effort.

2 Problem solving using objects and types

OBJECTIVE

To show you how to solve a problem for implementation on a computer using an object-oriented approach by:

- introducing a top-down approach to problem solving, as a first step in designing a program;
- introducing the concepts of data and control-flow abstractions, and notations to capture these aspects of design;
- identifing the key features of object-oriented design;
- showing the importance of types in problem solving, program design and implementation.

Problem solving doesn't start here

2.0 THE PROBLEM OF PROBLEM SOLVING

> Please construct a software system to simulate the operation of a nuclear reactor, to calculate the stresses on the reactor vessel, and to draw the plans for the reactor.

Off you go then – start writing some C++ code to solve the above problem. Ah, you don't yet know any C++? OK, well write a program in English that will permit a human to do the necessary work on a calculator and draw the plans by hand. You still don't think you can do this? Probably not, and of course we wouldn't really want you to try. (The answer is not in the back of the book either!)

While you might understand roughly what it was you were being asked to do, it's probably not immediately clear to you how you should go about it; you don't know how to solve the problem. Even if you knew all there was to know about C++, this knowledge is unlikely to help you solve the problem. The problem of solving the problem is separate from the problem of writing a solution in a programming language.

Many people are confounded about where to start when they are given even a simple problem specification and asked to write a program that provides a solution. This difficulty is hardly surprising, and the purpose of this chapter is to address this issue. Starting is not as hard as it may seem at first glance, but it's important to realize that even experienced programmers do not (and should not) dive straight into writing code.

Why are we introducing problem solving so early in the book, even before we've introduced any C++? The answer is twofold:

1. So that we can demonstrate the independence of the problem-solving and programming activities.
2. To emphasize that problem-solving activities should *always* precede programming.

A "good" program will generally follow easily from a "good" design produced at the problem-solving stage. Would you like to fly in an airliner that someone just built without having first produced and analyzed some plans for that plane? Poor programs generally result when the implementer starts problem solving by starting to type in programs at a computer keyboard. Unfortunately, this seems to be a lesson that some only learn with experience (and regrettably, some never seem to learn it at all).

Where does a problem specification come from?

In the real world, problems that require a solution come from many sources.

EXAMPLE:

A manager of a business might request some analysis to be performed on the sales in the month of December over the last ten years.

There's no mention of computers or software in this request. A person trying to satisfy the request might be aware that all of the sales information is held on a computer, and hence the request can be respecified as a problem requiring some software to access and analyze this information.

The process of going from a general statement of a problem to a more exact specification of what is required is often the first stage in problem solving, a stage called **systems analysis**. This stage can involve becoming familiarized with the problem domain (for example, the company and business of the manager mentioned earlier), and hence with the problem itself. Systems analysis is beyond the scope of this book, and we'll proceed on the assumption that you have specifications for the problems you have to solve.

An overview of the problem-solving process

Given the specification of some problem, how do you go about designing a solution (that is, producing a design) which can eventually be transformed into a computer program? This is the process of problem solving, a key part of software engineering.

The first thing to recognize is that a problem specification usually indicates *what* is required as a result, not *how* to achieve that result. For example, a problem specification that's a touch simpler than that posed at the start of this chapter might be the following.

PROBLEM:

My computer is attached to the compact disc (CD) player of my stereo system, and the player can be controlled by the computer. There are no buttons on the CD player to allow me to control it by hand. Please build me a software system that I can use on my computer to play a compact disc on the CD player.

This specification tells you what result is required (a software system to operate the CD player) but not how to achieve it. You have to decide how to achieve the result (and eventually implement a program in C++ to do it). How should you set about this?

The overall problem-solving process is illustrated in Figure 2.1. Essentially you have to go from the *problem specification* to a *design*, and then from the design to *C++ code*. Of course, the design and the coding stages are only part of the overall software engineering picture, as we discussed in Chapter 1 (see Figures 1.1 and 1.2), but let's concentrate on just these stages for the moment.

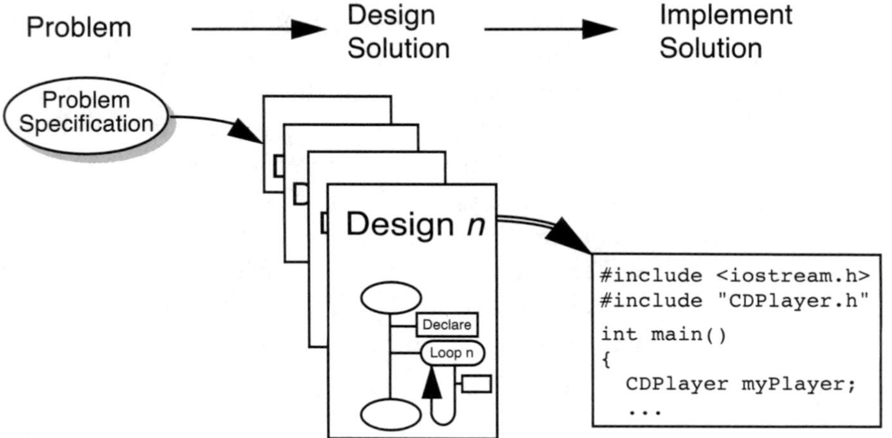

Figure 2.1 An overview of the problem-solving process

It's important to note that you can't expect to sit down and produce the final design for a software system at the first go (unless it's a trivial system).

Lesson: The design stage is the starting point for problem solving.

You will need to produce a number of designs during the problem-solving stage, increasing in size and complexity as you get to grips with the problem and its potential solution, until you get to the point that you feel you can stop designing and start implementing.

How do you know when to stop designing? What characteristics should a design have at this point? These are good questions to think about. The answers come up later in the chapter.

But first you ask "How do I start on a design? How do I deal with all of the complexity of controlling the CD player? How could I start on the design for a program to calculate the forces in a reactor?" Read on ...

Top-down design

The key to starting the design process is to realize that it isn't necessary to understand everything at once. Design normally proceeds in a **top-down** fashion. You:

1. Start with a very high-level, abstract view of the problem and its solution.
2. Gradually break down (or refine) this high-level view into more detailed, less-abstract (or more concrete if you prefer) parts.
3. At a final step the design can be translated into a program written in some programming language.

This is shown in Figure 2.2.

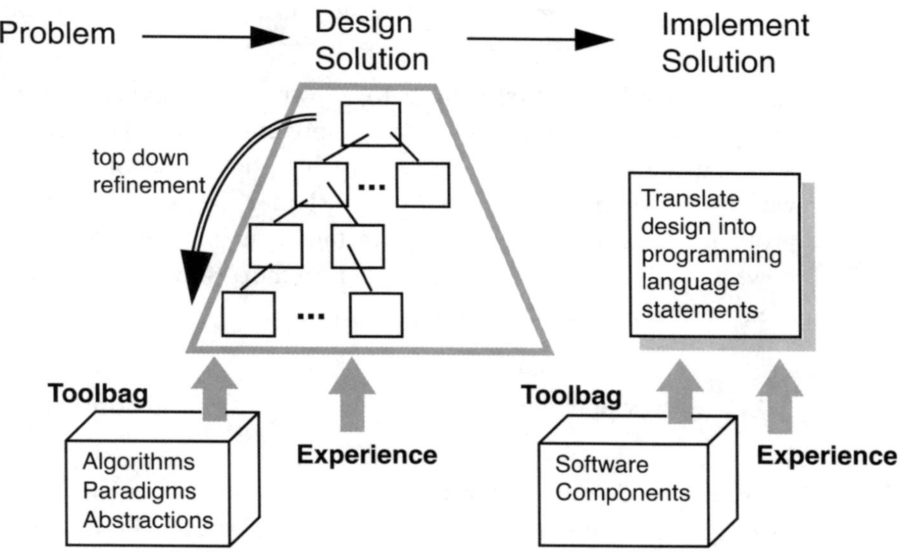

Figure 2.2 From specification to program

As Figure 2.2 indicates, other factors necessarily feed into the design and implementation phases:

- tools and techniques from your toolbag;
- experience.

Of course, these are factors that you might not possess at this very early stage in your career and hence make this design process appear even more of a black art than it really is. Just as solving the problem of designing a nuclear reactor is not suitable for a first-year mechanical engineer, so the problem of solving large complex programming problems is beyond the ability of an apprentice software engineer. You need to start by concentrating on problem solving "in-the-small," and thus on designing "in-the-small."

Nevertheless, there are three fundamental steps in top-down design, as given in Figure 2.3.

1. Identify a set of high-level components that a solution can be expressed in.
2. Express a solution to the problem using that set of components. If this cannot be achieved, return to step 1.
3. For each component, consider its design and implementation. That is, apply these three steps to each component in turn.

Figure 2.3 Three key steps in top-down design

In other words, the first step in top-down design involves providing a solution to a problem as a set of high-level components that can be used together to form a design that solves the problem. At this point you don't need to worry about where the components come from, just that they could form a solution to the problem. However, this is a step in the right direction. You've begun to break down the complexity of the problem into more solvable parts, each of which can then be considered separately.

Lesson: Apply top-down design as an approach to problem solving.

Now, how do you design these components? By applying the same principle: treating each component as a problem to be solved by designing a set of subcomponents and so on, until you reach problems that you can easily express the implementation of.

PROBLEM:

Construct a new automobile.

DESIGN:

Step 1: Identify some useful high-level components: an engine, a body, four wheels, and perhaps a few more things. How do you provide an engine? Identify some useful components: . . . . . . and so on.

Each component you identify is an **abstraction** that helps you in the design. We'll discuss abstraction in much more detail in the next section, but perhaps you can see that abstractions hide complexity and detail. An engine is an abstraction that provides motive power: you can understand that abstraction even if you don't understand how it provides that power.

Lesson: Identify abstractions/components appropriate to the problem being solved.

Identifying and designing components, however, is not sufficient for solving a problem. If a top-down design for an automobile finishes up with say 51,724 individual components, would you be happy to be given a large box containing just those parts (with the comment that the customer is going to collect the final product after coffee)? Probably not! To help you in the construction, you would expect to receive some plan or instructions showing how the components should fit together. A **design notation** is required to capture the design showing what components are used, where, in which order, and how they are connected. You'll discover later that you need a design notation for software with precisely these characteristics.

While we're on the topic of implementation think briefly about the following questions. Would it be easier to assemble an automobile by being given the 51,724 parts and the plan, or by being given a much smaller number of "bigger" components (an engine, a body, etc.) and a plan? What strategy might you use to test the thing you're building? For example, it would be annoying to find the automobile didn't work because some little component deep inside the engine didn't work as expected. These are questions that we'll come back to when we're considering the engineering of software systems.

In a later section of this chapter we'll go through an example of producing a top-down design for the CD player problem mentioned earlier. For the moment, take note of two things in the stage-by-stage approach to design:

1. At each stage you can use *abstractions* as a way of hiding complexity and detail, allowing you to concentrate on a smaller set of issues.

2. You need some *notation* for expressing the design that's emerging. A programming language is the final notation you'll use to express the solution to the problem, but additional notations are needed to capture higher-level design details.

These two concepts, namely abstraction and design notation, are key parts of your apprenticeship and will be introduced in more detail in the next sections of this chapter, and also in later chapters in the book.

The importance of these concepts doesn't diminish at the end of your apprenticeship. Indeed, these are perhaps the key skills that a successful software engineer possesses. The forms of abstractions used or the actual design notations adopted might change, but identifying useful abstractions and expressing solutions to complex problems in some notation will remain as vital skills.

But what is abstraction? What are appropriate components or abstractions for use in designing software systems? What's this got to do with object-oriented software systems? This is the next set of issues to be addressed.

EXERCISE FOR SECTION 2.0

1 Apply top-down design to identify the components you might need to provide:

(a) supper for a friend you are trying to impress;
(b) music in your college room.

2.1 ABSTRACTION

If you look up the term "abstraction" in a dictionary, you'll find definitions like:

> Separation of an idea from its concrete accompaniments.
>
> The principle of ignoring those aspects of the subject not relevant to the current purpose in order to concentrate solely on those that are.
>
> Separation by the action of the mind, as in forming a general concept from consideration of particular instances.

These definitions contain some very interesting and important ideas, though you probably won't appreciate the significance of them yet. What abstraction is and why it's important is easy to write about, but difficult to appreciate. Your appreciation will come later, as you gain experience. At the end of your programming apprenticeship you should come back to this section and reread it.

The power of abstraction is the ability to think about something via its external *interface* without concern for its internal workings or construction. This is the key part of the first two dictionary definitions given earlier. The interface describes what behavior that something provides, or how it should be used. Why is this important?

The answer is that applying this principle is the main weapon for handling complexity. Abstractions allow complexity to be mastered by hiding unnecessary detail.

EXAMPLE:

If people had to understand all of the electronics inside a video recorder in order to record a TV program, not many video recorders would be sold. Fortunately, you only have to deal with an abstraction of the functioning of the electronics as provided by the buttons on the front of the recorder or on the remote control. The interface to the video is provided by these buttons and described in the instruction manual that tells you what the controls do.

How can the forms of abstraction in this example be applied to design? For the video recorder, the interface provided by the buttons is hiding the details of an already designed and constructed system. However, you can start the design for a new system by considering the interface of that system, following the three key steps identified previously in Figure 2.3.

PROBLEM:

Design a new video recorder.

DESIGN:

Start by considering the interface – the set of abstract controls you might need and what each control does. The overall use (or functioning) of the recorder can then be expressed as sequences of operations on these controls. When you are satisfied with this high level of design, you can then move to the next stage of detail: considering how the controls and their functionality can be provided.

Lesson: Abstractions hide unnecessary detail.

Lesson: The interface is an important part of an abstraction.

Of course, when you're solving problems for eventual implementation in software, it's important to identify abstractions appropriate for software in the design phase. Appropriate abstractions are identified later in this section.

If you examine the dictionary definitions of abstraction in detail, you'll see that there are two different facets to abstraction:

1. Hiding detail.
2. Forming generalizations by studying specific instances.

The hiding-detail facet we've already considered above. The idea of forming generalizations by studying specific instances is also regarded as abstraction, and is a vital part of the object-oriented philosophy. Let's examine this form of abstraction with an example.

EXAMPLE:

Do you know what a merganser is?

(If you do know then consider how you would explain what it is to a friend.)

If you don't know what a merganser is then think for a moment about what questions you might pose to someone who did know what it is (but who is not prepared to tell you directly). For example, you might start by asking: "Is it animal, vegetable, or mineral?"

If you were given the answer "vegetable" to this question then a model of some of the overall characteristics of a merganser would begin to form in your mind. Unfortunately, this model would be wrong since the answer is wrong. In fact the answer should have been "animal," and a further refinement would be "bird." Now you are getting some idea of what a merganser is, and a further abstraction "duck" is all we need to provide in a book on programming.

The biological classification system (birds, mammals, amphibians, students, etc.) is a superb example of the second use of the term abstraction, where abstractions are used to provide an organized view of the world by providing a set of *types* that provide generalized models of behaviors for all things that are *instances of those types*.

Biologists have developed their classification system by studying animal examples and defining appropriate abstractions, and this is an example of the second meaning of abstraction, as specified in the third dictionary definition given at the beginning of this section.

Don't forget these terms: **types** and **instances of types**. You're going to be seeing them used a lot in the not-too-distant future.

EXAMPLE:

A pet called Donald is an instance of the type merganser. By knowing what the type merganser is you have an immediate idea of some of the characteristics of Donald.

Earlier in this section we identified that the *interface* provided by an abstraction is important for design. Does this have anything to do with types and instances? In fact it does, and the link is very important. If you think about it, you'll see that the type can be regarded as defining the interface of something.

EXAMPLE:

The type "video recorder" defines a set of things you can do to an instance of a video recorder that you've just purchased.

Lesson: Types are useful abstractions, defining the interface for all of the things that are instances of that type.

Abstractions formed as a general concept from a study of particular instances can assist in design. These abstractions identify general components that help to provide high-level models for the problem at hand, and are especially important in software terms for identifying types.

While abstractions help you handle complexity by hiding detail and by providing models of behavior, there's a third reason why abstractions are useful in complex situations. It has been shown that humans have two types of memory: short-term and long-term. Short-term memory has the following characteristics:

1. It decays rapidly compared to long-term memory.
2. Its capacity is limited – an often-quoted figure is that the capacity is seven "things" (± 2), independent of the size of a "thing." Our experience is that this capacity decreases with age :–(

Thus, the capacity of short-term memory is increased through the use of abstractions. An abstraction hides detail and hence removes "things" that would otherwise occupy the short-term memory. Problem solving primarily involves the use of short-term memory, and thus the ability to increase its capacity must be useful.

To summarize, there are two main ways of handling complexity using abstractions:

1. Understanding complex issues: organization of views of the problem domain by building conceptual models (or types) of the area being studied, for example, the biological classification system.
2. Solving complex problems: decomposition of a complex problem into smaller, less-complex problems, and so on until manageable entities are reached.

You'll see that both forms are heavily used in problem solving for software solutions. But first, what do abstractions relate to in programming languages?

Abstractions: in programming language terms

If you're following a programming course, where are you heading when you're applying problem solving and design? The answer is, of course, towards a programming language implementation. It therefore follows that overall characteristics of programming languages inevitably must have an influence on a design and the way it's expressed. Details from the actual programming language eventually used shouldn't have an effect on your design, but if you specify something in your design that can't be easily translated into a program, the design won't be much use. You've got to know a little about programming paradigms. Unfortunately, if you've not programmed before, this poses a bit of a problem.

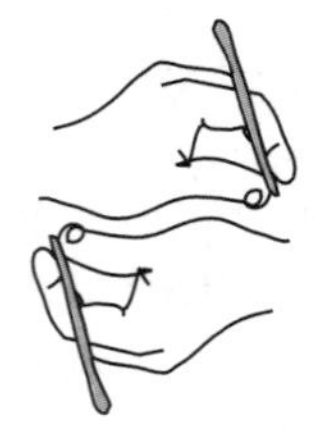

You can't design until you know some programming paradigms; but

You can't write programs until you know how to design.

One way of solving this circular problem is to leave this chapter and read several of the chapters in Part 2 on C++ programming language features, and then come back to this point later. Indeed, those itching to start programming may have done this already, unfortunately.

A better solution comes from the observation that you probably already know some of the basics of programming, albeit not in a programming language. Recall the discussion in Section 1.3 where the recipe program and the car repair program were introduced (Figure 1.3). If you understand those "programs" then you understand some of the basics of programming paradigms, and you can use that understanding to begin to consider how to solve problems for eventual implementation in a programming language.

In Chapter 1 we identified that, in general, programs consist of:

1. Some *objects* that represent the types of data to be manipulated.
2. An *algorithm* that gives a set of steps performing the manipulation, together with the proper sequencing of those steps.

Computer programs are no different. They follow a sequence of steps during which data is manipulated. For designing in the software arena you need appropriate abstractions and design notations for both of these. You need:

1. **Data abstractions**: identifying components for the design that can be used to represent the data that has to be manipulated, specifically objects and their type.
2. **Control-flow abstractions**: for the steps and their sequencing, as well as for using components the details of which are expressed elsewhere.

EXAMPLE:

The everyday use of the term data is in the context of facts or values that someone needs. "Give me the data on the number of students buying this book" you might ask, to determine a fact that you might use to evaluate the quality of this book. The way you evaluate the quality is the algorithm using control-flow abstractions such as "if more than N have been sold it must be a great book," but the things being manipulated by the algorithm are the data.

The data might be presented to you in the form "M have been sold in the last 12 months," representing a data abstraction. Why is it an abstraction?

One reason may be that you don't know how these values were actually derived. Maybe it was based on the number of copies shipped from a warehouse. Maybe it was based on actual sales in a shop. Either way, the implementation is not relevant to your design, since given this data abstraction you can specify the design of a program that determines the quality measure you were after.

The two forms of abstraction identified above are the fundamental abstractions that a software engineer uses, and the next three sections examine them in detail. You can use these two forms of abstraction in the key design steps identified in Figure 2.3. The control-flow abstractions to be discussed are common to the majority of programming languages. In contrast, data abstractions are a key part of the programming language C++ and of the object-oriented philosophy we're following in this book, so let's continue by first examining what we mean by data abstractions.

EXERCISES FOR SECTION 2.1

1 Look up the definitions of "abstraction" and "type" in a dictionary. Can you relate any of these definitions to concepts described in this section?

2 Examine the contents of a room. Identify some types, what interface those types provide, and instances of those types.

3 Say you were given the following problem to solve. Design a "program" that a person must follow in order to make a phone call, given that only the name of the person to be called is known. Follow a top-down design strategy and identify some data abstractions and control-flow abstractions that might be useful in helping you solve this problem. Outline the use of these abstractions in a "program."

2.2 DATA ABSTRACTIONS

The previous section introduced abstraction in general terms: an abstraction hides complexity and implementation detail, or provides a model of behavior, the latter we termed the **type**. How do these characteristics apply to data and design? Well, we want to come up with a design that solves a problem by specifying a set of steps that manipulate some data components. In software terms we use the term **object** to refer to these data components, and hence we refer to designing in this way as **object-oriented design**. Later, when you see how to translate such a design into a program using C++ you'll be applying object-oriented programming, but that step is for later.

If you're going to use objects in your designs, it's clearly important they have the desirable abstraction characteristics discussed above. In particular, you'll need to understand the interface provided by each object so you can figure out how to use it in a design. And what is it that defines such interfaces? The idea of "type" provides that definition. If you think about an object as being an instance of a type, you should be able to see that types also form a vital part of object-oriented design.

Types are a very useful component for use in a design. If you have types that are appropriate to the domain of the problem you are trying to solve then your design task will be much simplified. Conversely, if you have a set of types that provide abstractions that are a long way from the domain of the problem then you'll have a lot of work to do to use those types to express a design to solve that problem. If you were faced with having to use a fixed set of types then your problem solving is likely to be much more difficult than if you are free to design new types to match the problem at hand. Fortunately for software systems you have the freedom to design new types (that's part of the reason why these systems are "soft" or not fixed), and thus designing new types is the key aspect of object-oriented design.

Lesson: Object-oriented design is concerned with identifying types and objects as components for use in solving a problem.

Got all that? Do you now understand all about object-oriented design? We'd be (pleasantly) surprised if you answered "yes, no problem" or (unpleasantly) surprised if you couldn't relate any of the previous sentences to the earlier discussions about design and abstractions. We hope your reaction is somewhere in between; you have some sort of idea about the general points being discussed but you have lots of questions. These are complex issues to grasp, let alone to try to explain clearly in a few sentences.

Let's provide a problem specification that can be used for exemplification. To do this we need a problem that's relatively straightforward and comprehensible. We want you to concentrate on the use of abstractions for problem solving, rather than on the problem itself. Thus we've chosen a variation on the problem discussed earlier, namely a problem involving compact disc (CD) players, whose use we hope you're familiar with.[1]

PROBLEM:

Design a program that a (human) computer can execute in order to play a CD.

DESIGN:

What objects would be useful in solving this problem? Given a set of possible electronic types, a set of objects such as silicon chips, wires, buttons, etc., could be used to express the design of the desired program.

IMPLEMENTATION:

First, connect a wire to pin 3 of chip NC3047, and then . . .
. . . lots and lots and lots of steps later . . .
you can play the disc.

This set of components clearly doesn't have the characteristics leading to a high-level design to solve the problem. They are too low-level. There's too much detail to be dealt with. There's not enough use of abstraction. Not many people could (or would want to) follow such a design in order to play a CD.

What you really need are some higher-level (more abstract) components: objects whose type matches the problem at hand – an instance of a *compact disc*

[1] If you've never used a CD player, don't panic. It's very similar to a record player, or even an audio or video tape player. If you've never used any of these, do some background research in your nearest department store.

player type together with one or more instances of a *compact disc* type. These are types and objects that match the problem domain and, as you might imagine, lead more readily to a simple program than the electronic types and objects being used above. This is precisely the use of abstraction discussed earlier.

Lesson: Identify and use types appropriate to the problem domain for use in your design.

Even though there are already CD players and CDs in the real world, we're still thinking of objects in the design as abstractions. You should design a program that will work for any CD player, and hence remain divorced from the particular features of a specific manufacturer's model.

Just having a CD player object isn't much use unless you can identify what can be done with it – after all, the human executing the program you're trying to design has to do something with the player, even if they don't need to know about all of the detail inside the player! What you need to know (or design) is the interface.

If you've used a real CD player think for a moment about the *set of operations* that you can apply to a player. You'd probably come up with a list like that shown in Figure 2.4. If you've never used a CD player, examine the list in this figure. Does it help you begin to understand how a CD player behaves?

Switch On	**Switch Off**
Open Disc Drawer	**Close Disc Drawer**
Load a CD	**Unload a CD**
Play	**Stop**
Go to Next Track	**Go to Previous Track**
Read Display	

Figure 2.4 Operations on a compact disc player

The list captures the main operations that a CD player can perform. There may be other operations that some real CD players provide, but for our purposes this list will suffice.

These operations are part of the interface provided by a CD player abstraction; in other words, these operations are part of the type CD player. Turning this around you can note the following lesson:

Lesson: A type defines a set of operations that can be applied to instances of that type.

Why isn't there an operation **Bake a Cake** in the above list? A dumb question, you might think; would anyone want a CD player that could bake a cake? They wouldn't of course. The point of the question is to emphasize the importance of matching the data abstractions being contemplated with the problem at hand. The CD player type provides a model of some behavior, for which culinary activities do not seem a natural part.

There's another aspect to the abstraction provided by a CD player type. This concerns any **states** or **values** that an instance of a CD player might have. For a real-world CD player, the term **value** is a little misleading since we are not interested in the fact that it might have cost $169.37 or that second-hand it's worth $1.95. (Later you'll see why the terms value and state can be used synonymously.) There are other abstract states that are of interest to the design.

EXAMPLE:

In terms of the states that a CD player might be in, you could use descriptions like:

"The CD player is OFF"

"The CD player is ON and the drawer is OPEN"

"The CD player is ON and the drawer is CLOSED and a disc is LOADED"

The words ON, OFF, OPEN, CLOSED, LOADED all indicate various states that the player can be in. Of course, which state (or combination of states) the CD player is in affects what any "program" using that player has to do.

The various states or values are abstractions of some underlying implementation detail. For instance, ON means that electricity is present. Again, you don't want to be bogged down with implementation detail, and hence having a set of possible abstract states associated with the abstract object makes sense.

Lesson: A type may define a set of abstract states that instances of that type can exhibit.

The (abstract) states for the CD player are dynamic, in the sense that they can change as operations are applied to the CD player. An object may also have some static values associated with it; for a CD player these could be things like its price, its serial number, and its model number. As these values are not relevant to the process of using the player, we won't consider them further here.

To summarize, we've identified two important aspects of data abstractions:

1. The set of type-specific operations that are supported.
2. The set of abstract values that an instance of a type might take.

Given the description of these aspects for a CD player type, you could begin to solve the problem stated at the beginning of the section, namely to create a program for a human to execute to play a CD. However, before you do, let's elaborate further on the distinction between a *type* and an *object* (an instance of a type) since it's vital that you understand this distinction fully.

Type versus object

Reexamine the list of operations on a CD player given in Figure 2.4. Does this set of operations apply to just one particular CD player, or does it have more general applicability? Similarly, does the instruction manual for a real CD player work only for the one you've purchased, or is it common to all CD players of the same type?

The answer to the above questions is of course that the set of operations and the instruction manual are general and apply to all CD players of the type; the manufacturer wouldn't write a manual just for you.

We are making a distinction here between two kinds of things. The **type** which is a model of behavior and is applicable to all of the **objects** that are instances of that type.

We can identify the following properties of the type of something. A type defines:

1. A set of legal operations.
2. A set of abstract values.

These two properties define what we've called the **interface** of the type. The interface defines the externally-visible properties, the things that someone needs to know if they wish to use the type. As a user you're interested only in using the type as an abstraction. You're not interested in all of the details that comprise the implementation of the type.

A set of types supplies a set of abstractions that can be used in problem solving and design. Earlier we identified an abstract CD player type, giving its operations and possible abstract values. However, when you come to design a C++ program to control the CD player, it's not types that the program is going to manipulate. The program manipulates objects that are instances of a type. Thus an object is an instance of a type and has the following properties:

1. *The object has an identity:* identifying the object allows it to be referred to and hence manipulated by a program.
2. *The object has a type:* the type defines the set of legal operations that can be performed on the object. These operations permit the state of the object to be manipulated and changed.
3. *The object has an abstract state:* one of the values defined by the type.

EXAMPLE:

The CD player type defines a set of operations and abstract values. If you bought a CD player it would have an identity (for example, its serial number), or a name you might give it (for example, Lindsay's player). During its lifetime it would assume various abstract states (for example, ON). Its states are completely independent of the state of any other instance (Pete's player might be OFF). You couldn't bake a cake using the CD player since that isn't defined as a legal operation by the type.

It's important that you understand the distinction between type and object (or instance of a type), as this distinction is fundamental to what follows.

Type design notation

If you want to identify types to help at the design stage then you need some form of design notation to represent the interface of the types. For the moment, let's introduce an example of the use of a notation for the CD player type. We'll define the design notation in more detail in Section 2.7.

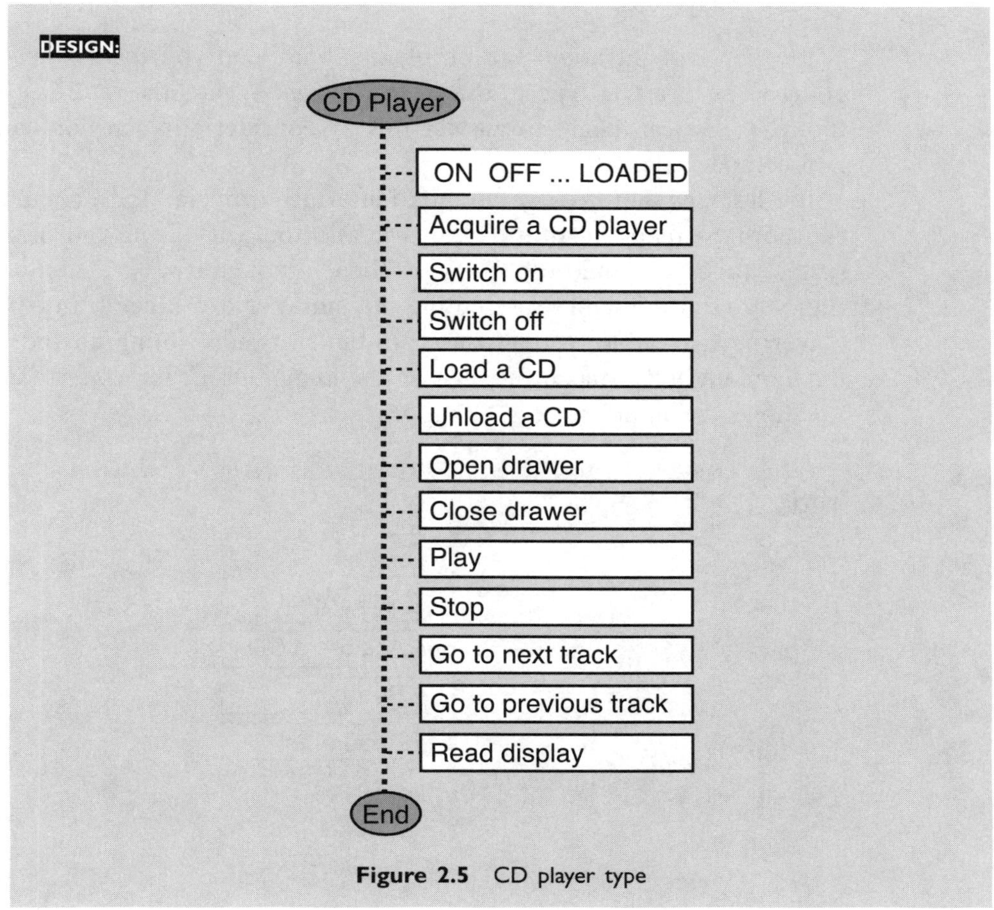

Figure 2.5 CD player type

Figure 2.5 captures graphically some abstract states together with the operations of the CD player type identified in Figure 2.4. You may note that there's an extra operation: Acquire a CD player. This operation has been added because you'll need to get an instance of a type to be manipulated in a program; you can't use a CD player at home until you've acquired (bought) one. Types generally provide an operation with this characteristic.

You might think that Figure 2.5 gives no more information (apart from the additional operation) than that provided earlier, and you'd be right. We'll be extending the design notation later to provide additional interface information.

Are there any other types you might find useful in solving the problem which, to remind you, is to design a program that a (human) computer can execute in order to play a CD?

Further thought about the problem should lead you to the idea that you're going to need a CD type to use in the design. What's the interface to this type though? You can begin to answer this by considering what you can do with a real compact disc.

For humans there is a very limited interface provided for a compact disc; you can perhaps read the title of the disc and the artist from the printing on the surface (and you could use it as a Frisbee, although it wasn't intended for that). Can you read the data representing the music? No you can't. In contrast, a CD player must be able to read this data but not the printing on the surface. For the moment, let's concentrate just on the human user's interface to a CD. Figure 2.6 shows the interface to a CD type.

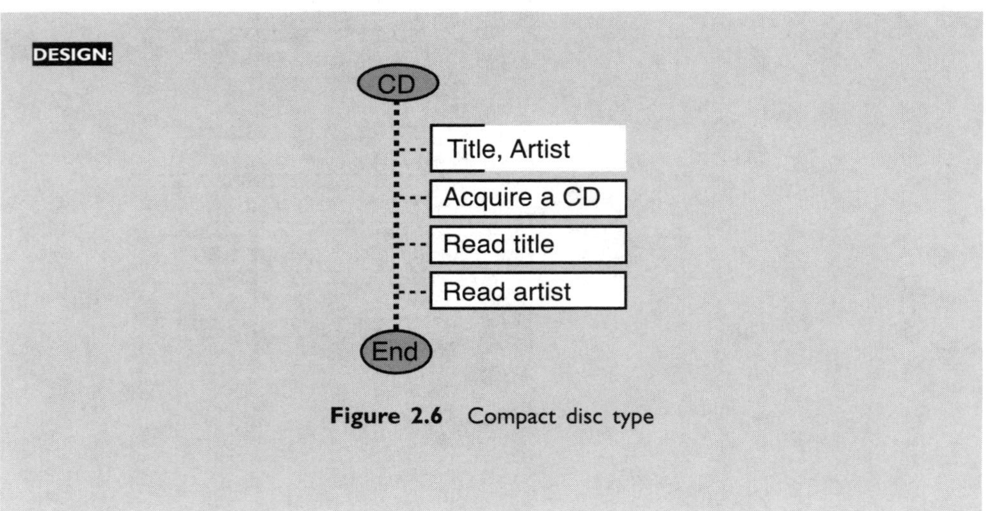

Figure 2.6 Compact disc type

If you're familiar with CDs and CD players, you're probably wondering why all this fuss? "Isn't it all obvious?" you might think. Let's just remind you that we've chosen a real-world problem that we hope you have some familiarity with – we're introducing and concentrating on some important principles, not trying to get you to re-design CDs and CD players! Nevertheless, studying real-world examples or descriptions of things in order to derive types for use in software systems is important, and comes up again in Section 2.8.

For the moment, given the CD player and CD types that you've now identified and specified, what's next in the design of the program? Using those types to specify the **algorithm** is the answer. What's "the algorithm"? Section 2.3 gives the answer as well as the principles involved.

EXERCISES FOR SECTION 2.2

1 There are a number of operations that you can do with the mouse attached to your computer system. Write down a list of these operations and the set of possible abstract states that the mouse might be in.

2 Express the interface to a telephone using the type design notation – that is, regarding a telephone as a type. What are the differences between this type and instances of the type (e.g. the telephone in your home)?

3 Consider a pocket calculator. Regarding your choice as a type, describe the interface to that type using the type design notation. Identify the differences between your type and instances of the type.

4 In Exercise 4 in Section 1.3 you wrote a "program" for using a pocket calculator to calculate a person's body mass index. Compare the operations on the calculator specified in that program with the operations you've defined in Exercise 3 for a pocket calculator type, and think about the reasons for any differences.

5 If you had to design a computer program to calculate a person's body mass index, can you identify any types and objects that might be useful in this design? What operations would those types define?

6 You're faced with the problem of describing how to find the phone number of someone whose name you know. Design a phone book directory type, expressed in the design notation, that would be useful in solving this problem.

2.3 CONTROL-FLOW ABSTRACTION

A set of types provides some components from which you can begin to think about constructing the design of a program. In other words, you now need to specify the **algorithm** – the sequence of steps that represent a solution to the problem. To do this you need to be concerned with *control-flow abstractions* and an associated *design notation*.

Here we'll be concerned just with using the interface of the types identified in the previous section. We won't worry about constructing the types themselves. Who is going to design how the CD player's operations are actually constructed (involving all sorts of electrical types and sub-components)? Assume it's someone else's responsibility to do that. Note however that the type is a separate component, the construction of which is simply a new problem to be solved using all of these wonderful techniques you're learning about. (You'll see later that implementing types in C++ just involves writing programs.)

In Figure 1.3 in Chapter 1 you saw one method that can be used to indicate steps and their sequencing. Both the recipe and the car repair programs identify the steps to be taken in numerical order, assuming that the "computer" (that is, the human) executing those programs would first do step 1, followed by step 2, and so on. There are two important things here:

1. The identification of the steps themselves.
2. The identification of the sequencing of the steps.

For the program to work correctly it's vital that the proper sequence of steps is followed. Just imagine what the recipe would turn out like if the steps were not followed in the correct order. Equivalent disasters can occur in computer programs.

We could use the approach demonstrated in Figure 1.3 to represent the control flow abstractions needed for a design. However, computer programs in general have a much more sophisticated and complex sequencing structure than that exhibited by either the recipe or the car repair programs. It's therefore useful to have a more graphical notation to capture the sequence of steps in an algorithm. An example of the design notation we'll be using is given in Figure 2.7.

Figure 2.7 illustrates the design for a simple program with three steps called A, B and C. The sequence is that the program starts at Start, then does step A, followed by step B, followed by step C, and then Stops. In a real design it's important to give the steps more informative names, but the purpose here is to introduce the notation and its interpretation.

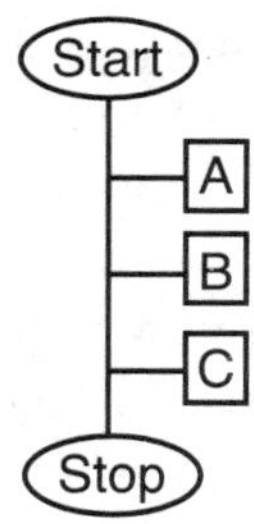

Figure 2.7 A simple design

PROBLEM:

Design a program to calculate a person's body mass index.

DESIGN:

You recall from Exercise 4 of Section 1.3 that the body mass index is defined as the person's weight in kilograms divided by the square of their height in meters. Concentrating on the steps in this algorithm rather than on any objects or types, the design for this calculation is straightforward:

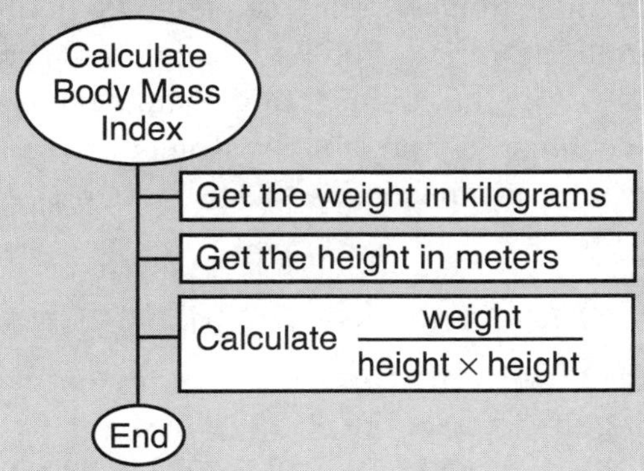

You might think that having to draw such design diagrams is far more complex than just writing a list of the three steps, and for this simple example you'd be correct. Unfortunately, computer programs rarely have a simple, sequential form of control flow. As we introduce more complex control-flow abstractions and designs, the advantages of a graphical notation over a textual notation will become clear.

You may have observed that the control-flow design notation is similar to that used earlier for a type (for example, in Figure 2.5). The similarity is intentional, but it's important to note that the type notation has no idea of sequencing associated with it, since it's used merely to express the interface defined by a type. In contrast, the control-flow notation *is* expressing the sequence of the steps in the algorithm, and hence the sequence of steps that a program derived from the design will need to follow when executed. The lines joining boxes in the type design notation are drawn as dotted lines to highlight this difference.

At this stage you may be wondering "Why is this sequencing called control-flow?" The answer has to do with the way that computers execute programs. An executing program controls what the computer does; the program "tells" the computer which instruction to execute next. We therefore talk about the control "flowing" through the program following the instruction sequence specified by that program.

In a computer, the flow of control is implemented by something called the program counter; this doesn't count programs, as its name might suggest, but indicates the next instruction to be executed by the computer (see Figure 1.6). When the computer is sequentially executing instructions, the program counter is effectively increased by one each time to get to the next instruction, just like following the numerical steps in a recipe. Changing the program counter to do something other than increase sequentially permits the flow of control through a program to be varied. You'll be seeing some control-flow abstractions that are implemented (by the compiler and computer) as changes to the program counter of the executing program, but you won't need to worry about this low-level detail when writing programs in C++. Abstraction is going to help you again!

Sequencing rules for the design notation

We need to give precise rules for determining the interpretation of the sequencing of steps specified in our design notation before more complex variations of the notation are used. Figure 2.8 indicates the terms used in these rules. Note that the directions "left" and "right" in the figure are from the viewpoint of someone traveling along the arcs in the directions indicated by the arrows.

The sequence of steps is given by the following sequence-algorithm: commence at the first input path, normally at the top of the diagram, and move to the first node. Nodes occur at the points indicated by the black dots in Figure 2.8, although these dots aren't used in the design notation.

For each node in the diagram, the following node-algorithm is applied: the left-hand output path is followed until the end of that path is reached. When

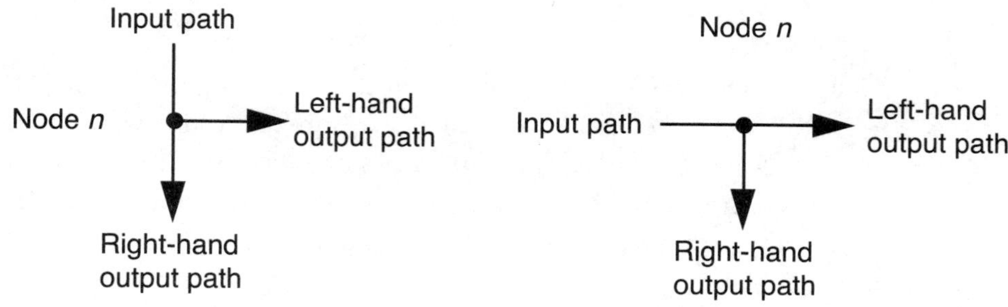

Figure 2.8 Sequencing notation

the end is reached, the right-hand output path is then followed. Whenever a new node is reached by following a path, the node-algorithm is reapplied. Whenever a node is reached for which the details are specified on a separate diagram, the sequence-algorithm is applied to the separate diagram, and at the end of that diagram, control returns to the originating node.

Did you understand that textual description? It's a description of two algorithms that you need to follow to identify the sequence of nodes reached when following a design expressed in the design notation. The description is complex because there isn't a simple sequence of steps to be followed. Can these algorithms be expressed more clearly using the design notation itself? Yes they can, and when you've learned more about control-flow abstractions and their associated design notation, you might just come across an appropriate exercise to try.

Designator box

Part of the top-down problem-solving process introduced in Section 2.1 is concerned with breaking a problem down into a set of smaller problems, each of which is easier to solve than the larger problem of which they are a part (see Figure 2.3). This is something we need to capture in the design notation. We need the ability to indicate that a box in the notation is actually an abstraction representing (or hiding) some of the detail that makes up that abstraction. We call this type of box a **designator box**. A rectangle with cut-off corners is used to represent a designator box.

EXAMPLE:

In Figure 2.9, step A is drawn as a designator box, indicating that A is an abstraction, the details of which are shown by the boxes underneath A. Thus A itself represents an abstract step which is actually composed of the steps E, S, I, G and N. In contrast, the box enclosing S is a regular rectangle, indicating that S is a step in its own right, but it also has some related parts (I and G).

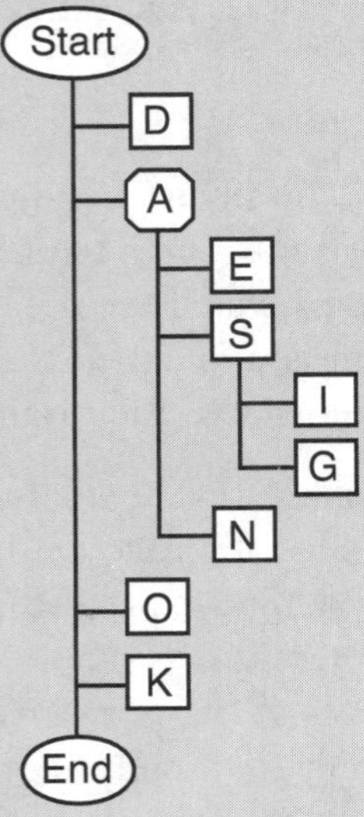

Figure 2.9 Design with expanded designator box

What is the sequence of steps produced by an execution of the program specified in Figure 2.9?

The sequence produced is DESIGNOK. Step A is a designator box, so we don't show it in the sequence. In contrast, step S is not a designator box, and is included in the sequence. If this isn't clear, there's another example coming up when the CD-playing program is designed.

Often in a design there isn't enough room on a page to show the expansion of all of the abstractions represented by designator boxes. Indeed, sometimes it's useful to deliberately hide the detailed expansion of an abstraction represented by a designator box. This is easily achieved simply by drawing a designator box where it's required, and providing a separate diagram giving the details of the expansion.

EXAMPLE:

Figure 2.10 shows a use of a designator box, and represents a simple version of the design process.

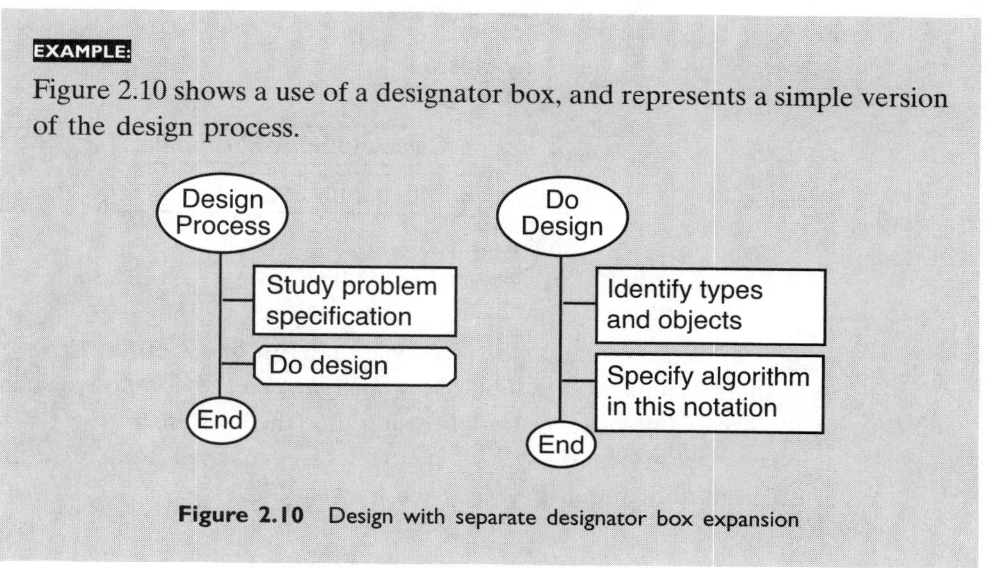

Figure 2.10 Design with separate designator box expansion

Functional abstractions

A designator box can be used in the control-flow design notation to represent an abstract step, or **function**. A function is a component of the design, the details for which will be provided by another design diagram that shows the actual sequence of steps in the component.

PROBLEM:

We can use the body mass calculation component designed earlier to illustrate the use of designator boxes and functions. Say you were given the following problem to solve:

> Print out a person's body mass index.

DESIGN:

You've already got a component designed to perform the calculation of the index, so a design for the new problem simply needs to use that component as follows:

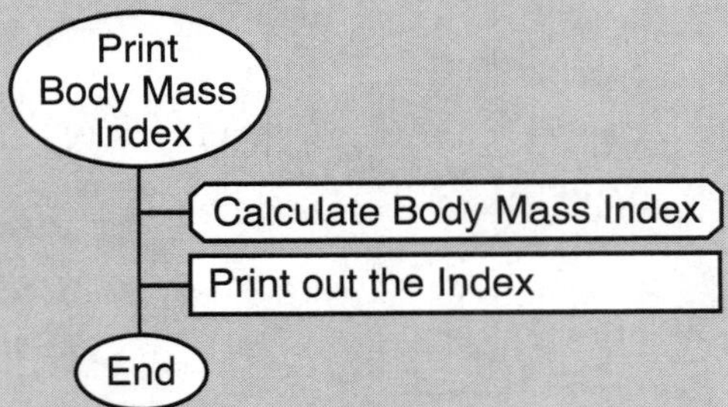

The interpretation of this design is that the first step is represented by a designator box, so the flow of control goes to the component identified by the box. Control then flows through the (three) steps of the Calculate Body Mass Index function, and when the end is reached control returns to the diagram above and the Print step is executed.

While this is a simple example, note that we've gained some benefit from reusing a component that's already been designed.

Using a designator box in this way provides an important form of control-flow abstraction, called **functional abstraction**. A functional abstraction is one that captures some general functionality, general in the sense that it's not tied to a specific type. If it was associated with one type, it would be part of that data abstraction rather than being a separate "stand-alone" functional abstraction.

Lesson: Functional abstractions generally are not type-specific operations.

Functional abstractions are often a useful starting point for a top-down design. They also form a vital role at the program implementation stage, and programming languages like C++ provide language constructs to permit a software engineer to write functional abstractions. Details of these constructs will be covered in Part 2.

CD player example: design 1

We've now established the two main types of abstractions we intend to use for design, namely *data abstractions* in the form of types (and objects), and *control-flow abstractions*, and we've presented design notations that can be used to represent them. Let's return again to solving the CD-playing problem:

PROBLEM:

Design a program that a (human) computer can execute in order to play a CD.

DESIGN 1:

You can start to capture an algorithm using the CD and CD player types identified in Section 2.2 in an algorithm to solve the problem. A first design you might come up with is shown in Figure 2.11.

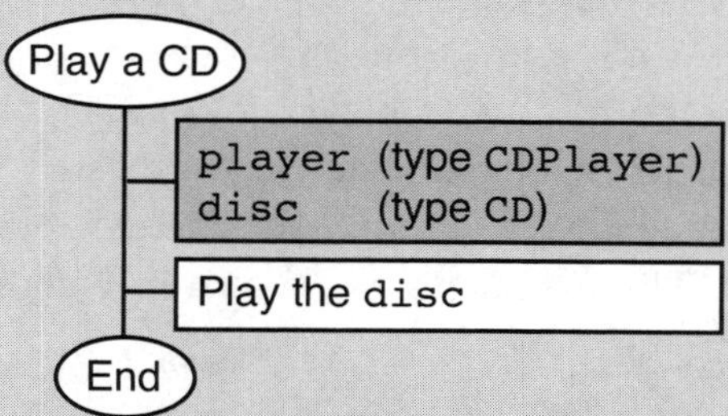

Figure 2.11 First design for Play a CD problem

This design gives a solution to the problem – a high-level solution, but a solution nonetheless. The shaded box indicates creation of the objects that the solution uses, giving each object a name (`player` and `disc`) by which they can be referred to in subsequent steps, and indicating the type (`CDPlayer` and `CD`) of each object. The other box indicates the single step of "Play the `disc`".

Ask yourself the following questions. "Is this design sufficient as a solution to the problem? Could someone who didn't know about CD players follow this design to play a CD? Do you play a CD by blowing on it, like you would a musical instrument?"

The answer to each of these questions is "no." By applying some human intelligence and prior knowledge of CD players or something similar, a human could perhaps get a disc to play. But for a dumb automaton (like a computer or a Computer Science Professor) the design is nowhere near sufficient. There is simply not enough detail. What's needed is to develop this first design diagram further, by supplying more detail in the form of additional steps.

CD player example: design 2

A first observation about Design 1 is that a CD player will do nothing until it has been switched on. A second observation is that it ought to be switched off at the end. A third observation is that the step Play the `disc` itself will consist of several substeps; it's a functional abstraction, since it describes a high-level function involving both the CD player and a CD object. You need to change the representation of this abstraction in the design to be that of a designator box, and design a separate diagram and solution representing the expansion of this abstract step. These changes are shown in Figure 2.12.

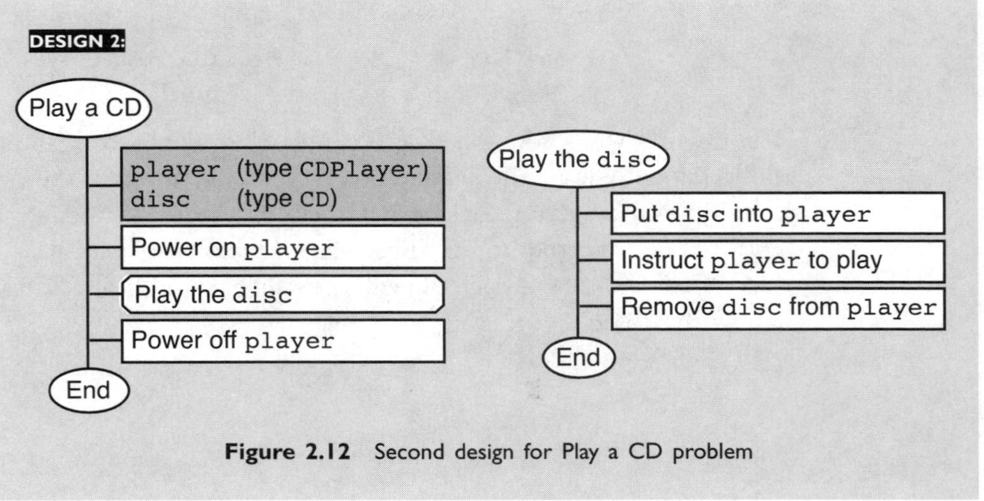

Figure 2.12 Second design for Play a CD problem

Again ask yourself the question "Could someone who didn't know about CD players follow this design to play a CD?"

The answer is still "no." This second design is better than the first (better in that it provides more detail), but further refinements of parts of it are required to ensure that the design provides a complete and precise solution.

CD player example: design 3

You need to expand the steps in the Play the disc design in Figure 2.12. This expansion is shown in Figure 2.13.

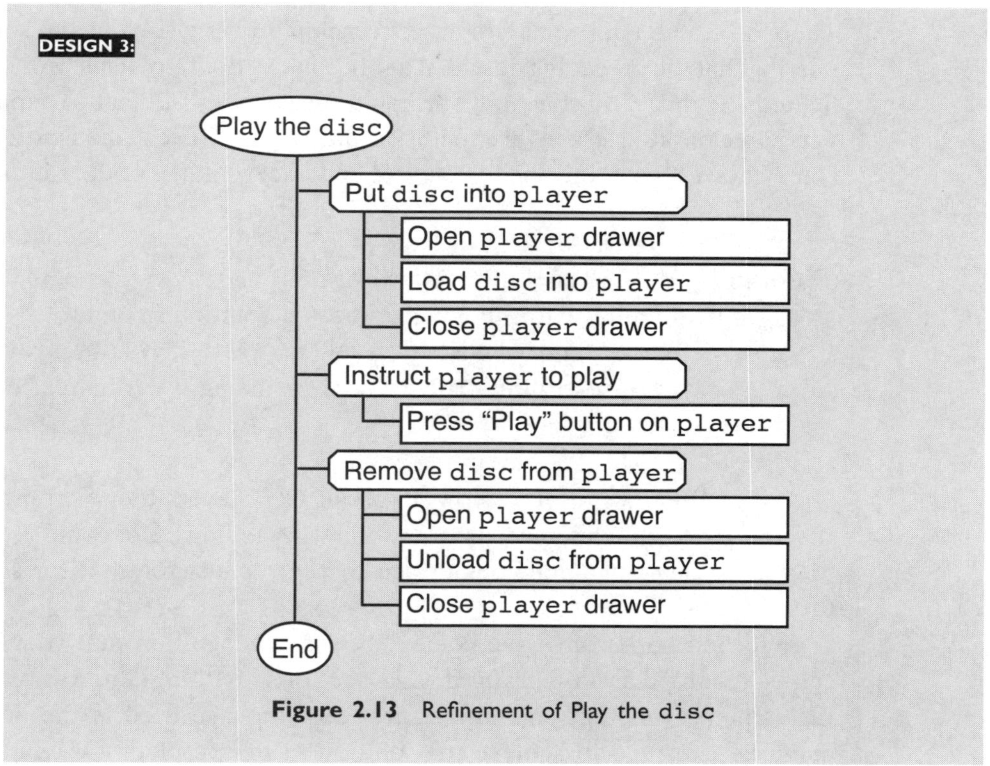

Figure 2.13 Refinement of Play the disc

In this new refinement of Play the disc the boxes from the previous design have been changed into designator boxes, and expansions of these boxes provided as part of the diagram. So for example, the step Put disc into player is now shown as being an abstract step composed from three substeps.

Because the abstract step Put `disc` into `player` is represented as a designator box, you don't execute the step Put `disc` into `player`, as well as the three substeps of Open `player` drawer, Load `disc` into `player`, and Close `player` drawer. These three substeps are a replacement for (an expansion of) the abstract step. This emphasizes the point discussed earlier (see Figure 2.9).

Given this refinement to the design, again ask yourself whether the design is now sufficient to provide a solution to the problem. If you feel the answer is still "no" then further refinement of the design diagrams is necessary. For the moment, we'll go no further. (Perhaps you can identify some steps in the above designs that are not as clear as they might be.)

Lessons for problem solving

There are some important lessons concerning problem solving and software engineering that the preceding design of a solution to the CD-playing problem has highlighted. At this early stage in your apprenticeship it's difficult to explain in detail why some of these lessons are so important. When you've gained more experience, come back to the points made below to convince yourself of their importance!

> **Lesson:** When you are faced with a problem, even one that you are familiar with, moving towards a solution in small, easily-understood steps from a high-level (abstract) view allows you to tackle (and solve) the problem without being overwhelmed.

As noted earlier, if you know all about CD players then you probably think that the preceding design steps were somewhat tedious. But could you have come up with a clear, unambiguous design to represent a solution for someone else to follow?

A second important issue comes from the recognition that your design itself can be regarded as a program. If someone (or something) knows how to generate the sequence of steps and to interpret the language used in the boxes, designs could be executed to achieve the solution to the problem. Of course, this form of program is not one a computer can execute directly, and you'll need to translate the design into a program specified in a programming language such as C++ when a software solution to a problem is required.

Designs are meant primarily for human interpretation (for example, so a software engineer can produce C++ code from a design), but nevertheless a human can "execute" an algorithm represented by a design to check whether any ambiguities or errors can be detected.

It's better from a software engineering point of view to detect errors at an early stage, before code has been produced. Can you think of any reasons why this might be so?

One reason is that trying to find errors by examining the code suffers from the "separating the forest from the trees" problem. Having translated the faulty design into a faulty C++ program, there will be much more low-level detail in the program than there was in the design, and hence the original design fault will have been obscured and will be much more difficult to find. Another reason is cost-related, in that it will require much more work to throw some code away, go back to the design, fix the design and reengineer the relevant parts of the C++ program, compared to the cost of fixing the design before the code was produced (which means there was no code to discard).

Later in this chapter we discuss some of the types of errors that might exist in a design. For the moment, the following lesson should be learned:

Lesson: Check a design for faults by hand-executing it, that is, by going through the program represented by the design in the sequence specified by the design.

Is the design in Figures 2.12 and 2.13 specific to one particular model of CD player, or is it more general than that? Of course, it's the latter, since the CD player type designed captures features common to most CD players. You could have designed a solution for one specific manufacturer's model, but a more general design is desirable. A specific implementation of a design will have to be more closely targeted at a specific model, but such a level of detail does not necessarily have to be shown in a design, and certainly not in the early stages of a design when the detail is likely to obscure matters.

Note also that if you were required to translate the design into a computer program, there's nothing in the design that relates it to a specific programming language. This is a good feature of a design. It has to be based on some overall programming paradigms that will also be part of the programming language, but it should be at a higher level of abstraction than programming language details, and should thus be language independent. When you don't know any C++ details, this is easy to achieve. However, even after you have learned some C++ you should try to keep C++ specific details out of your designs.

> **Lesson:** Designs should be general and abstract, and independent of any programming language.

When should you stop designing and start implementing a design in a programming language? The easy answer is:

> **Lesson:** Stop refining your designs when it's relatively easy to translate your design into programming language statements.

The difficult part is to define what is "relatively easy." The definition depends on many factors, such as:

- your experience;
- your familiarity with the problem;
- your familiarity with the programming language to be used;
- your familiarity with other things in your software engineer's toolbag, such as the existence of types or other software components you could reuse;
- how closely you've read this book :-).

What is relatively difficult now may become relatively easy after you've gained some experience, and thus the way you tackle a design is likely to change over time.

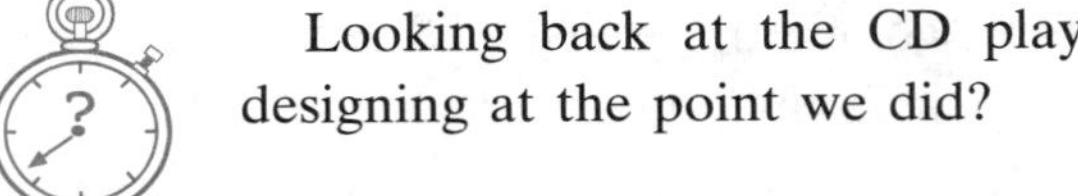

Looking back at the CD player problem, why do you think we stopped designing at the point we did?

One reason is that we felt the design was "good enough" for its purpose. Another reason is that the steps identified as the final abstractions match the operations identified earlier as appropriate for a CD player type (compare Figures 2.4 and 2.5). Given this type there is no need to provide further details in the design. Also note that the existence of the type made the design relatively straightforward.

> **Lesson:** Appropriate types help with problem solving and design.

As you gain familiarity with programming, you'll gain confidence in your ability to translate higher-level (more abstract) design steps into programming language statements without further design refinements. This may be highlighted in some student groups, where those who have programmed before may produce designs much faster than those who have not. If you are a relative novice, don't worry. Those who think they know it all may even believe they don't need to bother with a design at all. Such a strategy is doomed to failure!

Lesson: Always produce a design for a problem you're trying to solve before you start writing a program.

Finally, you should note that there may be many different possible designs and algorithms to solve a particular problem. This is perhaps not obvious for the CD player problem, since it was chosen because it leads to an obvious design. However, for more complex problems there may be several designs that all lead to perfectly acceptable solutions.

Lesson: There may be several different designs and algorithms that solve a particular problem.

One of the attractions of designing software systems is the level of innovation that can be applied to solving a problem; it's rare that you can look up the answer in a book, and it can be very satisfying to come up with your own solution to a problem.

However, if there are alternatives how do you decide which is "the best"? This is where software engineering comes in; you'll have to determine which is the best algorithm for a particular problem or set of data by applying engineering considerations to your design; for example, asking yourself if a particular design will produce a program which has a fast enough execution time. We'll return to the lesson to be learned from this in a later section of this chapter.

CD-playing program in C++

Although the CD-playing problem requested a program for a human to execute, given the availability of the right types it's relatively straightforward to implement the final design in C++. A program that does this is shown below in Figure 2.14. We haven't covered any C++ statements yet, so some of the details in this (incomplete) program may look rather strange to you. You aren't expected to understand the code yet. However, understanding all of the C++ details is not the point here. What you should be able to recognize is some similarity between the C++ code and the designs given earlier and be able to relate various lines in the C++ program to the equivalent parts of the design.

IMPLEMENTATION:

```
CDPlayer  myPlayer;
CDisc     aDisc;

myPlayer.on();               // Power On
                             // Play disc
                                 // Put disc into player
myPlayer.open();                     // Open drawer
myPlayer.load(aDisc);                // Load disc
myPlayer.close();                    // Close drawer
                                 // Instruct player to play
myPlayer.play();                     // Press "Play" button
                                 // Remove disc from player
myPlayer.open();                     // Open drawer
aDisc = myPlayer.unload();           // Unload disc
myPlayer.close();                    // Close drawer
myPlayer.off();              // Power off
```

Figure 2.14 C++ implementation of the Play a CD design

Summary

Look back at the key top-down design steps that were identified in Figure 2.3. These are the steps you've applied to solve this CD-playing problem. Components useful for solving the problem were identified, namely *types*, *objects*, and *functional abstractions* that permitted the algorithm to be developed in a top-down fashion until a suitably detailed sequence of steps emerged. Your first design: congratulations!

We'll have a lot more to say about types, as they're fundamental to object-oriented software. But before we do that, let's identify some further useful control-flow abstractions.

EXERCISES FOR SECTION 2.3

1 Identify any types, objects and functional abstractions used in the recipe and car repair programs in Figure 1.3.

2 While you haven't yet been introduced to any C++ language details, can you identify any types, objects and functional abstractions in Figure 2.14?

3 Design functional components for the following problems:

(a) Convert a weight in pounds to a weight in kilograms (assume there are 2.2 pounds in a kilogram).
(b) Convert a height given in feet and inches to a height in meters (feet can be converted to meters by multiplying by 0.3048).
(c) The older generation of people in the UK still think of their weight in terms of stones and pounds, where there are 14 pounds in one stone. Convert a weight in this form to a weight in kilograms.

For each of these problems identify any types you think will be used.

4 Construct a design using the design notation that specifies the sequence of steps that someone must follow to make a telephone call. You should use the telephone type you designed in Exercise 2 in Section 2.2. Assume that the telephone number is given.

2.4 MORE COMPLEX CONTROL-FLOW ABSTRACTIONS

It's useful to introduce some more complex control-flow abstractions and their design notation, as these allow us to examine problems with more complex solutions and designs.

So far, we've only considered simple sequences of steps. However, such simple flows of control are very limiting by themselves. Additional constructs are needed to cover situations such as executing part of an algorithm only if some condition is true, and for repeating parts of an algorithm. We need additional control-flow abstractions and appropriate design notations for:

1. Selection.
2. Repetition.

Selection

Consider the two lists of instructions (programs) shown in Figure 2.15. Both programs have the characteristic that the execution of some of the instructions is dependent upon some condition. If you're executing these programs, you first have to evaluate the appropriate condition to see whether it's true or false. The result of that evaluation then dictates which instructions are executed and which are not.

If the pancakes are to be stored, wrap in foil. Otherwise, slice the lemon and then ...	If the oil is at or below the MIN mark on the dipstick, add 1 litre of oil

Figure 2.15 Selection statements

This is a very common programming paradigm. You'll be making use of this kind of behavior in many designs and programs, and you need a design notation to capture the concept.

Design notation

An extension of the control-flow design notation for capturing selection is shown in Figure 2.16. The step representing the condition is shown as a rectangular box with an output path leading down to the diamond-shaped **decision box**. If the condition evaluates to "yes" the boxes on the path labeled YES are to be followed;

if the condition evaluates to "no" the boxes on the path labeled NO are to be followed (if there are any such boxes). Only one of the paths emanating from the decision box is selected.

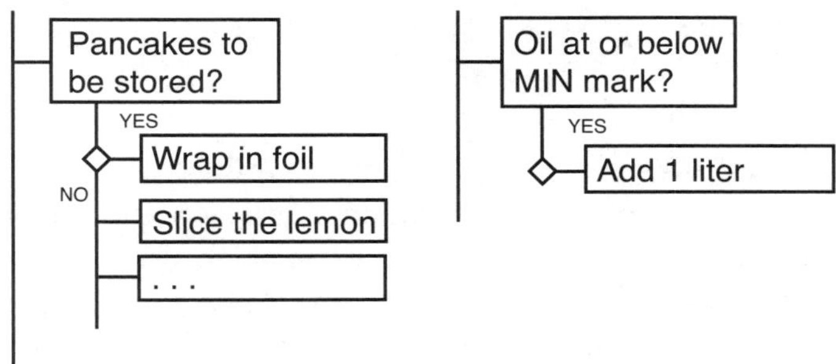

Figure 2.16 Examples of selection design notation

EXAMPLE:

Figure 2.17 gives an example design (of a meaningless algorithm) to test your understanding of the selection design notation. What steps are executed if `number` has the value 3?

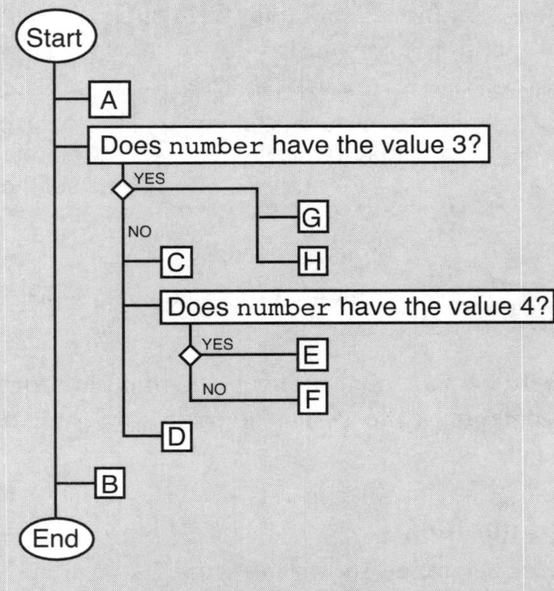

Figure 2.17 Selection design example

When `number` has the value 3, the following sequence of steps is executed:

A; Does `number` have the value 3? (answer YES); G; H; B;

where a semicolon ";" is used to separate the steps.

Repetition

Another common programming paradigm and form of control-flow abstraction comes from the requirement to be able to repeat a set of instructions a number of times. You could achieve this behavior by replicating the instructions the number of times required; for instance, you could extend the previous design for playing one CD to produce one for playing ten CDs by replicating the appropriate part of the design ten times. However, providing a control-flow abstraction for this situation is much more appropriate, especially if the number of repetitions required is not known in advance.

EXAMPLE:

Such a situation is illustrated by Figure 2.18(a), where the step continue to mix is continued while a condition (the mixture is lumpy) is true. Figure 2.18(b) demonstrates another form of repetition, where the number of times the repetition steps must occur is known.

While the mixture is lumpy continue to mix it.	For each of the 4 spark plugs clean the electrodes set the gap to 0.025 in
(a)	(b)

Figure 2.18 Two forms of repetition statement

Repetition statements are very common in programming, so you need further enhancements to the design notation to permit these paradigms to be clearly expressed.

Design notation

The design notation shown in Figure 2.19 can be used to express the two kinds of repetition identified by the examples in Figure 2.18. The notation in Figure 2.19(a), called a **while** repetition abstraction, is used to capture the idea that

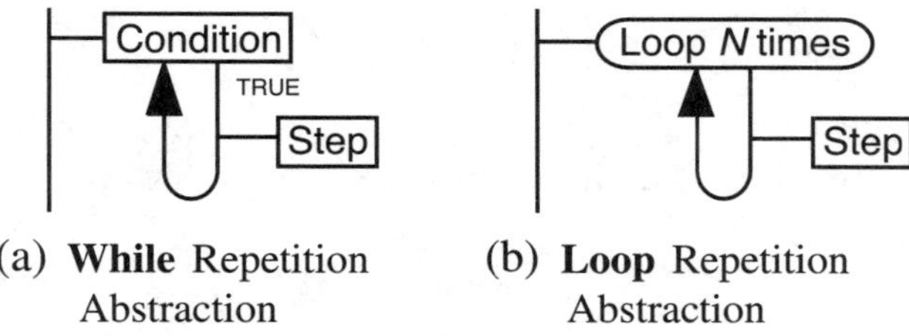

(a) **While** Repetition Abstraction

(b) **Loop** Repetition Abstraction

Figure 2.19 Repetition design notations

some steps need to be repeated while some condition is true, as indicated by the word TRUE appearing on the output path from the condition box. When the condition becomes false the repetition is terminated. This behavior may be contrasted with that represented by the notation in Figure 2.19(b) that captures the idea that some steps have to be repeated a fixed number of times. This is called a **loop** repetition abstraction, where the quantity *N* indicates the number of repetitions desired.

There's flexibility in how you express designs using these notations. For example, you don't have to use the word TRUE on the path from the condition box; you can use whatever makes your design clear to indicate the conditions under which the repetition proceeds. You'll see an example of this in Figure 2.22. There are some additional subtleties associated with these control-flow abstractions that will be described later. You may wonder, for example, how you use either abstraction to capture the idea of repeating an action until some condition is satisfied.

EXAMPLE:

A simple example of the use of these design notations is given in Figure 2.20 which translates the repetition statements of Figure 2.18 into the appropriate notation.

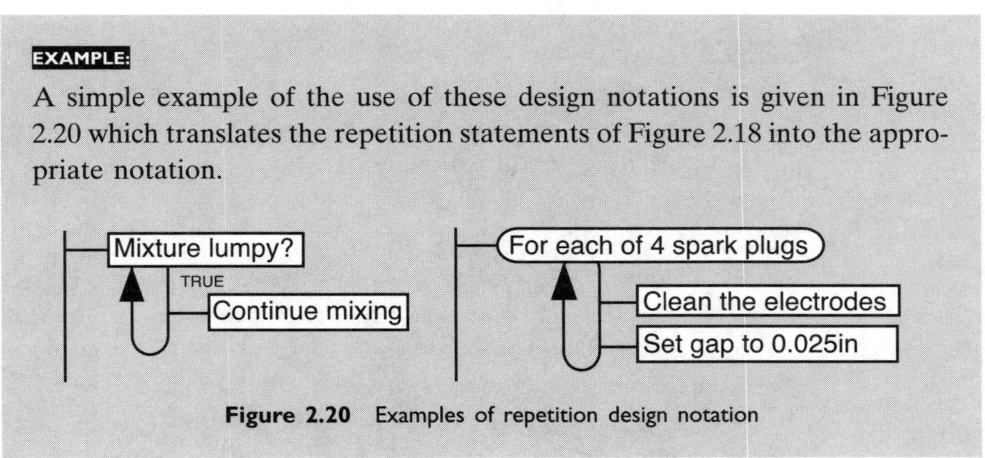

Figure 2.20 Examples of repetition design notation

EXAMPLE:

To test your understanding of loop repetition, what sequence of steps will be executed if the design in Figure 2.21 is executed and the value given to `number` is 3?

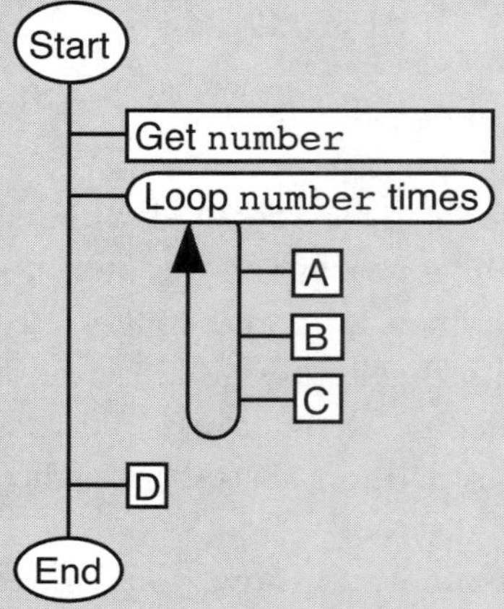

Figure 2.21 Repetition example 1

The sequence is: Get a number (3); A; B; C; A; B; C; A; B; C; D;

Here's an example of the need to repeat something until some condition becomes satisfied:

PROBLEM:

You are an instructor who has been asked to give a message to a particular student whose surname is Lee (you don't know this student). Design an algorithm to solve this problem.

DESIGN:

Figure 2.22 gives a design intended to solve this problem. This design uses a while repetition abstraction that terminates when a student with the correct name is found. Since it can't be known how many times the step Move on to next student needs to occur, a while abstraction is the appropriate repetition abstraction for this problem, with the condition indicating that the repetition continues while the student's name is not Lee.

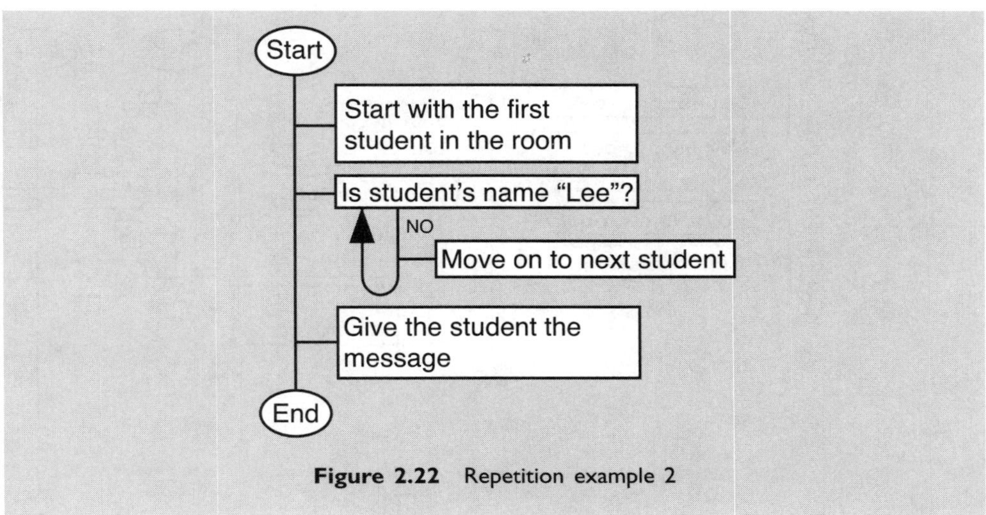

Figure 2.22 Repetition example 2

The design in Figure 2.22 may raise some questions about what some of the steps actually mean (the steps are not sufficiently descriptive). However, there are other things you should notice about this design. In particular, there are some potential faults in it that may lead to undesirable behavior if the design (or a program derived from this design) is executed. Can you identify any of these faults? Check for the answers in the next section.

EXERCISES FOR SECTION 2.4

1 Consider Figure 2.17. Work out what sequences would be executed if `number` has the values 4 and 1 respectively.

2 For each of the designs labeled **Start**, interpret the design and write out either the value of the number that's calculated or the sequence of letters produced as appropriate. When asked to supply a number *N*, use the value 15.

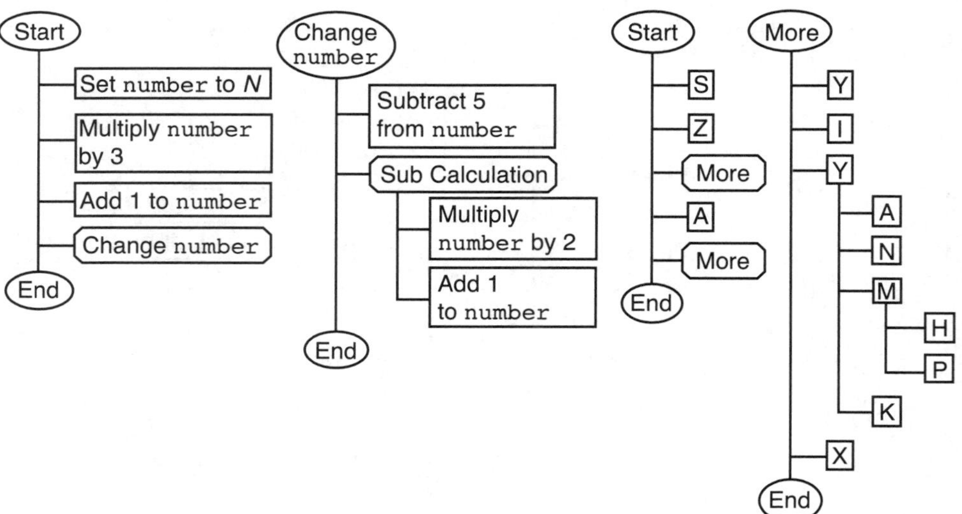

3 Design components that input a number and:

(a) if the number is odd then add one to its value;
(b) print out all multiples of the number from 1 to 12.

4 Reconsider the telephone call design you produced in Exercise 4 in Section 2.3. Change this design to deal with two additional conditions:

(a) someone else in the house is using the phone line. In this case your design should just give up trying to make the call;
(b) the number being called is busy. In this case your program should keep trying until it's successful.

5 Produce a design for making a telephone call to a person whose phone number may not be known. Produce one design that uses the directory type you designed in Exercise 6 in Section 2.2 to find the person's number, and a second design that calls the phone company's service that will get you the number. (Hint: in both cases use the component you designed in Exercise 4.)

6 Telling someone their body mass index (as defined earlier) is 22 may not be much use to them. In fact there are some medical terms that relate such values to more meaningful (abstract) concepts, defined as follows. If a person's body mass index is less than 20, they are underweight; between 20 and 25 their weight is OK; between 25 and 30 they are overweight; and above 30 they are what the medics refer to as obese. Using the design notation, design a program that asks a person for their height and weight, performs the body mass index calculation, and then prints out a message indicating their weight category.

2.5 DESIRABLE PROPERTIES FOR DESIGNS

One of the lessons highlighted in Section 2.3 was that any design you produce should be checked for faults, although we didn't identify what kinds of faults you should be checking for. With the more complex control-flow abstractions you've just seen there are several new chances for producing a wrong design.

We can identify four properties that are desirable in a design:

1. The design must produce the desired result.
2. Execution of the algorithm must terminate in a finite time.
3. The design must generate the same result given the same starting conditions; that is, it must be deterministic.
4. The design must be easily translatable into a program.

This set of properties identifies four main types of problem to look for when a design is being checked.

The first property is obvious. If the design doesn't produce the correct result then you haven't solved the problem properly.

The second property requires the algorithm to complete and to produce the results in a timely fashion. Using repetition in algorithms is one source of problem that can lead to an algorithm never terminating; for example, the use of a while repetition abstraction for which the terminating condition never becomes satisfied leads to infinite repetition of the steps inside the repetition. The second part of the property (finite time) is necessary since an algorithm that is correct but takes too long to execute isn't much use. An example would be a weather forecasting program that's required to provide a forecast for the next 24 hours but takes 48 hours to generate its results.

The third property, determinism, can be absent in computer programs, although it's not so easy to demonstrate at the design stage. An example of a design demonstrating the problem would be Figure 2.21 if the action "`Get number`" had been missed out. In this situation you couldn't predict how many times the loop would be repeated. Determinism is usually desirable, but not always necessary. Not every program needs to produce the same results each time it's executed.

EXAMPLE:

A program to draw random lines on a screen wouldn't be expected to be deterministic; a program that generates winning (random) numbers for a lottery is also required to be non-deterministic, unfortunately!

You should note, however, that computers (and compilers) rarely behave non-deterministically. When faced with a program that doesn't compile or doesn't produce the correct answers, many students will "try it again" just to see if it was the computer's fault rather than theirs. Of course, they'll get exactly the same outcome. Compile-time errors or wrong results will occur because you got something wrong, not because the computer or compiler behaved non-deterministically.

Lesson: The computer or compiler rarely lie (or behave non-deterministically).

Finally, the fourth property (that a design can be easily translated into a program) is difficult to check when you don't yet know any C++ details. But this property goes back to a point made earlier about knowing when you should stop designing in the abstract and start writing programs in a programming language. If a design you've produced is difficult to translate into programming language statements, then this probably indicates that your design is at too high a level (too abstract) and you should attempt further refinements of your design. At early stages in your apprenticeship your designs will need to specify quite a lot of detail; as you gain experience, the need to refine your designs to the same level of detail will diminish.

Lesson: Apply the four properties to each design to help you identify faults or to help you decide between alternative designs.

EXAMPLE:

To see the use of the properties in helping to uncover design errors, let's return to the design given in Figure 2.22 as a solution to the problem of finding the student in a room to give a message to. There are four main faults in this design – can the four properties above help identify these faults?

First, does the design produce the right result? The answer is: not necessarily. What would this design produce if there were two or more students named Lee in the class? If you examine the design you'll see that it may not identify the right student in this situation. This is the first main fault.

Second, does the design terminate in a finite time? It's not clear that the repetition statement expressed in the design will terminate if no student named Lee is in the room; there isn't a check that the last student in the room has been reached. This is the second main fault we're looking for. We also might be worried that the algorithm will take so long to execute that it won't have finished by the time the students have to leave the room. This is the third fault in the design.

The third property (determinism), or rather the lack of it, is demonstrated by this design, coupled with the first problem identified above. If there are two students named Lee in the class then the design could give different answers if the step Move on to next student was dependent upon where the students were sitting in the room. This is the fourth problem, although this can be eliminated by fixing the problem of there possibly being multiple Lees in the room (the first fault).

Can the algorithm be easily translated into C++? We'll have to leave answering that question until we've covered some C++ :-).

To conclude this example, think about what changes you could make to the design to fix the faults identified above.

Problem solving by brute force

The need to consider the time an algorithm may require to produce a result, and hence by implication the need to consider the time it will take a program to execute, is an important engineering consideration. Nevertheless, computers can execute millions of instructions every second, and worrying about the execution time of a program may not be appropriate for some problems.

The speed of computers can be used to advantage; it gives rise to the **brute-force** strategy for deriving a solution to a problem. This strategy, stated simply, is to work through a set of possible answers, checking to see if each possibility is the right answer to the problem. An example illustrates this strategy.

PROBLEM:

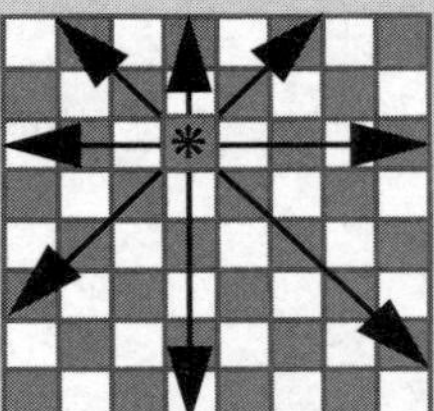

Design a program that determines whether eight queens can be placed on a chessboard such that, following the usual chess rules, no queen can capture any other queen. Chess rules, for the purpose of this problem, dictate that a queen can capture any queen that lies on a horizontal, vertical or diagonal line of squares centered on the first queen.

What strategy would you use to solve this problem? One strategy would be to think about the capture rules and to derive an algorithm for placing queens such that the rules are not violated. The brute-force approach suggests that you simply try all combinations of the placement of eight queens, and for each combination test whether that combination is a solution to the problem. The first strategy is likely to produce the more efficient (but complex) solution than the second strategy (which is simpler and hence easier to produce). But you also need to answer the following question: is the brute-force strategy feasible for execution?

To answer this question, you might care to consider the subsidiary question: ignoring the capture rules, how many ways can eight pieces be placed on a chessboard of 64 squares? The first queen can be placed on any of 64 squares, the second on any of the 63 remaining squares, and so on. For placing eight queens the total number of combinations works out to be $64 \times 63 \times 62 \times \ldots \times 57$, which evaluates to over 178 billion. You can see that the total number of possibilities for the eight queens problem is a very large number, and even if a computer could check one million possibilities a second, the program would still take 178 million seconds to execute (about five years). This solution to the problem is going to breach the second property (that is, to complete in a reasonable time) and thus is not a feasible solution.

A slightly more refined brute-force approach comes from the recognition that once a queen is placed on a row of the chessboard, no other queen can be placed on that row. This observation dramatically cuts down the total number of possibilities to 8^8, or 16.7 million, and this approach is likely to be feasible in terms of total execution time. Try Exercise 1 below. (We'll tackle the eight queens problem as a complete C++ problem in Chapter 16 after you've covered the necessary C++ language constructs.)

There are two problem-solving lessons to be remembered here:

Lesson: The brute-force approach can be an effective problem-solving strategy.

But:

Lesson: Brute-force techniques are not feasible for some problems, nor appropriate for others.

An example of the application of the brute-force problem-solving strategy is given in the next section.

EXERCISES FOR SECTION 2.5

1 Produce a design for an algorithm that solves the eight queens problem using the refined brute-force approach described above.

2 Can you think of any strategies for the eight queens problem that would reduce the total number of possibilities to be checked even further below 16.7 million?

3 Enciphering is a process that disguises text by converting the original (plain) text into an encoded form that can't be easily understood. A simple text enciphering strategy is to replace systematically every letter in the plain text by another letter; for example, replace A by Y, B by Z, C by A, . . ., Y by W, and Z by X. Given a section of text enciphered using this strategy but with unknown substitutions, outline a program that applies brute force to try to find the plain text. Is this approach likely to be feasible?

4 In general for English text, the letter E is the most frequently used letter. Adapt your outline program from Exercise 3 to use this fact so that the program can reject the results of an attempt to decipher the enciphered text if the result doesn't appear to be English.

2.6 ANOTHER PROBLEM-SOLVING EXAMPLE

The first problem-solving example tackled in earnest (the CD-playing program) didn't require much in the way of control-flow abstractions in its design. Let's examine a second problem that requires some of the more complex control-flow abstractions introduced in Section 2.4, together with an application of the brute-force problem-solving strategy.

PROBLEM:

Design a program that prints out the prime numbers that occur in the first *N* positive numbers. You may assume that the numbers 2 and 3 are prime numbers.

DESIGN:

For those who don't know (or who have forgotten) what a prime number is, it's a number that's exactly divisible only by itself and 1. Thus, 4 is not a prime number as it can be exactly divided by 2, whereas 17 is a prime number.

The first thing you need to consider is what types and objects are needed to help solve this problem. If you had a prime-number type then the solution would be relatively trivial. However, assume that there isn't such a type (there certainly isn't one in C++). Examining the problem specification doesn't provide much idea about what other types you might need, except for the idea of a *number*. Thus, you need to think some more about the algorithms you might employ to solve the problem before you can further identify any types.

Applying the brute-force approach, you might come up with a first design as shown in Figure 2.23.

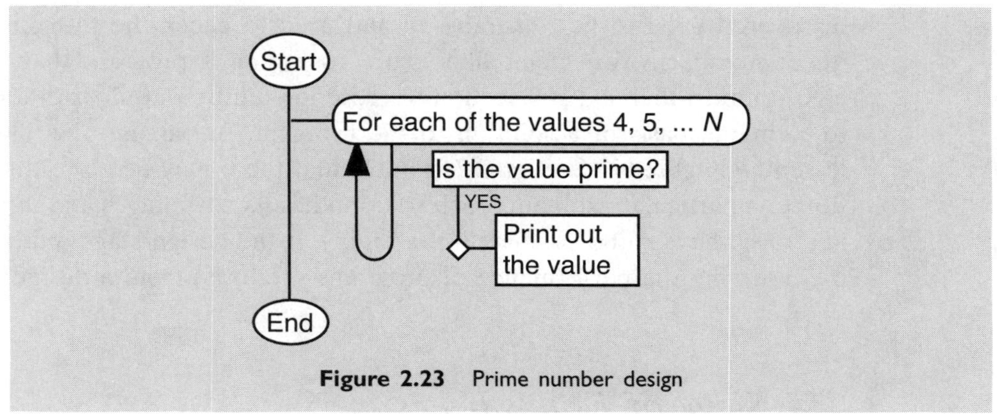

Figure 2.23 Prime number design

While Figure 2.23 captures what's needed to solve the problem, the abstract step Is the value prime? needs further elaboration, partly because this is the crux of the problem, but mainly because it doesn't provide enough detail. How do you determine if a number is prime?

One algorithm to determine whether a number i is a prime number is suggested by the definition of what a prime number is. If i can be exactly divided by any other number then it isn't prime. Thus you could try dividing i by all other numbers less than itself to see if it's prime. But can you do better than this?

This initial brute-force strategy can be refined, since you don't need to try dividing i by all other numbers:

Refinement 1: you don't need to try any number greater than the square root of i (since if i is divisible then at least one of its factors must be less than or equal to the square root of i);

Refinement 2: if i is exactly divisible by some factor then it must be divisible by at least one of the prime numbers that are less than the square root of i.

We'd like to claim credit for these refinements, but others have beaten us to it. In particular, refinement 1 is due to Leonardo of Pisa (who is otherwise known as Fibonacci; you may have heard of his number series 1, 1, 2, 3, 5, 8, . . . where the next term in the series is obtained by adding the previous two terms).

Note that an algorithm based on refinement 2 would be partly defined in terms of itself; that is, you need to work up from the small numbers towards the high numbers determining which numbers are prime, and the prime numbers discovered need to be remembered and used to check the primality of subsequent numbers. You might like to try to design a program that follows this algorithm. In the next sub-section we describe a different algorithm that's going to form the basis of a solution to the problem. In passing, this illustrates the lesson highlighted in Section 2.3, namely that there may be more than one solution to a particular problem. Each solution has its advantages and disadvantages, and these have to be evaluated, preferably at the design stage, but maybe even by observing the performance of programs produced from a design.

The Sieve of Eratosthenes

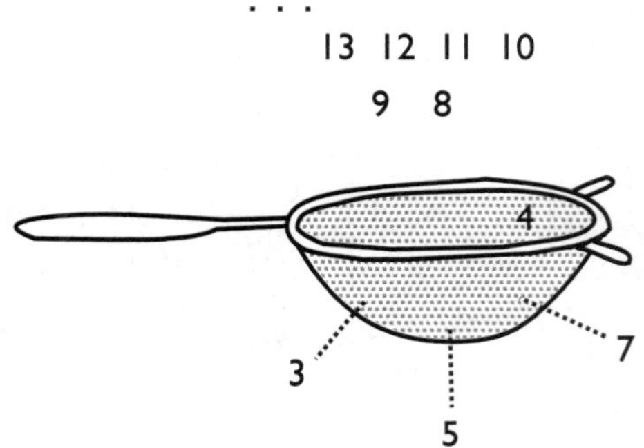

The following brute-force algorithm for determining the primality of a number is due to the mathematician Eratosthenes from the 3rd century BC. The algorithm is based on canceling out numbers that cannot be primes from a list of possible numbers, such that the numbers left uncanceled are the prime numbers.

The operation of Eratosthenes' algorithm is illustrated in Figure 2.24. The list of numbers being examined is shown in (a). Given the assumption that 2 is a prime number, the algorithm proceeds by canceling all numbers in the list that 2 is a factor of. These numbers are identified by "hopping" down the list in a step size of 2, and canceling out the number encountered. This process is shown in (b). When the end of the list is reached with a step size of 2, the algorithm repeats, starting with the next uncanceled number in the list (3), and hopping down the list with a step size of 3, as shown in (c). The algorithm is repeated until there are no further numbers left to cancel, and the remaining numbers in the list are the required prime numbers.

The canceling of the "next" number from the list has to be terminated at some point. Above we suggest terminating when there are no further numbers left to cancel. However, one of the refinements identified above could also be applied to indicate this terminating condition. Similarly, one of the refinements could also be used to terminate the "hopping" down the list activity before the end of the list has been reached. Both changes would result in a more efficient algorithm, as they would eliminate unnecessary processing. However, to keep things

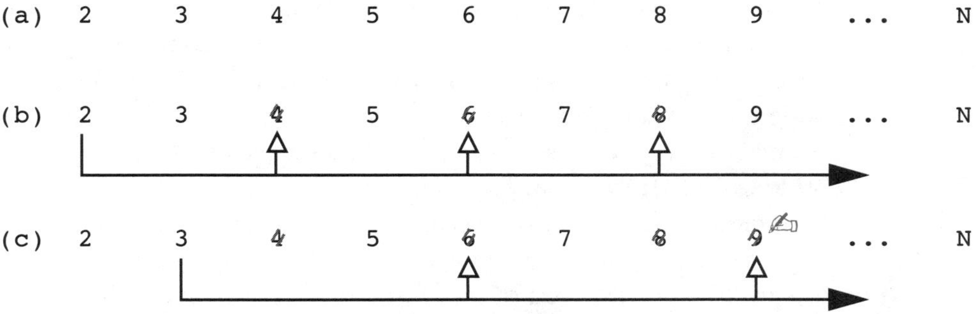

Figure 2.24 Sieve of Eratosthenes

simple at this early stage in your apprenticeship, we'll leave these refinements out of the designs coming up. Try changing the following designs to take account of these refinements.

Design for the Sieve

Examination of the Sieve algorithm suggests that you need a number type as well as a type to contain the list of numbers. Clearly the container type will use the memory of the computer to retain the values of interest. You also need to indicate the difference between canceled and uncanceled numbers.

Before trying to identify further any operations required for types "number" and "container", let's derive some designs for the algorithm. A first design is illustrated in Figure 2.25.

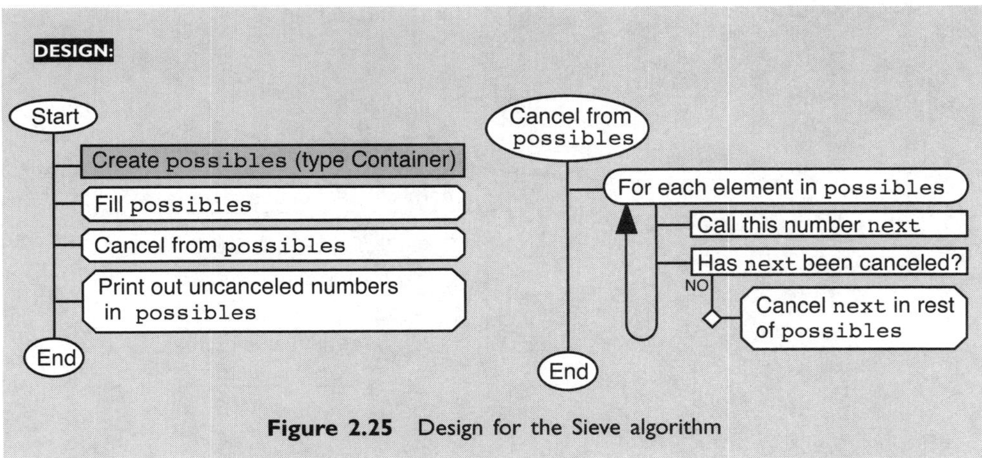

Figure 2.25 Design for the Sieve algorithm

This first design for the Sieve starts by creating an object for the algorithm to manipulate. This object is an instance of the container type, and since we need to express "do something to the container object" several times in the design, it's useful to provide a name to identify this object: `possibles` (`courier font` is used to highlight these names). Names have been given to other objects for the same reason.

Some of the steps in the design given in Figure 2.25 have already been identified as designator boxes, indicating that their expansion is required (and some are given later). But you should first check that the design has the desired properties identified in the previous section. Also, note the use of the loop repetition abstraction that goes through each element in `possibles`.

The remaining parts of the design are given in Figures 2.26 and 2.27. (Some of the designator boxes in these figures have been left as an exercise for you to design.)

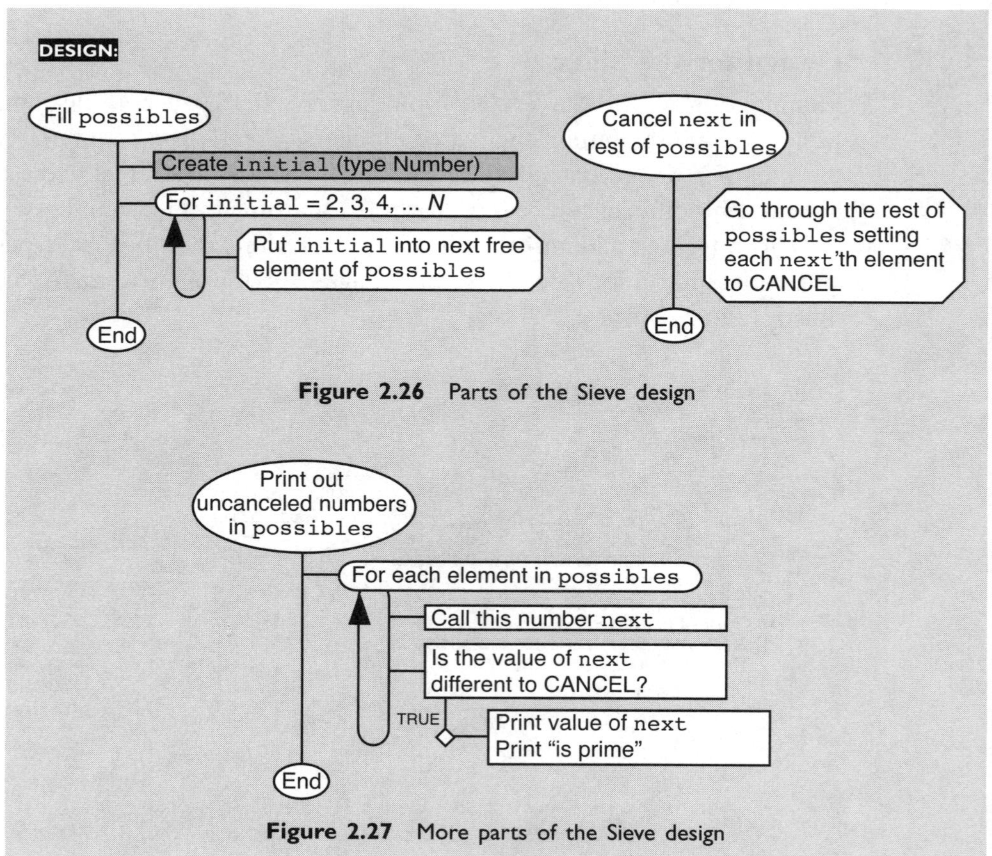

Figure 2.26 Parts of the Sieve design

Figure 2.27 More parts of the Sieve design

Types for the Sieve

As there is now more detail of the design for the program, you can again examine the types needed, and the operations that these types need to provide. From studying Figures 2.26 and 2.27, it should be apparent that the operations that the container type must provide are those shown in Figure 2.28(a).

Examination of the designs also suggests that a number type is needed to represent the *N* positive numbers being tested for primality. You need to create instances of these numbers, and an addition operator is required to enable the sequence of values 2, 3, . . . *N* to be generated. You also need to represent the abstract value CANCEL expressed in the design. Knowing that 0 is not used in this problem, you can use it to represent a canceled number. A comparison operation is then needed so the final list of numbers can be checked for the prime numbers, and a printing operation is required to print out those numbers. This leads to the interface for the Number type shown in Figure 2.28 (b).

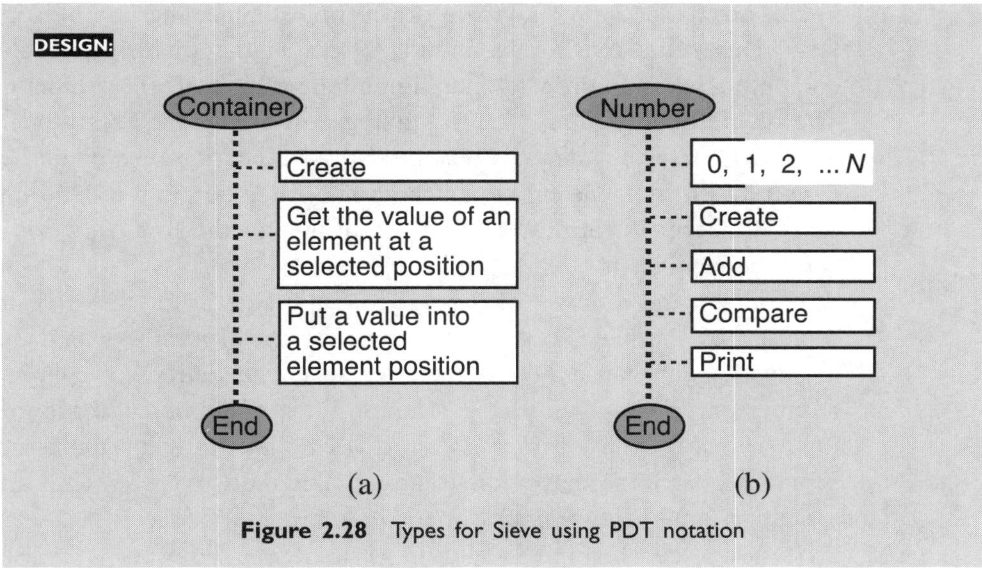

Figure 2.28 Types for Sieve using PDT notation

At this point, you should be able to check the design to see if it's correct. (The C++ program that implements this design is examined briefly in Chapter 3 and in more depth in Chapter 14 when the array data structure has been introduced.)

Note that the Number type has all of the properties of a type discussed in Section 2.2. The type defines a set of operations and a set of abstract values. An instance of this type will have a particular abstract value (for example, the value 3).

While the Sieve design only uses the addition operator, a swift look at your pocket calculator will suggest some additional operations that a Number type could support; you might even think of a slightly different type that provides different mathematical features (hint: not all numbers are positive, or even whole). As you'll see, more than one number type is provided in C++, and details of these are given in Chapter 5.

Software engineering considerations for the Sieve

Why should you use the Sieve algorithm for determining primes, as opposed to some other algorithm? Any algorithm inevitably has pros and cons, and these have to be evaluated in an engineering sense to determine whether the algorithm is appropriate. Such evaluations of necessity depend upon your experience.

One advantage of the Sieve algorithm is that it doesn't need to use a divide operation; the action of hopping down the list canceling numbers performs this task. This turns out to be an advantage as the divide operation on many computers takes an order of magnitude longer than other arithmetic operations. The divide operation is still fast (taking only microseconds to evaluate), but if a problem involves many divides the overall execution time could be a problem. If you had to find the primes in the first 50 numbers, the divide time wouldn't be of concern. If you had to find the primes in the first 5 million numbers, it could be significant.

However, the removal of the need for a divide in the Sieve design has been replaced by the need to store the complete list of numbers, and this may be a disadvantage because of the memory space needed on a computer. If each number occupies 4 bytes, as is common, then you'd need 20 Mbytes of storage for a list of 5 million numbers alone. (This illustrates a common trade-off in program design: the space/time trade-off. You'll discover that you can often trade execution time in a program for increased memory space.)

As you'll see when the Sieve design is implemented in C++, the list of numbers doesn't actually need to be stored. In effect a single bit can be used to represent each possible number, reducing the space requirements by a factor of 32 on a computer using 4 bytes (32 bits) for storing each number.

EXERCISES FOR SECTION 2.6

1 Complete the design for the Sieve program by adding additional detail to the design component `Cancel next in rest of possibles`. Several designs are possible depending on the way you choose to terminate the canceling sequence.

2 Can you think of a way in which the memory requirements of the Sieve algorithm (for storing the list of numbers) can be halved, or reduced further still?

3 An alternative Sieve algorithm for finding prime numbers works as follows. As each prime number is found, it's added to the end of a list of all prime numbers found so far. Each new number is then checked to see whether it's exactly divisible by each prime number in the list. If it's not divisible, the new number is also prime and is added to the end of the list. Numbers that aren't prime "fall out" of this sieve and you're left with a list of the prime numbers at the end. Design a program that follows this algorithm. Identify the space/time trade-offs of this algorithm compared with the algorithm presented above.

2.7 TYPES REVISITED

Because of the importance of types in the approach we're taking to problem solving and in the object-oriented approach to programming, it's worth summarizing what you've learned so far about types and objects.

Types: in general terms

A type characterizes the behavior of all objects that are instances of the type. This characterization includes:

1. The set of "things you can do to" (or operations on) objects that are instances of the type.
2. The total set of abstract values that instances can take.

These two characteristics define the **interface** of the type – the characteristics that a user of the type can make use of.

Thus a type is a software component providing a data abstraction; details of how a type is actually implemented can be hidden so that the complexity of the implementation need not be known by a user of the type. The user can simply concentrate on using a type via its interface. A type provides an abstraction (or model) of the behavior of the objects that are instances of the type. Note also that in order to be able to talk about a type, or to use a type, it's necessary for a type to have a name by which you can refer to it (like CD Player).

An **object** is an instance of a type. The "things you can do to" that object are defined by the type of the object, and the object has an abstract state that is one of the values from the set defined by the type. An object's state may be changed through the application of operations (supported by the type) to the object. An object must have a name so that it can be identified and hence manipulated.

EXAMPLE:

Real-world examples of types and instances abound. Try listing some types and instances of these types. For example, a car could be a type; what is its interface, and how do you separate the notion of a car type from the idea of an instance of a car?

It's important to observe that in the real world new types continue to get invented. We're not constrained to having to operate with a fixed set of types. CDs are an example of a new type that has been invented relatively recently. Instances of such types don't contain anything new; after all they have to be constructed from existing things. But providing a new type to describe some new abstraction is useful, otherwise we'd have to talk about "a shiny disk of material that contains invisible data in the form of 0s and 1s that magically can be used to represent music . . ." rather than saying "it's a CD."

The importance of abstraction cannot be over-emphasized. Abstraction is the key feature in software engineering. The usefulness of type abstractions in the real world is something that is important to replicate in the software engineering world.

Types: in programming language terms

Given that a design makes use of types and objects, it makes sense that these types and objects are carried forward into the implementation of the design in a programming language. If this isn't easy then you haven't satisfied the fourth property identified earlier – namely that a design must be easily translatable into a program.

So, where do the types that can be used in a programming language come from?

Most programming languages define a set of **built-in types**. These types are an integral part of the programming language; they are built into the language definition, and hence are understood by the compiler of that programming language.

EXAMPLES:

Examples of built-in types include the types that represent numbers such as integers (for example, 34, -197, 0, 32767) and decimals (for example, 3.14159, -0.0000345, 129342543.35). Most programming languages provide such number types, and thus programs that use only these types can be written without the programmer having to worry where the types come from and how they are implemented.

In many older programming languages (such as Pascal, Fortran 77, Basic) these built-in types are basically all you get. Such languages give you little or no support for defining new type abstractions relevant to the problem being solved. All problems have to be mapped into a solution involving just the built-in types. This is a bit like trying to define a CD-playing program by dealing with all of the separate hardware components directly. Not very easy! There has to be a better way.

Types: in C++ terms

Modern programming languages like C++ allow the software engineer to design and introduce new data type components to help implement a solution to the problem being tackled. Since such types can be defined by a programmer, we'll refer to them as **Programmer-Defined Types (PDTs)**. Once defined, these new types can be used in a program as if they were built-in types; that is, a programmer need not be aware of the difference between the built-in types and the programmer-defined types.

Defining new types is basically extending the programming language to suit the problem at hand. The closer the language is to the problem domain, the easier it's going to be to write programs that are solutions to problems in that domain.

Of course, at some stage the new PDTs themselves have to be implemented. They have to be constructed out of the programming language statements and the types already defined (both built-in and programmer-defined). Fortunately, this task can be completely divorced from the task of writing the program that solves a problem. This clear separation permits the complexity of constructing a type to be removed completely from the problem of constructing a solution using that type. With this separation, the complexity can be made more manageable – essentially:

Complexity of problem solution	=	Complexity of type definitions	+	Complexity of program

Without this clear separation, the complexity is likely to be more like:

Complexity of problem solution	=	Complexity of type definitions	×	Complexity of program

If types provide useful abstractions that can be separated from any program using those abstractions then you can *reuse* those types, once defined, in other programs. One of the main problems with software engineering in the past has been the need to "reinvent the wheel" for every new problem. This was often due to the difficulty of separating out type abstractions from the rest of a program in the older programming languages. This aspect of software reuse is a key problem in software engineering, which languages like C++ can help tackle. Types are components to load into your toolbag.

PDT notation

In Section 2.2 we informally introduced a notation for representing the interface provided by the type CD player. You can use this notation for representing any type, to express some of the details of the interface provided by the type. The general form of the notation is given in Figure 2.29.

In general terms, a type is identified by a name, and the interface provided by the type is described by the abstract value set and the four boxes identified in Figure 2.29. You may find the terms used in these boxes (constructors, etc.) a little strange at first. These terms are the actual terms used in later chapters where you begin using and constructing PDTs in C++. Eventually a PDT's interface has to be described completely in C++ terms (so it can be used in C++ programs), but such a description involves language details not yet covered. For the moment, these C++ terms capture the following ideas.

Constructors These are concerned with creating objects that are an instance of the type. Acquire a CD player is an example from the CD player type.

Member Functions These are the functions provided by the type, that is, the

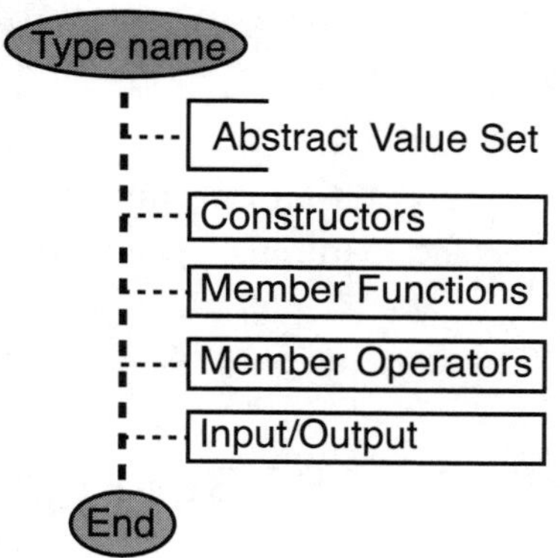

Figure 2.29 PDT interface notation

operations that can be applied to instances of the type – the "things you can do to" instances (for example, Switch on).

Member Operators These are also operations provided by the type, with a slightly different way of writing them. You haven't seen any operators yet, but the standard mathematical symbols such as + and × are examples.

Input/Output These are also operations. They allow you to input values to objects, and to output the value of an object (for example, to print a number, as in the Sieve design).

These four groupings give the general categories into which the features provided by a PDT's interface can be fitted. The ability to create an object by using a constructor is clearly fundamental. However, it isn't a requirement that all PDTs have features that map into all of the other sections. For example, the CD player description (see Figure 2.5) doesn't have the Member Operators or Input/Output sections.

With the control-flow notation, any rectangular box can be changed into a designator box and additional information provided. Such expansions can also be used with PDT designs. Examples of this can be found in Chapter 5 which gives the PDT notations for a number of C++ types that you'll be using.

EXERCISE FOR SECTION 2.7

1 In Exercise 3 in Section 2.2 you designed a pocket calculator type. Recast that design into the PDT notation introduced above, identifying which of the various categories each of the features of your type fits into (constructors, member functions, etc.).

2.8 TYPES IN PROBLEM SOLVING AND DESIGN

Types and objects are (or should be) used extensively in problem solving and design. A solution to a problem will consist of a design capturing the creation and manipulation of a set of objects, together with the identification of appropriate types for each object. A design, and programs that follow from the design, don't manipulate the types themselves; only objects that are instances of types are manipulated by the design/programs.

Identifying types is clearly an important part of problem solving. So, how do you do that?

A simple approach to identifying types

The following informal approach to identifying types is based on that described by Abbott (1983). The idea of this approach is to examine an English description of the problem or a design, looking for syntactic elements that are indicative of the need for a type or object. The main elements to be searched for, and what they suggest, are as follows.

Syntactic element	**Suggests**
Common nouns	Types
Proper nouns	Objects
Verbs, predicates and descriptive expressions	Operations
Attributes	Abstract values

Before we examine these elements in more detail (in case you've forgotten what a noun is) it's worth stressing the importance of the word "suggest" in this list. There are no hard-and-fast rules for applying this informal technique; English is never used in a manner precise enough to make the rules more than suggestions. Indeed, the main problem with the approach is the flexibility with which English can be used in a descriptive manner. Nevertheless, if these syntactic elements can be identified, the approach provides you with an algorithm to apply in identifying types and objects. Let's examine these syntactic elements in more detail.

A **noun** (or noun-clause) is a word (or clause) used to name something. Because of the descriptive nature of the use of English, distinguishing different types of nouns can be difficult.

Common nouns are nouns that apply to all members of a class of things, and thus suggest types. These nouns are often used with the indefinite article "a/an," or "this," or "every." Common nouns are also used in the possessive form; for instance, Samantha's CD player indicates that Samantha (a proper noun) owns an instance of a common noun (type) CD player.

One way you can determine whether a noun *xxx* is a common noun is to try the following questions. Can you say "A/An *xxx*"? Or can you ask "What is a/an *xxx?*" If the answer to such questions is "yes" then the noun is probably a common noun.

Proper nouns have some idea of identity associated with them, implying a specific instance and hence an object. Often proper nouns are used with the definite article "the," or via a direct reference using "my" or "this." The possessive form is a proper noun, although it implies a common noun too; Samantha's CD player is a proper noun (the CD player that belongs to Samantha) but, as you've seen, also implies the common noun CD player.

EXAMPLE:

Which of the following nouns are common nouns or proper nouns: student; the date; C++; a chair; car; CD player; Monday; bank account; the chair; programming language; the student's name; teachers; my car; a bank; the count of the number of people; this prime number.

Proper nouns that identify objects must have some idea of type associated with them. This association can be expressed as an "is-a" relationship that can help separate proper and common nouns. This relationship can be used to ask a question to help identify this separation. If you can say that "*xxx* is-a *yyy*" then *xxx* is an object and *yyy* is its type.

EXAMPLE:

Samantha's player is-a CD player; my car is-a Ford; Donald is-a merganser; the name is-a noun; Hexham is-a town.

Verbs are those parts of a sentence concerned with actions, and hence verbs identify operations.

Predicates are relationships between two objects, often giving rise to a yes/no answer.

Descriptive expressions are expressions that describe additional properties associated with the noun to which they are applied.

Attributes are qualities or properties of the thing to which they are being applied.

EXAMPLE:

Verbs: *add* the two prices together; *load* the CD.

Predicates: if the two dates *are the same* (a comparison operation).

Descriptive expressions: the *earliest* time; the *most expensive* price; the *same* time (also implying comparison operations).

Attributes: The graph can be drawn in four colors: *RED*, *GREEN*, *BLUE* and *YELLOW*; the *canceled* number; the CD player is *OFF*; the CD player is *ON* and a disc has been *LOADED*.

Again, it must be emphasized that the approach is informal, and the syntactic elements you're searching for in a real English description of a problem or its design are often not as easily identified as the above might suggest.

Components of types

When analyzing descriptions it's important to note that proper nouns are often used in a manner that identifies the object as being a "part-of" some type. Thus the analysis will identify not only the types needed in a problem solution, but may also begin to indicate what the constituent parts of those types are.

Various key words in the description can point out such part-of relationships directly: "is part of . . ." (obviously), "contains," "encloses," and "includes" are all obvious pointers. Sometimes phrases like "the balance of an account" are encountered: the indefinite preposition "an" indicating a common noun and hence a possible type (for example, an account) while the phrase "the balance of" suggests that the object "balance" is a part of an account.

Such part-of relationships often identify characteristics that are part of the interface of the type; for example, showing that part of the abstract state of an account type is the balance. Although the analysis of the words would suggest that "the balance" should be regarded as an object in its own right (with its own type and operations), you have to ask the question whether an object really appears as part of the interface of the enclosing type (account), or whether it should just be regarded as an abstract component.

EXAMPLE:

A complex number[2] has a real part and an imaginary part, both of which are decimal numbers. You can perform the standard mathematical operations of addition, subtraction, multiplication and division with complex numbers, and the values of the real and imaginary parts can be extracted.

The above description identifies two types (complex number and decimal number) and potentially two objects (real part and imaginary part) that are instances of decimal numbers. The real and imaginary parts are abstract parts-of a complex number. Note the importance of the word abstract here. While the abstraction of a complex number object having real and imaginary parts must be supported, there's no requirement that an implementation of the type actually uses two decimal numbers to hold these abstract parts – the type implementer could decide to use polar representation[3] for the actual implementation of complex numbers. Whichever implementation is chosen, a type designer should be careful to separate interface issues from implementation issues, and part-of relationships are where the potential for confusion may arise.

[2] If you don't know what a complex number is, think instead about representing a point on a graph that requires both x and y coordinates to identify it.

[3] A complex number can be represented in polar coordinates by a distance r and an angle θ.

Often part-of relationships have to appear in a type's interface, since access to the parts may be required. In the complex number example, it's required that the value of the real and imaginary parts can be extracted. In situations like this it's better to provide access to the abstract parts that the type is comprised of via operations provided by the type, rather than give the appearance of allowing direct access to internal components of a type. Thus, the PDT for the complex number type should be designed as shown in Figure 2.30, where the extraction of the real and imaginary parts is provided by member functions.

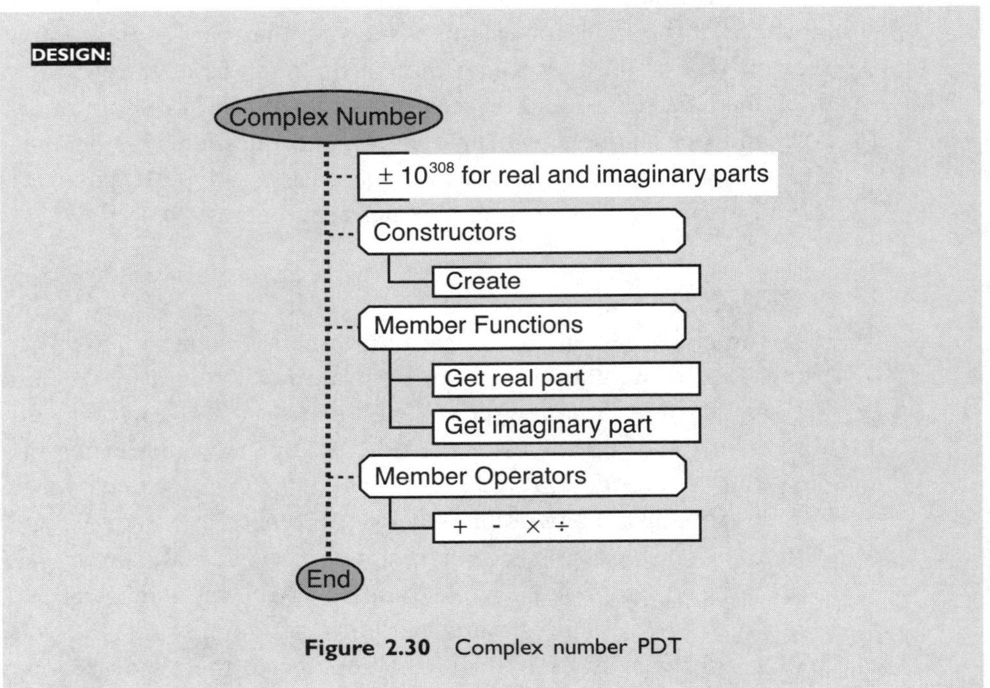

Figure 2.30 Complex number PDT

Let's go through a problem specification trying to analyze the English in order to identify types and objects that can be used to help solve the problem. In the following description the first occurrence of each of the important common nouns is highlighted using *italics*, proper nouns using <u>*underlined italics*</u>, verbs, predicates and descriptive expressions using **bold**, and attributes using <u>**underlined bold**</u>.

PROBLEM:

The Fiddlers Bank has decided to computerize its customers' accounts, and has provided the following description of the way accounts are used. (The Fiddlers Bank is a much simplified version of a real bank, so base your PDT designs on the information provided in the description below, rather than anything you know about real bank accounts.)

An account has a number of pieces of information associated with it: the <u>*account number*</u>; <u>*current balance*</u>; <u>*overdraft limit*</u>; and <u>*account state*</u>. The *state* of an account can be <u>**open**</u>, <u>**closed**</u>, <u>**overdrawn**</u>, <u>**stopped**</u> or <u>**special**</u>, and these states **can be set** by the Bank's officials. *Money* can be **deposited** in an account to increase the current balance. *An amount of money* can be **withdrawn** from an account as long as the amount does not cause the current balance to become **less than** the overdraft limit. However, **if an account is in** the special state, any withdrawal is permitted. The overdraft limit can be **altered**. Customers can also **ask** what the current balance in their account is. At regular intervals, the Bank **prints out** brief summaries of each account, showing just the pieces of information identified at the beginning of this paragraph.

DESIGN:

The first type to be identified by a common noun is *account* – clearly, a successful bank will have lots of instances of accounts (one for each customer). Two other types suggested are *money* and an account's *state* (for which a set of abstract values has been specified). Note however, that other types aren't specified explicitly in this description. What's the type of the proper nouns <u>*account number*</u> and <u>*current balance*</u>? You can't complete the is-a relationship for these objects, except by applying your intuition (account number is-a *number*; current balance is-an amount of *money*). The operations that can be applied to an account type are determined in a straightforward fashion from the verbs identified above.

For the type *account state* the description identifies the set of abstract values that such a type defines – <u>**open**</u>, <u>**closed**</u>, etc. One operation identified is a comparison (if an account is in the <u>**special**</u> state . . .). A comparison operation is also required for whatever the types of <u>*current balance*</u> and <u>*overdraft limit*</u> are.

The description also identifies some proper nouns and hence objects: the account number, the current balance, etc. However, you should have noted that these objects are described as being part-of an *account*; in other words, these proper nouns are actually identifying (abstract) components of the type *account*. Thus, part of the abstract state of an account must include these features. However, applying ideas from the discussion above suggests that we don't permit direct manipulation of these component quantities. Instead, the interface to *account* should provide appropriate operations.

For example, the current balance of an account is effectively a number (representing an amount of money) but should you be able to increase a balance simply by adding to that number?

The answer is "no": the balance should only be able to be increased via the **deposit** operation provided by type *account*. While the description "increase the current balance" suggests an addition, there may be much more to it than that. Maybe part of the implementation of the operation requires the amount to be added to the bank's reserves also; maybe an entry needs to be made in a ledger so that a statement for the account can record the fact that a deposit has been made. The point is that the abstract operation (increase the current balance) may have to be implemented by more than the abstract behavior requires. Thus hiding all of this implementation detail by encapsulating the behavior in the interface of the enclosing type *account* has much merit.

The fact that software engineers working for the Fiddlers Bank can't write a program that simply multiplies their current balance by two (or ten) may be something that would make sense to you if you were the bank's manager, but maybe not if you were one of those software engineers!

The results of this analysis can now be described using the PDT notation, as shown in Figure 2.31. Some of the types have been left for you to specify.

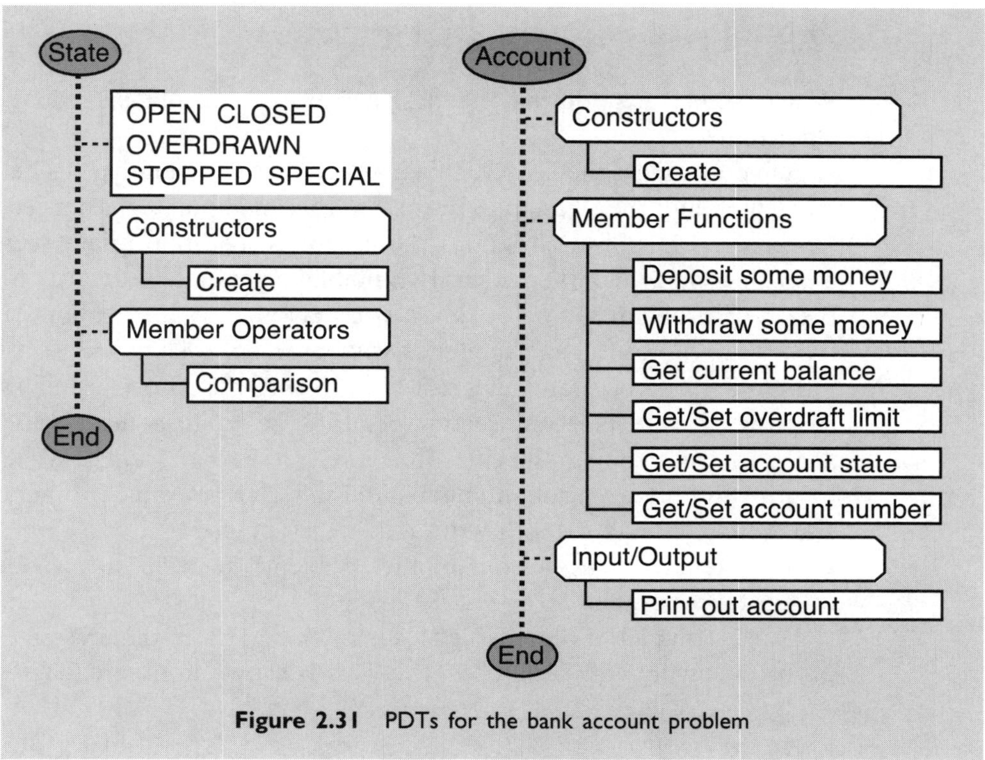

Figure 2.31 PDTs for the bank account problem

EXERCISES FOR SECTION 2.8

1 Write a description of the operation of an everyday object like a telephone. Analyze the description to find the types and objects, using the approach described in this section. Present the type(s) using the PDT notation, and contrast with the telephone type you designed in Exercise 2 of Section 2.2.

2 Examine a user manual for your computer system and identify sections that relate to the mouse and its operation. Analyze these descriptions to identify the interface for a mouse type, and express this using the PDT notation. Does this PDT differ from the one you produced in Exercise 1 of Section 2.2?

3 Write an English description of what you have to do to borrow a book from a library. Analyze this description to identify types that would be useful if you were being asked to computerize a library's operations.

2.9 THE DESIGN PROCESS

Which comes first during the design process: the objects, the types, or the algorithm?

As you've seen, there isn't a fixed answer here. Sometimes it's best to identify types first, and then design the program that manipulates instances of the types (as in the CD player program). Other times it's appropriate to work on the algorithm first, and then identify suitable types, the sequence followed with the Sieve problem. At other times, you may already know about some existing types that you can use to influence your problem solving.

Identifying types (and objects) by applying the informal analysis approach described in the previous section requires an English description for you to analyze. The problem specification may not be sufficient; "Write a program to print the first *N* prime numbers" doesn't give you much to analyze. In such situations you may need to write an English description of a first design (or of a more detailed specification of the problem) in order to provide something of substance to analyze.

Considering all of these issues leads to an algorithm that describes the overall problem-solving and design process. This is shown in Figure 2.32.

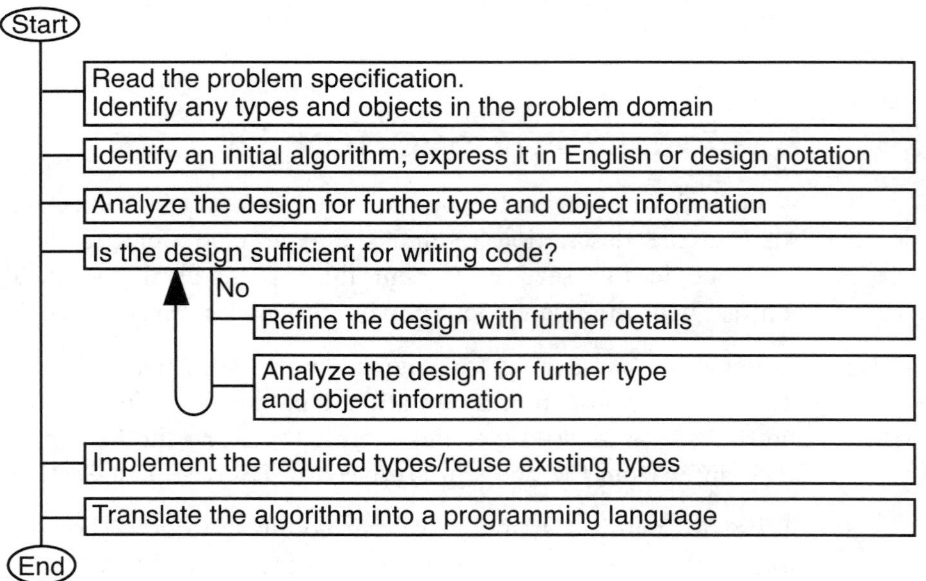

Figure 2.32 Problem-solving and design process

Inevitably, when designing there's a lot of to-ing and fro-ing between thinking about types, objects, and algorithms. As you gain more experience in identifying and using types you'll find it easier to specify a type's interface and get it right first time (well, maybe on the second or third time!), but problem solving and design are generally iterative processes.

Don't worry if you have to keep changing your design – often a first design will be discarded when you discover better solutions as you become more familiar with the problem you are tackling. Often a first design should be discarded for this reason. But if you get to the stage that the design just "falls out" given the types you have identified, you can feel confident you've got it close to being right!

Lesson: Design and problem solving are iterative processes that rarely produce ideal results the first time around.

SUMMARY

You've probably found the material in this chapter heavy going if you're new to computer programming. The material will take a while to sink in! Many important elements concerned with solving problems for software implementation have been covered, and in doing this we've touched on some important software engineering and programming aspects. You've learned:

- **problem solving** is a separate activity from writing programs;
- **the design stage** is the starting point for the problem-solving process; always produce a design before you produce C++ code;
- **a design notation** allows you to capture aspects of your design in a standard way;
- **top-down design** starts with a high-level abstract view of the problem and gradually refines (or decomposes) this view into more detailed components;
- **abstraction** is a powerful problem-solving technique concerned with separating an idea from the implementation of that idea; an abstraction hides detail; identifying abstractions appropriate to the problem domain simplifies problem solving;

- **a type** is a form of data abstraction appropriate for software engineering; types identify operations and abstract states; a design notation for representing types has been introduced;
- **an object** is an instance of a type; the type defines the object's permissable behavior; an object has an identity;
- **object-oriented design** is concerned with identifying types and objects to solve a problem;
- **an algorithm** is a sequence of steps (including operations on objects), the execution of which will produce a solution to a problem;
- **control-flow abstractions** are used to represent algorithms; a design notation for representing algorithms has been introduced;
- **selection** is a control-flow abstraction permitting the conditional execution of (parts of) algorithms;
- **repetition** is a control-flow abstraction that permits (parts of) algorithms to be repeated;
- **brute force** is a problem-solving strategy involving evaluating a large set of possible solutions for the required answer; it's not a feasible strategy for all problems;
- **Eratosthenes** lived a long time ago :-);
- **Programmer Defined Types** (PDTs) are types identified at the design stage for eventual implementation in C++;
- **identifying types** involves analyzing an English description of a problem; identifying common nouns, proper nouns, verbs and attributes can help you identify types and objects;
- **the design process** is generally iterative and rarely produces the correct design the first time around.

You should now have some idea about problem solving and design; that is, given a problem specification, you should be able to start putting a design together. However, designing software systems isn't something you can just learn from a book. You need to try out the ideas in practice, and keep on trying.

You may find it appropriate to keep returning to this chapter to reread some of the ideas introduced that didn't register the first time you encountered them. Take heart; you won't be the only one!

END-OF-CHAPTER EXERCISES

1 Why is it important to design a solution to a problem before you write C++ code to implement that solution? Explain why the top-down design process allows you to tackle complex problems.

2 You may have one or more software applications on your computer system that you can use to construct designs in the graphical design notation – for example, a graphics package or a feature of your word processor. Investigate such applications and try constructing some designs – for example, copying some from this chapter. Can you construct some reusable graphical components that you can use as templates for designs? This exercise will increase your familiarity with your computer system, as well as be useful for the designs you construct later.

3 Draw a design diagram showing how the sequencing rules explained in Section 2.3 (see Figure 2.8) can be represented using the control-flow design notation.

4 Using the design notation, express the design of a program to operate a washing machine, or some similar device.

5 Design a program that counts the number of people in a class with the same birthday. Identify types (and their interfaces) that assist you in solving this problem.

6 Identify the different types that a cell in a spreadsheet can represent.

7 Consider the design specified below. Work out what this design will produce for values for `number` in the range 0 to 16. Notice that the design for Check `number` against *N* is generalized, and is used with various values for *N* as indicated in the main design.

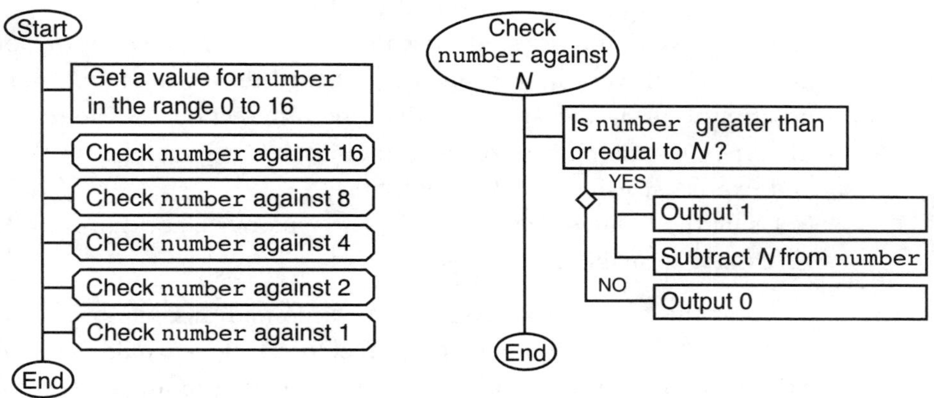

8 The design in Exercise 7 expresses a decimal-to-binary conversion routine for numbers less than or equal to 16. Redesign this solution, using repetition abstractions, so that it will work for any number.

9 Redesign the solution to Exercise 8 to provide a program that converts a number specified in decimal (base 10) to a number in a specified base in the range 2 to 9.

10 Consider the design for the CD-playing problem specified in Figures 2.12 and 2.13. Modify this design to handle the following situations:

(a) If a "bad" disc is loaded you don't want to play it (assume there's an additional operation that can indicate the status of a disc loaded into the player).
(b) So that it can skip to track N of a compact disc.
(c) So that it can count the number of tracks on a compact disc.

11 Using repetition, design an algorithm that will cause the turtle introduced in Exercise 4 at the end of Chapter 1 to draw a circle. Can you identify a new command or set of commands that would be useful to add to the turtle's repertoir to permit you to translate this design into a turtle program?

12 Design an algorithm for a game of tic-tac-toe (noughts-and-crosses), and express the algorithm using the design notation. Use a top-down approach to this design. One of the abstract steps in this algorithm will be something like Find next best square. It's not necessary to provide the optimal algorithm for this abstraction, although you could provide several variations of increasing complexity, starting with one that simply chooses the next available square.

13 Design a "better" algorithm for the abstraction Find next best square introduced in Exercise 12.

14 Each of the squares of the board used in tic-tac-toe needs to be examined, or have things "done" to it, during the course of a game. Write out an English description of what may happen to a board during a game. Then analyze your description using the approach described in Section 2.8 to see if you can identify types, components of types, and objects. Design a type for the game's board, and express it using the PDT notation.

Using the type you've designed, redesign your algorithm from Exercise 12, as necessary, to make use of this type.

15 Say that the turtles from Exercise 4 at the end of Chapter 1 were represented by a type `Turtle`. Creating an instance of `Turtle` would give you a turtle that can move around on a piece of paper. Creating multiple instances of `Turtle` would give you multiple turtles on the paper. Given this, and the turtle programs you wrote in Exercise 4 in Chapter 1 or Exercise 11 above, are there any problems with those programs now that you've got multiple turtles? Think of some ways of overcoming these problems.

16 Exercises in Sections 2.2, 2.3, and 2.4 have considered various aspects of the body mass index problem. While the calculation of the index requires metric units, namely the weight in kilograms and the height in meters, people in different countries may use different units of measurement. For example: in the US weight is measured in pounds, and height in feet and inches; in the UK the older generation know their weight in stones and pounds (there are 14 pounds in each stone) and their height in feet and inches, while the younger generation are happy with the metric units of kilograms and meters; in the rest of Europe the metric system is used.

Design one program (specified using the design notation) that takes account of these variations in the way people may wish to specify their measurements, and prints out a message giving the weight category of the person using the program. If you've attempted the previous exercises, you'll have lots of experience in this problem domain and a few useful components in your toolbag that you can reuse in this exercise!

17 The purpose of this exercise, and the one that follows, is to give you some experience with using your C++ compilation system.

This example program searches through a large text file to find a word that you specify. Using your C++ system, compile this program and then execute it (it should compile and execute without problems). The executing program gives some instructions at the start. Take a quick look at the source code that comprises this program. You aren't expected to understand it at this stage, but see if you can relate some of the statements to the actions you see on your screen when the program runs.

18 This exercise also involves you using your C++ system to compile the indicated program.

This program makes use of some graphics to draw what are called Hilbert space-filling curves. Produce an executable version of this program using your C++ system. Run this program and experiment with the input data that the program requests in order to generate different patterns on your screen. Have a quick look at the source code for this program to see if you can identify features that correspond to the graphics that appears on the screen.

FURTHER READING

Abbott, R.J. (1983) Program Design by Informal English Descriptions. *Communications of the ACM*, **26**(11), 882–94.

A detailed description of how to identify types and their interfaces by examining English descriptions of the problem. The approach is targeted at implementing types in the Ada programming language, which provides similar features to the parts of C++ covered in this book.

Booch, G. (1994) *Object-Oriented Analysis And Design With Applications*, Benjamin/Cummings, Reading, Massachusetts.

Designing real object-oriented software systems requires a much more sophisticated design notation than that used in this chapter. Booch describes one of the popular notations.

Conger, S. (1994) *The New Software Engineering*, Wadsworth, Belmont, California.

In spite of its title, this book is concerned with systems analysis – analyzing problem specifications to identify types and objects.

3 Overview of programming language features

OBJECTIVE

To develop further an understanding of the transition from the design phase to the program development phase by looking at:

- languages in general, and programming languages in particular;
- the relationship between the design notation introduced in the previous chapter, and the facilities that mirror this notation in a modern programming language.

Different languages

3.0 FROM PROBLEM SOLVING TO PROGRAM

In Chapter 2 we looked at the problem-solving process in detail:

- taking a specification of a problem to be solved;
- from the specification generating a design for an implementation of a solution to that problem.

The design will be used to achieve the ultimate goal: the production of a correct piece of software. Knowledge of what a programming language can offer is useful at the design stage; it's no use producing a design that can't be readily translated into a program, but you can't appreciate how difficult or easy that translation might be until you understand what programs might look like. To understand what a program might look like, you need to know what features are available.

Fortunately most programming languages have some common structure, and you can reasonably assume that the particular language you are using (C++, of course) conforms to this standard model. You can assume that there are concepts of types and objects, that there are selection and repetition statements, and so on. Indeed, it was the assumption of this basic model that allowed us to introduce some design notation in Chapter 2. The design notation itself is in terms of a "language." This design language supports the representation of types, has the notion of a program consisting of a sequence of operations, has a notation for selection and repetition statements, and so on; all the things normally found in a programming language. Hence the transition from design to program should be straightforward.

This chapter looks at the concept of a programming language in more detail, to tie in the design notation with the implementation of that design as a program. The chapter is written in general terms; a study of actual C++ programming doesn't come until Part 2. This is deliberate, since it's important that you learn general programming principles here without becoming aware of the peculiarities of any specific language. However, later on in this chapter we include a lengthy C++ program to give you some practice in recognizing general language features as expressed in the specific language you're going to learn.

In the previous chapter it was noted that an understanding of the design notation is useful for an overall perspective of what you might expect to find in a design for software to control a nuclear reactor, or anything else for that matter. Similarly, an understanding of what programming languages have to offer is useful for comprehension of what a program to control that reactor might be constructed from. Of course, you won't be writing such programs yet; you need to have much more than just a superficial knowledge of a language before you can even contemplate doing that.

EXERCISE FOR SECTION 3.0

1 The idea of a good design is that it readily leads to an implementation in a programming language. Given the various design notations introduced in Chapter 2, what features do you expect a programming language to support?

3.1 LANGUAGES: IN GENERAL TERMS

The way that children learn to speak and write in their native language is a complex matter. From an early age they simply learn to imitate the sounds they hear; in particular they associate words with objects. Gradually they come to recognize that there are various rules associated with the language.

If someone breaks the rules of the language only slightly then it's still possible that anything said or written will be understood by the recipient, who may be able to translate the words into a grammatically correct sentence. However, the interpretation assumed may be completely at odds with what was intended. More serious transgressions of the rules may result in the recipient not being able to understand what was meant at all. Following the rules to the letter is important to be sure that the correct message is transmitted, and is essential if you wish to gain a gold star for your essay submissions.

The rules that must be obeyed for correct sentence construction vary from language to language. There isn't even a guarantee of a common character set. The symbols (letters) used to express words in English (the alphabet) are not sufficient, without modification, for French (with acute and grave accents, and cedillas), or for German (which has ß for a double-s sound), and certainly not appropriate for Russian, Chinese, or Arabic. Even putting this aside, the rules for word construction vary; for example, in English the personal pronoun (I) is always capitalized while in German all nouns start with a capital letter. Rules vary with sentence construction; for example, the placement of adjectives with respect to the nouns they are describing (before with English, but usually after in French), or the placement of verbs (in-between subject and object in English, but at the end of the sentence in Latin). To be added to all this is punctuation – the use of periods, commas, semicolons, question marks, and so on.

To use a language successfully and with confidence you therefore need to master:

- the components (syntactic elements) of the language;
- the (syntax) rules for putting the components together;
- the precise meaning of collections of components (semantics).

Let's investigate these aspects a little further.

Syntax rules

The rules of a language are encompassed by the terms **grammar** (the accepted usage of the language) and **syntax** (the rules for sentence construction). To use a language correctly you need to understand the syntax of the language, its grammar and **vocabulary** (the set of valid words in the language).

The rules for a "word" in English are reasonably straightforward; a word can be any sequence of alphabetical letters. Rules such as this can conveniently be expressed using a diagram; we'll use the term **syntax diagram**, even though here we're discussing word, rather than sentence construction. Syntax diagrams often have an advantage over the written word in that they can be used to express a concept succinctly and without (or at least with less) ambiguity.

The syntax diagram for a word in English could be expressed as

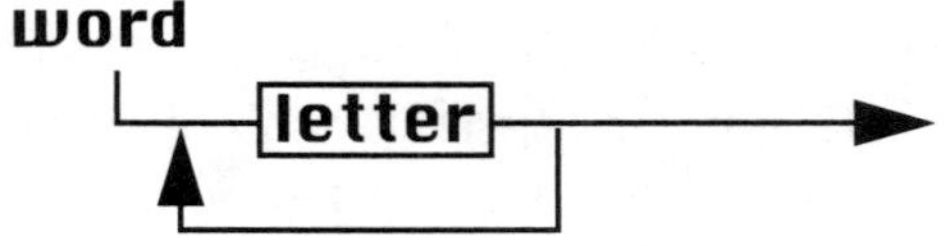

The way to read this diagram is to follow the lines and arrows. There are some implied arrows here that have been omitted for simplicity. The "token" at the top left of the diagram indicates the item (syntactic element) whose rules are being captured in the diagram, here a **word**. Following the line down, and then horizontally to the right, you come across a box with **letter** in it, so you know that a legal word must start with a letter. The diagram can now be followed horizontally to the right and off the end of the diagram, indicating that a single letter constitutes a word. Alternatively, the line can be followed down, left and up, and then horizontally right to come across the **letter** box again, indicating that a word can consist of two letters. The cycle can be repeated as many times as required, suggesting that a **word** can be any number of letters (possibly an infinite number).

What the syntax diagram doesn't specify is what a **letter** is. This is another syntactic element that requires its own syntax diagram. An abbreviated version is:

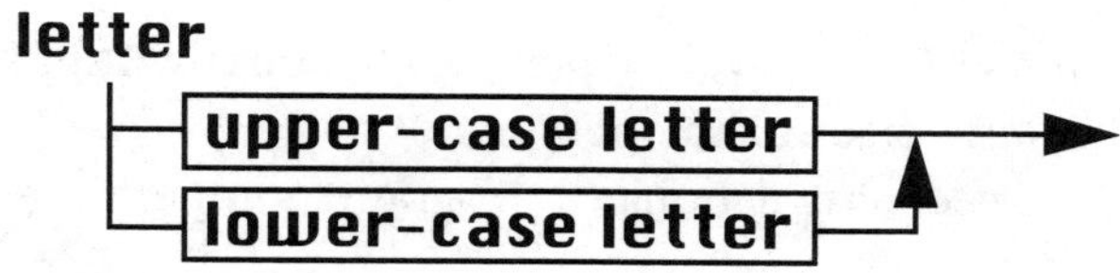

This says that a **letter** is either a **lower-case letter** (and this, itself, needs defining as meaning one of the characters `a` to `z`) or an **upper-case letter** (`A` to `Z`). Note that there isn't necessarily a unique way of producing a syntax diagram. The token **letter** could have been expressed directly in terms of the characters `a` to `z` and `A` to `Z`. Whether one way is better than another depends on its usefulness in support of other syntax diagrams.

Unfortunately, there are still some deficiencies associated with the syntax diagram for a **word**. Taking the diagram literally `ugladumph` is a word, as is `qazwsxedc`, neither of which is likely to be found in any dictionary. This is much to the chagrin of Scrabble players who would find this literal interpretation of the syntax diagram somewhat appealing. The diagram also allows `sArSaPaRiLlA`, and while you'd be quite happy with a capital letter to start the first word of a sentence or a proper noun, it's hard to picture a situation in which every other letter is capitalized.

The syntax diagram is just as deficient as the original description, in English, of what a **word** is. Both description and diagram fail to tell the whole story. Hence either the diagram must be refined (which here would be less than trivial), or we put up with such limitations, and say that the diagram defines all potential words, even if not all of them are recognized as being legitimate words. Without listing an entire dictionary it would be impossible to give a completely accurate syntax diagram for a valid **word**.

Lesson: The ability to read a syntax diagram is an important skill. Ideally, there should be no ambiguity in a syntax diagram, but the use of simplified versions can be a helpful way to explain new topics. Where a syntax diagram is not strictly accurate you need to be aware of its limitations.

Putting words together

To learn a language, vocabulary alone (the set of valid words) is not sufficient. You need to know how to construct syntactically-correct legal collections of words. Examples of the use of collections of words in a natural language are:

- prose (in a novel or piece of fictional writing);
- plain verse or limerick;
- a set of instructions (a program) to operate a video recorder;

and different rules have to be obeyed depending on which form is being used.

A section of prose in English consists of a collection of sentences (in groups of paragraphs, chapters, and so on). Encapsulating this in a syntax diagram, we have:

To read a section of prose we read each sentence in turn from left-to-right and top-to-bottom. The layout of the sentences (the way sentences appear on paper) is unimportant, but a section of prose in which

the text to
be read is laid out sequentially but in a
rather haphazard fashion

would not be easy to read. So rules are imposed that say that each word is separated from the next by some white space, but not too much.

What's a sentence? It's surprisingly difficult to answer this question precisely. A simple, effective (but not very helpful) definition is the so-called popular definition, which says: "A sentence is anything that extends from one period to another."

This isn't strictly true, since not all sentences are terminated by a period; some are terminated by question or exclamation marks! Does the terminating punctuation mark form part of the sentence? At the risk of offending our colleagues in the English Department, we'll assume that it does, and that the collection of words in front of the punctuation mark is termed an **English language construct**. Thus we have:

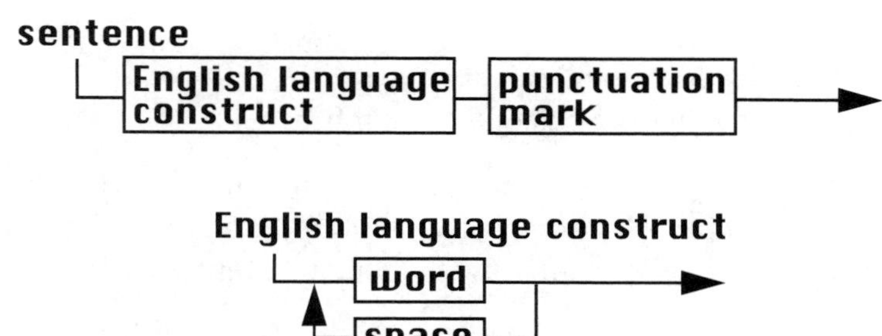

Of course, we've avoided the fact that within an English language construct there may be punctuation marks, but there's no point here in complicating matters. Furthermore, there are different types of English language construct that we could go into, but don't intend to. This is a book on programming after all, not the English language! We've gone far enough with prose to be able to draw analogies with programming languages in the next section.

For verse there is usually even more structure, especially for styles such as limericks.

EXAMPLE:

Some people are making a fuss
Which makes us so eager to cuss
When the answer's quite clear
And we're giving it here
Buy this book and use C++

A limerick consists of five lines in which the ends rhyme in the order *aabba*. Furthermore, the construction of the lines must follow a definite pattern, which is dictated by the meter of the limerick.

A set of instructions is also usually well structured. You've already seen two examples in Chapter 2 – a recipe and a description of how to remove a car engine. Here's another one.

EXAMPLE:

To make an international phone call:

1. Dial the international code.
2. Then the country code.

3. Followed by the city code.
4. Finally the customer's number.

For example, to dial London from San Francisco, dial 011 (the international code), then 44 (the UK country code), followed by 171 (the city code for London), followed by the customer's number.

With a set of instructions there's usually a preamble indicating what the operation is, followed by a bulleted or numbered list of instructions. Often, as here, the instructions are **parameterized**. The instructions to make an international phone call are expressed in terms of unspecified international, country and city codes, and the number of the customer. It's not necessary for the description to involve specific values, but of course you do have to use specific values when you make an actual call.

Grouping

The idea of grouping is used extensively in natural languages. For example, sentences are grouped into paragraphs. The start and end of each paragraph have to be clearly identified, like leaving extra interline spacing between paragraphs or indenting at the start of a paragraph and not right-justifying the last line of a paragraph. Poetry often involves grouping; for example a set number of lines in a verse. Again, extra space is used to indicate the break between one verse and another.

EXAMPLE:

Another form of grouping is exemplified by the engine removal program of Section 1.3. Some of the instructions, such as "Remove the radiator" are high-level descriptions (or abstractions) of component operations whose details are found elsewhere. Not only have these detailed operations been grouped together, they have also been identified by a simple but descriptive title. In the engine removal program it's sufficient merely to refer to this title to indicate that the radiator has to be removed, rather than go into details about removing hoses, radiator mounting bolts, etc.

EXAMPLE:

"Make an international phone call" is another high-level description of an operation with a number of sub-operations. As observed earlier, the operation has been parameterized in the sense that the basic operations of dialing the various codes are common to all international calls. The operation "to dial" is itself a high-level operation that has been parameterized in terms of a particular collection of digits that make up the appropriate code. Of course, specific values have to be used to make an actual call, and to dial a particular code, but it's not necessary to know these values to provide a generic list of instructions for making a call.

Lesson: Grouping a set of instructions under a simple descriptive title means that you can describe even higher-level operations in a succinct manner. It has the effect of localizing any changes that have to be made. Parameterizing an operation makes it general-purpose and applicable in a variety of situations. There's an important analogy with programming; write general-purpose reusable code.

EXAMPLE:

To fax a letter to another country requires, among other things, making an international call. If you already have a description of how to make an international phone call, then you can make use of it in the instructions to send an international fax message. If the international code changes, then you only have to change the "make an international phone call" set of instructions; the fax instructions remain unchanged.

Syntax versus semantics

In natural languages it's important to distinguish carefully between the concepts of syntax and semantics. To paraphrase from the *Concise Oxford English Dictionary*:

> Syntax is the grammatical arrangement of words in speech and writing to show their connection and relation; the set of rules governing this arrangement.

while

> Semantics relate to meaning in language.

Let's look at syntax again. Typically a sentence has a subject, a verb and an object, so

> I like a wee dram of malt whisky.

is syntactically correct; the sentence follows an acceptable pattern and the individual words are spelled correctly.

Where do semantics come into this? To answer this question it's necessary to have some understanding of what the sentence is trying to convey – its meaning. It makes sense for the subject of the verb "to like" to be a person (and a pronoun will do for this) and for the object to be, well, almost anything. A drink of malt whisky certainly fits the bill as a suitable object for many people. The sentence "I like a wee dram of malt whisky." is syntactically correct; it also makes sense – it is semantically correct. The sentence:

> My Apple Macintosh likes a wee dram of malt whisky.

is also syntactically correct but the sentence is semantically incorrect since it's wrong to associate feelings with an object that is supposedly inanimate. In summary, the sentence isn't meaningful.

> **Lesson:** Just because something is syntactically correct, doesn't mean that it makes sense. Adhering to syntax rules is an important step, but you've got to put the syntactic elements together so that they are both syntactically and semantically correct.

EXERCISES FOR SECTION 3.1

1 Construct a syntax diagram for a someone's surname. This should be valid for hyphenated names such as Temple-Black and allow extensions such as Jr. and III. Similarly, construct a syntax diagram for a person's forename allowing hyphenated names such as Mary-Joe and abbreviations such as D. Use these diagrams to construct a syntax diagram for a person's full name. This should be valid for names such as Mary Temple-Black, Franklin D. Roosevelt, Loudon Wainwright III, Sammy Davis Jr., but not the symbol for the artist formerly known as Prince.

2 In French the (singular) definite article may be *le*, *la* or *l'*. A verb's subject may be a definite article, followed by zero or more adjectives, followed by a noun, followed by zero or more adjectives. Express the French terms for **definite article** and **verb subject** using syntax diagrams.

3 Complete the limerick that begins:

I've just been to buy a PC

4 Write a set of instructions that cover the things that you have to do on a typical morning before you set out for college. Do any of these instructions provide an illustration of grouping? In what way are the instructions parameterized?

3.2 PROGRAMMING LANGUAGE BUILDING BLOCKS

Many modern (imperative) programming languages, such as Fortran 90, Pascal, Modula-3, C++ and Ada are, at a superficial level, very similar in their basic features. It therefore makes sense to talk about these features in an abstract sense so that you can gain an overview of what a programming language is likely to offer before looking at C++ in detail. In the following we initially assume a hypothetical language that is no language in particular, but which supports all the good features that we would expect to find in a modern programming language. At the end of the section we give a complete C++ program that exhibits those features.

Fundamentally a programming language is just like any other language. Much of what we've said about a natural language can be applied to a programming language. In particular, the concept of syntax carries over – you have to understand the syntax rules of a language to be able to converse in the language. Sometimes you may wish to converse in a programming language with (show your program to) another human, but more typically you'll be presenting your program to a compiler.

A compiler reads your program (the source code) and attempts to recognize its syntactic elements; by so doing the compiler can check if the source is syntactically correct. If there's something wrong with the syntax the compiler will tell you that the transition to object code cannot be achieved. (The translation steps from source to executable were covered in Section 1.5.) It's important that you understand the syntax of the language if you're going to be able to employ the language successfully.

However, you also need to understand how to express your intentions in a computer language – how to use the language to produce a program that does what you want it to. Just as a sentence in English may be syntactically correct but not semantically correct, a syntactically correct program may not necessarily give the expected results.

Program statements and execution

Of the various forms in which English is used, perhaps the best analogy with a computer program is a set of instructions, like the set to make an international call given in the previous section. In its basic form a program is just a set of instructions; we use the term **statement** for instruction. Using a syntax diagram, we have:

This is a gross oversimplification, but it will do for now.

The basic building block for a **program** is the **statement**; it corresponds to a sentence in English. The use of the term "statement" in the context of a program is arguably a little misleading. A program statement is active; it's an instruction to perform some action, whereas a statement in English is passive; it's more of an observation. Just as we chose to divide a sentence into an English language construct and a punctuation mark, so a programming statement has two components: a programming language construct and a terminating character, such as a semicolon. Extending the analogy using syntax diagrams, we have:

Just as there are different forms of English language construct, so there are different forms of **programming language construct** and, in turn, different types of program statement.

Simple categories of program statement

In an attempt to simplify matters, let's start by introducing the following four categories of statement:

- statements that introduce new types – **type definitions**
- statements that introduce new objects – **variable declarations**
- statements that involve a change of value of an object – **assignment statements**
- statements that involve **I**nput or **O**utput – **I/O statements**

The concepts of types and objects were introduced in Chapter 2, and if you've forgotten the distinction, go back now and remind yourself. The notions of types and objects are of fundamental importance. At the problem-solving stage you need to identify types and then use the design notation to capture the desired behavior of those types. Objects, or variables, are instances of types and you need to indicate where objects are required. This analysis carries over to the programming phase where you need to write statements that represent the behavior of types (PDT definitions) and statements that introduce objects (variable declarations).

The concept of assignment might appear new, but it was indirectly touched upon in Chapter 2. Since an object is an instance of a type, it may have one of the states (or abstract values) of that type.

EXAMPLE:

In the Sieve of Eratosthenes problem, the collection of possible primes must be capable of holding integer values.

The potential to possess a value then begs the question “How can an object be given one of these values?” One answer is “by using an assignment.” Another valid answer is “by using an input statement.”

It’s rare for a (useful) program not to require some input or output. Input may be from the user via a keyboard, a file, or a touch screen. Output may be to a screen, to a file, or cause a lathe to drill a hole of 1 inch diameter. When you’ve finished reading this book see if you can come up with a useful program that doesn’t involve input or output in one form or another. We bet you can’t.

Because we frequently need to refer to input and output, it’s common to use the acronym I/O (pronounced eye-oh) in text and speech. So now you can go around safe in the knowledge that when you talk about I/O only software engineers will understand what you mean and the rest of the population won’t understand you.

Grouping in programs

Just as grouping is used in English prose or verse, so grouping is also useful in programs to collect together a group of statements with some common theme. Such a collection is called a **compound statement**, or a **block**. Some mechanism is required to indicate the start and end of a compound statement, just as some extra space may be used to indicate the start and end of a paragraph. The following syntax diagram captures this concept in general terms.

A compound statement is, in programming language terms, equivalent to a statement. So wherever we use the term “statement” in the context of a program you can legitimately read “compound statement.”

Control-flow statements

Are there any other types of statement? At the problem-solving phase you will often identify operations that are to be followed only if some condition is satisfied, and operations that have to be followed repeatedly. There’s a design notation that captures this (Section 2.4). Programming languages have types of statement that control the sequence of statements to be executed according to whether certain conditions are satisfied, and other types of statement that execute some other statement repeatedly. It's therefore useful to introduce two further categories of statement:

- statements that determine which of one or more other statements should be executed – **selection statements**;
- statements that repeatedly execute some other statement – **repetition statements**.

Collectively, we refer to these as **control-flow statements**.

Functions

When considering an operation consisting of a list of instructions, we noted that it's useful to form a functional abstraction by:

- grouping the detailed instructions;
- providing a high-level description (name) that can be used to refer to the operation;
- parameterizing the operation so that it can be employed in a variety of situations.

The idea of grouping instructions in this way is also supported in programming languages. A group of statements is combined to form a compound statement, and the compound statement is then given a name. The concept is known as a **function** and the specification of what the function does (the compound statement that constitutes the **function body**) is called a **function definition**. Given that a function definition exists somewhere, a reference to the name of the function can be made in a program and this will cause the statements that make up the function body to be executed. This is known as a **function call**.

Functions can be parameterized in that they can be supplied with specific values that can be used in place of the generic values the function is written in terms of. Further more, as the term "function" might suggest, functions can be used to derive new values, and some languages (but not C++) make a clear distinction between functions that return values, and functions that do not return values. The term used for a function that does not return a value is **procedure**.

Recognizing programming constructs

Now you've made some progress. You know what a program is – it's a list of statements. In addition, you know in general terms something about the types of statements that can be found in a program, and you also know a little about functions. It's still quite likely that if you were now presented with a program you wouldn't be able to understand it completely, although you might be able to recognize some things. Let's return to a problem that you looked at in Chapter 2. Don't worry if the program coming up is all gobbledygook to you at the moment. In the next two sections (and also in Part 2) we'll be looking at the components of programs in more detail. By the time you've read those sections you'll be able to recognize some of the syntactic elements of the program.

PROBLEM:

Use the Sieve of Eratosthenes to find the prime numbers in the range 1 to *N* and print out a frequency histogram showing their distribution.

DESIGN:

A design for the Sieve of Eratosthenes was given in Section 2.6. For the frequency histogram, assume a division of the numbers 1 to *N* in blocks of

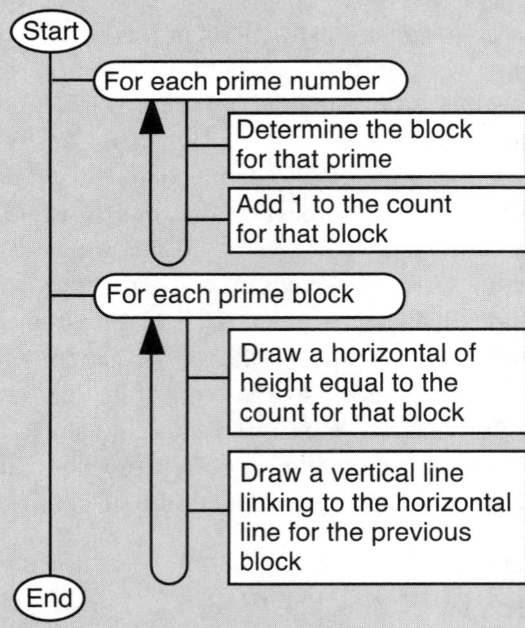

Figure 3.1 Design for the Sieve frequency histogram

width b and form a count of the number of primes within each block. Then for each block draw a horizontal line of height equal to the number of primes in that block, and a vertical line linking the start of the horizontal line with the end of the horizontal line in the previous block. Figure 3.1 summarizes these actions.

IMPLEMENTATION:

```
//////////////////////////////////////////////////////////////////
//                          sieve.c                             //
// Purpose                                                      //
// =======                                                      //
// This program is a simple implementation of the sieve         //
// of Eratosthenes for finding prime numbers                    //
//                                                              //
// Author              Creation Date                            //
// ======              =============                            //
// Eratosthenes        13 September 3BC                         //
//                                                              //
// Input/Output                                                 //
// ============                                                 //
// Input:  The last natural number to be checked                //
// Output: The prime numbers identified and a graph of          //
//            frequencies (if possible to draw)                 //
//                                                              //
//////////////////////////////////////////////////////////////////

#include <iostream.h>
#include "Array.h"
#include "bool.h"
#include "Canvas.h"
#include "error.h"
#include "Text.h"

void fillPossibles(Array<bool>& possibles);
void cancelPossibles(Array<bool>& possibles);
void printPossibles(Array<bool> possibles);
void drawFrequencies(Array<bool> possibles);
Text intToText(int i);

int main()
{
  int         n;
  Array<bool> possibles;        // Create possibles
```

```
  cout << "Type the number to stop at: ";
  cin  >> n;
  if (n <= 1)
  {
    cout << "Error: number must be greater than 1" << endl;
    return -1;                      // Terminate the program
                                    // with error flag
  }
  possibles.setSize(n);
  fillPossibles(possibles);         // Fill possibles
  cancelPossibles(possibles);       // Cancel non-primes in
                                    //   possibles
  printPossibles(possibles);        // Print out uncanceled
                                    //   elements
  drawFrequencies(possibles);       // Draw frequency graph

  return 0;                         // Terminate the program
} // end main()

void fillPossibles(Array<bool>& possibles)
{
  for (int initial = 0;
           initial < possibles.size();
           initial += 1)
  {
    possibles(initial) = true;
  }
  return;
} // end fillPossibles()

void cancelPossibles(Array<bool>& possibles)
{                                // For each element in possibles
  for (int nextCheck = 2;
       nextCheck < possibles.size();
       nextCheck += 1)
  {
    if (possibles(nextCheck))     // Has it been canceled?
    {                               // No: cancel in rest
                                    //  of possibles.
     for (int cancel = nextCheck + nextCheck;
          cancel < possibles.size();
          cancel += nextCheck)
      {
        possibles(cancel) = false;  // Set to CANCEL
      } // end for cancel
    } // end if possibles
  } // end for nextCheck
```

```
    return;
  } // end cancelPossibles()

  void printPossibles(Array<bool> possibles)
  {
    int count = 0;
    cout << "The primes are:" << endl;
    for (int prime = 1; prime < possibles.size(); prime += 1)
    {
      if (possibles(prime))       // Has element been canceled?
      {
        cout << prime << ' ';         // No - print value
        count += 1;
      }
    }
    cout << endl << endl << "The total number was "
         << count << endl;
    return;
  } // end printPossibles()

  void drawFrequencies(Array<bool> possibles)
  {
    const int XMAX      = 200;              // Size of picture
    const int YMAX      = XMAX;
    const int MARGIN    = 1;
    const int BLOCKSIZE = 10;

    int roundUp = 0;
    int freq;
    Array<int> frequencies;

    if (possibles.size() % BLOCKSIZE != 0)    // Valid size?
    {
      roundUp = 1;    // To round up number of blocks to be drawn
    }

    frequencies.setSize((possibles.size() / BLOCKSIZE) +
                        roundUp);

    // Set scaling factors
    const int XSCALE = XMAX / frequencies.size();
    const int YSCALE = YMAX / BLOCKSIZE;

    // The columns must be at least one pixel wide for the
    //   frequency graph to be drawn. If XSCALE is zero they
    //   aren't, and either the window size or the BLOCKSIZE
    //   need to be increased for this range of numbers.
```

```
  if (XSCALE == 0)
  {
    cout << "Sorry: This range of numbers is too large "
         << "to be plotted" << endl;
    return;
  }
  for (freq = 0; freq < frequencies.size(); freq += 1)
  {
    frequencies(freq) = 0;           // Initialize counts
  }
  for (int prime = 1; prime < possibles.size(); prime += 1)
  {
    if (possibles(prime))            // Is element a prime?
    {                                      // Yes - add 1 to
      frequencies(prime / BLOCKSIZE) += 1; // block's count
    }
  }
  Canvas frequencyGraph;            // Create Canvas

  // Set Canvas size and then draw the frequency graph
  frequencyGraph.setSize(XMAX + MARGIN, YMAX + MARGIN);
  frequencyGraph.penDown();
  for (freq = 0; freq < frequencies.size(); freq += 1)
  {
    frequencyGraph.moveTo(freq * XSCALE,
                          frequencies(freq) * YSCALE);
    frequencyGraph.moveTo((freq + 1) * XSCALE,
                          frequencies(freq) * YSCALE);
  }
  frequencyGraph.moveTo(frequencies.size() * XSCALE, 0);

  // Add a title
  Text graphTitle = "Plot of frequencies of primes";

  frequencyGraph.penUp();
  frequencyGraph.moveTo(20, YMAX - 20);
  frequencyGraph.displayText(graphTitle);
  graphTitle = "in the range 1 to " +
               intToText(possibles.size());
  frequencyGraph.moveTo(20, YMAX - 40);
  frequencyGraph.displayText(graphTitle);
  return;
} // end drawFrequencies()
```

```
        // Convert an integer to a string of characters
Text intToText(int i)
{
  Text message = "";

  // Generate digits, starting with the least significant
  while (i > 0)
  {
    char nextDigit = char((i % 10) + int('0'));

    message =  Text(nextDigit) + message;
    i /= 10;
  }
  return message;
} // end intToText()
```

Figure 3.2 A C++ implementation of the Sieve of Eratosthenes

OUTPUT:

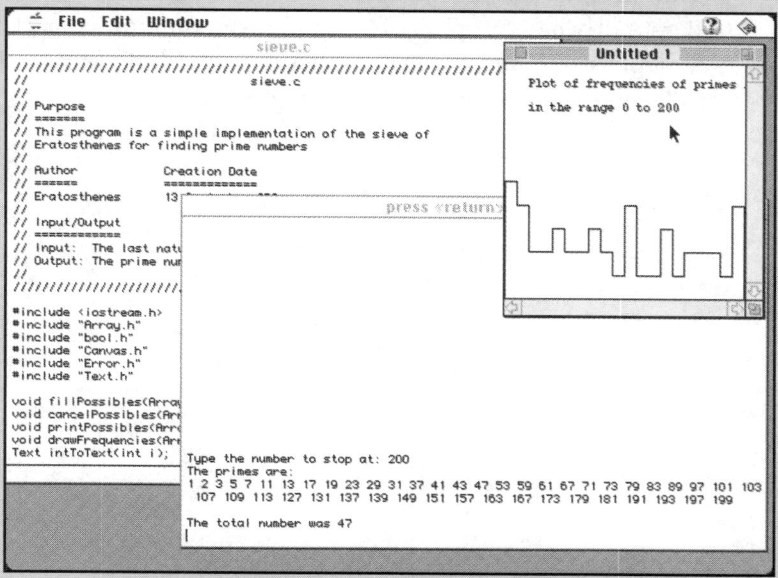

Figure 3.3 Results of the Sieve frequency histogram program

Where are the statements in the program? Are there any type definition statements? Which are declaration statements and which assignment statements? Which are the control-flow (selection and repetition) statements? Are you able to answer any of these questions yet? We expect the answer to this last question to be "no," so we'll give you some help in the next two sections.

EXERCISES FOR SECTION 3.2

1 Attempt a match between the design for the Sieve of Eratosthenes problem given in Figure 2.25, and the program of Figure 3.2. Try compiling and running the Sieve program.

2 At the end of this book there's an alphabetical list of C++ syntax diagrams. What is the **terminating character** for a **statement** in C++?

3 Several of the lines in Figure 3.2 contain comments. Comments don't affect the execution behavior of the program; they're there to help the human reader understand what the purpose of the programming constructs is. The start of a comment is denoted by the character pair `//`. Try to work out the C++ rules for placement of comments in a program.

3.3 DECLARATION, ASSIGNMENT AND I/O

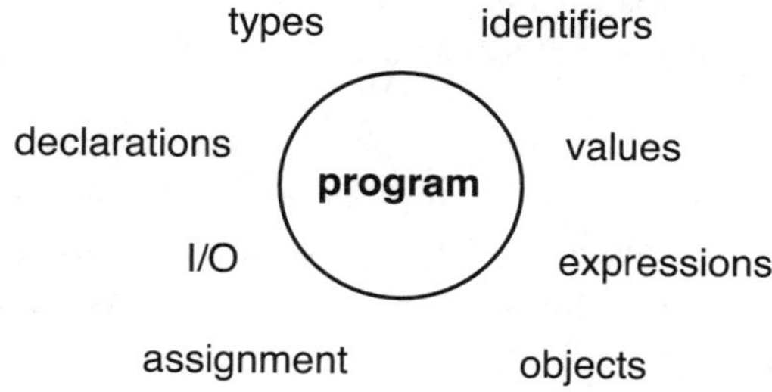

In order to know about types you need to know about declarations; this in turn means you need to know about identifiers. In order to know about identifiers, you need to know something about their use in connection with types. This, in turn, means you need to know about objects, values and expressions, but to understand expressions properly you need to know about identifiers and types. You have to do something to the result of an expression, which means it's useful to know something about assignment and I/O. Confused? You should be!

Declarations, assignment, identifiers, types, objects, values, expressions, assignment and I/O are all inextricably interlinked. How then in Part 2 can we justify introducing types first, followed by declarations, and so on, until I/O is covered in Chapter 15? The short answer is that we don't follow this format to the letter. For example, there's some I/O in Chapter 4, and some features of expressions and assignment in Chapter 6. In the meantime, it's useful to have a general feel for what the various concepts are. This will help to prepare the groundwork for what comes in Part 2.

Identifiers

When reading a book you're used to recognizing names as representing characters (such as Queequeg in *Moby Dick* and Bilbo Baggins in *The Lord of The Rings*). Once these characters have been introduced, a mere mention of their name is enough to invoke an image of who is being referred to. It's not necessary for the author to write "The Ship's Captain who has a wooden leg and a parrot on his shoulder and frequents the Admiral Benbow Inn" every time – Long John Silver is sufficient. Often names are attached to inanimate objects too: for example, Air Force 1, or The Flying Dutchman. These names give a mechanism for referring to an object, and as you saw in the previous chapter there's a type associated with each object. Using the guidelines set out in Section 2.8 you could look for "is-a" to establish the relationship between object and type.

EXAMPLE:

Moby Dick is-a whale; Robert E. Lee is-a Confederate general (or maybe is-a steamboat); Leonardo is-an artist (or maybe is-a Ninja Turtle).

What about whale, steamboat, artist, and so on? Aren't these names too? Not in English terms, no. They are common nouns, rather than proper nouns, but it's not unreasonable to think about them as names of types, rather than names of instances of types.

In a programming language, names or **identifiers** are used to represent objects and types (and functions too – wait until the next section for more on this). An identifier is a convenient way of providing a handle on an object; it allows the programmer to refer to an object, just as the name Long John Silver is repeatedly used in *Treasure Island* to refer to a particular person. It's a convenient way of providing a handle on a type too, just as "whale" refers to a particular type of animal.

The precise rules for what constitutes a valid identifier varies from language to language, but the simple rule of:

> An identifier is any sequence of letters and digits, with the restriction that the first character must be a letter

is usually sufficient, and will certainly do here. We can represent the rule for an identifier using a syntax diagram:

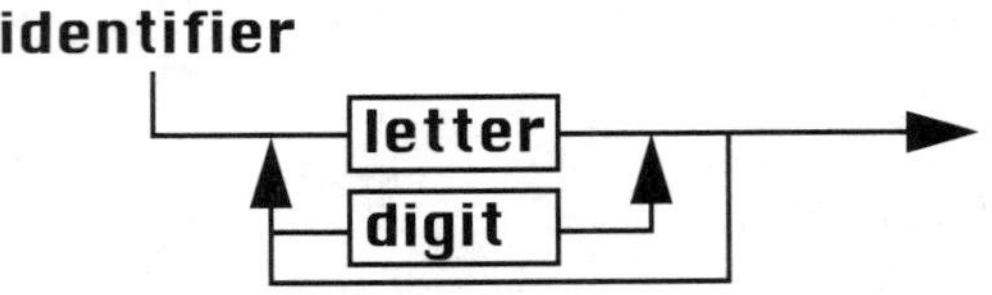

So `X` is a valid identifier, as is `A69` and `qwerty`. But what do these identifiers represent? It's useful to employ a sensible naming strategy that gives a visual clue, like `CDPlayer` for a CD Player type, and `myPlayer` for an instance of that type.

Lesson: You'll be using identifiers a lot in programs. Use sensible naming strategies. It'll help you to understand their purpose, and will also guarantee good style marks from your course tutor.

Now see if you can recognize the identifiers in Figure 3.2. We've not given the precise syntax rules for an identifier in C++ – you'll have to wait until Part 2 for that – but you should be able to recognize that `possibles` is an identifier, as are `fillPossibles` and `frequencyGraph`. Do these names give you any clue as to what they represent? You may think it strange that for one identifier a lower-case "`p`" is used while for another identifier an upper-case "`P`" is used. This is all to do with C++ style rules which are covered in Part 2.

Types

In films and in books you're familiar with the concept of types, such as lawmen, outlaws and bar girls in a Western movie, or Hobbits and Orcs in *The Lord of the Rings*. Types tell you something about the characteristics of the characters of that type; they obey stereotypes.

EXAMPLE:

Lawmen are always clean shaven; outlaws have permanent 5 o'clock shadows, chew tobacco and have a limited vocabulary; bar girls wear voluminous dresses and are proficient at hitting outlaws over the head with a bottle.

Computer programs involve types too, such as the basic numeric types for representing integer (whole) and floating-point (real) numbers, and for characters (no, not that sort; we mean alphanumeric characters, punctuation marks, and so on). We refer to these as **built-in types** since they are provided as part of the language. You don't have to introduce these as new types; they're there and you can just make use of them.

Modern languages additionally provide a facility for programmers to define their own types; the PDTs introduced in Chapter 2. In essence this facility allows programmers to extend the language, to tailor it to the requirements of the problem. The new types supplement the built-in types, and in principle are "first-class citizens" of the extended language; it's as though they had been provided as built-in types in the first place.

Types in a programming language tell you something about instances of that type in two respects: values/states and operations.

EXAMPLE:

A CD player type might have a set of recognized states such as `ON`, `OFF`, and so on, and a set of operations such as `on`, to switch it on, and `load`, to load a CD. The integer type will consist of whole numbers (confined to a certain range of values). The ability to add, subtract, multiply and divide integers, to compare integers, and to input and output integers, are all operations that you would expect to be supported. It's quite likely that you're not going to want a full set of these operations for a character type (is there any sense in dividing one character by another?); the ability to compare, and input and output are likely to be sufficient.

EXAMPLE:

Since there's the possibility that the execution path of a program may be conditional, it's likely that there will be a type whose values can only be `true` or `false` – a logical, or Boolean, type. Again, you're unlikely to expect to find arithmetic operations of much use for this type, but you might find it useful to have the ability to combine values (using `AND` or `OR`) or to complement a value (switch from `true` to `false` or *vice versa* using `NOT`). Conversely, you wouldn't expect a `NOT` operation for integers.

Now go back to Figure 3.2. Can you identify any types yet? We expect the answer to this question to be "no" (although you might be able to hazard a guess at what `int` refers to). It's not entirely clear which identifiers are the names of types and which are the names of objects, even for a program as clearly written as this example :–). By relating back to Section 2.7 you may be able to figure out that `possibles` must be an object, but what is its type? An easy way to recognize which identifiers are types and which are objects is to look for declarations.

Objects and declarations

Imagine reading *War and Peace* starting at page 284. You become aware that there is an object (a person in the book) called Pierre. But is Pierre Russian or French? Does he belong to the aristocracy or to the peasantry? You have a name but no clue as to any generic characteristics. You need defining is-a sentences, something that classifies the characters.

EXAMPLE:

- Pierre is-a Bezuhov
- Spock is-a Vulcan
- Superman is-a superhero

The fact that Pierre belongs to the Bezuhov family means that he is a member of the Russian aristocracy. As a Trekkie (a fan of Star Trek) it's sufficient that you know that Spock is a Vulcan to be aware that he can't experience emotions and that he has pointed ears. The superhero type is general and indicates that an individual of the type can be expected to come from a planet in some other solar system, to possess special physical prowess, and will wear strange clothes when undertaking feats of superheroism. These are all characteristics of an instance of the type. Instances of the superhero type can be introduced, and already you know a fair bit about them in general terms. It takes a little more to fill in the specific details: Superman is from the planet Krypton, he can fly, he wears a cape and underpants outside his trousers, and so on.

In programming terms the introduction of an object (the equivalent of a defining is-a in English) is termed a **declaration**. A declaration is an example of a programming language construct. In the previous section we introduced the idea that a construct can be turned into a statement by the addition of a terminating punctuation mark. Here a declaration can be turned into a statement (a **declaration statement**) by the addition of a terminating character of some form. If you've tried Exercise 2 of the previous section you should have worked out that in C++ the terminating character is a semicolon.

A declaration serves to indicate two things:

- the name of the object being introduced – an identifier;
- the type of that object – another identifier.

What does the type tell you? Just as you know that an instance of a superhero will have particular characteristics, so the indication of the type of an object tells you something about that object in general terms. Of course, it tells you (or, what is more important, the compiler) something about the potential operations involving that object: the type interface (Section 2.4). It also tells you something about the potential values/states of the object.

Programming languages require a variable to be declared before it's used in any other statements. Unfortunately, there's no agreement between programming languages as to which order the type identifier and object identifier appear in a declaration. For some languages (including C++) it's the type identifier followed by the object identifier, for other languages it's the other way round. C++ allows declarations to appear almost anywhere within a program, as long as the declaration-before-use rule is obeyed; other languages are more restrictive and require declarations to appear in groups, and only in specific places in a program.

Given that the following syntax diagram represents a simple C++ **declaration**, go back to Figure 3.2 and try to identify declarations, types, and objects/variables. Note that in the syntax diagram the token **identifier** on its own refers to a variable identifier.

You should have been able to work out that int is a type, as are Array<bool> and Canvas. Examples of objects include frequencyGraph, possibles, count and initial.

Values and expressions

As you've seen, characters in books are identified by names and are often associated with types that indicate general characteristics (Superman is-a superhero). These characters are given specific values that may be subject to change (Superman wears his underpants outside of his trousers only after he's been in the phone booth and before he gets back to the *Daily Planet*). A type governs what the valid values are. It's no good saying that the color of Superman's cape is 42, or that the number of days before the vacation is red. This would be semantically incorrect.

EXAMPLE:

The word "red" is a perfectly valid value, as is 42, but they have to be used in the correct context. They are both examples of **literals**. Literals are explicit values that cannot be changed; 42 is 42 is 42, no matter which way you look at it. Further, literals have a type associated with them; 42 is an example of an integer literal, while "red" is an example of a color literal.

So what's the big deal about literals with respect to programming? A literal is the way of expressing an explicit value in a program. Since a literal has a type it can be used in combination with operators of that type. For example, you can add two integer literals, multiply two integer literals, and so on. The result of adding two integer literals is an integer value, and so you can build up really complicated combinations of integer literals and operator symbols if you've got nothing better to do on a wet Sunday afternoon.

Can you use only literals in combination with operator symbols? If you were so restricted then this would severely limit the usefulness of the programs you could write. You can use literals *and* objects to build up **expressions**. Often these expressions are derived from mathematical formulas, or from a formula expressed in English.

EXAMPLE:

The amount of money taken in one day for admissions to the Roman fort of Housesteads on Hadrian's Wall in Northern England could be expressed as:

> the number of adults multiplied by the adult rate plus the number of children multiplied by the reduced rate;

or, in a programming language, as

```
numAdults * adultRate + numChildren * reducedRate
```

Here `*` is the operator symbol for multiplication and + is the symbol for addition. The identifiers `numAdults`, `adultRate`, `numChildren` and `reducedRate` are all names assumed for objects that have been declared to be of some integer type. It's obvious what they represent, isn't it?

If the reduction for children is 50%, here's another way of writing the above expression using objects and a literal:

```
(numAdults + numChildren / 2) * adultRate
```

Here / denotes division, and 2 is an integer literal.

It should be noted that there is implicit in the first expression a concept of priority – which operations take place first. The use of brackets, as in the second expression, can be used to enforce the priority intended.

Values combined using an operator symbol are known as **operands**. In the last example above, the operands of the division operator are the value of `numChildren` and the value of the literal `2`. The result of the division is then used as one of the operands for the addition operator.

What do you think the result of the expression would be if the brackets were left out?

Without the brackets, the expression would evaluate as dividing the number of children by 2, multiplying the result by the adult rate, and then adding this to the number of adults. If the number of adults is 500, the number of children is 200, and the adult rate is £3, the expression with the brackets gives £1,800; leaving the brackets out gives £800.

An expression computes a result value and, like any other value, the result has a type associated with it. Precisely what this type is will depend on the operators and, in turn, on the types of the values of the operands. You'd naturally expect the addition of two integer numbers to give another integer number, and the addition of two floating-point numbers to give a floating-point number. Note that the symbol used for addition is always the same (+) regardless of whether the operands are integers or floating-point numbers, a concept known as **operator overloading**.

Assignment and state change statements

Once you have a value, what do you do with it? Sometimes the result of a mathematical expression is an end in itself, such as the need to record in a ledger the takings for one day at Housesteads. Other times a value needs to be recorded and then later reused (for example, to determine the total takings for the year, or the average per day over the past seven consecutive days). It's useful to introduce a name (in practice, often a collection of words, such as "Takings for January 13th") that represents the value computed, and refer to this name in subsequent expressions (the sum of the Takings for January 9th, the Takings for January 10th, . . ., the Takings for January 15th, all divided by 7).

In a program you might choose simply to output the value of an expression or to store the value for later reuse. You know from the previous sub-section that types define a range of potential values, that identifiers are used to label a particular instance of a type (a variable), and that a declaration statement introduces a variable of a type. The use of the term **variable** suggests an important concept: the value of a variable is not fixed; it can vary. Once a declaration has been made the variable can be given a value using an **assignment operator** in an **assignment statement**, and can subsequently be given a new value in another assignment statement.

The combination of a variable, an assignment operator and a value is known as an assignment, with syntax:

The effect of an **assignment** is to assign the value of the **expression** on the right-hand side of the **assignment operator** to the variable referred to on the left-hand side of the assignment operator by its identifier. The value of the expression on the right-hand side is recorded in the memory of the computer and the variable identifier is used to refer to the location in memory where the value is stored. (The idea of a memory model was outlined in Section 1.4.) Any value held by the variable before the assignment was executed is lost.

To complete the description we have to indicate what represents an assignment operator. Unfortunately, as with all things, this varies from language to language. A symbol, or combination of symbols, is usually employed: either "=" or ":=". The colon-equals combination is usually pronounced "becomes equal to," which is a good description of what is going on. We say:

> The value of the variable whose identifier appears on the left-hand side of the assignment operator **becomes equal to** the value represented by the expression on the right-hand side.

With languages for which the assignment operator is the equals symbol the tendency is to say:

> The value of the variable whose identifier appears on the left-hand side of the assignment operator **is equal to** the value represented by the expression on the right-hand side.

which unfortunately sounds more like an assertion or a question than an action.

Hence we recommend that you always say "becomes equal to" even for languages like C++ for which the assignment operator is the equals sign.

Lesson: The assignment operator is a shorthand for **becomes equal to**.

Refer again to Figure 3.2. Where are the expressions? Where are the assignments?

You should be able to spot expressions involving the operators `+`, `-` and `*`. Less obvious is that `%`, `+=`, `/=`, `>` and even `=` are operators too.

New values can be assigned to instances of PDTs using the assignment operator, just as they can for the built-in types. More likely, you'll want to change just a component of an instance of a PDT (Section 2.8).

EXAMPLE:

You may wish to simulate the payment of cash into an instance of a Bank Account PDT. The effect will be to update the current balance, but the overdraft limit must remain unchanged.

The effect is not so much assignment but more a change of state, and consequently it would be wrong to use an assignment operator for this. Clearly the PDT must support an operation that will permit such a change of state, rather than employ an assignment.

I/O statements

It's a rare program (a computer program, or otherwise) that doesn't have some form of I/O. Following a set of instructions usually has some effect.

EXAMPLE:

If you follow the recipe program of Section 1.3 then you should have a sumptuous meal that will give pleasure to your senses of sight, smell and taste. If you follow the instructions to make an international call in Section 3.1 then a link will be established, and provided the person you're after picks up the phone the other end, you'll be able to talk to them.

A computer program often involves input from a keyboard or file, and output to a monitor or file. To achieve these effects you require special forms of statements: I/O statements.

An input statement reads a value into a variable. It's like assignment, except that the value on the right-hand side of the assignment is obtained from some external device. An input statement therefore needs an identifier indicating which variable the value read is to be assigned to. It also requires an indication as to where the value is to be obtained from. In many languages a default device, such as a keyboard, is often implicit as a source of input.

An output statement is also like an assignment, except that the value of the right-hand side (an expression) is sent to an external device. The statement therefore needs to have a value to be output – the result of an expression – and needs to know where to send the value to. Again, many languages implicitly assume a default device for output, such as a monitor screen.

In C++ I/O is achieved using operators; the operators >> for input and << for output.

From Figure 3.2 can you identify any I/O statements?

Output statements are used in the program to produce on the monitor the list of prime numbers and the total number of primes. Note that any numbers output are identified by some additional textual description. There's an output statement prompting the user to type in the upper limit on the primes to be found, and a corresponding input statement to read in a value typed by the user at the keyboard.

Compound statements

As indicated in the previous section, a compound statement is just a collection of statements. There must be some sense in grouping statements – some common thread – and we'll provide some motivation in the next two sections. For now all you need to be aware of is the notion of a compound statement and that there is an analogy with the concept of a designator box as used in a program design (Section 2.3). A compound statement corresponds to a designator box and the individual statements that make up the compound statement correspond to an expansion of the designator box.

What's the notation that programming languages use to indicate the start and end of a compound statement? One style is to use `begin` and `end`. C++ uses braces; the curly brackets `{` and `}`.

Are there any compound statements in Figure 3.2?

Yes, there are lots of compound statements in Figure 3.2 and they appear in a variety of situations; after a line that begins with `for`, `while`, and `if`, and `void` and `Text`. At variance with the other types of statement we've looked at so far, a compound statement has no terminating character. Why should it? It's pretty clear where the compound statement ends.

Now that you know something about some simple forms of statement you can begin to contemplate identifying more complex statements in programs in general, and in Figure 3.2 in particular. These more complex statements we generically refer to as control-flow statements.

EXERCISES FOR SECTION 3.3

1 Next time you watch your favorite soaps on TV (as a temporary diversion from reading this book) identify the stereotypes represented in these programs. Others may care to dive into Thomas Hardy's *Tess of the D'Urbervilles*, or F. Scott Fitzgerald's *The Great Gatsby* to identify stereotypes. How would you describe the type "College Professor"?

2 The alphabetical syntax list given at the end of this book shows that the syntactic element **statement** can take one of many forms. Try to identify and categorize the statements in Figure 3.2.

3.4 CONTROL-FLOW STATEMENTS

The program for making an international call defines a set of operations that have to be followed. It also defines the sequence in which those instructions must be obeyed. It's no good dialing the customer's number before the country code; you may end up speaking to someone in Outer Mongolia, rather than London! This is not to say that all programs obey a sequential pattern. Some employ selection and/or repetition, as you saw in Section 2.4. How are these concepts implemented in a programming language?

Selection statements

You'd like to think that your chance of winning at Monopoly™, Risk™, or any other board game depends on your skill in making the right decisions. Chance must come into play, since these games rely on the throwing of dice, and the action to be taken will depend on the throw of the dice. But the decision whether or not to buy the Electric Company, to trade your Get Out Of Jail card, or to invade Central America, is something the player has to take.

EXAMPLE:

A simplified version of the instructions for a "turn" in Monopoly could be written as follows.

1. Throw the dice.
2. Move your piece the required number of squares.
3. If by so doing you pass Go, collect an amount of money from the Bank.
4. If you've landed on a property:
   (a) if someone owns the property pay them the required rent;
   (b) otherwise:
      (i) buy the property; or
      (ii) auction the property.
5. Otherwise, if you've landed on Chance or Community Chest, pick up the card and follow the instructions on it.
6. Otherwise, if you've landed on a fine (Income Tax) pay it.
7. Otherwise, if you've landed on "Go to Jail" then do it!
8. Otherwise, since you're on either Go, Just Visiting (Jail) or Free Parking, do nothing.

The precise nature of the action you take is dependent on which square you land on.

Chance is not something that you would naturally associate with a computer program since determinism is a fundamental property of any "good" program However, the possibility of the action to be taken being dependent on some condition is a common feature of many programs.

EXAMPLE:

A program will continue to execute if you type a "Y" at the keyboard, and terminate otherwise; or the square root of an expression will be formed only if the value of that expression is positive.

Programming languages provide a selection statement – an **if statement** – that supports this mode of operation. An if statement consists of three principal parts:

1. A test – a Boolean expression (one that gives a true or false value) that controls which compound statement is to be executed.
2. A then branch – the compound statement to be obeyed if the Boolean expression evaluates to true.
3. An else branch – the compound statement to be obeyed if the Boolean expression evaluates to false.

Often the else branch is not required, when it can be omitted altogether.

Sometimes we want to say (in English and in a program) "if some condition is satisfied then do one thing, else if some other condition is satisfied then do something else, else . . . and if none of these conditions is satisfied then do the last thing."

EXAMPLE:

If today is Monday, then there's a C++ lecture at 2:00 and 4:00, but if today is Tuesday or Thursday, there's a lecture at 9:00, but for every other day there's no lecture (so you'd better do some practical work).

Situations like this can be readily catered for using multiple if statements, but languages often provide a special construct – a **multiway selection** – for cases where there are several tests of the same basic form but involving different values.

To indicate that a particular statement is a selection statement, certain special words are used. These are examples of **keywords**, words that have some special significance in the language and that in no circumstances can be used as an identifier. Typical keywords used for selection statements are `if`, `then` and `else`, and for a multiway selection words like `switch`, `case`, `default` and `otherwise`. Not all languages use all these words (in particular, C++ doesn't use `then`) but if you see any of them in a program, there's a fair chance that a selection statement is involved.

Have another look at Figure 3.2. Can you identify any selection statements in it?

The keyword `if` is used in several places in Figure 3.2 as part of a selection statement. Note that since the last part of an if statement is a compound statement there's no terminating character.

Repetition statements

On a long car or bus journey children often try to amuse themselves singing songs such as *10 Green Bottles*, or *One Man Went to Mow*.[1] These songs are simple in structure. They consist of the same lines repeated with some variation each time round, or **iteration,** and (thankfully) some way of terminating.

EXAMPLE:

The first verse of *10 Green Bottles* goes:

10 green bottles standing on the wall
10 green bottles standing on the wall
And if 1 green bottle should accidentally fall
There'd be 9 green bottles standing on the wall

The second verse repeats this with the 10 in the first two lines replaced by 9, and the 9 in the last line replaced by 8, and so on. Eventually, you come to the situation in which there is 1 bottle only, and its demise results in no bottles, the end of the song, and hopefully some peace and quiet for the rest of the journey.

Imagine having to write the song out in full. Yes, it would be easy with a word processor, since you can copy-and-paste the lines and make minor amendments. But what if the song started with 100 bottles, and you had to write the song out using pen-and-paper only? We suspect that you'd write the first four lines as above and then add at the top something like "Repeat these lines 10 times but at the end of each cycle reduce the number of bottles by 1."

In other words, you'd write a repetition instruction. It's a feature of this repetition that you know in advance how many times it has to be cycled: 10. You could use a counter, counting downwards from 10 to 1, to indicate the variations in the lines on each cycle. In other words, instead of "10 green bottles standing on the wall" you'd write "`count` green bottles standing on the wall" and the value used for `count` would reduce by one each time round. You'd additionally change the last line to "There'd be `count-1` green bottles standing on the wall." You can also use the counter to specify the termination criterion – when there are no bottles left; that is, when `count` is equal to zero.

[1] Or any other similar counting songs such as *100 Bottles of Beer* or *The Song That Never Ends*.

EXAMPLE:

Contrast *10 Green Bottles* with *One Man Went To Mow*. The fourth cycle of *One Man Went To Mow* goes something like:

4 men went to mow
Went to mow a meadow
4 men, 3 men, 2 men, 1 man and his dog
Went to mow a meadow

On each cycle the number of men who went to mow in the first line is increased by 1, with a corresponding increase in the length of the count down in the third line (a repetition within a repetition).

The fact that you count upwards for the main cycle is not particularly significant, but it does rather leave things open-ended. When do you stop? When the bus reaches your destination? When someone in the bus throws their shoe at you? Or when you're too tired to bother going on? The difference between *One Man Went To Mow* and *10 Green Bottles* is not large, but it does illustrate a slightly different form of repetition. With *One Man Went To Mow* you don't know at the outset how many cycles are to be performed, but some event happens that eventually causes the repetition to terminate.

Repetition is an important feature of any programming language and is often found in a design. Reflecting the examples above and in Section 2.4, many languages provide more than one repetition construct:

- a **loop repetition** usually refers to a repetition in which there is a counter that counts either up or down. Each time around the repetition the counter is either increased or decreased by a constant amount (often 1). When the value of the counter is greater than (when counting up) or less than (when counting down) some value known at the start of the repetition, the loop terminates.
- a **while repetition** cycles while some Boolean condition holds. It's important that something happens at some stage to make the value of the Boolean expression false, otherwise the repetition will cycle indefinitely.

A repetition statement controls a compound statement, the statements of which are executed on each cycle.

As with selection statements, certain keywords are used to indicate that a particular statement is a repetition statement. Words like `for`, `do`, `while`, `repeat` and `until` are often used.

Have another look at Figure 3.2. Does it contain any repetition statements? If so, are they for or while repetitions?

The program of Figure 3.2 contains several for repetitions and a while loop. There's a for repetition to fill the collection of possible primes, and another for repetition to go through this collection to print the uncanceled values. A while repetition is used in the section of the program that converts an integer to a string of characters.

Now you know about the concepts of certain types of control-flow statements: selection and repetition. There's another feature of programming languages evident in Figure 3.2 that you need to know about: the ability to define and call functions.

EXERCISES FOR SECTION 3.4

1 Write a sequence of statements that describe a "turn" in a board game such as Risk, or a card game such as Solitaire. Do these instructions involve any selection or repetition statements?

2 Think back to your formative years and those counting songs you learned as a youngster. Classify them as for repetitions or while repetitions.

3 Take a sneak look at the alphabetical syntax list for C++ given at the end of this book. Match the syntactic element **for statement** with the corresponding repetition statements in Figure 3.2. Do likewise for the syntactic element **if statement**.

3.5 FUNCTIONS

We frequently employ high-level abstractions to describe complex operations.

EXAMPLE:

The statement "make an international call" represents a complex operation whose details were given in Section 3.1.

The advantages of encapsulating high-level descriptions are:

1. Other operations can be described in a succinct fashion using the abstraction.
2. A high-level description can be parameterized so that it can be used in a variety of ways.
3. Just one copy is required of the low-level description of the high-level operation. If any changes are to be made then these changes are localized to one place only.

EXAMPLE:

1. To send a fax to your friend in Iceland you need to load the document to be sent into the tray, make an international call, press the SEND button, and so on. At this level it's not necessary to worry about details, such as precisely how you might make an international call, that might otherwise obscure what is required.
2. The actions required to make an international call to your friend in India are essentially the same as those for a call to Iceland, but the values (country code, area code, friend's local number) will vary.
3. The telephone company might, in its infinite wisdom, require the sequence "before international code, country code, city code, local number"; to be reversed. Make the appropriate changes to the operation "make an international call" and then all other operations that involve an international call remain valid.

Making use of such control-flow abstractions will make your initial stab at a design more straightforward than if you had to worry about all of the details of the components.

We distinguish carefully between:

1. The invocation of a high-level operation.
2. The definition of that function, corresponding to the expansion of the related designator box in the design.

EXAMPLE:

1. The overall action of making a call to your friend in Iceland is an invocation of the "make an international call" operation. It requires specific numbers to be dialed.
2. The "make an international call" operation is expressed as a sequence of steps that have to be performed, but it's only when an actual call is made that those steps are carried out.

The distinction may appear a little subtle, but it's an important one that you need to understand.

Function calls

To invoke (call) an operation it's sufficient to know what the interface is. You need to know the name of the operation, what information to supply, and what you get back from the operation.

EXAMPLE:

The name of the operation might be "make an international call" or "remove a radiator." The information to supply might be a set of dialing codes, or the make and model of a car. You expect to get a connection to the number you've dialed, rather than a car-minus-radiator, when you make an international call.

The detailed implementation of the operation is irrelevant to the person who just wants to make use of that operation. The high-level operation acts as a black box; you put something in and get something out, but don't care about what goes on in the box as long as the outcome matches the specification of the operation. All the user needs to know is that someone or something, somewhere, will establish that phone connection, or remove the radiator.

In programming language terms the encapsulation of a parameterized high-level operation using a name is known as a **function**. In Section 3.2 you saw that a compound statement is equivalent to the design concept of a designator box. Rather than expand a designator box in-line as in Figure 2.13 of Section 2.2, the precise details of what operations a designator box represents can be specified in a separate diagram, as illustrated by Figure 2.12. The latter situation corresponds to the way that functions are used in a programming language. The invocation of a high-level operation encapsulated in a function is known as a **function call** and corresponds to a designator box. A **function definition** corresponds to the expansion of the designator box in a separate diagram.

To establish the connection between the function call and a function definition, a function has a name associated with it: a **function identifier**. This is just a standard identifier, as discussed in Section 3.1. A function call consists of the name of the function followed by a **parameter** (or **argument**) **list** enclosed in round brackets. The parameter list is the mechanism by which the user of a function can pass values to a function (and even get values back). This description of a function call is summarized by the following syntax diagrams.

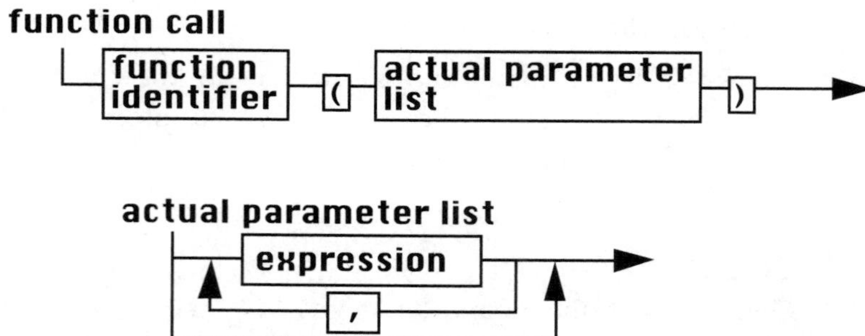

When describing how to make a function call we qualify the term "parameter list" by the addition of the adjective "actual." The **actual parameter list** says what parameters the function is "actually" being supplied with. Depending on circumstances, these may be expressions or variable names (which are simple forms of expressions anyway, but there may be a clear distinction as you'll see).

A function returns a value, and so associated with a function is a **result type**. A function call can appear in any position that is valid for a value of the result type. The result value could be output, an operand in an expression, or an actual parameter to some other function.

To make a call to a function you therefore need to know:

- the name of the function;
- what type of values have to be supplied to the function as actual parameters;
- the type of value that you get back.

Collectively these three items constitute the function **interface**.

Mathematical functions

Programming languages usually come with a standard library of mathematical functions for working out square roots, trigonometric quantities (sines and cosines), or logarithms. When you make a call to any of these functions you don't care how the desired quantity is evaluated; maybe there's some extremely complicated formula to work it out; maybe there's a table of values to look up. You just need to know the interface.

EXAMPLE:

For the square root function the name is usually `sqrt`; the value whose square root is required is a floating-point number, and the function computes a floating-point result.

More general functions

Many of the standard mathematical functions are used in an identical way to that in which the square root function is used. There's a single parameter, and a single value being computed. The parameter might be an angle expressed in radians and the value returned the tangent of that angle. Are all functions like this? Is this the only way you can use functions? The answer is, of course, "no" (otherwise we wouldn't be making such a big deal about functions in the first place). As indicated before, a function is like a black box; you put values in and you get values out. We need to look more carefully at this information exchange.

EXAMPLE:

Suppose that you want to make a call to a function, let's call it `deductions(...)`, that, given a person's gross monthly income, works out the deductions for that month. These deductions might be the amount of tax payable, pension contributions and health care payments, all of which are calculated using complicated formulas that don't concern you. There's only one value (the monthly income) going into the function but there are several to be computed and returned, one for each deduction category.

Very few languages allow a function to return more than one value in the way that the square root function returns its single result, and so some alternative mechanism has to be employed.

The square root function uses the parameter-passing mechanism to allow you to specify the number whose square root you require. Can you use the same mechanism to get values back? The answer is "yes" – but how?

EXAMPLE:

The effect of a call to the function `deductions(...)` will be similar to multiple assignments:

- one assignment to a variable that records the tax;
- a second assignment to a variable that records the pension contributions;
- a third assignment to a variable that records the health care payments.

Since you want the function to do the assignments for you it's reasonable to expect that all you have to do is to specify the names of variables to which three values are to be assigned. You also need to supply a value for the gross income. This could be a variable name too, but it's only the value held by that variable before the function call is made that's important.

To proceed, it's useful to introduce the following three ways in which values can be passed to/from a function using the parameter-passing mechanism.

1. In-parameters are used in a function call to supply a value to a function. The actual parameter may be a variable name. More generally, the parameter may be an expression.
2. Out-parameters are used to get a value back from a function call. The actual parameter must be a variable name since a value will be assigned to it by the function.
3. In/out-parameters can supply a value to a function and can also be used to obtain a value from a function. The actual parameter must be a variable name.

Are you confused by all this in, out, in/out, shake-it-all-about stuff?

Let's try to simplify matters by first of all saying that not many languages give you out-parameters, so you've usually only got a choice of in-parameters and in/out-parameters. If you know that a parameter is an in-parameter then you know that you must supply a value. If it's an in/out-parameter then you must supply a variable name. It's reasonable to assume that the variable represented by this identifier has a new value when the function call is complete, since otherwise why isn't it an in-parameter? Whether the variable needs to have a value before the function call is made depends on the particular function being called.

So a function can return a value in the way that the square root function does, and it can also return values back through the parameter list. Can a function return values both through the parameter list and through the return type? Technically, yes, although it's often the case that a function returns values back only through the parameter list.

Procedural abstraction

Many programming languages use a special terminology – **procedure** – for functions that don't use the return type to return a value. For languages that don't make this distinction it's up to the programmer to make the distinction explicit by indicating that the return type for the equivalent of a procedure is a special type. In C++ this special type is `void`. Since there's no value being returned, there's no value to output, or use as an operand in an expression, or use as an actual parameter to some other function. For a procedural abstraction, a call followed by an appropriate statement terminator is a statement.

Function definitions

We return now to the concept of a function's interface, which tells you how to make a function call. To make a correct function call it's necessary to know:

- the name of the function (the function identifier);
- the return type (none if it's a procedure);
- the number, type (data type and category – in or in/out) of the parameters.

This interface needs to be specified in a program; a typical order in which the individual items might appear in such a specification is:

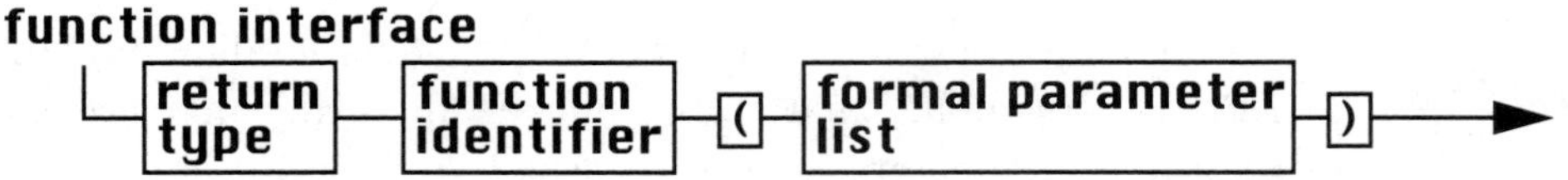

where the **formal parameter list** might be defined by:

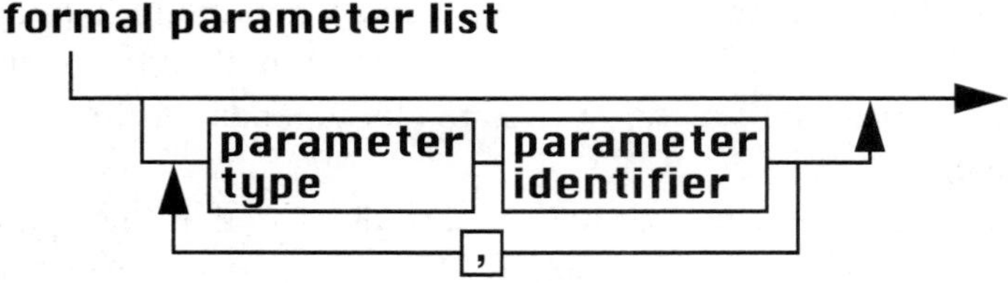

When describing what the interface is we qualify the term "parameter list" by the addition of the adjective "formal." The formal parameter list indicates what parameters the function expects, not what they actually are (the actual parameters). For each parameter there's a parameter type and a parameter name. You may recall that taken together these two entities constitute a declaration (here, a declaration for a local variable that can be referred to only in the function's **body** – the statements that are executed when a function call is made).

When the in-parameter-passing mechanism is used the formal parameter variable assumes the value of the corresponding actual parameter. Any change made by the function to the formal parameter has no effect on the actual parameter. When the in/out-parameter-passing mechanism is employed the actual and formal parameters refer to the same object, not just the same value. Any changes made by the function to a formal parameter automatically results in the same change to the actual parameter. Just how this is achieved depends on the compiler and is of no consequence to you, so you don't have to worry about it.

Now you know how to make a function call, what a function interface is, and the difference between in- and in/out-parameters. All that's left is how to specify the function body. In fact a function body is just a compound statement. It can contain declaration statements, I/O statements, selection and repetition statements, and even function calls. There's nothing particularly special about it at all, so that's a relief!

Have yet another look at Figure 3.2 and try to find the function calls. What are the actual parameters? Now find the function definitions. This is slightly more difficult. Some languages use keywords, such as `function` or `procedure` to indicate function definitions, but C++ doesn't use any special keywords. If you can spot the function calls then you know that there must be a definition somewhere for a function of that name. Why does the specification of the function interface appear twice? Are any of the functions "procedures"?

In the program in Figure 3.2 `fill Possibles(...)`, `cancelPossibles (...)`, `printPossibles(...)`, `drawFrequencies(...)` and `intToText(...)` are all functions. The first three are called with the actual parameter `possibles` from the body of the function `main()`. `intToText(...)` is called from the body of `drawFrequencies(...)` with the actual parameter `possibles.size()`. The usual use-before-definition rule means that the function interface (name of function, number and type of parameters) must be known to the compiler before a function call can be made, but it's not necessary to have access to the function body yet. The definition of each function appears after the definition of `main()`. Of the function definitions shown, `intToText(...)` and `main()` don't represent procedural abstractions.

How can you tell which are in-parameters and which are in/out-parameters? The latter are sometimes indicated in the formal parameter list using keywords such as `VAR`, `INOUT`, or `REF`. C++ uses the symbol `&`. Another clue is to look at the function call. If the actual parameter is not a variable then the parameter must be an in-parameter. If it's a variable then it could be either an in-parameter or an in/out-parameter.

Which are in-parameters in Figure 3.2, and which are in/out-parameters?

Since `fillPossibles(...)` and `cancelPossibles(...)` both alter the contents of their parameter, it must be an in/out-parameter. On the other hand, `printPossibles(...)`, `drawFrequencies(...)` and `intToText(...)` don't change the value of their parameter at all, so in-parameters are OK here.

Finally, we return to the concept of types. You may recall from Section 2.7 that a type has associated with it a number of operations, and that to invoke these operations you make calls to member functions. Is there anything special about a member function as opposed to the sort of functions discussed above? In general terms, not much at all. It's just a function, like any other function, even though the function is inextricably linked with a particular type (it's a member of that type, after all). Since a call of a member function is associated with an object, that is, an instance of the type, a member function call must involve the identifier of the function *and* the identifier of the object.

Are there any member-function calls in Figure 3.2? To answer this question you first need to identify the PDTs in the program and instances of those PDTs. How is the name of an instance of a PDT separated from the name of a function in a member-function call? Where are the definitions of the member functions?

`Canvas` is a PDT and `frequencyGraph` is an instance of that PDT. So `frequencyGraph.penDown()` is a call to the member function `penDown()`. This function has no parameters. A period is used as a separator between the name of an object and the name of a member function. The definitions of the member functions of PDT `Canvas` don't appear in the code shown, but rest assured that the definitions need to be somewhere and eventually linked in.

Now you have some overall view of what a program might look like. There's a lot more detail that we could fill in, and other things that we could tell you about, but we'll leave all that for Part 2.

EXERCISES FOR SECTION 3.5

1 Match the function definitions in Figure 3.2 with the design diagrams in Figures 2.26 and 2.27.

2 For each of the function definitions in Figure 3.2 add a brief comment (see Exercise 3 of Section 3.2) that describes the purpose of that function.

SUMMARY

From reading this chapter you should have picked up some idea of what programming languages and C++ in particular, are all about. You should understand:

- **syntax** – the rules that govern the construction of programming elements;
- **semantics** – putting syntactic elements together so that they make sense;
- **syntax diagrams** – a visual representation of syntax rules (and how to read them).

You've seen some C++ language building blocks:

- **identifiers** – names used to refer to types and variables;
- **declarations** – introduce variables;
- **expression** – combinations of program elements that produce values, and operator symbols that combine those values;
- **statements** – instructions to perform actions.

Programming statements come in various forms:

- **assignment** – used to assign a value to a variable;
- **input/output** – used to communicate with the program user;
- **compound** – a group of statements;
- **control flow** – selection and repetition that changes the normal sequential flow of control.

You've seen how a functional abstraction is translated into program statements, and the difference between:

- **a function call** – the invocation of a functional abstraction;
- **a function definition** – the detailed specification of the functional abstraction expressed as a compound statement.

In the context of functions you've seen the importance of parameters, and the difference between:

- **in parameters** – used to supply values to a function;
- **in-out parameters** – used to supply values and get values back.

You're also aware of the difference between:

- **functions that return a value** – a function call can be used in an expression;
- **functions that return no value** – a function call is a statement.

You should be able to relate all of these ideas to the problem-solving process, and in particular, how designs can be turned into programs.

In summary, you should be able to look at a simple program written in almost any programming language and have some understanding of what's going on. This doesn't mean that you'll be able to write your own C++ programs yet, but it does mean that you're ready to start to learn how. Part 2 beckons.

END-OF-CHAPTER EXERCISES

1 What is meant by the terms "selection statement" and "repetition statement"?

2 Produce syntax diagrams for the English language terms **paragraph**, **chapter** and **book**.

3 The terms **semi-quaver**, **quaver**, **minim**, **semi-breve** and **breve** are notes in music. Notes are grouped into **bar**s, and a **twelve-bar blues** song consists of, well, 12 bars. Produce syntax diagrams that summarize these terms.

4 Go to a library and find a book on animal classification. Use it to produce syntax diagrams that can be used to classify a variety of animals. The list needn't be exhaustive, but should include the syntactic element **merganser**.

5 Write a set of instructions for making an international call from a public phone booth that accepts coins only.

6 Pick up a textbook on some language other than C++ (Fortran, Pascal, Modula, Ada – we suggest you don't try Motorola M68000 Assembler or a functional language such as Miranda). Try to find some large complete programs. Can you identify the items discussed in Sections 3.3–3.5 (identifiers, declarations, expressions, loops, function calls, and so on)?

7 You'll find plenty of complete, and part-complete programs throughout this book, and on the accompanying disk. Again, can you identify the items discussed in Sections 3.3–3.5?

8 The following diagrams define some C++ syntactic elements. Interpret them.

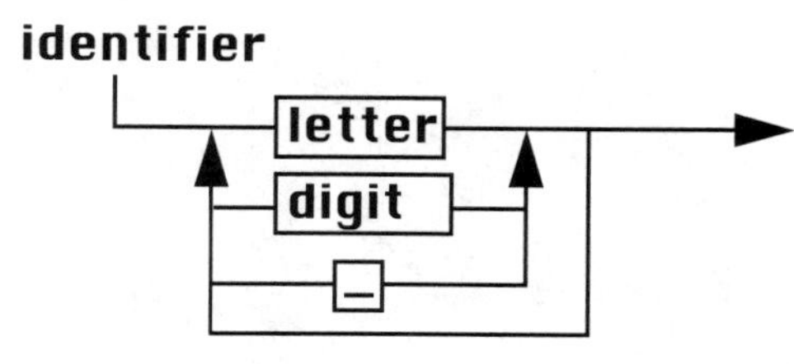

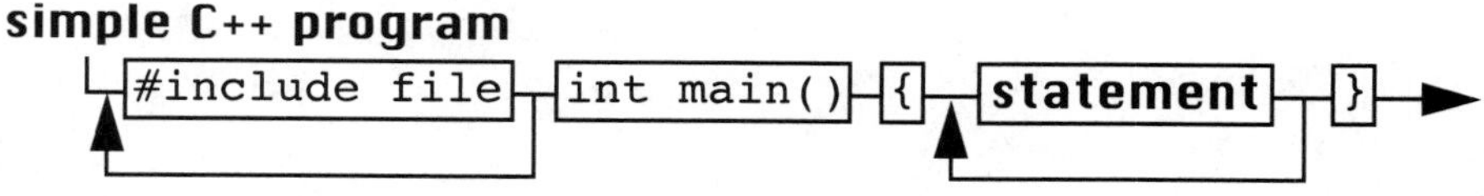

9 Computer language X-- has a while repetition construct but no loop repetition. Does this mean that in X-- you cannot write a loop that cycles a predetermined number of times?

10 No program is complete without a full set of documentation that includes, among other things, a user manual for a potential user of the program. A user manual should cover the purpose of the program and its I/O requirements in more detail than shown in Figure 3.2. Write a detailed user manual for the program of Figure 3.2.

PART 2

Learning to use your C++ toolbag

4 Starting C++ programming

OBJECTIVE

To get started on programming in C++ and introduce:

- simple C++ statements;
- example programs;
- program layout and style;
- simple input and output in C++;
- comments in C++ including syntax and style rules.

Off we go++

4.0 INTRODUCTION

For you to be able to produce a C++ program there are a few skills that you have to acquire. First, of course, you need to know how to write C++ programs! Second, you have to be able to type in the program and to correct any mistakes you make while doing this typing; this requires you to be familiar with an editor on your computer system. Third, you'll want to compile the program, for which you'll need to know how to invoke the compilation system on your computer. And finally, when your program has compiled with no compile-time errors, you'll want to run the program.

The prospect of acquiring all of these skills simultaneously can be a little daunting (and frustrating when things don't work). To minimize your learning curve, this chapter concentrates on working with some small complete programs, allowing you to concentrate on acquiring skills with the editing and compilation tools. Some of the C++ features in these programs are introduced as "magic" in that they are not explained in detail yet. Nevertheless, some important features of programming in general, and in C++ in particular, will be introduced.

Right; let's make a start. Let's solve the following simple problem.

PROBLEM:

Write a program to display a greeting to you on your computer.

DESIGN:

The design for solving this problem is straightforward.

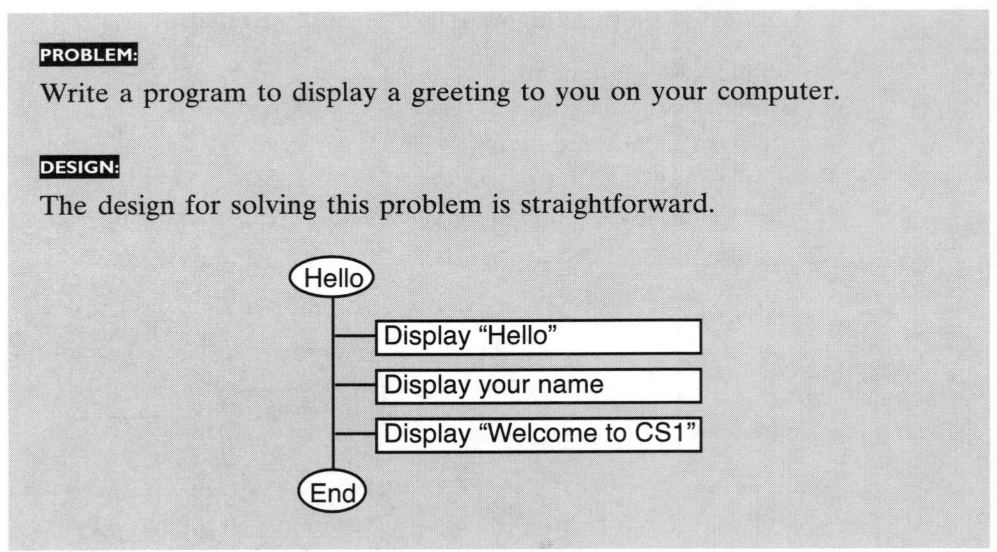

Take a look at the C++ program in Figure 4.1. This simple program is the translation of the above design into C++. Don't worry about all of the C++ gobbledygook for the moment. The program will compile and run as it stands, although you can use the editor on your system to modify the program so that it prints out your name and the name/number of the programming course you are taking. Try making these changes and running the modified program.

IMPLEMENTATION:

```
#include <iostream.h>

int main()
{
  cout << "Hello ";
  cout << "Your name" << endl;
  cout << "Welcome to CS1" << endl;
  return 0;
}
```

Figure 4.1 Hello program in C++

The exact details of how to use an editor and compiler will depend upon the system that you're using, and hence we can't cover them in detail here. Refer to your system's manuals to find out exactly how you do these things. After all of this you'll have edited, compiled and executed your first C++ program. Well done!

Note the style we adopt for displaying programs. In particular, note the use of `courier font` when C++ is being presented, enabling you to distinguish C++ text from the normal prose.

Running the program should produce output something like that shown in Figure 4.2.[1] This figure shows a window on the left (with the title **hello.c**) containing the source of the Hello program, while the window on the right (titled **press «return» to exit**) shows the output produced by executing the program (after it has been compiled).

Let's examine this simple C++ program and the output it produces in more detail. Chapter 3 introduced the basic form of a program as consisting of a set of statements, where each statement is an action that the program must obey. Although you haven't been told the syntax of any C++ statements yet, can you identify any statements in the above program?

[1] The fact that this screen shot is from a Macintosh isn't important, and your system may differ in some of the details shown on your screen. All we want to do here is establish the link between the program and the output produced.

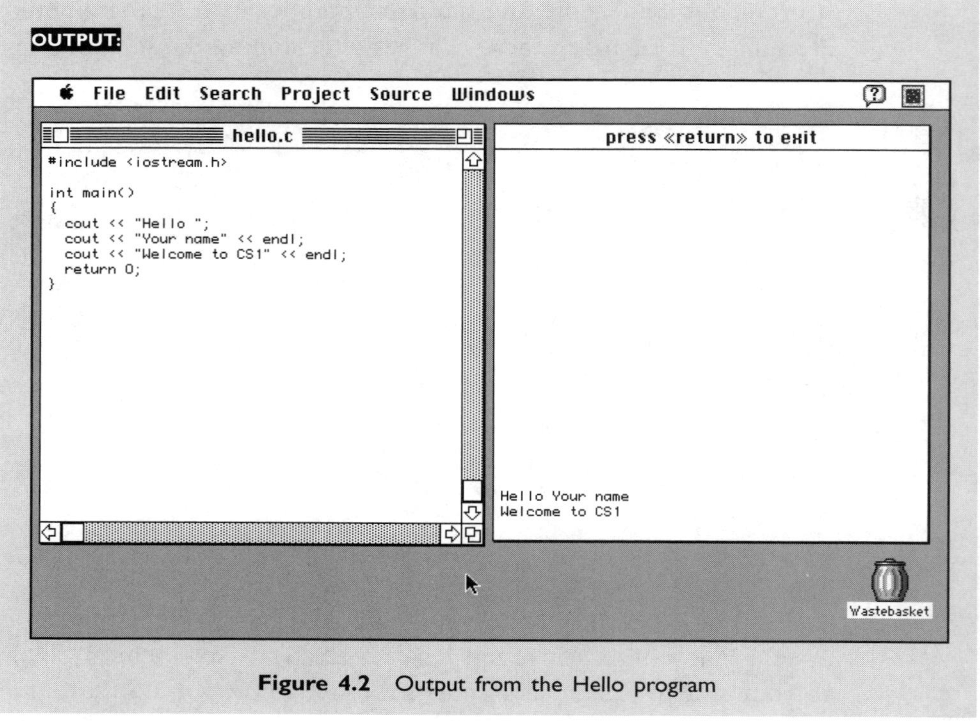

Figure 4.2 Output from the Hello program

Most of the C++ statements in Figure 4.1 are lines terminated by semicolons. Several of the lines are statements of the form

```
cout << "...";
```

These are C++ statements that, when executed, cause messages to be displayed on your computer's screen. If you've executed the program you'll have seen that the messages displayed consist of the string of characters enclosed in the double quotation marks (`"..."`) in those statements. These messages can be seen in the right-hand window in Figure 4.2. Change the characters inside the quotation marks in the program and you change the messages produced when the program is executed.

The name `cout` (pronounced "see-out") is used to denote an object that is an instance of an output type, and the characters << represent the output operator that means "do some output." So

```
cout << "Hello ";
```

is an output statement and means send the characters `Hello` (without the enclosing quotation marks but with the space that appears just before the second quotation mark) to `cout`. Since `cout` is normally linked to your computer's screen, these characters will be printed on the screen.[2]

One of the things you might be wondering about is the purpose of the quotation marks and the semicolon in the C++ statements. Their purpose will be explained shortly (although Chapter 3 gave some hints), but for now just take it that these things are needed.

You've probably noticed that two of the output statements in the program contain two occurrences of the output operator <<. In each case the second occurrence is followed by the word `endl` (which isn't enclosed in quotation marks). Did you also notice that the word `endl` isn't printed on your screen? What's going on here?

One way of finding out is for you to experiment with the program to see if you can identify the behavior caused by `endl`. Edit the program to delete just the characters `<< endl` (don't delete any others!) from each of the lines on which they occur. Then try executing the edited program. Having done this, can you determine the behavior of `<< endl`?

Lesson: Try things out in small test C++ programs as a means of determining what certain C++ features do. This isn't a substitute for looking things up in this book, but it can help you to understand what's going on. Test your understanding of a feature by writing a small test program, predicting what that program will do, and then executing the program and comparing the actual result with that predicted.

The word `endl` means **end** of **l**ine, and its output causes a newline to be output; that is, the current line on the screen has been completed, and any characters output; after the `endl` will be printed on the line below starting at the beginning of the line. If you experimented as suggested by removing the `<< endl`s from the program, you'll have seen that the characters are then displayed on a single line of your screen.

In fact you can use the output operator << multiple times in a single output statement, not only with `endl` but with other strings of characters that you wish to output.

[2] We often talk about "printing" something, even though a printer may not be involved. We use the verb "print" as a generic verb meaning to output something.

EXAMPLE:

The output statements from Figure 4.1 could be combined into a single statement:

```
cout << "Hello " << "Your name" << endl << "Welcome to CS1" << endl;
```

This statement has the obvious meaning: first, send the characters `Hello` to `cout`, then send the characters `Your name` to `cout`, then output a newline, ... and so on. Whether you use this form of output statement, or the form shown in Figure 4.1 with multiple output statements, will be influenced by issues of program layout and style, as you'll see in Section 4.2.

How do the characters produced by the output operator << get to the screen? Well, the output operator has to obtain the characters, one at a time, from the program and then place them into a buffer memory and eventually pass them in some form to the operating system, which has to convert them from one encoding into a form suitable for displaying on the screen, which involves ... Do you need to know all of this excruciating detail and complexity? Of course not. You just need to understand the abstraction provided by the object `cout` and the operations provided by its type. Isn't that a relief! Could you ever write a C++ program if you had to deal with all of the complexities of how output occurs? (Well, not yet anyway.) Would you ever want to write programs if it involved that much work every time? We wouldn't, and we expect that you wouldn't either! However, someone has had to implement the output operator.

If you think back, you'll recall the discussion of software reuse and software libraries (see Figure 1.8 in Chapter 1), and the discussions about types in Chapter 2. The object `cout` is an instance of a PDT provided for you to use. It's part of the `iostream` library that normally comes as part of the C++ system. If you need to use the PDTs contained in this library, you have to indicate this explicitly in your program. This is the purpose of the line:

```
#include <iostream.h>
```

in the program. This line tells the compiler to include the `iostream` PDTs when it's compiling your program. The library also has to be included at the link stage of building an executable program – see Figure 1.8 if you can't remember what linking is. Arranging for the link stage to pick up the `iostream` library is another system-dependent activity that you may need to look up in your system's manuals.

In changing the program you may have accidentally made some illegal changes that prevented the program from compiling successfully. If this happened, you were probably baffled by the error messages that the compiler produced. (If you didn't hit any compile-time errors, try deleting just one of the semicolons, or one of the quotation marks and then recompiling.) Before we can discuss such error messages further, we need to present some of the language details of C++ to identify what constitutes a legal C++ program.

EXERCISES FOR SECTION 4.0

1 Modify the Hello program (Figure 4.1) so that it prints out your name and the number of the course that you are taking.

2 Modify the Hello program so that each word is printed on a separate line.

3 Predict the output that these C++ fragments will produce:

(a)
```
cout << "——————————————";
cout << endl << endl;
cout << "——————————————";
```

(b)
```
cout << "  *";
cout << " ***";
cout << "*****";
cout << "  |";
cout << "—————";
```

Modify a copy of the Hello program (Figure 4.1) to replace its output statements with those shown in (a) and (b), and compile and execute the resulting programs to see whether your predictions were correct. If the output isn't what you feel was intended, change the statements to obtain the desired behavior.

4 What (if anything) is wrong with the following C++ statements:

```
(a) cout << endl
(b) cout << "BANG!!!!!!;
(c) cout << "End of Section 4.0" < < endl;
```

5 Modify the Hello program to inform the world of your name, age, birthday, favorite meal and anything else you might care to divulge (within reason :-).

6 What's wrong with the following statement that's meant to be a one-statement equivalent to the statements shown in 3 (b) above?

```
cout << "  *"; << " ***"; "*****";<< "  |";"—————";
```

Make changes to fix the errors in this statement, and also to mirror any changes you made to 3 (b) to obtain the desired output behavior. Contrast the appearance of the single statement you finish up with to the multiple-statement version. Which do you think looks best?

4.1 STRUCTURE OF SIMPLE C++ PROGRAMS

Chapter 3 introduced the basic structure of a program in a programming language, including the notions of syntax and syntax diagrams. It's very important that you understand these concepts and what they mean for writing legal computer programs. In this section you'll be introduced to the first of many C++ syntax diagrams.

What does a legal C++ program consist of? For the simple C++ programs that you'll be starting off with, the following syntax diagram captures all of the rules:

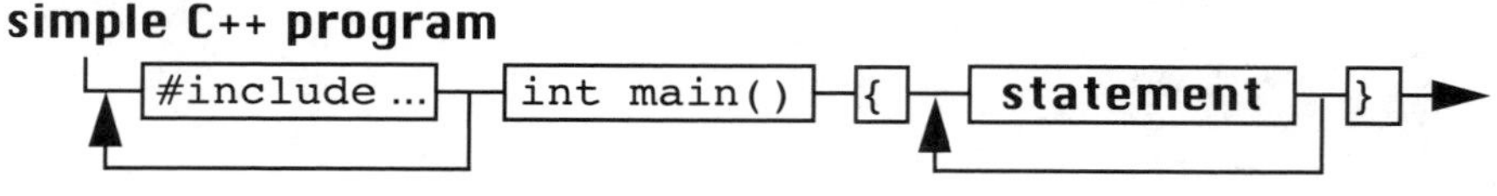

Figure 4.3 Syntax diagram for a simple C++ program

This diagram defines the syntactic element **simple C++ program**. A legal program consists of possibly multiple `#include` lines, followed by `int main()`, followed by one or more **statement**s enclosed by the characters `{` and `}`.

We haven't defined the C++ syntactic element **statement** yet. In fact, we'll describe several different forms of **statement** in subsequent chapters. The full syntax diagram for **statement** is given in Appendix A if you want a sneak preview. However, each of the "`cout << ... ;`" lines in the program in Figure 4.1 is an example of a statement, as mentioned before.

The text `int main()` is telling the compiler that what follows is the main part (or function) of the program. The name `main` has a special significance in a C++ program in that the computer will start executing the statements inside `main()` when it starts executing your program. We'll explain the reasons for the word `int` and the parentheses `()` later. For the moment just note that they're required.

The characters { and } are called braces and enclose the set of statements that form the main function of the program. The braces help the compiler figure out where the set of statements that constitute the main function begin and end.

For the first programs you write, the syntax diagram in Figure 4.3 will help you get your program's overall structure right. Your simple programs must contain all of the elements identified. However, if they don't or if you get something wrong, you'll need to find out about compile-time errors.

C++ compile-time errors

What happens if you try to compile a C++ program that contains syntax errors? The answer is that the compiler will report syntax errors to you, and it won't produce an executable program (Figure 4.4). You have to fix the faults in your program that caused these compilation errors before you can proceed.

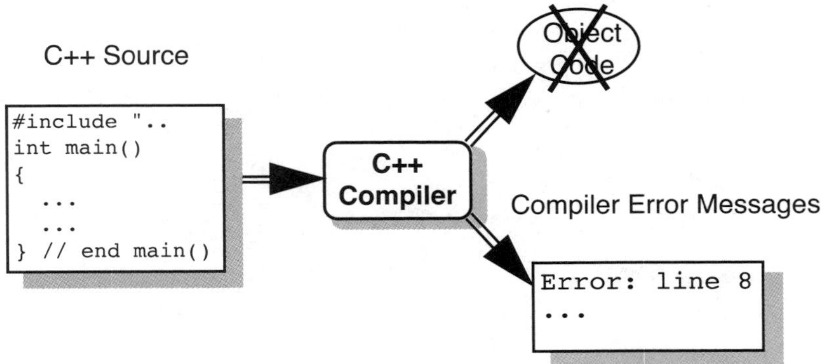

Figure 4.4 C++ compile-time errors

Ideally, a compiler's error messages would tell you exactly what is wrong with your program, on which lines the errors exist, and provide some suggestions on how to fix them (or even fix them for you!). In practice, a C++ compiler is rarely this helpful. This isn't because the compiler has a nasty streak. It's because C++ is a complicated programming language. Even though you'll only be using a subset of the language, the compiler doesn't know this and it has to report syntax errors with respect to the language's full syntax.

It's difficult for the C++ compiler to identify the exact line in your source file that needs to be fixed, as an error may not become apparent to the compiler until it has looked at a few more lines in your program. The compiler will often report a syntax error on a particular line number where in fact the actual error occurred on a previous line. Moreover, a mistake on one line can lead the compiler to generate messages about subsequent lines that may in fact be error-free.

Lesson: A single error in your program may give rise to multiple error messages.

Lesson: You'll have to get used to the form of the compiler's error messages, and to looking closely at the lines reported by the compiler, as well as at lines that precede them, in order to identify errors.

EXAMPLE:

The following error messages were generated by a C++ compiler when the opening brace { was deleted from the program shown in Figure 4.1.

```
File "hello.c"; Line 5
Error:    'cout' is not in function parameter list

File "hello.c"; Line 6
Error:    'cout' is not in function parameter list

File "hello.c"; Line 7
Error:    'cout' is not in function parameter list

File "hello.c"; Line 8
Error:    '=', ';' or ',' expected

File "hello.c"; Line 9
Error:    '=', ';' or ',' expected

File "hello.c"; Line 10
Error:   premature end of source file
```

These error messages seem a trifle severe for such a simple syntax error. The messages don't even identify that a { is missing! Since some errors produce a follow-on effect where the compiler flags error-free lines as being suspect, you may find it useful to identify and fix the first few syntax errors and then try recompiling, rather than attempting to deal with all of the cascaded effects of the first error.

Lesson: For some syntax errors it may be worth finding and fixing the first source-code error and then recompiling.

As your experience with your C++ system develops, you'll get used to applying the lessons above in order to find the syntax errors that cause compile-time error messages.

Syntax diagrams for C++ in this book

Because C++ has complex syntax rules and many features that you won't be needing in this apprenticeship, we're left in somewhat of a dilemma for using C++ to teach programming. We want to use C++ as our programming language, yet introducing the complete C++ syntax rules would be overwhelmingly complicated, especially in the early stages of your apprenticeship. We've therefore chosen to present you with a subset of C++ syntax where appropriate. The subset is valid C++ (as it has to be) but it doesn't tell the complete (and, in places, gory) C++ story.

As a case in point, consider the syntax diagram shown in Figure 4.3. The syntactic element that this diagram introduces (**simple C++ program**) is not actually a syntactic element recognized by C++ compilers. Moreover, a `#include` line is not strictly a C++ syntactic element, and you can define a valid C++ program without any `#include` lines or any statements. However, no useful programs can be so defined, and we've chosen not to show these possibilities in the syntax diagram. If you try to compare some of the syntax diagrams in this book with the syntax as defined for the full C++ language, you'll find some differences. Regard our syntax as an abstraction of the full syntax. Believe us, we're doing you a favor.

When you construct your C++ programs you must get the syntax right, unless you want to get some nice, (un)friendly messages from your compiler. But are there any rules for how you should layout your program on the page or screen? Does the compiler care how your program looks? These are topics for the next section.

EXERCISES FOR SECTION 4.1

1 The purpose of this exercise is to find out a bit more about the error messages your compilation system may produce. Take a copy of the syntactically correct Hello program illustrated in Figure 4.1, change the copy with each of the following alterations and try compiling the resulting program. Edit the program to remove one change and to restore the original before moving on to the next change. Observe the error messages that the compilation system produces.

(a) Delete `int main()`
(b) Change `#include` to `#incrude`
(c) Try deleting other characters in the program (e.g. `;` or `"`)
(d) Change the word `Hello` to `GobbledeGook`.

2 Given the syntax diagram in Figure 4.3, identify the errors in the following simple C++ programs (you may assume that `return 0;` is a valid **statement**).

```
#include <iostream.h"
int main[]
{
  return 0;
)
```

```
#Include <iostream.h>
imt main()
{
  return 0;
};
```

3 Try typing each of the C++ programs of Exercise 2 into your computer and compiling them. Can you relate the error messages produced by the C++ compiler to the errors you predicted in Exercise 2?

4.2 PROGRAM LAYOUT AND STYLE

Which of the following four line styles do you prefer to read, and why?

1. whatiswrongwithwritingsentenceslikethisafteralltheycontainallofthe rightletters
2. what is wrong with writing sentences like this after all they contain all of the right letters
3. what/is/wrong/with/writing/sentences/like/this/after/all/they/contain/all/of/the/right/letters
4. What is wrong with writing sentences like this? After all, they contain all of the right letters.

Example 1 is very difficult to read because there are no spaces separating the tokens (words). Example 2 partially fixes this problem, but while you can now identify the tokens, the lack of sentence structure (normally indicated by capital letters and punctuation marks) complicates matters. You'd find this book very difficult to read if we'd adopted style 2! Example 3 also partially fixes the problem, but looks a little unusual in that the character "/" has been used to separate the words. Finally, there's nothing wrong with example 4. It contains punctuation marks, extra spaces, and styles such as capitalizing the first letter in a sentence, all of which help you to read and understand what the writer meant to convey.

The last three examples illustrate the need for **separators** to allow you to identify the individual tokens in a sentence, while the final example also illustrates how other separators (such as punctuation marks) can add additional meaning to the tokens you are reading; for example, adding a question mark indicates that a question is being asked.

The principles illustrated by 1 to 4 apply equally well to the reading and writing of programs as they do to the reading and writing of English. Consider the following two fragments derived from the C++ program in Figure 4.1.

1. `intmain(){cout<<"Hello ";cout<<"Your name"`
   `<<endl;cout<<"Welcome to CS1"<<endl;return0;}`

2. `int main(){cout<<"Hello ";cout<<"Your name"`
   `<<endl;cout<<"Welcome to CS1"<<endl;return 0;}`

The first fragment is illegal, one reason being that the compiler won't be able to find the name `main` when it reads that text. It will only find the name `intmain`. The space acting as a separator between `int` and `main` was removed, and the compiler can't identify the separation.

Fragment 2 fixes this problem by adding just two separator spaces. Did you note where these spaces were placed? Do you think the compiler will complain about the second fragment – after all, not everything has been space-separated?

The answer is that the compiler won't report any compile-time errors for the second code fragment. This fragment is legitimate C++. Characters such as `{` and `}` and `;` act as separators for C++, just as spaces and punctuation marks act as separators in English. The compiler can identify the separators in fragment 2, and hence the syntactic elements and the structure of the program.

Moreover, just as in English where different separators such as punctuation marks add additional meaning to what is being read, so in C++ the different characters act as separators with different meanings for the compiler. For instance, C++ uses semicolons to terminate certain kinds of statements. Hence by looking for semicolons, the compiler can find the ends of statements, regardless of how the program appears to the human eye.

Should a human reader complain about the legitimate C++ code shown in the second fragment? The answer is "yes"! The program fragment is very hard for a human to read. Does this matter? You bet it matters! It's absolutely vital that humans can easily read a program. Your programs will need to be read by you, when you are looking for errors; they'll need to be read by others (for example, to help you look for errors); they'll need to be read by the person who has to mark your programs set as assignments; and in the real world, when you are working with a team of software engineers, you'll all need to be able to read and understand each other's programs.

Lesson: The aesthetics of your program's appearance to the human eye are VERY important.

What can you do to make your C++ programs more readable and comprehensible? There are lots of things you can do, and we regard these as a very important part of the process of software engineering. These things are all **style** issues. Adopting a good style can help to overcome inadequacies in a programming language. Equally, adopting a bad style can counteract the beneficial features of a good programming language!

For many of the C++ language features introduced, we'll also suggest some **style rules** for using those features. Failure to adopt these style rules won't prevent you from writing C++ programs that produce correct results, but won't help you either! The style rules will help you produce readable programs, which can only be a positive software engineering advantage. We'll introduce style rules in the following manner:

✓ *This bullet introduces a good style rule that you should adopt.*

✗ *Whereas this bullet introduces a bad style that you should avoid.*

One of the problems in proposing style rules is that they involve a measure of personal preference (even if the compiler doesn't care about such things!). If you look at different books, you may find different style rules being adopted.[3] We have good reasons for choosing the styles you'll see in this book, and we'll

[3] The instructor on your course may wish to use different styles to those we have used, but if they do ask them why - they'd better have a good reason :-)

explain these reasons as we go along. If you (or your instructor) can suggest counter-arguments and different styles, that's OK (we won't change the book though!). What is most important is to be consistent – adopt a style and stick with it. Using multiple styles **for** things in *one* program IS **as** `confusing` *as* the USE ***of*** the multiple ***font*** ***styles*** in this sentence!

Lesson: Adopt sensible style rules when writing your programs and stick with them.

One of the major aspects of how a program looks to the human eye is its layout on the page or screen, and this is a first area where style rules have a part to play. But what freedom do you have in laying out a C++ program? Is it required that syntactic elements appear in fixed places? What rules govern the overall layout? Good questions to ask. They lead us nicely to the next sub-section.

The overall layout of C++ programs

C++ is a **free-format** programming language. This means that you are free to format your program however you like (so long as you obey the syntax rules). The compiler ignores **white space** (spaces, tabs, ends of lines, blank lines) in programs in most situations. Sometimes one "unit" of white space is needed to separate one word from another (for example, to separate `int` and `main` as discussed earlier), but apart from this you are free to layout your C++ program as you please. You should use white space to make your programs look neat and tidy.

✓ *Use indentation and white space to make your programs more readable. The compiler doesn't care about white space.*

EXAMPLE:

Figure 4.1 showed how we used indentation[4] and white space to make this simple program readable (at least, more readable than the two-line fragments shown in the previous section). Here's a slightly differently formatted, but equally acceptable, version of that figure.

[4] To indent means to move in the lines from the margin. This is not to be confused with indenture, which is a contract binding a (software) apprentice to a company.

```
#include <iostream.h>

int main()
{
  cout << "Hello ";
  cout << "Your name"
       << endl;
  cout << "Welcome to CS1"
       << endl;
  return 0;
}
```

Figure 4.5 Alternative Hello program in C++

The only difference between the programs in Figures 4.1 and 4.5 is the different use of white space. If you don't believe us, try changing your program to the format shown in Figure 4.5 and recompiling and executing it. Try adding additional white space to convince yourself that the compiler doesn't care about white space in certain places.

What style conventions can you identify from studying Figures 4.1 and 4.5?

First, note the vertical alignment of the opening brace `{` and its closing partner `}`, making it easy for the eye to match this pair up. If braces don't occur in matching pairs the compiler will generate lots of compilation errors, as shown earlier. Second, note how the statements inside the braces have all been indented from the braces, to show they are all inside the pair of braces. Finally, note how you can spread a statement over multiple lines if necessary. All of these style issues are introduced in more detail later in the book, so we'll leave specifying and justifying them until then.

EXERCISES FOR SECTION 4.2

1 Try the following two C++ programs, which you saw earlier. Do they compile, and if they do, does their execution produce the results you expect?

```
intmain(){cout<<"Hello ";cout<<"Your name"
<<endl;cout<<"Welcome to CS1"<<endl;return0;}
```

```
int main(){cout<<"Hello ";cout<<"Your name"
<<endl;cout<<"Welcome to CS1"<<endl;return 0;}
```

2 Design and write a C++ program that uses a single output statement to print out your address with each item of the address on a separate line and with a blank line before the zip code (postal code). Experiment with this program (or with the earlier Hello program) by formatting this program in various ways. Try adding white space at various places in the statements. Are there places in your program where adding white space affects compilation or your program's output?

3 In Exercise 6 in Section 4.0 you wrote a single output statement that drew a textual representation of a tree. We noted that it wasn't clear from this version that it was actually a tree that was being drawn. Using white space, reformat the single output statement so that it's more apparent what the output should be.

4 Predict the result of trying to compile a program with the following output statement in it, and then see if your prediction is borne out in practice.

```
cout << "Your
        name" <<endl;
```

4.3 SIMPLE INPUT AND OUTPUT IN C++

So far you've experimented with C++ programs that just generate some output. There are equivalent facilities for providing **input** to a program; that is, for you to provide data to a program from your keyboard. To illustrate some of the input features of C++, let's solve the following problem.

PROBLEM:

Design and write a program that asks the user to input their first name followed by their age in years, and then calculates and prints out their age in hours.

DESIGN:

You can construct a design for this problem even though you don't yet know how to write input statements in C++.

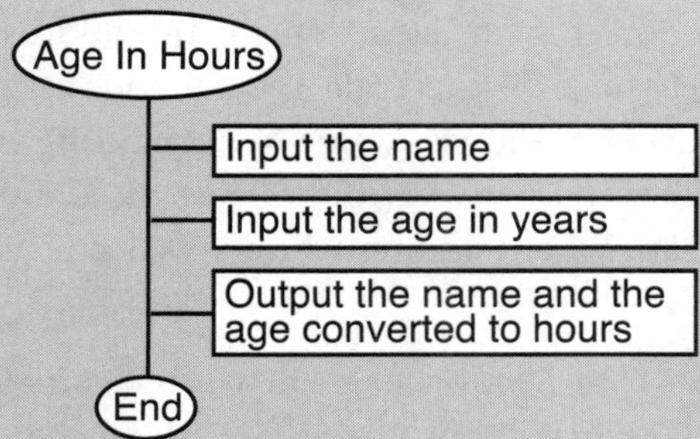

This is a rather simple design, but nevertheless provides a useful first cut at a solution to the problem.

If you were given an age in years, how would you convert that to an age in hours? OK, you'd use a calculator, but what algorithm would you use?

The conversion requires a straightforward *algorithm*: you'd multiply the number of years by the number of days in a year and by the number of hours in a day. You could expand the above design to include this additional detail, and then all you need to know is how to express this algorithm in C++.

IMPLEMENTATION:

Figure 4.6 shows a translation of the design for the Age-In-Hours problem into C++. You should be able to recognize the output statements this program uses, so let's concentrate on the input statements. The user of this program has to provide some input, by typing at the keyboard when the program is executed.

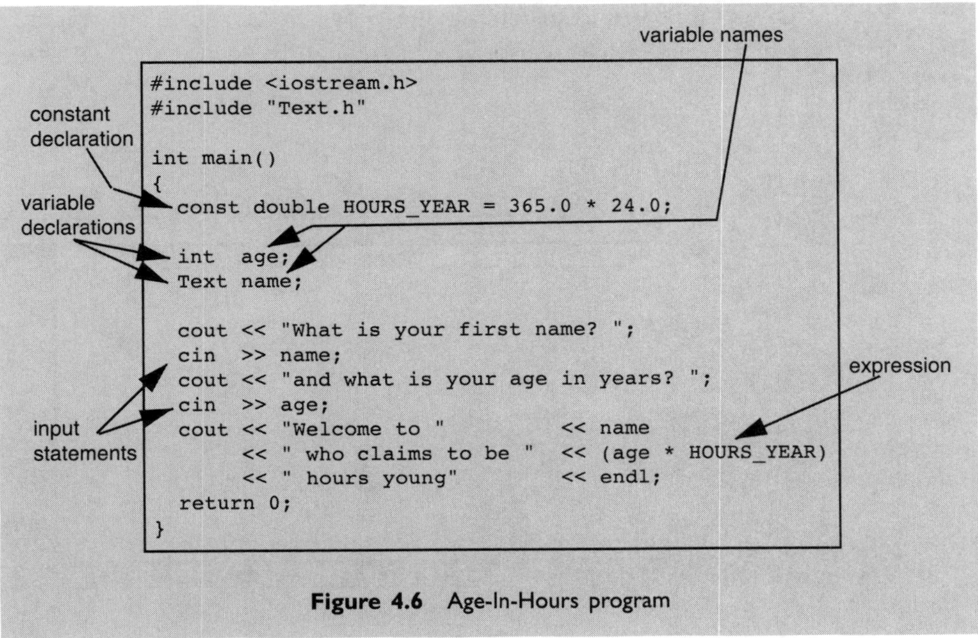

```
#include <iostream.h>
#include "Text.h"

int main()
{
   const double HOURS_YEAR = 365.0 * 24.0;

   int  age;
   Text name;

   cout << "What is your first name? ";
   cin  >> name;
   cout << "and what is your age in years? ";
   cin  >> age;
   cout << "Welcome to "          << name
        << " who claims to be "   << (age * HOURS_YEAR)
        << " hours young"         << endl;
   return 0;
}
```


Figure 4.6 Age-In-Hours program

We want to rely on your intuition in understanding some of the features of this program, since we don't want to overwhelm you with all of the explanations just yet. Compared with the earlier examples, this program has an additional `#include` line. It also declares a constant (`HOURS_YEAR` – set to be equal to the number of hours in a year) and two variables (named `age` and `name`) used in subsequent statements. The program uses output statements "`cout <<` ..." which you've already seen, and input statements "`cin >>` ..."[5] which you haven't.

As you might guess, `cin` is an object of an input type, and `>>` is the input operator. When executed, a statement of the form

`cin >>` *xxx*

means "get some input data from the keyboard." This data has to be put somewhere and the *xxx* provides the name of a variable into which the data can be put, essentially putting the data into the computer's memory for subsequent use.

So, the statement "`cin >> name;`" says "get the characters typed by the user at the keyboard and store them in the variable called `name`." The next input statement "`cin >> age;`" says "get a number typed by the user and store that number in a variable called `age`."

[5] We pronounce `cin` as "see-in."

Try compiling and executing the program of Figure 4.6. Figure 4.7 shows a typical run, even if this user has been slightly economical with the truth about their age!

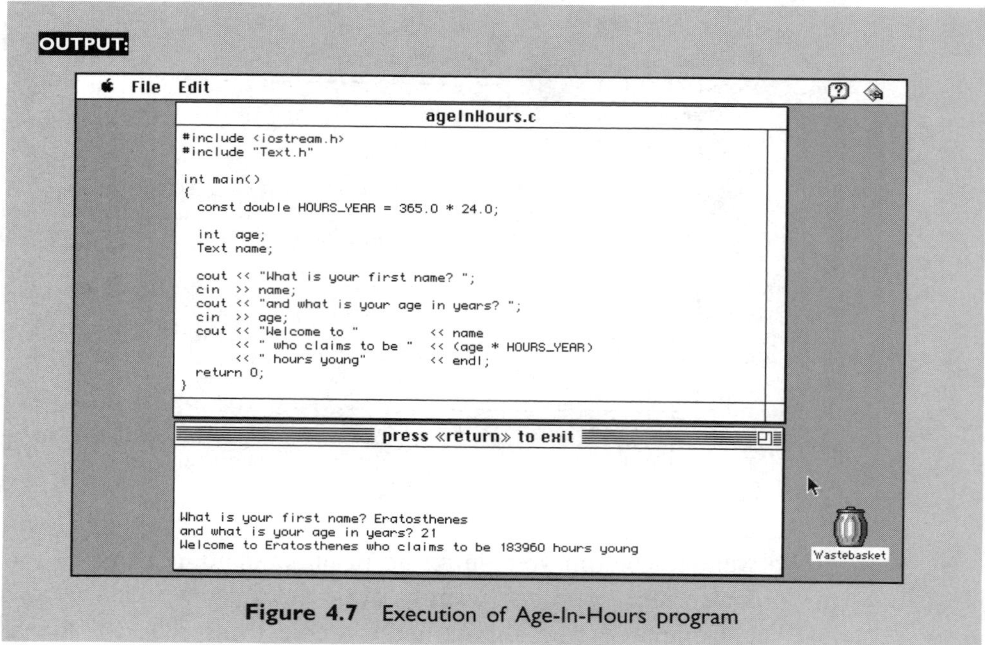

Figure 4.7 Execution of Age-In-Hours program

In this program you can only input a single name. Trying to enter your first name followed by a space and then your surname would cause the computer to attempt to read your surname as your age, and an error situation would ensue.

How can the computer tell when you've finished typing the name and also when you've finished typing the number? The answer is: when you type some white space. White space is used to indicate the end of an input token. Very often you'll type this white space using the <Return> key on your keyboard, which is pressed to mark the end of a line. This is what happened in the run shown in Figure 4.7.

You might want to experiment with white space and input with this program, and this would be a good way to learn a bit more about how C++ input behaves. For example, try typing in something like:

```
Eratosthenes   21 <Return>
```

While you can use any white space character to mark the end of an input item, using <Return> is normally advisable, as without a <Return> your program won't receive any of the data you've typed. This feature of the input system, where input is buffered, is explained in more detail in Chapter 15.

You should note that the above program has no provision to deal with unexpected inputs (for example, if it's expecting to read a number but you type your surname), and it may therefore go wrong in unexpected ways. You should look up in your system manual how to interrupt or stop a running program before you do too much experimentation.

> **Lesson:** It's important to know how you can stop an executing program from executing further. It's often some combination of keys that you have to press. Pressing the <CTRL> key in conjunction with the letter C key is always worth a try.

The final `cout` statement in the Age-In-Hours program extends over four lines, and is used to output some messages as well as the values held by the variables `name` and `age`. The statement also contains an expression (`age * HOURS_YEAR`) that calculates the number of hours corresponding to the number of years, before outputting this value. (You'll be learning a lot more about expressions in Chapter 8.) Of course the person may be more hours older than that calculated, since you only input the age in years and thus ignore any fractions of a year. Also, leap years aren't taken into account, but we'll ignore those potential program refinements.

Note also how you get the value of a variable printed. What would happen if the variable names were enclosed in quotation marks (for example, << "`name` ")? If you can't provide an answer, try editing and executing the program and interpreting the outcome. If you have an answer, try editing the program and see if it produces what you predicted.

The input operator >> and the output operator << are similar, but different, and are easily confused. Here's a tip about how to remember which is which. Think of the operators as arrowheads pointing to the destination of the data. Then a statement of the form

```
cin >> name;
```

means "get data *from* `cin` and direct it *to* the variable `name`." Similarly,

```
cout << name;
```

means "get data *from* the variable `name` and send it *to* `cout`."

Lesson: The input and output operators >> and << point to the destination of the data.

Finally, note the layout of the program. We've used indentation and white space to line things up in the program. The white space used to align the output operators doesn't appear on the screen when the program is run, although any white space within any double quotation marks does. Again, experiment with the program if you're not quite sure of what has just been stated.

EXERCISES FOR SECTION 4.3

1 Change the Age-In-Hours program in Figure 4.6 so that it calculates and outputs the number of minutes (or seconds or days) corresponding to the number of years that were input.

2 Assume that a variable `iq` has the value 150. What output will the following C++ fragment produce?

```
cout << "Their " << iq << " is " << iq << "." << endl;
```

3 How do you know whether the Age-In-Hours program or your program from Exercise 1 are producing the right answers? What should you do to check that the answers seem correct?

4 You know you have to use the correct input and output operators with `cin` and `cout`, respectively, and you've been given a lesson to remember which is which. What will happen if you use the wrong operator? Try it and see.

5 Find out for your computer system how you can stop an executing program. (Switching off the power is not a good answer!) This usually involves the keyboard or possibly using the mouse. Try out your answer by running the Age-In-Hours program and stopping it before you type in the name. Try compiling, running, and stopping the following C++ program (there are some language features used here that you'll meet in later chapters).

```
#include <iostream.h>

int main()
{
  for (;;)
  {
    cout << "You'd better stop this program ..." << endl;
  }
  return 0;
}
```

4.4 COMMENTS

Comments: in general terms

To make a program more readable you often want to introduce some additional words in a natural language to help the reader understand what the program is about.

EXAMPLE:

Recall the recipe program introduced in Chapter 1, the outline of which was:

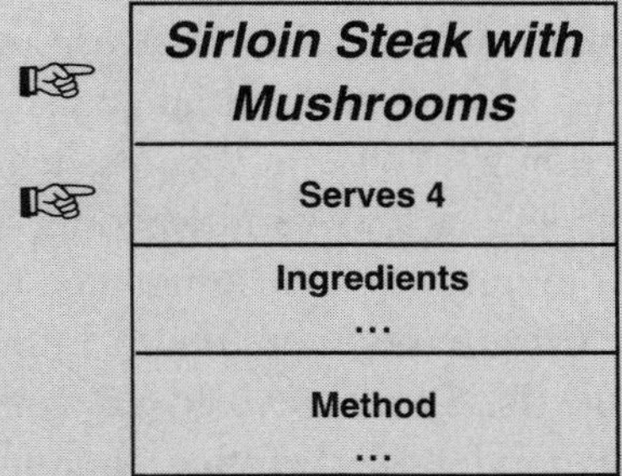

The words being pointed to are **comments**, the first giving an overall (abstract) description of the recipe, and the second indicating that the recipe is intended for four people. You could have figured out both pieces of information by looking at the list of ingredients (which provides a lot more low-level detail) but it's more convenient to see the comments. Note that neither comment is an instruction to the chef. You could use the same recipe program to serve two hungry C++ programmers (or eight ancient Pascal programmers :-)!

C++ comments are also something you need to get your teeth into.

Comments: in C++ terms

Looking back at the program in Figure 4.6, could you have figured out what it was doing without the explanation given? If you'd previously programmed in C or C++ you might reply "Whey aye man, nay bother"[6] but otherwise the program is fairly incomprehensible.

Program statements by themselves aren't very readable for a human. The language statements may be precise and unambiguous, but they're not English. Even when you're familiar with a programming language and its hieroglyphics, the meaning of a program may not leap out at you instantly. The program statements will, of course, define exactly what the program will do when executed, but this definition can be rather low-level. What you need is a higher-level description or overview of what's supposed to be going on.

We've already stressed the importance of programs being readable (can you remember the reasons?). So, how can you incorporate additional descriptions in a program, in the form of natural language commentary, that help explain what the program is doing? You don't want such comments to change the execution behavior of a program; they're not adding anything that the compiler will take note of, they're merely for the human reader of the code.

C++ allows you to put comments into a program, interspersed with the language statements. There have to be syntax rules that permit the comments in a program to be identified so the compiler can ignore them. A simple syntax diagram for a comment follows.

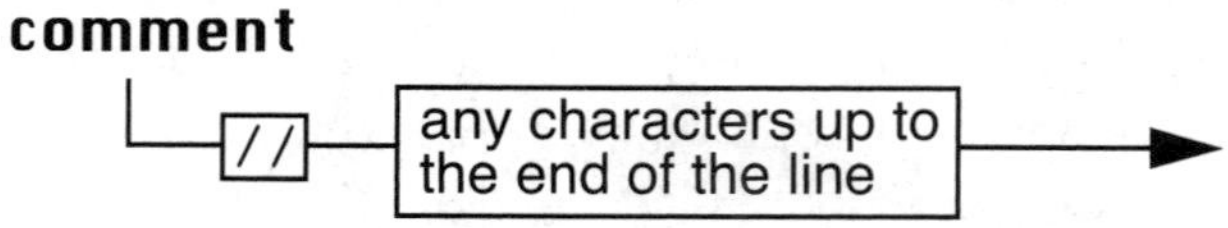

comment

// → any characters up to the end of the line →

In words, the start of a C++ comment is identified by the pair of characters // and the end of the comment is the end of the line on which the comment occurs. All characters after the start-of-comment pair // are ignored by the compiler. Note that there cannot be a space between the two / characters.

EXAMPLE:

Figure 4.8 shows comments in use: it's the Hello program you saw earlier with some comments added.

[6] Slang from Newcastle upon Tyne meaning "Of course sir, no problem."

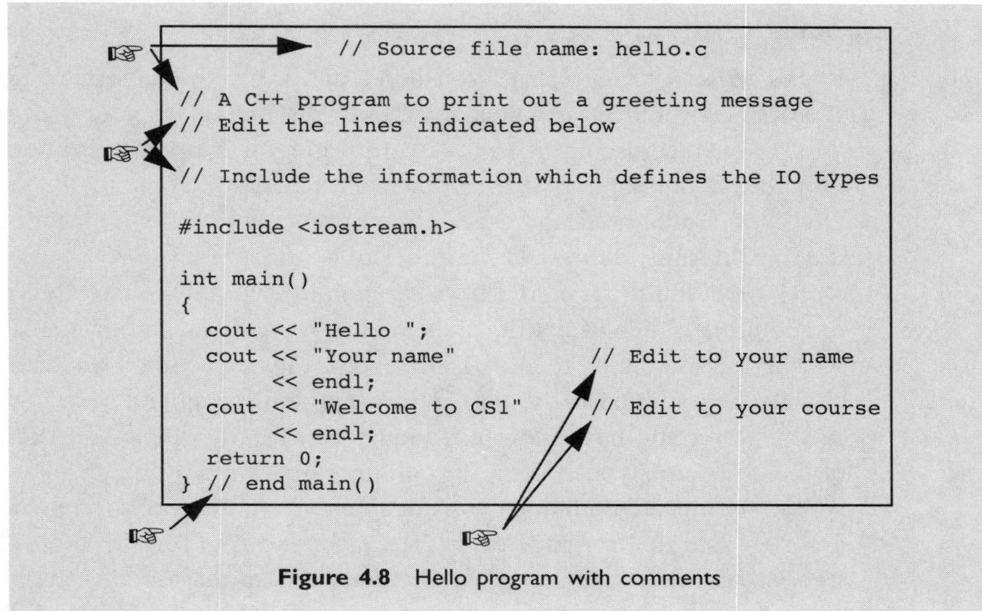

```
                 // Source file name: hello.c

// A C++ program to print out a greeting message
// Edit the lines indicated below

// Include the information which defines the IO types

#include <iostream.h>

int main()
{
  cout << "Hello ";
  cout << "Your name"            // Edit to your name
       << endl;
  cout << "Welcome to CS1"       // Edit to your course
       << endl;
  return 0;
} // end main()
```

Figure 4.8 Hello program with comments

You can see from this example that a comment can appear on a line by itself, or on the same line as a program statement. Remember, though, that all characters on a line after // are ignored by the compiler, so make sure that none of the syntactically important or executable parts of your program follow the // pair.

EXAMPLE:

```
int main(    // Make sure there is a matching  )
{
  cout       // Output a greeting << "Hello ";
  return 0; // Exit the program
} // end main()
```

is read by the compiler as:

```
int main(
{
  cout
  return 0;
}
```

and would result in a few compile-time errors.

Style rules

If you write a program and you don't put any comments in it, expect to get shouted at by someone – your instructor, the marker of your assignment, your boss, or anyone else trying to read your program! A program without comments is indicative of poor engineering practice, and thus of a potentially poor program. However, a program that has so many comments that the C++ code is obscured is probably going too far in the other direction.

Try to view your program from the point of view of someone else reading it; the comments should help explain what's going on in the program. Comments should add something to a program, and not just expand on the obvious. What's obvious to you at an early stage in your apprenticeship and what will be obvious to you when you have more experience will clearly differ, and thus the nature of the comments you add to a program may change over time.

You should add comments to your source code while you're implementing the program, and not five minutes before you hand it in for marking. When you're translating a design expressed in the design notation into C++ code, it makes a lot of sense to use comments to transfer some of the high-level descriptions or abstractions from your design into your source code. This will provide some high-level comments for your program, as well as indicating the link between your design and the C++ code you eventually write.

Lesson: A useful starting point for a C++ program is first to write the program as a set of comments that express the design, to form a template for the code that is to follow.

Let's show an example of this lesson in action. Say you were asked to solve the following problem.

PROBLEM:

Design and implement a program to draw a square on your computer's screen.

DESIGN:

The first step to solving this problem, as always, is to come up with a design. Even though you may not yet have much idea about the eventual C++

code, you can express the design in a high-level manner reflecting how you'd draw a square on a piece of paper. Assuming some graphics-window type was available, you'd come up with a design like that shown in Figure 4.9.

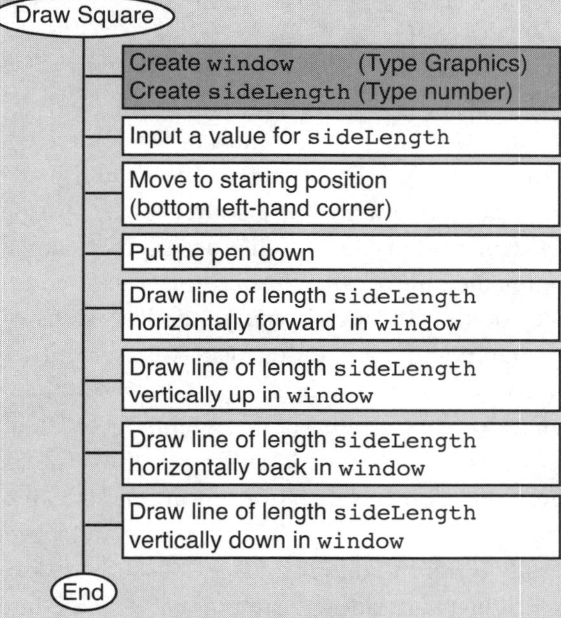

Figure 4.9 Design for Draw Square

IMPLEMENTATION:

Applying the above lesson you could then construct the following skeleton C++ program for drawing a square. This program doesn't yet solve the problem, but it's a good start.

```
int main()
{
  // Create window and sideLength

  // Input a value for sideLength
  // Move to starting position (bottom left-hand corner)
  // Put the pen down
  // Draw line of length sideLength horizontally
  //   forward in window
  // Draw line of length sideLength vertically
  //   up in window
```

```
    // Draw line of length sideLength horizontally
    //   back in window
    // Draw line of length sideLength vertically
    //   down in window

    return 0; // exit the program
} //end main()
```

Comments in the first few lines of any source code can provide useful information for the reader. These comments should provide a descriptive name for the software component that the source code represents, and indicate the purpose of the component. Often the descriptive name relates to the name of the computer file where you can find the source code. This information is useful for anyone looking through some printed versions of source code in order to find some components for reuse, just as it's useful to have a descriptive title for a recipe to help you search for something suitable for a vegetarian. Other useful information to be given via comments includes a component's author, the date it was created, and the dates and authors of any subsequent changes. Some information regarding the I/O requirements can also be useful.

Of course you can, and should, use white space to make comments look neat and easily differentiable from the C++ code. It looks neat if the comments added to the right-hand side of statements are all lined up vertically, as shown in Figure 4.8. Since your computer screen and printer don't have an infinite width, such aesthetics often conflict with practical considerations. We have a particular problem in this book where the page width often prevents us from showing a program exactly as we would like it to appear, particularly with respect to comments. So do as we say, not as we sometimes do in the examples in the book! The source codes accompanying the book provide better examples of the use of comments.

Summarizing these points, we have the following style rules.

- ✗ *A program without any comments is a bad program.*
- ✓ *A comment should add something to the program.*
- ✗ *A comment should not just expand on the obvious.*
- ✓ *Use white space to improve the readability of your comments.*
- ✓ *Add comments while you are implementing your program.*
- ✓ *Capture design abstractions in your source code using comments.*
- ✓ *A source file should identify the name and purpose of the program, its author and date, and I/O requirements.*

Program template

To promote the last style point, you can use a template as the starting point for all of your programs. Our standard template is illustrated in Figure 4.10 and is used in all of our example programs. You might like to create your own version of this template.

Chapter Hello

```
/////////////////////////////////////////////////////////////////
//                    descriptiveName.c                        //
// Purpose                                                     //
// =======                                                     //
// What is this program supposed to do? What problem is        //
//   it supposed to be a solution for?                         //
//                                                             //
// Author            Creation Date                             //
// ======            =============                             //
// Your Name         1 April 1999                              //
//                                                             //
// Input/Output                                                //
// ============                                                //
// What input data does the program expect? What format?       //
// What output does your program produce?                      //
/////////////////////////////////////////////////////////////////

#include <iostream.h>

int main()
{
  // Insert your program here
  return 0;
} // end main()
```

Figure 4.10 Template for C++ programs

EXERCISES FOR SECTION 4.4

1 Identify which of the following lines contain a syntactically valid C++ comment, and for the other lines explain why they are not valid.

(a) `int age;       // Holds the user's age in years`
(b) `// Start of program    void main()`
(c) `{       \\ Ask user for name and age`
(d) `/ / Program created 1st April 2010`
(e) `////////////// What a great book! //////////////`
(f) `cout << "The characters // introduce a comment in C++";`

2 Consider the Hello program (Figure 4.1). Put `//` in front of the statement:

```
cout << "Your name" << endl;
```

Predict what will happen if you compile and execute this modified program. Confirm your prediction by compiling and running the modified program.

SUMMARY

You've now compiled and executed some simple C++ programs. You've taken your first steps as a C++ programmer and learned some basic concepts:

- **syntax rules and diagrams** define how you can construct legal programs in C++;
- **compile-time errors** occur when a program contains syntax errors, and a single syntax error may give rise to multiple compile-time error messages;
- **simple C++ programs** follow a common pattern that can be succinctly described using a syntax diagram;
- **I/O** can involve the use of `cin`, `cout` and `endl`;
- >> **and** << are the input and output operators respectively (pointing to the destination of the data);
- **comments** are totally ignored by the compiler.

You've also taken your first steps as a C++ software engineer. You've been introduced to several software engineering issues:

- **layout** – the importance of formatting your source programs to help the reader;
- **style rules** – our suggestions for helping your program's layout;
- **indenting** – the use of indentation and white space to make a program readable;
- **comments** – add an explanation for the reader;
- **capturing the design** – how to use C++ comments to capture aspects of your designs in C++ code;
- **test programs** – constructing small test programs to determine what C++ features do.

Programs that just consist of simple I/O statements aren't very interesting, and programs that just contain comments are even more boring to execute! What you need are some PDTs and some additional types of statements in C++ that enable you to tackle more complex problems.

END-OF-CHAPTER EXERCISES

1 Explain the difference between syntax rules and style rules. The C++ template in Figure 4.10 contains a number of different items in the comments at the top. Describe what you think the importance of each of these items is.

2 Change the Age-In-Hours program in Figure 4.6 to ask the user for both a surname and a first name, as well as the user's age. Hint: you'll need to declare another variable to hold the surname.

3 Consider the following fragment of a C++ program:

```
int number1;
int number2;
cin  >> number1;
cin  >> number2;
cout << (number1 + number2) << endl;
```

What output will this fragment produce when executed with each of the following typed as input at the keyboard?

(i) `12 13`
(ii) `12                13`
(iii) `13`
`12`
(iv) `twelve thirteen`

4 This exercise involves you using the given program to learn some additional features about the input system. (Beware: it assumes you've completed Exercise 5 of Section 4.3.) Don't worry about some of the unfamiliar C++ features this program contains.

```
#include <iostream.h>

int main()
{
  int aNumber;

  // Repeat the following set of statements continuously
  //   until the user types the number 0
  do
  {
    cout << "Input a number (0 to terminate the program): ";
    cin  >> aNumber;
    cout << endl << "The number was " << aNumber << endl;
  }
  while (aNumber != 0);
  return 0;
} // end main()
```

This program executes the `cout/cin/cout` statements repeatedly until you type a 0 at the keyboard. Experiment with this program and with various uses of white space in your input, identifying some of the characteristics of the input system that you uncover from these experiments. For example, try inputs such as the following, predicting what you think the program will do.

```
1                                        683
32767
-33
1  2  3  4        5  6
Sue
10    15    Bob    20    25
```

5 Design and implement a program that asks the user for their height in feet and their weight in pounds and outputs these measurements converted to meters and kilograms respectively. (Assume there are 2.2 pounds in a kilogram and feet can be converted to meters by multiplying by 0.3048.)

6 Without using the compiler, identify all the syntax errors in the following program.

```
#include iostream.h

int main()
{
  cout << "cout is used to output items << endl;
  cout << "The output appears on the screen" >> endl
  return ;
}
```

Type in this program exactly as given and see what error messages the compiler produces. Edit the file to remove the errors you identified earlier. Does the program now compile?

7 In Section 2.2, the following design was produced for the simple body mass index problem:

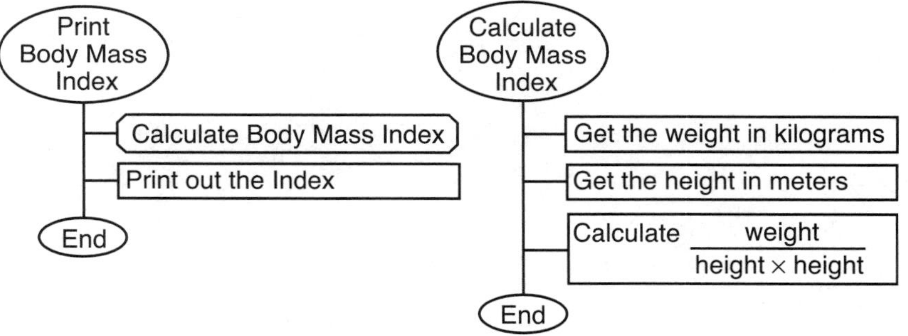

Translate this design into a template C++ program containing just the steps in the design expressed as C++ comments. Check to see if you've made any errors by trying to compile this template program; it should be valid C++ even though there aren't any executable statements in it yet. (Keep this skeleton program around as you'll be adding to it in exercises in later chapters.)

In addition, you could add statements to the template for the input of the weight and height. (Writing an expression to perform the calculation needs some details that will be covered in Chapters 5 and 8.)

5 Types in C++

OBJECTIVE

To develop an understanding of the interface details of a number of types by:

- introducing terminology for type interfaces;
- introducing some important C++ built-in types;
- specifying the interface of some useful PDTs used in the book;
- examining the C++ mechanism for including types in a program.

Programs manipulate objects

5.0 INTRODUCTION

You should have realized by now that *types* are a seriously important concept as far as this book is concerned. Types are one of the major abstraction mechanisms you use when designing a software system. Types are a fundamental part of the object-oriented programming languages we are interested in implementing our systems with, since every object is an instance of a type. Types are where it's at, they're the real thing, one ought to attach a modicum of importance to types. Are you convinced yet?

In Chapters 2 and 3 we introduced the basics of types as used in software engineering. Chapter 2 concentrated on types as an abstraction mechanism that can be vital for the problem-solving and design stages, while Chapter 3 touched upon the use of types in programs. Later chapters will tell you how to construct new Programmer Defined Types (PDTs) in C++, but for the moment we want to concentrate on some of the basics of programming since we'll need these basics later to define new PDTs.

So, what's this chapter all about? Well, programs manipulate objects, and objects are instances of types. If you want to construct programs that contain more than just I/O and comments, you'll need some types to use. The purpose of this chapter is to introduce a number of types that we'll use in the following chapters to illustrate C++ programming basics. The initial emphasis is on *using* types in programs, and thus benefiting from the abstractions these types provide. To use a type you'll need to know the type's *interface,* which as you recall from Chapter 2 consists of a set of abstract values and a set of operations.

A type hides implementation complexity; indeed, this is one of the aspects you'll benefit from in terms of making your programming life easier. However, this doesn't necessarily mean that the interface of every type is simple to understand and use.

EXAMPLE:

Say we gave you a type that accurately models the economy of a country. While the details of the modeling process could be kept from you, the details of how you use an instance of the type to model, say, the economy of the USA, would be enormously complicated. Just think of all of the parameters that need to be controlled: the money supply, the rate of inflation, the growth rate, the price of pork bellies, and so on.

Using the economy-type to illustrate some programming basics would hinder rather than help you; the complexity of the type, as well as the abstraction it represents, would prevent you from concentrating on understanding the basics of programming. You probably wouldn't find much interest in using such a type either (unless you are a budding finance officer). So, to allow you to concentrate on the basic features of programming, we provide a set of readily-understandable types with simple interfaces, yet which allow the construction of interesting programs. The types introduced here include those representing numbers, a PDT that simulates a CD player, and one that permits you to draw graphics on your computer's screen. You won't need to read all of this chapter at one go; you can keep coming back to it to uncover the details of various types as the need arises in following chapters. But first, let's go over some of the background information concerning types in C++.

5.1 TYPES: IN C++ TERMS

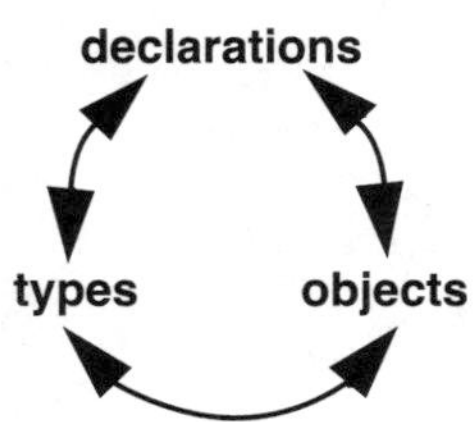

C++ programs manipulate *objects*. How do these objects get created by a program? The answer is by being declared in a declaration statement. But what is a declaration statement? Well, we haven't told you yet (this is the topic of the next chapter) but declarations involve *types*. Here we're faced with the circularity problem mentioned in Chapter 3. Declarations need types, to provide objects whose behavior is defined by their type – an object is an instance of a type. Which one should we tell you about first: types or declarations? We've chosen to tell you about types first. For the moment, just take it for granted that you need to use types in your programs.

The types that you can use in a C++ program come from two main sources:

1. *Built-in* types that are built into the C++ language definition and implemented by a C++ compiler.
2. *Programmer Defined Types* (PDTs) that have been defined and implemented in C++ by software engineers.

The built-in types are always available for use in a program. Every time the compiler runs, it already "knows" about the built-in types as they are an inherent part of C++. In contrast, you have to include PDTs explicitly in a program as needed. These normally come from a library of types that has been set up for you to use and reuse. As we mentioned earlier, a subject for later chapters is how you can define new PDTs to add to a library of useful types. But first, let's see how a type's interface is presented.

Interface to types

To use a type you need to know two things:

1. The name of the type.
2. The interface of the type.

Section 2.7 in Chapter 2 introduced a notation for describing types, which is shown in Figure 5.1. Now might be a good time to revisit that section to refresh your memory if necessary.

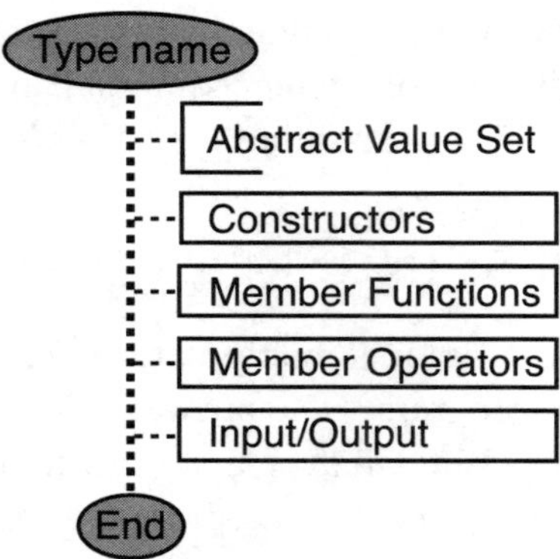

Figure 5.1 PDT interface notation

Recall that:

> **Abstract Value Set** records the set of abstract values that instances of the type can assume;
> **Constructors** tell you how to create an instance;
> **Member Functions** are the operations that can be applied to an instance;
> **Member Operators** are used in expressions involving the instance;
> **Input/Output** means just what it says!

We used this notation in Chapter 2 to capture interface details of types identified during problem solving, with these details being represented mainly by English phrases; for example, see Figures 2.5, 2.6, 2.30 and 2.31 in Chapter 2. Here we're interested in the specific details of how to use a type when programming in C++. To do this we need to present interface details in terms of the way that you would use them in a C++ program. However, it's not imperative that you completely understand all of the features described in the interface diagrams at this point, as you'll see examples of using the features in subsequent chapters.

While the notation in Figure 5.1 has been introduced specifically as a notation for PDTs, we can also use it to describe the built-in types as well. So, this is what we'll do in the next section.

5.2 BUILT-IN TYPES

Many people regard computers as being "number crunchers" that are able to do vast amounts of calculations in unimaginably small amounts of time. Performing calculations was a principal *raison d'être* (reason for existence) for computers, and it's not surprising therefore that types representing numbers were the only types of importance in early programming languages. Nowadays, computers are used less for purely numeric calculations and more for processing symbolic data such as letters and words. Nevertheless, number types are an inherent and necessary part of all programming languages, and C++ is no exception to this.

It's important, therefore, to describe the C++ built-in number types you'll need to use. Their names are `int` and `double`, and they represent integer numbers and floating-point numbers respectively. You'll be using these number types a lot in some programs. But don't worry, this doesn't mean you're going to be covering a lot of mathematics.

The data-processing aspects of programming means that types other than numbers are also important. C++ provides a character type as a built-in type (named `char`), permitting you to deal with characters in programs.

EXAMPLE:

Increasing the pay of someone by a factor of 2 will involve numbers, but finding the payroll record for a person named Eratosthenes could involve a program checking: in this record is the first character of the name an "E" and is the next character an "r," . . . and so on.

You've seen in Chapters 2 and 3 that certain statements such as selection statements and repetition statements have a need for true/false (or Boolean) values, with these values determining the flow of control in your programs. Programming languages provide a means for recognizing and acting upon Boolean values, and C++ has the type `bool`.

C++ has other built-in types, particularly for representing numbers, to reflect the types generally supported by computer hardware. Two floating-point types are named `float` and `double`. The `float` type doesn't provide as big a range of values as the `double` type, although `float` values occupy less memory space than their `double` counterparts. However, some compilers require the use of extra libraries when using `doubles`. We'll just concentrate on `double`'s interface, although that of `float` is very similar.

There are about 20 different ways of specifying an integer type in C++. These allow a programmer to get at integers that have different ranges (and therefore occupy different numbers of bytes of memory), with signed or unsigned ranges. There are even multiple ways of specifying the same integer type! This is a level of complexity you can do without in your apprenticeship, and we'll use only one of these variations: the C++ type named `int`. You'll rarely want or need to use an integer type other than `int`.

C++ integer type

−999 0 42 −3 1024

What type do you think you'll use most often in your C++ programs? The answer is the type that represents integer numbers, namely `int`.

Before describing the interface of `int` in more detail, we need to provide some additional background on what this type represents. The `int` type is actually a shorthand for "the most convenient/efficient integer type for the computer on which you are running your C++ programs." Implicit in this statement is the idea that different computers may have different convenient integer types, normally reflected in the range of values available.

EXAMPLE:

The range of values for `int` on some PCs and their C++ compilation systems is -32768 → 32767, while the range on Macintosh and most Unix systems is -2147483648 → 2147483647.

The C++ language standard permits `int` to provide different ranges on different machines. Note, however, that the only effect of the variation in `ints` across computers or compilers is with respect to the range of values that an `int` type can represent. All other aspects of the interface are identical. Later in your software engineering career you may be faced with having to write programs that work on a variety of systems, and the issue of portability becomes important. But we'll stick with good old `int` for the moment.

While sitting and watching TV
Wondering: is the `int` *type right for me?*
While the bits used may change
You won't feel deranged
As abstraction will help you, you'll see.

C++ `int` *interface*

Figure 5.2 depicts the main features provided by the `int` type. The ranges shown are the two most common ranges; most systems use one of these ranges for its `int`s.

If the range matters to you, you'll need to find out the values for your system. Look them up in your manuals. Alternatively, standard C++ systems include a header file named `<limits.h>` that defines the values appropriate for your system; check your system's manuals to locate this file. However, you may discover if you look at this file that it's not easy to identify the numbers you are looking for as the file usually contains a large amount of low-level (and incomprehensible) detail.

Let's just comment on a couple of features concerning the use of the design notation for the `int` type. The overall interface consists of the main `int` chart (in Figure 5.2) together with the three subsidiary diagrams that provide the details of the operators available with the `int` type. The designator boxes in the main chart refer to the subsidiary charts in the standard manner.

The rectangular boxes on all charts provide the C++ details of what you need to write in your programs to specify a particular operator. For example, the character `*` means multiplication. C++ comments are also provided in the boxes to help you understand some of the C++ notation. All we're doing here is telling you what operators are available, not how to use them. Chapter 8 covers how you use the operators in a C++ program.

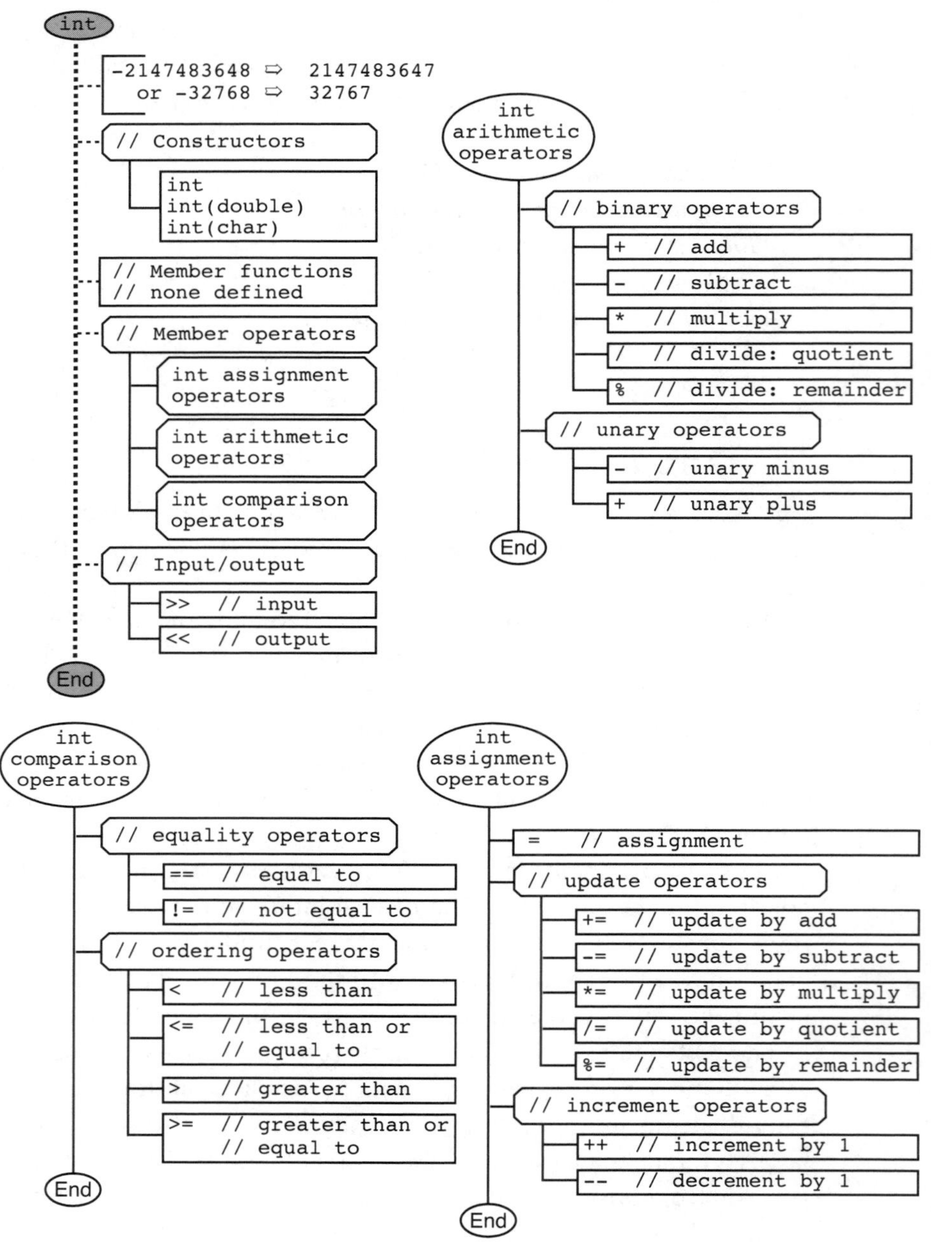

Figure 5.2 C++ int interface

C++ `double` *interface*

3.14 Figure 5.3 shows the interface provided by `double`. In many respects the interface is similar to that provided by `int`, which isn't surprising as both types represent forms of numbers, although `double` has fewer operators.

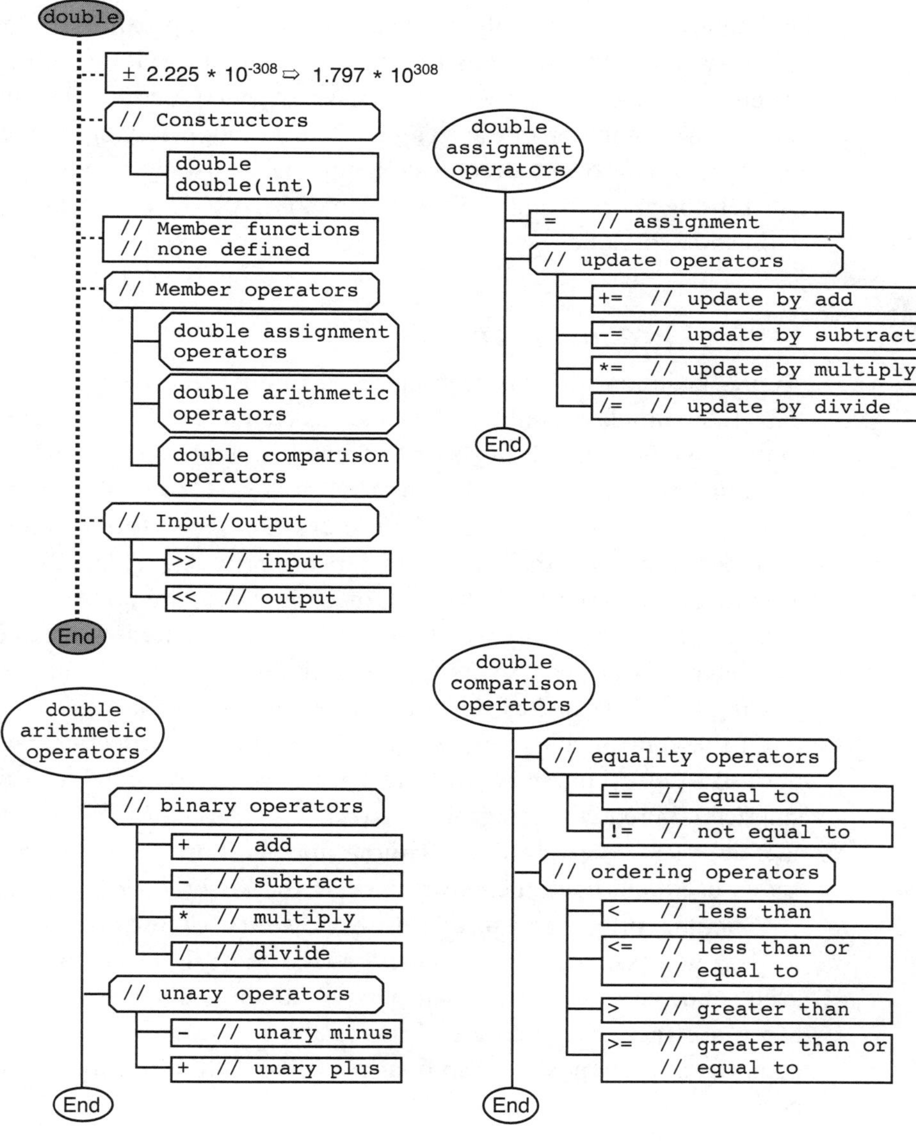

Figure 5.3 C++ `double` interface

The range shown in this figure for `double` may be different for your computer so you should check your system manuals to find the exact values for your system. Standard C++ systems provide a header file named `<float.h>` that provides low-level details for your system, but as with the `<limits.h>` file mentioned earlier you may not find this file especially illuminating.

Note that `double` supports an enormous range of abstract values, although the values quoted are only approximate. Why "approximate" you may ask? A full answer would require us to reveal the implementation of the `double` type, which is a set of details you don't have to worry about. The simple answer is that as the computer doesn't use decimal notation to store values, there's only an approximate decimal equivalent for the actual set of values. Normally you can rely on there being the equivalent of about 15 decimal digits of precision with `double` values.

C++ character type

K A ? " $ m

At the beginning of this section we mentioned that computers are commonly used to manipulate symbolic data such as **characters**. Each letter, digit and punctuation symbol on the keyboard of your computer is a character. Other keys on your keyboard modify this basic set of keys to generate other characters; for example, the <Caps Lock> or <Shift> keys can be used to turn lower-case letters to upper-case. Most of these characters are printable in that, when printed, they are visible on the print medium.[1] Other characters are non-printable in that they don't have a visible representation, and these are generally referred to as **control-characters**. These characters are sometimes generated from the keyboard by holding the <CTRL> key down and pressing another key.

Of the control characters, some are called **print control characters** since they have some effect on, or control over, printing. You've probably used print control characters already when typing in your C++ programs. White space characters such as <Tab>, <Space> and <Return> are the most common print control characters used and have their own keys on the keyboard to represent them.

Programs often need to deal with individual characters. Programs also need to deal with sequences of characters (for example, a person's name), treating such sequences as a single object rather than as a set of individual characters. More abstract types are usually available for such sequences; the `Text` PDT coming up in the next section is such a type. Here we need to discuss the simple character type.

[1] Recall that we use "print" to refer generically to outputting in some fashion.

Most computers provide instructions for storing character values efficiently. Why? Because such symbolic information is the most common form of data that people want to store and it therefore makes sense to store such values using the minimum number of bits. What does the computer store in these bits for a character's value? Well, this is something you normally don't need to know (abstraction to the rescue again), as you can deal with the abstract values in your programs (such as an `A` or an `n`).

C++ provides the built-in type `char` for characters. The underlying implementation for this type uses 8 bits for the storage of character values, thus permitting a range of 256 different characters to be identified. This is enough for most simple alphabets, although these days with increasing internationalization and different alphabets 256 is nowhere near enough values to permit every different character in the world to be represented. The range of abstract character values that C++'s `char` type represents is the simple Roman character set.

C++ `char` *interface*

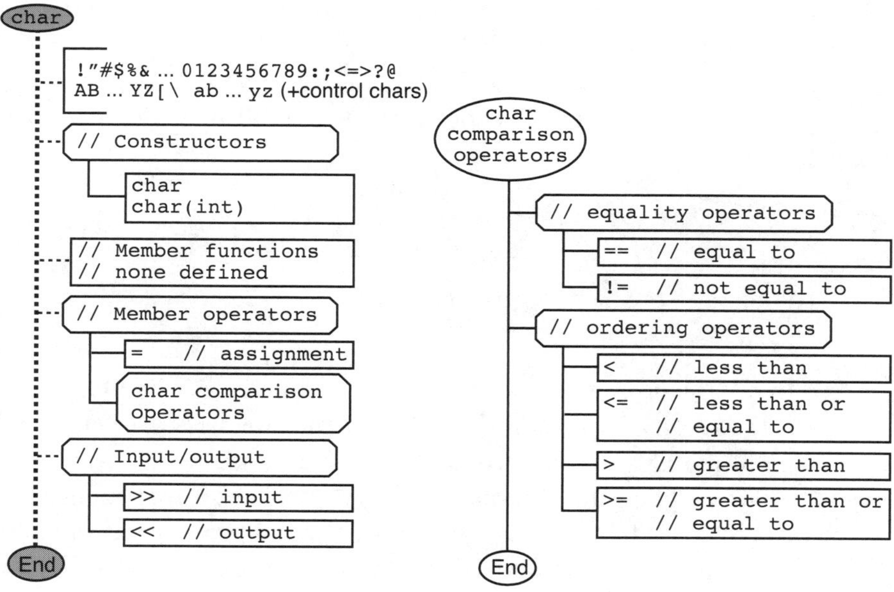

Figure 5.4 C++ `char` interface

OK, so we've cheated a little in the abstract value box in not listing every character, relying on your intuition instead!

You'll see from Figure 5.4 that there are no arithmetic operators defined by the `char` type. Does this seem right to you? Do you think you'd ever want to add an `A` to a `B`?

At first glance this lack of arithmetic operators may seem fine. You'll find out later that there are occasions when you do need to perform addition and subtraction on character values, and we'll explain how you can achieve this.

The semantics of some of the `char` comparison operators require further elaboration. The equality and inequality operators behave as expected, unless you expect the character '`A`' to be equal to the character '`a`' (because it isn't!). But what about the ordering operators? Is the character '`A`' less than the character '`B`'? In fact an ordering of the whole abstract character set is defined, so such questions do have an answer, but we'll address these answers in Chapter 8.

C++ Boolean type

You've already seen the need for the Boolean values *true* and *false.* In Chapter 2, Booleans were employed in the design of programs involving selection and repetition. When you translate the selection and repetition parts of a design into selection and repetition statements in C++, you'll need Boolean values.

Boolean values are generated as the result of asking questions.

EXAMPLES:

"Is one number less than some other number?"

"Is one character equal to another character?"

In other words, when two objects are compared in some fashion, a Boolean value is the result of that comparison. Thus the **comparison operators** that you've seen in all the C++ types introduced so far produce true/false answers.

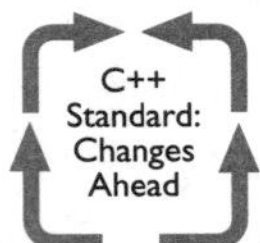

We're going to describe the `bool` type that implements the abstraction of Booleans. While we treat this as being a built-in type, at the time of writing this is a white lie. However, the `bool` type has been proposed and accepted for the version of C++ that is to become an internationally recognized standard in the not-too-distant future. We've taken the liberty of pretending that `bool` is built-in, even though it currently has to be supported as a PDT.[2] It's just that we're ahead of our time!

[2] A `bool` PDT is provided with the programs distributed with this book.

How does the current version of C++ manage without a Boolean type? The answer is that it (mis)uses integer values to represent Boolean values: an integer value 0 represents false while all other integer values represent true. This is adequate, but it's not a very good abstraction, and we prefer the abstraction provided by the `bool` type described in the following section.

C++ `bool` *interface*

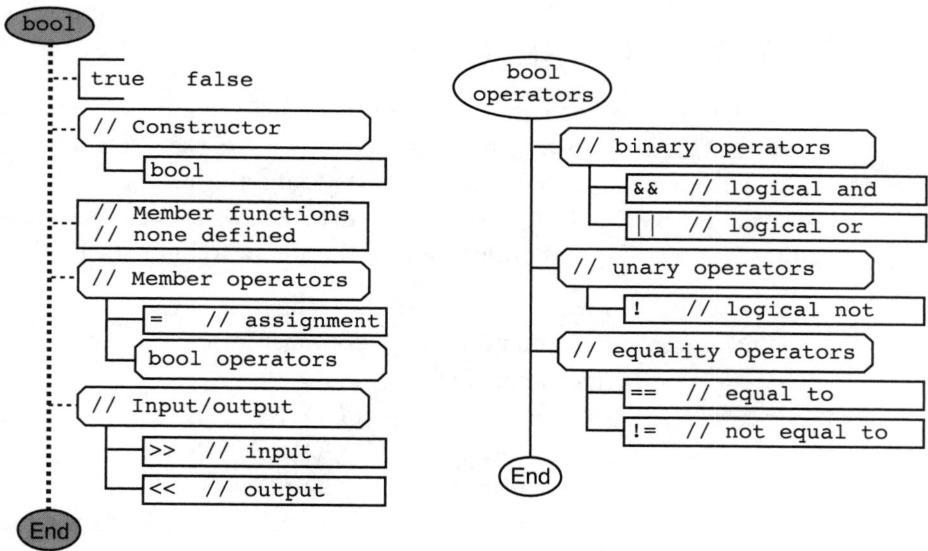

Figure 5.5 C++ `bool` interface

With only two abstract values, `true` and `false`, it doesn't make sense to have any ordering operators, so none are defined in `bool`'s interface. Later you'll see that there's a need to express certain combinations of Boolean values and that's where the binary and unary operators identified in Figure 5.5 come in. Arithmetic operators aren't required for Booleans – it doesn't make sense to multiply `true` by `false`. Instead, you'll need ... but this story can wait until Chapter 8.

EXERCISES FOR SECTION 5.2

1 Determine the range of values for the `int` and `double` built-in types on your machine. The answers should be in your system's documentation.

2 If you're interested in finding out more about how computers work (this isn't necessary for your programming apprenticeship though) look up number representation in a book on computer organization in your library.

5.3 SOME USEFUL PDTs

Now that you've seen the built-in types, this section presents the interface of some PDTs that we've implemented for you to use. You don't need to know how we've implemented these PDTs – that's the power of the object-oriented abstraction mechanism. You just need to know how to use instances of these PDTs in your C++ programs. So, on the menu tonight we have:

`Text`	for strings of text characters;	
`CDPlayer`	a simulation of a compact disc (CD) player, with some associated PDTs:	
	`CDisc`	a CD
	`CSDiscSet`	a CD collection
	`PlayerStatus`	a CD player's status
	`DisplayMode`	the modes for the display on a `CDPlayer;`
`Canvas`	for drawing simple graphics on your computer's screen, with:	
	`Palette`	a PDT that represents a color on the screen.

You don't have to understand all of the features of these interfaces just yet; we'll be using them in the chapters that follow, and that's where all will be revealed.

`Text` *interface*

When the `char` type was introduced we noted that while it represents symbolic information such as letters, there are other useful abstractions that can be provided. The `Text` PDT is one of them.

Often in a program you want to manipulate textual information; for example, someone's name or their address. The `Text` PDT is a useful abstraction for this.

Instances of type `Text` represent a sequence of characters that are grouped together and can be treated as a single object, rather than forcing you to deal with the individual characters in the sequence.

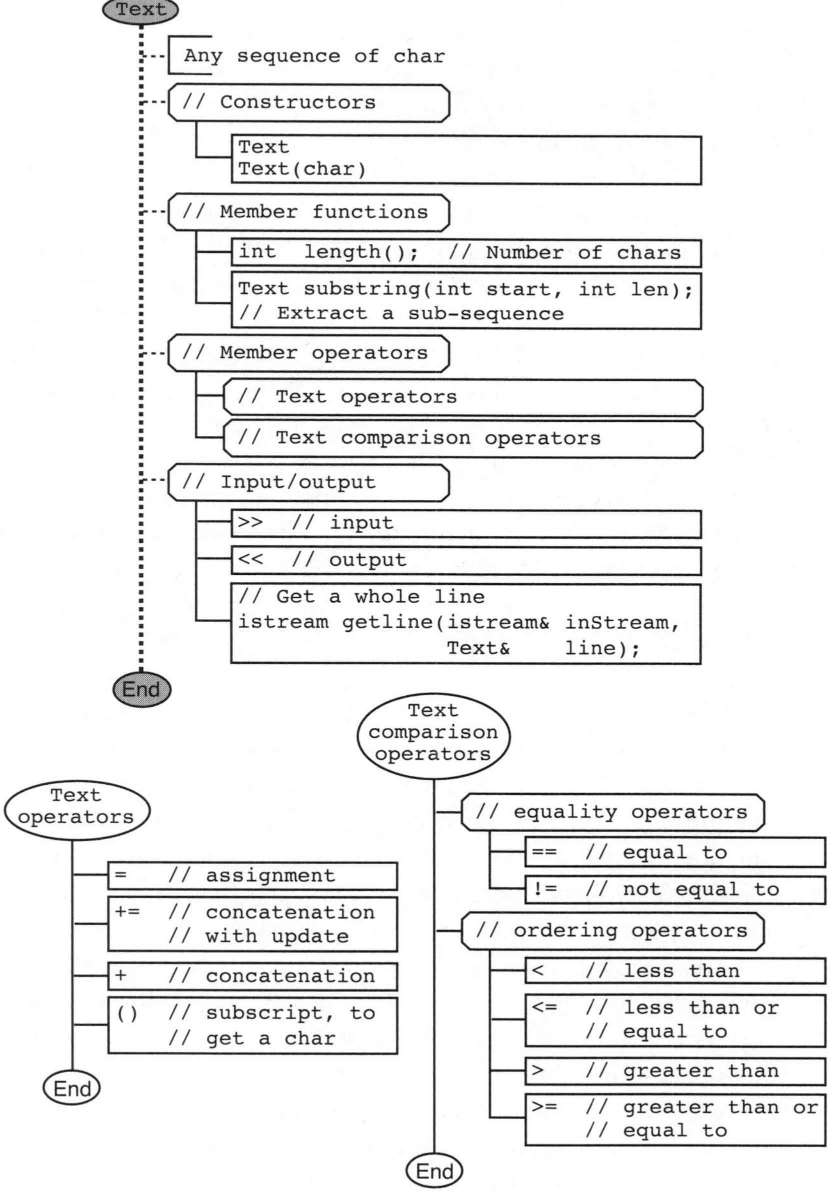

Figure 5.6 `Text` PDT interface

Contrast the `Text` interface in Figure 5.6 with that of some of the interfaces of the built-in types presented earlier. What differences can you notice?

First, the range of abstract values for a `Text` object is specified only in general terms. Second, there are no member functions in `int` but `Text` has two member functions that use some C++ syntax we haven't explained. Third, `Text` has a number of operators: two of them, `+` and `+=`, look like they involve addition (what does it mean to add two `Text` objects together?) while the other operator `()` looks a bit strange. Fourth, `Text` has an extra operation `getline(...)` in its I/O section, also with some syntax we'll explain later. Finally, the comparison operators look the same for both `Text` and `int`, but what does it mean to compare two `Text` values? Did you spot all of those differences?

Let's briefly address some of the differences. First, it's impossible to specify precisely the range of abstract values for a `Text` object, as there can be an infinite number. Second, this is the first time you've come across member functions in a PDT's interface. You'll be seeing lots more member functions in the PDTs coming up. Ignoring the C++ syntax for the moment, recall that member functions are operations you can apply to instances of a type. Thus for the `Text` type there's a member function that will tell you the number of characters in an instance, and one that will extract a specified part (or sub-string) from an instance; for example, you might use the latter member function with a `Text` object that contained someone's full name to extract just their surname.

Third, turning briefly to the operators defined in `Text`'s interface, we often have two separate `Text` instances that we would like to turn into a single object; for example, if we had someone's first and second names as separate objects. This operation of concatenating (joining) two strings could be provided by a member function, however it's common in computer science to use the `+` operator in this context. So this is what the `Text` PDT provides. In addition the subscript operator `()` permits you to extract a single character from a `Text` object.

In passing, let's highlight another C++ feature shown by the availability of the `+` operator in the `Text` PDT. Why can we use `+` for `int` objects, for `double` objects and now for `Text` objects? Doesn't the compiler get confused by using the same symbol with all these different types? No: the compiler doesn't get confused as it can figure out from the types of objects whether an `int` addition or a `Text` concatenation is required, and it will "do the right thing." This is a very important feature of object-oriented systems. It's called **overloading** in C++ parlance – the (re)use of names and operator symbols in multiple contexts. Not clear? Don't worry, we just want to provide a taste here of another neat feature that's described in depth later. We've got to give you some reasons for looking forward to forthcoming chapters!

`CDPlayer` *interface*

As mentioned earlier, this PDT provides a simulation of a CD player that you can control in your C++ programs. Here we'll just provide the definition of the interface for this type (and its associated PDTs in the next sub-sections) as following chapters are going to be using this type and providing detailed explanations of what the various parts of the interface do.

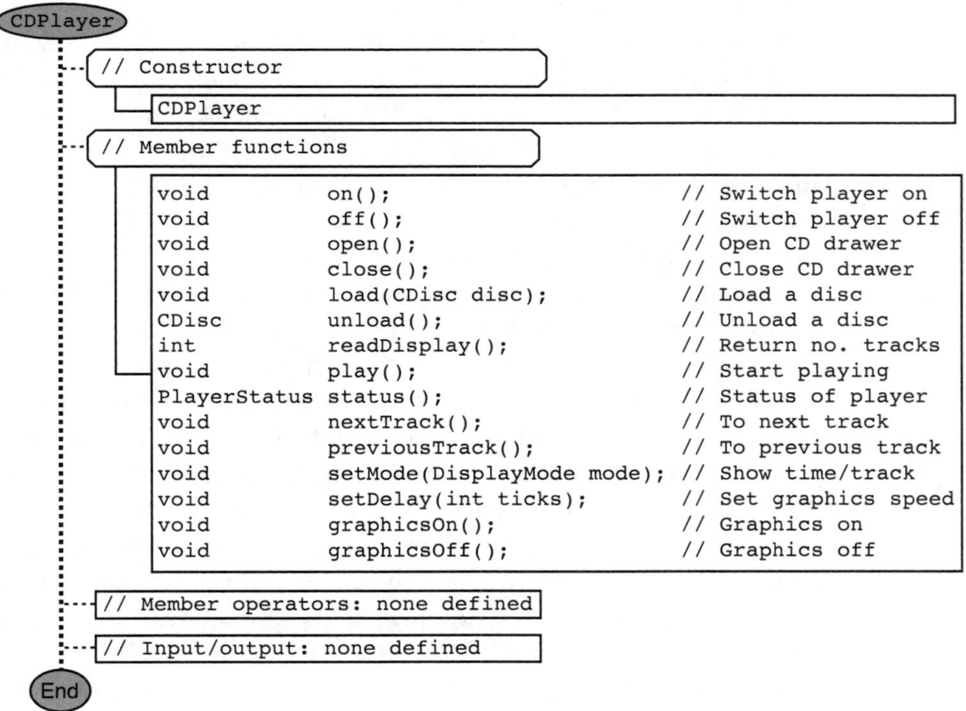

Figure 5.7 `CDPlayer` PDT interface

We haven't shown an "Abstract Values" box for this PDT. This is to emphasize that the abstract values of instances of this PDT aren't normally referred to directly in a program. An instance of `CDPlayer` will have abstract state, such as whether it's switched on and whether a CD has been loaded, but this state is manipulated indirectly by the member functions.

`CDPlayer` has a constructor and member functions but no member operators. This means you can't add two `CDPlayers` together, or compare one with another. The member functions have been specified in their full C++ syntactic form (that is, giving all of the details you'll need when using them in a program), although they've been given names that indicate their purpose. The names, such as `on()` and `play()`, are in the second column in the member functions box in Figure 5.7. A C++ comment adds an explanation to each member function.

A brief explanation of the member functions follows, although detailed descriptions are provided in the chapters that use them. We don't expect you to be able to understand some of the following C++ details yet, but it's useful reference material for looking back at later.

Most of the member functions simulate functions of a real CD player: the ability to load and unload CDs, to play a CD, and to skip to the next track or previous track. There's also a member function `status()` to return the status of the simulated player. Member functions such as `load(...)`, `nextTrack()` and `previousTrack()` set the player's status (see PDT `PlayerStatus`), for example, to indicate an error condition such as trying to play a faulty CD or trying to skip past the final track on the CD.

Most real CD players contain a small display in which information, such as the track number or the length of a track, can be displayed. The simulated CD player provided by this PDT also has such a display, and the value being shown in the display can be obtained using the member function `readDisplay()`. The `setMode(...)` member function can be used to set the display to show track numbers (`TRACK_DISPLAY`) or track time in seconds (`TIME_DISPLAY`). Finally, there are three member functions to control the graphic representation of the simulated CD player. The graphics can be turned on (the default) or off using the `graphicsOn()` and `graphicsOff()` member functions, while `setDelay()` can be used to slow down or speed up the graphics (0 is the minimum delay).

You may be thinking that there's a lot to this PDT and that the above interface description doesn't provide you with all of the detail, and you'd be right. Syntax details are captured in the interface diagram, but the semantics of what goes on in, say, a member function requires further documentation, such as in the descriptions above.

You may be wondering what `void` is. In fact it's a built-in type in C++, but it's not very interesting; it has no values nor any operations. It's needed as part of the syntax for these member functions.

`CDisc` *interface*

The `CDPlayer` PDT needs a simulated CD upon which to operate. This PDT provides that simulation.

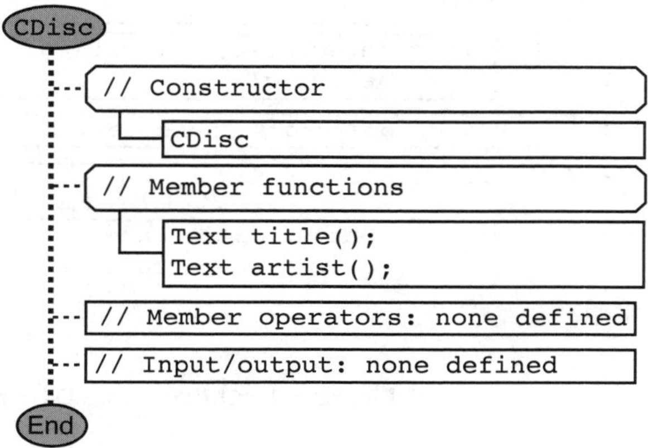

Figure 5.8 `CDisc` PDT interface

The aim of this PDT is to simulate a CD as seen by a person. Since a person can't read the music on a CD, there isn't a member function to do this; the only member functions are those that simulate reading the title and artist (objects of type `Text`) printed on the surface of a real CD. However, a CD player has to be able to read the music even if a human can't, and this is true in our simulated types also.

`CSDiscSet` *interface*

This PDT simulates a particular collection of CDs (Figure 5.9). In other words, an instance of this PDT will behave like someone's CD collection, a collection of `CDisc`s that are sitting on a shelf or in a cupboard, just waiting to be selected and played. For simplicity it's not a simulation of a general collection that you can add more CDs to; it contains no member functions for such operations. The "CS" in the name of this PDT is short for Computer Science, to indicate the specific nature of this PDT.

The member function `selectDisc(...)` permits you to supply the title of a CD and simulates the extraction of the CD with that title from the collection. The `nextDisc()` member function allows you to cycle through the whole collection one disc at a time.

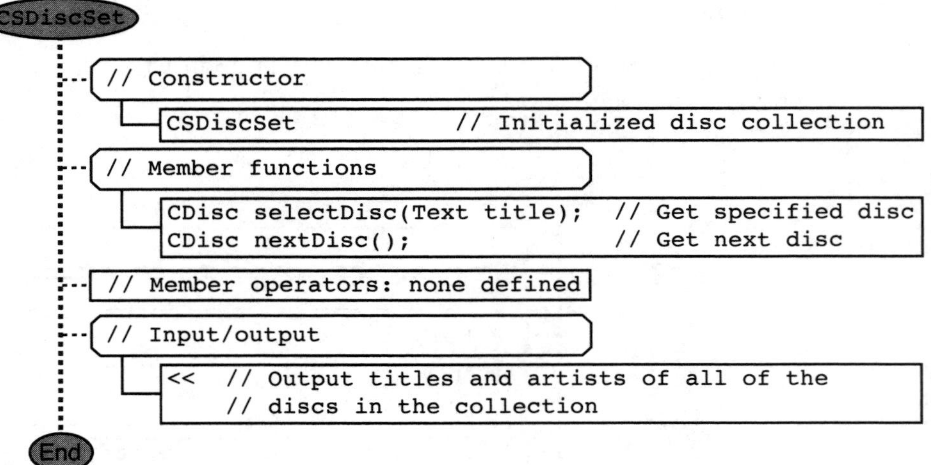

Figure 5.9 `CSDiscSet` PDT interface

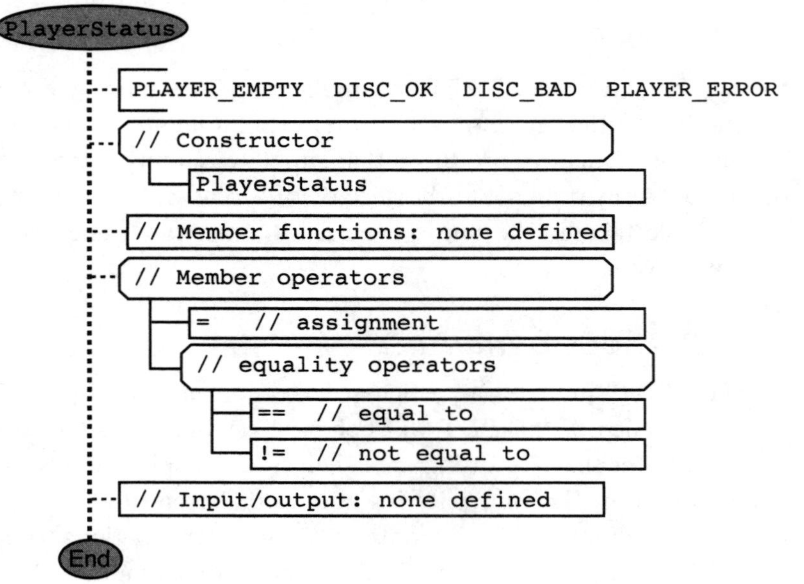

Figure 5.10 `PlayerStatus` PDT interface

Notice that `CSDiscSet` provides an output operator (<<) that prints out a list of all of the `CDiscs` contained in the collection.

`PlayerStatus` *interface*

One of the components of a `CDPlayer` object is a `PlayerStatus` object that represents some of the aspects of the status of the player: whether it has a `CDisc` loaded or not, whether a loaded `CDisc` is OK or bad, whether an error has occurred in the operation of the player. These statuses are represented by the abstract values that an instance of `PlayerStatus` may take. The `PlayerStatus` PDT interface is shown in Figure 5.10. How do you find out the status of a `CDPlayer` object? That's not part of the `PlayerStatus` interface, but you may find the answer if you look back at the interface of `CDPlayer`.

`DisplayMode` *interface*

The last PDT associated with `CDPlayer` is `DisplayMode` (Figure 5.11). Instances of this type are used with the `CDPlayer` member function `setMode(...)` to change the mode of the display on a simulated `CDPlayer` to display the track number or the length of a track in seconds.

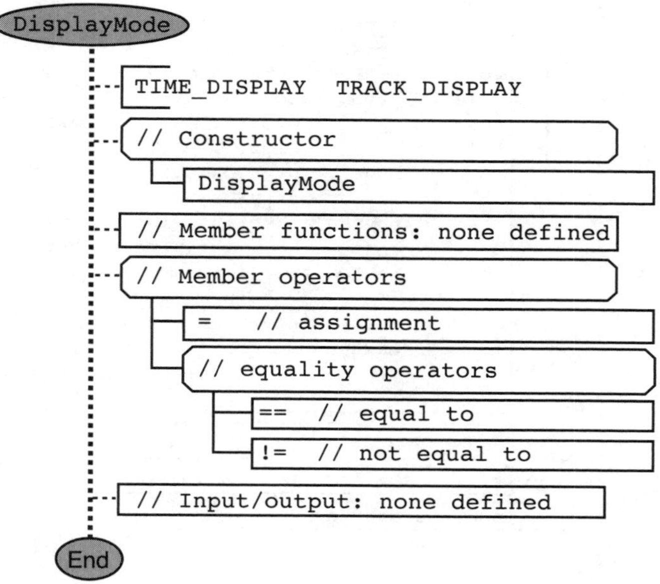

Figure 5.11 `DisplayMode` PDT interface

`Canvas` *interface*

This PDT provides you with the ability to draw simple graphics in a window on your computer's screen. Each instance of `Canvas` has a pen as a component, and by controlling and moving the pen you can cause drawing to take place. Using the terminology established in Chapter 2, we say that the pen is part-of the `Canvas` PDT. The `Canvas` PDT interface is shown in Figure 5.12.

The first thing you have to do to an instance of `Canvas` is to set its size, that is, the number of units (or pixels) in the *x* direction and in the *y* direction. Nothing can be displayed on your computer's screen until the size required is specified. You use the member function `setSize(...)` for this operation. The two member functions `sizeX()` and `sizeY()` allow you determine the values of these sizes.

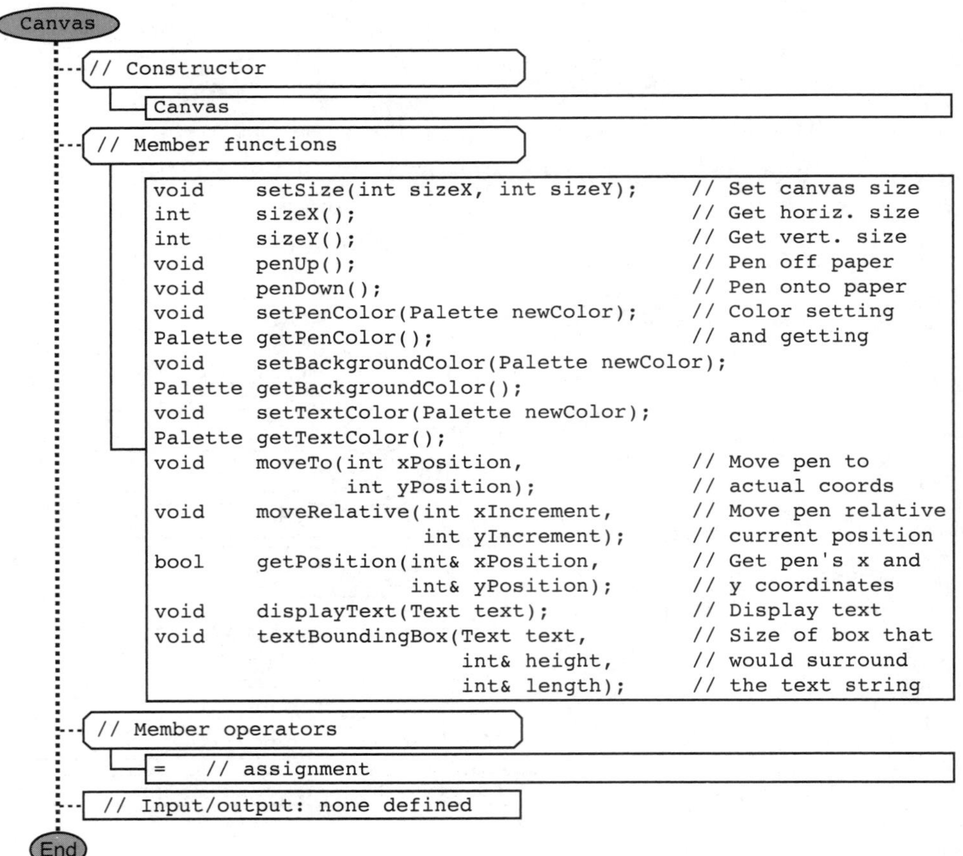

Figure 5.12 `Canvas` PDT interface

Like a piece of graph paper, you can address each point on the canvas by using a pair of values, the *x*-coordinate, and the *y*-coordinate, with the origin being at the bottom left-hand corner. The origin is always at coordinates (0,0). For example, for a `Canvas` instance that has had its size in the *x* direction set to 300 units and the size in the *y* direction set to 200 units, the following diagram shows the coordinates of the corners of the window.

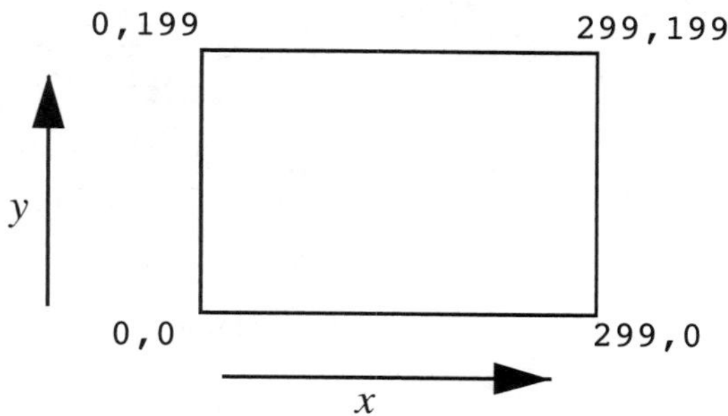

The `moveTo(...)` member function moves the pen to the specified coordinate position from its current position. If the pen is down a line is drawn; if the pen is up no line is drawn. The `moveRelative(...)` member function permits you to move a distance in the *x* and *y* directions by a specified amount. The purpose of the other member functions should be fairly self-explanatory; further explanations and examples of their use come later.

`Palette` *interface*

A pen is part-of a `Canvas`, and one aspect of the pen that you can control is the color of the "ink" that it draws with. The colors you can select for the pen are defined as abstract values in this `Palette` PDT. Did you notice the part of the `Canvas` interface in Figure 5.12 that looked like it could be used to control a pen's color or to tell you what the current color is?

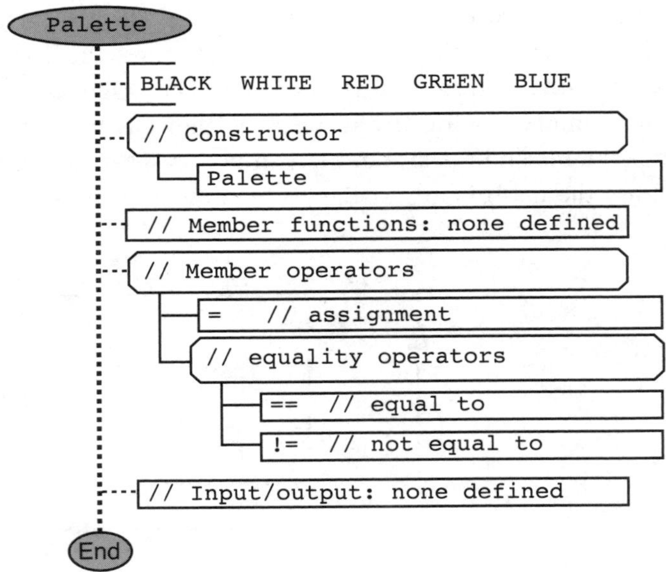

Figure 5.13 `Palette` PDT interface

EXERCISES FOR SECTION 5.3

1 The following fragment of code uses the `Text` + operator. What do you think this fragment produces when executed? (Try it and see also.)

```
#include <iostream.h>
#include "Text.h"

int main()
{
  Text firstName;
  Text surname;

  cout << "What is your first name: ";
  cin  >> firstName;
  cout << "What is your surname: ";
  cin  >> surname;
  cout << "Hello " << firstName << " " << surname << endl;
  cout << "Hello " +  firstName +  " "  + surname << endl;
  return 0;
} // end main()
```

2 Think of some examples in which the `Text` PDT would be useful.

5.4 USING PDTS IN YOUR C++ PROGRAMS

When you've written a C++ program making use of built-in types and PDTs, you'll want to compile that program of course. The compiler has to know all of the details of the interfaces of each type you have used, for two reasons:

1. So that it can compile your program correctly.
2. So it can check that a type's interface is being used properly by your program. If you are attempting to misuse a type's interface then the compiler will generate a compile-time error message to indicate that there's something wrong with your program.

EXAMPLE:

Consider trying to add two `CDPlayer` objects together, or trying to `play` an `int` object, or trying to `bakeACake()` using the `CDPlayer` PDT. In each case the operation is not supported by the type of the object. Hence, the compiler will generate an error message.

For the built-in types the C++ compiler already has all of the information concerning their interfaces; this is part of what being "built-in" means. However, the compiler can't implicitly have all of the information about the PDTs your program uses. Instead, you've got to inform the compiler explicitly about what PDTs you've used, and the compiler can then include the interfaces of the appropriate PDTs as your program is being compiled. This is the purpose of the `#include` lines in a C++ program. You may recall seeing examples of `#include` lines in some of the earlier C++ programs. To describe what goes on in C++ systems with `#include` lines we've got to provide some description of the way PDTs are implemented.

A PDT in C++ generally consists of two parts:

1. Definition of the *interface* supported by the PDT.
2. Definition of the *implementation* of the PDT.

The first of these parts provides the PDT interface information that you've been looking at in the diagrams in this chapter. However, the compiler can't read diagrams, so the interface information has to be provided in a purely textual form giving the exact details of the member functions, operators, and so on. (We've taken some liberties in earlier figures to simplify PDT interfaces at this early stage in your apprenticeship.) The normal convention is to put this textual information into a separate file on your computer. This file is called the **header file** for the PDT. The `#include` lines tell the compiler to include a named header file as part of its compilation process, and in reading the header file all of the information concerning a PDT's interface becomes known to the compiler.

The second part identified above is also generally kept in a separate computer file, and is normally referred to as the **source file** for the PDT. The source file contains all of the C++ code that implements the abstractions described in the header file. To keep this code separate from any program that's using the PDT, it's normal to have this source file separately compiled and stored in a library for use. By now you know that compilation is only part of the process of building an executable program, so if you've used a PDT, the compiled implementation of that PDT has to be extracted from the library to be connected with your program, a process called **linking** (see Figure 1.8 in Chapter 1 to refresh your memory). We'll tell you a bit more about this mechanism when we cover defining new PDTs (in Chapter 12). For the moment, you shouldn't need to worry about this stage. Your C++ compilation system should have been set up to link to the libraries that contain the compiled versions of the PDTs described in this chapter. All you have do is write some programs to use these PDTs, but using them does involve you using `#include` lines, so there's a bit more stuff to cover.

`#include` *files*

Each of the PDTs we've described in this chapter has its own separate header file. The convention used to name header files in C++ is that they have a "`.h`" suffix (guess what the "`h`" stands for), so the full name for a PDT header file is given by combining the name of the type (the type identifier) with the "`.h`" suffix:

```
Text.h
CDPlayer.h      CDisc.h         PlayerStatus.h
                DisplayMode.h   CSDiscSet.h
Canvas.h        Palette.h
```

If your compilation system doesn't support `bool` as a built-in then there's `bool.h` to add to this list.

To use any of the PDTs in your program requires you to use the appropriate header file names.

EXAMPLE:

```
#include "Text.h"
#include "CDPlayer.h"
#include "PlayerStatus.h"
#include "Canvas.h"
```

Thinking back to Chapter 4 and the C++ programs it contains, you may recall the line

```
#include <iostream.h>
```

How come this line uses the symbols < > around the header file name instead of the double quotes used for the other PDTs? The answer is that there is a set of header files that should be common across all C++ compilation systems, and the use of the characters < > tells the compilation system to look for the named file in the set of standard header files. Thus filenames you see enclosed in < > will be common to all C++ systems. In contrast, header files whose names are enclosed by " " are specific to one environment and will not necessarily be available in other environments unless someone has explicitly made them available.

As different computer systems have different file directory hierarchies, each C++ system has rules that govern precisely where in the hierarchy the compiler looks for include files. This avoids you having to specify the full hierarchy of names to get to a header file when you include it. Ideally, the systems you'll be using in support of this book will have been set up correctly so you don't need to worry about the details of what has just been said. If you're trying to set up your own system with the include files for the PDTs, you'll have to read the documentation to find out exactly where the files need to go. Without the include files installed in the place where the compiler can find them, you're going to have trouble compiling the programs that use the associated PDTs.

Syntax diagram

Let's capture the rules just stated for include files in a syntax diagram. An include line is part of a syntax element called **pre-processor line**, since they are read before the compiler processes the rest of the file. The full syntax element follows, with the parts relevant to this section highlighted.

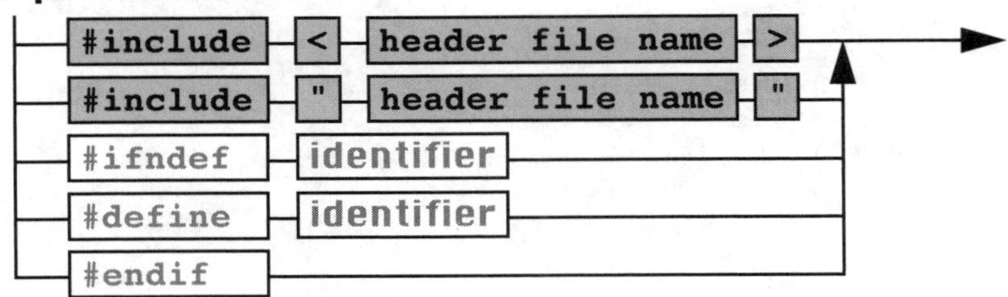

Style rules

Where should you put the #include lines in your C++ programs? The compiler needs to know the interface of a PDT before that PDT can be used (otherwise you'll get compile-time errors), and therefore any include must at least precede any use of the PDTs it contains. We recommend the following style rules to ensure you don't get into trouble with including header files.

✓ *Put all of the* #include *lines at the beginning of your source program,* <System includes> *first, followed by* "Other includes"

✗ *Don't* #include *a file more than once.*

Putting the include files at the beginning of your programs ensures that all of the types are known before your program is compiled. You don't need to include a header file more than once. If the header file has been set up correctly, multiple inclusions won't cause any problems, they just waste compilation time.

EXERCISES FOR SECTION 5.4

1 Try to find the header (.h) files for the PDTs introduced in this chapter and take a look at them. Try to correlate the information in the header file with the description of the type's interface as presented in the figures in this chapter.

2 Take a program from Chapter 4 and move the #include <iostream.h> line to the end, and observe the form of error messages produced by the compiler.

SUMMARY

This chapter has introduced the interface details of a number of types. Put these types into your apprentice's toolbag; you'll be using them a lot in subsequent chapters.

Providing all of the information about these types in one chapter means you know where to find the information when you need to refresh your memory in later chapters.

You now know:

- **built-in types** – are types that are an inherent part of the C++ language, including the number types `int` and `double` (and their limited ranges), `char` for characters, and `bool` for Boolean values `true` and `false`;
- **PDTs** – are Programmer Defined Types that a software engineer has provided, such as `Text` and `CDPlayer`;
- **interface diagrams** – describe the abstract values instances of a type can take, and the operations that can be applied to instances;
- `#include` **files** – are the header files for each PDT that have to be included in your program whenever you use the associated PDT.
- `<file.h>` **and** – `"file.h"` distinguish between system header files and other header files respectively.

So what comes next? Using these types to declare some variables in C++ programs. On we go . . .

END-OF-CHAPTER EXERCISES

1 The two built-in number types have some limitations. Can you think of any problems you should be careful of if you're using these types in programs?

2 Did you understand the icons attached to the `double` and Boolean sub-sections? Did you see double or note the leaning Bool :-)

3 Exercise 4 at the end of Chapter 1 and Exercise 11 in Chapter 2 introduced some designs using "turtles." Translate those designs into a design that uses the `Canvas` PDT described above. The aim is not to generate correct C++ or to understand all of the details of using the PDT, but just to observe how you'd map the turtle abstractions into a next lower-level of detail (i.e. following top-down design as introduced in Chapter 2). (Hint: a first approach might be to design functional abstractions that correspond to the basic turtle commands.)

4 Exercise 16 at the end of Chapter 2 and Exercise 5 at the end of Chapter 4 considered different designs involving a person's body mass index. Given only the types given in this chapter, consider those designs and identify which types are likely to be of use in an eventual C++ implementation of those designs.

6 Variable declarations

Objective

To develop an understanding of variable declarations by:

- describing the purpose of declarations;
- introducing the C++ syntax for declarations;
- introducing style rules for declarations;
- looking at the software engineering issues of scope, global variables, uninitialized variables, and constants.

A declaration

6.0 VARIABLE DECLARATIONS: IN GENERAL TERMS

Sirloin Steak with Mushrooms
Serves 4
Ingredients **4 Sirloin Steaks** **1 oz (30g) Butter** **1 tsp (5 ml) Olive Oil** **8 oz (225g) Mushrooms, sliced** **1/2 cup (125ml) Cream** ***Method*** **1 Brush the steaks with oil, season and place on a wire rack.** **2 Melt the butter and toss the mushrooms in it. ...**

Say you were going to cook the delectable dish defined by the recipe given above. Or, stating this more technically, say you were going to execute this recipe program. What would be the first thing you would do? Brush the steaks with oil? OK, but what steaks? What oil? It's late on a Sunday night and you haven't got any steaks, and you probably don't want to get some oil out of your car to use.

So, you wouldn't start to follow the steps in the method; instead you'd begin by ensuring you had all of the ingredients available. How do you know what ingredients you need?

You could identify what you need by reading through the method steps and identifying the objects that you need, identifying the nouns, as you saw from the methodology in Chapter 2. You'd then see that you need steaks, oil, and so on. But these are just names for the things that you need. These are sensible names and help you understand what to do, but do these names really give you all of the information you need? What kind of steaks? How many steaks? Will a gallon of engine oil be OK? The problem is that the method is using descriptive names that don't give all of the information you need about the types of the objects and the quantities of each required.

Fortunately, the ingredients list does give all of the information you need. The ingredients list *declares* the objects that the recipe program requires. This list comes before the method steps so that when you get to those steps you know what the ingredients are and you have them ready.

Does the list tell you everything you need, though?

It doesn't. In fact, there are some objects referred to in the method that aren't part of the ingredients list (for example, a wire rack, and the container and heat source implicitly referred to in step 2). Of course, they aren't ingredients to eat, but they are things that the recipe is implicitly assuming you have available. If you wanted to provide a truly accurate recipe there would have to be a list of all of the objects you need (a brush, a pan, a stove, . . .). Like a dumb chef, dumb computers require their programs to be "truly" accurate. They can't rely on human intelligence to infer which objects are needed to execute a program. So, a first point to note is:

1. Every object (variable) used in a recipe (program) must be declared and the declaration must occur before any use of that object (variable).

In the next section we'll discuss further the programming equivalent of this and subsequent notes, although some hints are given in the parenthesized terms.

Let's return to the ingredients list in the recipe. Each item in the list is a declaration of something you're going to use when following the method. In addition, each declaration provides an initial value for the item. Thus, when you reach a statement in the method like **Brush the steaks with the oil**, you have the relevant objects (steaks and oil) ready and available in the right quantities and of the right type (4 sirloin steaks and 1 tsp. of olive). What you should note from this is:

2. The ingredients (variables) must be declared and prepared (initialized) before they are used in the recipe steps (program statements).

Because of the flexibility there is in the use of English and the additional interpretation that the human intellect can sometimes provide, the ingredients list above is not a precise example of what you'll find in programs. To make it more apparent what the individual parts of declarations are, let's rewrite the ingredients list in a manner that highlights the important programming aspects, and we'll refer to this modified ingredients list in what follows.

Type of Ingredient	*Name*	*Initialization*
Sirloin-Steaks	steaks	= 4
Butter	butter	= 1 oz (30g)
Olive-Oil	oil	= 1 tsp (5 ml)
Button-Mushrooms	mushrooms	= 8 oz (225 gm)
Cream	cream	= 1/2 cup (125 ml)

Consider further the recipe step **Brush the steaks with the oil**. It could have been stated as **Brush the 4 sirloin steaks with the 1 tsp (5 ml) of olive oil** but there's no need for this elaboration. You know that **the steaks** refers to "the 4 sirloin steaks" and that the oil refers to "the 1 tsp (5 ml) of olive oil". In other words the name of something used in the method relates to an object declared in the ingredients list. Can you think of some advantages of this?

An obvious first advantage is that you can express the method more succinctly by just using the name of an object, for which further detail is given in the ingredients list. You don't have to keep repeating the 4 sirloin steaks in the method: the steaks will do.

A second advantage might become apparent if you think about the following. Say you had to cook this recipe for eight people instead of four. The quantity of ingredients would have to change, but would the method description also have to change? No, it wouldn't; Brush the steaks with the oil is sufficient for either 4 or 8 steaks and 1 or 2 tsp of oil. In other words, the method is expressed in a general manner that doesn't depend on the actual number of steaks, the amount of oil, etc. It would be a real pain if every recipe had to be written out multiple times: one for a single person, one for two people, one for three people, and so on. We say that the method has been **parameterized**, and we look at the wider implications of this in Chapters 9 and 11.

This level of generality in a recipe (program) is a good thing. What did we do to achieve it? We used a name in the method as a general way of specifying something that is to be manipulated, and the name ties up with some specific object declared in the ingredients list. In other words, what we've noted is:

3. The ingredients list (declarations) introduces names (identifiers) for the objects (variables) – steaks, butter, oil, etc. – and these names can be used in the method (program statements).

Let's examine further some of the features of the objects declared in the modified ingredients list. The declaration:

```
Sirloin-Steaks steaks = 4
```

is actually telling you two things in addition to introducing the name of the object. First, it's telling you something about the type of the steaks used in this recipe – the type is Sirloin-Steaks. Second, as mentioned earlier, it's giving a value for the number of steaks. (Other values could also have been provided for example, Sirloin-Steaks, each of weight 8 oz.) We'll return to the notion of the value of an object in Chapter 8. Here, let's concentrate on the type information since this is more relevant to declarations.

As discussed in Chapter 2, types are a very important abstraction mechanism. Sirloin-Steaks as a type of steak is a useful abstraction for "a piece of meat without bone cut from hindquarter of a bovine animal." You don't even need to know what the implementation of this abstraction is as long as you have a butcher you can trust.

Types dictate what operations can be performed on instances of the type, so if one of the steps in the recipe was:

Put the steaks into the dishwasher

you'd be a little confused. Of course in this real-world example the type doesn't actually prevent you from doing such a silly thing, but you'd have to admit it wouldn't really make sense to apply this operation to a steak. In the programming world, each type has a finite set of valid operations associated with it, and the compiler will prevent you from applying invalid operations to objects, but for the moment let's just note:

4. A declaration provides information about the *type* of an ingredient (object or variable) that's being declared, and the type defines the operations appropriate for that object.

There's a final general point about declarations and object names worth noting. Having read the Sirloin Steak with Mushrooms recipe in your cookbook, if you then turned to another page and read the instruction:

Poach the steaks in milk until cooked

would you expect the steaks to be referring to sirloin steaks? Ugh, we hope not. This instruction is probably part of a new recipe, with its own ingredients list in which the steaks now refers to an instance of a different type, namely Fish-Steaks. You expect:

- each recipe to have its own ingredients list immediately preceding the steps in the method – it would be a strange cookbook that listed the ingredients for all recipes in one big long list at the start of the book;
- the object names used in the recipe steps are applicable only to that recipe, although:
- the names can be reused in other recipes (it would be a strange cookbook that tried to use a different name for "steak" in each different recipe that involved steaks). You might get confused if you were trying to cook the fish and meat dishes simultaneously, but in general you would keep the contexts of the two recipes separate ("now I'll switch to the fish dish so steaks in the method refers to the fish steaks").

In other words:

5. Each recipe (component) will have its own ingredients list (declarations); the ingredients are relevant only in the context of the associated recipe (variables have a well-defined scope); ingredient names (object or variable identifiers) may be reused.

If you can understand the points 1–5 that are being made above with respect to recipes and their ingredients then you are well on the way to understanding all of the general points about declarations in C++. Maybe we're whetting your appetite for becoming an apprentice chef instead of an apprentice software engineer, so we'd better get into some C++ . . .

EXERCISE FOR SECTION 6.0

1 The car repair program in Figure 1.3 of Chapter 1 doesn't contain anything that relates to the ingredients list of the recipe. Should it? What "declarations" might be useful for this program, or for a list of instructions for assembling a piece of furniture.

6.1 VARIABLE DECLARATIONS: IN C++ TERMS

The C++ programs that you execute will always be manipulating variables of one type or another. Even a simple program that just consists of output operations is manipulating a variable that is an instance of an output type. Take a look at Figure 4.1 in Chapter 4 and see if you can identify this variable.

Variables play a fundamental role in programming; you can't get away from them, and it's vital that you understand what a variable is.

- The term **variable** refers to a data object that the program can manipulate.
- Variables occupy space in the memory of a computer, and hence can retain information.

Where do variables come from? Clearly they have to be created somehow, somewhere, but are they created as needed by the computer? Of course not, computers are far too dumb for that. You, the programmer, have to instruct the computer when to create variables so that when your program executes, the right variables are available at the right time for your program to manipulate. How do you instruct the computer to create variables? Using declaration statements is the answer.

Declaration statements are the statements you write in your C++ program to introduce the compiler to the variables that your program is going to use. As with all statements, the compiler is responsible for translating your declaration statements into actions at run-time to make the variables available. Declarations thus have a compile-time role and a run-time role, and we need to examine both of these roles. But before describing all of the necessary syntactic and semantic details concerning declarations in C++, let's look at a simple example of a C++ program that contains some declarations to give you a feel for what's going on.

DESIGN:

Say you've designed a program that requires two variables: one to represent a simulated CD player and the other to hold an integer number. Translate this part of the design into a C++ program with appropriate variable declarations.

IMPLEMENTATION:

Recall that Chapter 5 described the PDT called `CDPlayer` for simulating the behavior of a CD player on your computer's screen, and the built-in type called `int` for integer numbers. Here's a C++ program that declares two variables, one an instance of `CDPlayer` and the other an `int`.

```
#include "CDPlayer.h"

int main()
{
  CDPlayer myPlayer;
  int      count;

    // manipulation of variables myPlayer and count in here
  return 0;
} // end main()
```

Figure 6.1 Program with declaration statements

Figure 6.1 shows a valid C++ program. As a declaration statement is a syntactically valid form of **statement**, the program fits the syntax of a **simple C++ program** introduced in Figure 4.3 of Chapter 4. Even though we've yet to describe the C++ details, can you identify the declaration statements and do you recognize anything in their constituent parts?

Have you identified two declaration statements? They are the two lines following the opening brace (`{`), and are terminated by semicolons (`;`) just as you saw with the I/O statements in Chapter 4. If you go back to the previous section and remind yourself of the notes made there, some aspects of declarations might also begin to fall into place. Let's pick a couple of those notes.

3. The declarations introduce identifiers for the variables . . .
4. A declaration provides information about the type of a variable that's being declared . . .

You know about some types (from Chapter 5), so you should be able to identify the two types being used in the declarations (`CDPlayer` and `int`), and hence the names or identifiers being used (`myPlayer` and `count`).

You can begin to see some of the C++ rules for declarations:

Lesson: There are two parts to a variable declaration:

type identifier – to indicate the type of the variable (and hence the valid set of operations you can perform on it together with the set of possible abstract values);

variable identifier – to provide a uniquely-recognizable "name" for a particular instance.

EXAMPLE:

With respect to the program shown in Figure 6.1 we say that `myPlayer` is a variable that's an instance of type `CDPlayer`, and `count` is a variable that's an instance of type `int`. As `CDPlayer` is a PDT you need the `#include` line in the program for the reasons described in Chapter 5.

Two questions for you to ponder.

Why isn't the following line present in the program?

```
#include <int.h>
```

What do the C++ declaration statements in the program in Figure 6.1 cause to happen at run-time? (Why don't you try running the program and see what happens, before you move on to read the answer to this last question.)

The reason that there's no `#include <int.h>` line is because `int` is a built-in type.

With respect to the run-time behavior of the variable declarations, if you've executed the program you'll have seen the following: a window containing a picture of a CD player popped up, and then disappeared. What's going on here? Well, when your program is executed, the computer reaches the declaration statement:

```
CDPlayer myPlayer;
```

Executing this statement causes an object of type `CDPlayer` to be created; in fact, the constructor you saw in `CDPlayer`'s interface is invoked to create the object. Creating the object causes the graphical representation of a CD player to appear on your screen, since that's the behavior that the constructor of this type provides. A similar sequence occurs for the declaration of the variable `count` of type `int`, except there's no visual representation of this variable.

When the end of the program is reached, which is immediately after `count` has been created, there's no further use for these objects so they're deleted; hence the CD player window disappears. Objects have a lifetime, defined by their *scope*, something else we need to explain further, but first let's introduce the link between declarations and the use of variables in a program.

PROBLEM:

Determine which compact discs are represented in an instance of `CSDiscSet`.

DESIGN:

Take a look at the interface provided by PDT `CSDiscSet` (Figure 5.9). Does this type provide any operations useful for solving this problem?

In fact, this type supports an output operator that seems to provide all that's needed to solve this problem. So, all you'll need to do is declare an instance of the type and use the output operator on that instance. We won't bother doing a design diagram for this simple problem, but construct one for yourself if you feel it's necessary for you.

IMPLEMENTATION:

The C++ program shown in the top window of Figure 6.2 is attempting to use a variable `myCollection` in the highlighted output statement. Note that we've commented out the two potential declaration statements in the program (that is, turned those statements into comments) and hence they're not seen by the compiler. As you can see from the compiler's error message in the bottom window, the program hasn't compiled. Incidentally, there are several lines in the source window not visible since they've scrolled off the top of the window; the error really is on line 28! Can you guess what the missing lines are? (See Figure 4.10 in Chapter 4 for a hint.)

OUTPUT:

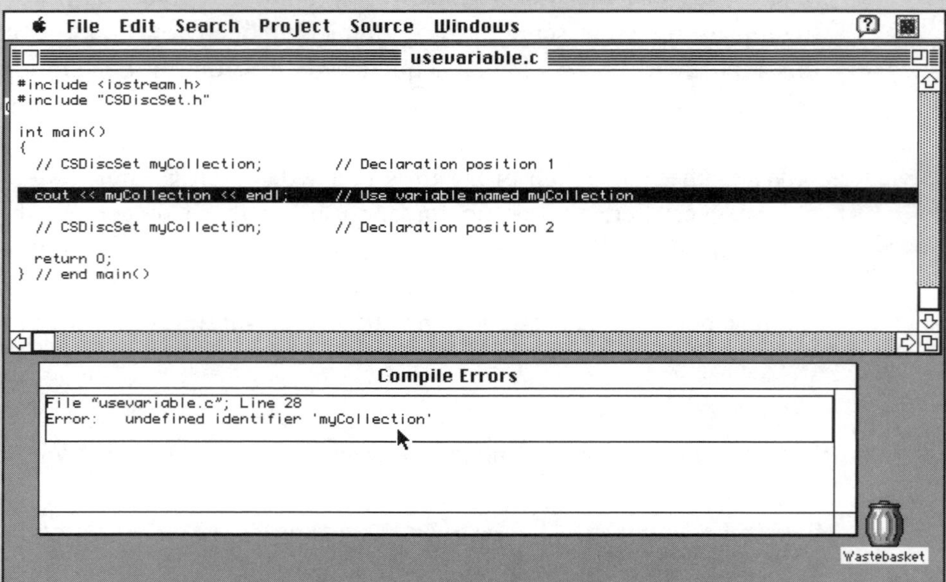

Figure 6.2 Using a variable before its declaration

The reason for the compile-time error is that when the compiler reaches the statement

```
cout << myCollection << endl;
```

it has no idea what `myCollection` is since it hasn't been told. The compiler therefore complains that the identifier `myCollection` hasn't been defined.

The purpose of a declaration is to inform the compiler about the identifiers being used, and their type. The above program demonstrates a lesson that you saw (note 1) in the previous section.

Lesson: It's a requirement that all variables used in a C++ program are declared.

Does it matter where in the program the declaration is found in relation to any use? Yes, it does matter. A declaration of a variable must precede any use of that variable. In the above program, which of the two declarations commented out should be made an active part of the program by removing the comment symbol?

The answer is the declaration in position 1. Try removing the comment symbol (`//`) before this declaration and compiling the resulting program. It should compile and run now.

To convince yourself that a declaration must precede use, also try the following. Reinstate the comment symbol to the declaration in position 1 (so it's again as shown in Figure 6.2) and instead remove the comment symbol from the (identical) declaration in position 2. Then try compiling the resulting program. The compile-time messages will again be as shown in Figure 6.2, indicating the following lesson.

Lesson: A declaration of a variable must precede any use of that variable.

There's a final lesson that the program in Figure 6.2 demonstrates. Did you notice that the first lesson (there are two parts to a declaration ...) states that the variable identifier must be "uniquely recognizable"? You can demonstrate this requirement in action by removing the comment symbols from the declarations in both positions 1 and 2. In effect, the program now contains two declarations, both introducing the same variable identifier. This isn't allowed, as the compiler will happily tell you when it attempts to compile this version.

How could you change this version of the program to be legal? One way is by changing one of the variable names to be different from the other. It's quite legal to have multiple declarations in a program of variables of the same type, so long as the variable identifiers are uniquely recognizable. Try it and see.

We've now covered the majority of the important points about variable declarations in C++, albeit in an informal manner. Let's be a little more precise by introducing the syntax rules for some of these points.

Syntax diagrams

The syntax diagrams in Figure 6.3 and Figure 6.4 capture the first set of C++ rules for declarations and declaration statements. So far we've been looking at the (highlighted) element **variable declaration**.

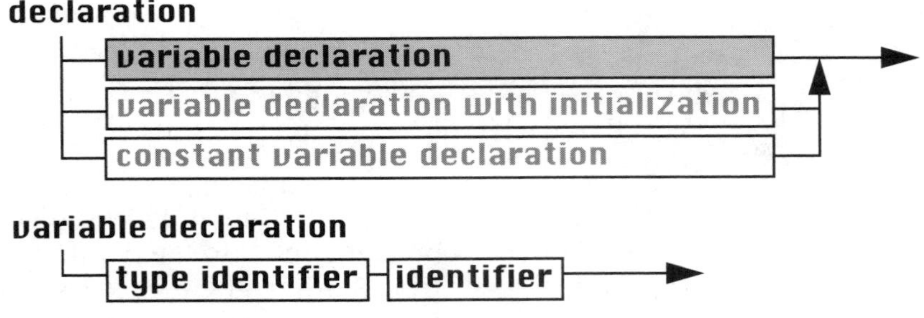

Figure 6.3 Declaration syntax diagram I

As these syntax diagrams show, there are other forms of declaration that you're going to meet later in this chapter.

Variables are declared in a program using a **declaration statement**, which is a **declaration** terminated by a semicolon. So, we introduce the syntactic element **statement** that was mentioned in Chapter 4. (You'll see that there are a few more forms of statement to cover in up-coming chapters.)

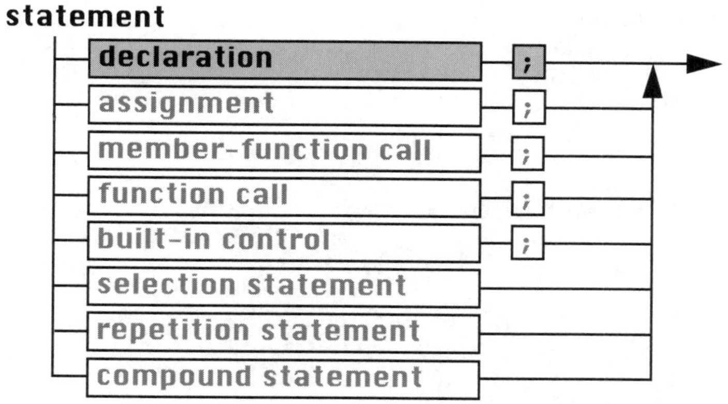

statement

declaration ;
assignment ;
member-function call ;
function call ;
built-in control ;
selection statement
repetition statement
compound statement

Figure 6.4 Statement syntax diagram

"What are the syntax rules for **type identifier** and **variable identifier**?" you may well ask. In fact, identifiers are so important that we've devoted a whole section to them.

EXERCISES FOR SECTION 6.1

1 Write a C++ program that declares a variable of type `Canvas`. What happens when you execute the program? Can you explain this behavior? (Hint: read the `Canvas` description in Chapter 5.)

2 Identify the type identifiers and variable identifiers in the following C++ declaration statements.

```
int            count;           bool      isPlaying;
PlayerStatus   status;          Palette   forText;
double         salary;          Text      address;
Duration       cdLength;        Product   packetOfSoap;
```

Can you identify any style rules being used here?

3 Write a program that declares three variables of type `CDPlayer` and two `double` variables. What happens when you execute this program?

4 Will the following C++ program compile without errors? If not, what is required to fix any problem?

```
#include <iostream.h>

int main()
{
  Canvas drawing;

  return 0;
} // end main()
```

6.2 IDENTIFIERS

Identifiers are the human-readable names you give to items that you introduce in your C++ programs. You've already seen two uses for identifiers in the previous section, namely variable identifiers and type identifiers. Later you'll be introduced to other uses for identifiers, but the rules for all uses are the same and are covered here.

Figure 6.5 shows the syntax diagram for an **identifier** in C++.

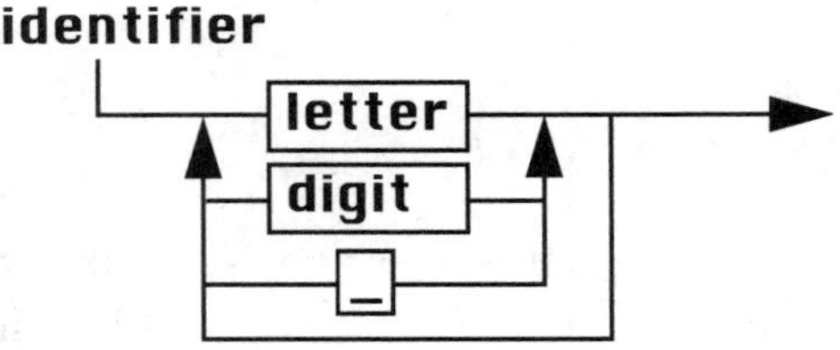

Figure 6.5 Identifier syntax diagram

In words, an identifier must start with a letter but can be an arbitrary-length sequence of the following characters.

letters: a b c d e f g h i j k l m n o p q r s t u v w x y z
A B C D E F G H I J K L M N O P Q R S T U V W X Y Z
digits: 0 1 2 3 4 5 6 7 8 9
the underscore character: _

When the compiler is reading your program, how does it tell when it has reached the end of an identifier? The answer is "When it reads a character that isn't a valid identifier character." Often some form of white space terminates an identifier, although you'll also find semicolons as terminators in C++ programs when a variable identifier is used at the end of a statement. You can see examples of both forms of termination of an identifier in Figure 6.1.

Two other rules you should note aren't shown in the syntax diagram. First, in identifiers the case of a letter is significant; the compiler treats UPPER-CASE letters as being different from their lower-case counterparts.

Second, there are some words that you cannot use as identifiers. This isn't a

EXAMPLE:

The compiler treats all of the following identifiers as being different:

```
pete    Pete    PETE    peTe    peTE    PeTe    pEtE
```

form of censorship (although this might be a good idea for some words), but rather that some words have already been reserved for a specific use in the language. These are the *keywords* of C++.

C++ keywords

Keywords are specially reserved words in a programming language that have a predefined meaning in the language and can't be used for any other purpose. For example, they can't be used as identifiers. You haven't seen many keywords yet, but several will be introduced as different features of C++ are presented. The names of the built-in types, such as `int` and `double`, are keywords that you have seen. We've highlighted the built-in types in ***bold italics*** in Figure 6.6.

There are approximately 70 keywords in C++. The following table lists these (and includes the new keywords proposed for the next version of C++). Even though you won't be using all of the keywords during your apprenticeship, you need to know which words not to use as identifiers. If you try to use any of these keywords as an identifier (for example, as a variable identifier), you'll get compile-time errors for that program. (Some C++ systems help you identify keywords by highlighting them in some fashion whenever you type them into a program.)

`and`	`do`	`new`	`switch`
`and_eq`	***`double`***	`not`	`template`
`asm`	`dynamic_cast`	`not_eq`	`this`
`auto`	`else`	`operator`	`throw`
`bitand`	`enum`	`or`	`true`
`bitor`	`explicit`	`or_eq`	`try`
`bool`	`extern`	`private`	`typedef`
`break`	`false`	`protected`	`typeid`
`case`	***`float`***	`public`	`typename`
`catch`	`for`	`register`	`union`
`char`	`friend`	`reinterpret_cast`	***`unsigned`***
`class`	`goto`	`return`	`using`
`compl`	`if`	***`short`***	`virtual`
`const`	`inline`	***`signed`***	`void`
`const_cast`	***`int`***	`sizeof`	`volatile`
`continue`	***`long`***	`static`	***`wchar_t`***
`default`	`mutable`	`static_cast`	`while`
`delete`	`namespace`	`struct`	`xor`
			`xor_eq`

Figure 6.6 C++ keywords

EXAMPLE:

Here are some examples of legal identifiers.

```
myPlayer  CDPlayer   stopBox   timeOfDay
sum_1     count      x         a_very_long_identifier_1234
```

The examples below present some identifiers that would not be legal. Use Figures 6.5 and 6.6 to identify why each of the following is illegal.

```
2Sum   "AName"   friend   Sum-1   finished?   class
```

Identifiers: General style rules

You have a reasonably free choice over the identifiers you can use in your programs. You now know the syntax rules you have to follow, and that you must avoid using a keyword. Anything else you should know? Well, you need to use meaningful and sensible identifiers.

EXAMPLE:

Say the recipe you saw at the start of this chapter had the following declaration for one of the ingredients:

Sirloin-steaks a = 4

A step in the method would then read:

Brush the a with the oil, season and place on a wire rack.

This method step now looks a little strange. If you knew that **a** is a synonym for steaks it's not so bad, but you'd probably be confused if you just looked at the method. The identifier **a** is not as meaningful to a reader as the identifier steaks. You'd be even more confused if, because of a different declaration, the method step read:

Brush the computer with the oil, season and place on a wire rack.

The important point is that an identifier is something that a human is going to read (either in a recipe or, more relevantly, in your C++ program) and thus the identifier should be readable and help convey some meaning to the reader about the purpose of that identifier. Can you feel some style rules coming on?

✓ *A program should be readable.*
✓ *Use meaningful identifiers for your variables.*
✓ *Make an identifier long enough to be readable and to give some indication of its use; for example,*

`countOfItems`   `CDPlayer`

✗ *Make an identifier no longer than necessary*

`countOfTheNumberOfItemsInThisContainer`

✗ *An identifier should not be as short as possible either*

`c`

✓ *Use established abbreviations (e.g.* `noOfItems`*), or add comments to your program to explain your abbreviation scheme.*

To reemphasize, the compiler doesn't care whether your identifiers are human-readable or not. The compiler would be perfectly happy with an identifier such as `dchRbaXSsSsGhanJsKiLoWQadQokPxZ`. A human reader would be puzzled and confused if they came across such an identifier in your program.

Identifiers are needed for several different purposes in C++ programs. Before we started examining identifiers we identified the need for a **type identifier** and a **variable identifier** as part of a **declaration**. It's useful when reading a program if the style adopted for an identifier gives the reader some indication of the use of that identifier; for example, to differentiate between a type identifier and a variable identifier. So, in addition to the general style rules given above we can usefully introduce some extra style rules specific to each particular use of identifiers.

Type identifiers: style rules

When a programmer defines a type (a PDT), that type has to be given a name, or identifier, to be used in declaring variables that are instances of that type. Look back at the PDTs defined in Chapter 5, and Exercise 2 of the previous section. You'll see that all of the PDT identifiers follow the identifier syntax rules as well as the general style rules, but can you identify any other styles that have been adopted?

The following are the style rules adopted in this book for PDT identifiers.

- ✓ *Begin the type identifier with an UPPER-CASE letter.*
- ✓ *With identifiers that use multiple words, start the second and subsequent words with an UPPER-CASE letter; use lower-case letters elsewhere.*
- ✗ *Avoid using underscores (_) to separate words.*

While an underscore character is a legal character to use in an identifier, our preference is to avoid its use since it tends to make multiword identifiers that much longer. Capitalizing at word boundaries serves the purpose of delineating the separate words for the human eye.

The identifiers for the built-in types don't follow these style rules (they're not PDTs). In addition, you'll see that any PDTs provided as part of the standard C++ libraries don't follow our PDT identifier style rules either. We're afraid you'll have to live with these inconsistencies. We think our style rules serve a useful purpose, but we can't easily change the identifiers used in the standard libraries.

EXAMPLE:

Here are some examples of PDT identifiers as we'd write them.

```
CDPlayer  CDisc   PlayerStatus  Text      BankAccount
Complex   Canvas  Duration      Palette   Library
```

Variable identifiers: style rules

The most frequent use you'll have for identifiers is for giving names to the variables in your program. Here are the style rules we adopt for variable identifiers.

- ✓ *Begin the variable identifier with a lower-case letter.*
- ✓ *With identifiers that use multiple words, start the second and subsequent words with an UPPER-CASE letter; use lower-case letters elsewhere.*
- ✗ *Avoid using underscores (_) to separate words.*

The difference between the capitalization of the first letter in a type identifier versus the non-capitalization of the first letter of a variable identifier helps you to distinguish between these two kinds of identifier when writing and reading programs.

EXAMPLE:

Here are some examples of good variable identifiers:

```
count    xPosition  yPosition    window1   window2
drawing  noOfEs     trackLength  myPlayer  penInk
```

Declarations: style rules

Even though our syntax diagram for declarations doesn't allow it, the following is a legal C++ variable declaration statement that declares three `int` variables.

```
int xPosition, yPosition, count;
```

Normally we don't bother you with the more complex C++ syntax for something we've provided a simpler syntax for, but the above form of declaration is something you're likely to come across in other books or in other people's code. We don't like the above form, as there are several C++ pitfalls that you could fall into. While such declarations are syntactically legal, there are other language features used in declarations that are much less intuitive and error prone. So, we recommend that you follow our declaration syntax and style rules to avoid these future pitfalls.

✓ *Follow the style rules for variable identifiers and type identifiers.*
✓ *Use a separate declaration statement for each variable.*

We're not done with declarations yet. There are some more important points to cover, as well as those additional forms of declaration statement shown in Figure 6.3. However, at this point, now that you know the basics of C++ variable declarations, you should experiment further with using variables in a program. Thus, we recommend that you leave this chapter temporarily and move on to Chapter 7 which declares and uses several variables in a program that simulates playing a CD on a CD player. After that, Section 6.3 awaits you.

EXERCISES FOR SECTION 6.2

1 Which of the following could be used as syntactically legal type identifiers? For those you think are illegal explain why.

```
RecordPlayer        Floppy-DiskType        switch
integer             double                 Vinyl_Record_Player
ReCoRdPlAyEr        Boolean                Aaaaaaaaaaaaa
Floating.Point      2ndTrack               C_D_P_l_a_y_e_r
RecordPlayerWithSpeedControlFor78RPMVinylDisks
```

2 For those type identifiers from Exercise 1 that you identified as legal, which would you reject on style or other grounds?

3 Considering style rules as well as syntax rules, which of the following do you think would be suitable for use as variable identifiers?

```
RecordPlayer      x            count
complex           3rdWindow    sideLength
weightKG          try          repeat
speed-RPM         window       name
```

6.3 SCOPE AND VISIBILITY

Variable declarations in the source code of a program introduce new identifiers that are recognized by the compiler. Two questions arise. First, how long does this recognition last? In other words, what is the scope or validity of these identifiers? Second, what is the visibility of an identifier? In other words, which parts of a program can use the new identifiers without compile-time errors?

How long should a newly introduced identifier be valid?

- forever?
- just for your source file?
- for some smaller unit?

If the identifiers were valid forever, you could never reuse an identifier. Once someone has used a particular identifier, the compiler would remember that identifier and prevent anyone else from using it. This would be a strange state of affairs. Just imagine the compiler's error message.

> Sorry, the identifier `direction` cannot be used. It has already been used by Stroustrup in 1991.

The world would quickly run out of sensible identifiers. It would be like requiring every person to have a unique name. Clearly, we need some way of restricting the lifetime, and hence validity, of an identifier. This is the issue of the **scope of an identifier**. An associated issue is the scope, or lifetime, of a variable when a program is executed. We discussed this earlier in Section 6.1, so for the moment let's concentrate on the compile-time issues.

Having identifiers in scope just for the source file (that is, while the compiler is compiling that file) would be an improvement on "forever"; at least the variable identifiers in one file would then be independent of the identifiers used in other files. Having even more restricted levels of scope turns out to be useful in programming languages for at least two good software engineering reasons:

1. It permits the visibility of names to be restricted to just those software components that need to know those identifiers.
2. It allows you to reuse identifiers.

Let's illustrate these points with a real-world analogy.

EXAMPLE:

Say an instructor wishes to contact a particular student in a class. They could announce "Would Bill Major come and see me at the end of the class." They wouldn't expect every Bill Major in the world to come running. They wouldn't even expect every Bill Major in the university to come. They would expect that the scope and visibility of their request was just the class present at that time. The question could be asked again in the next class with a different set of students. The identifier "Bill Major" could be reused (multiple students with the same name) and the question would be equally valid in the scope of the next class, although a different result (student) would be expected.

If there are two Bill Majors in the class, the instructor (and the Bill Majors) may have a problem. Which one does the instructor want? This is the problem you run into if identifiers are not uniquely-recognizable as suggested in an earlier lesson.

In C++ variable identifiers come into scope when the compiler reads the declaration introducing that identifier. An identifier goes out of scope, that is the compiler forgets about the identifier, at some other point in the source file. Once a variable identifier has gone out of scope you can reuse that identifier without any complaints from the compiler.

There's equivalent run-time behavior that we've already discussed in Section 6.1 with respect to the `CDPlayer` instance. Objects are created when they come into scope (when the declaration statement is executed) and they are destroyed when the object goes out of scope.

EXAMPLE:

The example in Section 6.1 described the `CDPlayer` object `myPlayer` being created and appearing on the computer's screen, with that image being deleted when the end of the program was reached. You can infer that the end of the program is one of the points at which a variable's scope may end.

The idea of variables being destroyed when they go out of scope has some practical benefits. At run-time, a variable will occupy some of your computer's resources; usually some amount of memory is occupied by a variable to hold its (abstract) state. When variables go out of scope the resources they occupied can be reclaimed by the system. This probably doesn't appear to you to be of much significance given the small programs you've come across so far, but it does become an important issue with more complex programs.

Of course, implicit in the idea of objects going out of scope, and thus being destroyed, is the idea that you've finished with the variable and its destruction is of no consequence to the continued execution of your program.

If you tried to use a variable after it had gone out of scope what kind of error do you think you'd get? A compile-time error? A run-time error?

The answer is a compile-time error. If you try to use a variable outside its scope, the compiler will generate an error message. It's essentially the same rule as before: a variable must be declared before it's used in a program, and using a variable outside its scope is equivalent to using a variable that hasn't been declared.

Now that you're convinced that the ability to have multiple levels of scope in a program is a good thing, let's examine the C++ details of how scope levels are opened and closed.

Identifier scope and visibility in C++

In a C++ source program the braces { and } can be used to open and close new levels of scope in a program. In fact we can introduce you to a new syntactic element, a **compound statement**, to represent a particular level of scope (Figure 6.7).

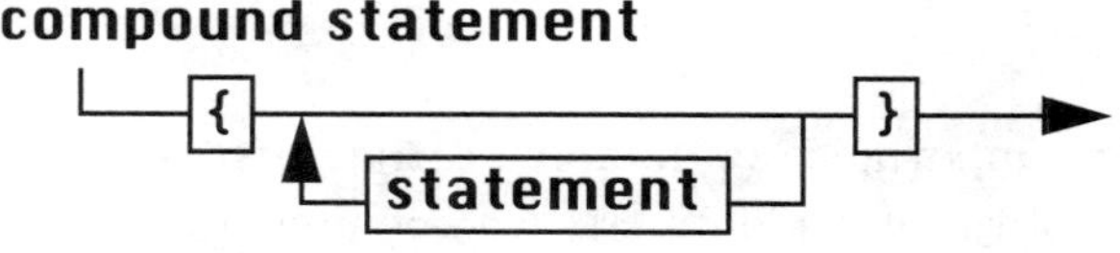

Figure 6.7 Compound statement syntax diagram

In words, a set of statements enclosed in a pair of braces { and } is called a **compound statement**, Furthermore, a compound statement is itself a form of **statement**, which implies that compound statements can be nested, or written, inside each other.

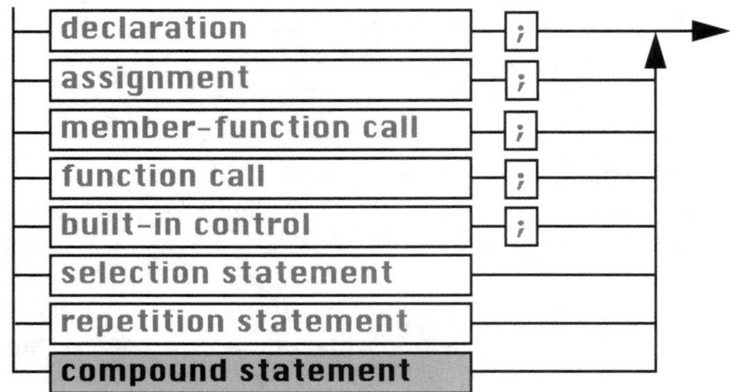

EXAMPLE:

The following is a syntactically legal statement (it's a compound statement), even though all of the extra braces aren't doing anything useful.

```
{
  {
    {
      {
        cout << "A deeply nested statement" << endl;
      }
    }
  }
}
```

The importance of compound statements in this chapter is in identifying the scope of variable identifiers. An opening brace { opens a new level of local scope into your program while the corresponding closing brace } closes that scope. As compound statements can be nested in a source file, you can have local scopes within local scopes, providing further flexibility in the use of variable declarations.

A variable declaration that follows a { is said to be **local** to that compound statement. There's another level of scope in C++ called **global scope**. Can you declare variables at global scope? You can, although we don't want you to do this so the answer should be "No you can't!", but let's first give an example of different levels of scope.

EXAMPLE:

```
int count;          // Global scope

int main()
{                         // Compound statement 1
  CDPlayer myPlayer;         // Local scope 1
  {                             // Compound statement 2
    Canvas drawing;                // Local scope 2
  }                             // End compound statement 2
  return 0;
} // end main()           // End compound statement 1
```

Variable identifiers introduced at global scope are normally visible in all other scopes. If the variable `count` was used inside `Compound statement 1` or inside `Compound statement 2` when the compiler was compiling the above fragment, the variable would have been declared by the time those usages were reached. There would be no compile-time errors.

Identifiers introduced in a local scope are not visible outside that scope, although they may be visible in any nested scopes that this local scope encloses. Thus, variable `myPlayer` is visible within `Compound statements 1 and 2`, while `drawing` is visible only within `Compound statement 2`.

We've already said that one of the advantages of scope is that identifiers can be reused. Does this mean that two variables can be declared using the same variable identifier? Well yes, and no.

Examine the code fragment in Figure 6.8. First question: do you think these variable declarations will cause any compile-time errors (after all, the same identifier is being reused)? Second question: if there are no compile-time errors, which variable would be changed at the different points identified in the figure?

```
int main()
{
  int count;          // Declaration 1
  ...                 // First change to count
  {
    int count;        // Declaration 2
    ...               // Second change to count
  }
  ...                 // Third change to count
  {
    int count;        // Declaration 3
    ...               // Fourth change to count
  }
  return 0;
} // end main()
```

Figure 6.8 Reuse of variable identifiers

The answer to the first question is that there won't be any compile-time errors. Variables declared at one scope level must have unique identifiers; however, the identifiers can be reused at other scope levels.

When identifiers are reused the compiler needs a rule to figure out the answer to the second question above. Its rule is given in the following lesson.

Lesson: The most local identifier "wins."

EXAMPLE:

In Figure 6.8 `First change to count` refers to the variable declared at `Declaration 1` and `Second change to count` refers to `Declaration 2`. These variables are the most local.

What about `Third change to count`? At this point in the program the variable declared in `Declaration 2` has gone out of scope (at run-time, the variable would have been destroyed by the time `Third change to count` is reached) and `Declaration 3` hasn't been reached yet. Thus, `Third change to count` uses the variable declared in `Declaration 1`. When `Fourth change to count` is executed, it also refers to the most local variable, that is `Declaration 3`.

You might question whether it's sensible to have several variables with the same identifier as shown in Figure 6.8. There isn't an easy answer here. In general, using different identifiers will remove any potential source of (human) confusion and thus is to be recommended. However, in practice it's sometimes convenient to reuse variable identifiers. So, *caveat actor* (let the doer beware).

Restricting variable declarations to the most local scope possible makes sense from a software engineering point of view. If in Figure 6.8 you'd forgotten to redeclare variable `count` at `Declaration 2` then `Second change to count` would not cause a compile-time error. The compiler would happily use the variable declared at `Declaration 1` even though this may be a bug in your program as it's not what you intended.

Global variables are the most extreme version of this problem. Experience has taught us that global variables are a bad thing and that unanticipated use of global variables is a significant cause of problems in programs. Further, these problems can be very difficult to track down. So, we say that global variables are a pitfall to be avoided. Don't use them.

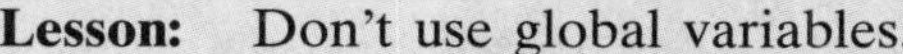

Lesson: Don't use global variables.

Compound statement style rules

Have you noticed any style rules in the way we've used compound statements? You should have noted the following.

- ✓ *A closing* `}` *should appear in the same column as (that is, vertically below) the matching opening* `{`.
- ✓ *Indent all statements inside the* `{ }` *pair by two spaces.*

The reason for these style rules is to make it easy for the eye to see the extent of each compound statement: where it starts, which statements it encompasses, and where it ends. You could use <Tabs> to indent statements, but you'll find you quickly run out of space on a line when nested compound statements are used.

Declaration statement placement style rules

Let's summarize the points we've been making about the placement of variable declarations.

- ✗ *The use of global variables is not recommended.*
- ✓ *Declare variables as and when they are needed; that is, within the smallest scope identified by* `{` *and* `}`.
- ✓ *A variable declaration statement can occur anywhere that any other form of statement can, so long as the declaration precedes use.*
- ✓ *Declarations grouped together at the beginning of a compound statement make it easy to see which identifiers have been used.*
- ✓ *However, declarations placed close to the declared variable's usage are easy to find when examining that usage.*
- ✓ *Generally, place all variable declaration statements together at the start of a compound statement.*
- ✓ *Use blank lines to separate declarations from other statements.*

The syntax rules of C++ allow you to write a declaration statement anywhere inside a compound statement. However, notice from the above style rules that our preference is for all declarations to appear together as the first statements in a compound statement. Sometimes you may wish to ignore this style rule and instead to place a variable declaration closer to the variable's usage. In a very long compound statement, for example, it may be preferable to have a variable declaration close to where that variable is being used, rather than a large number of lines earlier at the start of the compound statement. But it's then sometimes easy to overlook such declarations; if you wish to declare an additional variable, it's more difficult to find the set of existing declarations.

To conclude this description of scope and visibility, let's consider one more aspect of C++ that we've already introduced you to. Recall the syntax of a simple C++ program introduced in Chapter 4, which indicated that all of the `#include` lines should be at the start of your source code. Any identifiers included into your program as a consequence of the source code inside the include files will therefore be at global scope. One of the main purposes of include files is to define the PDTs that you're going to use in your program, and having the identifiers for these types globally available makes sense. Similarly, global constants can be useful in some situations. Unlike global variables, your program cannot inadvertently damage a global type or a global constant. But what if an include file does contain a variable declaration statement? Then you'll get a global variable.

In fact, you've already used a couple of global variables. Cast your mind back to I/O statements using `cin` and `cout`. We said that `cin` and `cout` are instances of I/O types, so when you've used them in your program you've been using two variables with identifiers `cin` and `cout` respectively. Why can you use these variables without any visible declarations and without compile-time errors? The answer is that they're declared as global variables (as part of the file `<iostream.h>`) but you've never seen their declarations.

So global declarations are of some use, despite our warnings above? OK, we'll admit that, just occasionally, global variables do have legitimate uses. You expect input from your computer's keyboard and output to your computer's screen to be possible from anywhere in your program; a global declaration of variables representing these resources therefore makes sense. But our general style rule for global variables still stands: if you were thinking of declaring a global variable, think again! Using global variables is a bad habit to get into. Their use may not trip you up for the small programs you construct during your apprenticeship, but it can be a major problem in real-world software systems involving many software engineers.

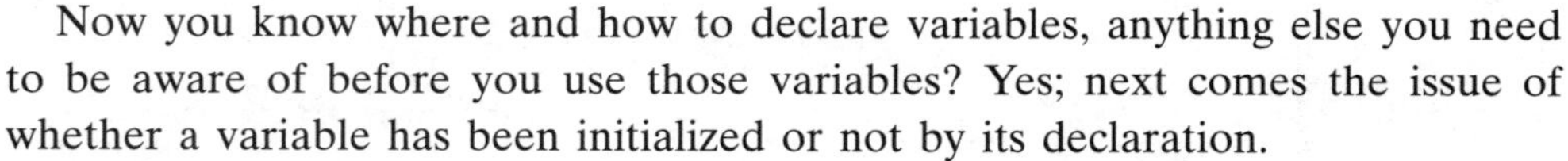

Now you know where and how to declare variables, anything else you need to be aware of before you use those variables? Yes; next comes the issue of whether a variable has been initialized or not by its declaration.

EXERCISES FOR SECTION 6.3

1 Which of the following are valid compound statements, and for those that you think are invalid explain why. (We haven't followed our style rules in these examples to save space.)

```
(a) {{{{{cout "Hell"; {cout << "o"; }}}}}}
(b) { cout << "Hello"; )
(c)   cout << "Hello";
(d) {}
(e) {{{ cout << "Hello"; }}
```

2 Take a look at some other C++ books in the library. Identify whether they use other styles for the layout of compound statements and, if they do, whether you think their style has advantages or disadvantages over our style rules.

6.4 VARIABLE INITIALIZATION

Take a look at the two C++ programs in Figure 6.9. The program on the left-hand side declares two variables and then attempts to print the values of each. The output from running this program is shown below the source code window. The program on the right-hand side is a version of a program you experimented with earlier in this chapter. The output from this program is also given below the source. In both of these programs, where are the output values coming from and why was there a run-time error in one of the programs?

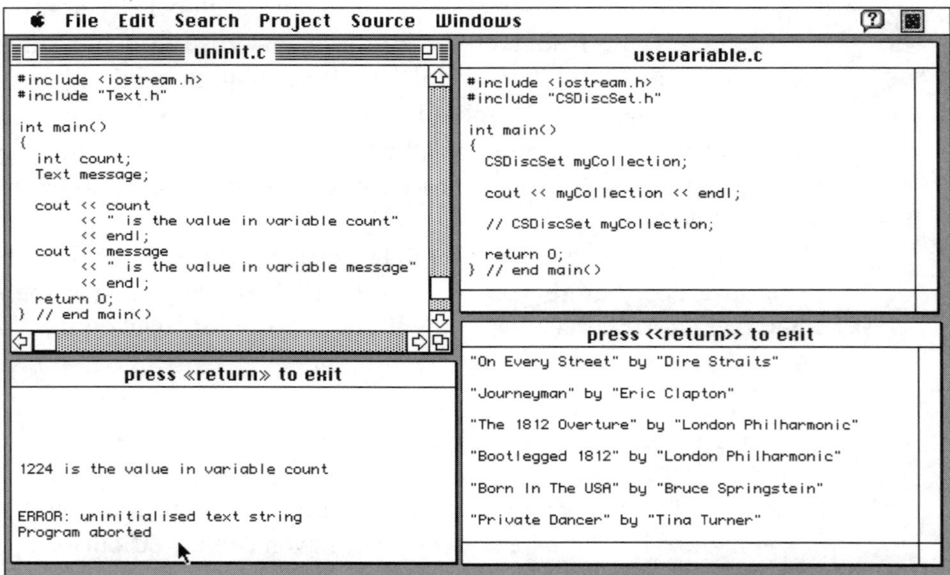

Figure 6.9 Output of uninitialized variables

The execution of the left-hand program seems to have produced a value `1224` for `count`, although there's no such value expressed in the source code of the program. (It's not in any parts of the source code window that you can't see either, honest.) Try this program on your computer, and you may well get a different value printed. However, the output statement that attempts to print out the value of the variable `message` has produced a run-time error. In contrast, the right-hand program has produced what looks like sensible output as the value of the variable `myCollection`.

What's going on here? The declaration of a variable followed by use of that variable (in an output statement) has produced three different effects for the value of the variable:

1. A sensible value (`myCollection`).
2. A random value (`count`).
3. A run-time error (`message`).

The cause of these differing effects is the initial state of the variable following its declaration. What value does a variable have once it has been declared?

In general, when a variable declaration statement is executed all the system does is to allocate memory for that variable and no initial value is stored in the memory. In other words, the variable is said to be **uninitialized**. The memory space occupied by the variable may contain random binary values, so you can make no assumptions about a variable's value following its declaration. For these variables you'd better do something about a variable's value before you do something that uses the value; you need to **initialize** the variable.

So effects 2 and 3 are both the result of an uninitialized variable. For the `int` variable, its uninitialized state hasn't been detected whereas for the `Text` variable, it has been detected and a run-time error has been flagged, a far more useful state of affairs than the behavior with the `int` variable where you might never know that an uninitialized variable has been used in your program. If the variable was part of a program's calculation of how strong an airplane's wing ought to be perhaps you'd care about uninitialized variables being used!

It's a characteristic of all of the built-in types that variables declared in local scope using these types will at first be uninitialized. Not very helpful you might think, but that's the way it is. For PDTs, it depends on what the implementer of that type has chosen to do. For the `Text` type there are checks on the use of an uninitialized state and a run-time error reported accordingly. For the `CSDiscSet` type it turns out that a declaration of a variable of this type additionally initializes that variable, as we noted in the interface diagram in Chapter 5. However, this behavior cannot be guaranteed for all PDTs, and there's a lesson here.

Lesson: All variables should be initialized before they are used. When in doubt, initialize the variable, to be on the safe side.

Fine you say, but:

1. What do I initialize a variable with? And
2. How do I do it?

The answer to (1) is: with a value of the appropriate type. "And how do I express that in my C++ program" you ask? Well, the answer to this is in Chapter 8, which describes values and their expression. Chapter 8 also covers assignment statements that are one answer to question (2).

There's another answer to question (2) which is to initialize a variable as part of its declaration (a good time to do it so you don't forget). This clearly belongs in this chapter on declarations. So, we'd suggest another break in your reading sequence at this point; leave this chapter and come back to it after you've learned all about values and assignment from Chapter 8.

EXERCISES FOR SECTION 6.4

1 Compile and execute the two programs seen in this section to confirm the behavior shown in Figure 6.9.

2 Modify the program `uninit.c` in "Uninit Variable" to output an uninitialized `char`, `double`, `bool` and `CDisc` variable. What behavior do you observe?

6.5 DECLARATIONS WITH INITIALIZATIONS

Let's now see how you can extend a declaration in C++ to include initialization of the variable. Here are some examples of declarations with initialization.

EXAMPLES:

```
int    numberItems   = 0;
Text   sellingHype   = "The world's best C++ book";
double pi            = 3.14159;
```

Figure 6.10 shows the syntax diagram for **variable declaration with initalization**, the second of the forms of **declaration** to be examined.

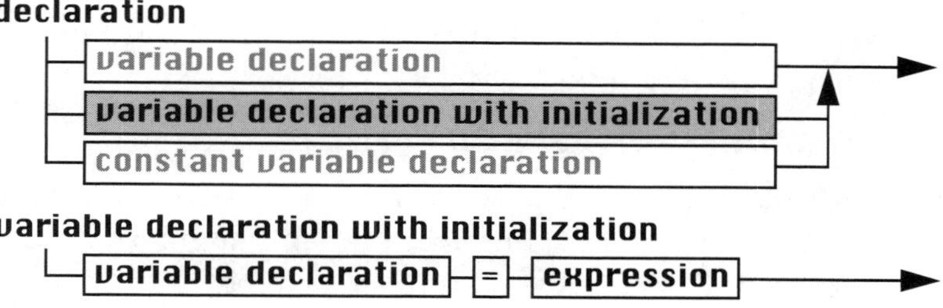

Figure 6.10 Declaration syntax diagram 2

The syntactic element **expression** is defined in Chapter 8. However, note that the type of the expression must be compatible with the type involved in the declaration, otherwise you'll get a compile-time error.

So, there's one form of declaration left to cover: a constant variable declaration. A constant variable? Doesn't that sound a bit of a contradiction in terms? The next section explains all.

EXERCISE FOR SECTION 6.5

The following exercise depends on material from Chapter 8.

1 Considering each of the following declarations as an independent declaration statement (that is, not depending on any other statements), indicate which statements would give rise to a compile-time error and which would not. Assume that the relevant header files have been included. For those statements that would result in an error, indicate what you think is the cause of the problem.

(a) `double minusPi = -3.14159;`
(b) `char letters = "C++";`
(c) `Text digits = 1234567890;`
(d) `bool end = FALSE;`
(e) `int fourHundred = 4 * 10;`
(f) `char letterP = 'P';`
(g) `Text name = "Debbie";`
(h) `int nine = 9;`

6.6 DECLARATION OF CONSTANTS

Constants: in general terms

Some objects in the real world have a value that can be read or changed. For example, a blank cassette tape, the tax rate, or your bank balance. However, other things in the real world can only be read and cannot be changed, for example, the numbers 3, π, Euler's constant, or a specific CD. Variables are used in programs to represent objects that can be varied, so is there a useful programming parallel to constants? Would we ask the question if the answer was "no"?

Constants: in C++ terms

If you've read Chapter 8 before reaching this point (like we suggested) then you'll know what literals are. You know you can write constants in a C++ program as literals, and often you need to use a constant several times within a program.

PROBLEM:

Given the radius of a circle, calculate and print out the radius and area of a circle whose circumference is one third that of the original circle.

DESIGN:

For this design we've used the generic type `Number` for some of the quantities needed. Think about what types might be used in the C++ implementation of this design.

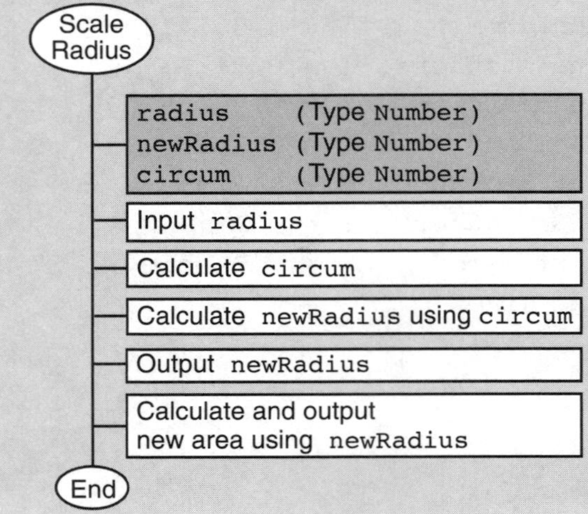

IMPLEMENTATION:

Remembering a bit of school mathematics for the circumference of a circle ($2\pi r$) and for the area of a circle (πr^2) we derive the following C++ code fragment. The problem specification wasn't precise about whether the input radius was an integer or floating-point number; we've chosen the latter, especially as the type of the other "numbers" being calculated is unlikely to be integer.

```
double radius;
double newRadius;
double circum;

cout << "Radius: ";
cin  >> radius;
circum    = 2.0 * 3.14159 * radius;
newRadius = (circum/3.0) / (2.0 * 3.13159);
cout << "New radius is " << newRadius     << endl;
cout << "New area is "
     << (3.14159 * newRadius * newRadius) << endl;
```

The multiple uses of the literal `3.14159` as the value of π for this program are syntactically correct, but there are several software engineering disadvantages of this approach:

1. You have to type the value several times.
2. You may make a non-obvious mistake; did you spot the typing mistake in the one instance of the literal: `3.13159`?
3. It may not be clear to a reader of the program what this magic constant represents.
4. It's some work to change the constant; you have to edit all occurrences of it.

How could you overcome these disadvantages? One suggestion might be to use a variable initialized to the correct value:

IMPLEMENTATION:

```
double radius;
double newRadius;
double circum;
double pi = 3.14159;

cout << "Radius: ";
cin  >> radius;
circum    = 2.0 * pi * radius;
newRadius = (circum/3.0) / (2.0 * pi);
cout << "New radius is " << newRadius << endl;
cout << "New area is "
     << (pi * newRadius * newRadius)  << endl;
```

Using a variable overcomes all of the disadvantages of using a literal. However, there's a new disadvantage; somewhere in your program you could erroneously write:

```
pi = 27.546
```

You won't make such a mistake will you? Of course you will, and even if you don't, someone else who might have the responsibility of maintaining your program could make the mistake for you!

What's needed is the facility to declare and initialize a variable but to indicate that the value of the variable can't be changed subsequently. So we want a "fixed" variable; a bit of a contradiction in terms, but C++ has just the thing...

`const` *prefix in C++*

C++ provides a facility for declaring "fixed" (that is, constant) variables. You can prefix any declaration-with-initialization by the keyword `const` to indicate that, once initialized, the value of the variable cannot be changed. Just the job! Here's the previous example done properly at last.

IMPLEMENTATION:

```
const double PI     = 3.14159;
const double TWO_PI = PI * 2.0;
double radius;
double newRadius;
double circum;

cout << "Radius: ";
cin  >> radius;
circum    = TWO_PI * radius;
newRadius = (circum/3.0) / (TWO_PI);
cout << "New radius is " << newRadius << endl;
cout << "New area is "
    << (PI * newRadius * newRadius)  << endl;
```

Given the above code fragment, what do you think would happen if you tried to compile it with the following line added after the declarations?

```
PI = 27.546
```

Do you think you'd hear from the compiler? You'd be right; a compile-time error message would ensue.

Figure 6.11 shows the final part of the syntax diagram for a declaration.

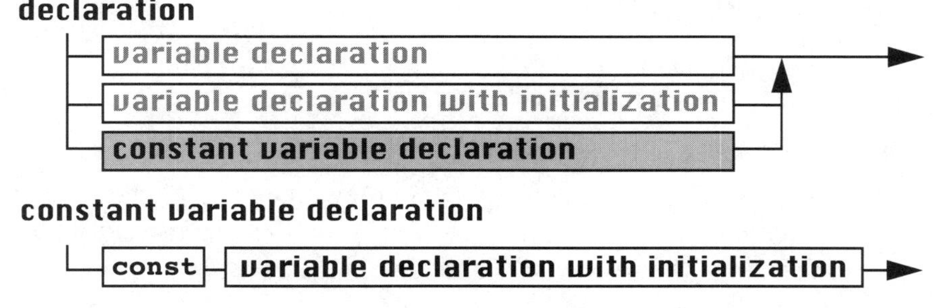

Figure 6.11 Declaration syntax diagram 3

Don't forget how you turn a declaration into a declaration statement (that pesky "**;**").

Style rules for using constants

You may have noticed something fishy about the `const` variable declarations in the last code fragment. Did you notice that the variable identifiers for the constants didn't follow the usual variable identifier style rules. You did notice? Well done! You didn't notice? Shame on you!

Since constants are subtly different to variables, it's worth having a different style rule for constants. This reinforces the idea that you can get some feeling of what an identifier represents merely by looking at a program. The style rule is embedded in the following set of style rules for the use of constants in general.

- ✗ *Never repeatedly use literal constants (magic numbers) in your program.*
- ✓ *Always use* `const` *declarations to provide a meaningful name for a single constant with a particular value.*
- ✗ *Don't overuse* `const` *declarations; for example for numbers like* `2.0` *and* `3`.
- ✓ *Use a separate declaration for each constant declaration.*
- ✓ *Follow the style guide for declaration placement.*
- ✓ *Use UPPER-CASE only for the constant identifier. This gives a visual clue to the reader of the program.*
- ✓ *Use underscores to separate multiple words in constant identifiers.*

If you need to use a constant in a program that's comprised of several different source files, it also makes sense sometimes for the declarations of constant values to be global, as a constant value is something that can only be read from other parts of your program. The constant value cannot be updated by the executing program, and it is undetected updates of global variables that cause software engineering problems.

EXERCISE FOR SECTION 6.6

1 Consider each of the following constant declarations as an independent declaration statement (that is, not depending on any other statements). Indicate which statements would give rise to a compile-time error and which would not. For those that would result in an error, indicate what you think is the cause of the problem.

(a) `const double MINUS_PI = -3.14159;`
(b) `const Text COPYRIGHT "Copyright (c) 1996";`
(c) `const int ANSWER = "Forty two";`
(d) `const bool = true;`
(e) `const char OPEN_BRACE = '{';`
(f) `const 2PI = 6.28318;`

SUMMARY

In this chapter you've covered variable declarations. You now know:

- **variable** is the term given to the data objects that a program manipulates;
- **declaration statements** instruct the computer to create variables, and consist of a type identifier and a variable identifier;
- **a variable declaration** must precede any use of the variable in the program, and all variables must be declared;
- **identifiers** are the human-readable names you give to variables; they start with a letter, generally followed by a sequence of letters and digits;
- **case** – the C++ compiler is case-sensitive – UPPER-CASE letters are different from lower-case letters;
- **keywords** are identifiers with reserved meanings and can't be used as identifiers;
- **scope** – an identifier (variable) has a compile-time (run-time) life-time;
- **compound statements** introduce a new level of scope;
- **initialization** – variables can be initialized as part of a declaration statement;
- **constants** can be declared to provide human-readable identifiers for literals.

Software engineering issues that you've been introduced to in this chapter include:

- **identifier style rules** – for `variableIdentifiers` and `TypeIdentifiers`;
- **global variables** – should not be used;
- **initialization** – beware of using uninitialized variables; built-in types are initialized to random values; some PDTs automatically initialize instances, some don't.

We do declare: you are now an expert on C++ declarations. Well, a budding expert maybe.

You've seen lots of style rules in this chapter. Style rules are an important adjunct to the C++ syntax rules. Sure, you could write C++ programs that work without following these style rules, but trust us, it's important that you follow these rules. Hopefully, we've explained the purpose of the rules and thus you're convinced. If you aren't convinced yet then "just follow 'em."

END-OF-CHAPTER EXERCISES

1 Why is it useful to be able to have local variable declarations and how do you obtain different scope levels in C++? What's wrong with using global variables? Name 70 C++ keywords from memory (only kidding!).

2 Assuming vigorous application of the style rules presented in this chapter, which of the following identifiers are legal variable identifiers, which are legal PDT identifiers, which are legal constant identifiers, and which are illegal identifiers?

```
countOfNs          Dictionary          spoon
LibraryCard        xCoordinate         Y_OFFSET
Duration           found?              BankAccount
Address            distance            speed-in-KPH
Speed              speed               SPEED
```

3 Predict the output that this C++ fragment will produce.

```
int eighteen;
int answer;

answer = eighteen / 3;
cout << answer << endl;
```

4 In Exercise 4 at the end of Chapter 5 you thought about which types might be used in the Body Mass Index calculating program, and for Exercise 5 in Chapter 4 you constructed a skeleton C++ program for this calculation. Add appropriate declarations for the variables to that skeleton. You'll then be ready to add the final pieces of C++ to do the actual calculation in Chapter 8.

5 Identify the compile-time errors in the following C++ program:

```
#include <iostream.h>
#include "Text.h"
const Text CHAR = "Burn";
int main()
{
  int    aNumber;
  double circumference;
  Text   aNumber;
  {
    double circumference;
    text   message;
  }
  int aNumber;
  {
    char circumference;
  }
  return 0;
} // end main()
```

6 The following program illustrates some of the issues of scope and visibility. Before running the program, try to predict what output it will produce. If your predictions are correct, you clearly have some understanding of the C++ scope and visibility rules.

Try the following.

(a) Comment out different declaration statements and predict the result of running (or compiling) the program.

(b) Starting with the program in its original form can you get the contents of the `Text` variable which contains "`Global variable`" printed after the second declaration `Text string;` by adding `cout` statements?

(c) Starting with the original program, which declaration statements have to be deleted so that the contents of the global `Text` variable are printed by each and every `cout` statement? You may wish to delete some of the assignment statements as well as some declaration statements to help make this clear.

```
#include <iostream.h>
#include "Text.h"

Text string;        // A global variable, for illustrative
                    //   purposes only. Remember,
                    //   global variables are NOT recommended.
int main()
{
  string = "Global variable";
  cout << string << endl;

  Text string;      // Also try the program commenting out
                    //   this declaration

  string = "Variable in main";
  cout << string << endl;
  {
    cout << string << endl;

    Text string;    // Also try the program commenting out
                    //   this declaration

    string = "Another variable declaration";
    cout << string << endl;
  }
  // Which message will the following cout produce?
  cout << string << endl;

  return 0;
} // end main()
```

7 A CD-playing program

OBJECTIVE

To construct a C++ program, working from problem specification to implementation, in order to:

- demonstrate the control flow through a sequential C++ program;
- show how to use PDTs to develop an object-oriented program;
- introduce the syntax of member-function calls;
- illustrate the software engineering issues of bugs in programs.

A CD-playing program

7.0 CD-PLAYING PROBLEM AND DESIGN

In this chapter we're going to get you to construct a C++ program to simulate the playing of a CD on a CD player. In fact, you're going to complete your first pass through the software development process from problem specification to implementation. You'll:

- take the CD player problem posed in Chapter 2 together with the design derived as a solution to this problem;
- use some C++ comments, as defined in Chapter 4;
- add a dash of some of the PDTs introduced in Chapter 5;
- mix in some declarations, as covered in Chapter 6;

and with a few new C++ features thrown in, out will pop the desired solution.

In constructing the C++ program you'll be introduced to the C++ syntax for invoking operations on objects, a vital part of the object-oriented programming paradigm. You'll use the PDT interface descriptions to identify the particular operations, or *member functions*, that each PDT provides.

There's another important aim for this chapter. In executing the program you'll be learning about the simple sequential execution of the operations in your program, a vital part of the understanding of how computers execute programs. And you'll begin to address some of the software engineering issues of getting your software to produce the right results. So, let's get cracking.

EXERCISES FOR SECTION 7.0

1 How is sequential execution denoted in the design notation?

2 Are you reading this book in a sequential fashion?

7.1 DEVELOPING THE C++ CD-PLAYING PROGRAM

In Chapter 2 we tackled the following problem.

PROBLEM:

Design a program that a (human) computer can execute in order to play a CD on a CD player.

DESIGN:

We came up with the design in Figure 7.1 as the solution to this problem.

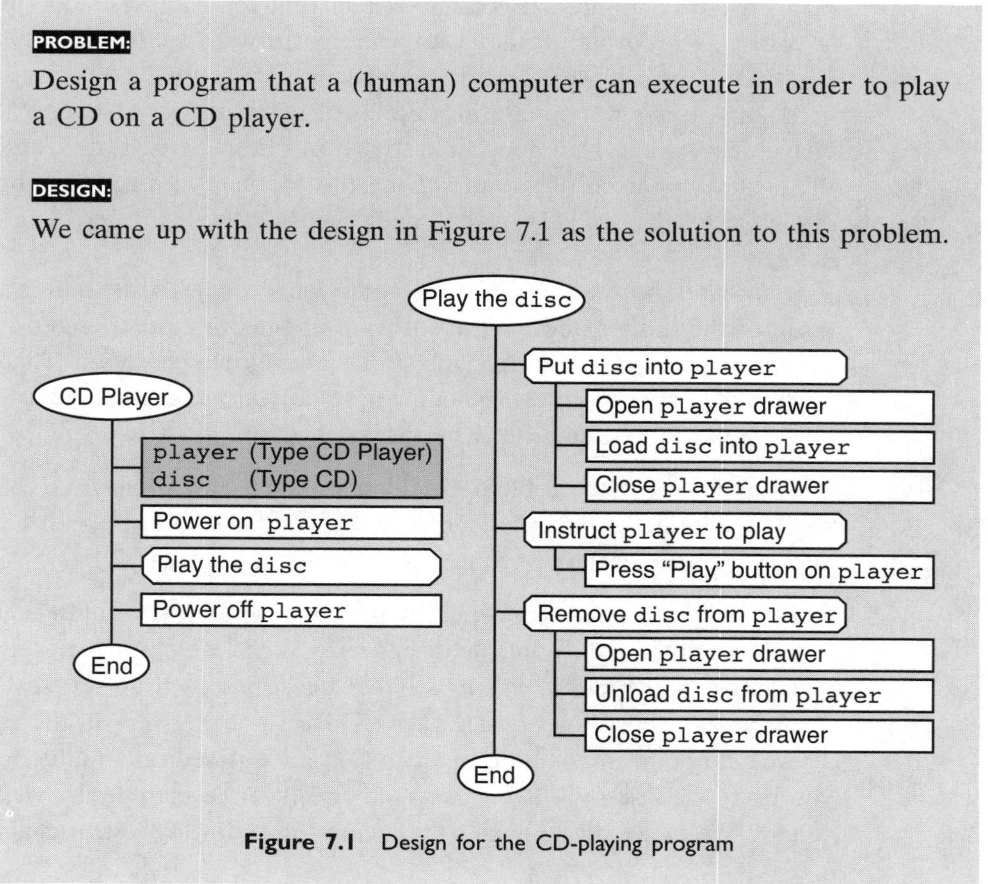

Figure 7.1 Design for the CD-playing program

This design was originally produced for a human computer to execute, but here we want to implement a C++ program for a real computer to execute. We therefore have to translate this design into C++.

Recall that a design not only records the operations that must be performed to solve the problem, but also specifies the order in which those operations must be executed. You know that it's no good pressing the "play" button before the power has been turned on, and this requirement is captured in the design. The sequencing rules given in Section 2.3 specify the execution order of the various boxes in the design, and it might be a good idea to remind yourself of these rules. You'll want the C++ program to exhibit the same ordering of operations in its execution if you want the program to work as expected.

Take another look at the design. Notice that it consists primarily of a set of operations applied to the `player` object identified at the start of the design as being of type CD Player. If you had a PDT that you could use in a similar fashion in your C++ program, wouldn't it be straightforward to translate this design into C++? Of course it would, and you've seen such a PDT (`CDPlayer`), together with some other potentially appropriate PDTs such as `CDisc`. What a coincidence! This would be a good time to return briefly to Section 5.3 to identify the PDTs that might be of use in solving the problem and remind yourself of the interfaces of those PDTs, since you'll be using those interfaces in the sections below.

Before we move on to the implementation stage, let's just reiterate the importance of the design stage in the software engineering process. It's critical to the success of your programs that you start by developing a design. This permits you to get to grips with the problem you're solving, and engenders the precision that's going to be necessary when translation into C++ takes place.

Think back to the problem of telling a person how to play a CD. If you'd just tried to write down the instructions, would you have come up with such a detailed and precise set as the above design indicates is necessary?

Probably not, and your person-program probably wouldn't have worked exactly as intended. While a design is a high-level, abstract solution to the problem it does permit you to address questions such as "Have I got enough detail in the steps in my design?" or "Have I got the steps in the right order?". There's no point in going on to write C++ code based on a faulty design. Would you want a house built if you weren't sure that the plan/design was structurally sound? We make no apologies for giving the following lesson again.

> **Lesson:** The design stage is a vital part of the software engineering process.

Even with a good design to work from, it can be a little daunting to embark on writing C++ code. This is especially so in the early days of your apprenticeship when you're not familiar or confident with constructing software systems. Without a good design it's much harder of course, and that's why we emphasize the design step as the first vital part of the software engineering process. But just as a design is often developed incrementally, so you can apply the same technique to developing your C++ program. Take it in simple incremental stages, testing each stage as you go along, at least to check for compilation errors.

Lesson: Develop your programs in small incremental steps that you can test as you go along.

During this incremental development, it isn't possible to produce the program that solves the problem immediately; if this were possible it wouldn't be incremental development! Nevertheless, at each stage you can progress towards the final solution, gradually building up the C++ code. You can make a start in this incremental development for version 1 of the CD-playing program by capturing, in C++ notation, the overall design as expressed above.

C++ program: version 1

The design captures the algorithm that's a solution to the problem, and expresses that algorithm as a sequence of high-level abstract steps. Naturally, your C++ program will closely reflect the design (if it doesn't there's something wrong either with your design or your implementation). So why not construct a first C++ program that's a skeleton program reflecting the design, and you can hang the additional detail onto this skeleton in subsequent steps. How should you reflect the design in C++? Why not use *comments*?

Applying this technique to the CD-playing design, you can easily come up with the following first version of a C++ program.

IMPLEMENTATION:

```
int main()
{
  // Declare the objects
  // player and disc

  // Power on player
```

```
    // Play the disc
        // Put disc into player
              // Open drawer
              // Load disc
              // Close drawer
        // Instruct player to play
              // Press "Play" button
        // Remove disc from player
              // Open drawer
              // Unload disc
              // Close drawer

  // Power off player
  return 0;
} // end main()
```

This C++ program reflects the structure of the design; indeed, the design is captured completely in the comments. There's nothing else in the program except comments, but of course this isn't the final solution. You can check that you've made no syntax errors by trying to compile this program. You can even execute it, but it won't do very much!

Now you have a skeleton program to which you can add detail, as you'll do in a moment. Although we're recommending this technique as a starting point, there's an important software engineering lesson here.

Lesson: Capture aspects of a design in your C++ program by using comments. This will help you to construct the program, and will also help document your program for others who have to read your code to understand it.

C++ program: version 2

The first flesh to add to the bones of Version 1 is something you learned about in the previous chapter, namely *declarations*. You need to declare variables of appropriate types, and these variables will be manipulated in the program. Have you identified appropriate PDTs from Chapter 5? If you have, you'll recognize the use of those PDTs in the following fragment of C++ code.

IMPLEMENTATION:

```
int main()
{
  CDPlayer  myPlayer;      // Declare the objects
  CDisc     aDisc;

  // Power on player
```

... rest as before

Two variable declaration statements have been added to the skeleton. What are their identifiers and types? You've two pieces of knowledge, either of which will permit you to answer this question (one piece is the syntax of variable declarations; the other is the style rules specified for type identifiers and for variable identifiers).

The first declaration statement declares a variable with the name `myPlayer` that's an instance of the PDT `CDPlayer`. The second declaration introduces a variable named `aDisc` that's an instance of the PDT `CDisc`. These two declarations are the translation into C++ of the objects identified in the design, and to emphasize this translation aspect we've given the variables slightly different names to those used in the design. We could have given the variables the identifiers `a` and `b`, but that wouldn't be following the style rule of giving variables meaningful names.

With the declaration statements added to the skeleton, can you compile this new version? Well, you can try, but you'll get compile-time errors (try it and see). Is there anything else you need to `include` in the program? (There's a hint here :-)

The answer is that you need to tell the compiler about the two PDTs that the declarations use. You need to add the relevant `#include` lines to the program, as follows.

IMPLEMENTATION:

```
#include "CDPlayer.h"
#include "CDisc.h"

int main()
{
  CDPlayer  myPlayer;      // Declare the objects
```

```
CDisc    aDisc;
// Power on player
                                ... rest as before
```

Now the compiler will be happy with the declaration statements. The include files provide the compiler with all of the information it needs to compile the declaration statements. You can even execute the program (with all of the additional comments and closing } that are not shown in the above fragment) – can you predict what it will do? You've already executed a similar program in the previous chapter.

C++ program: version 3

The next stage requires you to provide C++ for all of the actions identified in the design. Let's examine the first action in detail. Once you see how this is translated into C++, the rest follow easily. The first action is:

Power on `player`

This design action is stating that you need to take the `player` object and switch its power on. Obvious, eh? But we're spelling out this obviousness because there's an important point here. Why didn't the design just say Power on? Because you want to turn the power on just for the object `player` and not on any other object. While this might be obvious in this design, what if the design identified two CD player objects? Say you had a `backupPlayer` just in case `player` didn't work. You might wish to control the power to each separately, and this couldn't be achieve by just stating Power on. You need to specify the object to which an operation is to be applied in order to obtain the necessary control, not only in the design but also in the C++ code that's a translation of the design. This is a very important aspect of object-oriented programming.

Lesson: In object-oriented programming, actions are generally specified by naming the operation that's required as well as the name of the variable to which that operation is to be applied.

In words, the C++ equivalent of the first design action is that you need to apply the operation to switch the power on to the variable `myPlayer`.

Do you recall what defines the operations that can be applied to a variable?

The answer is another vital part of the object-oriented paradigm: it's the *type* of the variable. The interface of the type defines the set of legal operations. In C++ a PDT interface defines the syntax for the operations supported by that type, so you've got to look at the PDT interface for `CDPlayer` to find out how to write the C++ code that switches the power on. The interface is given in Figure 5.7 in Chapter 5, so go take a look.

In Chapter 5 you should have found the following member function as part of the interface of `CDPlayer`.

```
void   on();          // Switch player on
```

This may be just what you're looking for, at least according to the comment. But what is "`void`"? It's a C++ keyword (which of course you've remembered from Chapter 6); in fact it's a built-in type, a null type that doesn't have any values or any operations defined. Just take it for granted at the moment that it's needed as part of the interface definition, although it doesn't affect the C++ statement you're going to write. All you need to know for now is how to apply this `on()` operation to the variable `myPlayer`. This application introduces a new C++ feature, the **dot notation**, used in the following manner:

```
myPlayer.on();
```

You'll be seeing an awful lot of this notation so it will soon become second nature to you. This statement is saying:

> To the variable named `myPlayer` apply the `on()` member function that's defined in the interface of the PDT `CDPlayer` of which `myPlayer` is an instance.

A bit of a mouthful, but an accurate specification of what the statement means. Since "`.`" is not a legal character for an identifier, it acts as a punctuation mark allowing the compiler to distinguish a variable name from a member-function name.

A C++ statement such as the one above is termed a **member-function call** since the statement, when executed, results in the identified member function being called/invoked. Yes, this is another form of C++ statement and the syntax rules are stated shortly. For the moment let's continue with the construction of the C++ CD-playing program. You now know how to translate another part of the design into C++ code.

IMPLEMENTATION:

```
#include "CDPlayer.h"
#include "CDisc.h"

int main()
{
  CDPlayer  myPlayer;       // Declare the objects
  CDisc     aDisc;

  myPlayer.on();            // Power on player

  ...rest as before
```

Notice how in the above fragment we've kept the comments, associating them with the appropriate statements by placing them on the right-hand side of those statements.

Having added this member-function call to your skeleton you can again try compiling the program and executing it. Can you predict what it will do when executed?

The answer is that `myPlayer` will be turned on, and there will be an appropriate change to the CD player graphic that represents this visually.

C++ program: version 4

You've now seen how to translate one design action into the relevant C++ code. So, you should be able to translate most of the rest of the actions specified in the design into member-function calls, once you've identified the relevant member functions from the `CDPlayer` interface. Most of the member-function calls are written in a manner similar to the `on()` call. Figure 7.2 shows the complete C++ program.

We hope you can see the direct correspondence between the design you started with and the code in Figure 7.2, although there are a couple of new features to explain. First, look at the C++ statement:

```
myPlayer.load(aDisc);
```

This statement is applying the `load(...)` member function of `CDPlayer` to the variable `myPlayer`, but you have to indicate which CD you wish to load. In other

IMPLEMENTATION:

```
#include "CDPlayer.h"
#include "CDisc.h"

int main()
{
  CDPlayer  myPlayer;              // Declare the objects
  CDisc     aDisc;

  myPlayer.on();                   // Power on player
                                   // Play the disc
                                        // Put disc into player
  myPlayer.open();                           // Open drawer
  myPlayer.load(aDisc);                      // Load disc
  myPlayer.close();                          // Close drawer
                                        // Instruct player to play
  myPlayer.play();                           // Press "Play" button
                                        // Remove disc from player
  myPlayer.open();                           // Open drawer
  aDisc = myPlayer.unload();                 // Unload disc
  myPlayer.close();                          // Close drawer

  myPlayer.off();                  // Power off player

  return 0;
} // end main()
```

Figure 7.2 Version 4 of the CD-playing program in C++

words you have to specify the name of the variable that identifies the compact disc you want to play, that is, `aDisc`. In C++ terms this behavior of passing something to a member function is called **parameter passing**. This is a very important part of programming. Here we hope that it's intuitively obvious what's going on, although you might like to note that the type of `aDisc` and the type of the parameter in the member-function description in `CDPlayer`'s interface (`void load(CDisc disc);`) are the same. Rather than disrupt our discussion of the CD-playing program we postpone detailed discussion of parameters to Chapter 9.

The `unload()` member function "gives you back" the disc that had been loaded into the player, just as happens with a real CD player. In the program you have to do something with the disc that's unloaded, so you can put it back into the variable `aDisc`. (This is called **assignment** and is discussed in more detail in the next chapter.) The fact that this member function returns a `CDisc` result is indicated by the description of the member function (`CDisc unload();`) in `CDPlayer`'s interface, but more on that in Chapter 9. Lots of things to look forward to!

Again, note how the comments expressing the design are retained in the above program. We've also tried to maintain the hierarchical structure of the design in the comments; for example, using indentation to show that "`Remove disc from player`" has three sub-steps.

Executing the program

Is Version 4 of the program syntactically correct? Yes it is, but you should try compiling it to confirm this. What's going to happen when you execute the program? To understand this you have to understand how the computer interprets the flow of control in a program and whether this interpretation matches what's specified in the design.

In the above program this flow of control is straightforward, straight down the program, so to speak. The computer starts executing the statements inside the `main()` function. The first statement it reaches is the declaration of `myPlayer` (which results in the image of a CD player appearing on your screen). The next statement is the declaration of `aDisc` (which has no visual representation). The next statement is the member-function call to switch `myPlayer` on. Having executed this statement, the next statement is the member-function call to `open()` the player's drawer. And so on; the computer will execute each statement in turn, in the order in which they appear in the program.

To confirm this behavior, execute the program and you will see changes to the graphical representation of the player as each member function is called in sequence.

However, there's a problem with this program. It's syntactically correct, but it's faulty. Can you see what the problem is? If you've executed the program you may have a better idea what's wrong.

C++ program: version 5

The problem with the program in Figure 7.2 is that it hasn't actually specified which compact disc is to be played. You've declared a variable `aDisc` but haven't initialized this variable to anything. Hence this variable doesn't contain a proper abstract value, so when the variable is used in the member function `load(...)` a run-time error is detected and reported, and the program aborts.

Forgetting to initialize variables is a very common programming mistake. This is something that's discussed in more detail in Section 6.4, which you'll be going back to if you're following the suggested reading plan.

Lesson: All variables must be initialized before they are used.

Unfortunately, the design for the CD-playing program is deficient with respect to choosing a compact disc. The design didn't specify that we had to select a disc and we faithfully reproduced this error in the C++ program. We need to correct the design by adding an action of the form:

Choose a disc

We'll leave it as an exercise for you to think about where this action should go in the design, but we'll translate this design action into C++ below.

"What about the variable `myPlayer`?" you may ask. Does this variable need initializing? Think back to your previous use of PDT `CDPlayer`. Recall that the execution of a declaration of a variable using this PDT results in the graphic appearing on your screen with no "uninitialized" errors being reported. In fact, this PDT deals with initialization as part of the declaration. However, the `CDisc` PDT doesn't. Some types provide initialization as part of a declaration, some don't. Further discussion of this topic is in Section 6.4.

To fix the problem in the C++ program, have you come across any PDTs that might be useful? Do you recall PDT `CSDiscSet` in Chapter 5? Use of an instance of this PDT allows you to choose a particular CD, and the final C++ solution is given in Figure 7.3. To initialize the variable `aDisc` we've added another declaration (`someDiscs`) and used PDT `CSDiscSet` that provides a collection of CDs. One of the operations supported by `CSDiscSet` is the `selectDisc(...)` member function that allows your program to specify the title of the disc you wish to select (as a `Text` string). This member function "gives back" a `CDisc` just like the `unload()` member function seen earlier. The instance of `CDisc` given back is then used to initialize the variable `aDisc`. `"The 1812 Overture"` is one valid title, and if you ran the program in Section 6.1 that used `CSDiscSet` you'll have seen the titles of other CDs in the collection that could be used.

IMPLEMENTATION:

```
#include "CDPlayer.h"
#include "CDisc.h"
#include "CSDiscSet.h"

int main()
{
  CDPlayer  myPlayer;      // Declare the objects
  CDisc     aDisc;
  CSDiscSet someDiscs;

  aDisc = someDiscs.selectDisc("The 1812 Overture");

  myPlayer.on();           // Power on player
                           // Play the disc
                                // Put disc into player
  myPlayer.open();                    // Open drawer
  myPlayer.load(aDisc);               // Load disc
  myPlayer.close();                   // Close drawer
                                // Instruct player to play
  myPlayer.play();                    // Press "Play" button
                                // Remove disc from player
  myPlayer.open();                    // Open drawer
  aDisc = myPlayer.unload();          // Unload disc
  myPlayer.close();                   // Close drawer

  myPlayer.off();          // Power off player

  return 0;
} // end main()
```

Figure 7.3 Final version (V5) of the CD-playing program in C++

We've now fixed the problem in the earlier version, so you can try compiling and executing this final version. You'll see the whole program execute from start to finish as reflected in the changes to the CD player graphic when each statement in the program is executed in the order defined by the program.

No music? We're afraid not; that's one part of the operation of a CD player we decided not to simulate. Copyright laws prevent us from freely capturing music recorded by others, but the pragmatic consideration of being deafened by hundreds of students simultaneously executing the program in class was a factor in choosing a quiet option. Besides, you didn't want to hear the 1812 Overture, did you?

Wasn't this an easy program to implement?

The final program is a straightforward mapping from the design to the code, simplified by the PDTs that were available for use. "Isn't this a bit of a cheat?" you may ask. "Weren't we fortunate in having the right types around?"

It's true of course that the PDTs used were designed specifically for problems like this, but this is what object-oriented design is all about. The fact that the PDTs matched the problem domain is what made the program's implementation straightforward. But this is always true, and that's why this book places so much emphasis on types and their importance to the software engineering process. Take the following lesson to heart.

Lesson: Having PDTs to match the problem domain makes a software engineer's life so much easier!

EXERCISES FOR SECTION 7.1

1 Write a program that declares two instances of PDT `CDPlayer` and then switches both instances on before switching them both off.

2 If you've successfully run the program Use Variable in Section 6.1, you'll have seen the set of CD titles that are provided by the PDT `CSDiscSet`. Modify the design for the CD-playing program (Figure 7.1) to (a) output the contents of the collection of `CDiscs`; and (b) add a Choose a `disc` step. This step should ask the user to specify the title required (typed using the keyboard) and then the `CDisc` with that title can be selected from the collection. Finally, modify a copy of the final version of the CD-playing program (Figure 7.3) to implement your design.

You'll notice that the titles of many CDs consist of multiple words separated by spaces, and you remember from the exercises in Chapter 4 that white space terminates a `cin` operation. So, how do you read in multiple words from the keyboard into, say, a `Text` variable? If you look at `Text`'s interface (Figure 5.6), you'll see there's an I/O operation `getline(...)`. This operation gets a complete line from the keyboard, white spaces and all but terminated by typing <Return>, and places all of the characters except the <Return> into a `Text` variable. As `getline(...)` isn't a member function it's not invoked using the dot operator. In fact it's a function, something that's discussed in Chapters 9 and 11. But you can use this operation in the following manner to get a complete line of text from the keyboard:

```
Text title;
getline(cin, title); // Get a line from cin and assign to title
```

7.2 MEMBER–FUNCTION CALL SYNTAX

Now you've some familiarity with member-function calls through their use in the CD-playing program, you should be ready for the appropriate syntax rules.

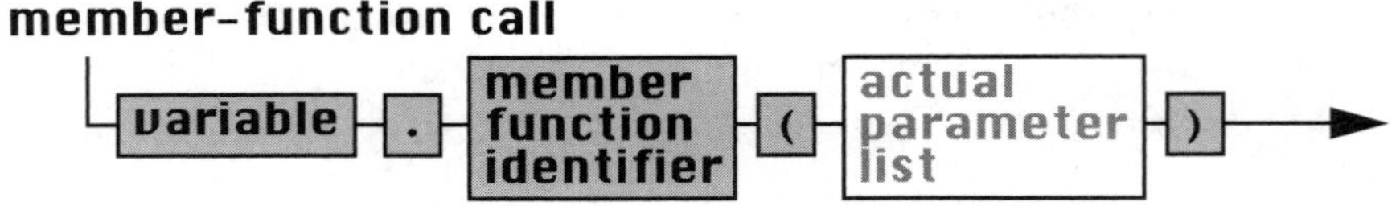

One form of **statement** consists of a **member-function call** followed by a semicolon, although member-function calls can be used in other statements (for example, in an **assignment**). However, we'll leave these additional syntax details together with the details of **actual parameter list** until later in the book.

EXERCISES FOR SECTION 7.2

1 In Section 4.4 a design for drawing a square was presented (Figure 4.9) and a skeleton C++ program was derived from this design as a first implementation. Using this design and skeleton, together with the PDT `Canvas`, refine this skeleton program to be a complete C++ program that draws a square of a size specified by the user, starting from coordinate position (10, 10) on a `Canvas` that has been set to a size of 200 by 200.

2 This exercise depends on you having covered Section 6.6. Consider the program you generated in Exercise 1 above (or the specimen answer for this exercise). How might you make use of constant variable declarations in this program? What software engineering advantages come from the use of constants in this way?

3 Modify your CD-playing program to select a disc with the title "`No such disc`". What behavior occurs when you run this program?

7.3 SOFTWARE ENGINEERING ISSUES: GETTING THE RIGHT ANSWERS

It's a fact of life that mistakes are often made when programs are writttten. As an apprentice software engineer you will make mistakes, but hopefully you'll learn from these mistakes and not repeat them too often! Software systems can be very complex, and it's not surprising that, despite your best efforts, some faults will creep through.

How can you uncover any faults? First, let's remind you of the stages that you go through to construct an executable program. These stages are captured in Figure 7.4, which you've already seen in Chapter 1.

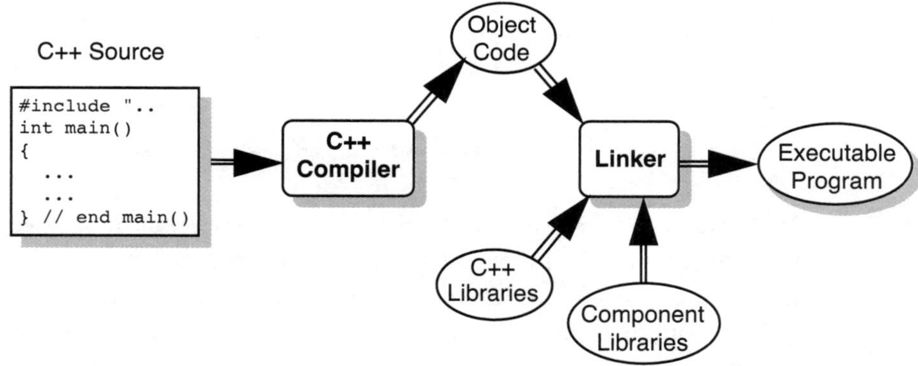

Figure 7.4 Compiling and linking process

Five situations can be identified during the compilation and execution of a program where errors can raise their ugly heads. Some of these situations result in you being explicitly told about the errors by the C++ system, which can be useful! However, two situations require you to be alert and to detect problems. The five situations are:

1. Compile-time errors.
2. Link-time errors.
3. Run-time errors.
4. No explicit errors.
5. Style errors.

In all five cases you've got to find the cause of the error, and to fix it in order to be able to proceed.

Compile-time errors

You already know what compile-time errors are – you met them first in Chapter 4. They're reported by the compiler when you've transgressed the syntax rules of the language (Figure 7.5). There are syntax errors in your source code that you have to fix. (Also, recall the lessons in Chapter 4 pertaining to the helpfulness, or otherwise, of the compiler's error messages!)

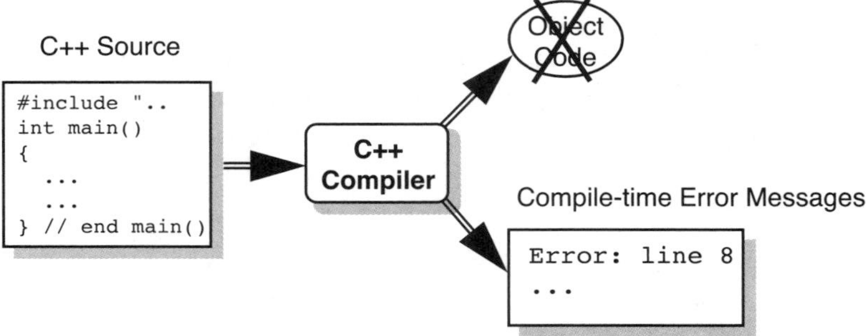

Figure 7.5 Compile-time errors

Now that you've started to use PDTs, there are some new compile-time errors that can occur. It's important for you to understand these errors so you can fix them (or avoid making the mistakes in the first place).

What operations can be applied to a variable? The answer, as always, is any operation defined in the interface of the type of which that variable is an instance. If you try to apply an operation that isn't part of the type's interface then you'll get a compile-time error.

EXAMPLE:

Given the declaration

```
CDPlayer myPlayer;
```

what would happen if you wrote something like:

```
myPlayer.bakeACake();
```

There isn't a member function named `bakeACake()` defined in the interface of `CDPlayer`, so if you try to compile this statement the compiler will report a compile-time error indicating that this is not a valid operation for a variable of this type. Of course, you wouldn't try something as silly as trying to bake a cake using a CD player would you?

Most commonly this form of compile-time error arises because you've misspelled a member-function nmae.

Other type-related errors are also detected by the compiler.

EXAMPLE:

If you tried the statement:

```
myPlayer.load(myPlayer);
```

the compiler would generate a compile-time error, since the member function was expecting to load something that was of type `CDisc` whereas `myPlayer` is of type `CDPlayer`. You'd have trouble getting a CD player into the CD drawer in the real world too!

It's extremely useful that the compiler applies these checks, and that your program is checked against any constraints imposed by the types it's using. In programming language terms we say that C++ is a **strongly-typed programming language**. Such languages are now regarded as being of significant benefit to the engineering of good quality software.

Link-time errors

Sometimes, your source code will compile without errors but the link stage will report some problems. Most commonly, this situation occurs because one or more C++ libraries have been omitted from the link stage, and hence the linker cannot find some of the code it needs to complete your program (Figure 7.6).

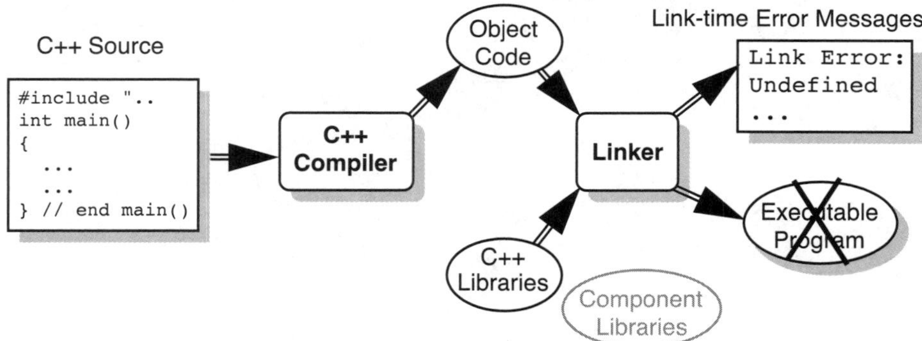

Figure 7.6 Link-time errors

The linker, and where it searches for libraries, are system dependent, so you may have to refer to your system manuals if link-time errors occur.

Run-time errors

If there are no compile-time or link-time errors, you've produced an executable program that will produce the correct answers. Right?

Not necessarily! There are still some error situations that may show up when you execute the program.

EXAMPLE:

Consider what would happen if the following two statements were in the CD-playing program immediately following the variable declaration statements.

```
myPlayer.play();
myPlayer.on();
```

The compiler won't complain about these statements as they're both syntactically correct, and assuming the correct library has been specified, the linker will be happy as well. Unfortunately, this ordering of statements doesn't make sense semantically; it doesn't make sense to try to play anything before the player has been switched on. So if you try to execute a program containing these two statements in this order, the `CDPlayer` type will detect the error, print out a message and halt your program. This is called a **run-time error**, and this particular example is shown in Figure 7.7.

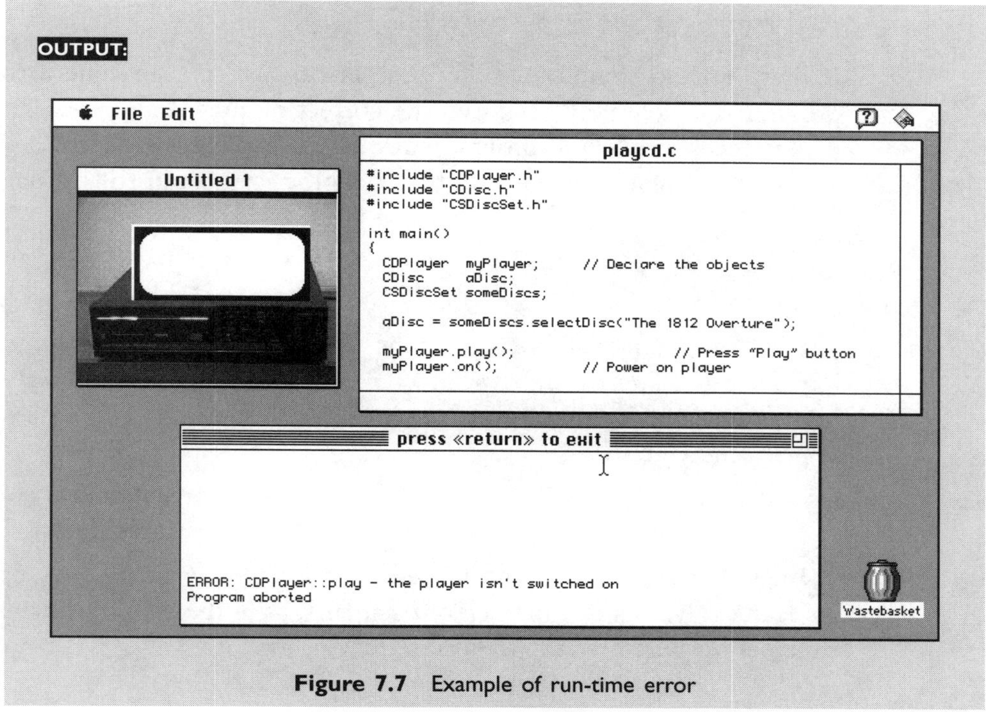

Figure 7.7 Example of run-time error

Of course, if you've not made this mistake in your design then you're unlikely to make this error in your C++ code. Nevertheless, it's not unknown for a design or a program to contain faults, but the detection of errors at run-time is dependent upon the PDT providing the necessary checks. Some PDTs provide such checks; others don't. Earlier you saw the design mistake of not choosing a disc, and the use of an uninitialized `CDisc` variable was detected and resulted in a run-time error. You won't be so lucky with all uninitialized variables.

What causes a run-time error? It's caused by a fault in your program; such faults are traditionally known as "bugs."[1] Maybe the bug was present because you mistranslated something from your design. Maybe there was something you overlooked in your design which therefore appeared as a bug in your code. Maybe you just got something wrong.

Whatever the reason, a bug may result in a run-time error which at least shows that there is a problem in the program. It will be necessary for you to study the program and any output to identify the bug, and then to repair the program. This is a process called (surprise, surprise) **debugging,** about which we'll have more to say later.

[1] Originating from early days of computers when a real bug (a moth) stopped a relay in a computer from working.

No explicit errors

If there are no compile- or link-time errors, and no run-time errors then the program has definitely produced the correct output. Right?

Not necessarily! Your program may have completed its execution without any apparent problems yet the results it has produced could still be incorrect.

EXAMPLE:

Say you'd omitted the statement `myPlayer.play();` from the CD-playing program. The program would run to completion without error, but the program wouldn't have achieved its desired result. There's a bug in the program.

Bugs that result in a run-time error at least show themselves up. However, you can't rely on a run-time error occurring, as in the case of the missing "play" statement. There's a very important lesson here.

Lesson: You cannot assume that a program that executes normally will produce error-free results. You must always test your programs extensively and check the results they produce.

Testing is thus a vital part of the software engineering process, and merely getting your program to compile and to execute without any run-time errors isn't normally regarded as being a stringent test! Testing is the software engineering process of verifying that a program behaves as its specification says it should. In the CD-playing program in this chapter testing isn't a big issue as the program has such a simple structure. You'll soon be learning additional programming constructs that allow you to make much more complex mistakes. So, other upcoming attractions in later chapters are the issues of *testing* to detect errors and *debugging* to identify the fault that led to those errors.

Style errors

Finally, no compile-, link- or run-time errors, and the output produced by the program looks OK. Anything else to check? Just one thing …

The final thing to check is whether you've properly applied all of the style rules. We've said that style rules are important for software engineering reasons, and if your program is a project that's going to be marked, the marker will certainly be checking for style errors. In the real world, your programs are inevitably going to be read by others, and you wouldn't want them criticizing your code's style, would you! Get into the habit of always following the style rules when you write code.

EXERCISES FOR SECTION 7.3

1 Experiment with inserting faults into the final version of the CD-playing program (Figure 7.3) in order to generate compile-time errors. For each fault, note the form of the error message that the compiler produces. The error messages often relate to statements other than the one where you inserted the fault, but it's useful to be able to acquaint yourself with error messages and what can cause particular messages.

2 Consider the following program with the deliberately misspelled "`main`":

```
#include <iostream.h>

int man()
{
  cout << "Hello " << endl;
  return 0;
} // end main()
```

Predict what type of error would occur if you tried to get this program to execute (compile-, link- or run-time error). Then try the program to see what happens. Can you explain the results you observe?

3 In Exercise 1 in Section 7.2 you constructed a program for drawing a square. Try running this program specifying a size for the square that won't fit into the `Canvas` instance (e.g. a size greater than 190). What sort of error ensues? What about side lengths of 0, –5, and –20?

SUMMARY

In this chapter you've developed and implemented an object-oriented program from a design. You now know:

- **object-oriented programming** involves naming an operation and the variable to which the operation is to be applied, using the dot operator;
- **a variable's type** defines the set of legal operations that can be applied to that variable;
- **sequential control-flow** occurs as the computer executes each statement in your program in turn, enabling you to translate the (sequential) sequence of steps expressed in your design into C++.

Developing the CD-playing program has highlighted several software engineering issues:

- **the design stage** is a vital part of the software engineering process;
- **appropriate PDTs** simplify the implementation task significantly, thus demonstrating the advantages of software reuse;
- **errors** are reported to you in some situations and are not reported in others;
- **compile-time errors** are reported by the compiler when your program contains syntax errors or type-misuse errors;
- **link-time errors** occur if a software component has been omitted when the linker is trying to build an executable program;
- **run-time errors** are caused by bugs in your program, although not all bugs will result in a run-time error;
- **appropriate PDTs** simplify the implementation task significantly. OK, we've already stated this, but it's important and worth repeating!

You now know how, in C++, to apply operations to objects, one of the key features of object-oriented programming. You've also been exposed to a little more of the software development process, and where errors can show up. If you're beginning to see that compile-time errors are an assistance to you, you're on the right track.

Where to next? If you're following our reading plan, you should go back to Section 6.3 to learn a little more about declarations. After that, the delights of expressions await you in Chapter 8 :-)

END-OF-CHAPTER EXERCISES

1 Explain (i) what the following C++ statement is; (ii) what the constituent parts are; (iii) what checks the compiler performs when compiling the statement; and (iv) assuming successful compilation, what happens to the program's flow of control when the statement is executed.

```
varId.fnName();
```

2 Identify (by hand) the syntax errors in the following program.

```
#include <iostream.h>
#include <CDisc.h>

int main()
{
  CDisc ADisc;

  Cout << "This disc contains " << aDisc << endl;
  return aDisc;
} // end main()
```

3 Explain what causes run-time errors. What is the benefit of a language being strongly typed?

4 Modify the design and implementation of the program from Exercise 1 in Section 7.2 to draw each side of the square in a different color, in the order RED, GREEN, BLUE and BLACK.

5 Taking your program from Exercise 1 in Section 7.2, design and write a program that draws a face of the following form:

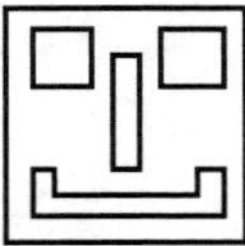

Hint: Use a piece of graph paper to plot the coordinates of the features on the face.

8 Values and expressions

OBJECTIVE

To discuss the notions of values and expressions in order to see:

- how values can be combined to produce new values using expressions that involve:
  - literals that explicitly represent values;
  - variables that represent values;
  - operator symbols;
- how new values can be retained by a variable using assignment.

Facial expressions

8.0 VALUES

In Chapters 5 and 6 we introduced the concepts of types and declarations. To recap, a declaration in a program introduces a variable by giving it a name and specifying what the type of that variable is. The type defines the possible operations that can be performed on the variable and the potential abstract values that the variable may possess.

In itself a declaration doesn't necessarily give a variable any values at all, and a declaration certainly doesn't perform any operations other than the actual declaration itself. So although declarations are essential, a program that consists of declarations only isn't going to be of much use. Not only have you got to introduce variables, you've also got to do something with them.

In this chapter we look at what you can do with the values of variables. To do this it's necessary to investigate:

- what is meant by a value;
- how values can be explicitly incorporated into programs;
- how values can be assigned to variables;
- how new values can be computed from existing values.

Values: in general terms

The concept of the value of an item is something you're very familiar with in real life.

EXAMPLE:

By value we might mean the total value of the coins in your pocket, the price of a theater ticket, or the price of a packet of Sudzo washing powder. Often, as here, value means monetary value that formally has to be qualified in terms of the unit of currency (GB Pounds, US dollars, Indian Rupees, and so on). However, other notions of value are also important. If you're fitting new spark plugs to your car engine, another value that is likely to be of just as much interest is the gap between the electrodes (in thousandths of an inch); when cooking a soufflé an important value is the oven temperature; and so on. Other examples of values are the attendance at a football game (expressed in units of people), the altitude of a plane (measured in feet), and the time it has taken you to read to this point in the book (in days or weeks, rather than years we hope).

With all the examples mentioned so far values are measured in numerical terms, but this isn't always the case. The color of a car is a value, as is the model number of a CD player. Your name, address, title of degree, and so on, are all examples of values.

It's important to distinguish carefully between a range of potential values that an item can possess, as defined by its type, and the actual value of the item. Given the range of potential values of an item, it would clearly be wrong to attribute to that item a value outside the permitted range.

EXAMPLE:

You know that Everest, at 29,028 feet, is the highest mountain in the world. Therefore if you have a type for the height of a mountain you know that any instance of that type is restricted to be in the range 0 to 29,028. Similarly, if you have a type for oven temperature, the temperature of a particular oven is restricted to some range (say up to 550°F), as is the attendance at a particular stadium (which is limited by the number of seats), and so on. So if someone tells you that they cooked their soufflé at 1000°F, be suspicious.

Just as the concepts of value and range are an essential feature of everyday speech, so the concepts of value and range are an integral part of the variables used in most computer programs.

Values: in C++ terms

Chapter 5 showed how a built-in type in C++ governs the potential values that an instance of that type can have.

EXAMPLE:

The value of an `int` is finite, although system-dependent. Permitted values of `char` variables include the upper-case letters `'A'` to `'Z'` and the digits `'0'` to `'9'`. Instances of type `bool` can have the value `true` or `false`.

Of course, all these are abstract values in the sense that they have to be represented in the computer by some combination of 0s and 1s. Fortunately you don't have to worry about this representation to use abstract values in your programs.

What about PDTs? Can PDT variables have values, like variables of the built-in types? For some PDTs the answer is an unqualified "yes."

EXAMPLE:

The `Palette` PDT admits the abstract values `WHITE`, `RED`, etc.

Each of these values somehow has to be represented in the computer, but you don't need to know how. You just need to know that you can use these abstract values in your program.

With other PDTs the question as to whether they have values is less clear, even if the answer is still "yes." For example, what is the value of an instance of type `CDPlayer`? Is it the amount of money you'd pay for one in a shop? Or the make and model number? Or its power consumption? In Chapter 2 we introduced the idea of a type having several components, and clearly instances of types, such as `Text` for make and model number, and `int` for power consumption, could form components of the `CDPlayer` type. Since these components are all fixed, constant values they're not all that interesting but other variable, components are.

EXAMPLE:

A component of the `CDPlayer` type is the state of the player (with potential values `PLAYER_EMPTY`, `DISC_OK`, `DISC_BAD`, and `PLAYER_ERROR`).

An instance of a `BankAccount` PDT will typically have components for the current balance, the overdraft limit, a list of regular payments, and so on. An instance of a `BankAccount` PDT collectively represents these values as a single object.

By now you should have some idea of what "values" are and even what they look like. How do you express values in a C++ program? By using literals.

EXERCISES FOR SECTION 8.0

1 What values would you associate with each of the playing cards in a hand of poker or bridge?

2 For each of the following potential types indicate ranges of values you might associate with them.

(a) a personal computer;
(b) a washing machine;
(c) a car.

8.1 LITERALS

Literals: in general terms

Within a text document you're used to seeing literals that express some absolute, constant value.

EXAMPLE:

Literal numbers such as 100, 98.4 and 66 represent fixed quantities. Often literal numbers are represented by a sequence of digits forming an integer; the inclusion of a decimal point indicates that the literal is a floating-point number. Sometimes literal numbers are represented using words, such as one hundred, ninety-eight point four, and sixty six. And sometimes literal numbers are represented using an entirely different number system, such as MCMXCVI (1996 in Roman numerals). Sometimes a literal is not numerical; for example, the points of the compass have the literal values North, East, South and West; and literal values for the primary colors (for painting) are red, blue and yellow.

Literals: in C++ terms

When you want to express values explicitly in a program you use literals.

EXAMPLE:

Examples of literals in C++ are:

`1000`	is-an	`int`	literal
`98.4`	is-a	`double`	literal
`'X'`	is-a	`char`	literal
`true`	is-a	`bool`	literal
`"Yahoo"`	is-a	`Text`	literal
`RED`	is-a	`Palette`	literal

It should be noted that while there are literal values for all the built-in types, PDTs won't necessarily have literal values. You'll see later (Chapter 12) that PDTs such as `Palette` and `Canvas` have some fundamental differences that explain why there are literal values for one PDT and not for the other. That's a little way off yet. For the moment let's look in detail at the syntax of C++ literal values for the built-in types, and look at literals associated with some of the PDTs you've seen in earlier chapters.

`int` *literals*

In a C++ source file `int` literals are expressed as in ordinary arithmetic, except that commas are not permitted. An `int` literal is any sequence of decimal digits, as expressed by the following syntax diagram.

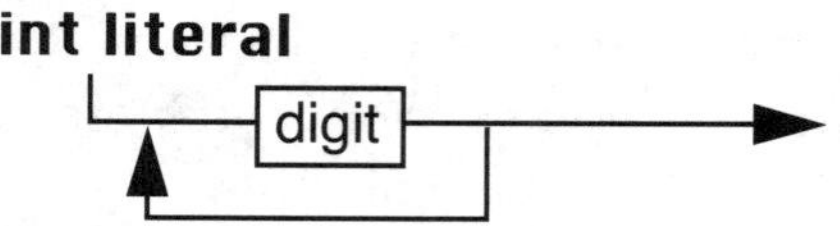

To complete the definition, a syntax diagram for a digit is really required; we'll assume that you can figure that out.

EXAMPLE:

Legal `int` literals	`1   15   32   23842`
Illegal `int` literals	`32,376   32.0   32K`

As with several of the syntax diagrams in this book, the diagram for an `int` literal is correct, but it doesn't tell the whole story. A particular case in point is if the number of digits is at least 2 and the initial digit is a zero, as in `0123`. This is still a legal `int` literal and it represents an integer value, but unfortunately it's interpreted as octal (base 8) representation, which may not be quite what you intended. In fact the C++ literals `0123` (octal) and `83` (decimal) are equivalent. If the literal starts with `0X` or `0x` (and such a situation isn't even covered by the diagram) then it's in hexadecimal (base 16) format; so `0X53` is equivalent to `83` too. The syntax diagram we've given doesn't capture these subtleties. We could have introduced syntactic elements for **base 10 int literal, base 8 int literal,** and **base 16 int literal**. However, we assume that you're unlikely to want to use octal or hexadecimal notation and so you'll carefully avoid using a leading zero for an `int` literal (unless the literal is `0` itself).

There's one further limitation of the syntax diagram that arises from the fact that the `int` type restricts values to lie within a given range, as indicated in Chapter 5. The syntax diagram doesn't convey a range limitation at all; it even suggests that an infinite sequence of digits is a valid `int` literal, which clearly can't be right. It's unlikely that you're going to want to use really big integer values, but if you do you'll first have to find out whether such values are representable as `int` literals on your C++ system, by looking up some documentation to find out what range applies.

What about negative integers? Is `-272` a valid `int` literal? No; it's an `int` literal preceded by a minus sign. Let's put this to one side for the moment; we'll return to it in Section 8.3.

`double` *literals*

`double` literals are expressed in a C++ program in floating-point format, which consists of two parts:

- a **fixed-point** `double` literal, which we'll refer to as the **mantissa**, consisting of an integer part, a decimal point, and a fractional part;
- an optional **exponent**, which expresses a shift to be applied to the decimal point in the mantissa; that is, the exponent indicates the power of 10 by which the mantissa has to be multiplied.

The exponent is expressed using an `e` or `E` (meaning "times 10 to the power of"), followed by an optional sign, followed by an `int` literal.

EXAMPLE:

Legal `double` literals

```
3.14159   0.314159e1   .00314159e+3   314159.e-5
```

Illegal `double` literals

```
3,14159   0.314159x10^1   42
```

Additionally note that C++ allows `314159e-5` as a floating-point `double` literal, that is, an `int` literal followed by an exponent.

Constructing a syntax diagram for an `int` literal was straightforward. For a `double` literal it's not so easy.

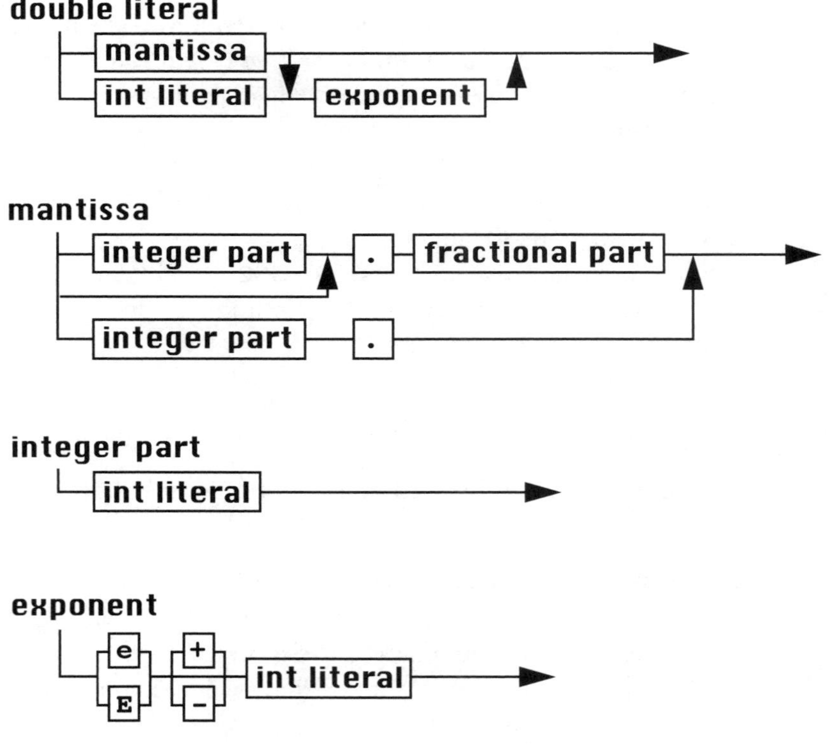

Wow! Four diagrams required for just one syntactic element. Of course, you don't necessarily need all the potential flexibility afforded by the diagrams, and it might be better to adopt the following style rules for `double` literals.

✓ *Always include an integer part (even if zero).*
✓ *Always include a decimal point.*
✓ *Always include a fractional part (even if zero).*
✓ *If an exponent is present* use `e`, *not* `E`.

Taking into account the limitations in the syntax diagram for an `int` literal, is the syntax diagram for a `double` literal entirely correct? Almost, but the problem lies with our use of the **int literal** syntactic element. For example, the ranges of values permitted for the exponent and mantissa are not the same as for an `int` literal. A typical range for the mantissa would give you about 18 digits in total for the integer and fractional parts, while a typical range for the exponent is -308 to 308.

`char` *literals*

In a C++ program a `char` literal is normally written as a single character surrounded by single quotation marks. The quotes are needed to differentiate a `char` literal from any other text in a program, such as an identifier, and don't form part of the literal itself. It's essential for the compiler to be able to recognize which (if any) characters in a program are `char` literals and which aren't.

EXAMPLE:

Legal character literals `'A'` `'a'` `'7'` `'?'` `'@'` `'('`

We used the word "normally" above because there are a few exceptions to the single-character rule. There are non-printable characters and other special characters that are specified as a literal using a combination of two or more actual characters.

EXAMPLE:

`'\n'`	is the literal for the new line (NL) character.
`'\t'`	is the literal for the horizontal tab (HT) character.
`'\a'`	is the literal for the bell (BEL) character (which, when output, should cause your machine to utter some sound[1]).
`'\''`	is the literal for the single quote character.
`'\\'`	is the literal for the back-slash character.

[1] On old equipment, such as a teletype, output of the `bell` character would, indeed, cause a bell to be rung.

These sequences, which all start with a back-slash after the opening single quote, are termed **escape sequences**. Since the single quote character is itself used to denote a character literal, an escape sequence has to be used to denote the single quote character. And since the back-slash character is used to denote an escape sequence, an escape sequence is needed in a literal for the back-slash character. You'll meet another escape sequence shortly.

Here are syntax diagrams that capture the rules for a **char literal** and an **escape sequence**.

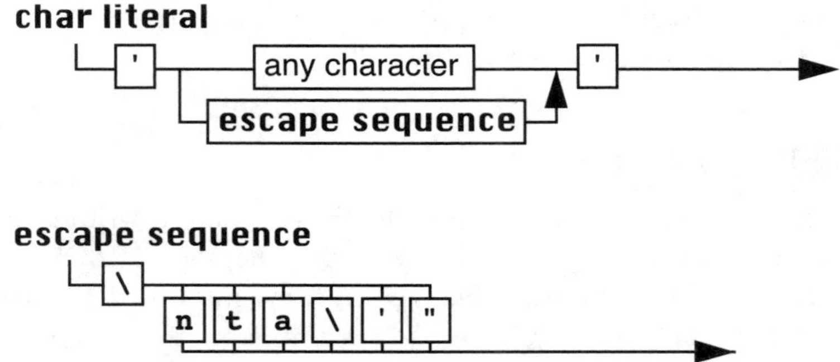

In the first of these diagrams we should really qualify "any character" by "other than the single quote character and the back-slash character," but we're sure you can remember this.

`bool` *literals*

Chapter 5 introduced the `bool` (Boolean) type for which literals are restricted to just two values, `true` and `false`. That's it; there aren't any more. You might be tempted to think that, like `char` literals, some special notation is required to indicate that `true` and `false` are `bool` literals rather than identifiers. This is not an unreasonable assumption, but in fact no special notation is required (and therefore you can't use `true` and `false` as identifiers).

Here's a syntax diagram for a **bool literal**. We hope that by now you would have been able to construct this one with ease.

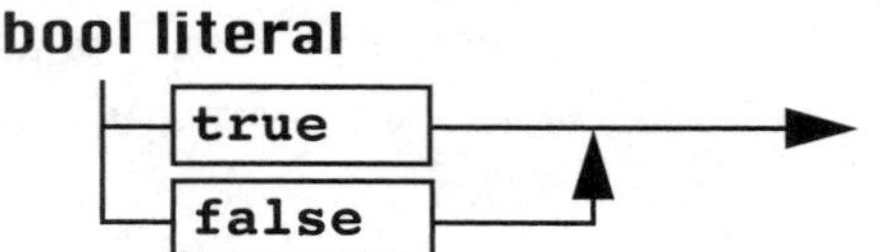

Text *literals*

A Text literal is any sequence of characters enclosed by double quotes.

EXAMPLE:

Legal Text literals

```
""
"This is a text string"
"And this is another one"
"String 1\n String 2 on a new line"
"\"A text string in double quotes\""
```

In all these examples the double quotes are there just to denote a Text string; they don't form part of the string itself. They allow the compiler to detect the start and end of a Text literal.

All valid characters are permitted in a string, including non-printable characters that have to be denoted using an escape sequence, such as \n for a new line. Note that the first example indicates an empty string (a string with no characters in it).

You'll note that in the last example an escape sequence has twice been used to indicate the double quotes character. Why?

Because in ""A text string in double quotes"" the second double quotes symbol terminates an empty string, which is then followed by what the compiler would interpret as an identifier A. Expect a compile-time error.

The syntax diagram for a **Text literal** is similar to that for a **char literal**, except that the delimiters for a **Text literal** are double quotes, rather than single quotes, and multiple characters and escape sequences are allowed, rather than just one.

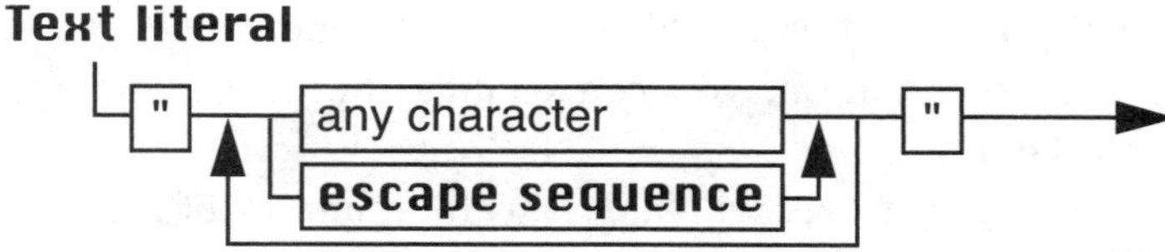

Other PDT literals

You've seen that there are literal values for the `Text` PDT. What about other PDTs? These may, or may not, have literal forms. For PDTs such as `Palette` and `PlayerStatus` there are indeed literal values.

EXAMPLE:

Legal `Palette` literals	`RED WHITE GREEN`
Legal `PlayerStatus` literals	`PLAYER_EMPTY DISC_OK` `PLAYER_ERROR`

What can you do with literals? Well, one thing you can do is assign a literal to a variable using assignment, the topic for the next section.

EXERCISES FOR SECTION 8.1

1 What is the range of valid `int` literals for your machine? For a `double` literal how many digits can you specify for the mantissa and what is the range of the exponent?

2 What would you expect the valid literal values for the PDT `CompassPoint` to be?

3 Produce a syntax diagram for a **Palette literal**.

8.2 ASSIGNMENT

Assignment: in general terms

In real life you're used to the idea of storing values, as in writing down a shopping list, a set of train times, a set of appointments in a diary, or the details of an assignment you have to complete. The storage medium you use might be paper, a blackboard, or some electronic medium such as video or audio cassette. Usually you start with a blank piece of paper, tape, and so on, and record information. In addition, you can change the information that's been recorded at some later stage.

The ability to record values in the memory of a computer is of fundamental importance in programming. The process is similar to writing a shopping list on a memo pad, or recording your favorite TV show on video tape. The process of saving values is termed **assignment**, and it's a rare program that doesn't involve some form of assignment.

To understand assignment fully you need to know a little more about the memory of your computer. But as you saw in Chapter 1, the power of abstraction is that you don't need to worry about the details. If you can start by thinking of memory as a filing cabinet you won't go far wrong.

EXAMPLE:

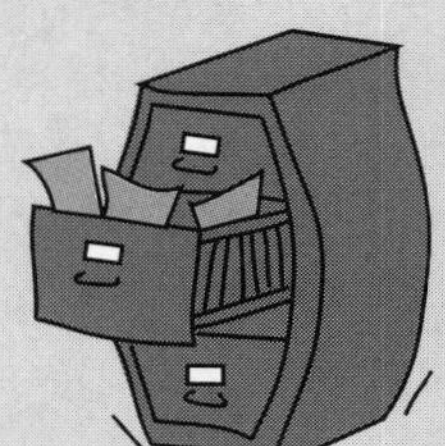

How do you organize a filing cabinet? Well, you could just shove papers in anywhere and hope that when you come to retrieve something you'll be able to find it. Alternatively, you could label the sections in your cabinet using an identifier; maybe one section marked "C++" and another marked "Discrete Mathematics."

You could also have different sections for different types of information, such as a section for your jars of coffee and powdered milk, a section for back-up disks, and so on. In other words, you'll have different sections for storing different types of things. You wouldn't expect to find a jar of coffee in the section labeled "C++". To make the analogy with programming meaningful, it's important to recognize each section as a named variable that has a fixed capacity; each section has a type and an identifier.

Further, assume that the way you use the filing cabinet is a little unconventional. Let's suppose that a particular section is capable of holding a single "value" only at any one time; you can't expand the capacity. The value may be a floating-point number, a sequence of characters, or all the details of a bank account. You can put a value into an initially empty section, and you can subsequently look at that value without actually removing it. In addition you have the ability to replace a value already stored in a section. Once a value has been placed in a section, there's always a value in that section, although the value may change over time.

But how can you physically place a floating-point number into a section of a filing cabinet? We're stretching the real-world analogy a little, so let's look at assignment in C++ terms, since you already know what a C++ value is.

Assignment: in C++ terms

Each variable in a C++ program acts like a section of a filing cabinet. The variable has a name – an identifier – that allows you to refer to it, just as the section of your filing cabinet has a name. The variable also has a fixed capacity for holding a certain type of information, and that type might be `int`, `double`, or `Text`, or any other built-in type or PDT. Just as you don't put your important C++ lecture notes in the section of your filing cabinet marked "Coffee", so you shouldn't expect to be able to put – **assign** – an integer value into a `Text` variable.

Assignment to a variable works in a manner equivalent to initializing or replacing the contents of a section of your filing cabinet with a new piece of information. On completion of the assignment, the old information (if any) that was in the section/variable before the assignment took place is no longer available; the effect is that you've simply replaced that information.

Assignment in a program is specified using an **assignment operator**. In C++ the symbol = is the assignment operator.

EXAMPLE:

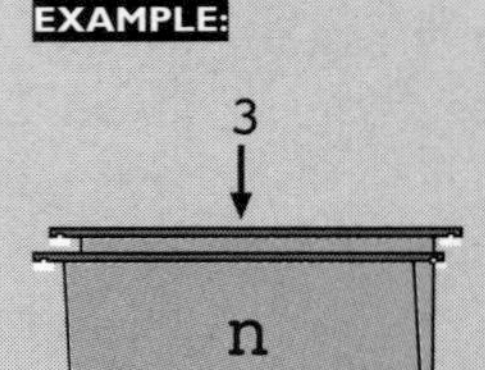

A simple form of an assignment statement (an assignment followed by a semicolon) is:

```
n = 3;
```

which says "the value remembered by the (integer) variable whose name is `n` becomes equal to the value represented by the integer literal `3`." You might like to say "assign `3` to `n`," or "write `3` into `n`," or anything else that conveys the semantics of what's going on here. However, we advise you not to say "`n` equals `3`" since this could be misconstrued as a question that requires a true or false answer. We'll stick to "becomes equal to" and expect you to recognize that the effect is equivalent to putting the value `3` into a section in your filing cabinet labeled `n` that is capable of holding an integer value (and only one value). In so doing, any value that was previously held in that section is discarded.

Lesson: To make it clear what the effect of assignment is, say (the left-hand side) becomes equal to (the right-hand side).

Let's look at assignment in more detail and break it down into its constituent parts:

- the item on the left-hand side of the assignment operator;
- the assignment operator symbol itself;
- the item on the right-hand side of the assignment operator.

The item on the left-hand side is usually a variable identifier. It's a name for a variable capable of holding a value of the appropriate type. The item on the right-hand side must be capable of realizing a value, and a literal is certainly one such item. Of course, the type of the value on the right-hand side must be compatible with the type of the variable on the left-hand side. It's no good trying to assign a `Text` literal to an `int` variable, or an `int` literal to an instance of type `Canvas`.

EXAMPLE:

Figure 8.1 shows what happens if you try to assign an `int` literal to a `CDPlayer` variable.

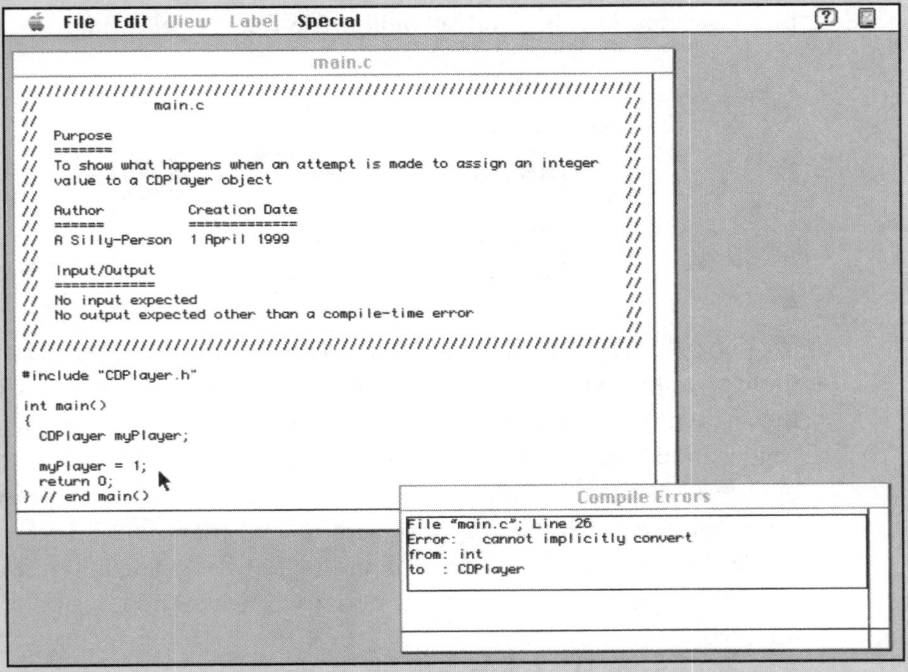

File Edit View Label Special

main.c

```
///////////////////////////////////////////////////////////////////////////
//                main.c                                                 //
//                                                                       //
//  Purpose                                                              //
//  =======                                                              //
//  To show what happens when an attempt is made to assign an integer    //
//  value to a CDPlayer object                                           //
//                                                                       //
//  Author            Creation Date                                      //
//  ======            =============                                      //
//  A Silly-Person    1 April 1999                                       //
//                                                                       //
//  Input/Output                                                         //
//  ============                                                         //
//  No input expected                                                    //
//  No output expected other than a compile-time error                   //
//                                                                       //
///////////////////////////////////////////////////////////////////////////

#include "CDPlayer.h"

int main()
{
  CDPlayer myPlayer;

  myPlayer = 1;
  return 0;
} // end main()
```

Compile Errors

```
File "main.c"; Line 26
Error:   cannot implicitly convert
from: int
to  : CDPlayer
```

Figure 8.1 Attempt at invalid assignment

In an assignment the left- and right-hand sides must be *type-compatible*, otherwise you'll get a compile-time error. We'll go so far as to say that the type of the left- and right-hand sides must be the same, and if you stick to this rule you won't go far wrong.

> **Lesson:** In an assignment statement, the type of the value on the right-hand side of an assignment operator should be the same as the type of the variable on the left-hand side.

In practice, you can relax this rule in certain circumstances since the compiler will try to perform a **type coercion** – to treat a value of one type as being of some other type. You'll see later that type coercions can be performed by the compiler for numeric types (although we recommend that you don't rely on this), but treating an `int` as a `CDPlayer` in Figure 8.1 was just too much.

The concept of type-compatibility in an assignment is not easy to incorporate into a syntax diagram, and so we'll settle for the following.

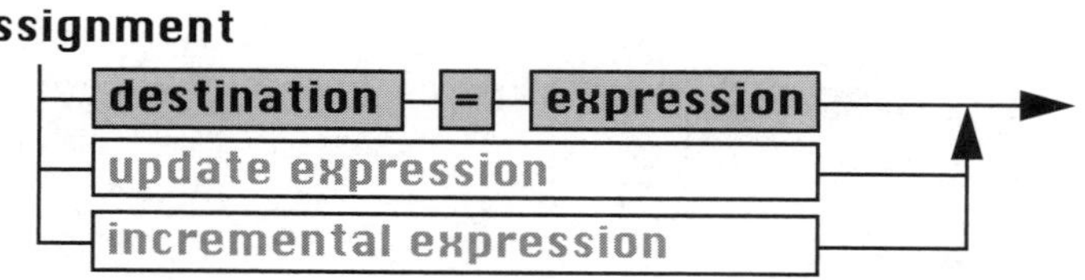

We'll be dealing with the syntactic elements **update expression** and **incremental expression** later in this chapter, so for now we'll just concentrate on the shaded part of the above diagram. For the moment we're being deliberately vague about the token **expression** on the right-hand side of the assignment operator. A literal is an acceptable expression, but an expression may take a much more general form. Stay with us and more will be revealed in Section 8.4. We've also been a little coy about the left-hand side and just called it **destination**. A variable identifier is a permitted destination, so we'll stick with that for now.

An **assignment statement** is just an assignment terminated by a semicolon. It's time to update our syntax diagram for a **statement** again.

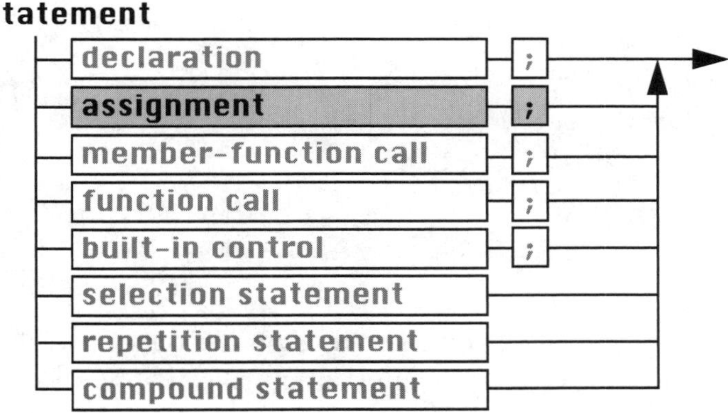

In the assignment statement:

```
n = 3;
```

where does the variable n come from? In Chapter 6 you saw that the rules of C++ state that the use of a variable identifier in a program must be preceded by a declaration of that variable. So somewhere in the program, and prior to this assignment statement, there must be a declaration statement of the form:

```
int n;
```

otherwise the compiler will complain when it reaches the assignment statement. By now, you should be entirely familiar with the idea that such a declaration introduces the name of a variable and indicates its type, but it doesn't necessarily assign a value to that variable. We say that the very first assignment to such a variable using an assignment statement **initializes** that variable.

But is the value of a variable such as n restricted to be the first value you give it? No, you can use a second (third, fourth, and so on) assignment to change the value of n. What then happens to any previous value held by n? It's simply been discarded. The new value assigned to n is retained until another assignment to the variable takes place.

EXAMPLE:

The following code fragment shows some more examples of assignments involving literals.

```
int    numberOfStudents;
double litresInTank;
```

```
bool   test;
Text   tuttiFrutti;

numberOfStudents = 144;
litresInTank     = 28.3;
test             = true;
tuttiFrutti      = "A-wop-bop-a-loop-bop-a-wop-bam-boom";
```

Assignments involving literals on the right-hand sides are often used in (but not restricted to) the context of initialization of a variable. There's a short-hand notation for this that we cover in Chapter 6. If you've followed our reading plan you won't have read that bit yet, so now is the time to go back and read Section 6.5.

Welcome back from Section 6.5, where you found out about the use of variable declaration with initialization.

EXAMPLE:

Here are some more examples of a variable declaration with initialization.

```
int     numberOfStudents = 144;
double  litresInTank     = 28.3;
```

In an assignment the right-hand side must be something that produces a value and a literal does this. What else can appear on the right-hand side of an assignment? What about using a variable on the right-hand side? Surely a variable can produce a value too?

Yes, of course a variable can appear on the right-hand side of an assignment, but it's important that you recognize what's going on in an assignment statement of the form:

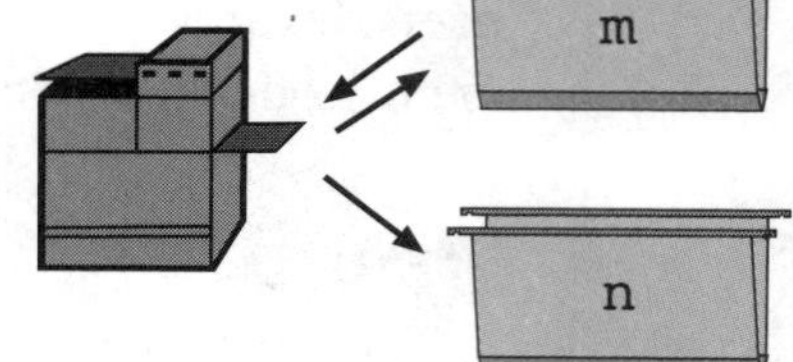


```
n = m;
```

In this assignment statement there are two variables with rather different roles to play; `m` is the *source* of a value, while `n` is the *destination* to which the value is assigned. So is it like moving the contents of the section labeled `m` to the section labeled `n`? Not really. The effect is equivalent to taking a copy of the contents of a section labeled `m` and placing that copy in the section labeled `n`. The section labeled `m` is unaffected. A variable on the right-hand side of an assignment operator acts as a *source*, or *producer* of a value; a variable on the left-hand side of an assignment operator acts as a *destination*, or *consumer* of a value. It's important that any variable on the right-hand side of an assignment has a value as otherwise the value on the left-hand side is indeterminate.

> **Lesson:** When a variable appears on the right-hand side of an assignment, make sure that it has a value.

Now you know that the token **expression** can be a literal and it can be a variable identifier. Can it be anything else? Can you construct new values by combining values represented by literals and identifiers in some way? Would we ask such a question if the answer was "no"? Of course not. You now need to see how expressions can be constructed.

EXERCISES FOR SECTION 8.2

1 Which of the following are valid C++ numeric literals, and what is their type?

(a) `6`	(b) `+85.27`	(c) `6.25e-4`
(d) `.24`	(e) `24.000`	(f) `24.`
(g) `21474836470`	(h) `e7`	(i) `3e4`
(j) `6,000`	(k) `5e.1`	(l) `-4.e2`
(m) `007`	(n) `+7777`	(o) `0.666e-17`

2 Identify the type of the following literals. If you cannot determine the type of the literal, mark it as "unknown."

(a) `57943`	(b) `false`	(c) `'?'`
(d) `DISC_OK`	(e) `One`	(f) `"Hello"`
(g) `error`	(h) `59.16`	(i) `TRUE`
(j) `"A string that is \nquite long"`		(k) `'\''`
(l) `"X"`	(m) `GREEN`	

3 For each of the following declarations-with-initialization, replace the question mark with a suitable literal value.

```
int           pageNumber    = ?;
double        weight        = ?;
bool          test          = ?;
char          terminator    = ?;
Text          message       = ?;
Palette       brushColor    = ?;
PlayerStatus  currentStatus = ?;
```

4 Assuming the declarations-with-initialization of Exercise 3, which of the following assignments are valid in the sense that the variable on the left-hand side has the same type as the literal on the right-hand side?

```
pageNumber    = "33";
weight        = 145.0;
test          = 1;
message       = " ";
brushColor    = PINK_WITH_WHITE_SPOTS;
currentStatus = YES;
```

8.3 EXPRESSIONS, OPERATORS AND OPERANDS

Expressions: in general terms

In mathematical terms an expression is often known as a **formula**. Formulae are composed from literals, names representing values and operator symbols. In mathematics the four basic operator symbols are + (addition), – (subtraction), × (multiplication) and ÷ (division). However, it's conventional to omit the multiplication operator wherever possible.

EXAMPLE:

The length of the circumference of a circle with radius r is $2\pi r$.

If T represents a temperature in °C the temperature in °F is $32 + \frac{9}{5}T$.

Expressions: in C++ terms

In the context of a C++ program an expression is just a representation of a formula. A C++ expression:

- produces a value;
- can appear on the right-hand side of an assignment operator;
- consists of literals, names representing values, and operator symbols.

Having reached this far you know what literals are, and names representing values are, of course, variable identifiers. So we're just left with having to explain what operators are and how to use them.

In C++ the four basic operator symbols are + (addition), – (subtraction), * (multiplication) and / (division). There are always two values, or **operands**, involved in a multiplication or division operation, and so the * and / operators are termed **binary** operators. You can use the addition and subtraction operators as binary operators too. However, the + and - symbols have a dual role. You can also use them as **unary** operators with just a single operand placed after the operator symbol.

EXAMPLE:

```
const double PI = 3.14159;

int    degreesF;
int    degreesC;
int    degreesAbsolute;
double radius;
double volume;
double side1;
double side2;
double side3;

// Assign values to degreesAbsolute, radius,
//   side1, side2 and side3

degreesC = -273 + degreesAbsolute;
degreesF = 32 + (9 * degreesC) / 5;
volume   = 4.0 * PI * radius * radius * radius / 3.0;

cout << "Semi-perimeter of the triangle with sides"
     << side1 << ", "  << side2 << " and "
     << side3 << endl  << "is "
     << (side1 + side2 + side3) / 2.0 << endl;
```

In the three assignment statements, there's an expression on the right-hand side of the assignment operator. At run-time the expression is evaluated to give a value, and that value is then assigned to the variable on the left-hand side. How does a computer evaluate the expression? It applies the operators to the operands. If an operand is a variable identifier, the value represented by that variable is used as the operand.

The fourth statement also requires an expression to be evaluated, but instead of the value being assigned to a variable it's printed on the screen using `cout`.

Note the use of a unary minus in the second assignment statement. The assignment could have been written

```
degreesC = degreesAbsolute - 273;
```

where now the binary minus operator is being used.

Order of evaluation

When you look at a C++ expression you'll probably have some preconceived idea about how it will be evaluated.

EXAMPLE:

In the expression to convert °A (absolute) to °C you expect the answer to be arrived at by adding the number of °A to –273, rather than adding the number of °A to 273 and then negating the result.

Have a look at the expression that converts °C to °F.

```
32 + (9 * degreesC) / 5
```

In what order do you expect the operations to take place?

Say `degreesC` has the value 10 then you expect 10 to be multiplied by 9 to give 90, 90 to be divided by 5 to give 18, and 18 added to 32 to give 50.

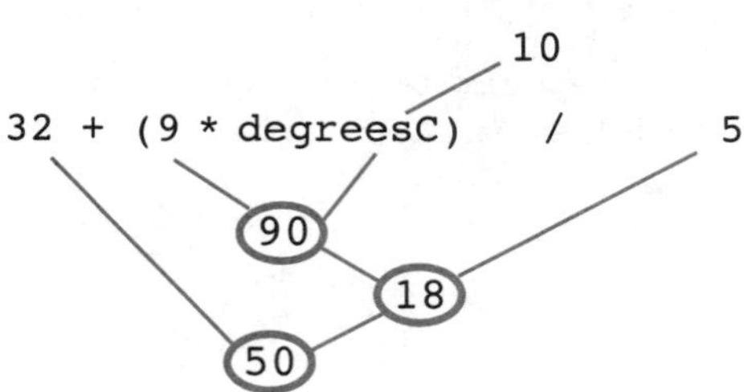

The order in which you evaluate expressions in a mathematical formula is pretty intuitive, but unconsciously you're using some rules that dictate the order in which operations should take place. Expressions within parentheses are evaluated first, and multiplications and divisions take precedence over additions and subtractions. A programming language has rules too, and we've already assumed some of the C++ rules in analyzing the behavior of some simple C++ expressions. It's time we had a look at these rules in detail. We'll use the following problem to exemplify the key points.

PROBLEM:

Write a program to calculate the total amount repayable on a loan subject to simple interest using the formula:

$$repay = loan + \frac{loan \times rate \times years}{100}$$

where *loan* is the amount borrowed over *years* years at an interest rate of *rate*. All quantities are whole numbers.

DESIGN:

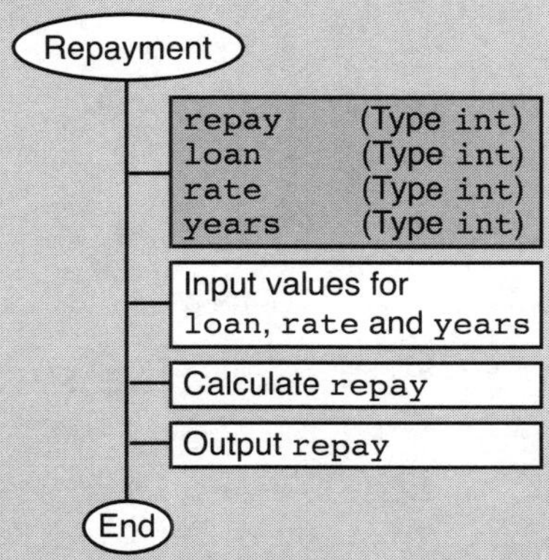

IMPLEMENTATION:

The implementation follows immediately from the design.

```
#include <iostream.h>

int main()
{
  int repay;
  int loan;
  int rate;
  int years;
```

```
  cout << "Provide integer values for the following."
       << endl << "The amount of the loan: ";
  cin  >> loan;
  cout << "The rate of interest (as a percentage): ";
  cin  >> rate;
  cout << "The number of years that the loan is to extend over: ";
  cin  >> years;
  repay = loan + loan * rate * years / 100;
  cout << endl << endl << "The total amount repayable on a loan of $"
       << loan << " over " << years << " years at a rate of "
       << rate << "%"
       << endl << "is $" << repay << endl;
   return 0;
} // end main()
```

OUTPUT:

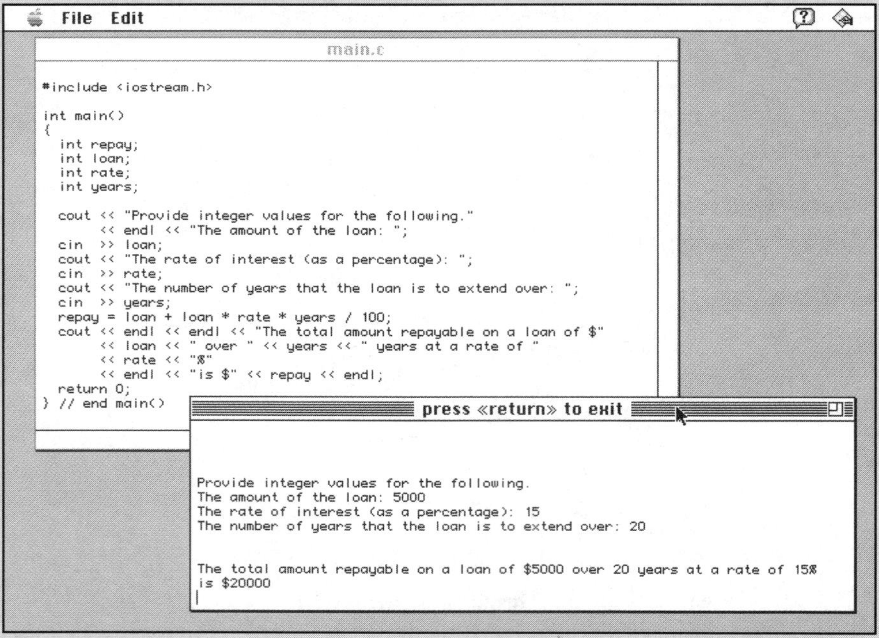

File Edit

main.c

```
#include <iostream.h>

int main()
{
  int repay;
  int loan;
  int rate;
  int years;

  cout << "Provide integer values for the following."
       << endl << "The amount of the loan: ";
  cin  >> loan;
  cout << "The rate of interest (as a percentage): ";
  cin  >> rate;
  cout << "The number of years that the loan is to extend over: ";
  cin  >> years;
  repay = loan + loan * rate * years / 100;
  cout << endl << endl << "The total amount repayable on a loan of $"
       << loan << " over " << years << " years at a rate of "
       << rate << "%"
       << endl << "is $" << repay << endl;
  return 0;
} // end main()
```

press «return» to exit

```
Provide integer values for the following.
The amount of the loan: 5000
The rate of interest (as a percentage): 15
The number of years that the loan is to extend over: 20


The total amount repayable on a loan of $5000 over 20 years at a rate of 15%
is $20000
```

Let's look at this problem in a little more detail, and in particular the expression

```
loan + loan * rate * years / 100
```

used to calculate the value of the total amount repayable.

No doubt Loan Sharks Inc. would expect you to read this expression as saying that the amount repayable is the original loan plus the interest, and that the interest is the loan multiplied by the rate multiplied by the number of years divided by 100. They'd expect a computer to evaluate the expression in this way too. You might hope for a different interpretation that says that the amount repayable is determined by performing an addition in which both operands are the value of the loan and then multiplying the result by the rate and number of years before dividing by 100. The difference on a loan of $20,000 at a rate of 15% over three years is that Loan Sharks Inc. expect a total repayment of $29,000, whereas your preferred evaluation order results in your paying back $18,000, which is less than the original loan!

The difference in the values obtained from the two interpretations of the expression for the loan repayment is a result of the different order in which the various operations were performed. To remove any possible ambiguity a compiler needs some rules to determine the order in which operations should be performed. These rules are expressed in terms of **precedence**, or priority, levels for the operators. Operators with the higher precedence "win" over operators with lower precedence in an expression. That is, operations involving operators with high precedence are performed before operations involving operators with low precedence.

Fortunately the precedence rules in C++ are the ones you're familiar with from mathematics.

> **Lesson:** Multiplications and divisions are performed before additions and subtractions, but unary plus and minus have higher precedence than any of these.

We say that multiplication and division have identical precedence levels. Addition and subtraction also have identical precedence levels, but lower than that of multiplication and division. The unary plus and minus operators have identical precedence levels that are the highest of all the arithmetic operators. In summary:

Operator			
+	−	(unary)	Highest Precedence
*	/		↕
+	−	(binary)	Lowest Precedence

Sometimes in an expression there's a tie: there are two or more operators with the same precedence level and the above lesson doesn't indicate which is executed first. Look at the subexpression

```
loan * rate * years / 100
```

that has been taken from the expression for the loan you took out with Loan Sharks Inc. Here all the operators have the same priority. In which order do the operations take place? In situations like this where there's a tie the operations are performed in a left-to-right order, so that here the value of `loan` is multiplied by the value of `rate` first, and the value of the result of this multiplication is then multiplied by the value of `years`. Finally the result of the two multiplications is divided by `100`.

Lesson: In the event of equal precedence levels, operators are evaluated in a left-to-right order.

All this is reasonably straightforward, but C++ supports many more operators than the basic ones considered so far, and there are no less than 17 precedence levels! It would be a real pain to have to remember all of these, but fortunately you don't, since you can force the order in which operations take place using parentheses.

Let's see how the use of parentheses, to enforce the order in which operations take place, works in practice. Your preferred repayment to Loan Sharks Inc. would be expressed as

```
(loan + loan) * rate * years / 100
```

but it's unlikely that Loan Sharks Inc. would allow you to get away with this.

The expression

```
loan + loan * rate * (years / 100)
```

looks (as far as Loan Sharks Inc. are concerned) like it ought to give the right result. Maybe it will, but more on that later. To be absolutely sure, Loan Sharks Inc. might insist on:

```
loan + (((loan * rate) * years) / 100)
```

even though the precedence rules say that

```
loan + loan * rate * years / 100
```

will give the same result. Which version do we recommend? It depends. Always include parentheses if they help you ensure that the operations are performed in the order you intend. But don't include parentheses unnecessarily, since the relationship between the expression and the original mathematical formula may be obscured. As a compromise we suggest

```
loan + (loan * rate * years / 100)
```

which combines clarity with simplicity.

Lesson: When writing a C++ expression, if you have to think twice about what the precedence level of an operator is, use parentheses to ensure that the operations take place in the order you intend.

Overuse of parentheses can lead to a very cluttered expression, one that's hard for a human reader to fathom what's going on. So it's useful if you can remember, and exploit, the precedence levels of some of the operators.

- ✗ *Don't overdo the use of parentheses.*
- ✓ *It's important that the meaning of an expression is legible.*
- ✓ *Where you can, use your knowledge of the precedence levels of the arithmetic operators to avoid overuse of parentheses.*
- ✓ *It's a good idea to use parentheses in all other cases.*
- ✓ *When in doubt, parenthesize.*

Of course, our model of interest is a simple version of what happens in practice.

The brackets are there so you see
What Loan Sharks are doing to me
But I'm really dumbfounded
That they haven't compounded
The interest rate on my course fee.

Now you have some idea of how to produce a new value using variables and operator symbols, let's have a look at the type of the value you get.

The type of the result of an operator

For the built-in numeric types `int` and `double`, the operator symbols `+`, `–`, `*` and `/` are defined for pairs of operands of the same type; that is, `int + int`, `double * double`, and so on. In each case the type of the result is the same as the type of the operands, so the result of `int + int` is of type `int`, which is what you might expect.

But what about `int / int`, you ask? What do you get when you use integer division as in `22 / 7`? You might expect the result of integer division to be a `double` value, but in fact in C++ `int / int` gives an `int` result. To work out what the result value of integer division is, do the division on your pocket calculator in floating-point arithmetic and then take the whole part of the floating-point result. In the case of `22 / 7` this means that the result is 3. What about the remainder of integer division? You can work this out using the `%` (modulo) operator. For example, the value of `22 % 7` is `1`.

Loss of accuracy as a result of integer division may, or may not, be a matter of great concern. Returning to the amount repayable on the loan you took out with Loan Sharks Inc., if in the expression

```
loan + loan * rate * (years / 100)
```

the `int` variables `loan`, `rate` and `years` have values of `20000`, `15` and `3` respectively, then the parentheses force the division to be evaluated first to give a value of `0`, and hence the amount repayable is just the original loan. No doubt you prefer this to the expression

```
loan + (loan * rate * years / 100)
```

Now the multiplications will be performed first, giving a value of `900000` before the division by `100` takes place, with no loss of accuracy in the final result.

Unfortunately, this calculation will not work correctly if `int` on your system is restricted to a maximum of `32767`. You could use `doubles` instead, as we do shortly for accuracy reasons.

Types and availability of operators

What about operators that apply to values of other types, you ask? Can you:

- subtract one instance of type `CDisc` from another
- divide one instance of type `CDPlayer` by another
- multiply one instance of type `Canvas` by another

In all of these cases the answer is a resounding "no!" There are clearly good reasons for this; these operations just don't make sense. But how do you (and the compiler) know which operations are valid for an instance of a particular type and which are not?

The answer lies in the type interface that, as you saw in Chapter 5, lists all member functions and operators supported by that type. In the type interfaces given in that chapter, as far as the operators are concerned, we've only indicated what the operator symbols are since to do otherwise would unnecessarily complicate matters. However, for each operator a full specification of the interface would indicate the types of the operands and the type of the result.

EXAMPLE:

If you look at the interface for `Text` (Figure 5.6) you'll see that the + operator is defined, but the arithmetic operators -, * and / are not supported by this type. When both operands of the + operator are of type `Text`, then the result type is `Text`. The operator implements string concatenation: the two string operands are joined together to form another string. For example `"Sam's " + "Diner"` gives the result `"Sam's Diner"`.

The interfaces for both `int` and `double` indicate that the four basic operations +, -, * and / are supported by these types. For `int` there's also the `%` operator. Are there any other operators for these built-in types? Yes, lots more and we'll be looking at these shortly, but first let's look at the issue of mixing numeric types in expressions, and problems with underflow and overflow.

Type coercion

In general, if you attempt to use an operator symbol with incorrect operand types, that is, the operator is not defined for the types of the operands you specify, then a compile-time error will occur. In all the examples you've seen so far the operands of binary operators have been of the same type (and the result type is the same as that of the operands). It doesn't have to be this way, it just so happens that for all the built-in types the operators take two operands of that type.

What if in the expression `loan * decimalRate`, `loan` is of type `int` and `decimalRate` is of type `double`? Given what we've just said about operand types, would such an expression cause a compile-time error? This sounds somewhat severe but a strict interpretation of the interfaces of the built-in types `int` and `double` says that this is how it is. So how do you multiply an `int` by a `double`? First think about what you expect the type of the result to be: a `double`, even if you eventually want to express it as a whole number (of $). You know that there's a multiplication operator for `double * double` that gives a `double`, so that's what should be used. Since `loan` is of type `int` you need a **type coercion** to change an `int` value to a `double` value before it's used in the multiplication.

A type coercion converts a value of one type to a value of another type. A type coercion consists of the name of the type to be converted *to* followed, in parentheses, by an expression giving a value of the type you want to convert *from*.

EXAMPLE:

`double(loan)` gives the value of `loan` as a floating-point number, without affecting the value of `loan` itself.

Hence you can write `double(loan) * decimalRate` and get a `double` result. If you're working out the amount of interest repayable on a loan, you're going to have to do a few more type coercions as a result of just one variable being of type `double` instead of `int`.

PROBLEM:

Write a program to calculate the total amount repayable on a loan subject to simple interest as before, but this time with the interest rate being a floating-point number.

DESIGN:

The design is as before, but this time the `int` variable `rate` is replaced by the `double` variable `decimalRate`.

IMPLEMENTATION:

```
#include <iostream.h>

int main()
{
  int    repay;
  int    loan;
  double decimalRate;
  int    years;

  cout << "Provide values for "
       << endl << "The amount of the loan (integer) ";
  cin  >> loan;
  cout << "The rate of interest "
       << "(as a percentage, floating-point): ";
  cin  >> decimalRate;
  cout << "The number of years that the "
       << "loan is to extend over (integer): ";
  cin  >> years;
  repay = int(double(loan) +
              (double(loan) * decimalRate * double(years)
               / 100.0));
  cout << endl << endl
       << "The total amount repayable on a loan of $"
       << loan << " over " << years
       << " years at a rate of " << rate << "%" << endl
       << "is $" << repay << endl;
  return 0;
} // end main()
```

Since the result of:

```
double(loan) * decimalRate * double(years) / 100.0
```

is of type `double` a final type coercion is used before the assignment to the `int` variable `repay` takes place. The effect of this final coercion is to discard the fractional part. This means that Loan Sharks Inc. may miss out on a few cents, but they probably won't mind too much about that if the loan is large.

EXAMPLE:

If the loan is $1,000 at a rate of 12.575% over two years then the interest is $251.5, so a type coercion to $251 saves you 50 cents. In contrast, to borrow $1 under the same terms gives an interest repayable of $0.2515, so a type coercion results in Loan Sharks Inc. getting no interest at all.

Given a particular type, how do you know what other types can be coerced to that type? Take a look back at the type interfaces given in Chapter 5 and you'll see that a type coercion corresponds to a constructor call. For a given type, the types you can convert from are shown enclosed in parentheses in the constructor section of the interface.

Lesson: Type coercion is achieved using a constructor. A type coercion consists of the type to be converted to followed, in parentheses, by the type to be converted from.

What if you don't use a type coercion when you multiply an `int` by a `double`? Will you really get a compile-time error?

No, a type coercion from `int` to `double` will automatically be performed in an expression wherever and whenever necessary. This is an example of a process known as **widening**, and widening from `int` to `double` is a safe operation in that you'll get a sensible value.

What do you expect the result of the expression `'2' + '2'` to be?

Automatic coercion from `char` to `int` will take place where necessary. There's no addition operator for type `char`, but the compiler won't complain at all if you write an expression such as `'2' + '2'`. You won't get the character `'4'`, or even the integer 4. When a type coercion from char to int takes place the value returned is the position of the character in the ASCII character set. The value of int('2') is 50, so the value of '2' + '2' is the integer value 100.

As a general rule there are no significant problems in type coercisions in the widening direction char → int → double, although the value you end up with may not be quite what you intended (as in char → int).

Type coercion in the opposite direction are rather more problematic, and may even lead to garbage. For example, what do you expect the value of char(-3) to be? And what do you expect the value of int(99.9e99) to be? Write a simple program to find out what values you get.

Rather than leave the compiler to perform type coercions, it's best to make them all explicit. In particular, where a literal is used make sure that it won't be subject to an implicit type coercion. For example, if a literal is used as an operand for * and the other operand is of type double, make sure that the literal is a legal double literal (for example, 3.0 rather than 3).

Lesson: Never rely on implicit type coercion since they may not do what you want.

EXAMPLE:

Here are some examples of good style that avoid implicit type coercions.

```
const double PI = 3.14159;
double r;
double cash;

// Assign values to r and cash

double volume  = (4.0 / 3.0) * PI * r * r * r;
int    dollars = int(cash);
int    cents   = int((cash - double(dollars)) * 100.0);
```

✓ *Use explicit coercion wherever an implicit coercion would otherwise be performed.*

✓ *Always use a literal of the correct type in an expression.*

Overflow and underflow

Did you write a program to find out what happens when you write `int(99.9e99)`? What do you get when this value is output? It won't be the whole part of the floating-point number 99.9e99, since such a large integer is outside the range of permitted values for the `int` type.

Arithmetic that results in a value that lies outside the range of values for a particular type, as specified in the type interface, is known as **overflow**. As already indicated, you can sometimes get overflow when you perform a type coercion in a program, such as from `double` to `int`. You can also get overflow when you use the arithmetic operators. For example, you may get overflow when you add two very large positive `int` values together, or if you add two very large negative `int` values. You can sometimes get overflow when you're working with `doubles` too.

Unfortunately, if integer overflow occurs in your C++ program it won't cause that program to terminate with a run-time error. Integer overflow just happens "silently" and the value you end up with won't be the one you want. There's likely to be a follow on effect with the wrong value being used in some subsequent calculation. If you're diligent you'll detect that something has gone wrong when you look at the results your program produces. If you're not diligent then you may end up paying Loan Sharks Inc. a different amount than that which you anticipated.

Depending on the compiler you're working with, overflow of a floating-point number may or may not result in a run-time error. If it doesn't then, as with integer overflow, the value you end up with won't be the one you want and you won't find out about this unless you carefully check the output of any results your program produces. It's unlikely that you'll want to perform arithmetic involving very large numbers just yet, but you need to be aware of the possibility of overflow.

Lesson: Overflow is usually a catastrophic error.

A particular case in which overflow occurs is if you attempt to divide an `int` or `double` value by zero.

When working with very small floating-point numbers you may end up with a result that's outside of the range permitted by the `double` type, but this time a range error occurs because the number is too small, rather than too large. This situation is termed **underflow**, and when underflow occurs the value you get is `0.0`. Underflow is something that can usually be safely ignored.

Lesson: Underflow is not usually a catastrophic error.

Assignment and expression syntax

By now you should have a fair idea of what an assignment can look like, and what an expression can look like (but you don't know the whole story yet). You've also learned about type coercions, overflow and underflow. This is a good point to draw breath and look at some syntax diagrams.

Recall that one valid form for an **assignment** is a **destination**, followed by an = sign, followed by an **expression**. A definition for the syntactic element **destination** is, on the face of it, straightforward.

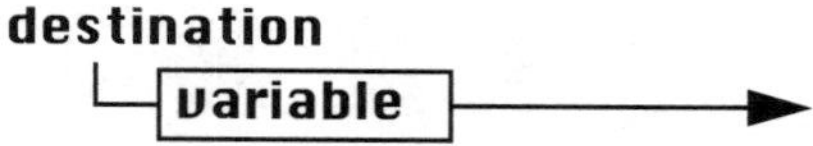

But what is a **variable**? Well, a **variable identifier** will do for now. You'll find out about other forms of **variable** in later chapters.

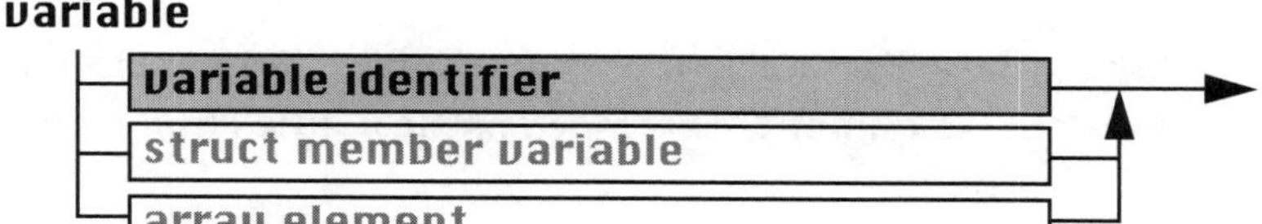

On the right-hand side of an assignment operator is an **expression**:

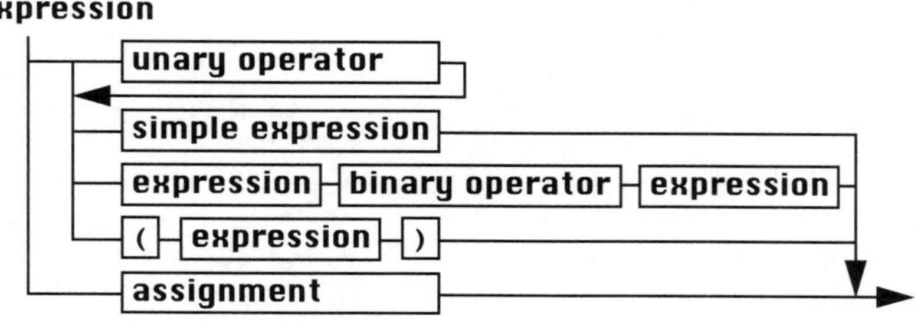

This diagram states, for example, that an expression can be an expression followed by a binary operator followed by an expression, and an expression can be... That is, an expression can be made up of two subexpressions either side of a binary operator, and each subexpression can be an expression in its own right. If you're not careful you'll end up going round in circles. You can terminate the cycle by taking one of the alternative routes through the diagram, in particular, by taking the **simple expression** route.

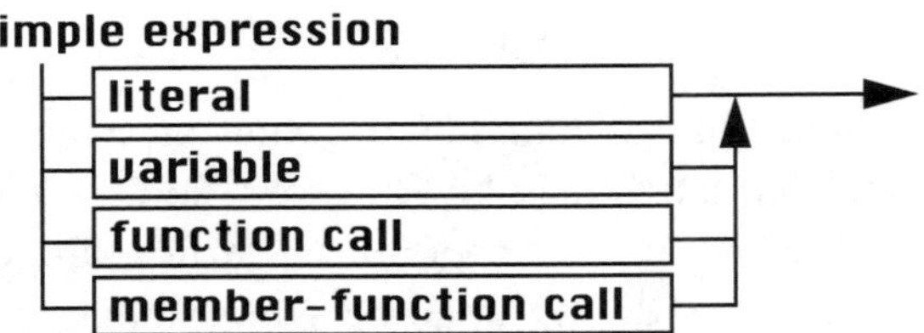

Note that the syntax diagram for **expression** indicates that an expression may be preceded by a unary operator. The syntax diagram for a unary operator is as follows.

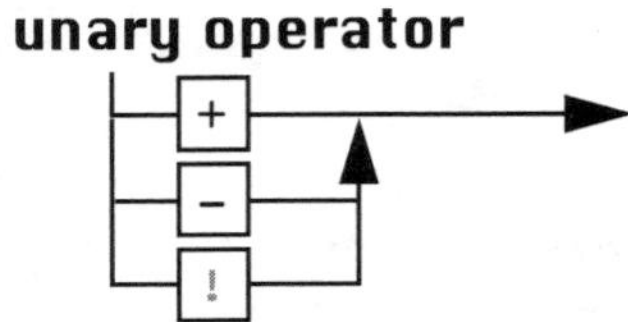

+ and - you've already met. You'll come across the unary operator `!` in Section 8.5.

The syntax diagram for an **expression** indicates that one form of an expression is an **assignment**. This may appear a little strange to you, and it's time we expanded on this.

EXERCISES FOR SECTION 8.3

1 Assuming appropriate declarations, write C++ expressions for the following algebraic formulas:

(a) $r + \frac{s - t}{v^2}$

(b) $\frac{a + b}{c + \frac{d}{e + f}}$

(c) $\frac{1}{6} n\,(n + 1)(2n + 1)$

(d) $\frac{4}{3}\,\pi r^3 h$

2 In what order are the operations performed in the following C++ expressions? Write these expressions in algebraic notation, using parentheses to express this order.

(a) `a * b / c + d * e - f`
(b) `a * b / (c + d) * e - f`

(c) `a * b / (c + d * (e - f))`
(d) `(a * b) / ((c + d * e) - f)`

3 Assume that `n` is of type `int`. Evaluate the following expressions under the assumption that (i) `n` has the value 7; (ii) `n` has the value 8.

(a) `n * (n + 1) / 2`
(b) `(n / 2) * (n + 1)`
(c) `n * ((n + 1) / 2)`
(d) `(1 / 2) * n * (n + 1)`

4 Making use of explicit type coercions, write the following expressions in such a way that no implicit type conversions would take place.

(a) `1000 / 8 + 9 * 6.0`
(b) `'A' + 'a'`
(c) `5 * (98.4 - 32 ) / 9`
(d) `"Hi" + ' ' + "Ho"`

5 On the Pacific island of Sans Serif, the unit of currency is the Sans Serif dollar ($SS), divided into 100 cents. Sans Serif islanders pay a tax to the government based on an islander's annual income according to the following scheme.

First $10,000SS	No tax payable	
$10,000SS to $20,000SS	Taxed at 5%	(Basic Rate)
$20,000SS to $50,000SS	Taxed at 10%	(Higher Rate)
$50,000SS+	Taxed at 20%	(Super Rate)

Given that a particular islander's annual income is in excess of $50,001SS, write expressions that determine (a) how much of the person's income is taxable; (b) what their taxable income is as a percentage of their overall income; (c) how much tax they pay at the Super Rate; and (d) their total tax bill.

8.4 ASSIGNMENT REVISITED

You recall that assignment involves the assignment operator =. The assignment operator is a binary operator with a precedence level lower than that of the arithmetic operators. Like all other binary operators, the assignment operator takes two operands and returns a result. The result happens to be the value of the right-hand side operand.

EXAMPLE:

The following statement has the effect of assigning the value 3 to the variable a and printing the value 3 (and a new line).

```
cout << (a = 3) << endl;
```

You can write statements like this because an assignment is just an expression. It follows that it's possible to write an expression of the form

```
i = j = j + 1
```

If `j` has the value 35 before the expression is evaluated, what values do `i` and `j` have after the expression is evaluated? In particular, is the value of `i` set equal to the value of `j` before 1 is added to it, or after?

It so happens that the = operator goes against the normal left-to-right rules for operators of equal precedence. In a multiple assignment like this the assignment operations get performed in a right-to-left order. So the value of `i` is set equal to the value of `j` after 1 has been added to it; that is, the value of `i` is changed to `36`.

Lesson: Assignments take place in a right-to-left order.

To avoid potential confusion, our advice is:

✗ *Don't use the result of an assignment as an operand for some other operation.*

Can you use anything other than the assignment operator for assignment? Yes, you can use the update and increment operators.

The update operators

It's common in programs to want to update the value of a variable in the sense of adding, say 2 to it, or multiplying it by 2. Since the idea of updating is such a common operation, C++ provides a special set of operators, the **binary update** operators.

The += operator is an example of an update operator. You use it just like you use the assignment operator. On the left-hand side there has to be a **destination** and on the right-hand side there's an **expression**. Assuming a variable name as the destination, the effect of the += operator is to add the value of the expression to that variable.

EXAMPLE:

If num is a `double` variable, then:

```
num += 2.0   is equivalent to   num = num + 2.0
num -= 2.0   is equivalent to   num = num - 2.0
num *= 2.0   is equivalent to   num = num * 2.0
num /= 2.0   is equivalent to   num = num / 2.0
```

Each update operator consists of an arithmetic operator (`+`, `-`, `*`, `/`) followed by an `=` symbol, with no space in between. The `int` type also supports these operators, as well as `%=`.

All the update operators involve assignment; they change the value of the left-hand operand (which must therefore be a **destination**). Hence they are all assignment operators, and in fact all have the same precedence level as the assignment operator `=`. However, in view of their particular effect, **update operators** is the term we'll use since it helps to convey the idea that their use updates the value originally held by a variable.

PROBLEM:

Write a program that reads in a set of positive values, counts how many numbers have been read in, and computes their product. The sequence of input values is terminated by zero.

DESIGN:

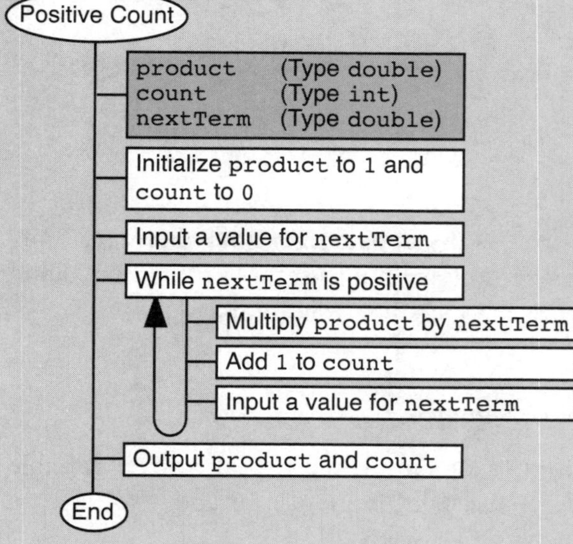

IMPLEMENTATION:

```
#include <iostream.h>

int main()
{
  double product = 1.0;
  int    count   = 0;
  double nextTerm;

  cout << "Type a sequence of positive values." << endl
       << "Terminate the sequence by a non-positive value."
       << endl << endl;

  cin  >> nextTerm;
  while (nextTerm >= 0)
  {
    product *= nextTerm;
    count   += 1;
    cin >> nextTerm;
  }
  cout << endl << endl << "The number of positive terms read is "
       << count << endl
       << "Their product is " << product << endl;
  return 0;
} // end main()
```

You'll formally meet the C++ `while` repetition statement in Chapter 10, but you may care to run this program to check that it satisfies the problem specification.

As well as the update operators, there are some other operators that involve assignment but again it's useful to categorize them separately. These other operators are the increment operators.

The increment operators

Adding 1 to, or subtracting 1 from, an `int` variable is an update operation that's frequently used in programs. To add 1 to an `int` variable it's easy enough to write `i = i + 1` or even `i += 1`. However, C++ provides a shorthand notation using the unary **increment** operator `++` which can be placed either after (**postfix** form) or before (**prefix** form) the name of an `int` variable. This means that there are no less than 4 ways that you can add 1 to `i`. There's a unary **decrement** operator `--` too, so there are 4 ways of subtracting 1 from `i`.

EXAMPLE:

On each of the following lines, the expressions are equivalent in terms of their effect on `i`.

```
i++        ++i        i += 1        i = i + 1
i--        --i        i -= 1        i = i - 1
```

You now should have some idea why C++ is so called; it's a step up from C.

Wait a minute. What's all this "equivalent in terms of their effect on `i`" stuff?

Why not just say that `i++`, `++i`, `i += 1` and `i = i + 1` are all equivalent? The answer is because only `++i`, `i += 1` and `i = i + 1` are entirely equivalent; `i++` is the odd one out. Eh? Let's think about this.

When the prefix form of `++` is used, as in `++i`, in syntactic terms there's a unary operator and an operand; when combined they form an expression. You expect `++i` to increase the value of `i` by one, and since `++i` is an expression it must yield a value. But what is this value? It's the value of `i` *after* the increment has taken place. The return value is the same as that returned by the expressions `i = i + 1` and `i += 1`. In contrast, the value of the expression `i++` is the value of `i` *before* the increment took place. Hence `i++` and `i = i + 1` aren't exactly equivalent.[2]

Does any of this matter to you? Yes, it does if you intend to use the result of one of these operators. No, it doesn't if you follow an extension to the last style rule we gave.

✗ *Don't use the result of an assignment, an update or an increment as an operand for some other operation.*

[2] There's an argument that C++ is misnamed – it should be ++C. The C language has been updated and you get the new version, not the old one.

Increment/decrement operations are most frequently found in repetition statements, such as the one we gave earlier for counting the number of positive floating-point numbers read in and outputting their product. We could have written `count++` instead of `count += 1`, and many books use the ++ and — operators extensively in situations such as this. In fact, we recommend that you use the += and -= operators in this context instead. The += and -= operators are more versatile than ++ and — in that they allow an increment other than 1.

✗ *Don't use the ++ or — operators to add 1 or subtract 1 from an* `int` *variable.*

✓ *Use += or -= instead.*

Let's now summarize in syntax diagrams what you've learned in this section.

Assignment syntax revisited

An **assignment** can involve the assignment operator, or it may take the form of an **update expression** or an **incremental expression**. An **incremental expression** involves either a prefix or postfix **increment operator** and a **destination**. (We'll use the term "increment" to cover both increment and decrement.)

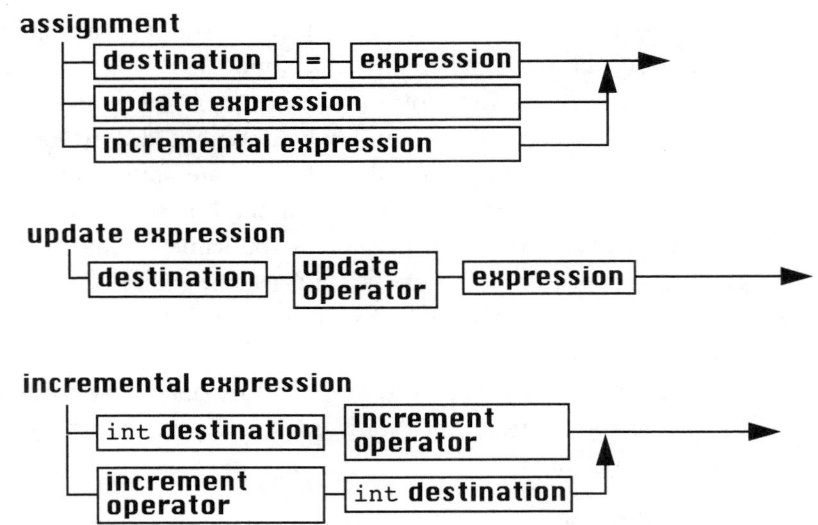

As before, these diagrams don't paint the whole picture. You know that the destination of an increment operator can be the identifier of an `int` variable, and there are a few other things that you'll meet later that it can be too. Look at the interface of a type to check whether or not the increment operators are supported by that type. You can be confident that the compiler will check, even if you don't.

It's time now to look at some other forms of expression and some other operators.

EXERCISES FOR SECTION 8.4

1 Given that `i` is an integer variable with the value 7, what are the values of the following expressions?

(a) `i++` (b) `++i` (c) `i += 1` (d) `i = i + 1`
(e) `i /= 2`

2 Modify the program that determines the product of positive numbers read so that it determines their sum.

8.5 BOOLEAN EXPRESSIONS

Boolean expressions: in general terms

Booleans are used in the context of specifying whether something is true or false, and situations like this often arise in the context of making comparisons of the form less than, equal to, greater than, and so on. Comparisons are often based on numerical values, but comparisons may be made between nonnumerical items too.

EXAMPLE:

Was yesterday's lunchtime temperature in Melbourne greater than or equal to that in Rio de Janeiro? Is the time it would take me to get to Tulsa equal to 24 hours? Is the name of this mountain I've just struggled up equal to Kilimanjaro?

In each case a question is being asked that requires a true or false answer, rather than a statement of fact being made.

When asking a question the answer may depend on a more complex relationship than a simple one concerning two values only.

EXAMPLE:

You might ask the question "is today Saturday and is it 5.00 pm, or is today Monday and is it 9:00 pm?"

Hence you need comparison operators (such as "less than" and "greater than") to determine Boolean values and Boolean operators (such as "and" and "or") to combine two Boolean values and produce a Boolean result.

Boolean expressions: in C++ terms

If you look back (yet again) to the interface for the `int` and `double` types given in Section 5.2 you'll see that there are a number of comparison (equality and ordering) operators associated with these types:

Comparison operator	Meaning
==	equal to
!=	not equal to
<	less than
<=	less than or equal to
>	greater than
>=	greater than or equal to

Since the = symbol is already reserved for assignment a different symbol has to be used to test for equality: it's the == symbol. We guarantee that at some time you'll erroneously use the = symbol where you really mean the == symbol.

If you can get used to the idea of saying "becomes equal to" every time you do an assignment and "equals-equals" every time you do an equality test, it'll help to minimize the confusion between the = and == operators. The compiler may even question your intentions in the form of giving a compile-time warning if it finds an assignment where it's expecting a Boolean expression.

For each of the comparison operators the types of the operands must be the same (again, don't rely on implicit type conversions) and may be any of the built-in types, or indeed any PDT that supports these operators. To determine whether a particular PDT supports comparison operators you're going to have to look at its interface.

Would you expect the `Canvas` PDT to support the comparison operators? Does it? What about `Text`?

The `Canvas` PDT doesn't support the comparison operators but the `Text` PDT does.

As with any operator, the operands in a comparison can take any of the possible forms of an expression given in the **expression** syntax diagram shown earlier. A comparison gives a result value of type `bool`.

EXAMPLE:

Given the following declaration-with-initialization statements:

```
int  i      = 15;
char ch     = 'P';
bool test   = true;
Text greet  = "Hi";
```

the following examples illustrate the use of some of the comparison operators and the results of the Boolean expressions:

Expression	Value
`i == 15`	`true`
`i != 15`	`false`
`i == 35`	`false`
`i != 35`	`true`
`i <  17`	`true`
`i >  17`	`false`
`i <= 15`	`true`
`i >= 15`	`true`
`ch == 'P'`	`true`

Expression	Value
`ch != 'P'`	`false`
`ch == 'p'`	`false`
`ch != 'p'`	`true`
`ch <= 'Z'`	`true`
`ch >= 'A'`	`true`
`greet == "Hi"`	`true`
`greet <  "Ho"`	`true`
`greet != "Hi"`	`false`
`test  != false`	`true`

The comparisons of `ch` against an upper-case `char` literal indicate that there's a natural ordering associated with the `char` values representing upper-case letters. `'A'` is less than `'B'`, which is less than `'C'`, and so on. There's an equivalent natural ordering for the lower-case letters too. Then there's the question of the relationship between the upper- and lower-case letters. Is `'a'` less than `'A'`? Or is it the other way round? The answer depends on the implementation of the `char` type that your system is using, but in ASCII the upper case letters come first, so `ch < 'p'` has the value `true`.

Lesson: You can safely rely on an alphabetical ordering of the upper-case letters, and of the lower-case letters, but don't assume any ordering between upper-case and lower-case.

Comparison of digit character literals works as you would expect. For example, the value of `'0' < '1'` is `true`.

Lesson: You can safely rely on an ordering of the characters representing digits.

For the `Text` PDT the two operands of a comparison operator are compared character by character to determine a lexicographic order.

EXAMPLE:

In ASCII `"Hi"` is less than `"Ho"` since `'i'` is less than `'o'`, while `"Hi"` is less than `"hi"` since `'H'` is less than `'h'`.

One final (in this chapter) glance back to Chapter 5 will show that the `bool` type has three Boolean operators:

Boolean operator	Meaning
`!`	NOT
`&&`	AND
`||`	OR

These Boolean operators are valid only for `bool` operands, and the type of the result of an operation using them is `bool`. The operators `&&` and `||` are both binary operators; `!` is a unary operator.

EXAMPLE:

Given the following declaration-with-initialization statements:

```
int  i     = 15;
char ch    = 'P';
bool test  = true;
Text greet = "Hi";
```

the following table gives some examples of the use of the comparison and Boolean operators, along with the result of the Boolean expression.

Expression	Value
`(0 < i) && (i < 20)`	`true`
`(i == 0) || (i == 15)`	`true`

Expression	Value
`!(ch <= 'Z')`	`false`
`test && !test`	`false`
`(greet != "Hi") && (greet != "Ho")`	`false`

Although the `&&` and `||` operators have two operands, if the result of an operation involving either of these operators can be determined by knowing the value of the left-hand operand only, the right-hand operand is not evaluated. For example, if the left-hand operand of `&&` is `false` then the result must be `false`, regardless of the value of the right-hand operand. Similarly, if the left-hand operand of `||` is `true` then the result of the operation must be `true`.

You might be tempted to think that the first of the Boolean expressions in the above example could be written `0 < i < 20`. Unfortunately although the compiler will accept an expression such as this it won't necessarily have the desired effect (why not?). Would you expect the Boolean expression `i > 0 < 20` to give the right result?

In `0 < i < 20` the first `<` operator gets evaluated before the second. The result is either `true` or `false`, and then `1` (`true`) or `0` (`false`), as appropriate, is used as the left-hand operand for the second `<` operator. Since we've assumed a value of 15 for `i` then, fortunately, you'll get the right result. If the value of `i` is greater than or equal to 20, however the value of the Boolean expression is still `true`. The same line of logic applies to `i > 0 < 20`.

Mistakenly writing an expression such as `0 < i < 20` can stem from an incorrect specification (in English) of what the test to be made is.

Which of the following possibilities is likely to give you the required C++ Boolean expression directly?

1. `i` lies between 0 and 20.
2. `i` is greater than 0 and less than 20.
3. `i` is greater than 0 and `i` is less than 20.
4. (`i` is greater than 0) and (`i` is less than 20).

The answer is versions 3 and 4, although version 3 requires you to know the appropriate precedence rules, so 4 is safest.

Lesson: When writing code involving Boolean expressions you may need to reword the English expression from which the test was derived to get a Boolean expression that does what you want it to do.

One way to check a Boolean expression is to look at the types of the operands of the comparison operators. The types should be the same.

Lesson: Ensure that the operands for the comparison operators are of the same type.

Of course, the operands of the Boolean operators must be of type `bool`.

As with all operators, the comparison and Boolean operators have precedence levels associated with them. The following table lists all operators you've met so far according to their precedence levels, including the input and output operators >> and <<. The operators with the highest precedence are at the top, while those with the lowest precedence are at the bottom. Operators within the areas separated by lines have the same precedence levels.

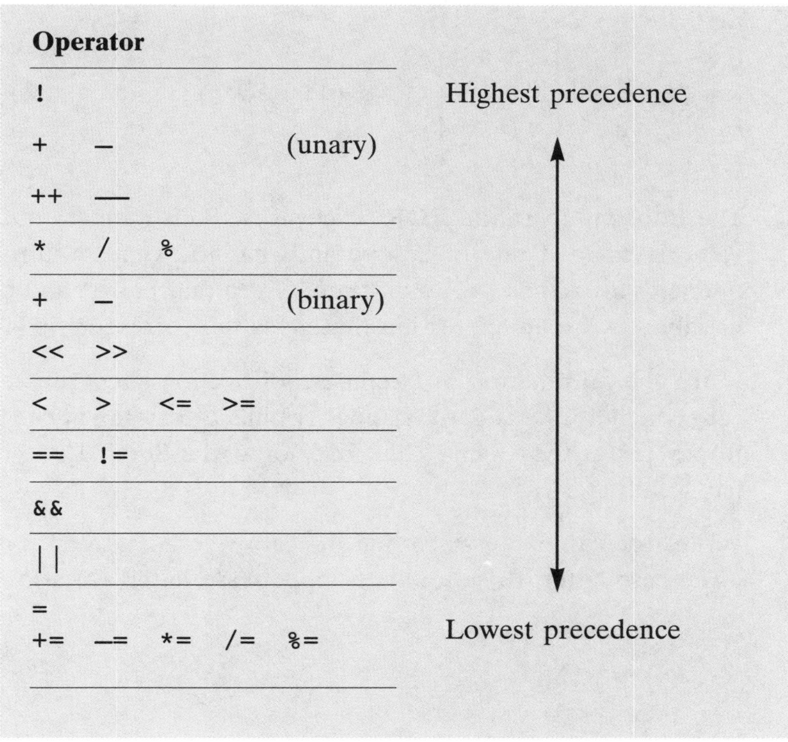

<table>
<tr><th>Operator</th><th></th><th></th></tr>
<tr><td>!
+ - (unary)
++ --</td><td></td><td>Highest precedence</td></tr>
<tr><td>* / %</td><td></td><td></td></tr>
<tr><td>+ -</td><td>(binary)</td><td></td></tr>
<tr><td><< >></td><td></td><td></td></tr>
<tr><td>< > <= >=</td><td></td><td></td></tr>
<tr><td>== !=</td><td></td><td></td></tr>
<tr><td>&&</td><td></td><td></td></tr>
<tr><td>||</td><td></td><td></td></tr>
<tr><td>=
+= -= *= /= %=</td><td></td><td>Lowest precedence</td></tr>
</table>

Remember, if in doubt (and you will almost certainly be in doubt at some stage) use parentheses to enforce the order in which you want operations to take place. You'll almost certainly have difficulty in remembering the precedence levels of the comparison and Boolean operators in relation to the other operators.

> **Lesson:** Be prepared to use parentheses liberally in a Boolean expression to ensure that the expression gives the expected value.

EXERCISES FOR SECTION 8.5

1 Given that the integers `i`, `j` and `k` have the values `2`, `-4` and `7`, what are the values of the following Boolean expressions?

(a) `(i < j) && (j < k )`
(b) `(i < j) || (j < k)`
(c) `(i < j) || ((j == k) && (!(j > k)))`
(d) `(j < i) && !(i < j)`
(e) `(i < j) || !(i < j)`

2 The Boolean operation XOR (exclusive OR) is a binary operation whose result value is `true` if one of its operands has the value `true`, and `false` if both operands are either `false` or `true`. Given that `test1` and `test2` are two `bool` variables, write an expression that gives the corresponding XOR value.

3 Using the information of Exercise 5 of Section 8.3, write expressions that indicate whether a Sans Serif islander (a) has to pay tax at the Super Rate, (b) has to pay tax at the Higher Rate but not at the Super Rate; or (c) has no tax to pay at all.

4 Write Boolean expressions that indicate whether the `char` variable `ch` is (a) a lower-case letter; (b) a lower- or upper-case letter; (c) a lower-case vowel.

SUMMARY

In this chapter, you've learned:

- **literals** are a way of expressing values within a program;
- **assignment** gives a value to a variable;
- **operator symbols** are used to combine values of their operands to produce new values;
- **unary operators** have a single operand;
- **binary operators** have two operands;
- **precedence levels** govern the order in which operations are evaluated;
- **expressions** are built using literals, variables and operator symbols;
- **update and increment operators** are a form of assignment;
- **explicit type coercion** uses a constructor to convert a value of one type to a value of another;
- **implicit type coercion** is used by the compiler where necessary.

Now you can build complex expressions in C++ that work out the speed you're reading this book (in pages per day), the value of your savings expressed in Polish zlotys, or whether this year is a leap year. However, you're not finished with expressions just yet. In the next chapter you'll see how the **simple expression** syntactic element can be extended to include function calls.

END-OF-CHAPTER EXERCISES

1 Write a program that prompts the user for two integer quantities representing amounts of money in dollars and cents and converts this to an amount in sterling (pounds and pence, with 100 pence to the pound). Use an exchange rate of 1.54 US dollars to the pound sterling.

2 Write a program that prompts the user for their weight (a floating-point number) in pounds and converts this to a weight in kilograms (see Exercise 3 of Section 2.3).

3 Write a program that prompts the user for their height in feet and inches (both integer quantities) and converts this to a height in meters (see Exercise 3 at the end of Section 2.3).

4 Write a program that computes a person's body mass index (see Exercise 4 at the end of Chapter 6).

5 The value of the `char` variable `digit` is known to be one of the digits `'0'` to `'9'`. Write an expression that gives the corresponding integer value in the range `0` to `9`.

6 Given that `a`, `b` and `c` are `doubles`, and `i` and `j` are `ints`, which of the following are valid C++ expressions?

(a) `-b / 4 * a *c`
(b) `b / -4 * a * c`
(c) `i *= j += 1`
(d) `i++++`
(e) `a && b || i`

7 Given values for `a`, `b` and `c` of 1.0, 2.0 and 3.0, and for `i` and `j` of 9 and 2, what are the values of the valid expressions in Exercise 6?

8 For each of the following write corresponding C++ expressions that will yield the defined quantity. (You're allowed to assume the existence of variables representing the values that quantities are defined in terms of.)

(a) The density of a solid is equal to its mass divided by its volume.
(b) The volume of a cuboid is equal to the product of its length, breadth and height.
(c) The perimeter of a rectangle is the sum of twice the length and twice the breadth.
(d) The surface area of a sphere of radius r is equal to $4\pi r^2$.
(e) The surface area of a cylinder of height h and base radius r is equal to $2\pi r(r + h)$.

9 Given that the variable `index` represents someone's body mass index, write Boolean expressions that indicate whether that person is (a) underweight, (b) OK, (c) overweight, or (d) obese. (The definition of this classification is given in Exercise 6 of Section 2.4.)

10 The `int` variables `mark1`, `mark2`, `mark3`, `mark4` and `mark5` represent the marks for your last five computing assignments. For reasons best known to themself, your instructor marked your first two assignments out of 20, your next two out of 50, and your last assignment out of 100. Write and test an expression that gives the average mark (as a floating-point number).

11 Write an expression that rounds your average assignment mark, defined in Exercise 10, to the nearest integer.

9 Using functions and member functions

OBJECTIVE

To introduce the concept of function calls in C++, covering:

- functional abstraction;
- how to interpret a function interface in order to make a function call;
- the parameter-passing mechanism;
- how to specify actual parameter values;
- the difference between value and reference parameters;
- the link between functions and operators.

Calling a function

9.0 FUNCTIONAL ABSTRACTION

Functional abstraction: in general terms

5 Engine – Removal

1 Remove the bonnet as described in Chapter 11
2 Disconnect the battery negative lead
3 Remove the air cleaner as described in Chapter 3
4 Remove the radiator as described in Chapter 2
5 Loosen the clip and disconnect the top hose from the thermostat housing
...

Think back to Chapter 1 and the list of instructions that you'd typically expect to find in a car maintenance manual for removing an engine. OK, the list is a long way back, so we've repeated part of it here. The analogy between this list of instructions and a program should be pretty clear to you by now. The actions have to be obeyed one-by-one in order for the desired outcome to be achieved (namely, to take the engine out of the car).

But wait a minute. There appear to be two different types of instruction here:

- detailed low-level instructions that tell you all you need to know in order to carry them out (for example, "Loosen the clip . . .");
- high-level skeleton descriptions that give only an abstraction of what the operation is (for example, "Remove the bonnet"); the detailed low-level instructions associated with these operations have to be found elsewhere (for example, Chapter 11[1]).

In the latter case it's sufficient to know that a detailed low-level description exists somewhere, and to use a high-level description to abstract from this. When you invoke (or call) the high-level instruction, the low-level instructions are carried out.

Step 4 "Remove the radiator as described in Chapter 2" is another example of a high-level description. When you reach this instruction you know that there's a switch of control to Chapter 2 where radiator removal is described in detail. Having completed the removal of the radiator you return to Chapter 5 and continue with engine removal. This sequence of events is captured in Figure 9.1. The light shaded arrow indicates the flow of control as seen at the top level, while the dark shaded arrows indicate a lower-level view of the flow of control.

The term used for this idea of packaging a set of instructions is **functional abstraction**. As you're aware, in the absence of instructions to the contrary, the normal sequence for executing a "program," computer or otherwise, is to follow the instructions one by one in order. However, when a function invocation is

[1] If you've read about scope in Chapter 6 of this book there's an interesting example of scope here. If you go to Chapter 11 of this book you won't find anything about bonnet removal, but you will find something about defining functions. In the context of the car maintenance manual, references to Chapter 11 mean Chapter 11 of the manual, not this book on C++.

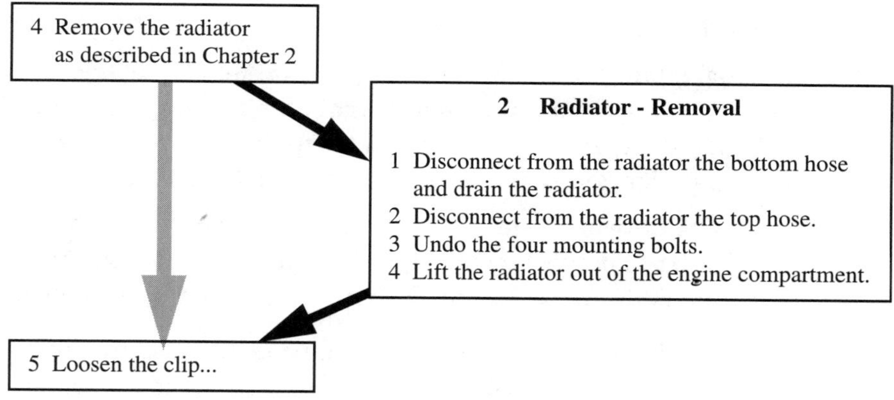

Figure 9.1 The sequencing of events in the Engine Removal example

encountered, the corresponding set of instructions defined elsewhere is followed. At the end of that sequence the original sequence is returned to and the instruction following that corresponding to the function invocation is obeyed next. We therefore say that functional abstraction is a form of **control abstraction**: there's a transfer of control.

When do you employ functional abstraction? When you use a designator box in a design. In Chapter 2 we stressed the importance of producing a design before you start writing any code. You start with a high-level design. Then you gradually refine this design by placing designator boxes around instructions that require expansion, and then provide that expansion. It's not necessary for such expansions to be in-line; in fact it's often better if they're not. Rather, the expansion can be provided elsewhere, just as the instructions for removing the radiator are found in a part of a car maintenance manual separate from that of the position of the call of this operation in the engine removal section.

Lesson: A designator box is equivalent to functional abstraction.

Functional abstraction: in programming language terms

In programming language terms, the invocation of a high-level instruction representing a functional abstraction is termed a **function call**. The expansion of the designator box used to represent a function call is termed a **function definition**. It follows that there are three aspects to functional abstraction:

1. **The designer's view**. The designer analyzes the problem description in order to derive functional abstractions. A functional abstraction is represented in the algorithm design diagram as a designator box.

2. **The implementer's view**. The implementer needs to provide the detailed instructions that constitute the definition of the function.

3. **The user's view**. The user needs to know, in abstract terms, what the function does and how to make a call.

These aspects are necessarily interrelated, but they can also be thought of as entirely separate concepts.

You won't be surprised to learn that we're taking the separatist stance and hence in this chapter we'll be considering the user's view only. As far as the user is concerned a function is just a black box that causes something to happen when it's called. The black box needs a name. Sometimes the black box will give the user something back. Sometimes the black box requires some information to be supplied – **parameters**. Maybe the box has "Fibonacci's Pizzeria" written on it and inside is the pizza you ordered earlier.[2]

EXAMPLE:

Consider the instruction (statement) "Call your local pizza parlor and ask for a pizza to be delivered to your home."

The act of ordering a pizza is an example of functional abstraction. You don't expect to have to tell the chef how to cook your pizza. You expect them to know how to prepare the base, to place the uncooked pizza in the oven, and to take it out when it's cooked. You just order the pizza and then wait for it to arrive. But what sort of pizza do you expect to be delivered? Deep pan? 12″? Four Cheese? It would be pretty boring if all pizzas were the same and, of course, you can vary the order to suit your own

[2] Or should that be Fibonnacci's Pisa-ria? The Italian mathematician Leonardo Fibonacci was born around 1170 in Pisa. You'll meet him again in Chapter 11.

tastes. This requires you to provide some information to the pizza parlor that dictates just what sort of pizza you require. You're also going to have to supply an address to which the pizza should be delivered. You need to supply some parameters to tailor the function call to your gastronomic and physical needs.

Parameterization: in general terms

Just as a program that doesn't involve any I/O is not a very interesting program, so a function that doesn't involve some form of information exchange when called is not very interesting either. Typically, the user of a function supplies zero or more input values to a function, and expects to get back zero or more values. For the moment we'll keep things simple and say that at most one value can be returned, as demonstrated in Figure 9.2. Precisely what output the function produces can then be made dependent on the values input. We say that the function has been **parameterized** in terms of input values.

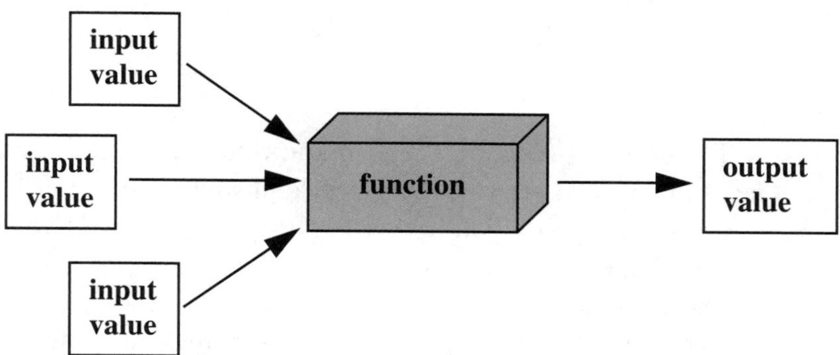

Figure 9.2 Function input and output values

EXAMPLE:

Input parameters for a functional abstraction to cook a pizza (the output) could be

- whether it's deep pan or thin and crispy;

- the size – 12″, 14″, etc.;
- what toppings are required – mushrooms, anchovies, ham, etc.

Are there any other examples of parameterized functions in the real world? Well, mathematicians and high school students use functions a lot.

EXAMPLE:

In the not too dim-and-distant past it was commonplace for every high school student to be armed with a set of mathematical tables, giving lists of values of the trigonometric functions (sines, cosines, etc.), of square roots, of natural logarithms, and so on. Nowadays students are armed with pocket calculators that make life much easier. To determine the square root of a number all you have to do is type in the number (an input parameter for the square root function) and then "call" the square root function by pressing the key labeled √. You don't care how the calculator works the result out, as long as the answer you get is correct. Simple calculators tend not to provide much more than a square root function key, but more advanced calculators have keys for the trigonometric functions, for exponentials and logarithms, and so on.

The user of a function needs to know how to interact with that function. They need to know what values to supply and what values they'll get back. When you go to order a pizza, you need to know what questions you might be asked and how to respond, and that you'll get a delicious pizza to eat before you get back to reading this book. When you want a square root you've got to indicate what number you want the square root of, and then do something with the number that's returned. The user of a function needs to know about the function's **interface**, and in particular what goes in and what comes out.

Who is responsible for specifying the function interface? In the first instance it's the designer, and thereafter it's the implementer who implements the design of the designer. We're not going to say anything about C++ function implementations until Chapter 11. You've been quite happy (at least we hope you have been) to make use of other "black boxes"; black boxes that involve operations and abstract values. That's right, you've been making use of PDTs knowing their interfaces only. The details of how PDTs work – what's inside the black boxes – we've deliberately left until Chapter 12, by which time you'll be completely familiar with the use of PDTs and in a position to consider their implementations. Similarly we're going to delay the details of implementations of functions – what's inside function black boxes – until Chapter 11, by which time you should be entirely familiar with using functions.

Fortunately, there are lots of functions around whose implementations have already been written, and therefore that you can call. What's a function call? In the calculator example above it's the action of pressing the square root key. Let's see how you express a function call in C++.

EXERCISES FOR SECTION 9.0

1 For each of the following functional abstractions identify the component parts of their interfaces.

(a) Given a number for a chapter in this book, determine how many pages are in that chapter.
(b) Given a key word or phrase (such as "function interface") determine the number of the first page in this book on which that word or phrase appears.

2 What parameters would be appropriate for a functional abstraction that draws a square?

9.1 CALLING A FUNCTION

Consider the following problem.

PROBLEM:

You've been contracted by the King Arthur Lottery Company to write a program that outputs the 6 numbers (in the range 1 to 50) for a weekly draw.

IMPLEMENTATION:

You might be tempted to write a program that includes the statement

```
cout << "This week's lucky numbers are  " << endl
     <<  2 << "    " << 15 << "    " << 21  << "    "
     << 33 << "    " << 41 << "    " << 49  << endl;
```

The fact that these numbers happen to coincide with those on your ticket is entirely coincidental, isn't it!

Being rather more honest than this you realize that you need some way of generating numbers that are in some sense "random" so that neither you nor anyone else can predict the numbers that will be generated. Fortunately there's a predefined C++ function available that provides a potential solution to your problem, and it's called `rand`. Unlike the member functions you saw in Chapter 7, you won't find `rand()` in the interface of any built-in type, or any PDT for that matter. `rand()` is a stand-alone function. A call to the function `rand()` produces a random `int` value, and you can use this `int` value in the same way that you use any other source of an `int` value. Here's a potential alternative solution to the statement that outputs 6 "random" numbers.

IMPLEMENTATION:

```
cout << "This week's lucky numbers are   " << endl
     << rand() % 50 + 1 << "     " << rand() % 50 + 1 << "     "
     << rand() % 50 + 1 << "     " << rand() % 50 + 1 << "     "
     << rand() % 50 + 1 << "     " << rand() % 50 + 1 << endl;
```

In the above code fragment each call of `rand()` produces a random number in the range 0 to `RAND_MAX`, a large positive integer (for example, 32,767). Hopefully you get a different number each time, otherwise the numbers wouldn't be very random. Using the `%` operator to calculate the remainder of integer division by 50 and then adding 1 is an expression giving a value in the range 1 to 50. Since the function call `rand()` produces an `int` value, you can place the function call any place that any other `int` value could appear, for example, as an operand for the + operator.

Despite your honesty, if you use the above modified output statement for the lottery draw you'll get the same sequence for each run of the program, which isn't very satisfactory. The sequence can be changed by making a call to `srand(...)` before any call to `rand()`. The function `srand(...)` initializes the sequence according to the value (or **seed**) provided as a value (a parameter) within the parentheses. Use a different seed and you get a different sequence.

IMPLEMENTATION:

```
int seed;

cout << "What value do you want to use as the seed?" << endl;
cin  >> seed;
srand(seed);
cout << "This week's lucky numbers are  " << endl
     << rand() % 50 + 1 << "    " << rand() % 50 + 1 << "    "
     << rand() % 50 + 1 << "    " << rand() % 50 + 1 << "    "
     << rand() % 50 + 1 << "    " << rand() % 50 + 1 << endl;
```

Note that `srand(...)` itself doesn't return a random number, or anything else for that matter. Hence you can't use a call to `srand(...)` as the source of a value. You can only use it in the context of a function call followed by a semi-colon – a statement.

What value should be input for the seed? Well, you could use the final number generated for the previous week's draw. However there's still scope here for you to cheat the system since the sequence is predictable. You need some way of generating a seed to start the sequence whose value you have no way of knowing.

One way of achieving the desired outcome is to use the system clock of your computer. The value of the clock should be different each time you access it. Hence if you can use the clock you should get a different set of random numbers each time. How do you find out the time? Make a call to the function `clock()`, which returns an `int` value.

IMPLEMENTATION:

```
srand(clock());
cout << "This week's lucky numbers are  " << endl
     << rand() % 50 + 1 << "    " << rand() % 50 + 1 << "    "
     << rand() % 50 + 1 << "    " << rand() % 50 + 1 << "    "
     << rand() % 50 + 1 << "    " << rand() % 50 + 1 << endl;
```

At this point we just want you to get a feel for what a function call looks like. We'll show you lots more function calls in the next section, and give you the syntax for a function call.

To make a function call you need to know what functions are available for you to call. The C++ system you're using comes with a standard set of function libraries, and you have to `#include` the header (`.h`) file for the appropriate library if you wish to make use of (that is, call) any of the functions in that library.

EXAMPLE:

To make a call to the `rand()` and `srand(...)` functions you need to `#include <stdlib.h>`. To make a call to `clock()` you need to `#include <time.h>`.

Inclusion of the header file is necessary for the compiler to check that you're using the functions correctly. Just as you need a variable declaration to precede any use of that variable, so a function "declaration" must precede any use (call) of a function. This "declaration" specifies the function's interface. Not only does the compiler need to know about the interface of any function that you call, you need to know about the interface to be able to make a successful call. So let's look at function interfaces.

EXERCISE FOR SECTION 9.1

1 Write a program that makes two calls to the `clock()` function, stores the values returned in two `int` variables, and then prints out their difference. Is there any difference? Why might there be?

Now try inserting the following code between the two calls of `clock()`.

```
int n = 10;
for (int i = 0; i < n; i += 1)
{
  cout << rand();
}
```

(This is a repetition statement that outputs 10 random numbers.) Does this affect the time difference? If not, how large does `n` have to be before there is a difference?

9.2 THE FUNCTION INTERFACE

The user of a C++ function needs to know three principal things that collectively form the function interface.

1. What is the name of the function?
2. What are the types of the input values, if any, that the function requires as parameters?
3. What is the type of any value that the function returns?

You should have some idea of what's required here. For the name of a function you should be expecting an identifier. And what about the types for the input values and the type of the return value? Well, any valid type you like, including the built-ins and PDTs you learned about in Chapter 5.

EXAMPLE:

The name of the function that can be used to determine a random number is `rand`. The function `rand()` has no parameters and the return value is of type `int`.

The name of the function that's used to initialize the random number sequence is `srand`. `srand(...)` has a single parameter of type `int` but has no return value.

To make a successful function call requires correct use of the function interface:

- a function call involves the name of the function, so just like any other identifier, you'd better spell it correctly;
- you need to supply parameters correctly, which means getting both the number of parameters right as well as the type of each parameter;
- if a function returns a value of a specified type, then something sensible must be done with that value.

A function call can appear in any location that any other value of the return type may appear; for example, on the right-hand side of an assignment, as a value to be output, or as an operand for an operator. Some functions don't return a value, in which case the function call is followed by a semicolon to form a statement.

EXAMPLE:

A call to `rand()` can appear anywhere an `int` value is required. `srand(...)` can only be used with a semicolon to form a statement.

Let's have a look at some more examples of predefined functions. By putting `#include <math.h>` at the top of your program you have access to a set of mathematical functions that includes the following:

Interface	Description
`double sqrt(double x)`	square root
`double log(double x)`	natural logarithm
`double exp(double x)`	exponentiation
`double sin(double x)`	trigonometric sine
`double cos(double x)`	trigonometric cosine
`double atan(double x)`	inverse tangent (arctangent)
`double fabs(double x)`	floating-point absolute value

In the first column above we've put the interface, or **prototype**, of each function. The interface of a function gives you sufficient information to enable you to call that function, specifying

- the result type – the first item that appears in a function interface;
- the function **signature**, which has two components:
  1. The function name, or **identifier** – the second item that appears in a function interface.
  2. The type of the parameter(s) – a list of parameter types (a **parameter list**), enclosed by parentheses, is the third item that appears in a function interface.

The compiler needs this information too, to check that you've written a correct function call. The compiler needs to know about:

- the function signature, so that it can check that your function call is syntactically correct, that it recognizes the identifier you've specified as the function name, and that the parameters you supply are correct in number and type;
- the function result type, so that it can check that your use of the result of a function call is correct.

Here's a diagram that shows an example of a function interface broken down into its constituent parts.

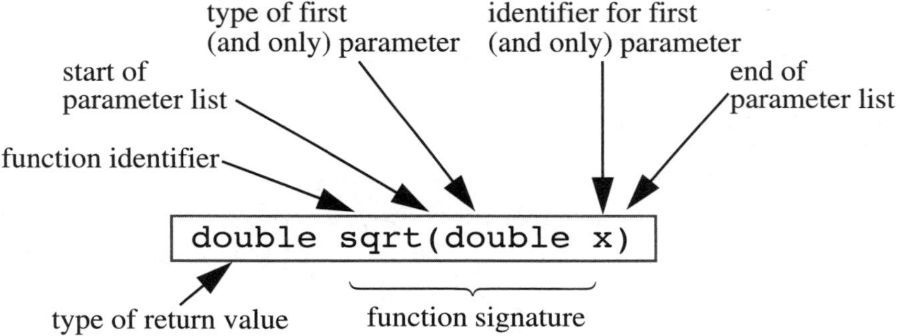

In fact, the signatures of all the mathematical functions listed earlier tell you a little more than just the types of the parameters, since there's a name for each parameter too. In a function signature the parameters are referred to as **formal parameters**, as opposed to the **actual parameters** that appear in a function call.

Lesson: Formal parameters are used in a function interface; actual parameters are used in a function call.

Here are example calls to some of the predefined mathematical functions.

EXAMPLE:

```
// Declare double variables x, y, s, a and theta
//   and assign them values
double hypotenuse = sqrt(x * x + y * y);
const  double PI  = 4.0 * atan(1.0);
```

```
double xToY        = exp(y * log(x));
cout << "Radius is " << (s - a) * tan(theta / 2.0) << endl;
```

Each function call produces a double value, and so the call may appear any place that any other source of a double value may appear; for example, on the right-hand side of an assignment as in the first three examples, or in an expression whose value is to be printed. The call of `exp(...)` demonstrates that the value returned by a function (here, `log(...)`) can be used in an expression that forms the actual parameter to some other function (here, `exp(...)`).

Lesson: A call of a function that returns a value is just a particular form of a simple expression. There's a type associated with the value, and the function call can appear in any position that any other expression that returns a value of that type may appear.

You should note that for the C++ trigonometric functions, angles must always be specified in terms of **radians**. 360° is equivalent to 2π radians.

All the mathematical functions we've looked at so far have the same format; they all have a `double` as a parameter, and return a `double` result. The parameter supplies a value to the function (such as the value whose square root is required). Just because the name of the formal parameter is `x`, doesn't mean that the corresponding actual parameter must be a variable of the same name. The name of a formal parameter just acts as a place holder for the value supplied as an actual parameter, allowing the function interface to be specified in a generic manner.

Lesson: The name of a formal parameter in a function signature is a place holder only for the corresponding actual parameter.

You'll find out more about the precise link between actual and formal parameters, and in particular the use of the name for a formal parameter, in Chapter 11, where we consider function definitions. The above examples illustrate that for the particular functions being considered here the actual parameter can be any expression that gives a `double` as a result.

The actual and formal parameters must be type-compatible. As we indicated in the previous chapter, you shouldn't rely on automatic type coercions, and hence for "type-compatible" you should read "of the same type."

Lesson: The type of an actual parameter must be the same as the type of the corresponding formal parameter.

There are also some predefined mathematical functions that return a `double` value but require more than one actual parameter.

EXAMPLE:

The function `pow(...)` with interface:

```
double pow(double x, double y)
```

can be used to perform exponentiation, that is it gives the value of x^y.

The function `pow(...)` has two formal parameters, both of type `double`, called `x` and `y`. You should note that a parameter list is just like a list of declaration statements, except that each "declaration" (apart from the last) is terminated by a comma, rather than a semicolon. We'll have more to say about what constitutes a legal function interface in Chapter 11. For now we just want you to be able to recognize a legal function interface when you see one and to know how to interpret it.

Since `pow(...)` has two formal parameters, there must be two actual parameters in a call to this function. Just as the formal parameters are separated by commas, so the actual parameters are separated by commas. It's important that you get the actual parameters in the correct order too.

EXAMPLE:

Here are some example calls to pow(...).

```
cout << pow(2.0, 3.0)              << endl;
cout << pow(pow(2.0, 2.0), 2.0) << endl;
```

The call pow(2.0, 3.0) will give a value of $2.0^{3.0} = 8.0$ (as a double), whereas the call pow(3.0, 2.0) will give a value of $3.0^{2.0} = 9.0$ (as a double).

Hence not only is it necessary to know how many parameters a function has and what their types are, it's also necessary to know what the order is. We could have said "the result of the pow(...) function is the value of the first actual parameter raised to the power of the value of the second actual parameter", but by providing names for these parameters we've been able to say "x^y" which is somewhat more succinct. Better still, the function definer could have come up with more meaningful names for the formal parameters that describe their purpose.

EXAMPLE:

Meaningful names for the formal parameters of the pow(...) function would be base and exponent, and the interface would then be defined as:

```
double pow(double base, double exponent)
```

Providing meaningful formal parameter names alone isn't a complete substitute for the description of the purpose of the function to be found in the system documentation, but it helps. Since we weren't responsible for defining the math.h library, you're going to have to make do with rather less helpful names than the ones we'd have chosen. The documentation for the libraries you'll be using is likely to have been written in terms of xs and ys, and so on. If you look at the function header files you may well find that no names at all are used. Does it matter whether or not any names are given for the formal parameters? And if names are used, are those names significant? In both cases the answer is "no."

As far as the function call is concerned, the actual names, if any, of any variables used as formal parameters is irrelevant, apart from possibly indicating their purpose. The principal matter of importance to you the user, and to the compiler, is what the types of the formal parameters are. The actual parameters needn't even be variables (at least, not for the functions you've seen so far); any form of expression that gives a result of the appropriate type will do. So when you make a function call you've got to ensure that:

- the expressions defining the actual parameters give results of the type required by the formal parameters;
- the actual parameters are in the right order.

Lesson: The actual parameters in a function call must agree in number and type with the formal parameters of a function signature. A positional convention is used to associate actual and formal parameters.

What if you don't supply the correct number of parameters? What if you get some of the types wrong? Expect the compiler to complain. To check that a function call is syntactically correct the compiler needs to know the signature of the function, as provided in the appropriate header file. Using the interface, and hence the signature, the compiler can check that:

- you've supplied the correct number of actual parameters;
- the parameters are of the correct type.

The compiler will additionally use the function interface to check that:

- you've done something valid with the result of the function call.

Precisely how the function arrives at the result it produces is not required at compile-time, and so, for example, you won't find the code that implements the square root function in `math.h`. In any case, as the user of a function you don't care how the desired effect is achieved.

For any function you call in a program, a function definition specifying the effect of a function call is required at run-time, so in between compilation and execution the linker must link to the code that implements that function. We'll talk about the source code for function implementations in Chapter 11. For the moment just take it that the source has to exist somewhere and the corresponding object code has to be linked in before your program can execute.

OK, so you know that you can use the `sqrt(...)`, `exp(...)`, `pow(...)`, etc. functions as long as you `#include` the `math.h` library (and link to the function implementations). Are there any other libraries of functions around? Yes, of course there are.

The following function interfaces can be found in `ctype.h`.

Interface	**Description**
`int isalpha(char c)`	test for an alphabetic character
`int isupper(char c)`	tests for an upper-case letter
`int islower(char c)`	tests for a lower-case letter
`int isdigit(char c)`	tests for a digit character
`int ispunct(char c)`	tests for a punctuation mark
`char tolower(char c)`	converts an upper-case letter to lower-case
`char toupper(char c)`	converts a lower-case letter to upper-case

The first five of these functions test the category of their `char` parameter and return a 1 (representing true) or 0 (false) value. The `math` library functions were designed and implemented in the year 5 BC (**B**efore **C**++) when `bool` wasn't heard of. Of course, when you call one of these functions you'll use an explicit type coercion to convert the result to a `bool`. The sixth function can be used to perform an upper-case to lower-case transformation, while the seventh function can be used to transform from lower-case to upper-case, each time giving the transformed character back as the function result.

Let's look at a problem that makes use of some of these character-test functions.

PROBLEM:

Read a sequence of characters until a punctuation mark is encountered, converting any upper-case letters to lower-case and forming a character string from the sequence for printing. An error needs to be flagged if a character read is not a letter or a punctuation mark.

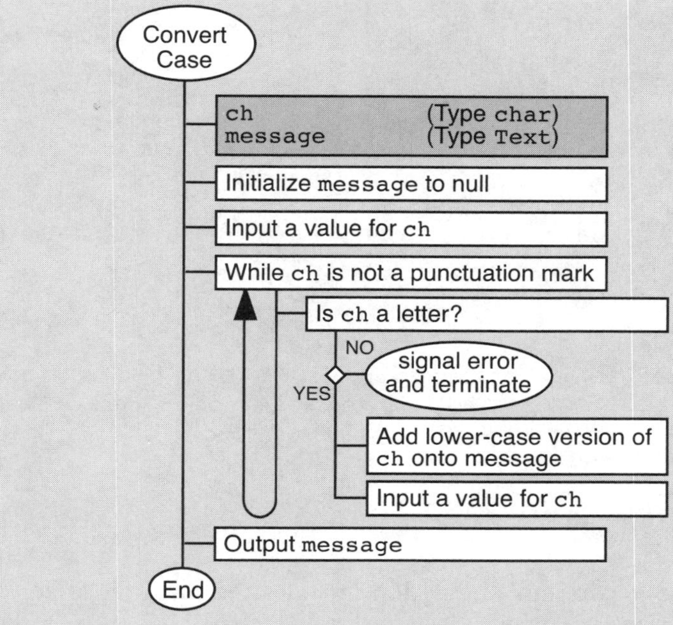

DESIGN:

The design employs repetition and selection, features of C++ that you won't formally meet until the next chapter. However, you should be able to understand what goes on in the implementation that follows, and it provides a tasty little appetizer for Chapter 10.

IMPLEMENTATION:

Can you match the following implementation with the design and therefore recognize the repetition and selection statements?

```
#include <iostream.h>
#include <ctype.h>
#include "Text.h"
#include "error.h"

int main()
{
  char ch;
  Text message = "";

  cout << "Type a sequence of letters, "
       << "terminated by a punctuation mark"   << endl
       << "All spaces will be ignored" << endl << endl;
  cin  >> ch;
  while (!ispunct(ch))
```

```
    {
      if (!isalpha(ch))
      {
        Text errorMessage = "Got: " + message +
                            " and then invalid character read: " +
                            Text(ch);
        error(errorMessage);
        return -1;                      // Terminate the program
      }
      message += Text(tolower(ch));
      cin >> ch;
    }
    cout << endl << endl
        << "The result of conversion is" << endl << endl
        << message << endl;
    return 0;
  } // end main()
```

The above implementation includes the function call:

```
error(errorMessage) ;
```

Is `error(...)` a C++ system library function? No, it's a function that we've provided to help you deal with circumstances like this. Its interface is:

```
void error(Text message)
```

To use the function `error(...)` you need to `#include "error.h"` at the top of your programs. Note that `error(...)` doesn't return a value; its return type is `void`. So you can't assign the result of a call to `error(...)` to a variable, or use a call as an operand, or output the result of a call. The only way to use a function that has a `void` return type is in a function call statement, a function call followed by a semicolon.

Lesson: A function that has a `void` return type returns no value and hence is not a valid expression.

In the previous section we introduced some predefined functions that can be used to generate random numbers. Let's have another look at them. The library `stdlib` has two functions that are useful for generating "random" test data.

Interface	Description
`int rand()`	produces a random number
`void srand(int seed)`	starts the random number sequence

The first of these functions, `rand()`, has no formal parameter – hence the empty parameter list. It follows that when you make a call to `rand()` you don't have to give any actual parameters, although the parentheses are still required. Note that `srand(...)` doesn't return a random number, or anything else for that matter, so its return type is `void` – that is, no result.

Lesson: Even if a function has no parameters, the parentheses must always be present in a function call (and also in a function interface).

The library `time` contains, among other things, an interface for a function `clock()`.

Interface	Description
`int clock()`	returns the time since system start-up

Like `rand()`, `clock()` has an empty parameter list and returns an `int` result.

Let's summarize what you've learned so far about function calls using syntax diagrams.

Function call syntax

Here's the syntax for a **function call**:

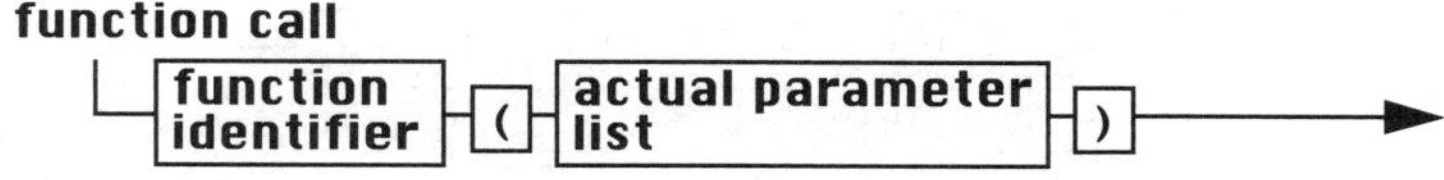

A **function identifier** is just an ordinary identifier that obeys all the syntax rules of any other identifier, and the style rules of a variable identifier.

In a function call the **actual parameter list** is just a (possibly empty) comma-separated list of **actual parameter**s.

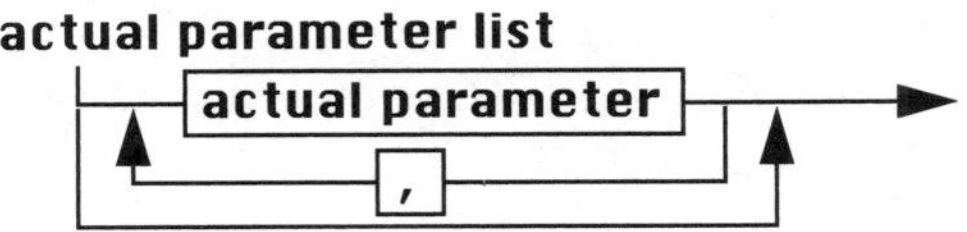

At present the only form of **actual parameter** that we've covered in this chapter is an **actual value parameter**. You'll meet actual **actual reference parameter**s in the next section.

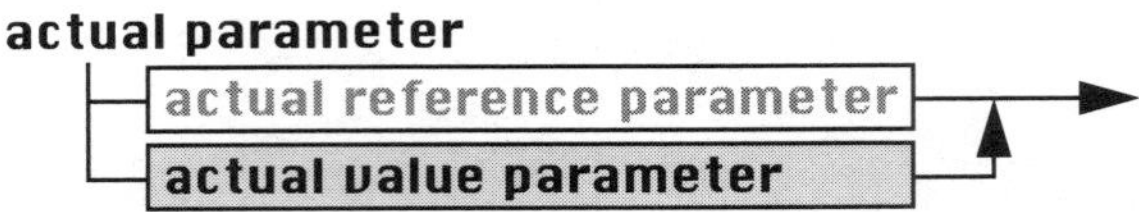

An **actual value parameter** can be any form of expression.

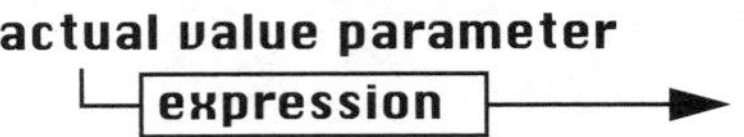

A function call is just a form of a **simple expression**:

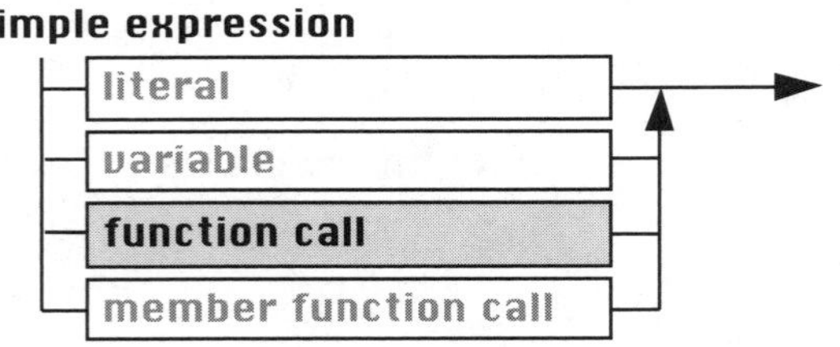

As mentioned earlier, the result type of the expression must be type compatible with the type of the formal parameter.

Don't forget that if a function returns a `void` result you can only use it in the context of a function call statement.

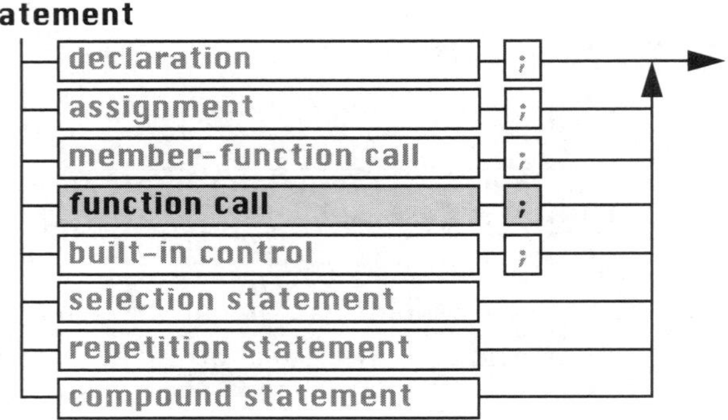

Now you have some idea about function names, actual parameters, and what you can do with the result of a function call. There are some style rules that we suggest you follow when making function calls.

- ✓ *The opening parenthesis should follow the function identifier with no space in between.*
- ✓ *There should be no space between the final actual parameter and the closing parenthesis.*
- ✓ *The comma separating one actual parameter from another should immediately follow the expression that precedes it. There should then be one space between the comma and the next actual parameter.*
- ✓ *Long parameter lists should be continued on following lines. Each line (except the last) should end with a comma separator. Subsequent lines should be indented so that the start lines up with the start of the first parameter on the first line.*

EXAMPLE:

Here are some examples of function calls that follow the above style rules.

```
double area          = triangleArea(side1, side2, side3);
Pizza myPizza        = orderAPizza(12, DEEP_PAN, ANCHOVIES);
ZodiacSign mySign    = signOfZodiac(dayOfBirth, monthOfBirth,
                                    yearOfBirth);
double myAgeInHours = ageInHours(dayOfBirth,  monthOfBirth,
                                 yearOfBirth, dayToday,
                                 monthToday,  yearToday);
```

But wait a minute. You've been following these style rules for some time now (at least, we hope you have). You've been making function calls prior to reaching this chapter. It's just that the function calls you've been making have been member-function calls, rather than plain, ordinary, run-of-the-mill function calls. So let's tie up what we've just covered about using functions with using member functions.

EXERCISES FOR SECTION 9.2

To answer several of the following questions you'll need either to run a simple test problem, or to look at your system documentation.

1 To obtain the absolute value of a `double` value, you use the function `fabs(...)`. For `int`s the equivalent function is `abs(...)`. What do you expect the value of `abs(-6.7)` to be?

2 The `math` library contains two functions for finding the angle (in radians) whose tangent is supplied; `double atan(double x)` and `double atan2(double y, double x)`. What is the range of values that can be returned by `atan(...)`? Why the extra parameter in `atan2(...)`?

3 Can a unary operator precede a function call?

4 What happens if the actual parameter to the square root function is an expression whose value is negative?

5 Find out for which characters the `ctype` function `ispunct(...)` returns `1`.

6 Find out for which characters the `ctype` function `isspace(...)` returns `1`.

7 Write an expression involving the `ctype` functions `isalpha(...)` and `islower(...)` such that the result of the expression is the same as the value of `isupper(ch)`.

8 What is the result value of `tolower(ch)` when `ch` is not an upper-case letter?

9 A function may return a value, in which case a **function call** is a **simple expression** and can therefore be used in a position that any other simple expression may appear (e.g. on the right-hand side of an **assignment** or as an **actual parameter**). If a function call doesn't return a value then a **function call** followed by a semicolon is a **statement**. What happens at compile-time if you treat a call to a function that doesn't return a value as a **simple expression** (for example, try outputting the result). What happens at compile-time if you make a call to a function that returns a value but do nothing with that value (the function call is just a statement)?

10 The function `silly(...)` has the interface `void silly(int i)`. You make a call to this function with an actual parameter the `int` variable `unSet`. There is no assignment to `unSet` prior to the call of `silly(...)`. Does this matter?

9.3 CALLING MEMBER FUNCTIONS

A member function is, in many respects, no different to the functions you looked at in the previous section. It's just that a member function happens to be a member of a PDT. It follows that to use (make a call to) a member function you need to know its interface, consisting of:

- the member function name;
- the number and type of the parameter(s);
- the result type;

just as you need to know the interface of a non-member function to make a function call. All of the lessons of the previous section apply here with "function" replaced by "member function," including:

Lesson: The actual parameters in a member-function call must agree in number and type with the formal parameters of a member-function signature. A positional convention is used to associate actual and formal parameters.

Lesson: A call of a member function that returns a value is just a particular form of a simple expression. There's a type associated with the value, and the member-function call can appear in any position that any other expression that returns a value of that type may appear.

Lesson: A member function that has a `void` return type returns no value and hence is not a valid expression.

The difference between a member function and a non-member function is that the former is inextricably linked to a PDT, and hence to a variable of that PDT.

EXAMPLE:

A quick glance at the interface for the `Text` PDT given in Chapter 5 indicates that it supports a member function with interface `int length()` that gives the length of an instance of the `Text` PDT. Thus, to print the length of a character string read from the keyboard you could use the following code.

```
Text message;

cin  >> message;
cout << "The message read consists of "
     << message.length() << " characters" << endl;
```

Since `length()` is a member function, the way to call it is to write the name of the `Text` variable, followed by the dot operator, followed by a (normal) function call.

Lesson: The only difference between a member-function call and a non-member-function call is that with a member-function call, the name of the function is preceded by an identifier for a variable of the type of which the function is a member. The dot operator separates the variable name from the member-function name.

In Chapter 4 you saw an outline program to draw a square on a `Canvas` variable. Let's see if you can improve your shape-drawing capabilities.

PROBLEM:

Write a program to draw a simple house shape on a `Canvas` object.

DESIGN:

For the simple house shape we'll draw a triangle on top of a rectangle. You saw a design for drawing a square in Chapter 4 (Figure 4.9). In summary, starting from the current pen position put the pen down. Draw a line horizontally forwards, then vertically up, then horizontally backwards, and finally vertically down, with each line being of the same length. Raise the pen up. The design to draw a rectangle is similar except that the length of the horizontal lines is different to that of the vertical lines. To draw the triangle (representing the roof) reposition the pen at the top left-hand corner of the rectangle, then draw a diagonal line right-and-up, followed by a diagonal line right-and-down.

IMPLEMENTATION:

The `Canvas` PDT supports the member functions `penUp()` and `penDown()`, with interfaces:

```
void penUp();
void penDown();
```

for lowering and raising the pen. The member function `moveRelative(...)`, with interface:

```
void moveRelative(int xIncrement, int yIncrement);
```

moves the pen by the amount specified by the two actual parameters in the two coordinate directions. If the pen is down, then a line is drawn as a result of that move. There's a `Canvas` member function:

```
void setSize(int sizeX, int sizeY);
```

that sets the size of the `Canvas` window that appears on the screen. Using these member functions, the following code fragment achieves the required result.

```
const int XMAX             = 200;
const int YMAX             = XMAX;
const int HOUSE_WIDTH      = 70;
const int HOUSE_HEIGHT     = 50;
const int ROOF_HEIGHT      = 15;
const int START_X_POSITION = 10;
const int START_Y_POSITION = START_X_POSITION;

Canvas picture;

// Get ready for drawing
picture.setSize(XMAX, YMAX);
picture.penUp();
picture.moveTo(START_X_POSITION, START_Y_POSITION);
```

```
// Draw the body of the picture
picture.penDown();
picture.moveRelative(HOUSE_WIDTH, 0);
picture.moveRelative(0, HOUSE_HEIGHT);
picture.moveRelative(-HOUSE_WIDTH, 0);
picture.moveRelative(0, -HOUSE_HEIGHT);
picture.penUp();

// Now draw the roof
picture.moveRelative(0, HOUSE_HEIGHT);
picture.penDown();
picture.moveRelative(HOUSE_WIDTH / 2, ROOF_HEIGHT);
picture.moveRelative(HOUSE_WIDTH / 2, -ROOF_HEIGHT);
picture.penUp();
```

In Chapter 11 you'll see how to write a definition for a function that will allow you to draw simple shapes using single function calls. If you had a function to draw a square you'd use it as follows.

```
Canvas myPicture;
// Set picture size
drawSquare(myPicture, SIDE_LENGTH);
```

With some justification you might argue that `drawSquare(...)` ought to be a member function of the `Canvas` class, just like `moveRelative(...)`, and that therefore you should be able to write:

```
Canvas myPicture;
// Set picture size
myPicture.drawSquare(SIDE_LENGTH);
```

But `drawSquare(...)` isn't a member function of the `Canvas` PDT (take a look back at Chapter 5 to check), so you can't draw a square using a single member-function call. But where should the line be drawn in terms of the range of member functions provided by the `Canvas` PDT? Would you expect us to have provided member functions to draw squares, rectangles, triangles, circles, Hilbert curves, images of John Wayne and Marilyn Monroe? No, we kept the `Canvas` PDT simple and expect you to write your own code to draw these and other shapes. The way to do this without changing the PDT is to write functions; we'll show you how to do this in Chapter 11. (At least, we'll show you how to draw squares, but don't expect artistic impressions of film stars.)

So when should a function be a member function, and when shouldn't it be? There's no simple answer, and in any case for the moment we're just looking at how you use functions, rather than how you design PDTs, which is what the question is really trying to address.

Time for some more syntax.

Member-function call syntax

The following syntax diagram indicates the essential features of a **member-function call**.

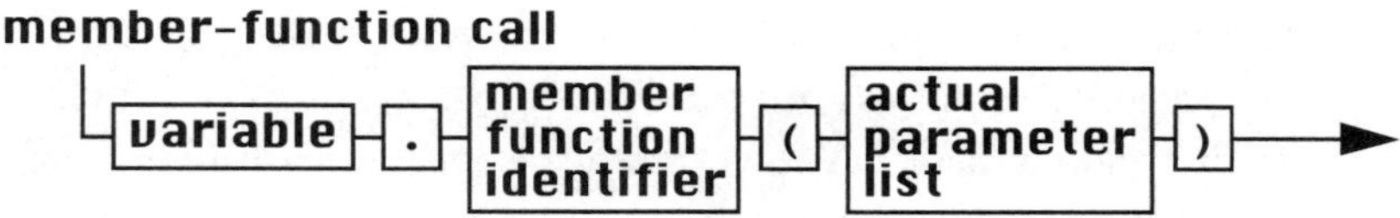

Details of what constitutes an **actual parameter list** were given in the previous section. As with a non-member function call, a call to a member function that returns a value is a form of **simple expression**:

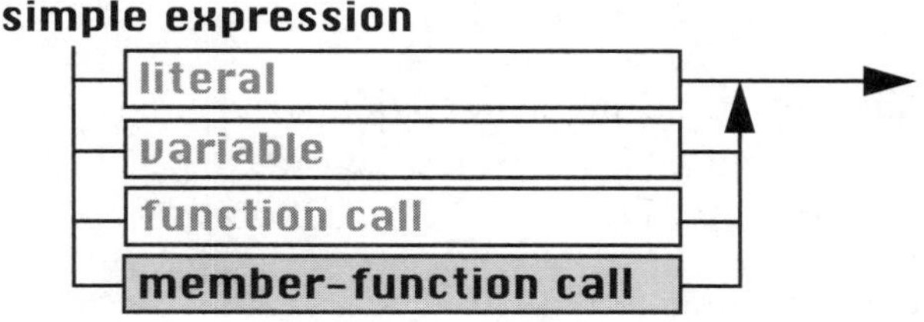

whereas a call to a member function that returns no value can only be used in the context of a **statement**.

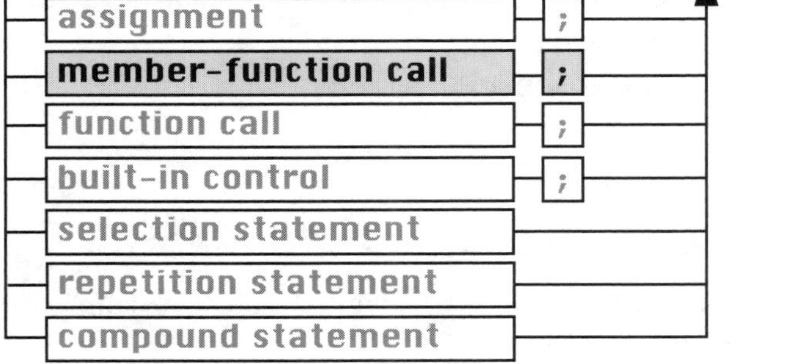

To use a function correctly you need to know, among other things, about its parameter list. Many of the functions we've looked at so far in this chapter use the parameter list as a mechanism to pass values to a function. But what about getting values back? You've already seen that a function can have a non-`void` return type and hence can return a single value, but often this mechanism alone is not sufficient. Is there any other way of getting a value back? We need to have another look at parameters.

EXERCISES FOR SECTION 9.3

1 This section introduced an implementation of a design to draw a house on a `Canvas` instance. What changes would you make to ensure that the center of the body of the house is at a specified coordinate position?

2 Adapt the house-drawing code so that it also draws a rectangle representing a door.

9.4 VALUE AND REFERENCE PARAMETERS

In the previous section you saw that a function can return a value, which is one way of getting a value back from a function. An alternative way of getting one or more values back in a function call is provided by the parameter-passing mechanism. This works by allowing a function call to change the value of an actual parameter.

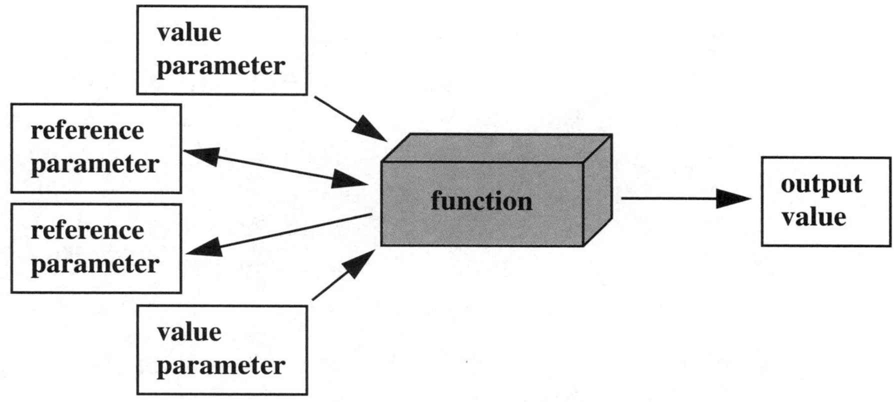

Figure 9.3 Value and reference parameters

A parameter that's used to supply a value to a function only is referred to as a **value parameter**, and the actual parameters that have been used in all the function calls you've seen so far in this chapter were all value parameters. However, there's another type of parameter that you can use to supply a value to a function and get a value back, or just to get a value back (Figure 9.3). Such a parameter is referred to as a **reference parameter**.

First, let's see how reference parameters are represented in a function interface. You've seen that value parameters in a function interface look like variable declarations, indicating the type of the parameter and giving the formal parameter a name. It should be obvious that a reference formal parameter is going to require much the same information, but in addition will need to be distinguishable from a value parameter. In C++ this distinction is achieved by placing an `&` (ampersand) after the type of the parameter.

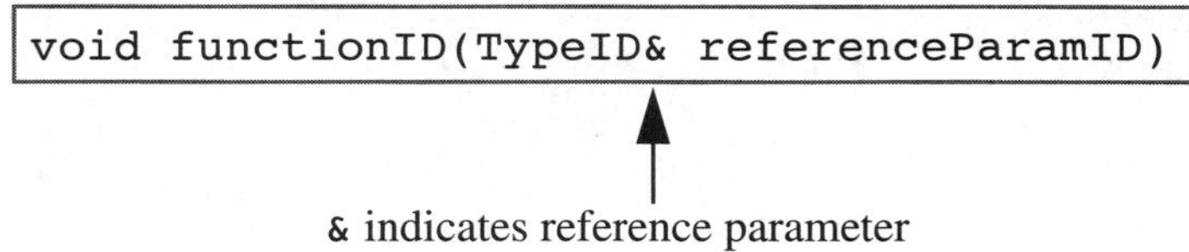

OK, so now you can recognize reference parameters. What behavior do they provide at run time? The behavior is best examined with a problem.

PROBLEM:

There's a member function `getPosition(...)` of PDT `Canvas` that can be used to find out where the pen is; that is, the *x*- and *y*-coordinates of the pen's current position. This member function thus has to provide its caller with two results: an `int` value representing the pen's *x*-coordinate and an `int` value for the *y*-coordinate. Reference parameters are used to allow this member function to return these two values. You'll see that the interface for this member function is:

```
void getPosition(int& xPosition, int& yPosition);
```

showing that the two formal parameters are reference parameters.

IMPLEMENTATION:

```
int currentX;
int currentY;
Canvas myPicture;
// Operations on myPicture
...
myPicture.getPosition(currentX, currentY);
```

As a result of the member-function call, the values of the variables `currentX` and `currentY` will be assigned the pen's coordinates by the member-function implementation code. That is, when the call has completed, these variables will contain new values, the current coordinates of the pen.

In effect, a reference parameter permits a function or member function to assign a value to an actual parameter. Contrast this behavior with what would happen if the parameters in `getPosition(...)` were value parameters. In this situation the values of the actual parameters `currentX` and `currentY` could not be changed by the member function.

Note that although the `&` notation is used to denote formal reference parameters in a (member or non-member) function signature, you don't use an `&` when you're specifying an actual reference parameter in a function call.

Lesson: An `&` is used in a function signature to indicate that a formal parameter is a reference parameter. An `&` is not used to indicate that an actual parameter is a reference parameter.

An actual value parameter can be an expression, but what about an actual reference parameter? Can an actual reference parameter be any form of expression?

Since a function call can result in a change in the value of an actual reference parameter, an actual reference parameter must be a **destination**, just as the item on the left-hand side of an assignment is a **destination**. Hence, an actual reference parameter may be a variable identifier, and as far as we're concerned here an actual reference parameter may not be any other form of expression.

Lesson: An actual reference parameter must be a **destination**, such as a variable identifier.

EXAMPLE:

As mentioned in the previous section, in Chapter 11 we'll show you how to write a function `drawSquare(...)` to draw a square on a `Canvas` variable.

```
Canvas myPicture;
const int SIDE_LENGTH = 100;
// Set the Canvas size and position the pen
drawSquare(myPicture, SIDE_LENGTH);
```

Should the first parameter of `drawSquare(...)` be a value parameter or a reference parameter?

After the call you expect the picture represented by the `Canvas` variable `myPicture` to have changed as a result of that call; the abstract value represented by the `Canvas` variable `myPicture` will have changed. Hence the first parameter of `drawSquare(...)` needs to be a reference parameter.

Is it necessary for an actual reference parameter to have a value before the function call is made? Since an actual reference parameter is just a destination, then an equivalent question is "Is it necessary for a variable to have a value before an assignment is made to it?" The answer to both questions is "no."

Now that you know something about the difference between value and reference parameters, we'll look again at the syntax for an actual parameter.

Actual parameter syntax

Look back to the previous two sections and remind yourself what constitutes a **function call**, a **member-function call**, and an **actual parameter list**. An **actual parameter** can be an **actual reference parameter**:

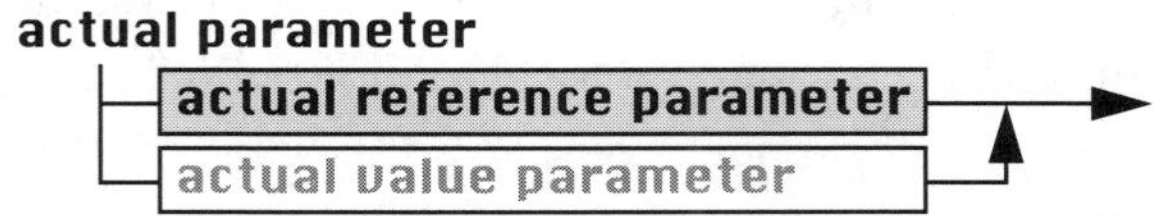

and an actual reference parameter can be any form of **destination**:

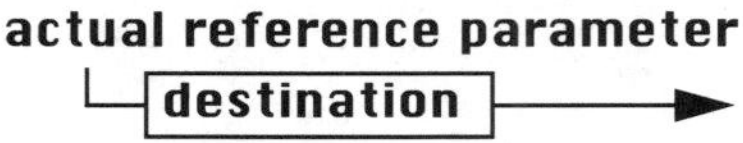

Typically the **destination** will be a variable identifier whose type must agree with the corresponding formal parameter. The diagram fails to spell out the type-compatibility requirement, but you'd better not forget it. A compiler will tell you if you get the types wrong.

Before we leave this chapter let's have one more look at functions, and in particular the choice of function name. You know that this must be a standard identifier, right? Well, yes, unless you think of operators as just special forms of functions.

EXERCISES FOR SECTION 9.4

1 The variable `GROSS` has been declared as:

```
const int GROSS = 144;
```

Can `GROSS` be used as an actual parameter where an `int` reference parameter is required?

2 The function `silly(...)` has the interface `void silly(int& i)`. Can the actual parameter to this function be a variable declared to be of type `double`?

3 The function `silly(...)` has the interface `void silly(int& i)`. Can the actual parameter to this function be a variable declared to be of type `Palette`?

4 The function `silly(...)` has the interface `void silly(int& i)`. You make a call to this function with actual parameter the `int` variable `unSet`. There's no assignment to `unSet` prior to the call of `silly(...)`. Does this matter?

5 Casually glancing at your classmate's code you come across the following fragment.

```
int numberOfCheers = 1;
multiplyByThree(numberOfCheers);
cout << numberOfCheers << "   cheers" << endl;
```

Assuming that `multiplyByThree(...)` achieves the outcome suggested by its name, what output would you expect to be produced if the interface of the function is `void multiplyByThree(int& parameter)`? If, however, the function interface is `void multiplyByThree(int parameter)`, what output would you expect?

9.5 OPERATORS AS FUNCTIONS

Although it may not be apparent at first sight, there's a strong connection between operators and functions, and therefore a chapter on using functions should naturally include a section on using operators. We'll limit the discussion to binary operators, since the most useful operators are of this form.

An operator acts like a black box in that you put (one or two) values in and you get a value back (Figure 9.4).

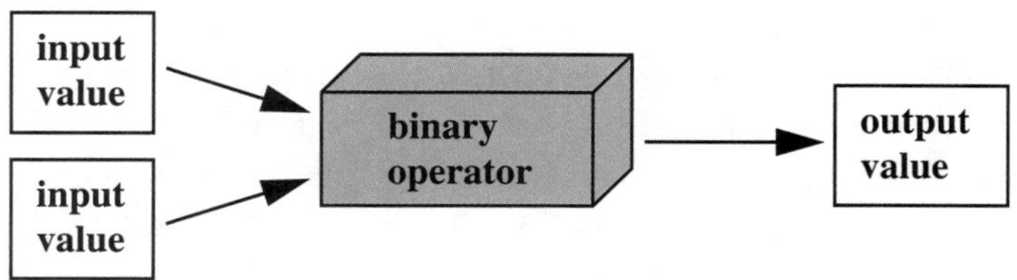

Figure 9.4 Binary operator as a function

The way you write an operator "call" is a little different to the way you write a function call. Normally an operator call is written in what is known as **infix notation**; the operands are placed either side of the operator symbol. In contrast, with a function call the actual parameters appear after the function identifier.

EXAMPLE:

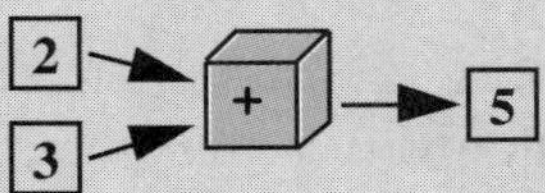

Suppose there's a function `add(...)` with interface `int add(int lhs, int rhs)` that returns the sum of its two parameters. Then the following output statements are equivalent:

```
cout << add(2, 3) << endl;
cout << 2 + 3     << endl;
```

In the second output statement the "name" of the addition operator is the symbol `+` and you place its two actual "parameters" (which we call operands) either side of the operator symbol. Can you write `2 add 3`? No. Can you write `+(2, 3)`? We'll delay a verdict on that one.

Associated with an operator, there's:

- a name, which is an operator symbol such as `+` or `*`, rather than an identifier;
- a set of parameters, which happen to be called operands, and the set is restricted in number to two (binary operators) or one (unary operators);
- a return value, the result of the operation.

So there's not a lot of difference between an operator and a function at all; an operator is just a particular form of a function.

Just as you need to know a function's interface to be able to form a correct call to that function, so you need to know an operator's interface to be able to form a correct "call" to that operator. However, the syntax of an operator call that you're used to using involves placing the operator symbol between the operands, rather than before. That is, you're happy with `a + b` and would find `+(a, b)` rather strange, wouldn't you?

Let's take this a little further by looking at some operators supported by the PDTs you've been using.

Take a look at the interfaces of the PDTs introduced in Chapter 5. Do any of them have operators or member operators? If they do, what do the interfaces of the operators look like? What's that, you say? "I don't know what an operator interface looks like and therefore what to look for. Do I really need to know what the C++ syntax for an operator interface is? Isn't it obvious how I make an operator call?"

In Chapter 5 we were content to provide you with only an abstraction of the operators. We just listed which infix operators were supported by a particular PDT, without bothering with the full details of what an operator interface looks like. Now it's time to come clean, since you really do need to know about an operator's interface in order to use it properly.

An operator interface consists of:

- the result type – the first item that appears in an operator interface;
- the operator signature, which has two components:
  1. The keyword `operator` followed by an operator symbol – the second item that appears in a function interface.
  2. The type of the parameter(s) – a list of parameter types (a parameter list), enclosed by parentheses, is the third item that appears in an operator interface.

You should be able to draw a direct analogy between this and the relevant discussion in Section 9.2 on function interfaces.

Can you find any operator interfaces in the header files for the PDTs introduced in Chapter 5? Here's a clue. The symbols >> and << represent I/O operators.

The `CSDiscSet` PDT has an output operator << with interface

```
ostream& operator<<(ostream& outStream, CSDiscSet value)
```

Here the return type is `ostream&` and the operator signature is `operator<<(ostream& outStream, CSDiscSet value)`. The "name" of the operator is `operator<<`, and the operator has two parameters (it's a binary operator).

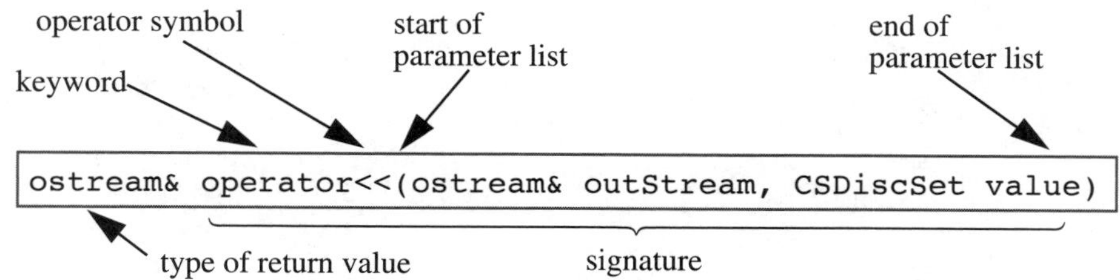

OK, so you now have some idea of what an operator signature looks like. You also know that a function signature indicates the form of a function call – the function name followed by an actual parameter list. What about an operator call?

So far you've been content to use infix notation to make an operator call, but can you make a direct analogy between the form of a function call and that of an operator call? As an alternative to infix notation, an operator call may take the form of the operator "name" (the keyword `operator` followed by the operator symbol) followed by an actual parameter list.

EXAMPLE:

Given the declaration

```
CSDiscSet myDiscs;
```

the following output statements are entirely equivalent.

```
cout << myDiscs;
operator<<(cout, myDiscs);
```

When the compiler encounters the first of these output statements, it will convert it to the second form. The fact that the return value of the operator is not being used is unimportant here.

What about member operators? Do any of the PDTs have member operators? What does a member-operator call look like? What does a member-operator interface look like? And is there an alternative form for a member-operator call that you can use?

A member-operator call can be expressed in infix notation, in which case there is no distinction between a stand-alone operator call and a member-operator call.

EXAMPLE:

There's a binary operator + that allows you to concatenate (join) two items of type `Text` as follows.

```
Text hi = "Hi ";
Text ho = "Ho";
hi = hi + ho
```

Is the + operator being used here a stand-alone operator, or a `Text` member operator? The operator call remains the same whatever the answer to this question is.

There's an alternative to infix notation that you can use to make a member-operator call. You write the name of the variable, the familiar dot operator, the "name" of the operator (again, the keyword `operator` followed by the operator symbol), and then an actual parameter list in parentheses. Since the use of the operator symbol as a member operator implicitly makes reference to the left-hand operand, only the right-hand operand appears as an operator parameter. It follows that the signature for a binary member operator has a single parameter only (and the signature for a unary member operator has no parameters at all).

EXAMPLE:

If the `Text` + operator is a stand-alone operator the alternative form of a call would be:

```
operator+(hi, ho)
```

If the `Text` + operator is a member operator the alternative form of a call would be:

```
hi.operator+(ho)
```

Try using both these forms. The compiler will indicate which is the correct one to use.

Now you know how to recognize member and non-member operator interfaces, and how to make operator calls using a form other than the familiar infix notation. But do you intend to carry on using infix notation and ignore the alternative form? We suggest that you do, since from the user's point of view infix notation can be used in a natural way regardless of whether the operator is a member or non-member operator.

Lesson: From the user's point of view there's no difference between a stand-alone operator call and a member-operator call when infix notation is used.

Whether operators are stand-alone operators or member operators does matter when you come to look for operator interfaces. The distinction also matters to the operator implementer, and so we'll show you how to implement both types of operator in Chapters 12 and 13.

One final point. Return to the problem of the addition of two integer values. Given two integer variables `a` and `b`, can you write `operator+(a, b)` (non-member-operator call), or `a.operator+(b)` (`int` member-operator call) as an alternative form to `a + b`?

The answer is "no." You can use only infix notation with the built-in types, but you didn't want to use anything else, did you?

EXERCISES FOR SECTION 9.5

1 Find out by experiment whether `operator>>` for an `int` is a member operator of the `istream` PDT, or a non-member operator.

2 The return type of the I/O operators >> and << is `istream&` and `ostream&` respectively. Why this and not `istream` and `ostream`? (Hint: take a look at Section 12.2.)

3 If the += operator for concatenating and updating one `Text` value with another were a stand-alone operator, what would you expect its interface to be? If the operator were a member operator, what form would you expect the interface to take? Write a program to see which is the correct interface.

SUMMARY

You now know about the terms:

- **function call** – a control abstraction that can be a form of expression or a statement in its own right, depending on whether the function does or does not return a value;
- **parameters** – used as a means of information exchange in a function call;
- **function signature** – written in terms of formal parameters, whereas a function call is written in terms of actual parameters. The actual parameters in a function call must agree in number and type with the formal parameters given in a function interface;

- **formal parameter** – used in a function interface to indicate both the type of the parameter and a name (a place holder only);
- **actual parameter** – appears in a function call;
- **value parameter** – used to supply values to a function; an actual value parameter can be any expression giving a value of the same type as the corresponding formal parameter;
- **reference parameter** – used to supply values to a function and/or get values back and is indicated by an `&` in a function interface; an actual reference parameter must be a destination;
- **operator** – a function with a restricted number of parameters (1 or 2) and a special syntax to indicate an operator call.

Function interfaces tell you all you need to know about how to make a function call. But how do you design a function interface in the first place? And how do you write a function that implements the abstraction represented by the interface? We'll be providing answers to these questions two chapters on. But first we're going to look at some other forms of control abstraction. We're going to tell you, among other things, about the repetition and selection constructs that we've referred to in this chapter.

END-OF-CHAPTER EXERCISES

1 In a function call what syntactic element can be used as (a) an actual value parameter, and (b) an actual reference parameter?

2 For each of the following functional abstractions identify the component parts of their interfaces.

(a) Given a person's height and weight, determine their body mass index.
(b) Given a person's body mass index determine whether they are underweight, OK, overweight or obese.

3 The `math` function `double floor(double x)` gives the largest integer (represented as a floating-point number) not greater than `x`. Similarly, `double ceil(double x)` gives the smallest integer not less than `x`. Print out the values these functions give for various values of `x` (both positive and negative) to observe their behavior. Can you obtain the same results as produced by `ceil(...)` and `floor(...)` using type coercions instead?

4 There are two logarithm functions in `math.h`, `log(...)` and `log10(...)`, whose interfaces are `double log(double x)` and `double log10(double x)`, respectively. `log(...)` gives the natural (base e) logarithm of a number, while `log10(...)` gives the logarithm to the base 10.

The value of x^y can be obtained using the identity $x^y = e^{y \log_e x}$. Use this formula in a C++ program to evaluate x^y for several values of x and y and compare your results with those given by the `pow(...)` function.

You can convert from one logarithm base to the other using the formula $\log_b x = \log_a x \log_b a$. Use this result in a C++ program with $a = 10$ to evaluate $\log_2 64$ and $\log_e 2.71828$.

5 If a, b and c represent the lengths of the three sides of a triangle, then the area of that triangle is given by the formula:

$$\text{Area} = \sqrt{[(s - a)(s - b)(s - c)]}$$

where s is the semiperimeter length, given by $s = (a + b + c)/2$. Write a program that reads in the lengths of the three sides of a triangle and outputs the area of that triangle.

6 The notation $n!$ is used in mathematics to denote the factorial of an integer number n. The factorial of an integer is another integer defined by the formula $n! = n \times (n - 1) \times \cdots \times 2 \times 1$. You can use Stirling's formula $n! \approx \sqrt{[(2\pi)n^{n+1/2} e^{-n}]}$ to obtain an approximation to $n!$. Write a program that reads in a value for n and prints out an approximate value for $n!$ using Stirling's formula.

7 Verify that the random number program of Section 9.1 generates a new sequence each time. Change the call to `srand(...)` so that the parameter is the same for each run of the program and verify that you get the same sequence of random numbers for each run.

8 Derive a syntax diagram for the syntactic element **operator call** that involves the syntactic elements **unary operator** call and **binary operator call**. Hence derive an alternative version of the syntax diagram for an **expression**.

9 Write a program that prints the character string `"A Rectangle"` on the screen image of a `Canvas` instance. Use the `Canvas` member function `textBoundingBox(...)` to determine the size of the rectangle that bounds the string and then adapt the code that draws a square so that it draws a rectangle enclosing the message.

10 Add windows and a chimney to the house you drew in Exercise 2 of Section 9.3.

11 Use the `Canvas` member functions to draw a (crude) image of a CD player.

10 Control-flow abstractions

OBJECTIVE

To introduce the selection and repetition control-flow abstractions in C++, covering:

- syntax and semantics of control-flow statements;
- design notation for selection and repetition;
- software engineering issues arising from using these control-flow abstractions.

Selection

10.0 DESIGN NOTATION RECAP

"Could you please tell me how to get to the Department of Computing Science, Claremont Road?" asked the stranger at Newcastle train station.

"Well, if you're going to walk then there's one set of instructions, otherwise if you're going to drive then there's another set of instructions, otherwise if you're going to go on the Metro then there's yet another set of instructions, else you could just take a taxi," replied the well-informed student.

"Decisions, decisions" replied the stranger. "OK, I'll walk. Can you now give me the right directions?" "No problem" came the reply. "In fact, I'll draw a design to help you. You are familiar with the algorithm design notation introduced in Chapter 2 of the book *The Apprentice C++ Programmer: A Touch of Class* aren't you? That will make things a lot easier." And the student proceeded to draw the following design.

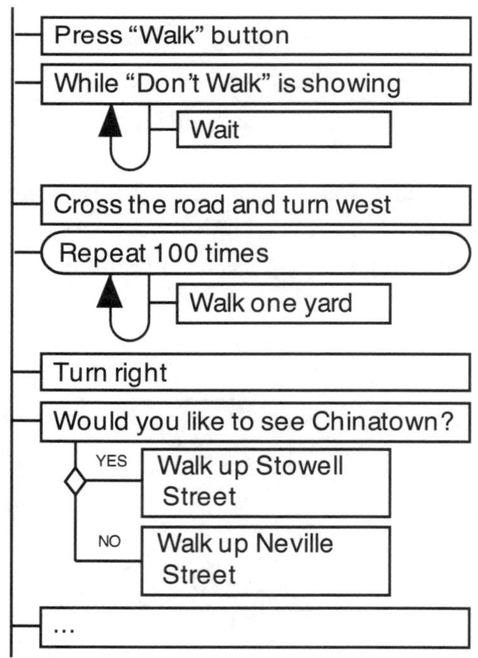

"That's a bit different from a map" exclaimed the stranger, but as he was familiar with the design notation he had no problem with the design. It shows the sequence of steps he would have to follow, together with the points at which he had to make a decision (selection) and follow different instructions based on the outcome of that decision, and points at which instructions were repeated until some condition became true (repetition). Useful things these control-flow abstractions, the stranger thought to himself. It would have been a real pain to describe the route just as a sequential set of instructions.

Selection and repetition are vital control-flow abstractions for programs. Most programs require the use of selection and/or repetition. You've already met the design notations for these control-flow abstractions. Some examples are given in the diagram above, but if you've forgotten which abstraction is which, why don't you revisit Chapter 2 to refresh your memory. Now, how do you express control-flow abstractions in C++?

Types of control-flow statement in C++

The primary purpose of this chapter is to introduce you to the syntax and semantics of the C++ *selection* and *repetition statements* that allow you to translate a design containing selection or repetition into an equivalent C++ program. But first, let's set the context by mentioning the four different kinds of control-flow statement provided in C++:

1. Selection statements.
2. Repetition statements.
3. Built-in control statements.
4. Function and member-function calls.

All of these types of statement have the characteristic that they change the flow of control in a program. You've already used member functions in Chapter 7 (in the CD-playing program) and functions in Chapter 9. Here we concentrate on items 1 and 2 although you'll also see the use of item 3. We can extend the syntactic element **statement** to add the new statement types that you'll be seeing.

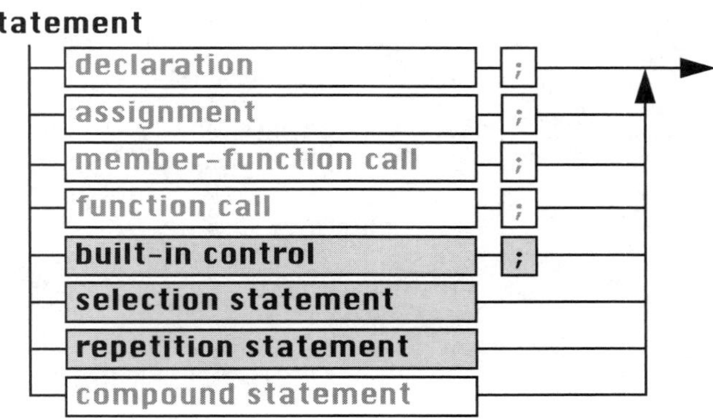

EXERCISES FOR SECTION 10.0

1 Each chapter in Part 1 of this book could be described by a short phrase that captures the main content of that chapter. For example, Chapter 1 could be described by "introduction," Chapter 2 by "problem-solving," and Chapter 3 by "programming language overview." Produce a design that allows a user to enter such a phrase in response to which the program will indicate which chapter to read to learn about that topic. The design should also set a Boolean variable to `true` if the user types a valid phrase, and `false` otherwise.

2 Using the software component you designed in Exercise 1, design a program that gives the user three tries at typing a valid phrase.

3 Design an algorithm that, given a number that represents the number of rows of stars that form the body of the tree, will generate a textual picture of a Christmas tree. The table below gives examples of the algorithmic relationships between the various elements that form the tree: the number of rows of stars, the number of stars in the maximum-sized row, the length of the trunk, and the height and width of the "box" forming the base of the tree. The example to the right of the table is a 5-row tree.

No. rows	Max. row	Trunk length	Base height	Base width
1	1	1	1	1
2	3	1	1	1
3	5	2	2	3
4	7	2	2	3
5	9	2	2	3
6	11	3	3	3
...				
9	17	4	4	5
and so on				

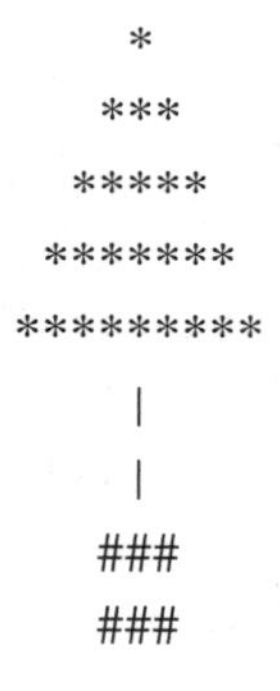

10.1 SELECTION STATEMENTS IN C++

Much of the flexibility of software systems comes from the ability to make run-time decisions and to select sets of statements for execution based on those decisions. Selection statements are thus a key part of a programming language.

There are two selection statements in C++: **if statements** and **switch statements**. Since if statements are the most fundamental form of selection statement we introduce these first.

`if` *statements*

Remember the CD-playing program designed in Chapter 2 and implemented in C++ in Chapter 7? Part of the design is shown below, although the expansions of the designator boxes have been omitted for brevity as you already know what these expansions are.

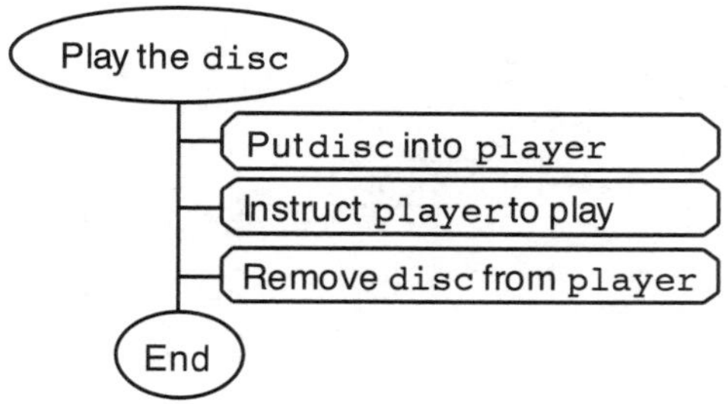

Let's consider some refinements for this design.

PROBLEM:

There's a possibility that the CD player will be damaged if an attempt is made to play a faulty CD. Modify the CD-playing program to prevent this damage from happening.

DESIGN:

To solve this problem you need to make the execution of the designator box "Instruct `player` to play" conditional upon the CD being OK. You need to add a selection box and associated actions to the design to accommodate this. A first refinement of the design that adds these features is given below, such that the action "Instruct `player` to play" is selected for execution only if the CD turns out to be OK. If the CD is not OK then no attempt will be made to play it.

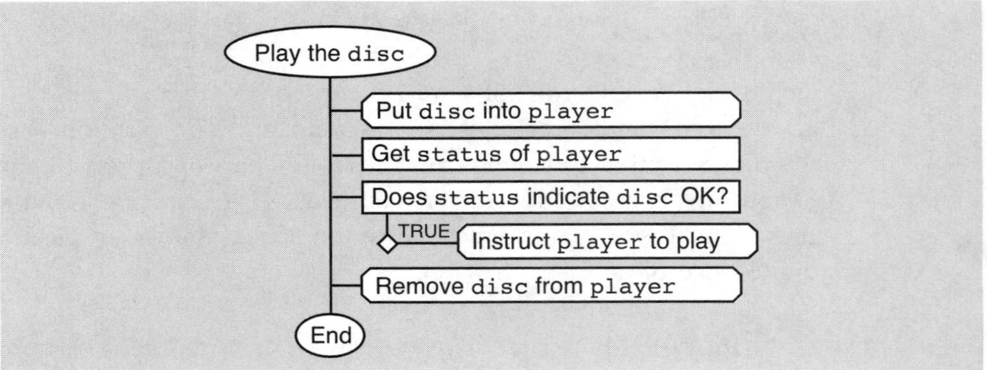

To translate this new design into C++ you need to use an `if` statement. Before completing the details needed to implement the design, let's consider the outline of a simple `if` statement in C++:

bool-expression
TRUE
statements

```
1. if (bool-expression)
2. {
3.   statements;
4. }
5. ...
```

The expression contained in the parentheses following the keyword `if` on line 1 is a Boolean expression. (You remember from Chapter 8 how to write these forms of expression and the type of the value produced – `bool`.) When the `if` statement is executed the Boolean expression is evaluated and the resulting value is examined:

- if the value is `true` then the compound statement immediately following is executed, after which the flow of control goes to the statement following the end of the compound statement (indicated here as line 5);
- if the value is `false` then the flow of control immediately goes to line 5 and the compound statement is *not* executed.

We'll cover the syntax details later, but for now let's continue with the CD-playing problem.

IMPLEMENTATION:

How do you write a Boolean expression to check whether a CD that has been loaded is OK? Check the interface for the PDT `CDPlayer` in Chapter 5. Can you find any useful member functions there?

Did you find the following member-function interface?

```
PlayerStatus status(); // Status of player
```

This interface tells you that the member function `status()` returns a value of type `PlayerStatus`; that is, one of the following abstract values (from Chapter 5).

```
PLAYER_EMPTY    DISC_OK    DISC_BAD    PLAYER_ERROR
```

The member function `status()` looks like just the thing you need, and leads to the following fragment of code for the new design.

```
                                  // Put disc into player
myPlayer.open();                    // Open drawer
myPlayer.load(aDisc);               // Load disc
myPlayer.close();                   // Close drawer
if (myPlayer.status() == DISC_OK) // Is disc OK?
{                                   // Instruct player to play
  myPlayer.play();                        // Press "Play" button
}
...                               // Remove disc from player
```

When this fragment is executed, if the value obtained by evaluating the Boolean expression `myPlayer.status() == DISC_OK` is `true` then the member function `play()` is executed. If, however, the value returned by the Boolean expression is `false` then `play()` isn't executed. Just what you wanted.

Why don't you try modifying your earlier CD-playing program to add these enhancements, and check its execution. Try your modified program with the disc title you used earlier. Then change your program to select the CD titled "`Bootlegged 1812`". This is a "faulty" CD that has been included in the `CSDiscSet` collection. Check to see whether your program does what you expect. (You could also try this bad CD in the original CD-playing program without the `if` statement.)

`else` clauses

If you tried the program modifications suggested above you should have noticed that the only visible effect of attempting to play a faulty CD is simply that it doesn't play. As the designer and implementer of this program you know that this behavior is as expected. However, someone else using your program might be confused by trying to play a CD and nothing happening. Can you fix the program to avoid this confusion?

PROBLEM:

Change the CD-playing program to provide an error message in the situation that a CD cannot be played.

DESIGN:

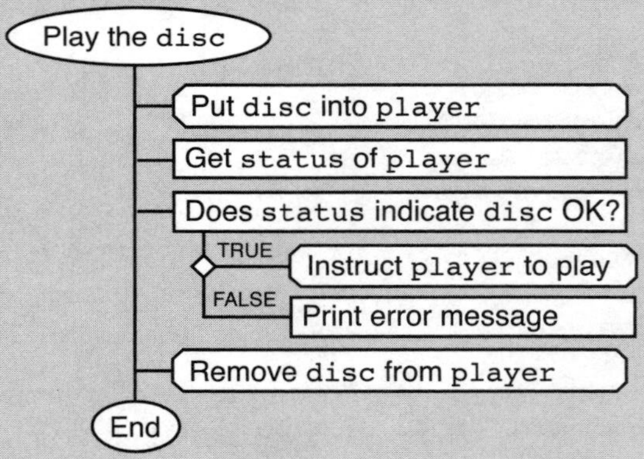

Play the disc
- Put disc into player
- Get status of player
- Does status indicate disc OK?
  - TRUE: Instruct player to play
  - FALSE: Print error message
- Remove disc from player

End

This design states that if the disc is OK then it should be played, but if the disc is not OK then an error message should be printed.

C++ provides a variation of the `if` statement that uses an `else` clause for precisely this kind of behavior. An `if-else` statement requires two compound statements: one for the case that the Boolean expression evaluates to `true`, and the second for the case that the expression evaluates to `false`. The keyword `else` introduces the second of the compound statements. One or other of the compound statements will be executed, but not both.

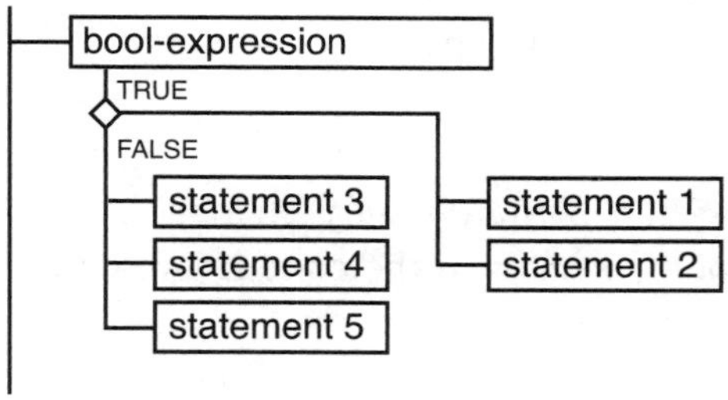

bool-expression
TRUE
FALSE
statement 3
statement 4
statement 5
statement 1
statement 2

```
if (bool-expression)
{
  statement 1;
  statement 2;
}
else
{
  statement 3;
  statement 4;
  statement 5;
}
```

The equivalence between the C++ statement and the design notation is shown above. There are two paths, or "arms" coming from the diamond-shaped decision box. That labelled TRUE represents the path to be followed when the `bool-expression` evaluates to TRUE. That labelled FALSE is followed when . . . we'll leave you to work that out!

In passing, note the usefulness of a compound statement in a selection statement. The grouping together of a set of statements in a compound statement is a way of representing in a textual form the two-dimensional form that may occur when using the design notation. For example, using compound statements above allows us to indicate to the compiler that `statement 1` and `statement 2` are grouped together, as are `statements 3-5`.

IMPLEMENTATION:

The `if-else` statement is just the ticket for implementing the earlier design. Here's the main fragment:

```
                                // Put disc into player
myPlayer.open();                  // Open drawer
myPlayer.load(aDisc);             // Load disc
myPlayer.close();                 // Close drawer
if (myPlayer.status() == DISC_OK) // Is disc OK?
{                               // Instruct player to play
  myPlayer.play();                // Press "Play" button
}
else
{
  cout << "This disc cannot be played." << endl;
}
...                             // Remove disc from player
```

As before, try the program out with a good disc as well as the faulty disc, and make sure the program does what you expect.

You might be wondering: What if there's only a single statement on one of the arms of a selection statement, such as in the code fragment above? Do I still need to use a compound statement?

The strict answer is that you could just write a single statement instead of a compound statement, and you may see this style used in other people's code. However, this is a style we strongly discourage, and never use. Why? Because it can lead to more problems than it's worth. Let's show you why. Consider the following fragment of code.

```
if (someCondition)
  statement;
else
  otherStatement;
```

This fragment is legal C++. However, what if the software engineer suddenly realizes that something is missing, and an extra statement needs to be added:

```
if (someCondition)
  statement;
  extraStatement;
else
  otherStatement;
```

Everything still OK? Unfortunately not. This fragment will lead to a compile-time error. (You don't believe us? Try it and see.) You'd have to go back and turn the two statements into a compound statement. Not the end of the world, but a nuisance nonetheless.

However, the following fragment is legal, but what would you expect it to do when executed?

```
if (someCondition)
  statement;
  extraStatement;
```

If `someCondition` is `true`, both `statement` and `extraStatement` are executed aren't they? The answer is "yes" (but maybe not for the reason you thought). If `someCondition` is `false` neither statement is executed, right?

Wrong – `statement` isn't executed but `extraStatement` *is* executed because the compiler doesn't treat it as being part of the "true" arm of the selection statement.

Why risk such confusing behavior? "Always use a compound statement" is our recommendation, and we suggest you follow this style. In fact, it must be time for some style rules.

- ✓ *Always use compound statements for the conditionally-executed parts of selection statements.*
- ✓ *Place the compound statement opening brace* `{` *on a separate line but in the same column as the start of the previous statement.*
- ✓ *Line up the matching* `}` *in the same column as the* `{`*.*
- ✓ *Use indentation to indent the statements inside the compound statement two spaces in from the column containing the* `{`*.*
- ✓ *Line up the statements that are part of the same compound statement.*
- ✓ *Leave one space between the keyword* `if` *and the opening parenthesis of the Boolean expression.*

As usual, we suggest the use of spaces to indent statements. You could use <Tab> but you'll find that with more complex structures, such as compound statements within compound statements, you'll quickly run out of space on a line.

`else if` clauses

The `if` statement permits you to construct one- and two-way selections (one-way without an `else` clause, two-way with an `else` clause). Sometimes in your designs and programs you'll want to construct **multi-way** selections, and C++ provides an `else if` clause to permit extensions to `if` statements for this effect. Here's an example of a multi-way selection expressed in the design notation, with the corresponding C++ code alongside.

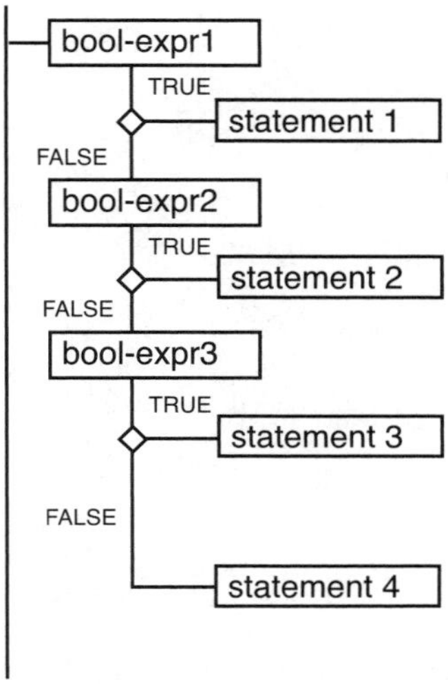

bool-expr1
TRUE
statement 1
FALSE
bool-expr2
TRUE
statement 2
FALSE
bool-expr3
TRUE
statement 3
FALSE
statement 4

```
if (bool-expr1)
{
  statement1;
}
else if (bool-expr2)
{
  statement2;
}
else if (bool-expr3)
{
  statement3;
}
else
{
  statement4;
}
...
```

The code fragment above contains a single `if` statement that's executed as follows. First `bool-expr1` is evaluated. If this gives the value `true` then `statement1` is executed, following which control goes to the statement indicated as line 17, that is, to the statement following the `if-else` statement. If `bool-expr1` is `false` then control goes to line 5 and `bool-expr2` is evaluated. If `bool-expr2` evaluates to `true` then `statement2` is executed and control then goes to line 17. However, if `bool-expr2` evaluates to `false` then control goes to line 9. And so on. The final `else` clause on line 13 is reached only if *all* of the Boolean expressions evaluate to `false`, whereupon `statement4` is executed and control then goes to line 17.

No more than one of the compound statements will be selected for execution – the first compound statement for which the associated Boolean expression evaluates to `true`. There can be as many `else if` parts as you need, and the final `else` clause is optional.

IMPLEMENTATION:

You can use this form of `if` statement to extend further the CD-playing program so that it deals with the complete set of values that the `status()` member function might return. You might like to construct the design for this extension. The C++ code appears in Figure 10.1.

```
PlayerStatus currentStatus = myPlayer.status();
if (currentStatus == DISC_OK)
{
  myPlayer.play();
}
else if (currentStatus == DISC_BAD)
{
  cout << "This disc cannot be played." << endl;
}
else if (currentStatus == PLAYER_EMPTY)
{
  cout << "No disc has been loaded." << endl;
}
else if (currentStatus == PLAYER_ERROR)
{
  cout << "PLAYER_ERROR status returned by the player." << endl;
}
else
{
  cout << "Unexpected status returned by the player." << endl;
}
```

Figure 10.1 CD-playing program with multi-way `if` statement

In this code fragment the variable `currentStatus` has been added and initialized to the value returned by `the status()` member-function call. This variable can then be used in each of the Boolean expressions in the `if` statement, so avoiding the member function being called each time.

Try out this code fragment in your CD-playing program. But think for a moment how you are going to test it, and what you want to achieve by testing.

You'll want the testing to exercise each part of the multi-way selection, so that you can have some increased confidence that the code is correct.

There's a software engineering lesson here.

Lesson: When testing a program try to ensure that every part of a selection statement is executed.

You can choose test data such that the parts of the selection statements will be selected and executed. For instance, you know how you can use a faulty CD (the data) to generate a status value that will exercise two of the arms in the code of Figure 10.1. How can you test the compound statement associated with the `PLAYER_EMPTY` or `PLAYER_ERROR` values though? In other words, try Exercise 2 at the end of this section :-)

The fragment in Figure 10.1 allows us to illustrate another C++ pitfall that we'd like you to avoid. You might have tried to use multiple `if` statements to achieve the same effect as the above code. Take a look at the code fragment in Figure 10.2. Does it produce equivalent behavior to that produced by the fragment in Figure 10.1?

```
PlayerStatus currentStatus = myPlayer.status();
if (currentStatus == DISC_OK)
{
  myPlayer.play();
}
if (currentStatus == DISC_BAD)
{
  cout << "This disc cannot be played." << endl;
}
if (currentStatus == PLAYER_EMPTY)
{
  cout << "No disc has been loaded." << endl;
}
if (currentStatus == PLAYER_ERROR)
{
  cout << "PLAYER_ERROR status returned by the player." << endl;
}
else
{
  cout << "Unexpected status returned by the player." << endl;
}
```

Figure 10.2 CD-playing program with multiple `if` statements

What will the fragment in Figure 10.2 produce if the `status()` member-function call returns one of the following values?

```
PLAYER_ERROR     DISC_BAD
```

For the `PLAYER_ERROR` value both fragments will print the message:

```
PLAYER_ERROR status returned by the player.
```

You got that right, didn't you? What about the value `DISC_BAD`? Both fragments will print the message

```
This disc cannot be played.
```

However, Figure 10.2 will produce the following message *as well*:

```
Unexpected status returned by the player.
```

We bet you didn't expect that – it certainly isn't the behavior required. There's a bug in this second fragment. Can you identify the problem? Note that the first fragment is a single `if` statement while the second contains four `if` statements. Spotted the mistake yet?

The problem is that in Figure 10.2 all four `if` statements are executed. For the final statement, `if (currentStatus == PLAYER_ERROR)` ..., any value that's not `PLAYER_ERROR` will cause the `else` arm to be executed and hence the unexpected message.

Lesson: Notice the difference in execution behavior between multiple `if` statements and multiple `else-if` clauses.

There's also another important software engineering lesson to be learned from these multi-way selection examples. Notice two things:

1. The `else if` code fragment explicitly tests for all of the known `PlayerStatus` values.
2. The final `else` clause "catches" any other value.

This is a style of programming known as **defensive programming**. With the current set of values provided by the PDT `PlayerStatus` the final `else` clause is redundant. It should never be needed. However, say someone decided to change the PDTs `CDPlayer` and `PlayerStatus` so that an additional status value could be returned (`PLAYING`, for instance). With the defensive programming version of the code, this additional value would be "caught" by the `else` clause and you'd get a sensible message indicating that something unexpected had occurred. Contrast this behavior with what would happen in a code fragment that didn't adopt this defensive programming approach, and instead relied upon:

```
...
else if (currentStatus == PLAYER_EMPTY)
{
  cout << "No disc has been loaded." << endl;
}
else   // The status must be PLAYER_ERROR, right??
{
  cout << "PLAYER_ERROR status returned by the player." << endl;
}
```

Here the unexpected value will be reported as the `PLAYER_ERROR` status, which would confuse the program's user or anybody who was trying to debug the code.

Lesson: Adopt defensive programming strategies wherever possible. Explicitly check for all known values in a multi-way selection and provide a clause to catch unexpected values.

Defensive programming sometimes requires you to add redundant code to your programs; that is, code that isn't needed if you can guarantee the code to be bug-free. But trust us: your code will rarely be bug-free, and certainly in its early days bugs will be lurking. Defensive programming strategies will help in the testing of your code; unexpected errors will be caught and reported. In the long term, where a piece of code in a system may have a long life and exist through many changes to the system, defensive programming will lead to more robust software systems. So, it's a good strategy to adopt now.

`switch` *statements*

While you can program multi-way selections using the `if` statement with multiple `else-if` clauses, the resulting code can become rather cumbersome if there are lots of different values to be catered for. C++ therefore provides another type of selection statement to cater for multi-way selections – the `switch` statement. Let's first look at some additional design notation that you can use to represent a multi-way selection more succinctly than through the use of multiple selection boxes, together with the C++ code that implements a multi-way selection using a `switch` statement.

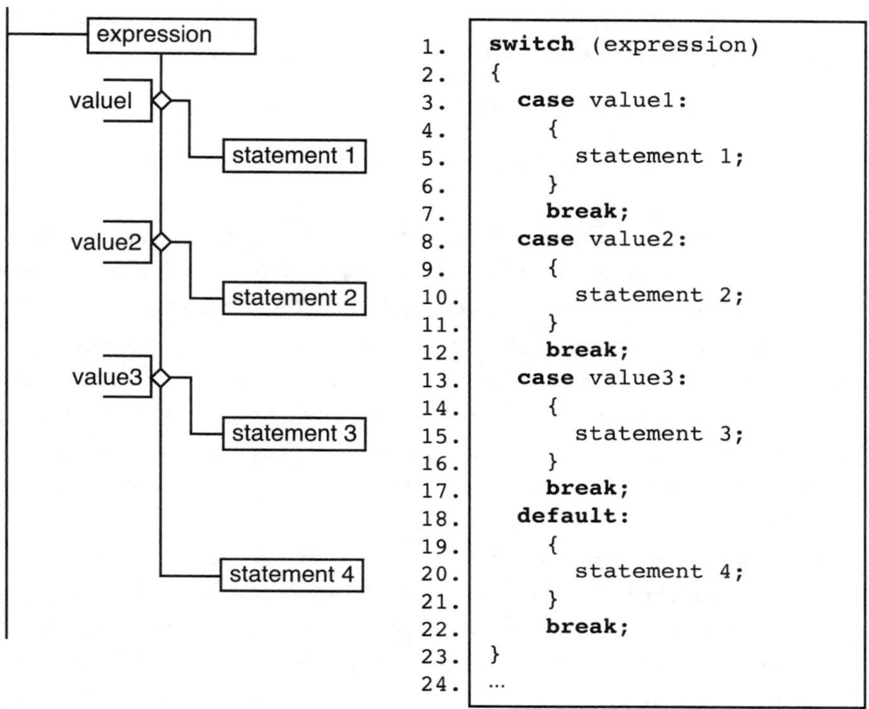


```
switch (expression)
{
  case value1:
    {
      statement 1;
    }
    break;
  case value2:
    {
      statement 2;
    }
    break;
  case value3:
    {
      statement 3;
    }
    break;
  default:
    {
      statement 4;
    }
    break;
}
...
```

The design notation expresses the following. First, expression is evaluated to produce a value. The value is then used to select one (and only one) of the arms for execution: if the value matches a label on the left-hand side of a diamond-shaped decision box then the statements on the path horizontally to the right are executed. For example, if the expression evaluates to value1 then statement 1 is executed. If the value matches none of the labels then the statement at the end (statement 4) is executed.

The horizontal paths to the right of the decision boxes could be labelled TRUE, but this is implicit and omitted to avoid cluttering up the diagram. In the design notation you can use any type of value in the expression. However, you'll see in a moment that C++ imposes restrictions on what the type can be.

While multi-way selections are a very useful design and programming-language feature, it has to be admitted that the C++ `switch` statement is less than perfect. As you can see above, you have to write several lines of C++ to implement even a simple multi-way selection using a `switch`, and there are a number of restrictions that you have to be aware of. But first, let's explain how a `switch` statement is constructed and then we'll examine how it operates.

The C++ `switch` statement introduces the use of four keywords (which have been highlighted in bold in the above diagram).

```
switch    case    break    default
```

The keyword `switch` is followed by an expression in parentheses. The compound statement (starting on line 2 and ending on line 23) represents the body of the `switch` statement and contains the set of alternatives that are selected from at run-time. Each alternative is introduced by the keyword `case` followed by a "label" terminated by a colon (:). There then follows a compound statement that contains the statements corresponding to one of the alternatives of the multi-way selection. After the compound statement of each alternative there's the keyword `break` followed by a semicolon. The final alternative within the switch's body is prefixed by the keyword `default` (without the keyword `case` preceding it). These are the syntactic details; now let's look at the semantics.

The execution of the C++ code fragment proceeds as follows. First the `expression` on line 1 is evaluated to produce a value. If this value is equal to the value of one of the `case` labels then the computer commences execution of the compound statement immediately following that `case` label. If none of the `case` labels match the value generated from the expression then the alternative labeled `default` is selected for execution. Got that so far?

The statement "`break;`" is a *built-in control statement.* When the computer executes this statement it causes the flow of control to break out of the `switch` statement and to go to the first statement after the `switch` statement (line 24 in the code). Most commonly, `break` is used to indicate the end of the statements in each `case` arm.

Let's redesign the CD-playing program to use a `switch` statement instead of multiple `else-if` clauses.

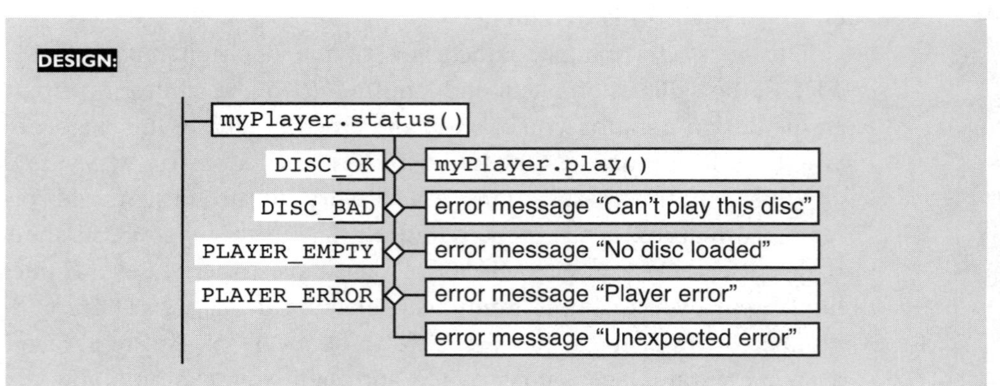

IMPLEMENTATION:

```
switch (myPlayer.status())
{
  case DISC_OK:
    {
      myPlayer.play();
    }
    break;
  case DISC_BAD:          // Bad disc
    {
      cout << "This disc cannot be played" << endl;
    }
    break;
  case PLAYER_EMPTY:      // Didn't load a disc
    {
      cout << "No disc has been loaded"   << endl;
    }
    break;
  case PLAYER_ERROR:      // Error status returned
    {
      cout << "PLAYER_ERROR status returned by the player." << endl;
    }
    break;
  default:                // Unexpected value
    {
      cout << "Unexpected status returned by the player." << endl;
    }
    break;
} // end switch (myPlayer.status())
```

C++ imposes restrictions on what the type of the value produced by the `expression`'s evaluation can be. This has a follow-on effect on what you can write as a label. Stated simply, the `expression` must evaluate to an `int` value. However, there are other types that can be converted into an `int` value and can also be used in `expression`, and there are other limitations you need to be aware of.

A first limitation on the labels that you can write in the `case` arms of one `switch` statement is that the label must be unique; this is sensible! However, each label must also be a **constant integral value**, meaning that it must be a value that:

1. Is known at compile time.
2. Can be converted into an `int` value.

You can use `int` literals or `int` literal expressions as labels without any problem, with `expression` producing an appropriate value. You can also use some abstract values as `case` labels, for example values of the PDTs `PlayerStatus` and `Palette`. In these cases evaluation of the expression must produce an abstract value of the appropriate type. The reason these can be used has to do with the way such types are implemented; there's a type mechanism in C++ called `enum` that you've not met yet, but `enum` values can be used as `case` labels as they can be implicitly converted to `int` literals by the compiler.

EXAMPLE:

Assuming the relevant PDT header files have been included, here are some examples of legal `case` labels.

```
case 1:            case 5 * 3:        case -42:
case DISC_BAD:     case DISC_OK:      case ERROR:
case RED:          case BLACK:        case int(3.2):
case 'a':          case 'Z':          case '\n':
```

Note the use of character literals as labels in the above example. Here we're relying on the compiler implicitly to coerce a `char` into an `int`, which is going against the style rule described in Chapter 8 that suggested explicit coercions should always be used. An explicit coercion would also result in a legal case label, but it's common in a simple `case` label like those above to omit the coercion as, unlike implicit coercions in expressions, no other values are involved.

EXAMPLE:

Given the variable declarations:

```
int       count;
const int LABEL_FOUR = 4;
Text      today;
```

here are some examples of `case` labels, only one of which is legal. Can you spot the odd-one-out?

```
case count:         case count + 1:         case count < 0:
case LABEL_FOUR:    case LABEL_FOUR == 4:   case LABEL_FOUR + count:
case today:         case "Monday":          case "3":
```

The only legal case label is `case LABEL_FOUR:` The rest will result in a compile-time error. Can you see why? Try Exercise 4 at the end of the section if you can. Be sure to try Exercise 4 if you can't :-)

When writing `case` labels you can't specify a range of values as a label. However, you can place multiple labels on an alternative to achieve this effect, as exemplified by the following problem.

PROBLEM:

Design and implement a fragment of code that asks the user to provide a yes/no response to a question in order to select different sets of statements for execution. The user can provide their response typed as "Y", "y", "n", or "N".

DESIGN:

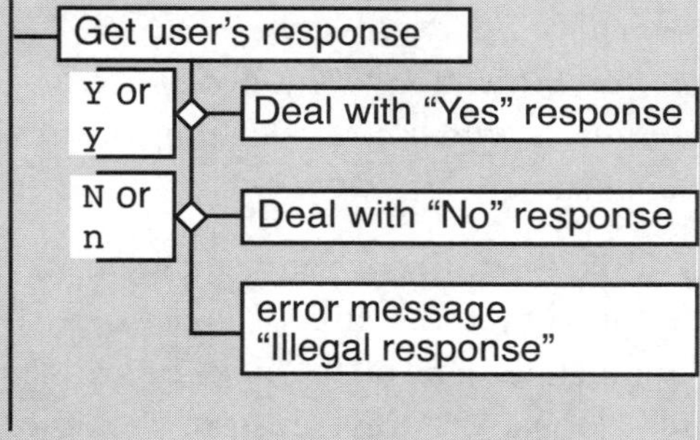

IMPLEMENTATION:

```
char response;

cout << "Respond Y or y for YES, and N or n for NO: ";
cin  >> response;
switch (response)
{
```

```
  case 'Y':
  case 'y':
    {
      cout << "User has indicated YES" << endl;
    }
    break;
  case 'n':
  case 'N':
    {
      cout << "User has indicated NO"  << endl;
    }
    break;
  default:
    {
      cout << "Illegal response"       << endl;
    }
    break;
} // end switch (response)
```

Are there style rules for the use of the `switch` selection statement?

You bet.

- ✓ *Leave one space between the* `switch` *keyword and the opening parenthesis before the expression.*
- ✓ *Indent each* `case` *label by two spaces.*
- ✓ *Indent the compound statement associated with a* `case` *arm by a further two spaces.*

Having looked at the given examples of the use of `switch` statements you might think that the use of `break` is unnecessary as either the end of the compound statement or the next `case` label would indicate where an alternative ends. However, this illustrates one of the foibles of C++'s `switch` statement: the use of `break` isn't mandatory and so the compiler won't warn you if you leave it out. If you don't use `break` your program's flow of control will just "fall through" from one alternative into the one below, without any test of the expression's value against that of the next alternative's `case` label. This is probably not the behavior you want or expect. So the syntax diagram at the end of this section will not admit to the absence of `break`s in a `switch` statement.

Another foible of the `switch` statement is that the `default` alternative isn't necessary for a legal `switch` statement. However, it's very good software engineering practice always to have a `default` arm, just in case you've forgotten a value or if a new value gets added. This is another example of defensive programming. Therefore, the syntax diagram will not admit to the possibility of omitting the `default` alternative.

Selection statement syntax

Let's conclude this introduction of selection statements with their syntax diagrams.

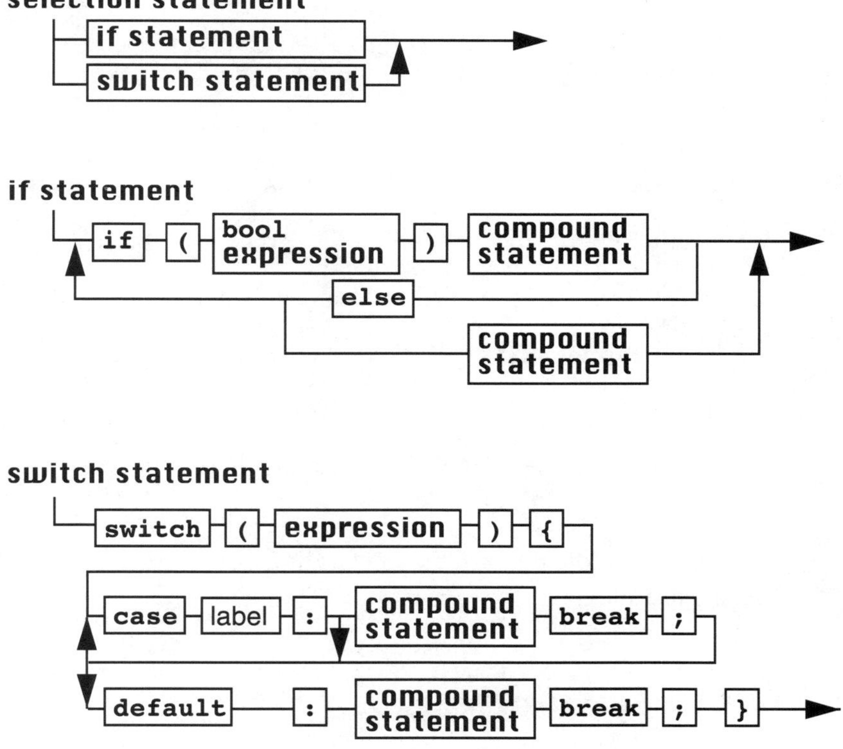

We've used **bool expression** above to indicate that an element should be an expression that produces a `bool` result. Also, we've not provided a syntax diagram for a label in a switch statement as it's rather complicated to specify clearly. Just remember that a label has to be an `int` literal or equivalent.

So, now you know how to get your C++ programs to select between different sets of instructions at run-time, the next control-flow abstraction you need to get to grips with is repetition repetition.

EXERCISES FOR SECTION 10.1

1 Implement the design you constructed in Exercise 1, Section 10.0.

2 How can you test the `PLAYER_EMPTY` and `PLAYER_ERROR` arms in the code fragment shown in Figure 10.1?

3 What output will each of these C++ fragments produce when executed, assuming that the `int` variable `number` has the value (i) `2`, (ii) `3`, and (iii) `4`:

```
// Fragment1
if (number == 3)
{
  cout << "Msg1";
}
if (number <= 3)
{
  cout " Msg2";
}
if (number == 4)
{
  cout << " Msg3";
}
else
{
  cout << " Msg4";
}
```

```
// Fragment 2
if (number == 3)
{
  cout << "Msg1";
}
else if (number <= 3)
{
  cout << " Msg2";
}
else if (number == 4)
{
  cout << " Msg3";
}
else
{
  cout << " Msg4";
}
```

4 Given the following variable declarations and case labels, identify why the case labels are illegal.

```
int        count;
const int LABEL_FOUR = 4;
Text       today;
```

```
case count:     case count + 1:       case case:
case :          case LABEL_FOUR + :   case LABEL_FOUR + count:
case today:     case "Monday":        case "3":
```

5 Given the following declarations and assuming the PDT `Palette`:

```
int         theAnswer = 42
const int ALABEL      = 24;
char        yes       = 'Y';
Palette     color     = RED;
```

consider each of the following as a `case` label. Indicate whether you think it's a legal or illegal label.

```
case int(3.3):      case 75:          case 3.14159:
case -53:           case yes:         case theAnswer:
case ALABEL:        case "Quit":      case 'N':
case color:         case RED:         case 3 + 4:
```

6 Write a program that asks the user to type in an integer in the range 1 to 10 and then prints out whether the number is even, odd or outside the requested range. Use a `switch` statement to separate the values. What values would you use to make sure all arms of the `switch` have been tested?

10.2 REPETITION STATEMENTS IN C++

You remember the design notation for repetition statements, don't you? You don't? Well, here's an algorithm for a parameterized function for getting to the Nth chapter of this book, to help you get back to Chapter 2 to refresh your memory (if you understand this design then maybe you don't need to go back :-).

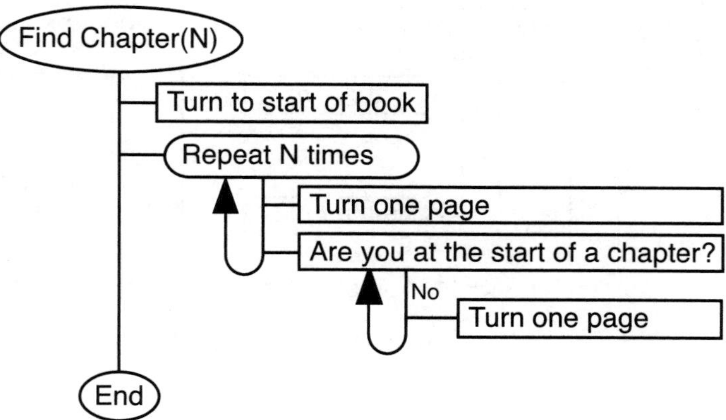

Now you remember: there are two kinds of repetition. The first is when you repeat some statements while some condition holds (**while** repetition abstraction); and the second kind is when you repeat some statements a known number of times (**loop** repetition abstraction). Examples of both types are shown above.

There are in fact three repetition statements in C++: the `while` statement; the `do` statement; and the `for` statement (you've now met three more C++ keywords). The `while` and `do` statements are similar and can be used to implement a while repetition. The `for` statement can be used for loop repetition. Let's first examine the need for two forms of while repetition.

While repetition: design notation refinement

The while form of repetition can be stated in two ways, with slightly different semantics:

1. While some condition holds, repeat a set of statements.
2. Repeat a set of statements while some condition holds.

At first sight there doesn't seem to be much difference between these two possibilities. The only difference is the position of the test to see whether the condition holds. In the former, the test is performed *before* the set of statements is executed, while in the latter the test is applied *after* the set of statements has been executed. Both forms can be useful in software systems, and it's therefore useful to distinguish between the two in the design notation. This can be achieved by adding something that indicates the position of the test. We'll use a pair of horizontal lines (=) to indicate the test's position, as shown in Figure 10.3.

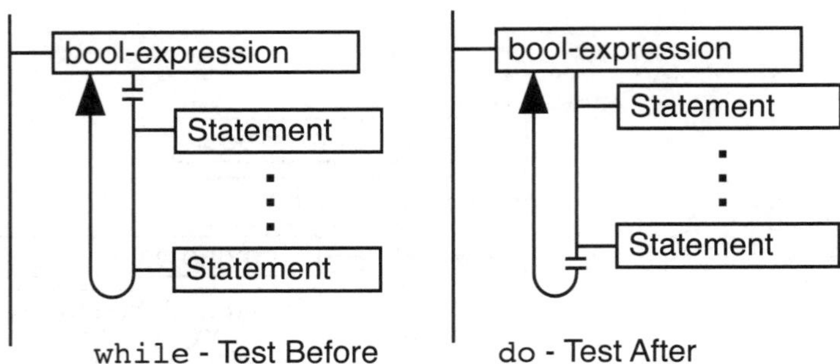

Figure 10.3 Design notations for while repetition

Let's now examine the C++ statements that correspond to these notations.

`while` statement

The `while` statement implements the "test-before" version of the repetition abstraction discussed above. There's a straightforward correspondence between the design notation and the C++ code:

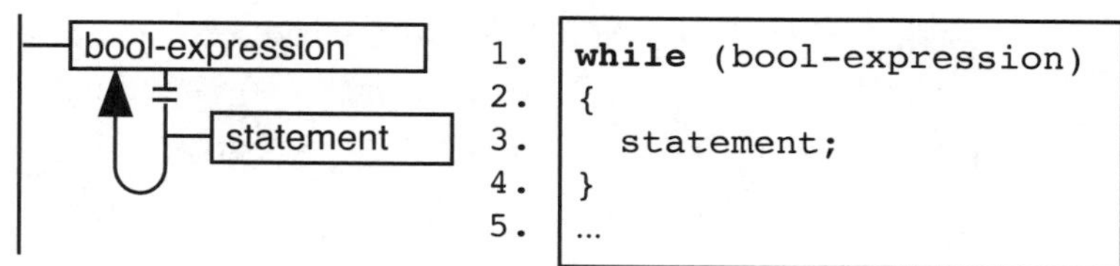

The execution of the `while` statement proceeds as follows.

1. The `bool-expression` following the keyword `while` (line 1) is evaluated.
2. If the value produced is `true` then the compound statement following (lines 2 to 4 – referred to as the **body** of the `while` statement) is executed, and the flow of control returns to step 1 to evaluate `bool-expression` again.
3. The sequence continues until `bool-expression` evaluates to `false`. When this happens, execution of the `while` statement is complete and the flow of control skips over the body and goes to the statement following the `while` statement (line 5).

So, the body of a `while` statement is repeatedly executed so long as the Boolean expression evaluates to `true` each time round. Note that the body may thus be executed zero or more times.

> **Lesson:** The Boolean expression controlling the execution of a `while` statement's body must evaluate to `true` for the repetition to continue, and to `false` for the repetition to terminate.

In your design you may have expressed the condition on a repetition in more abstract terms, but such terms have to be translated into the C++ semantics as described above.

EXAMPLE:

In Figure 2.22, the condition is written as:

Is the student's name "Lee"?

with the repetition continuing if the answer to this question is "no." Such descriptions have to be translated into C++ semantics with the repetition continuing while the equivalent `bool-expression` evaluates to `true`:

```
while (studentName != "Lee") // or (!(studentName == "Lee"))
{
  ... continue the repetition
}
```

What's the danger with `while` statements? Well, consider what happens if the Boolean expression never evaluates to `false`. The execution of your program will stay in the `while` statement forever – in an infinite loop. We guarantee that at some stage in your programming life this will happen to you! Typically, the statements in the body of a `while` statement will change the values of variables used in the Boolean expression such that it will eventually produce the value `false` and the repetition will terminate. Remember: one of the desirable properties of an algorithm that we discussed in Section 2.5 is that it should terminate in a finite time, and this property is equally desirable in a program!

We'll return to the software engineering lessons involved here in Section 10.4. However, this might be a good time for you to determine how you can halt a program that's executing on your system (if you didn't complete Exercise 5 in Section 4.3), just in case your program gets into an infinite loop. You'll need to refer to your system's manuals for this, but often there's some sequence you can type on the keyboard to halt a program. (Typing a "C" while holding down the <Ctrl> key is a common sequence.)

We give the syntax for all of the repetition statements at the end of this section, but you might care to have a quick look now to reinforce what you've learned so far.

Let's look at an example of the use of a `while` statement.

PROBLEM:

Design and implement a program that finds how many tracks there are on a CD (using PDTs you already know about).

DESIGN:

To solve this problem you'll first look at the interface provided by PDT `CDisc` since there may already be a member function that provides this information.

Unfortunately, there isn't anything relevant, but maybe the CD you're interested in could be loaded into a CD player and the player used to find out how many tracks there are. In other words, the relevant part of an initial design is:

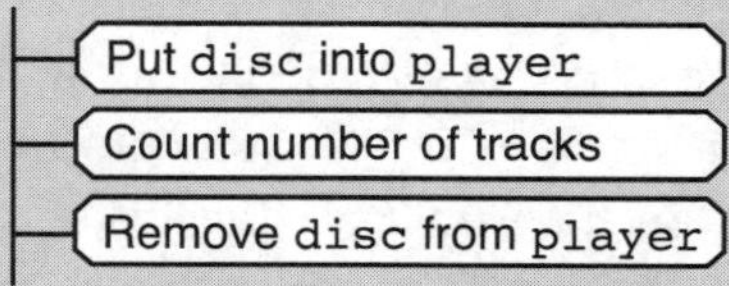

The next stage of the design is to expand the step **Count number of tracks**, since this is the crux of the problem to be solved. Take a look at the following design.

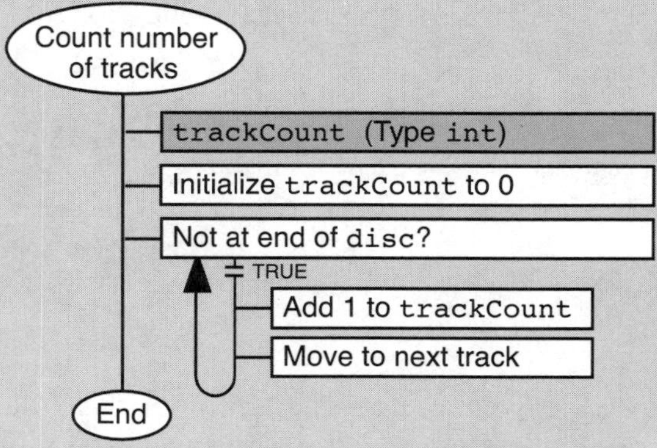

The test expressed in the repetition is a little clumsy to read in English (the repetition will continue while it's not at the end of the disc), but it's written this way to reflect the fact that in C++ the statements in the body will be executed while the Boolean expression is `true`. It would have been equally valid in the design to write the conditional as "At end of disc?" as long as we labeled the output path "FALSE" or "NO" to make it clear exactly what the condition for continuing the repetition is.

IMPLEMENTATION:

Now all you have to do is translate the design into C++. You've probably recognized that you're going to need a `while` statement, and if you've looked at the interface of PDT `CDPlayer` you'll have identified that there's a member function to move to the next track – `void nextTrack()`. But how can you determine whether the end of the disc has been reached?

When `nextTrack()` is executed it sets the status of the player to indicate whether it was able to move to the next track or not. If it succeeded then the player's status is set to `DISC_OK`. However, if it didn't succeed then the player's status is set to `PLAYER_ERROR`; for example, if the player is already on the last track of the disc when the member function is called. Hence you can use the `status()` member function to determine the player's status and to control the `while` statement's execution. You might like to evolve the above design to show the required steps. Here's the relevant fragment of C++ code.

```
// Count the number of tracks on a disc
int trackCount = 0;      // Declare and initialize trackCount

while (myPlayer.status() != PLAYER_ERROR)
{
  trackCount += 1;              // Add 1 to trackCount
  myPlayer.nextTrack();         // Try to move to next track.
                                //   This changes status
}
```

Before we leave this example, consider the following software engineering question: how could you check that the code produces the right result?

There are two answers. First, you could check the code by hand, executing the program as the computer would, pretending you have CDs with different numbers of tracks, such as 3 or 1. The second answer is you could check the result produced by executing the program with the information displayed in the graphical representation of the CD player when a disc has been loaded.

What's wrong with the following alternative implementation of the design?

```
int          trackCount    = 0;
PlayerStatus currentStatus = myPlayer.status();

while (currentStatus != PLAYER_ERROR)
{
  trackCount += 1;
  myPlayer.nextTrack();
}
```

Apart from the fact that there aren't any comments, the problem is that the `while` statement will repeat for ever. Can you spot why?

The bug is that the value of the player's status is recorded in the variable `currentStatus` before the `while` statement is entered, and the variable's value is never updated with the new status of the player. Beware of those infinite loops!

Lesson: Ensure that your repetition statements eventually terminate.

Here's another pitfall to avoid. What's wrong with the following `while` statement?

```
int count = 0;

while (count < 10);
{
  count += 1;
}
```

Did you spot the semicolon after the closing parenthesis of the Boolean expression? Is that legal C++? Unfortunately, it is legal, even though our upcoming syntax diagrams don't show it as being permissible. This fragment represents a one-line `while` statement (with no body) followed by a completely separate compound statement. This fragment will compile (although some compilers might, helpfully, give you a warning), and will give rise to an infinite loop if executed. So, we have the following style rules.

- ✓ *Always use a compound statement for the body of a repetition statement.*
- ✓ *Place the compound statement opening brace* `{` *on a separate line but in the same column as the start of the previous statement.*
- ✓ *Line up the matching* `}` *in the same column as the* `{`.

- ✓ *Use indentation to indent the statements inside the compound statement two spaces in from the column containing the* `{`.
- ✓ *Line up the statements that are part of the same compound statement.*
- ✓ *Leave one space between the keyword* `while` *and the opening parenthesis of the Boolean expression.*

The syntax diagrams for `while` statements are coming up shortly. First though let's cover the other C++ statement for repeating some statements while some condition holds: the `do` statement.

do statement

C++'s `do` statement is used to implement the form of while repetition that tests the Boolean expression after the body of the statement has been executed.

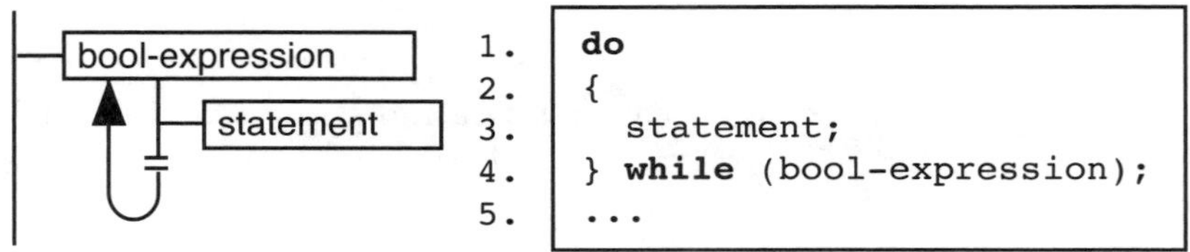

The execution of a `do` statement starts with the compound statement (for example, lines 2 to 4 above) following which `bool-expression` is evaluated. If a `true` value is produced the compound statement is executed again. A `false` value means that the `do` statement has terminated and the flow of control goes to the next statement (line 5).

> **Lesson:** The Boolean expression controlling the execution of a `do` statement's body must evaluate to `true` for the repetition to continue, and to `false` for the repetition to terminate.

With a `do` statement the compound statement is executed *one* or more times, in contrast to that of a `while` statement which may be executed *zero* or more times. This is the deciding factor that you must take into consideration when trying to decide whether to use a `while` statement or a `do` statement.

Here's a simple problem that requires the use of a `do` statement.

PROBLEM:

Write a code fragment that won't give up asking for an input value (in the range 1 to 10) until a value in the appropriate range has been entered. The input statement must be executed at least once.

DESIGN:

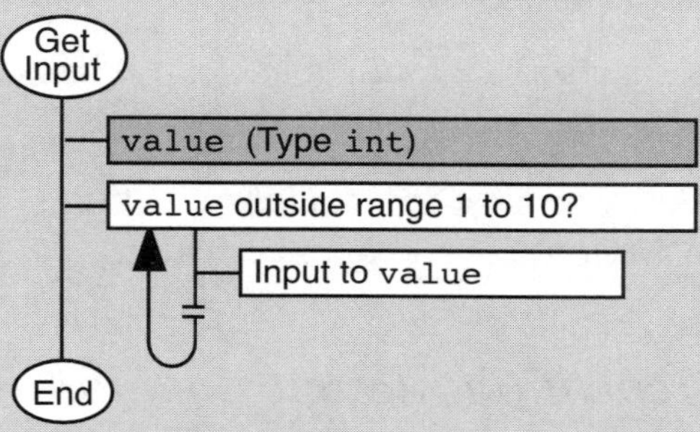

Recalling that the shaded box represents a variable declaration, are you concerned that there's a problem with the above design?

You might have thought that there's a bug since the design doesn't initialize the variable `value` before the condition is evaluated. You recall from Chapter 6 that an uninitialized `int` variable will have some random value. However, if you've remembered that the = indicates the point at which the condition is evaluated, you'll have realized that this bug doesn't exist. The input statement will have placed a value into `value` before the test is evaluated. So, you can now translate this design using a `do` statement.

IMPLEMENTATION:

```
int value;

do
{
  cout << "Input a value between 1 and 10: ";
  cin  >> value;
} while ((value < 1) || (value > 10));
```

Don't forget that pesky semicolon following the `while` part of a `do` statement. It's needed to tell the compiler that this is the end of the `do` statement. Note, however, that a semicolon isn't needed at the end of a `while` statement as the `}` of the compound statement is the terminator.

Notice also the potential confusion between a `while` clause as part of a `while` statement and a `while` clause as part of a `do` statement. To minimize this confusion, we suggest you adopt the following style rule in addition to the ones you saw earlier in the section on the `while` statement.

✓ *Place the* `while` *clause that's part of a* `do` *statement on the same line as the closing* `}`.

Is that all you have to `do for` repetition? `While` there's another repetition statement form to cover, continue reading.

Loop repetition: design notation refinement

Say you're faced with the following problem to be solved.

PROBLEM:

Design and implement a program that permits the user to indicate a start track number for a CD-playing program.

DESIGN:

A first design you might come up with is the following.

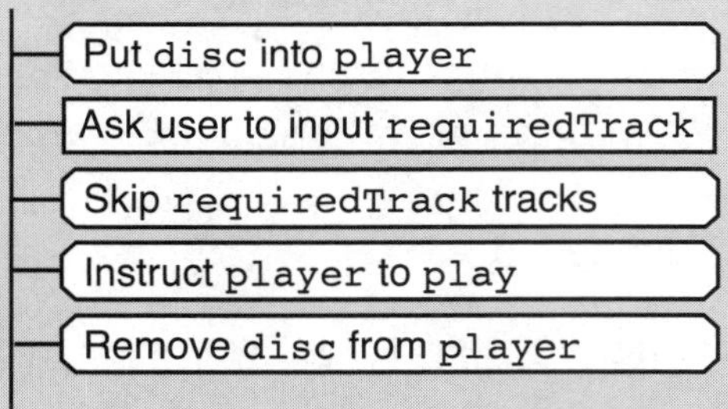

You're probably aware that the designator box "Skip `requiredTrack` tracks" is going to involve some repeated calls of the member function `nextTrack()`, but how should you design that repetition? You could use a `while` repetition:

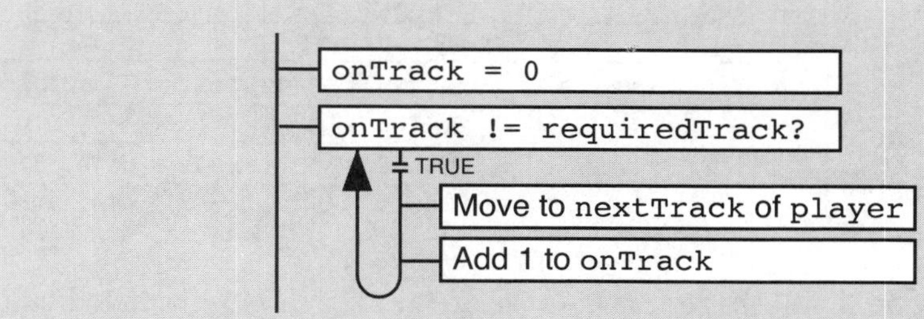

As long as you remember to declare the variable `onTrack`, initialize it, and update it each time through the body of the while repetition, this design is satisfactory. However, the structure represented in the design, of wishing to repeat some actions a known number of times, is so common in programming that the loop repetition abstraction is provided, which can be used as follows:

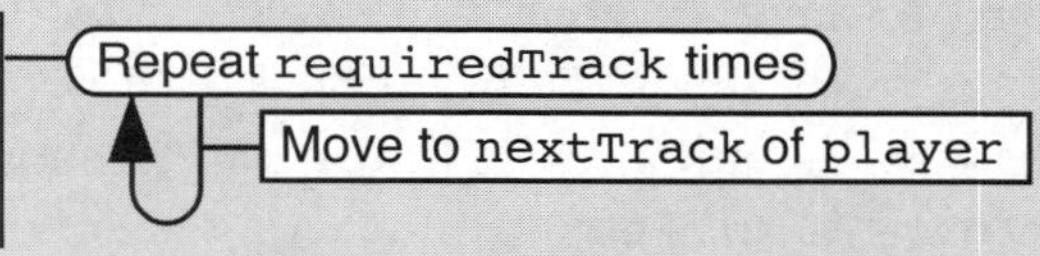

The `for` repetition statement in C++ directly implements the required behavior. In general, to repeat a compound statement a fixed number of times requires the use of a **loop control variable** that must be:

1. Initialized to a start value.
2. Tested against an upper- or lower-limit each time around the loop to see whether the end of the loop has been reached.
3. Updated (either increased or decreased in value) each time around the loop.

You saw all this detail in the `while` design above, where the loop control variable is `onTrack`. While the detail isn't needed in the design notation for a simple loop abstraction that effectively specifies "execute the loop body *N* times," additional programming flexibility is provided if the actions in steps 1–3 can be explicitly controlled by the programmer.

DESIGN:

To reflect this additional detail, we can refine the simple loop design notation you've seen so far, and respecify the simple example as follows.

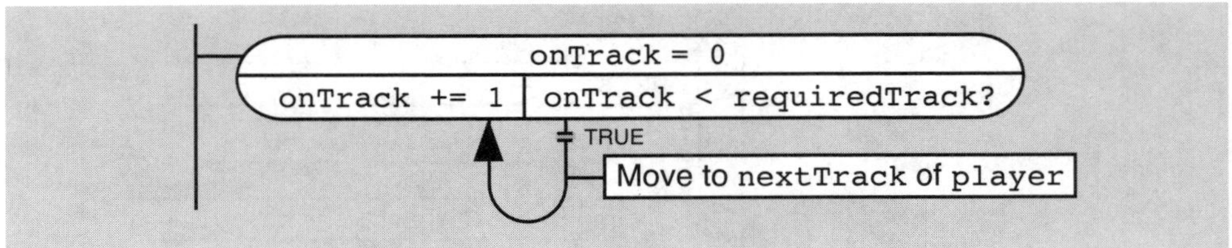

As you'll see shortly, this form of the design closely matches the C++ statement (the `for` statement) that's used for its implementation, and hence some C++ operators have been used in the design.

The three actions on the loop control variable are shown in a single box. At the top is the initialization of the loop control variable, with the test and update operations on the line below. We need to identify more precisely the ordering of the execution of these three parts. This is best done with respect to the C++ statement, although the notation shows the "input path" to the loop box going first to the initializing step. We've added the "=" to give you a hint about where the test action is performed (before the statements are executed). Although this notation doesn't provide anything additional to that shown in the version using a `while` repetition, it's easier to omit a box from the latter by mistake than it would be to omit the corresponding action from the loop design notation box.

`for` statement

The correspondence between the detailed design notation and the C++ `for` statement is shown by the following diagram.

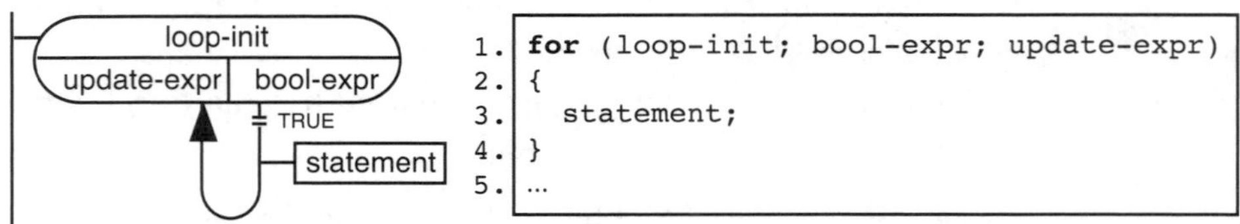

The `loop-init` part of the `for` statement is normally used to initialize a variable (the loop control variable) that controls the execution of the `for` statement. The Boolean expression `bool-expr` is used to determine whether or not the compound statement (the loop body) is executed – it normally tests the value of the loop control variable against a terminating value, and in this respect is very similar to the Boolean expressions that you've seen in `while` and `do` statements. The `update-expr` specifies the update to be made to the value of the control variable each time through the loop. Note the position of the semicolons in the `for` statement; they permit the compiler to recognize the separation of the three parts.

The `for` statement is executed as follows.

1. The `loop-init` following the `for` keyword is executed.
2. The `bool-expr` is evaluated:
   (a) if its value is `true` then the compound statement (lines 2 – 4) is executed, followed by the execution of `update-expr`. Then repeat from step 2;
   (b) if its value is `false` then the `for` statement has completed, and execution proceeds to the statement after the `for` statement (line 5).

Most commonly, the loop control variable is an integer and the update made each time through the loop is to increase its value by 1. However, the generality provided by C++ permits the loop control variable to be of any type and the update to be of any legitimate form.

EXAMPLE:

```
#include <iostream.h>

int main()
{
  int loopControl;

  cout << "Using a simple for statement to print numbers "
       << "1 to 10 inclusive" << endl;
  for (loopControl = 1; loopControl < 10; loopControl += 1)
  {
    cout << loopControl << " ";
  }
  cout << endl << endl;

  cout << "Using a for statement to print multiples of 13 "
       << endl << "between 1 to 1001 inclusive,"
       << " 5 to a line." << endl;

  int numOutput = 0;

  for (loopControl = 13; loopControl <= 1001; loopControl += 13)
  {
    if ((numOutput % 5) == 0)
    {
      cout << endl;
```

```
    }
    cout << loopControl << '\t';
    numOutput += 1;
  }
  cout << endl;

  return 0;
} // end main()
```

Go through this example by hand, pretending to execute it as the computer would and predict what the output from the first `for` statement will be.

Did you predict that the first `for` loop produces the following output:

```
1 2 3 4 5 6 7 8 9
```

or did you have `10` on the end of your predicted output? If you included the `10` you were wrong. The `bool-expr` returns `true` (and hence the loop continues) only while the value of `loopControl` is less than `10`. The comparison operator needs to be changed to `<=` to make the loop inclusive of the value `10`. This is a bug in the program, assuming that the comment indicating that "the numbers 1 to 10 inclusive" is accurate.

Note that the body of a `for` statement may be executed *zero* times, just like in a `while` statement. If the first evaluation of the Boolean expression returns `false`, the `for` statement will terminate without executing the compound statement.

Now return to the CD track selection design given earlier, for which the translation into C++ is straightforward.

IMPLEMENTATION:

```
int requiredTrack;
                    // Ask user to input requiredTrack
cout << "Type in start track number: ";
cin  >> requiredTrack;
```

```
                    // Skip requiredTrack tracks
for (int onTrack = 0;               // loop-initialization
     onTrack < requiredTrack;       // Boolean expression
     onTrack += 1)                  // update expression
{
  myPlayer.nextTrack();
}
...
```

Note how white space has been used in this fragment to lay out the `for` statement. Note also the loop-initialization part. Here it includes the declaration of the loop control variable as well as its initialization.

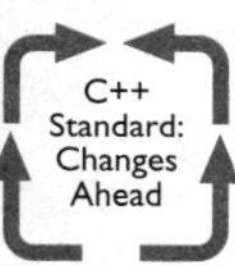

Including a declaration as part of the loop initialization is legal in C++, as you'll see later in the syntax diagrams. However, there's a potential "gotcha" here in the current versions of C++, although this is an area that's likely to change with the new C++ standard.

Can you see a syntax problem with the following piece of code?

```
int main()
{
  double i;

  for (int i = 10; i >= 0; i -= 1)
  {
    ...
  }
  return 0;
} // end main ()
```

If you compile this piece of code, the compiler will give you a syntax error indicating that `i` has been declared twice. The problem is that the declaration of `int i` in the `for` statement isn't local to the `for` statement; the scope of this `int` variable `i` is the same as that of the separate declaration of `double i`. The internationally-standardized version of C++ proposes a change here, so that `i` will be a local variable only for the scope of the `for` statement.

With the current version of C++ there's a bit of a "styles" dilemma here. On one hand, it's useful to declare the loop control variable as part of the `for` statement; this keeps the declaration close to the localized use of the variable (which is why the change to C++ has been proposed). On the other hand, there's the danger of the multiple declaration problem if two or more `for` statements are used at the same scope level with the same identifier for their loop control variable. (Of course, there isn't a problem if the `for` statements are at different scope levels.) At least in this situation the compiler currently provides an error message for the erroneous situation, so it isn't too dangerous. Our style rule is:

✓ *Declare the loop control variable as part of the loop initialization expression, except if there are multiple loops at the same scope level wishing to use the same identifier for their loop control variable.*

However, never do something like the following.

```
for (int i = 1; i < 100; i += 2)
{
  ...
}
...
// Some statements that use the value of i
...
for (i = 0; i != 10; i += 1)
{
  ...
}
```

Here the second and third uses of `i` depend on the declaration hidden away in the first `for` statement. Both are examples of bad style, and if you intend to reuse a variable in this fashion, the declaration should be given at the beginning of the relevant level of scope. Note also that this code won't work when the new version of C++ comes along, so if you don't use this bad style now you won't be getting into bad habits for later.

✓ *Don't use loop control variables for any other purpose in the part of the program in which they are in scope.*

You might also think that the use of the identifier `i` is going against our earlier style rule of having meaningful names. It is. However, it's very common in programs to use variables like `i` and `j` as loop control variables. But it's not worth another style rule.

Repetition statement syntax

Note that, as shown in the following syntax diagrams, the `do` statement requires a semicolon following the bracketed Boolean expression, whereas the `while` statement is terminated by the compound statement, the definition of which includes the terminating brace.

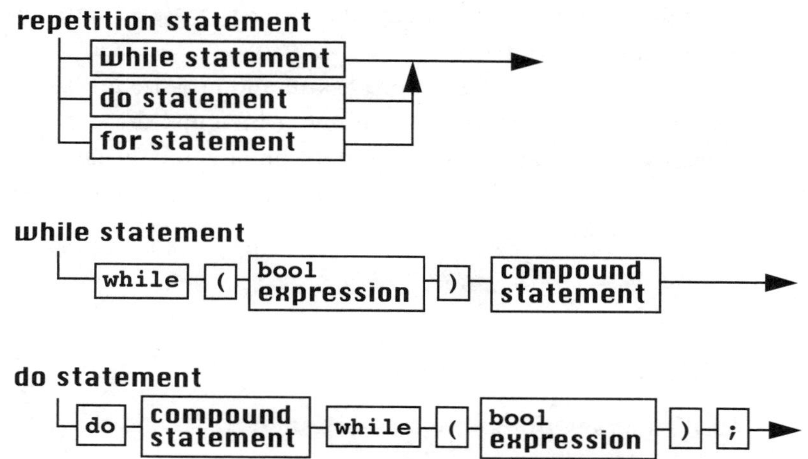

The following syntax diagrams for the **for statement** admit the possibility that any of the three parts of **loop init**, **loop b-expr** and **loop control var update** may in fact be null statements. This is legal C++, although only likely to be used in rather unusual circumstances (you'll see an example of an "unusual circumstance" in Chapter 14).

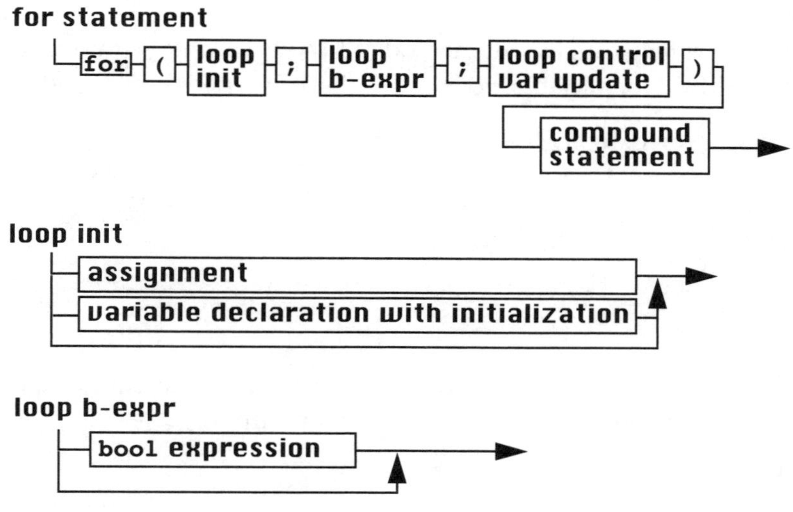

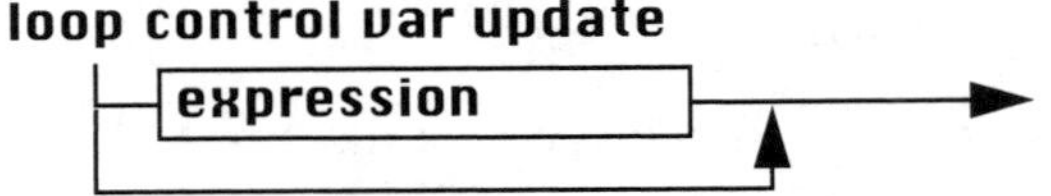

What statements can you write inside the compound statement that forms the body of a repetition statement? Well, any **statement** you like of course. It's not uncommon to find `for` statements inside `for` statements, or other combinations of repetition statements.

You may have noticed more "skull-and-crossbones" warnings in this chapter than in earlier chapters. As you might imagine, these are highlighting potential problem areas that the use of repetition statements can suffer from. In the next section we'll revisit some of the software engineering issues that we've already touched upon.

EXERCISES FOR SECTION 10.2

1 What's the key difference between the `while` and `do` statements in C++?

2 How many times will the body of the following two repetition statements be executed if the `int` variable `count` has the value (i) 1, (ii) 3, (iii) 0, and (iv) –1.

```
// Repetition statement 1
while (count != 0)
{
  count -= 1;
}
```

```
// Repetition statement 2
do
{
  count -= 1;
} while (count != 0);
```

3 How many times will the body of the following two `for` statements be executed if the `int` variable `count` has the value (i) 1, (ii) 2, (iii) 0, and (iv) –1?

```
// For statement 1
for (int  i = 0;
          i < count;
          i += 1)
{
  cout << "Hello ";
}
```

```
// For statement 2
for (int i =  count;
           i >= 0;
           i -= 3)
{
cout << "Hello ";
}
```

4 Write a `for` statement that prints out all of the multiples of 293 between 1 and 32,000 and indicates how many there are.

5 For Exercise 3 in Section 10.0 you produced a design to draw a textual "Christmas tree." Implement this design, and check that your code draws trees with the right dimensions.

10.3 SOFTWARE ENGINEERING ISSUES

The use of selection and repetition statements in your programs gives you lots more scope for making mistakes, especially during the early days of your apprenticeship. There's all the new complex syntax to master, let alone the complex semantics of the operation of the various C++ statements this chapter has introduced. As you've been going through this chapter, various software engineering issues have been raised, and it's worth going through some of them again.

When you use selection or repetition statements in a program, you naturally have a much more complicated program than the simple sequential programs you've seen earlier. A program that's just a sequential program only has a single control path through it. A program that contains a `for` statement that repeats 10 times has 10 distinct paths through it. If that program contains a simple `if-else` statement inside the body of the `for` statement then there are 1,024 possible distinct paths through it (that's 2^{10}). You can see that the total number of paths through a program increases rapidly as selection and repetition statements are used. So, aspects of design and testing are much more important than before, and defensive programming techniques such as those discussed earlier can play a very important role in preventing and detecting errors.

One of the most difficult things to get right when using repetition statements is their termination. Let's look at various paradigms that you can employ when designing repetitions.

Using sentinels and flags to terminate repetition statements

You know that, in general, `while` and `do` repetition statements are used when you don't know exactly how many times the repetition is required. How do you terminate the repetition? The short answer is "By ensuring that the Boolean expression controlling the loop evaluates to `false` at some stage," but how do you achieve this?

One method of terminating the repetition is by making use of a **sentinel**. This is just a data value that you choose as a loop terminating value, rather than a

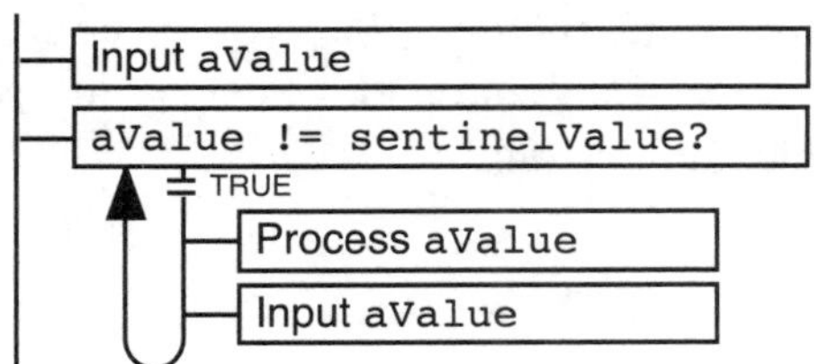

Figure 10.4 Using a sentinel to terminate a loop

value that requires further processing. You can then use the sentinel in the Boolean expression controlling the repetition. You test whether a value is the sentinel value: if it is, the repetition terminates; if it isn't, the program goes round the loop again.

Sentinels are commonly used with repetition loops processing input, where the number of input items isn't known and a sentinel can be used to terminate the input. The standard design for such processing is shown in Figure 10.4.

PROBLEM:

Design and implement a program that forms the average of a set of examination marks.

DESIGN:

The problem description doesn't tell you how many numbers there are going to be, so this should suggest to you that a while repetition is going to be needed. But how will your program know when the end of the set of input numbers has been reached? This is a situation where a sentinel can be used, and assuming that the value 0 isn't going to appear in the set of numbers, you could choose it as the value that, when input, terminates the repetition. This leads to the following part of the design.

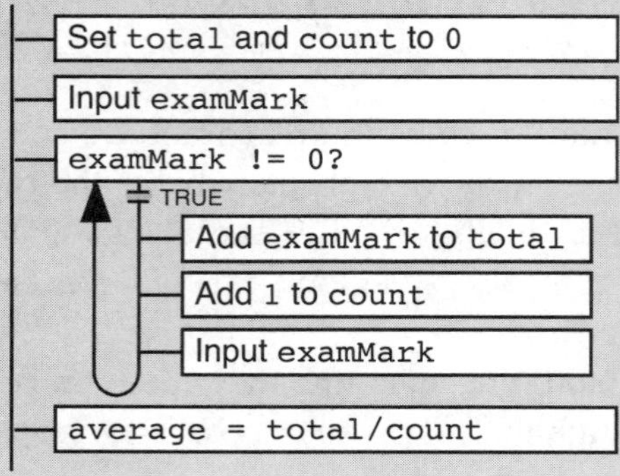

IMPLEMENTATION:

Here's a fragment of code implementing a solution to the problem.

```
const int STOP_INPUT = 0;
int examMark;
int count = 0;
int total = 0;

cout << "Enter exam mark (0 to terminate): ";
cin  >> examMark;

while (examMark != STOP_INPUT)
{
  total += examMark;
  count += 1;
  cout << "Enter exam mark (0 to terminate): ";
  cin  >> examMark;
} // end while

cout << "Average is " << total/count << endl;
```

Can you think of any problems with using sentinels?

The main problem is whether a special value that you can use as a sentinel exists. If all values can occur in the data you need to process, you won't be able to use a sentinel. Maybe it's just possible for one of your colleagues to get a zero mark in an exam even if you wouldn't :-). In the exam mark problem

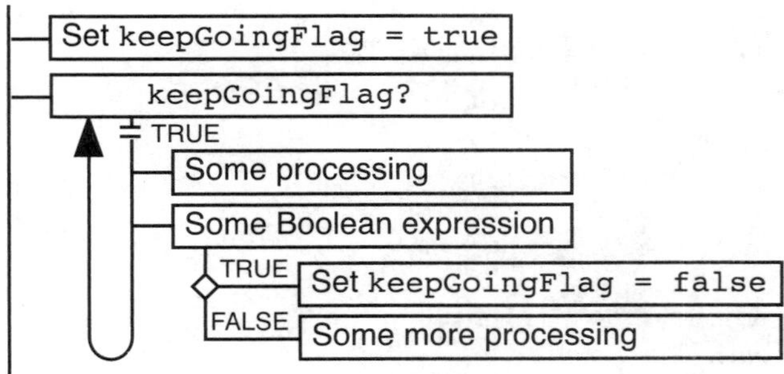

Figure 10.5 Using a flag to terminate a loop

you could perhaps choose another sentinel value (for example, -1), but in other situations you'll have to find an alternative method of terminating the repetition. One alternative is to use a **flag variable** (normally a Boolean) that can be set to indicate that the loop should be terminated. The general design for using a flag variable in a repetition is shown in Figure 10.5

To demonstrate this processing paradigm consider the following problem.

PROBLEM:

Write a program that generates a random integer value and asks the user to guess the nearest integer square root of this value. The guessing must continue until the user gets the right answer.

DESIGN:

The design for the repetition part of this problem closely matches the general design of Figure 10.5, so let's go to the implementation.

IMPLEMENTATION:

```
bool keepGoingFlag;            // Controls the while statement
int  number;
int  answer;
int  seed;

cout << "A number to seed the random number generator: ";
cin  >> seed;
srand(seed);
number = rand();
answer = int(sqrt(double(number)) + 0.5); // Add 0.5 to get
                                          //  to nearest
cout << "Guess the square root of "
     << number << endl << endl;

keepGoingFlag = true;
while (keepGoingFlag)
{
  int guess;

  cout << "Your guess: ";
  cin  >> guess;
  if (guess == answer)
```

```
    {
      cout << "You got it!"   << endl;
      keepGoingFlag = false;            // Flag terminates
                                        //   repetition
    }
    else if (guess < answer)
    {
      cout << "Too low ..."   << endl;
    }
    else
    {
      cout << "Too high ..."  << endl;
    }
  } // end while (...)
```

Terminating repetition statements using `break`

Sometimes when you're programming using `while` or `do` repetition statements, it's impossible to use sentinels to terminate the repetition (since a unique value isn't available), and the structure of your program is such that setting flag variables turns out to add significant complexity to the control flow. What you'd like is some other way of terminating the repetition.

At other times in `for` statements, you may need to terminate the repetition before the natural end of the loop has been reached. For example, if your program is using a `for` statement to search through a list of items for a particular item, you'll want to terminate the search either when the end of the list has been reached or when you've found the required item.

To represent a termination of a repetition or an early exit from a loop you can use the design notation in Figure 10.6, which includes an oval "exit box."

The oval exit loop box means the nearest enclosing repetition is terminated, as if that repetition had terminated normally. In the design in Figure 10.6, if exit loop is reached, the flow of control goes to the box More processing. Note that an exit box can be used with `while`/`do` repetitions as well as with `for` repetitions, as you'll see shortly.

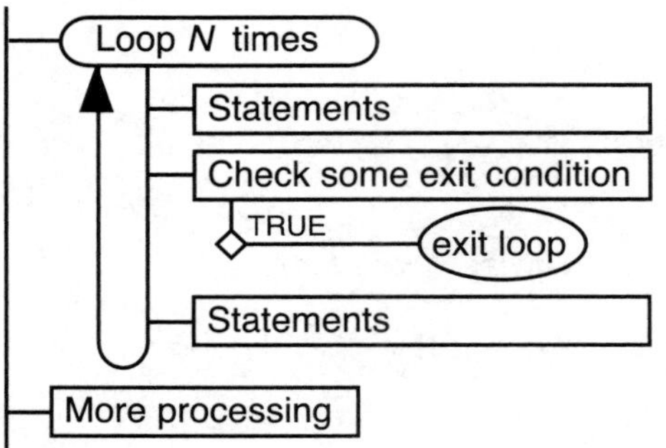

Figure 10.6 Using an exit box to terminate a repetition

Time to take a `break`? Well, time to look at the use of the *built-in* control statement "`break;`" in relation to exiting from repetition statements. You recall that `break` is used to indicate the end of a `case` arm in a `switch` statement, and its execution causes the `switch` statement to terminate and control to pass to the next statement. You can also use "`break;`" inside the compound statement forming the body of `while`, `do` and `for` statements to obtain an early exit from the repetition. If "`break;`" is executed in such a compound statement the repetition statement is terminated and control goes to the next statement after the repetition statement.

Translating the design in Figure 10.6 into pseudo C++ gives the following.

```
for (int i = 0; i < N; i += 1)
{
  Statements;
  if (someExitCondition)
  {
    break;
  }
  Statements;
} // end for
MoreProcessing;
```

Here's a more substantial example.

PROBLEM:

Design a simple program to input a sequence of numbers from the keyboard and to report whether each number is prime or not.

DESIGN:

Rather than use the Sieve algorithm of our old friend Eratosthenes that you saw in Chapters 2 and 3, let's just use a simple design that tries dividing each number to be tested by all integers less than the square root of that number. If an exact division results then the number being checked isn't a prime number. (Can you see why you can stop dividing when a potential divisor is greater than the square root of the number being tested?)

This algorithm is shown in the following design, where the sentinel of any value less than or equal to 2 is used to terminate the outer repetition loop which incorporates input from the keyboard.

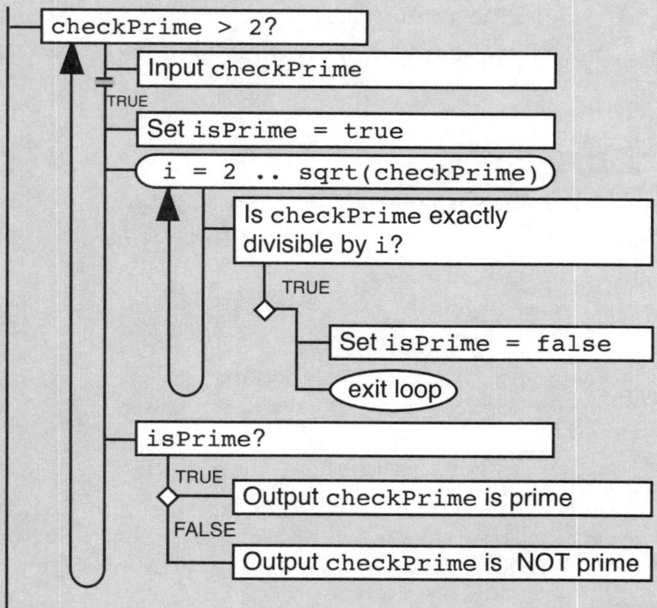

In looking at this design can you see any use of the notation that's different to what you've seen before? Can you see any problem with the first condition being tested (`checkPrime > 2`) and the position of the input action?

Did you notice the position of the lines indicating where the test (`checkPrime > 2`) is evaluated? Unlike all previous examples, it isn't at the start of the repetition (as it would be with a `while` statement) or at the end (as in a `do` statement). This design expresses the idea that the test isn't evaluated until *after* the input action has been completed, and hence there isn't a problem with the design: `checkPrime` isn't being tested before the input action gives it a value. But how do you translate these semantics into C++? The answer is that you can use `break`, as you'll see in a moment.

In the design, notice how the inner loop (trying all divisors less than the square root of the number being checked) has an early exit if an exact divisor is found. There's no point in this loop continuing once you've determined that a number isn't a prime number. However, you also want to test subsequently whether the inner loop has been exited because it terminated normally (in which case the number is prime) or because it terminated early (in which case the number isn't prime). A flag variable (`isPrime`) is set to indicate which of these two possibilities holds true.

IMPLEMENTATION:

Here's a C++ fragment that's the translation of the above design. Take a close look at how the position of the test in the outer repetition statement has been implemented.

```
int  checkPrime = 0;
bool isPrime;

cout << "Input a number <= 2 to terminate the program" << endl;

while (true)
{
  cout << "Input number (> 2) to check for primality: ";
  cin  >> checkPrime;
  if (!(checkPrime > 2))    // Terminate if not > 2
  {
    break;
  }
  isPrime = true;
  for (int i = 2; i <= int(sqrt(double(checkPrime))); i += 1)
  {
```

```
      if ((checkPrime % i) == 0)
      {
        isPrime = false;
        break;
      }
    } // end for (...)
    cout << checkPrime << " is ";
    if (!isPrime)
    {
      cout << "NOT ";
    }
    cout << "a prime number" << endl;
  } // end while (true)
```

Lesson: Use `break` to achieve early termination of a repetition statement.

Breaking out of a repetition statement early can be useful, but it's not a feature you should need to use very often. You may find that its use can be avoided by thinking carefully about the algorithm you're using. For example, its use above to exit from the loop requesting input (`while (true)` ...) could be avoided. We just wanted to show you how you can implement the differently-positioned test if a design really needed this feature.

It's very difficult to be precise about when you should and shouldn't use `break` for getting out of repetition statements. On one hand, when used in the right places, it can simplify your implementation. On the other hand, it's easy to fall into the trap of using `break` simply to cover up a badly-structured design. Sounds like a case for a style rule.

✓ *Use* `break` *for early exit from repetition statements minimally.*

Common programming mistakes

Selection and repetition statements are a common source of programming errors. The dangers of selection statements are associated with getting the Boolean expressions wrong. With multi-way selections, you risk forgetting some of the potential values. We've discussed some defensive programming steps you should take to minimize the effects of such errors.

With repetition statements there are two common mistakes:

1. Infinite loops – a repetition statement that never terminates because its Boolean expression never satisfies the termination condition.
2. Off-by-one errors – a repetition that goes around one too many, or one too few times.

EXAMPLE:

Here are three examples of infinite loops.

```
int i = 1;
while (i == 1)                           // Example 1
{
  cout << "Hello world" << endl;
}
for (;;)                                 // Example 2
{
  cout << "Hello world" << endl;
}
for (i = 1; i < 5; i += 1)               // Example 3
{
  cout << "Hello world" << endl;
  i -= 1;
}
```

Because of the flexibility you have for specifying the starting value and terminating condition in a `for` statement, it's easy to make an off-by-one error in your repetition statements.

EXAMPLE:

You're given the compound statement:

```
{
  cout << "This is a wonderful C++ book." << endl;
}
```

If you wanted the message to be printed out five times, which of the following `for` headings would achieve this effect when attached to the above compound statement?

1. `for (int i = 0; i <  5; i += 1)`
2. `for (int i = 0; i <= 5; i += 1)`
3. `for (int i = 1; i <  5; i += 1)`
4. `for (int i = 1; i <= 5; i += 1)`

If you're not sure of the answer, go through each variant by hand, executing it in the manner in which the computer would, albeit somewhat more slowly! The rules of execution were given in the previous section.

The answer is that loops 1 and 4 both give five executions of the output statement. Loop 2 gives six executions, while loop 3 gives four. Isn't it easy to make an off-by-one error?

So, when you've written a piece of code you should always . . . see the next sub-section for details!

Checking your program

One of the "laws" of software engineering is that the earlier in the engineering process you detect an error, the "cheaper" it's going to be to fix that bug. Detecting an error in your design is best fixed at the design stage rather than much later when you're testing the resulting program. Basically, it's "cheaper" because problems detected at program-testing time involve much more "scrap and rework" than is needed if you detect the problem earlier. While this may not be apparent to you at this stage in your apprenticeship, trust us: it's true in the real world.

EXAMPLE:

Memo From: SoftSoapSoftware Inc.
To: Sellalot Department Store

Please return all of those computer-controlled washing machines that you've sold, so we can fix a bug in Joe Blogg's code!

You should get into the habit of approaching a problem by first constructing a design and then checking that design for the four desirable properties introduced in Chapter 2, namely:

1. The design must produce the desired result.
2. Execution of the algorithm must terminate in a finite time.
3. The design must provide the same result given the same starting conditions – it must be deterministic.
4. The design must be easily translatable into a program.

Lesson: Check your design by going through it by hand, "executing" the actions in the order stated in the design.

Having detected (and fixed!) any mistakes in your design, you then translate your design into C++ (not forgetting to add comments that explain what's going on). It's worth doing some hand-checking again. Play at being a computer: with a piece of paper, draw a box for each variable as and when it's declared, and update the value contained in the variables as dictated by the statements you've written. Then execute the code by hand.

Lesson: Check your C++ code by going through it by hand, "executing" the actions in the order stated.

Once you're happy with the hand-checked version, it's time to compile. The compiler will also check some aspects of your program for you. Be careful when fixing syntax errors, so that you really fix the problem instead of just getting rid of the compiler's error messages. For example, if there's a missing "`}`" make sure that the one you add is in the right place!

EXAMPLE:

```
int total = 0;
for (int i = 1; i <= 3; i += 1)
{
  for (int j = 0; j < 6; j += 2)
  {
    total += i * j;
  }
}
```

total	0 0 2 6 6 10 18 18 24 36
i	1 2 3
j	0 2 4 0 2 4 0 2 4

Then you can do some run-time checking. Ideally, you should choose some test data so that when your program is run with that data, each and every potential path through the program has been executed. However, as you saw at the beginning of this section, there can be an awful lot of paths possible, and for many programs it can be infeasible to check all combinations of all paths. A compromise would be to ensure that each part of the program has been executed at least once. Again, choose input data to try to satisfy this requirement.

Lesson: Test your programs with test data that, ideally, exercises each part of your program (for example, each compound statement).

Finally, when your program is used with real data, don't assume that the answers it produces are correct. Check them to see if any residual bugs have reared their ugly heads.

Stopping your program

As part of your defensive programming strategy, it's often useful to build checks into your programs for unexpected situations. For example, in the selection statement section you saw the following important lesson.

Lesson: Adopt defensive programming strategies wherever possible. Explicitly check for all known values in a multi-way selection and provide a clause to catch unexpected values.

But what should the program do if an unexpected situation is detected? What you probably want is an early termination of the program. Just as you saw in the design notation for early termination of a loop, you can use an oval box to indicate early program termination (Figure 10.7).

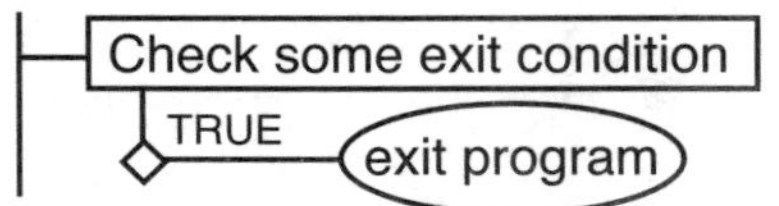

Figure 10.7 Using an exit box to exit a program

Most C++ systems provide a library function, with the following interface, that can be used to exit from a program and return control to the operating system (on some systems the parameter can be used to return an indication of the reason for the termination, a nonzero value indicating an error):

```
void exit(int status);
```

If you're going to use this function, you have to `#include <stdlib.h>` in your program.

Rather than just call this function, it's helpful if your program generates an error message to provide the user (and the person who has to debug the program) with some indication as to why the program has terminated prematurely. That's why you'll see in some of our programs that we use the following function as a means of printing an error message and terminating a program.

```
void error(Text message);
```

If you wish to use this function, you'll need to `#include "error.h"` in your program.

EXAMPLE:

```
#include "error.h"
...
while (someCondition)
```

```
{
  repeatCount += 1;
  if (repeatCount > LIMIT)
  {
    error("Repeated too many times");
  }
  moreProcessing;
}
```

EXERCISES FOR SECTION 10.3

1 A bank wishes to construct its account numbers so that errors in such numbers can be detected. The scheme it adopts is based on adding a check digit to each (unencoded) number, forming an encoded account number. The check digit is formed by treating each digit of the unencoded number as an integer, and adding them together. The check digit is then calculated as the integer that would need to be added to this total in order to make the remainder of dividing the total by 7 equal to 0. The check digit is then appended to the end of the unencoded number to form the encoded version. For example, an unencoded number 11 would be represented by the encoded number 115, since (1 + 1 + 5) is exactly divisible by 7.

Design and implement a program (encode) that permits a user to type in an unencoded number and then calculates and prints out the check digit. The unencoded number can have an unspecified number of digits, and you should read the input as a set of separate characters rather than as a number. Use the sentinel value of a newline character (`'\n'`) to terminate the loop reading the input characters. Assume that the user only types digits (and <Return> at the end of the digits – which is the newline character mentioned above). You might want to use some of the character-processing functions discussed in Chapter 9 (e.g. `isdigit(...)`), and you can use the following code fragments to assist you.

```
char ch;
cin.get(ch);            // Set ch to the next character from cin
                        //   Note: white space is NOT skipped
(int(ch) - int('0'))    // An int expression giving the integer
                        //   corresponding to the digit in ch
```

2 Identify some test values that you would use to test your encode program from Exercise 1.

3 Make your encode program more robust with respect to the characters typed as input, so that it uses a flag variable to terminate the repetition and to indicate whether or not an illegal character was typed by the user.

4 Design and implement a "decode" program that takes an encoded account number as input and reports whether or not that number is a valid number. The program should employ an infinite loop to repeat this task continuously, and should use `break` to exit from the repetition when a blank line is read as input. (Note that this latter requirement means that you'll have to read each encoded number in as separate digits rather than as a complete number.) Try out your decode program with the following two encoded account numbers: `7777` and `7770`. Does the output suggest that a problem has been identified?

5 Work out by hand what the following code sequence produces for various positive integer inputs.

```
int number;

cout << "Type in a number say between 4 and 20: ";
cin  >> number;

for (int step = 2; step <= (number / 2); step += 1)
{
  int cycle = 0;

  cout << "Step " << step << ": ";
  do
  {
    cout << cycle << ' ';
    cycle = (cycle + step) % number;
  } while (cycle != 0);
  cout << cycle << endl;
} // end for step
cout << endl;
```

Write a C++ program that incorporates the above fragment, and execute it to see if the actual sequences produced match the answers you worked out by hand. If there are differences, identify where (and why) you made mistakes in the "by-hand" version. Using the program, what do you notice in general about the sequences of values produced? Can you see any other patterns in the sequences when (a) the `step` value is not a factor of the input `number`; and (b) `number` is a prime number? (You may care to look at Exercise 8 at the end of the chapter after completing this exercise.)

SUMMARY

In this chapter we've introduced the syntax and semantics of the selection and repetition statements in C++. The language details you've covered include

- **selection** how to write single- and multi-way selection statements using `if` statements with/without `else` and `else if` clauses; and how to use the `switch` statement for multi-way selections;
- **while repetition** the `while` statement, which may execute its body zero or more times, being controlled by a Boolean expression that must evaluate to `true` for the repetition to continue; and the `do` statement, also controlled by a Boolean expression, which may execute its body one or more times;
- **for repetition** the `for` statement that provides a flexible construct for controlling loops, and that may execute its body zero or more times; generally controlled by a variable that counts up or down;
- **built-in control** the effects of executing `break;` in `switch` statements to indicate the end of a `case` arm, and to achieve early termination of a repetition statement.

You've seen the syntax for all of the above language features, and of course there have been style rules for you to think about as well. In addition, you've seen some refinements to the design notation to cover:

- **multi-way selections** for the `switch` statement;
- **test evaluation** to capture the exact semantics of the point at which the test controlling a repetition is evaluated (the "=" mark on the looping line);
- **loop box** to capture the three parts in a C++ `for` statement;
- **exit box** for the early termination of a repetition statement or a program.

We've introduced some important software engineering issues in this chapter. You now know about:

- **testing** – selecting test data so you can execute each and every part of a selection statement;

- **defensive programming** – explicitly checking for all known values in a multi-way selection, and providing a clause to catch unexpected values;
- **infinite loops** – the danger of constructing these using repetition statements;
- **off-by-one errors** – the problem of one-too-many or one-too-few repetitions.

Are you beginning to feel like a real software engineer yet? If you've understood selection and repetition statements, you're well on the way. You can now harness the power of a computer to do many more tasks than before. However, there are many more ways of getting your programs wrong! You will have noticed more skull-and-crossbones warnings in this chapter than in earlier chapters.

In fact, having reached this point in your apprenticeship, you've really covered all of the basics of programming. Is there anything left to cover? Well, a few things. In particular, you now need to be shown how to use all of these basics to construct useful software abstractions. So, onto the next chapter that describes how to define functional abstractions in C++.

END-OF-CHAPTER EXERCISES

1 Explain the similarities and differences between (a) a set of `if` statements, the Boolean expressions in which each test for a specific value in an `int` variable; (b) a single statement with a set of `else-if` arms with similar Boolean expressions; and (c) a `switch` statement using the `int` variable as its controlling expression. Describe the situations in which you might adopt one of these alternatives in preference to the others.

2 The C++ Repetition Appreciation Party has suggested that the three existing repetition statements in C++ are abolished and replaced with the following `loop` statement. The `loop` statement can be used in the following way.

```
loop
{
  statement1;
  exitwhen(bool-expression);
  statement2;
}
```

The execution of this statement would be as follows. On entering the compound statement, `statement1` is executed. Then the `bool-expression` of the `exitwhen` statement is evaluated. If the value is `true`, the `loop` statement terminates. If the value is `false`, `statement2` is executed before the flow of control returns to the start of the compound statement and the process repeats. Of course, `statement1` and `statement2` can consist of multiple statements, or be omitted completely, and the `exitwhen` statement can be placed anywhere between the `{` and `}` delineating the `loop` statement's body.

Draw a syntax diagram for this new statement. Can the existing C++ repetition statements be replaced totally by use of the `loop` statement? If they can, show how.

3 Reimplement the Count Tracks program using a `do` statement in place of the `while` statement.

Does this new program behave in exactly the same way as the original? Change the original program and the new implementation to use the CD titled "`Bootlegged 1812`". Do both versions now produce the same answers, and if their answers are different can you explain why?

4 A program is needed that asks the user for an integer number and then prints out that number of "`*`" characters. Before you start implementing, identify some test data, some numbers that you intend to use to test the behavior of any program designed to meet this specification. For each item of test data, specify what the expected output of the program should be. Then construct three versions of the program: a first version of the program that uses a `while` statement to achieve the repeated printing, a second version that uses a `do` statement, and finally, a third version that uses a `for` statement. Test these programs using the test data and report on the results.

5 Change the following piece of code so that the `while` statement is retained but changed from being potentially infinite to one that terminates the repetition after 5 tries.

```
int input = 0;

while (true)
{
  cout << "Type a number between 1 and 5: ";
  cin  >> input;
  if ((input >= 1) && (input <= 5))
  {
    break;              // Break out of the while loop
  }
} // end while (true)
```

6 Design and implement a program that finds the average length of the tracks on N CDs in the collection `CSDiscSet`, where N is an integer typed at the keyboard. (Hint: use member function `nextDisc()` of PDT `CSDiscSet` to obtain the N CDs.)

7 As you've seen in earlier exercises, if a person's body mass index is less than 20 they are underweight; between 20 and 25 their weight is OK; between 25 and 30 they are overweight; and above 30 they are referred to as obese. Extend the Body Mass Index calculating program you constructed in Exercise 4 at the end of Chapter 8 to print out a message indicating what a person's weight category is. You may have produced a design for this in answering Exercise 6 in Section 2.4. Given your new skills with selection statements you may wish to revise that design (or do it for the first time :-). In Exercise 9 at the end of Chapter 8 you produced Boolean expressions for categorizing a calculated index.

Also in Chapter 8's end-of-chapter exercises, you produced components for converting weights in pounds to kilograms, and heights in feet and inches to meters. Use those components to extend your program to allow the user to choose which units they wish to use, and to accept weight and height measurements given in either units.

8 Design and implement a program that uses PDT `Canvas` to draw rosettes. The program should prompt the user for the number of points in the rosette, and draw something like the following.

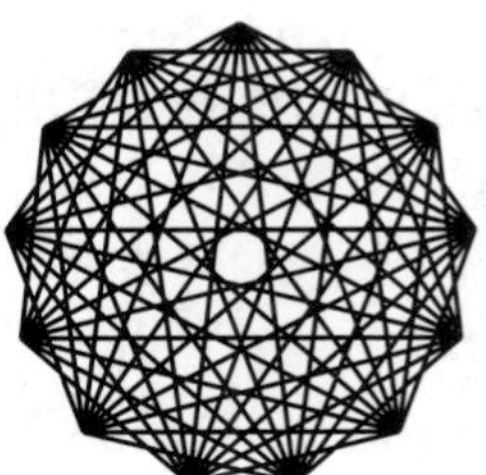

You'll need some elementary trigonometry to work out the coordinates of the points around the circumference of a circle. You then need to draw lines connecting one point to others to produce the effect. To see how you might do this, consider numbering the points in a clockwise direction from the top starting at zero. The first drawing cycle starts from point 0, draws a line from that point to the next-point-but-one, then from there to the next-point-but-one, and so on. If the point to be reached is the starting point, the cycle terminates. The cycle starts by drawing a line from the starting point to the next-point-but-two; the next cycle draws to the next-point-but three, and so on. (Hint: if you've not attempted Exercise 5 in Section 10.3, now might be a good time to do so, and to look at the sequences of numbers produced by the code fragment in that exercise.) Think about the effect you obtain when the number of points in the rosette is a prime number (so, those other programs that generate prime numbers may have some practical use after all!).

9 Design and implement a program that draws a user-specified number of lines on an instance of a `Canvas`, where the coordinates of the points are obtained by using the random number generator functions.

10 Modify your solution to Exercise 9 so that each line is drawn in a random color.

11 Function definitions

OBJECTIVE

To complete the coverage of functions by showing you how to define functions, looking at:

- the difference between a function interface and a function definition;
- how to provide a function definition;
- separation of concerns using header and implementation files;
- multiple uses of a function name;
- recursion.

Function call and implementation

11.0 FUNCTIONAL ABSTRACTION REVISITED

In Chapter 9 we took a detailed look at functional abstraction and used a car maintenance manual to illustrate what is meant by this term.

EXAMPLE:

> ...
> 3 Remove the air cleaner as described in Chapter 3.
> 4 Remove the radiator as described in Chapter 2.
> 5 Loosen the clip and disconnect the top hose from the thermostat housing
> ...

The description of the operations required to remove an engine included high-level-descriptions – functional abstractions – of detailed operations to be found elsewhere in the manual. For example, to take the engine out you need to remove the radiator, and the engine removal instructions included the high-level description "Remove the radiator." Associated with each high-level description there's an indication of where to find the details of that operation: "Remove the radiator as described in Chapter 2." You'd be pretty sore if, on turning to Chapter 2 of the car maintenance manual, you found that the description for radiator removal was missing. You'd expect to find in that chapter a detailed description of the steps you need to take to remove the radiator.

You also saw in Chapter 9 that there are three aspects to functional abstraction:

- *the designers view* – the designer analyzes the problem to recognize functional abstractions and the interfaces that need to be provided for those abstractions;
- *the implementer's view* – the implementer needs to implement the operations that the function should perform and provide a function interface;
- *the user's view* – the user needs to know how to make use of the function interface.

The user of a functional abstraction needs to know three principal things that collectively form the **function interface**:

1. The name of the function.
2. The types of the parameters that the function requires.
3. The type of the value the function returns.

In Chapter 9 we took the user's view and looked in detail at how to make a syntactically correct function call. We did this in the context of library functions, making calls to functions that exist in C++ libraries such as `math.h` and `time.h`. In this chapter we're going to take the implementer's view since you'll want to be able to implement your own functions.

Not surprisingly, there has to be some correlation between the user's view and that of the implementer. The implementer needs to:

1. Provide a sensible name for the operation.
2. Provide a parameter list for information exchange that indicates what is expected and what is returned.
3. Indicate the type of the value that will be returned (maybe `void`).

The user of a function doesn't really care how a function achieves its result, and needs just the details of the interface defined by the implementer. However, the implementer must provide an implementation (C++ code) that represents the detailed instructions of the functional abstraction. Hence the implementer must also:

4. Provide an implementation of the operation – a *function definition*.

This aspect is principally what this chapter is all about. However, there's some more work that the implementer must be prepared to do. There needs to be adequate documentation that describes the function interface and the effect of a function call. We won't be dealing with the documentation aspects of functions, but don't forget it.

We're principally concerned here with non-member (stand-alone) functions, but much of what follows is applicable to member functions too. Member functions will be dealt with formally in the next two chapters.

EXERCISES FOR SECTION 11.0

1 In Exercise 1 of Section 9.0 you were asked to provide interfaces for functional abstractions. Now write (in English) implementations of those abstractions.

2 Design an interface for a functional abstraction to produce a rudimentary drawing of a house. Outline a design for the implementation.

11.1 FUNCTION INTERFACES

As you saw in Chapter 9, a function interface consists of the function return type and the function signature, the latter consisting of the function name and a parameter list. A function signature gives just enough information, and no more, to ensure that any call to the function can be checked for legality by the compiler. The compiler will also use the return type to check that the position of the function call is legal with respect to that type.

EXAMPLE

You'll find the following function interfaces in `math.h`.

```
double sqrt(double x);
double log(double x);
double exp(double x);
double sin(double x);
double cos(double x);
double atan(double x);
double fabs(double x);
```

You've already seen plenty of function interfaces, so you should be ready to go straight into the syntax associated with them. Since you know that a function call must match a function signature, much of the syntax associated with a function signature mirrors the syntax for a function call.

A **function interface** followed by a semicolon is a form of **compilation unit**.

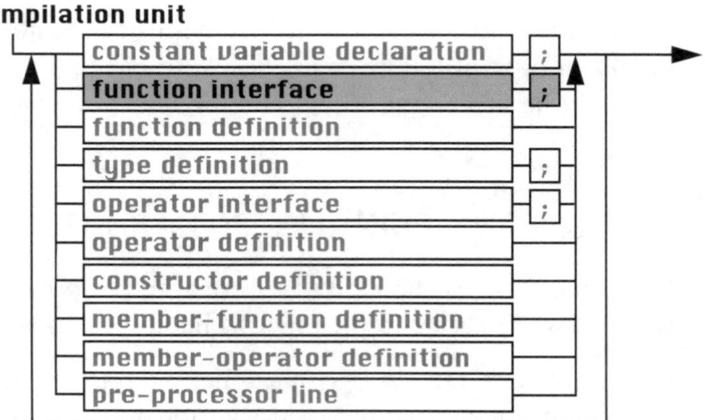

A **compilation unit** is a section of C++ code that, in the absence of syntax errors, will result in a successful compilation. You can submit a file containing function interfaces only to a compiler to check that the interfaces are syntactically correct. But can you run such a "program"? No; you'll recall that a **simple C++ program** requires, among other things, a `main()` program. You'll see later in this chapter just where `main()` fits into the picture and how compilation units are combined to produce a program that can be compiled, linked, and run.

A **function interface** consists of the return type followed by a **function signature**:

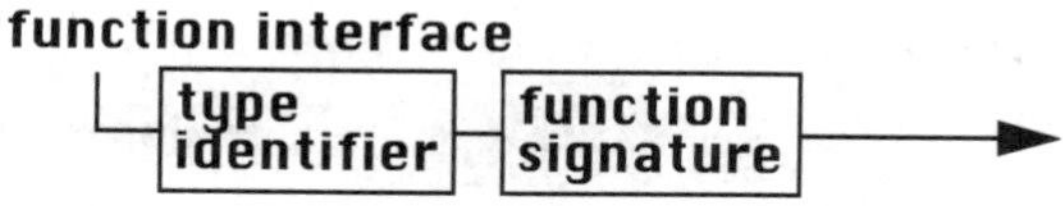

and a **function signature** consists of the function name followed by the **formal parameter list**:

So a **function signature** is similar to a **function call**, the syntax of which you saw in Chapter 9. The difference is that the **formal parameter list** in a **function signature** is replaced by the **actual parameter list** in a **function call**. An **actual parameter list** in a **function call** is just a (possibly empty) comma-separated list of **actual parameter**s; similarly, the **formal parameter list** in a **function signature** is just a (possibly empty) comma-separated list of **formal parameter**s:

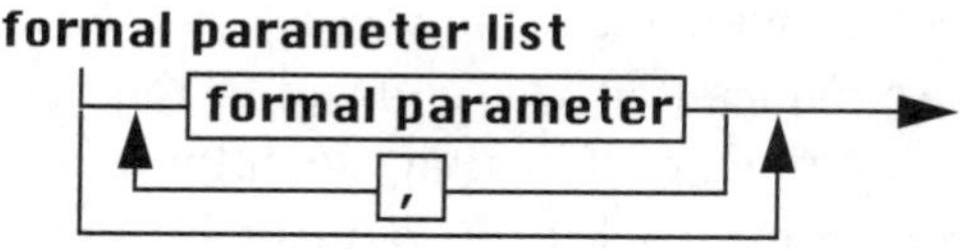

An **actual parameter** in a **function call** can be either an **actual value parameter** or an **actual reference parameter**, and it follows that a **formal parameter** can be either a **formal value parameter** or a **formal reference**

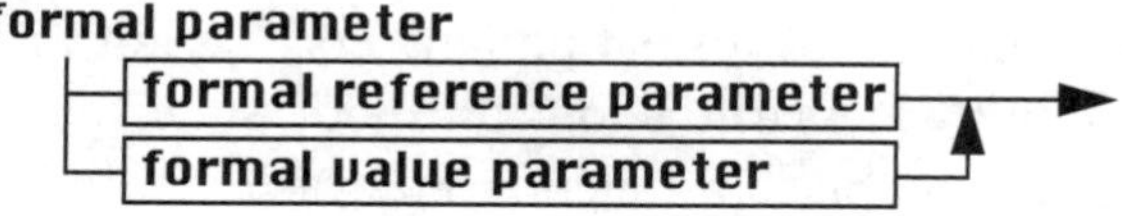

parameter.

From the signatures you've seen, you should be able to recognize that the form of a **formal value parameter** is identical to that of a **variable declara-**

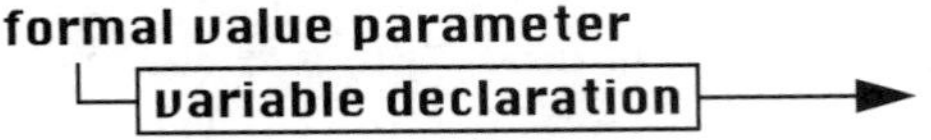

tion.

A **formal reference parameter** looks like a **variable declaration** too,

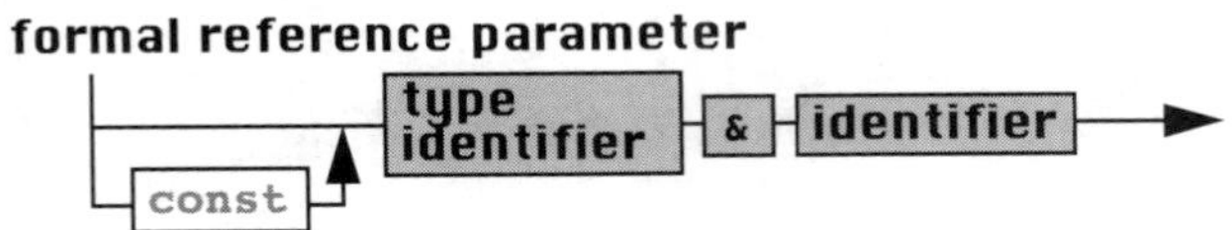

except that the type of the parameter is followed by an ampersand.

So the key, and only, difference between a **formal reference parameter** and a **formal value parameter** is the `&`.

What's the point of the formal parameter list? It indicates the number and type of the parameters that need to appear in an actual call, and indicates which are reference parameters and which are value parameters. It categorizes the form of the information exchange that takes place in a function call, and tells the user of the function what values to provide to the function and what values to expect back. Strictly speaking, this requires the specification of types only, but we've said that a formal parameter list should additionally provide a name for each parameter. This isn't absolutely necessary, as you may have noticed if you've looked at some of the standard library function header files but, as you'll see in the next section, you're going to have to provide names in a function definition, so you may as well provide names in a function interface too. This gives you the opportunity to use names that will indicate to the caller of the function (and to you, the implementer of the function) something about the information being exchanged, such as `radius`, for the radius of a circle, or `message` for a `Text` message, just as you would use meaningful names for any other identifiers.

✓ *Choose names for formal parameters that indicate the purpose of those parameters.*

Any function interfaces to be found in libraries we've provided always give meaningful names for formal parameters. It's not our fault if the standard C++ libraries don't necessarily adopt this good style rule.

Where do you place a function interface in your program? You know that a variable declaration must precede any use of that variable. Similarly, a function interface must precede any call to that function and the compiler will object if

Lesson: A function interface must precede any call to that function.

you don't follow this basic rule.

So a function interface can appear in any position that a variable declaration can appear? Strictly speaking, yes, but like constant variable declarations we suggest that you make all function interfaces global for reasons that we'll justify in Section 11.5.

✓ *A function interface should be placed in global scope above* `main()`.

Are there any other style rules associated with function interfaces that you should follow? Just as there are style rules for function calls (Section 9.2), so there are corresponding style rules for function interfaces too.

✓ *The opening parenthesis should follow the function identifier with no space in between.*

✓ *There should be no space between the final formal parameter and the closing parenthesis.*

✓ *There should be one space between the type of a formal parameter and the name of the parameter.*

✓ *The comma separating one formal parameter from another should immediately follow the identifier that precedes it. There should then be one space between the comma and the next formal parameter.*

✓ *Long parameter lists should be continued on following lines. Each line (except the last) should end with a comma separator. Subsequent lines should be indented so that the start lines up with the start of the first parameter on the first line.*

✓ *If a formal parameter is a formal reference parameter, the* `&` *should be regarded as part of the type of that parameter and hence placed imme-*

EXAMPLE:

Here are examples of some function interfaces that follow these style rules.

```
void   printMessage(Text message);
void   drawSquare(Canvas& picture, int sideLength);
```

```
void   swap(int& first, int& second);
double areaOfTriangle(double side1, double side2, double side3);
int    nFactorial(int n);
bool   drawLine(Canvas& picture, int startX, int startY,
                int endX, int endY);
```

diately after the type identifier.

By placing these function interfaces before `main()` you'll be able to make calls to these functions inside `main()`. That is, at least as far as the compiler is concerned you'll be able to make calls to these functions. But don't be surprised if you get an error at link time. A function interface introduces a function, but doesn't give it a "value." You need to make available at link time a *function definition* that defines what detailed instructions are to be performed when a function call is made.

1 EXERCISES FOR SECTION 11.1

Define a C++ interface for a function that produces a rudimentary drawing of
2 a house (Exercise 2 of Section 11.0).

Define an interface for a function that indicates if an integer is odd, and another function that indicates if a character is a lower-case vowel.

11.2 FUNCTION DEFINITIONS

A **function definition** in C++ has two components:

- a **function interface** – that specifies the function name, a formal parameter list indicating a name and type for each formal parameter, and the return type;
- a function body – a **compound statement** that specifies the set of statements to be executed when the function is called.

EXAMPLE:

Let's look at a simple example of a function definition by going all the way back to your first C++ program. Do you remember it? It's the one that performed some simple output. Here's a reminder of what the program looks like.

```
#include <iostream.h>

int main()
{
  cout << "Hello" << endl;
  cout << "Your name" << endl;
  cout << "Welcome to CS1" << endl;
  return 0;
} // end main()
```

We've modified the program a little so that each statement outputs a new line as well as a character string. Suppose that you want to ensure that every time you output a character string a new line is output. Here's a definition for a function that achieves the required result.

```
void printMessage(Text message)
{
  cout << message << endl;
  return;
} // end printMessage()
```

Here are some examples of calls to this function that could be used to replace the output statements in the above program.

```
printMessage("Hello");
printMessage("Your name");
printMessage("Welcome to CS1");
```

This is captured by the following syntax diagram.

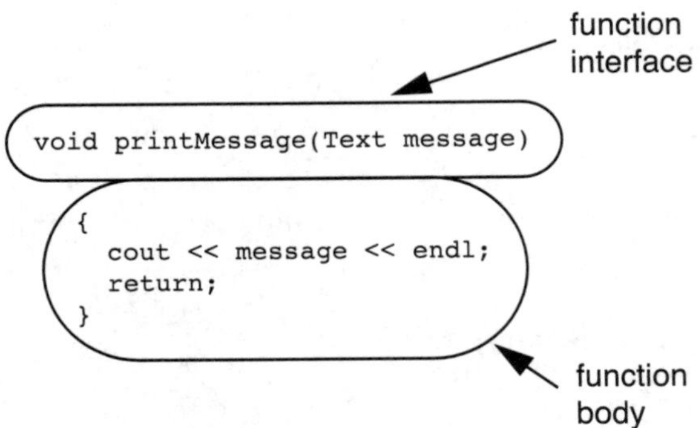

Figure 11.1 Function definition for `printMessage...`

As shown in Figure 11.1, the function definition for `printMessage (...)` contains a function interface:

```
void printMessage(Text message)
```

(without a semicolon) and a compound statement for the function body:

```
{
  cout << message << endl;
  return;
}
```

Disappointingly, a function body doesn't have arms and legs. A function body is just a boring old compound statement, a collection of statements bracketed by the braces `{` and `}`. As with any compound statement, any variables declared inside a function body go out of scope when the end of the function body is encountered. In our simple example, there aren't any locally declared variables in the compound statement. In fact, the formal parameter `message` is a local variable whose scope extends over the whole of the function body; we'll discuss this in depth shortly.

The function body of our example just contains two statements, the first of which:

```
cout << message << endl;
```

outputs the contents of the `Text` string identified by the formal parameter called `message`. When executed, the second statement:

```
return;
```

indicates that the function call has completed and that a return should be made to the point in your program at which the function call was made. Since the result type of `printMessage(...)` is `void`, the function call followed by a semicolon is a statement, and so completion of the function call simply transfers the flow of control to the statement following that call.

OK, so you now know what a function definition looks like, but where do you put it in your program? First observe that a **function definition** is another example of a **compilation unit**.

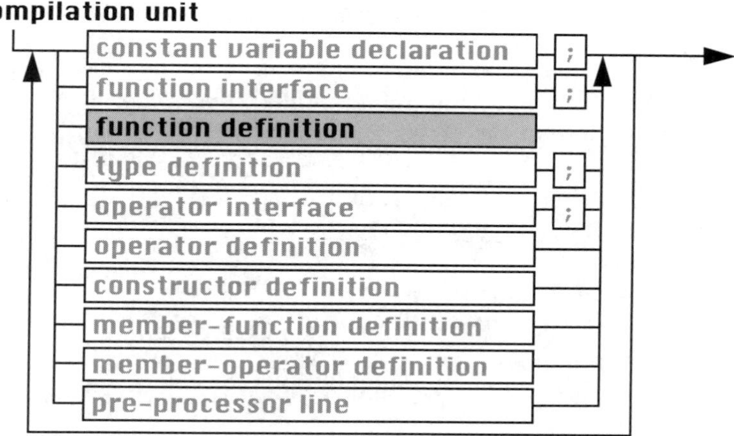

Since a function definition terminates with the closing brace } of a compound statement, there's no semicolon after that brace, just as there's no semicolon after the compound statement of a repetition or selection statement.

Because a function definition is just a compilation unit, in the absence of syntax errors you can successfully compile a function definition. In general, though, you still don't have a complete "program" that will successfully link and execute.

There's a single exception to "in general," though. Can you think what it is?

Every executable program must have a definition of the function `main()`, which is a rather special function, but it's a function for all that. So you've been writing function definitions all along, even if you weren't aware of the fact.

If you make a call to a function then C++ insists only that a function interface is available at compile-time; the corresponding function definition only needs to be available at link-time.

Lesson: Object code for function definitions is required at link-time only.

Does this mean that function definitions can't appear globally before `main()`? No. You can put them there if you want to, and then you don't need a separate function interface. However, there are good software engineering reasons, which we'll return to later, why you shouldn't put function definitions above `main()`. So where should a function definition go instead? After `main()` will do for now, even if this means that function definitions are available at compile-time.

✗ *Don't put function definitions above* `main()`.

EXAMPLE:

Applying the above style rule, an alternative version of that first program to print a simple message is:

```
#include <iostream.h>
#include "Text.h"

// Interface of printMessage
void printMessage(Text message);

int main()
{
  printMessage("Hello");
  printMessage("Your name");
  printMessage("Welcome to CS1");
  return 0;
} // end main()

// Definition of printMessage
void printMessage(Text message)
{
  cout << message << endl;
  return;
} // end printMessage()
```

Looks neat, huh? Not especially, but the point is to show you where function definitions may go, not to encourage you to output a new line after printing a text string.

As indicated in the previous section, our style rule for the placement of function interfaces implies that they should be global, but it's a style rule only, not a syntax rule. The compiler won't complain if you put a function interface inside a function definition. In particular you can put a function interface inside `main()`

if you really want to, as long as the interface is placed before any call to that function. But can a function definition be placed inside `main()`? No! The syntax rules of C++ say that a function definition cannot be placed inside the body of some other function definition. In particular, no function definition can be placed inside the definition of `main()`.

Lesson: Function definitions can't be nested. You can't have a function definition in the body of some other function definition.

Now you know what a function definition looks like, and where to place it. Are you ready to define your own functions yet? Well, since you've been writing definitions for `main()` right from the start you ought to be ready by now! However, there's an important feature of function definitions that you've not yet exploited: making use of the formal parameters in a function definition.

Parameters

You know from Chapter 9 that parameters provide a mechanism for information exchange between a function call and the function implementation. In particular, a value parameter provides a mechanism for a function call to pass information to a function.

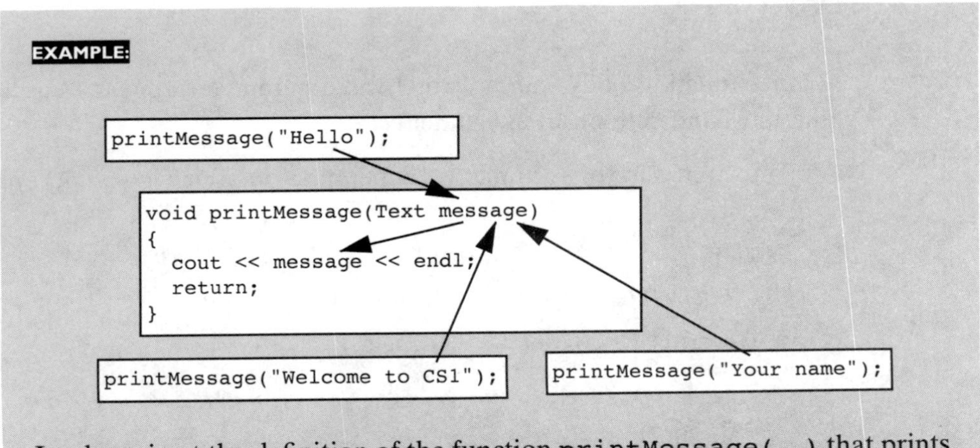

Look again at the definition of the function `printMessage(...)` that prints out the value of its `Text` formal parameter `message`. But what is this value? On the first call of `printMessage(...)` the actual parameter is the `Text` string `"Hello"`, and so this value is assumed by the formal parameter `message`. Hence the `Text` string `Hello` is printed. On the second call of `printMessage(...)` the formal parameter `message` is assigned a different value; this time it's `"Your name"`, and so it's this string that is output. The value of the actual parameter changes again on the third call, and so, correspondingly, does the value of the formal parameter `message`.

A formal value parameter acts like a local variable whose scope extends throughout the body of the function definition. When a function call is made this local variable is assigned a copy of the value of the actual parameter. Inside the body of a function you can write whatever code you like involving the identifier corresponding to a formal value parameter, subject to the constraints of the type of that parameter. For example, if there's an output operator for the type you can output the value represented by the identifier. In fact, the identifier may appear anywhere a normal variable identifier may appear.

Lesson: A formal value parameter is in scope throughout the function body.

Lesson: When a function call is made a formal value parameter is initialized to the value of the corresponding actual parameter.

In a function body, can a formal value parameter appear as a destination on the left-hand side of an assignment?

Unfortunately (or fortunately, depending on your viewpoint), yes, it can.

EXAMPLE:

The following function definition is perfectly valid, if a little bizarre.

```
void printFordColor(Text message)
{
  message = "Model T Ford: Color is Black";
  cout << message << endl;
  return;
} // end printFordColor()
```

No matter what the value of the actual parameter, any call to the function `printFordColor(...)` results in the message `Model T Ford: Color is Black` being printed.

So, the name of a formal value parameter may appear on the left-hand side of an assignment, but it's important to recognize that the effect of assignment is local to the function body only. There's a consequent change to the value of the variable representing the formal parameter, but the value of the actual parameter does not change.

Lesson: A statement in a function body can change the value of a formal value parameter but the effect is local to the function body.

EXAMPLE:

Consider the following sequence.

```
Text myCar = "Model T Ford: Color is Red";
cout << myCar << endl;
printFordColor(myCar);
cout << myCar << endl;
```

The character string `"Model T Ford: Color is Red"` is assigned to the variable `myCar` and then the value of `myCar` is printed. Although `myCar` is passed to `printFordColor(...)` as the actual parameter, the string `"Model T Ford: Color is Black"` is printed. On completion of the function call, the value of `myCar` is again printed. Since this variable remains unchanged as a result of the function call, the string `"Model T Ford: Color is Red"` is output.

OK, so now you know how to use value parameters in a function definition. What about reference parameters? A formal reference parameter is like a formal value parameter in that it's a variable with scope local to the function body. Anything you can do with a formal value parameter in the function body you can do with a formal reference parameter too. However, in Chapter 9 we said that an actual reference parameter must be a **destination**, such as the name of a variable. The reason for this is that an actual reference parameter and its associated formal reference parameter are synonymous; both the formal and actual parameters refer to the same variable. Any changes made in a function body to the value of a formal reference parameter are, automatically, also made to the value of the actual reference parameter.

EXAMPLE:

Suppose that you wanted a function to read a person's first name and their surname as a single character string, separated by a space. Let's define a function `readName(...)` with a single (reference) parameter of type `Text` that's used to get a value back. Here's the interface:

```
void readName(Text& name)
```

The ampersand is there to indicate a reference parameter, so any change made inside the function body to the formal parameter `name` is automatically made to the corresponding actual parameter. Hence the following code could be used to read in three names (each consisting of a first name and a surname).

```
Text firstPerson;
Text secondPerson;
Text thirdPerson;
readName(firstPerson);
readName(secondPerson);
readName(thirdPerson);
```

The function body for `readName(...)` needs to assign a value to the formal parameter `name`, leading to the function definition.

```
void readName(Text& name)
{
  Text firstName;
  Text surname;

  cin >> firstName >> surname;
  name = firstname + " " + surname;
  return;
} // end readName()
```

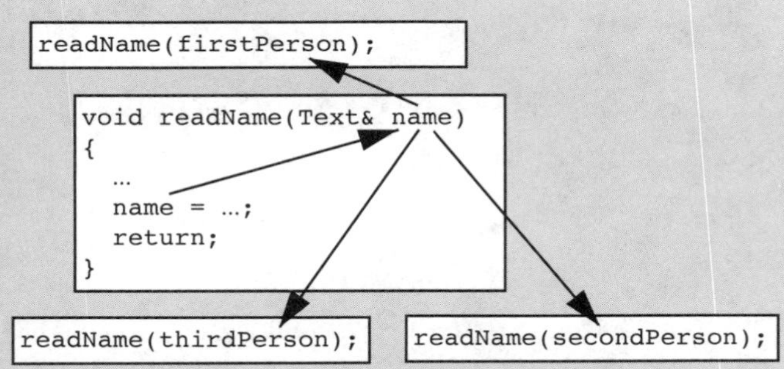

Look back at the three calls to the function `readName(...)` given above. In the first call, the identifier for the actual parameter is `firstPerson`. When the call is made the value assigned to the formal parameter `name` is a character string assembled from the first name and surname read from the keyboard. Since `firstPerson` and `name` represent the same variable during this call, `firstPerson` has this value when the function call is complete. On the second call, the name of the actual parameter is `secondPerson`. Now `secondPerson` and `name` are synonymous, and so when the function call terminates `secondPerson` has the value assigned to `name` in the function definition. A third call gives `thirdPerson` yet another value.

Lesson: A formal reference parameter and the corresponding actual reference parameter refer to the same variable.

The example function definitions we've given illustrate how parameters can be used to supply values to a function and return values from a function. With `printMessage(...)` the actual parameter is a value parameter and must be capable of giving a value of type `Text`. Hence the actual parameter could be a `Text` literal, or a variable of type `Text` that has previously been assigned a value, or any form of expression that gives a `Text` value. In contrast the actual parameter of `readMessage(...)` is a reference parameter and hence can only be a **destination** – a variable of type `Text`.

EXAMPLE:

The following calls to `printMessage(...)` are all valid.

```
Text  greeting = "Hi";
CDisc nextDisc;

printMessage("Hello");
printMessage(greeting);
printMessage("Hi" + " " + "Ho");
printMessage(Text('A'));
// Get a disc
printMessage(nextDisc.title());
```

However, the following function call will give rise to a compile-time error.

```
readMessage("Hello"); // error
```

With the function `readMessage(...)` it's not necessary for the actual parameter to have a value prior to the call. However, you may wish to write a function body that uses the value of the formal reference parameter before assigning a new value to it, in which case the corresponding actual parameter must have been assigned a value prior to the call.

EXAMPLE:

```
void multiplyByFactor(int& number, int factor)
{
  number *= factor;
  return;
} // end multiplyByFactor()
```

Here the value of the formal reference parameter is updated using multiplication by the value parameter, so the actual reference parameter is expected to have a value prior to the call.

The difference between value and reference parameters was summarized by a lesson in Chapter 9. The lesson is worth repeating.

Lesson: An actual value parameter may be any form of **expression**. An actual reference parameter must be a **destination**, such as a variable identifier.

In a function interface you can have as many formal/actual parameters as you need, using value/reference parameters as appropriate. Is the order in which the parameters appear important? No, in that you can have value and reference parameters in any order in a function interface, but yes, it does matter that the actual parameters used in a function call follow the same order.

EXAMPLE:

```
int n = 2;
int m = 3;

multiplyByFactor(n, m);
cout << n << " times "  << m << " is " << n << endl;
multiplyByFactor(m, n);
cout << m << " times "  << n << " is " << m << endl;
```

Let's have a look at a complete design and implementation of a functional abstraction.

Putting it all together: a worked example

PROBLEM:

Design and implement a function that draws a square on a `Canvas` variable.

DESIGN:

The design for drawing a square was given in Figure 4.9 in Chapter 4. There's some code in Section 9.2 that achieves the required result, so make use of that code. All you have to do is wrap the set of `Canvas` member-function calls up inside the compound statement of a function definition and then design and write an appropriate function interface. If you've completed Exercise 2 of Section 9.0 you may have deduced that a suitable interface would involve parameters for the `Canvas` variable on which the square is to be drawn and an `int` parameter specifying the length of the sides of the square. Since the effect of a function call is to change the "value" of the actual `Canvas` parameter it should be a reference parameter. In contrast the parameter specifying the side length is only providing information to the function, and therefore should be a value parameter.

IMPLEMENTATION:

```
void drawSquare(Canvas& picture, int sideLength)
{
  // Code to draw a square
  picture.penDown();
  picture.moveRelative(sideLength, 0);
  picture.moveRelative(0, sideLength);
  picture.moveRelative(-sideLength, 0);
  picture.moveRelative(0, -sideLength);
  picture.penUp();
  return;
} // end drawSquare()
```

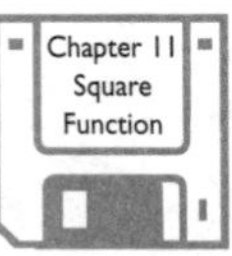

Having defined a function to draw a square on a `Canvas` variable, you can now use that function to draw some simple shapes.

PROBLEM:

Write a section of code that draws a square window with four square panes on a `Canvas` variable; that is, draw four squares symmetrically arranged within an enclosing square.

DESIGN:

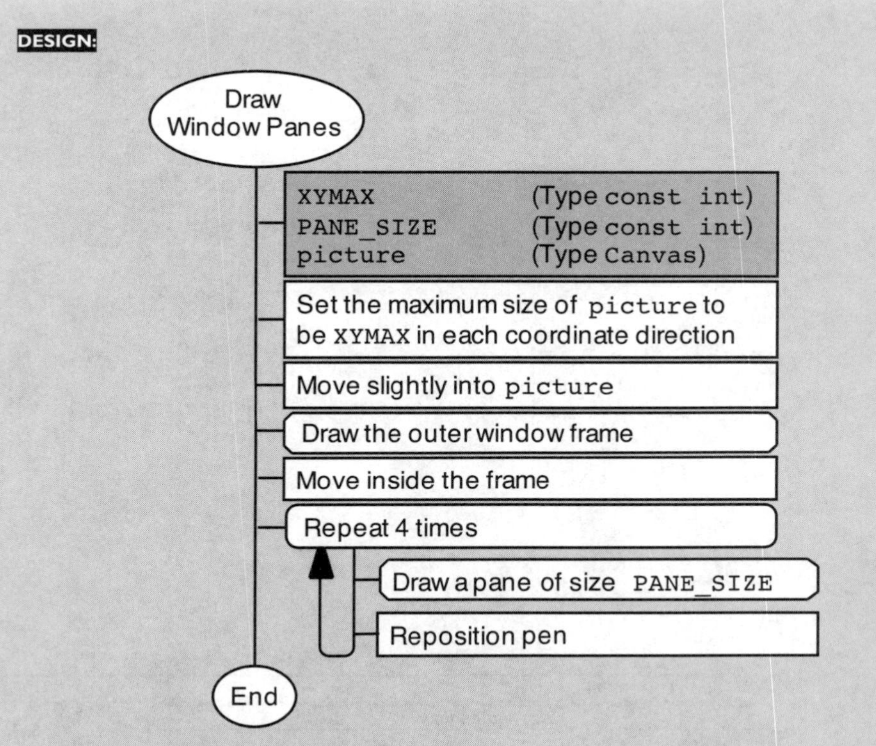

IMPLEMENTATION:

The key issues here are getting the sizes of the squares and the start positions right in each case.

```
const int BORDER    = 10;
const int XYMAX     = 200;
const int PANE_SIZE = (XYMAX - 5 * BORDER)/2;

Canvas myPicture;

picture.setSize(XYMAX, XYMAX);
picture.penUp();
picture.moveTo(BORDER, BORDER);          // Move slightly
                                         //   into the canvas
drawSquare(picture, XYMAX - 2 * BORDER); // Draw outer
                                         //   frame
picture.moveRelative(BORDER, BORDER);    // Move inside
                                         //   frame
for (int pane = 0, pane < 4; pane += 1)
```

```
{
  drawSquare(picture, PANE_SIZE);          // Draw a pane
                                           // Reposition pen
  if (pane == 0)                              // right
  {
    picture.moveRelative(PANE_SIZE + BORDER, 0);
  }
  else if (pane == 1)                        // up
  {
    picture.moveRelative(0, PANE_SIZE + BORDER);
  }
  else if (pane == 2)                        // left
  {
    picture.moveRelative(- (PANE_SIZE + BORDER), 0);
  }
} // end for (...)
```

OUTPUT:

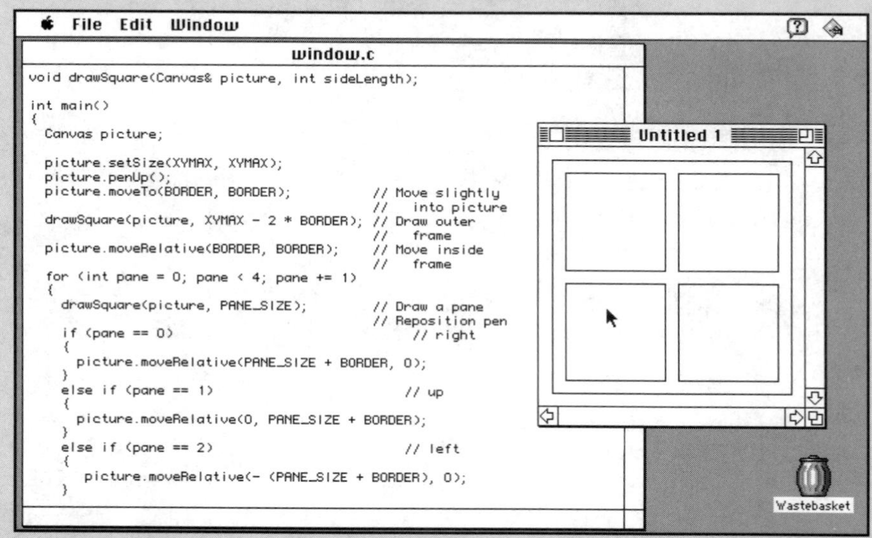

Software engineering issues

Since C++ is a strongly-typed language, you can rely on the compiler to check that the types of formal and actual parameters match, subject to implicit type coercions being used where necessary. But don't expect the compiler to be able to check that values supplied as actual parameters are sensible. You should build mechanisms into your code wherever possible so that invalid situations are recognized. Employ the software engineering technique of defensive programming that was introduced in the previous chapter. With respect to function definitions, one aspect of defensive programming is to build checks into your code that determine whether the values supplied to actual value parameters (and reference parameters, if appropriate) are suitable.

Lesson: A function definition should check values supplied as actual parameters.

DESIGN:

What if in the above code the second actual parameter to `drawSquare(...)` was wrong? Well, you'd get the wrong picture for a start. But what if you used a negative value as an actual parameter? Would `drawSquare(...)` draw a negative square? Should you regard passing a negative value as an error and recognize and report it?

As the implementer of `drawSquare(...)` you could check the value of `sideLength` and take appropriate action if it's negative. Let's add a third parameter (a reference parameter) to `drawSquare(...)` that, on completion of the function call, can be used to check that the call was "successful" in the sense that the value supplied as a second actual parameter was positive.

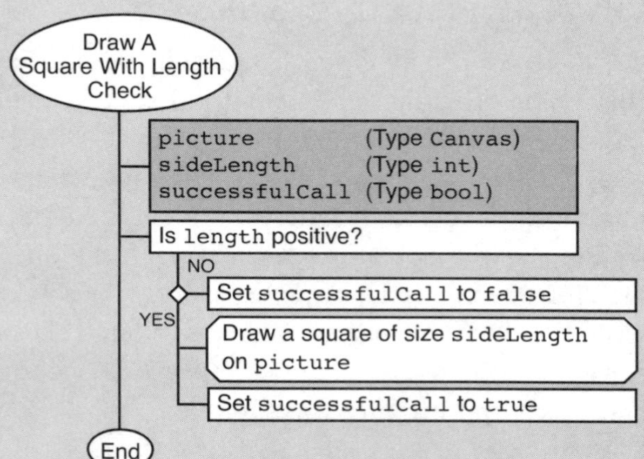

IMPLEMENTATION:

```
void drawSquare(Canvas& picture, int sideLength,
                bool& successfulCall)
{
  if (sideLength <= 0)
  {
    successfulCall = false;
  }
  else
  {
    picture.penDown();
    picture.moveRelative(sideLength, 0);
    picture.moveRelative(0, sideLength);
    picture.moveRelative(-sideLength, 0);
    picture.moveRelative(0, -sideLength);
    picture.penUp();
    successfulCall = true;
  }
  return;
} // end drawSquare()
```

In the above implementation, the third formal parameter, `successfulCall`, of `drawSquare (...)` is a reference parameter because it's returning a value: a Boolean flag indicating success or failure of the function call, where failure means an invalid value was provided for `sideLength`. After a call to `drawSquare (...)`, a test of the value of this parameter should be made before proceeding.

EXAMPLE:

Here's a section of code that makes a call to the latest version of `drawSquare(...)` and prints a message if the call was unsuccessful.

```
Canvas myPicture;
bool   success;
int    squareSideLength;

cin >> squareSideLength;
drawSquare(myPicture, squareSideLength, success);
if (!success)
{
  error("Call to drawSquare failed");
}
```

Reference parameters are clearly useful since they allow you to pass values back from a function body. Why not make `sideLength` a reference parameter in the interface to `drawSquare(...)` too? Wouldn't it simplify matters if all parameters were reference parameters?

There are some trade-offs associated with value and reference parameters that suggest both types are useful in appropriate circumstances.

Value versus reference parameters

There are good reasons for using value parameters. A value parameter:

- provides a safeguard in that a function body can't change a variable acting as an actual parameter;
- permits the use of a general expression (including a literal) as an actual parameter.

On the face of it, the rules of when to use a value parameter and when to use a reference parameter appear to be as follows.

✓ *If the parameter is being used to pass a value to a function only, make it a value parameter.*

✓ *If the parameter is being used to get a value back from a function (possibly in addition to passing a value to a function), make it a reference parameter.*

However, there's a potential drawback to using value parameters which won't become clear to you until you've covered a little more C++. To give you a flavor of what the difficulties are, recall that the use of a value parameter involves a copy of the value of the actual parameter being made. In contrast, with a reference parameter no copy is made since the actual and formal parameters represent the same variable. Copying of an actual value parameter incurs some overhead: a memory overhead for storing the copy, and a time overhead for making the copy. If the parameter is an `int`, these overheads aren't going to have much effect, but you'll see later, in Chapter 14 in particular, that sometimes the overheads can be considerable. So what do you do? Retain the security advantages of value parameters at the cost of space/time efficiency, or lose those advantages in pursuit of a program that has minimal demands on resources?

Fortunately, there's an alternative to value and reference parameters that can get you out of this dilemma; it's a **constant reference parameter**. In a function signature, a constant reference parameter is just like a reference parameter, but the type identifier is preceded by `const`. A constant reference parameter acts like a reference parameter in that no copy is made of the actual parameter. However, you're not allowed to change the value of the formal parameter in the function body; you'll get a compile-time error if, for example, the formal parameter appears on the left-hand side of an assignment operator in the function body.

EXAMPLE:

Return to the function:

```
void printMessage(Text message)
```

The fact that a value parameter has been used here means that when a function call is made, a copy of the actual parameter is made to the formal parameter. If the actual parameter is a very long message, then the overheads may be significant.

Let's make the parameter a constant reference parameter.

```
void printMessage(const Text& message)
```

Despite the fact that some form of reference parameter is involved here, you can still use any form of expression producing a `Text` value as an actual parameter.

We need another style rule.

✓ *If a parameter is being used to pass a value to a function only, and the overheads associated with making the parameter a value parameter are considerable, then use a constant reference parameter instead.*

Let's update the syntax diagram for a **reference parameter**, taking into account that the type identifier may be preceded by the keyword `const`.

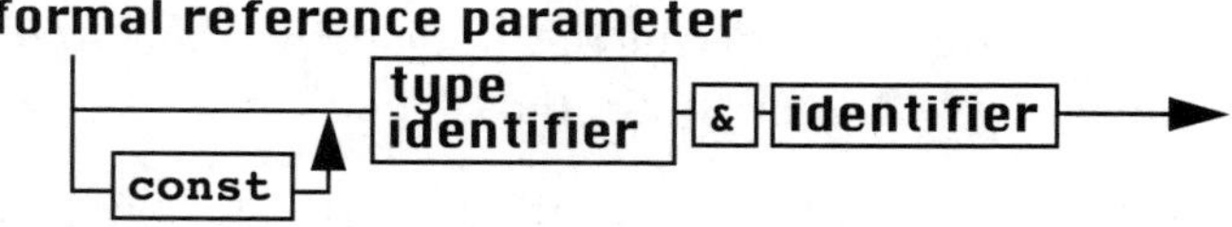

So far we've had very little to say about the `return;` statement, other than it terminates a function call. It's about time we looked at this programming construct in more detail, and explained the relationship between `return;` and the so-far mysterious `return 0;` statement that appears at the end of `main()`.

EXERCISES FOR SECTION 11.2

1 What happens to the window-drawing program of this section if you make the `Canvas` parameter of `drawSquare(...)` a value parameter?

2 Provide an implementation for the function `drawRectangle(...)`, with interface

```
void drawRectangle(Canvas& picture, int longSide,
                   int shortSide,   bool& successfulCall)
```

3 Consider the code fragments below. In these fragments the ####### are to be replaced by one of the following four formal parameter specifications.

(i) `int number` (ii) `int& aNumber` (iii) `int aNumber`
(iv) `const int& aNumber`

What will the program output for each of these?

```
void aFunction(#######);        // Function Interface

int main()
{
  int aNumber = 123;

  aFunction(aNumber);
  cout << "aNumber contains the value: " << aNumber << endl;
  return 0;
} // end main()
```

```
void aFunction(#######)
{
  aNumber = 456;
  return;
} // end aFunction()
```

4 In Exercise 5 at the end of Section 10.2 you implemented a program for drawing a textual "Christmas tree." Revisit that program and identify where you could use functions to assist in the implementation. Implement those functions and change the program to use those functions.

5 Add further checks to `drawSquare(...)` so that `successfulCall` is additionally set to `false` if an attempt to draw the square would go outside the `Canvas` window.

11.3 FUNCTION RETURN STATEMENT

What would happen if you left the `return` statement out of the function definitions of the previous section? Would you get a compile-time error? Or a run-time error? Or would the effect be "No effect"?

The correct answer is that when the return type of a function is `void` (as it is in all of the examples of the previous section, with the single exception of `main()`) and you leave the `return` statement out then it doesn't make any difference to the outcome. If inside a function definition the sequence of control reaches the end of the compound statement that forms the function body, a `return` statement is "assumed" and the function call terminates as if the `return` statement were there.

So why did we put a `return` statement at the end of each function body? Partly because we wanted to make it clear that termination of the execution of a function body returns the flow of control to the point at which the function call was made. Furthermore, there are certain situations that you'll see shortly in which termination must be via an explicit `return` statement, otherwise you'll get a compile-time error.

In addition, sometimes you'll want to terminate the execution sequence of a function body with a `return` statement that isn't the final statement of a function body, so making all points of exit clear is good practice. Getting into the habit of indicating where in the function body the function execution sequence should terminate is a good idea.

Lesson: The execution sequence of a function body should always be terminated by a `return` statement.

The effect of `return` is similar to `break`. Just as `break` can be used to terminate the execution of a loop or while repetition statement, or a multi-way selection statement, `return` can be used to terminate execution of a function. This can be represented using a variation of the design notation introduced in Figure 10.6 for exiting a program.

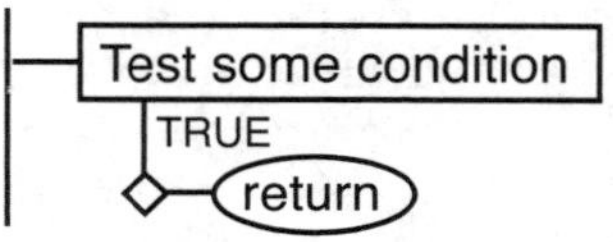

Let's return to the problem of drawing a square to illustrate some of these issues.

PROBLEM:

Redesign `drawSquare(...)` so that if the test that checks `sideLength` finds that a negative value has been supplied, then the execution of the function body terminates immediately.

DESIGN:

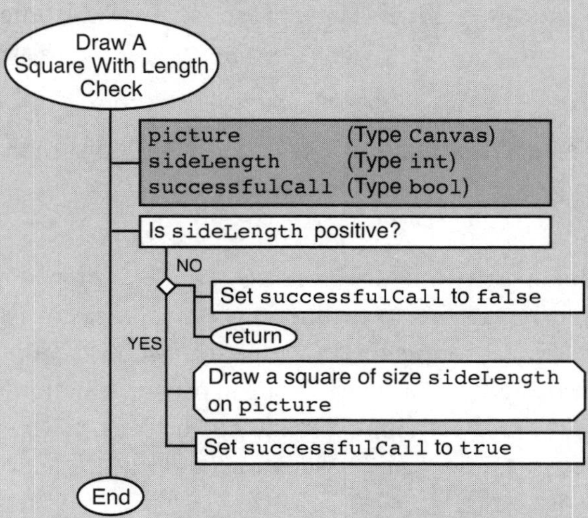

IMPLEMENTATION:

```
void drawSquare(Canvas& picture, int sideLength,
                bool& successfulCall)
{
  // Code to draw a square
  if (sideLength <= 0)
  {
    successfulCall = false;
    return;           // Terminate execution
  }
  picture.penDown();
  picture.moveRelative(sideLength, 0);
  picture.moveRelative(0, sideLength);
  picture.moveRelative(-sideLength, 0);
  picture.moveRelative(0, -sideLength);
  picture.penUp();
  successfulCall = true;
  return;
} // end drawSquare()
```

There's no particular advantage in writing the function definition this way, but it provides an example of the use of a `return` statement other than as the last statement of the function body. In addition this example shows that you're not limited to a single `return` statement in a function body.

Lesson: A function body may have more than one `return` statement.

From a software engineering point of view it's not good practice to have multiple returns from a function. At the very least the use of multiple returns can be very confusing to someone who's reading your code and trying to establish the flow of control through your function definitions. Sometimes you'll find that there are some "finalizing" actions that must be taken before the function returns, and you'll want to provide those actions in one place only. So our advice is:

✗ *Use multiple* `return` *statements in a function definition only in exceptional circumstances.*

✓ *Make sure that every possible path of control through a function body terminates with a* `return` *statement.*

We're willing to accept that "exceptional circumstances" covers termination of a function call because one or more invalid values have been passed to a function as actual parameters. Of course, for a particular function call only one of the `return` statements will ever be executed.

A `return` is a form of **built-in control** and so far you've only seen its use in a simple termination of a function; a `return` followed by a semicolon is a **statement**.

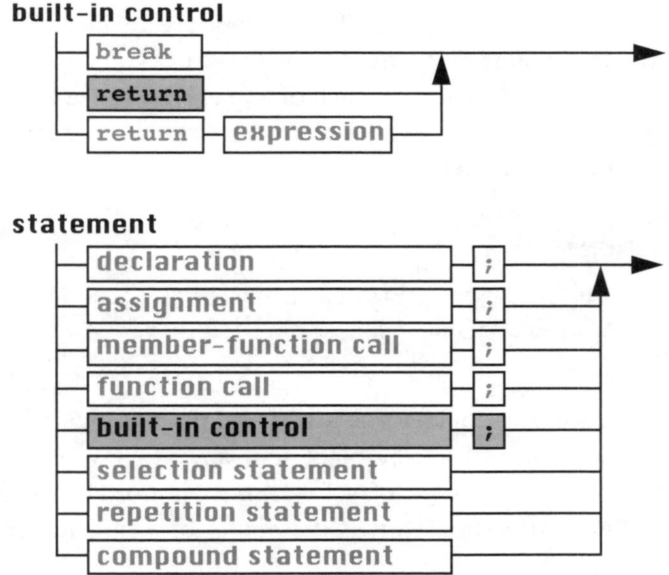

As with any built-in control statement you have to be careful with the use of `return`; `return` forces an unconditional termination of the function body at the point of the `return` statement. It could be that the position of a `return` statement makes some statements of the function "unreachable" in the sense that no matter what values are passed as actual parameters, the statements will never be executed. Some compilers will warn you if you make such a design/implementation error.

> **Lesson:** Use of multiple `return` statements could result in some statements in the function body becoming unreachable.

Our use so far of the return statement to terminate a function body is appropriate for functions for which the return type is `void`. But what if the return type is not `void`. Do you still use the return statement to terminate execution? Yes, but in addition to terminating execution of the function body, the return statement must also indicate what value must be returned.

Returning a value

In Chapter 9 you saw that there are lots of "standard" functions you can call provided you `#include` the appropriate header file. For example, including `math.h` means that you can make calls to mathematical functions such as `sqrt(...)` and `cos(...)`; including `ctype.h` means that you can make calls to the character test functions `isalpha(...)` and `isupper(...)`. For many of these functions the return type is non-`void`.

> **EXAMPLE:**
>
> The return type of `sqrt(...)` and `cos(...)` is `double`. The return type of `isalpha(...)` and `isupper(...)` is `int`.

When a function returns a non-`void` result, you can use the result produced by a function call in any place that any other value of that type may be used. When the return type of a function is non-`void`, a function call is a form of **simple expression**. How is the ability of a function to return a value reflected in a function definition?

Let's take another look at the syntax for a **function definition**.

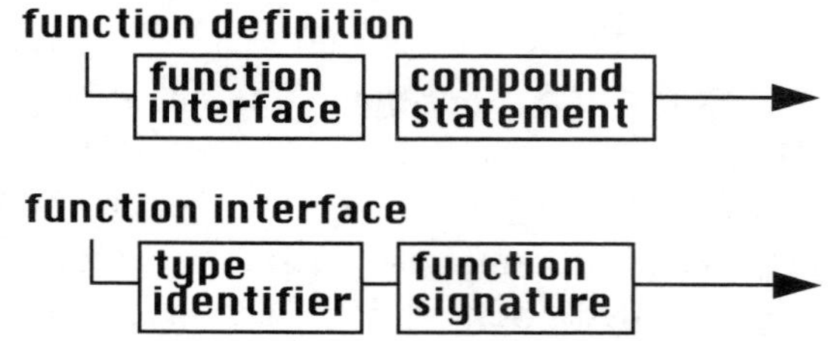

For all the functions that you've seen in this chapter, the **type identifier** happens to be `void`.

You know that for some functions the type identifier is `double`, `int` or `char`. What about other types? Can you define a function for which the type identifier is a PDT such as `Text`, `Palette`, or `CDPlayer`?

The answer is a resounding "yes." You've already met functions that return a value of type `CDisc`, such as the member function `unload (...)` of the `CDPlayer` PDT. Let's return to the function `readName (...)` of the previous section to see how you could define a function to return a value of type `Text`.

PROBLEM:

Provide a function that reads a person's first name and surname and uses the return type, rather than a formal parameter, to return the value of the full name.

DESIGN:

First let's look at the function interface. What should the return type be? The answer is `Text`. And what should the parameter list be? Since the formal parameter name is no longer to be used to return a value, the parameter list is empty. So the required function interface is:

```
Text readName()
```

Before we continue with the implementation of `readName()` let's look at how you would call a function that has a non-`void` return type. If a function returns a non-`void` result you need to do something with the value returned from a function call. Using the value on the right-hand side of an assignment is one thing you could do with the value.

EXAMPLE:

Using the interface `Text readName()`, a calling sequence to read three full names is:

```
Text firstPerson;
Text secondPerson;
Text thirdPerson;

firstPerson  = readName();
secondPerson = readName();
thirdPerson  = readName();
```

Even if a function has no formal or actual parameters, you still need the parentheses in both the function interface and in a function call. We repeat a lesson from Chapter 9.

Lesson: Even if a function has no parameters, the parentheses must always be present in a function call (and also in a function interface).

IMPLEMENTATION:

Now you know what the function interface for `readName()` looks like and how to make a call to this function. What about the implementation of the body of `readName()`? Most of the function body is as before. Declare variables for a person's first name and surname and use an input statement to read in appropriate values.

```
{
  Text firstName;
  Text surname;

  cin >> firstName >> surname;
  // Additional code to be inserted here
} // end readName()
```

For a function with a non-`void` return type there needs to be code that returns the required value. Let's look again at the syntax diagram for **built-in control**, this time highlighting the alternative use of the `return` that's needed.

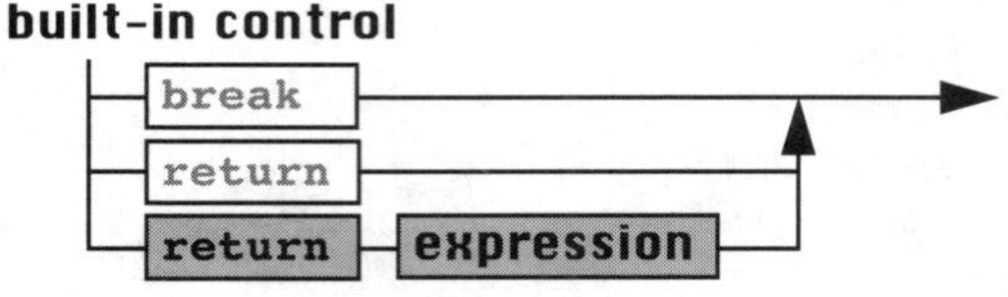

Now, what about that //Additional code to be inserted here?

IMPLEMENTATION:

For the version of readName(...) that used a formal parameter to return the result, the additional code was:

```
name = firstname + " " + surname;
return;
```

For the new version of readName() the return type is Text and the value of the **expression** to be returned is firstname + " " + surname. The definition of readName() can now be completed.

```
Text readName()
{
  Text firstName;
  Text surname;

  cin >> firstName >> surname;
  return (firstname + " " + surname);
} // end readName()
```

If the return type of a function is non-void, then any return statement in a function body must be capable of returning a value. Furthermore, the type of the value must be compatible with that of the return type of the function, otherwise you'll get a compile-time error. Given the comments we made in Chapter 8 about avoiding implicit coercions, we'd go as far as to say that the result type and return type should be identical.

Lesson: Any return statement in the body of a non-void function must be capable of returning a value of the same type as the result type of the function.

Now you should be able to understand why we've always included return 0; before the closing brace of main(). The function main() has no parameters but it does have a return type; it's int. Those return 0; statements indicate successful completion of the main program's execution.

You've already seen that you can use more than one `return` statement in a function body to terminate execution of a function with a `void` return type. Similarly, you can use more than one `return` statement to return a value when the function return type is non-`void`, but we repeat an earlier style rule.

✗ *Use multiple* `return` *statements in a function definition only in exceptional circumstances.*

If a potential path of control in the function body terminates without a `return` statement, you should expect to get a rebuke from the compiler. In the case of a function for which the return type is non-`void`, expect such a rebuke if there's a path of control that might reach the closing brace of the function body's compound statement without encountering a `return` statement.

Lesson: A function with a non-`void` return type must include at least one `return` statement.

EXAMPLE:

Suppose you want a function that determines an appropriate `Text` string for a `Palette` variable. Then you might be tempted to write the following definition.

```
Text paletteToText(Palette color)
{
  switch (color)
  {
    case BLACK:
      {
        return "Black";
      }
    case WHITE:
      {
        return "White";
      }
    // etc.
  }
} // end paletteToText()
```

As well as there being multiple `return` statements, if there's no `default` arm on the `switch` statement then potentially there's a route through the function body that doesn't return a value and so you'll get a compile-time error. We suggest that you write the definition as:

```
Text paletteToText(Palette color)
{
  Text textColor;

  switch (color)
  {
    case BLACK:
      {
        textColor = "Black";
      }
      break;
    case WHITE:
      {
        textColor = "White";
      }
      break;
    // etc.
  }
  return textColor;
} // end paletteToText()
```

(and also include a `default` arm!)

A function body is just a compound statement. It's a collection of statements that may involve declarations, assignments, expressions, etc. Oh! and a function body may involve a function call, of course. Now, you're forgiven for thinking that such function calls must involve other functions only. It would be pretty weird for a function body to involve a call to the function itself. Right? Actually, it can be perfectly natural for a function definition to include a call to the same function. This is known as *recursion*.

EXERCISES FOR SECTION 11.3

1 Provide definitions for a function that determines if an integer is odd, and a function that determines if a character is a lower-case vowel (see Exercise 2 of Section 11.1).

2 Provide a definition for a function that returns a random lottery number in the range 1 to 50 (see Section 9.1).

3 Complete the definition of `paletteToText(...)`. Make sure that your function will always return a value (the implementer of `Palette` may choose to add further colors).

11.4 RECURSION

A definition that includes the item being defined as part of the definition is known as a **recursive definition**.

EXAMPLE:

You know what an expression looks like, don't you? Here's a reminder of the syntax diagram for an **expression** that you saw in Chapter 8.

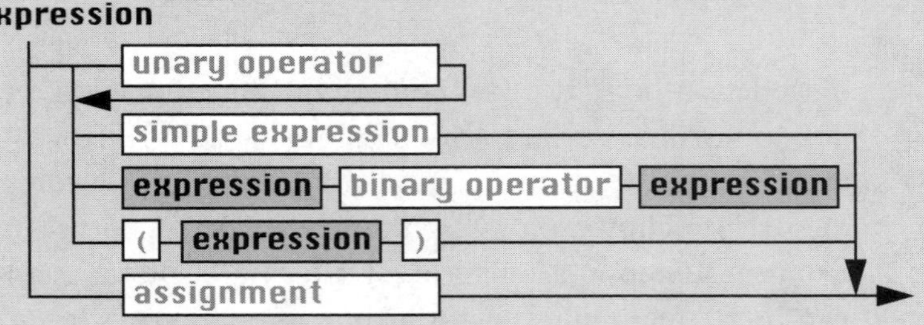

An **expression** is defined in terms of itself, an example of recursion.

You can use recursion in problem solving too.

PROBLEM:

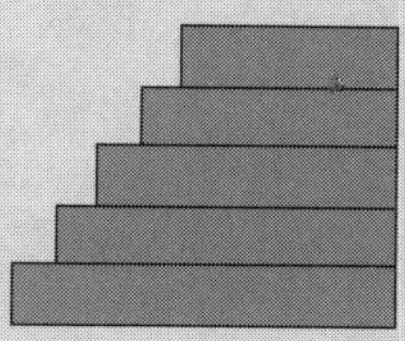

Imagine that you're at the bottom of a flight of stairs and you want to get to the top. What do you do?

DESIGN:

You could say that you climb the steps one at a time until you reach the top, an example of repetition. In C++ terms, you have a loop repetition if you know how many steps there are, and a `while` repetition if you don't. An alternative view is to say that to climb all the steps you climb to the last-but-one step, and then climb the last step. If you know that there are n steps, then the problem:

Climb n steps can be expressed as:

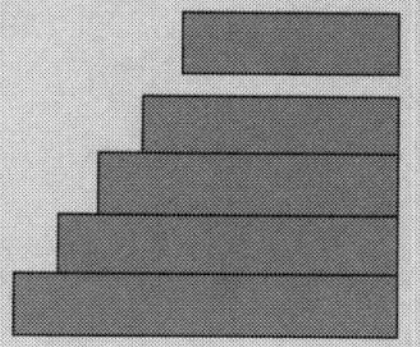

Climb $n - 1$ steps

Climb 1 step

or even as:

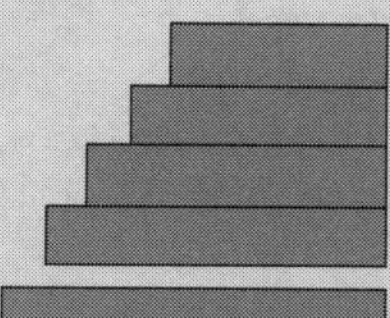

Climb 1 step

Climb $n - 1$ steps

Both are examples of a **recursive algorithm**: you've defined the solution in terms of itself.

PROBLEM:

Consider the following "Towers of Hanoi" problem.

You have a pile, or tower, of discs arranged in order of decreasing diameter size. The aim is to move the discs to form a new tower arranged in the same way. However, there are restrictions on the way you can proceed.

1. You are allowed to form at most three towers of discs at any one time.
2. Only one disc can be moved at a time.
3. Only the disc on top of a tower can be moved.
4. No disc can be placed on top of a smaller disc.

Rumor has it that there are a group of monks at the Temple of Brahma in Tibet who are trying to move a tower of 64 discs. They believe that the Universe will come to an end when they complete their task. Fortunately, this will take them a very long time.

DESIGN:

Assuming five discs, here's the situation after the first two discs have been moved. The smallest disc has been moved to Tower B, and the second-smallest to Tower C.

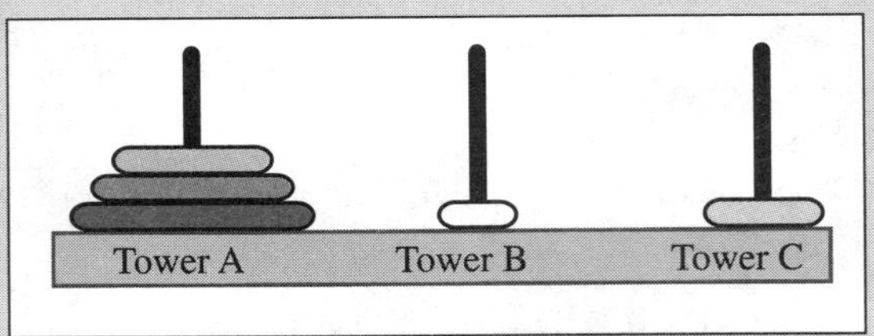

What's the next move? Which disc do you move next? Which discs can you move?

Well, you could move the smallest disc to Tower A, but that doesn't get you very far. And moving the second-smallest disc back to Tower A is hardly sensible. You can't move the second-smallest disc to Tower B since this breaks the rules. So move the smallest disc to Tower C? Yes, since that allows you to move the third-smallest disc off Tower A and onto Tower B. And then what? Can you see an obvious use of repetition here?

There's clearly some form of repetition here, and it would be possible to express a solution using one of the forms of repetition covered in the previous chapter. However, it's much easier to produce a recursive solution;

easier for us to write such a solution and easier for you to see what's going on. Using the design notation, here's our recursive solution.

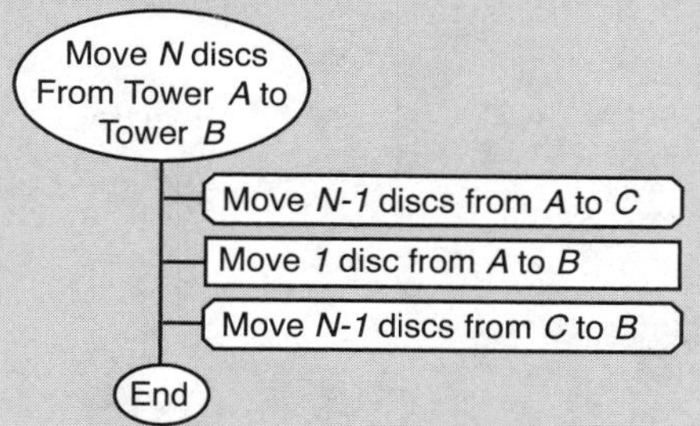

To move five discs from Tower A to Tower B, you first move the smallest four discs to Tower C (moving only one disc at a time). This allows you to move the largest disc from Tower A to Tower B, and then you move the discs from Tower C to Tower B. How do you move the discs from Tower A to Tower C? And from Tower C to Tower B? You just apply the algorithm recursively to each of these sub-problems, changing the labels of the towers as appropriate. Starting with a problem involving five discs you have to solve two sub-problems involving four discs. Each of those sub-problems will involve sub-problems involving three discs, and so on. Eventually you reach a situation in which the sub-problems involve movement of a single disc, and then there's no need to recurse any further.

How do you translate a recursive algorithm into C++? Well, you've seen that the step-climbing algorithm can be expressed in terms of both repetition and recursion. And if you're really prepared to work at it, you could even express the Towers of Hanoi problem in terms of repetition. So a possible solution is not to use recursion at all but simply rewrite a recursive algorithm in terms of repetition and then use the appropriate C++ repetition statements. But if you're tempted to skip the rest of this section we'd like to point out that there are direct ways of expressing recursion in C++. While the code you end up with may look a little strange, take our word for it that a recursive implementation can be much more elegant than a solution using repetition.

We'll leave the Towers of Hanoi problem to an exercise (Exercise 4) at the end of this section. When you've completed this section you should be able to tackle the problem with ease. To proceed, however, we'll take a somewhat simpler problem.

PROBLEM:

To illustrate the use of recursion in a program, have another look at the code from Chapter 10 that prints out the first ten integer numbers using a loop repetition. Now that you know how to define functions, you can define a function that achieves the same effect.

IMPLEMENTATION:

```
void printIntegers(int n)
{
  for (int loopControl = 1; loopControl <= n; loopControl += 1)
  {
    cout << loopControl << " ";
  }
  return;
} // end printIntegers()
```

We've generalized the function `printIntegers(...)` by specifying a formal value parameter `n` that indicates how many numbers are to be printed, so you can use a call to the same function to print the first ten integers, the first 20, or whatever, simply by specifying an appropriate actual parameter.

EXAMPLE:

```
cout << "Using repetition to print numbers 1 to 10 inclusive"
     << endl;
printIntegers(10);
cout << endl;
```

You're forgiven for thinking that a loop repetition is the perfectly natural way to ensure that an action is repeated. You wouldn't dream of doing anything else, would you? For such a simple problem as this we'd probably agree with you. A loop repetition provides a perfectly good solution to the problem. However, we want to try to persuade you that there is another way of solving the problem that's also natural.

Let's have another look at the problem, which we'll express in a generic style.

PROBLEM:

Print the integers 1 to n.

DESIGN:

The loop repetition solution was based on the premise that you know how to print one integer. So you embed a statement to output an integer inside a `for` loop and make sure that each time you go round the loop you increase a loop counter by one, since it's the value of the counter that you end up printing.

Let's now take a **divide and conquer** approach to the design of a solution.

> To print the integers 1 to n, print the integers 1 to $n - 1$ and then output n.

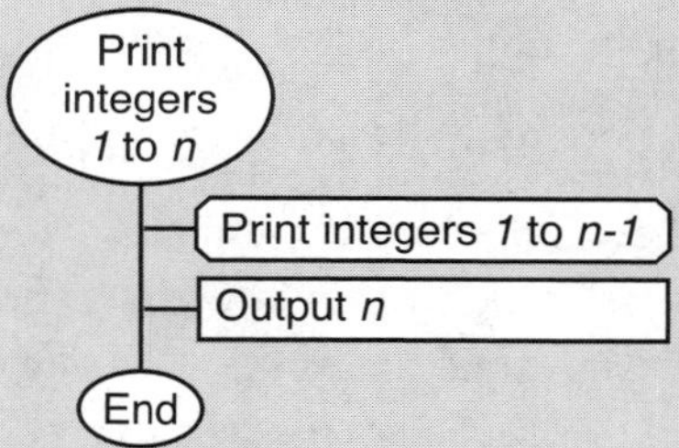

Can you see the similarity between this and the design for the solution to the Towers of Hanoi problem? The original problem has been replaced by two problems, one you know how to solve (output n), and one that is similar to the original problem (print the integers 1 to $n - 1$). Since you've been able to refine the original problem, you can refine the problem "print the integers 1 to $n - 1$" in a similar way.

> To print the integers 1 to $n - 1$, print the integers 1 to $n - 2$ and then output $n - 1$.

Again you've got a problem you know how to solve (output $n - 1$), and one that is similar to the original problem (print the integers 1 to $n - 2$). You can therefore refine the design.

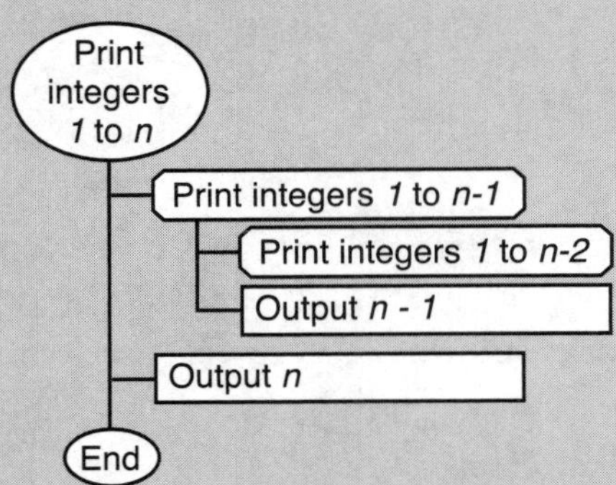

Then you can refine again, and again, and again ...

When do you stop? Eventually you end up with a problem that doesn't require refinement:

To print the integers 1 to 1, output 1.

You know how to write code to output 1, and so the design is complete.

In total, the number of statements executed that print a single integer is equal to n. In which order are these print statements executed? It's clear from the design that the value 1 is output first, followed by 2, and so on.

The process of refining a problem in such a way that you end up with a similar, but in some sense reduced, problem of the same form is an example of recursion. There clearly has to be some way of terminating the recursion. The refinement must stop somewhere, otherwise you'll go on for ever. So the aim of recursion is to work towards a **base case**, a problem that doesn't require further refinement.

Lesson: Whenever recursion is used to refine a problem the aim is to refine towards a base case, a simple problem that can be solved without recursing any further.

Recursion is a problem-solving technique, but fortunately C++ aids a direct translation from a recursive solution of a problem to C++ code by allowing *recursive function calls*. In other words, the body of a function definition may involve one or more statements that involve calls to the same function.

IMPLEMENTATION:

Here's a recursive definition of a function that solves the "print *n* numbers" problem that exactly matches the first design.

```
void printIntegers(int n)
{
  if (n > 1)
  {
    printIntegers(n - 1);
  }
  cout << n << " ";
  return;
} // end printIntegers()
```

Any call to the function `printIntegers(...)` with a value greater than 1 for the actual parameter results in a recursive call of the function. As the recursion is expanded, the value of the actual parameter decreases by one. Hence a situation is eventually reached at which no recursive call is made. The output statement is executed resulting in the value of 1 being output. The function call at the deepest level of recursion is now complete. This results in the output statement at the previous level being executed and the function call at that level terminating, and so on. Eventually the recursion unwinds to the top level, which corresponds to the initial call of the function, and the value supplied as an actual parameter at this level is printed.

DESIGN:

Although we've just completed a recursive solution to the problem of printing out the first *n* numbers, there are several alternative ways that you can tackle the same problem using recursion.

> To print the integers 1 to *n*, output 1 and then print the integers 2 to *n*.

The design diagram for this version looks similar to the first recursive solution in structure, but there are a few detailed differences, one of which is that the positions of the output statement and the designator box have been switched. In the diagram *start* is assumed to have a value less than *n*.

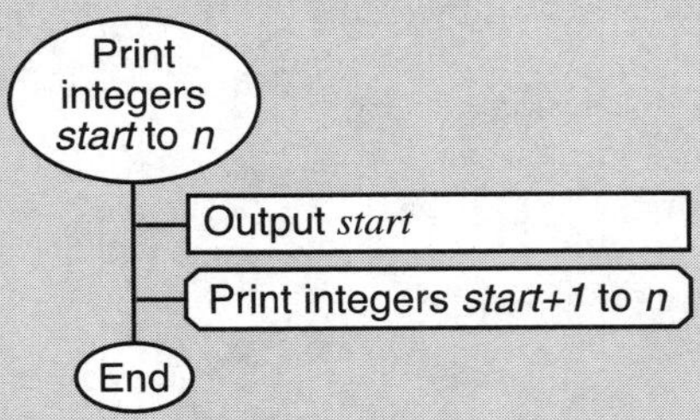

IMPLEMENTATION:

A function that solves the problem using this variant takes the following form.

```
void printIntegers(int start, int n)
{
  cout << start << " ";
  if (start < n)
  {
    printIntegers(start + 1, n);
  }
  return;
} // end printIntegers()
```

Here we've used a second parameter to `printIntegers (...)` that indicates where to start printing the sequence from. The base case now corresponds to the situation in which the start position and end position are the same (both equal to *n*).

DESIGN:

We've given two recursive solutions to the problem of printing out the first *n* integers, and there are plenty of others. For example:

> To print the integers 1 to *n*, print the integers 1 to *n*/2 and then print the integers n/2 + 1 to *n*.

When there are several possible recursive solutions to a problem, how do you decide which is best? Is recursion better than iteration? There are no simple answers, particularly to the last question. However, a recursive solution to a problem can sometimes be much more elegant, and more easily understood, than an iterative solution.

Lesson: Recursion can be a valuable problem-solving tool.

If a recursive design to a problem comes naturally then use that design to produce a recursive implementation. If a recursive design doesn't come naturally then use something else!

It's always possible to reformulate a recursive algorithm using iteration, and the converse is often true too. But is a recursive implementation going to be more efficient (measured both in terms of time and storage costs) than an iterative implementation? Again, it depends.

PROBLEM:

Write a function to calculate the *i*th number in the following sequence.

1 1 2 3 5 8 13 21 34 55

Starting with the first two numbers in the sequence, 1 and 1, every other number in the sequence can be obtained by adding its two predecessors. So 1+1 gives 2, 1+2 gives 3, 2+3 gives 5, and so on. If we use F_i to denote the *i*th number in the sequence (starting at zero), then it's easy to see that the numbers in the sequence are given by:

$$F_i = F_{i-1} + F_{i-2}$$

which is an example of a **recurrence relation**. (The *F* comes from Fibonacci whom the sequence is named after. You may recall reading about Fibonacci in Chapter 9.) The above definition of F_i is clearly a recursive definition, and a recursive design and implementation follow readily.

DESIGN:

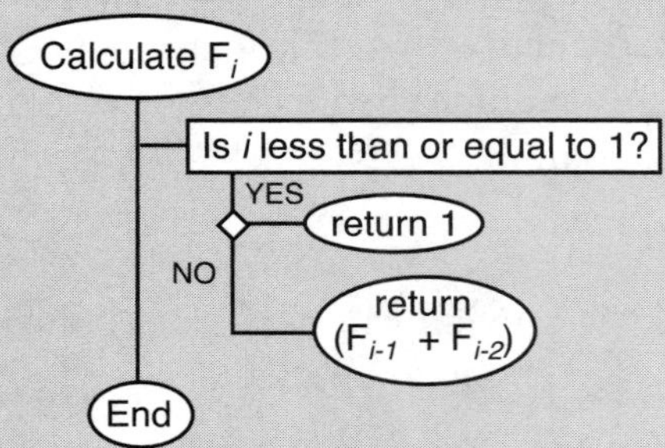

IMPLEMENTATION:

```
int fibonacci(int i)
{
  int number;

  if (i <= 1)
  {
    number = 1;
  }
  else
  {
    number = fibonacci(i - 1) + fibonacci(i - 2);
  }
  return number;
} // end fibonacci()
```

Chapter 11 Fibonacci Numbers

This is a perfectly natural solution to the problem since the design and implementation follow immediately from the problem description. However, a little thought shows that while you've got a very elegant solution here, using this implementation requires a large number of recursive calls and duplication of results.

EXAMPLE:

Think what happens when you make a call to `fibonacci(...)` with a value of the actual parameter equal to 10.

```
cout << "The 10th Fibonacci number is " << fibonacci(10) << endl;
```

The 10th Fibonacci number is the sum of the 9th and 8th Fibonacci numbers, so the call `fibonacci(10)` involves recursive calls of `fibonacci(9)` and `fibonacci(8)`. But the call `fibonacci(9)` involves the calls `fibonacci(8)` and `fibonacci(7)`; that is, the 8th Fibonacci number is computed twice. Taking the recursion further, you'll see that the 7th Fibonacci number is computed three times, and so on.

DESIGN:

An iterative implementation avoids the duplication of effort completely.

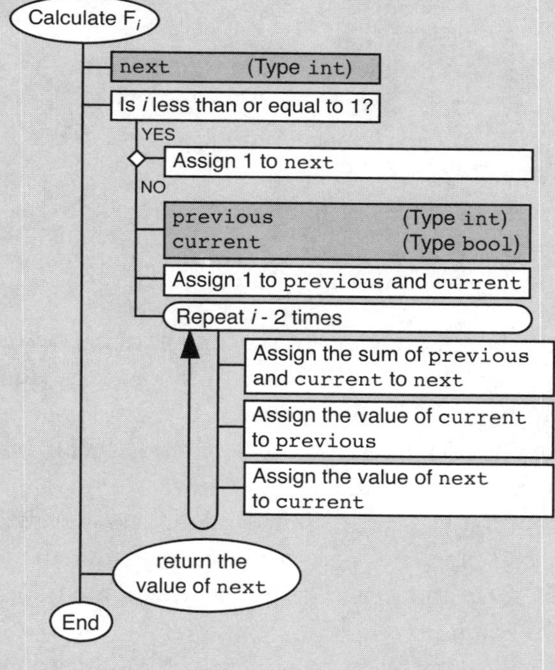

IMPLEMENTATION:

```
int fibonacci(int i)
{
  int next;

  if (i <= 1)
  {
```

```
      next = 1;
    }
    else
    {
      int previous = 1;
      int current  = 1;

      for (int count = 2; count < i; count += 1)
      {
        next     = current + previous;
        previous = current;
        current  = next;
      }
    }
    return next;
  } // end fibonacci()
```

This iterative implementation is more efficient but less elegant compared to the recursive implementation. The essential relationship between numbers in the Fibonacci sequence has been lost by the need to have three variables for three consecutive numbers in the sequence, and the need for a shuffle of values at the end of each iteration.

What about the recursive implementations of `printIntegers(...)` that you saw earlier? They don't appear to involve any duplication of effort so are they likely to be as efficient as an iterative implementation using a loop repetition? Probably not. Making a call to a function incurs both time and space overheads, and so an implementation that involves recursion can often be less efficient than a version that uses repetition. Trade-off time again. If a recursive solution comes readily and time and space resources are not a matter of concern, then use recursion. If time and space resources are limited, then you'll need to design an iterative solution.

We can't deny it; recursion can be a difficult concept to come to grips with at first, but with practice recursion should come to you naturally, maybe even more naturally than repetition. Let's complete this section on recursion with a look back at a problem you saw in Chapter 2 that lends itself naturally to a recursive solution.

PROBLEM:

Draw the Hilbert curve of order n.

DESIGN:

For a description of precisely what a Hilbert curve is, and an illustration of a Hilbert curve, see the discussion in Chapter 2. The salient points are that:

- each Hilbert curve consists of four copies of the Hilbert curve at the next level down;
- these four copies are drawn in different orientations;
- the four copies are linked by three straight lines.

At a particular level, a Hilbert curve is parameterized by:

- the order of the curve;
- four orthogonal directions, that we'll call right, left, down and up;
- a line size.

The four directions are with respect to the current orientation of the curve being drawn, not to physical directions. Hence for a particular value of the order of the curve being drawn, "right" might well mean "left," etc.

In the following description of how to draw a Hilbert curve, drawing always starts from the current pen position. Drawing takes place on a square of 1 unit in each coordinate direction. The initial pen position is $h/2$ units in from the top and left edges of a square, where $h=2^n$. Each connecting line is then of length h.

The curve is now drawn as follows.

1. In the top left-hand quadrant draw a first copy of the curve at the next order down but flipped about the diagonal linking top-left with bottom right (that is, swap the directions right and down, and the directions up and left).
2. Draw a line horizontally right.
3. In the top right-hand quadrant of the square draw a second copy of the curve at the next order down using the current orientation.

4. Draw a line vertically down.
5. In the bottom right-hand quadrant draw a third copy of the curve at the next order down using the current orientation.
6. Draw a line horizontally left.
7. In the bottom left-hand quadrant, draw a fourth and final copy of the curve at the next order down but flipped about the diagonal linking top-right with bottom-left (that is, swap the directions up and down, and the directions right and left).

Got that? No? Try some examples. A Hilbert curve of order 0 is just a point, so a Hilbert curve of order 1 is just the three connecting lines as shown in Figure 11.2.

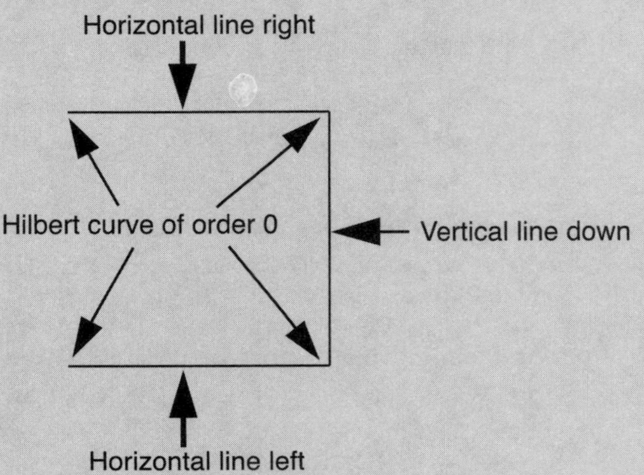

Figure 11.2 Hilbert curve of order 1

The Hilbert curve of order 2 consists of four copies of the Hilbert curve of order 1 plus the three joining lines, as shown in Figure 11.3.

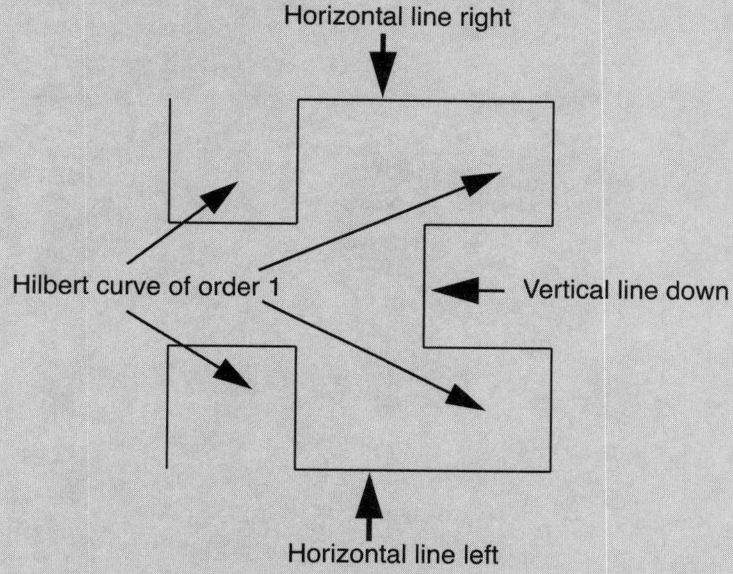

Figure 11.3 Hilbert curve of order 2

Now try matching the above description with the following design notation.

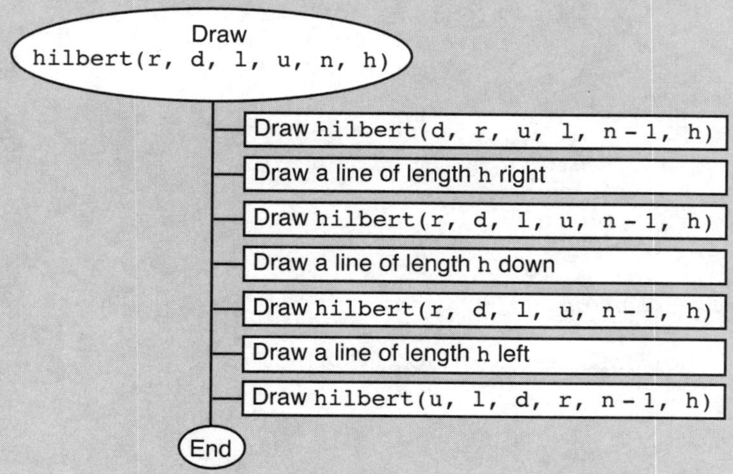

IMPLEMENTATION:

The following implementation employs a PDT `Direction` to represent moves right, down, left and up. You'll be seeing how to define your own PDTs in the next two chapters. For now just accept that `Direction` is similar to `Palette`. `Direction` has abstract values (`RIGHT`, `DOWN`, `LEFT` and `UP`) but no member functions or operators.

```
enum Direction {RIGHT, DOWN, LEFT, UP};

void move(Direction d, int h, Canvas& picture)
{
  switch (d)
  {
    case RIGHT:
      {
        picture.moveRelative(h, 0);
      }
      break;
    case DOWN:
      {
        picture.moveRelative(0, -h);
      }
      break;
    case LEFT:
      {
        picture.moveRelative(-h, 0);
      }
      break;
    case UP:
      {
        picture.moveRelative(0, h);
      }
      break;
    default:
      {
        error("Unknown direction");
      }
      break;
  }
  return;
} // end move()

void hilbert(Direction r, Direction d, Direction l, Direction u,
             int i, int h, Canvas& picture)
{
```

```
  if (i > 0)
  {
    hilbert(d, r, u, l, i - 1, h, picture);
    move(r, h, picture);
    hilbert(r, d, l, u, i - 1, h, picture);
    move(d, h, picture);
    hilbert(r, d, l, u, i - 1, h, picture);
    move(l, h, picture);
    hilbert(u, l, d, r, i - 1, h, picture);
  }
  return;
} // end hilbert()
```

OUTPUT:

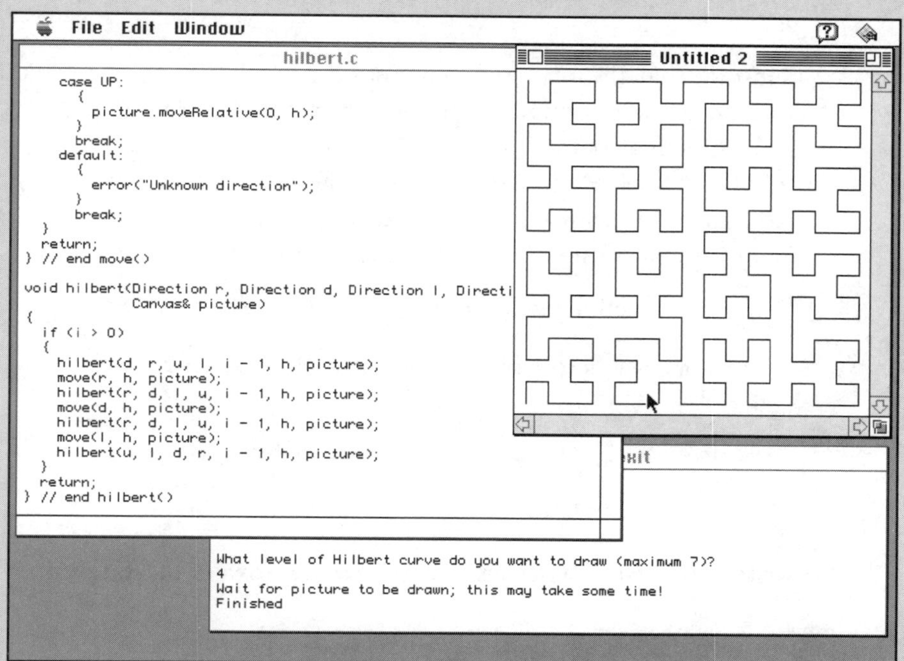

By now you should be convinced that whether it involves recursion or not, functional abstraction is a key problem-solving tool. Consequently the ability to use and define functions is an important skill to gain from your apprenticeship, a skill that you should gain lots of practice with. There are a number of software engineering issues related to defining functions that will help you become an accomplished user of functions, so let's take a look at them.

EXERCISES FOR SECTION 11.4

1 Produce a design based on recursion to sum the first n integers, and an implementation of this design.

2 Write a recursive function to print the first n integers based on the algorithm "To print the integers 1 to n, print the integers 1 to $n/2$ and then print the integers $n/2+$ 1 to n."

3 Suppose that the recursive version of `fibonacci(...)` is called from `main()` with an actual parameter of 5. How many calls to `fibonacci(...)` will be made with an actual parameter of 1, and how many with an actual parameter of 0? What happens when the actual parameter supplied in `main()` increases to 6? Add an `int& count` parameter to the interface of `fibonacci(...)` and increment `count` in the body of the function to check your results.

4 Using the function definition:

```
void moveADisc(char firstTower, char secondTower)
{
  cout << "Move a disc from tower  " << firstTower
       << "  to tower  " << secondTower << endl;
  return;
} // end moveADisc()
```

write a recursive function that solves the Towers of Hanoi problem.

11.5 SOFTWARE ENGINEERING ISSUES

In this section we discuss a number of software engineering issues associated with writing function definitions, covering:

- the provision of documentation in the form of user and maintenance manuals;
- the placement of function interfaces and function definitions;
- the use of the function return type as an error indicator;
- the reuse of function names.

Documentation

Functional abstraction begins at the design phase, and program documentation starts at the design phase too. The provision of design diagrams representing your functional abstractions is useful for the development of your implementations of those diagrams. In addition, including the design diagrams in a maintenance manual for your function implementations will mean that subsequent maintenance of those implementations will be more easily conducted, whether this is by yourself, or by some other programmer if you no longer work for the company you wrote the code for.

The provision of documentation can seem a tedious chore, much less interesting than actually designing and implementing software. But it's a necessary chore nonetheless. There's a tendency to leave documentation until the end; design, implement, then document as an afterthought. This is the wrong approach. Documentation should start at an early stage. If you're producing design diagrams then you're on your way to having the basis of a maintenance manual. As the implementation proceeds, document the components that you construct. By so doing you may identify errors that had previously been overlooked. By the time your program is complete, the maintenance manual should be complete too.

The design phase of functional abstraction involves establishing the interface for those abstractions, and the interface is something that has to be properly documented in the user manual. The user needs to be aware of the:

- **preconditions** – the set of conditions that must hold immediately prior to the function call;
- **postconditions** – the set of conditions that hold on completion of the function call.

Preconditions and postconditions are likely to involve the parameters of the functional abstraction.

EXAMPLE:

For a functional abstraction to draw a square on a `Canvas` variable, the preconditions would include the side length of the square being a positive value and the current pen position being such that drawing the square does not go outside the frame. The postconditions would include that the `Canvas` reference parameter has a square drawn on it (assuming the preconditions to hold) and the pen is in the up position and at the same coordinates as prior to the function call.

The mere presence of parameters in a function signature and the classification of the parameters as value, reference or constant reference parameters is a form of documentation. Comments added to the code summarizing the effect of the function and indicating the purpose of each parameter is another form of documentation. However, you shouldn't expect the user of your programs to have to read your code to be able to call your functions. Separate documentation indicating the function interface, the preconditions and postconditions, and containing a simple example that can be used as a template, are all things that the user will expect to see.

Lesson: Documentation in the form of maintenance and user manuals can give a professional feel to your software.

The user will also need to know how to access your functional abstractions, which brings us on nicely to header and implementation files.

Header and implementation files

Often you'll be asked to write a number of function definitions that are in some way related.

PROBLEM:

You've been contracted to design and test a number of stand-alone function definitions for drawing shapes on a `Canvas` object:

- a square
- a rectangle
- a circle
- a triangle.

If you're going to write a collection of related functions, it makes good sense to gather their interfaces together and place them in a header file. This makes it easy for your customer to access these functions; at compile-time they'll just need to `#include` the appropriate file.

✓ *Function interfaces that share a common theme should be placed in an appropriate header file.*

INTERFACES:

Since all the shape-drawing functions share a common theme (they all draw a shape on a `Canvas` variable) place their interfaces in the file `DrawShapes.h`. The contents of `DrawShapes.h` might look like the following.

```
#include "Canvas.h"

void drawSquare(Canvas& picture, int sideLength,
                bool& successfulCall);
void drawRectangle(Canvas& picture, int longSide, int shortSide,
                   bool& successfulCall);
void drawCircle(Canvas& picture, int radius,
                bool& successfulCall);
void drawTriangle(Canvas& picture, int side1, int side2,
                  int side3, bool& successfulCall);
```

Recall that a **function interface** and a **pre-processor line** are both examples of a **compilation unit**. You can compile header files containing function interfaces to check that the code is syntactically correct, but no executable code will be produced.

Just as it's good practice to group the interfaces of related functions in a single file (a `.h` file), so it is good practice to group the corresponding function definitions in a file too. This time it's called an implementation file since it contains implementations (definitions) of the functions.

IMPLEMENTATION:

Since the interfaces for the shape-drawing functions are in a file called `DrawShapes.h`, put the function definitions in the implementation, or source, file `DrawShapes.c`.

```
#include "bool.h"
#include "Canvas.h"
#include "DrawShapes.h"

bool drawSquare(Canvas& picture, int sideLength,
                bool& successfulCall)
{
  // Statements that constitute the body of drawSquare
} // end drawSquare()

bool drawRectangle(Canvas& picture, int longSide,
                   int shortSide, bool& successfulCall)
{
  // Statements that constitute the body of drawRectangle
} // end drawRectangle()

bool drawCircle(Canvas& picture, int radius,
                bool& successfulCall)
{
  // Statements that constitute the body of drawCircle
} // end drawCircle()

bool drawTriangle(Canvas& picture, int side1, int side2,
                  int side3, bool& successfulCall)
{
  // Statements that constitute the body of drawTriangle
} // end drawTriangle()
```

Just as the code in a header file doesn't constitute a legal C++ program, so the code in a function implementation file doesn't constitute a legal C++ program either. You can use the compiler to check for syntax errors in an implementation file and object code will be produced. However, since neither the header file nor the implementation file contains a `main()` function, all you have is a set of definitions, so no executable code will be produced. For a complete program you'll therefore need one further file, a file containing a test program with a definition for `main()` that involves calls to your functions, which will `#include` the header file.

By now you should realize that what you've done here is to define a function library, and that a user should be able to access this library just as they would any other library. The library has two parts to it; the library interface (the `.h` file) and the library implementation (the `.c` file). Access to the library interface is obtained at compile time using `#include`. You now need to indicate to your C++ system how to access at link-time the object code corresponding to the library function definitions. Unfortunately, the mechanism for doing this is system-dependent. The way you do it in the Symantec environment on an Apple Macintosh is significantly different to the way you do it in the Borland environment on an PC, which is different again to the way you do it in UNIX. We can't give you any detailed guidelines except that somehow, someway you've got to do something. Try looking at documentation for the C++ system you're using, or ask your instructor.

Let's have a look at the interfaces for the shape-drawing functions introduced above, and in particular the way those functions return values.

Returning more than one value from a function

You can use both a return statement and reference parameters to return values, but in general if you're returning more than one value, it's good practice to return them all through the parameter list. However, we're willing to permit using both a return value and reference parameters when the return value is a Boolean indicating some concept of success or failure of the function call.

EXAMPLE:

In Section 11.2 you developed several definitions for a function that draws a square on a `Canvas` variable. The final version had three parameters; a reference parameter for the `Canvas` variable, an `int` value parameter for the side length of the square, and a `bool` reference parameter to allow the function to report a failure of some description (for example, negative side length). Let's rewrite the function definition to use the return type to report the success/failure status of a function call.

```
bool drawSquare(Canvas& picture, int sideLength)
{
  // Code to draw a square
  if (sideLength <= 0)
  {
    return false; // Terminate execution
  }
  picture.penDown();
  picture.moveRelative(sideLength, 0);
  picture.moveRelative(0, sideLength);
  picture.moveRelative(-sideLength, 0);
  picture.moveRelative(0, -sideLength);
  picture.penUp();
  return true;
} // end drawSquare()
```

✗ *In general, if you want a function to return more than one value, don't use a* `return` *statement to return any of the values.*

✓ *A function that's designed to produce an indication of success or failure of a call should use a* `bool` *return type and a* `return` *statement to report that success/failure status.*

How do you ensure that a call to `drawSquare(...)` draws a square in the correct position? Well, you need to position the pen correctly. Would you like to be able to call a function that draws a square but has an additional two parameters indicating the start position? What would you like the name of that function to be? `drawSquare` again? C++ has just the mechanism for you!

Function overloading

You know that scope rules say that you can't use the same identifier at the same scope level more than once. Does this apply to function names? The answer is "yes" and it's also "no." Think back to Chapter 8 where you looked at expressions and the use of the same operator symbol + to add two `int`s, or two `doubles`, or two `Texts`. The ability to have multiple uses of the same operator symbol in this way was called operator overloading. In Section 9.5 you saw that an operator is just a very special form of function, so can the concept of overloading be applied to functions in general? In fact it can.

It's common in English to use the same word to describe a number of related actions.

EXAMPLE:

You use the word "load" when you refer to:

- loading a CD player with a CD;
- loading a VCR with a video tape;
- loading a plane with passengers;
- loading a car with groceries after a visit to the supermarket;
- loading the dice in your favor at exam time by buying this book.

It would be very clumsy indeed if you had to use a different word each time to describe what is essentially the same operation, and even the simplest of dictionaries would have to be very large if such name-proliferation was necessary. Fortunately the context of the word used to describe the operation makes it clear what the load operation involves.

EXAMPLE:

- Loading a CD player with a CD involves placing the CD onto the open tray.
- Loading groceries into a car involves placing the groceries into the trunk.

You wouldn't dream of trying to load your newly-purchased groceries into your CD player, would you. Essentially the operation "load" has been parameterized twice over:

1. Parameterized in the normal sense of function parameterization in that, for example, you're not restricted to loading the same CD into your CD player, which you'd soon get sick of doing.
2. Parameterized in terms of types in the sense that the same word is used to describe an operation that can involve CD Players, VCRs, or cars.

The second of these forms of parameterization is known as **function overloading**. Function overloading in C++ refers to the same identifier being used for two or more functions that can be uniquely defined in terms of the number and/or type of parameters in their parameter lists. Let's return to the idea of using the same name, `drawSquare`, for several functions that draw a square on a `Canvas` variable, but that have different numbers of parameters.

PROBLEM:

Extend your library of shape-drawing functions to include versions of `drawSquare(...)` that provide additional flexibility for the user.

DESIGN:

The last version of `drawSquare(...)` that you saw had the following interface.

```
bool drawSquare(Canvas& picture, int sideLength)
```

Suppose you wanted another function that draws a square but additionally allows you to specify the position at which to start drawing. You require a function with four parameters:

1. A `Canvas` (reference parameter) on which to draw the square.
2. An `int` (value parameter) to specify the length of the sides of the square.
3. An `int` (value parameter) to specify the distance along the horizontal axis from which to start drawing.
4. An `int` (value parameter) to specify the distance along the vertical axis from which to start drawing.

You could use a different function name to describe this operation, with the following interface.

```
bool drawSquare2(Canvas& picture, int sideLength,
                 int xPos,int yPos)
```

There's nothing particularly wrong with this approach, other than you've got to think of another name, and remember to use the appropriate name, `drawSquare` or `drawSquare2`, when you call either of these functions.

However, you can do better than using a different identifier for the two functions. Apart from the names you've chosen for the functions, the function signatures are recognizably different in that the parameter lists are recognizably different. You'll immediately agree with us by noting that `drawSquare(...)` and `drawSquare2(...)` have different numbers of parameters. Since it's easy enough for you to recognize this difference, you might expect a compiler to be able to recognize this difference too, even if the names of the functions were the same.

It's perfectly possible in a sophisticated language such as C++ to use the same name for a function twice or more, as long as the parameter lists of the functions are recognizably different.

DESIGN:

Rather than use the function identifier `drawSquare2`, reuse the name `drawSquare`.

```
bool drawSquare(Canvas& picture, int sideLength);
bool drawSquare(Canvas& picture, int sideLength, int xPos,
                int yPos);
```

Having included these two interfaces in `DrawShapes.h`, when you make a function call `drawSquare(...)` the compiler can work out which version you're referring to by matching the actual parameter list with one of the formal parameter lists.

EXAMPLE:

The following section of code uses the first version of `drawSquare( ...)` to draw the outside frame of a window and the second version to draw the window panes. The compiler will match each function call with the appropriate signature in the header file.

```
myPicture.moveTo(BORDER, BORDER);
drawSquare(picture, XYMAX - 2 * BORDER);
drawSquare(picture, PANE_SIZE, BORDER + BORDER,
           BORDER + BORDER);
drawSquare(picture, PANE_SIZE, 3 * BORDER + PANE_SIZE,
           BORDER + BORDER);
drawSquare(picture, PANE_SIZE, 3 * BORDER + PANE_SIZE,
           3 * BORDER + PANE_SIZE);
drawSquare(picture, PANE_SIZE, BORDER + BORDER,
           3 * BORDER + PANE_SIZE);
```

Why stop at just two versions?

You can have as many versions of a function as you like as long as their signatures are unique. Since you're using the same function identifier, this means that the parameter lists must be unique in the sense that either:

- the number of parameters in each version of the function is unique;
- if two or more versions of the function have the same number of parameters, then the type of at least one parameter in the parameter list differs from the corresponding parameter in the other versions.

Lesson: You can use the same name for a function identifier several times over as long as each function has a unique signature.

Let's extend the number of square-drawing functions further.

IMPLEMENTATION:

Replace the single function `drawSquare(...)` in `DrawShapes.h` with the following.

```
bool drawSquare(Canvas& picture);
bool drawSquare(Canvas& picture, int sideLength);
bool drawSquare(Canvas& picture, int sideLength,
                int xPos, int yPos);
bool drawSquare(Canvas& picture, int sideLength,
                int xPos, int yPos,
                int rotationAngle);       // Angle in degrees
```

```
bool drawSquare(Canvas& picture, int sideLength,
                int xPos, int yPos,
                double rotationAngle);    // Angle in radians
```

In the last two versions of `drawSquare(...)`, the parameter `rotationAngle` corresponds to a rotation about the left-hand corner of the square. These versions illustrate the use of the same name for a function with the same number of parameters, but with different types. The compiler recognizes these as entirely different functions.

In a function interface, specification of an identifier for a formal parameter is optional as long as the interface doesn't form part of a function definition. Our style rules say that you should always supply names for formal parameters, but the fact that you don't have to follow our style rules should suggest to you that trying to provide two versions of a function in which the only difference is the name(s) used for the formal parameters is going to incur the wrath of the compiler.

EXAMPLE:

Suppose you wanted to have a version of `drawSquare(...)` that draws a square of a default side length rotated by an angle specified as a parameter. In addition to the other versions, you'd like to have the following.

```
bool drawSquare(Canvas& picture, int rotationAngle);
```

This would be in conflict with the second version of `drawSquare(...)` given in the new version of `DrawShapes.h`. The fact that you've used `rotationAngle` here as the identifier for the second formal parameter instead of `sideLength` is irrelevant. Have some sympathy for that poor old compiler. In the call:

```
if (drawSquare(myPicture, 2))
{
   ...
}
```

how could it possibly be able to select between two versions of `drawSquare(...)` that both have a `Canvas&` as the first parameter and an `int` as the second?

Of course, there's nothing to stop you shuffling the parameter lists around to obtain a unique interface.

EXAMPLE:

The following two function interfaces can coexist.

```
bool drawSquare(Canvas& picture, int sideLength);
bool drawSquare(int rotationAngle, Canvas& picture);
```

The compiler would be able to distinguish between these two function definitions; the types of the parameters are the same in each case but the fact that they appear in a different order means that the function signatures are unique. However, shuffling the parameters around like this isn't a sensible thing to do from a software engineering point of view since it makes the user interface that much more complex.

The uniqueness of functions with the same identifier is determined by the parameter list only; the return type of the function has no role to play here. Let's reinforce the previous lesson.

Lesson: Two functions are unique only if their signatures are unique.

EXAMPLE:

The two functions:

```
bool drawSquare(Canvas& picture, int sideLength);
void drawSquare(Canvas& picture, int sideLength);
```

cannot coexist, despite the fact that one version has a `bool` return type and the other a `void` return type.

You could take the approach that for each version of an overloaded function you're going to need to supply a "self-contained" definition in that it doesn't involve a call to any other version of that function. However, there may be problems in maintaining consistency.

IMPLEMENTATION:

There's a collection of function interfaces in the header file `DrawShapes.h`. What do the implementations in `DrawShapes.c` look like? Suppose you take the "self-contained" approach. `DrawShapes.c` might contain the following.

```
bool drawSquare(Canvas& picture, int sideLength)
{
  if (sideLength <= 0 )
  {
    return false;
  }
  picture.penDown();
  picture.moveRelative(sideLength, 0);
  picture.moveRelative(0, sideLength);
  picture.moveRelative(-sideLength, 0);
  picture.moveRelative(0, -sideLength);
  picture.penUp();
  return true;
} // end drawSquare()

bool drawSquare(Canvas& picture, int sideLength,
                int xPos, int yPos)
{
  if (sideLength <= 0 )
  {
    return false;
  }
  picture.penUp();
  picture.moveTo(xPos, yPos);
  picture.penDown();
  picture.moveRelative(sideLength, 0);
  picture.moveRelative(0, sideLength);
  picture.moveRelative(-sideLength, 0);
  picture.moveRelative(sideLength, 0);
  picture.penUp();
  return true;
} // end drawSquare()
```

Can you see a potential problem with the above implementation? Well, for a start, you can't guarantee consistency between any two versions. You can see that the two versions of `drawSquare(...)` given here are very similar, but we've inadvertently made a mistake in the second. Can you spot it?

The error is that the final call to `moveRelative(...)` should be:

```
picture.moveRelative(0, -sideLength);
```

This is an easily-made mistake.

Replication of large chunks of code is always indicative of poor programming style, so how can you avoid it? By encapsulating those chunks in a function definition. In particular, this may involve defining one version of an overloaded function in terms of another version. You can build up a hierarchy of functions with, at the bottom level, an all-singing, all-dancing "comprehensive" version that takes all parameters possible.

Lesson: When you have a number of overloaded functions to define, consider using a hierarchical approach, if appropriate, to ease maintainability.

However, there are potential drawbacks here. If the effect of making one function call is that calls are made to several other overloaded versions of that function, then both time and space overheads will be incurred just by the function calls themselves. Furthermore, the comprehensive version may require the use of a considerable amount of time and space resources. If you make a call to a "simple" version of the program you'll incur these additional overheads, while a self-contained version might be more efficient.

Lesson: Adopting a hierarchical approach to providing definitions of overloaded functions may prove expensive in terms of time and space usage.

Let's return to the square-drawing functions to illustrate the above points.

DESIGN:

It's easy to see that the only difference between the two versions of `drawSquare(...)` relates to the shift of origin when four parameters are used. So the first version of `drawSquare(...)` is the same as the second, except that the shift of origin is 0 in both the *x* and *y* directions. You can make use of this fact by calling the second version of `drawSquare(...)` from the first.

IMPLEMENTATION:

```
bool drawSquare(Canvas& picture, int sideLength)
{
  return drawSquare(picture, sideLength, 0, 0);
} // end drawSquare()
```

Isn't that neat? Don't be confused that this function definition involves a call to a function of the same name. There's no recursion going on here. The two versions of `drawSquare(...)` are different functions since their interfaces are different.

Why stop here?

DESIGN:

Why not let the second version of `drawSquare(...)` with interface:

```
bool drawSquare(Canvas& picture, int sideLength, int xPos, int yPos)
```

call the version with interface:

```
bool drawSquare(Canvas& picture, int sideLength, int xPos,
               int yPos, int rotationAngle)
```

And that version could call the version with interface:

```
bool drawSquare(Canvas& picture, int sideLength, int xPos,
                int yPos, double rotationAngle)
```

IMPLEMENTATION:

```
bool drawSquare(Canvas& picture, int sideLength,
                int xPos, int yPos,
                double rotationAngle)
{
  const int DISTS = roundToInt(double(sideLength) *
                               sin(rotationAngle));
  const int DISTC = roundToInt(double(sideLength) *
                               cos(rotationAngle));
  if (sideLength <= 0)
  {
    return false;                     // Terminate execution
  }

  picture.penUp();
  picture.moveTo(xPos, yPos);
  picture.penDown();
  picture.moveRelative(DISTC, DISTS);
  picture.moveRelative(-DISTS, DISTC);
  picture.moveRelative(-DISTC, -DISTS);
  picture.moveRelative(DISTS, -DISTC);

  picture.penUp();
  return true;
} // end drawSquare()

int roundToInt(double value)  // Round double to nearest
{                             //   int value
  if (value < 0)
  {
    return int(value - 0.5);
  }
  else
  {
    return int(value + 0.5);
  }
} // end roundToInt()
```

There's some elementary trigonometry involved here. See if you can work out what's going on.

The shape-drawing functions include functions for drawing shapes other than squares; there are functions for drawing triangles and regular polygons. The "base" routine for drawing a square could have been implemented in terms of a call to a base version of `drawRegularPolygon`

(...). That way we could restrict the detailed code for drawing regular shapes to just one function. Maintaining that one function then avoids the duplication of effort in maintaining simpler, more specific implementations in other functions. However, our base version of `drawSquare(...)` doesn't call a base version of `drawRegularPolygon(...)` for two reasons:

1. The trigonometry involved in drawing a square is relatively straightforward; there's a lot of shifting between local/global polar/Cartesian coordinates in the base version of `drawRegularPolygon(...)` that we didn't want to expose you to.
2. Drawing a square using a base version of the function `drawRegularPolygon(...)` would require considerably more arithmetic to be performed than is actually needed to draw a square.

So there's a trade-off to be considered here; maintain detailed base versions of both `drawSquare(...)` and `drawRegularPolygon(...)` and preserve efficiency, or maintain just a detailed base version of `drawRegularPolygon(...)` and sacrifice some efficiency. You pay your money and take your choice. Our choice was to preserve some efficiency and limit the hierarchical structure to functions for drawing shapes with the same number of sides. So, for example, all the square-drawing functions ultimately result in a call to the base function for drawing a square.

Let's end this section by using the square-drawing functions to draw a pretty pattern.

EXAMPLE:

Try a repetition statement of the following form.

```
int angle;
for (angle = 0; angle < 360;
     angle += 10)
{
  drawSquare(myPicture, 25, 100, 100,
             angle);
}
```

This code fragment draws a series of squares rotated through an angle of 10°.

EXERCISES FOR SECTION 11.5

1 Given the function interfaces:

```
int    multiply(int    number, int    multiplier);
double multiply(double number, double multiplier);
```

suppose that the function body for the definition of each function takes the form:

```
{
  number *= multiplier;
  return number;
}
```

What output does the following code fragment produce?

```
int    n                = 5;
double r                = 7.5;
int    intMultiplier    = 3;
double doubleMultiplier = 2.5;

cout << n << "\t times "   << intMultiplier
     << "\t is equal to  " << multiply(n, intMultiplier)
     << endl;
cout << r << "\t times "   << doubleMultiplier
     << "\t is equal to  " << multiply(r, doubleMultiplier)
     << endl;
```

Which version of `multiply(...)` does each function call correspond to?

2 Given the function definitions and variable declarations of Exercise 1, what output does the following code fragment produce?

```
cout << n << "\t times "   << doubleMultiplier
     << "\t is equal to  " << multiply(n, doubleMultiplier)
     << endl;
cout << r << "\t times "   << intMultiplier
     << "\t is equal to  " << multiply(r, intMultiplier)
     << endl;
```

Which version of `multiply(...)` does each function call correspond to?

3 Design and implement a comprehensive set of functions for drawing rectangles.

SUMMARY

In this chapter, you've completed the description of functions by looking at function definitions. You now know that functional abstraction can be a powerful problem-solving tool. You know a lot more about the terms:

- **a function definition** comprises a function interface and a compound statement;
- **a `return` statement** is used to terminate execution of a function body and to return a value from a function call;
- **function overloading** allows you to use the same identifier for related functions with unique signatures.

You've also learned about some more software engineering issues.

- `bool` **return values** can be used to indicate success or failure of a function call;
- **a header file** is used to group a number of related function interfaces;
- **an implementation file** is used to provide the definitions of the functions whose interfaces are in a header file;
- **recursion** is a powerful problem-solving tool;
- **documentation** is an important feature of any good function library;
- **preconditions** indicate the conditions that are expected to hold prior to a function call;
- **postconditions** indicate the conditions that will hold after a function call.

We've concentrated in this chapter on non-member functions. It's time to come to grips with what are arguably the most important features of C++, the features that make it a suitable vehicle for object-oriented programming. Now that you know how to define functions, it's time you found out how to define your own PDTs.

END-OF-CHAPTER EXERCISES

1 Compare and contrast value parameters, reference parameters, constant reference parameters and the return value of a function as mechanisms for passing values to/getting values back in a function call, indicating the merits of each.

2 Provide an implementation for a function that has two value parameters indicating a person's height and weight and a reference parameter that, when a function call terminates, gives the person's body mass index. (See Exercise 4 at the end of Chapter 8).

3 Provide an implementation for a function that has a value parameter indicating a person's body mass index and a `Text` reference parameter that categorizes the index as underweight, OK, overweight or obese. (See Exercise 7 at the end of Chapter 10).

4 Use your solutions to Exercises 2 and 3 to produce an implementation of a function that has two value parameters indicating a person's height and weight and a `Text` reference parameter that is used by the function to categorize the person as underweight, OK, overweight or obese.

5 Adapt your solutions to Exercises 2, 3 and 4 so that they check for validity of all values supplied to your functions.

6 Rewrite the functions you developed in Exercises 2, 3 and 4 so that they use the return mechanism to return the value of the body mass index and weight category, as appropriate. Provide appropriate header and implementation files, and a user and maintenance manual.

7 Write your own functions for drawing squares without using a hierarchical structure; that is, no version of `drawSquare(...)` should invoke a call to any other version. What do you perceive to be the efficiency gains from this approach? Quantify these by performing some timing analysis using the timing functions introduced in Chapter 9.

8 Use `drawRegularPolygon(...)` in `DrawShapes.h` to draw patterns of decagons (10-sided figures) and dodecagons (12-sided figures) rotated through 360° in units of 10°.

9 Use `drawSquare(...)` and `drawTriangle(...)` to develop a definition for a function `drawHouse(...)`. (You're allowed to leave out the curtains and smoke coming out of the chimney, but not the garage.)

10 By making the side length small enough you can use `drawPolygon(...)` to give a passable image of a circle. Write a hierarchy of functions `drawCircle(...)` that make appropriate calls to `drawPolygon(...)`. Hence write a function `drawOlympicRings(...)` that produces the following picture.

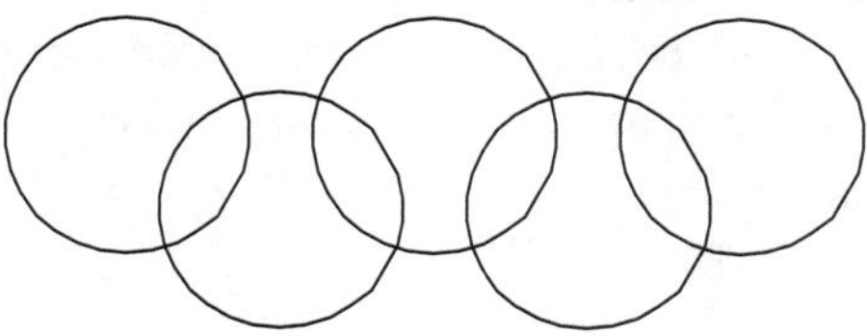

11 Write and test a function that takes an `int` parameter n and uses iteration to return the value of the factorial of that parameter. $n!$ is defined for non-negative values of n only as $n \times (n - 1) \times \cdots 2 \times 1$. How does your function deal with negative values? Write and test a recursive factorial function.

12 Write a recursive function to evaluate m^n for integers m and n using $m^n = m \times m^{n-1}$.

13 Ackerman's function is defined as

$$\begin{array}{ll} a(m,n) = n + 1 & m = 0 \\ a(m,n) = a(m-1,1) & m \neq 0,\ n = 0 \\ a(m,n) = a(m-1,a(m-1,1)) & m \neq 0,\ n \neq 0 \end{array}$$

Work out the value of $a(2,2)$ by hand and write a recursive implementation of this function to verify your answer.

14 Given the four letters A, B, C and D there are 24 ways of writing a three-letter sequence, such as ABC, DAB, etc. in which a letter is used once and once only. Each of these 24 possibilities is known as a permutation. In general, given r objects to be selected from n (with $n < r$) the number of possible permutations, written ${}^nP_r$ can be calculated using the formula

$${}^nP_r = \frac{n!}{(n - r)!}$$

Using your iterative or recursive solution to Exercise 11 to evaluate $n!$ and $(n - r)!$, write a program that reads in two integer values representing n and r and prints the value of ${}^nP_r$.

If the order the letters appear in is not significant then there are only four possible combinations of three letters taken from A, B, C and D, namely ABC, ABD, ACD and BCD. In general, given r objects to be selected from n (with $n > r$) the number of possible combinations, written ${}^nC_r$ can be calculated using the formula

$$ {}^nC_r = \frac{n!}{(n - r)!\, r!} $$

Write a program that reads in two integer values representing n and r and calculates and prints the value ${}^nC_r$.

15 Like the Hilbert curve, the Sierpinski curve is a space-filling curve, parameterized by a level, that has a natural recursive design and implementation. Here's an implementation.

```
void sierpinski(Direction r, Direction d, Direction l,
                Direction u, int i, int h, Canvas& picture)
{
  if (i > 0 )
  {
    sierpinski(r, d, l, u, i - 1, h, picture);
    move(d, r, h);
    sierpinski(d, l, u, r, i - 1, h, picture);
    move(r, r, 2 * h);
    sierpinski(u, r, d, l, i - 1, h, picture);
    move(u, r, h);
    sierpinski(r, d, l, u, i - 1, h, picture);
  }
  return;
} // end sierpinski()
```

The curve is drawn by the following call sequence in `main()`.

```
sierpinski(r, d, l, u, i, h, picture);
move(d, r, h, picture);
sierpinski(d, l, u, r, i, h, picture);
move(d, l, h, picture);
sierpinski(l, u, r, d, i, h, picture);
move(u, l, h, picture);
sierpinski(u, r, d, l, i, h, picture);
move(u, r, h, picture);
```

The function `move(...)` draws a line by making a diagonal move that corresponds to a move of length equal to the third parameter in each of the directions specified by the first and second parameters.

Draw the Sierpinski curves of orders 0, 1 and 2 on paper and then use a computer implementation to check your pen-and-paper results.

12 Constructing new types in C++

OBJECTIVE

To build an understanding of how to construct new types by:

- introducing the C++ constructs that permit you to define new types (PDTs);
  - `enum`
  - `struct`
  - `class`
- showing how I/O operators can be defined for new types;
- examining the software engineering issues associated with testing your newly-constructed PDTs.

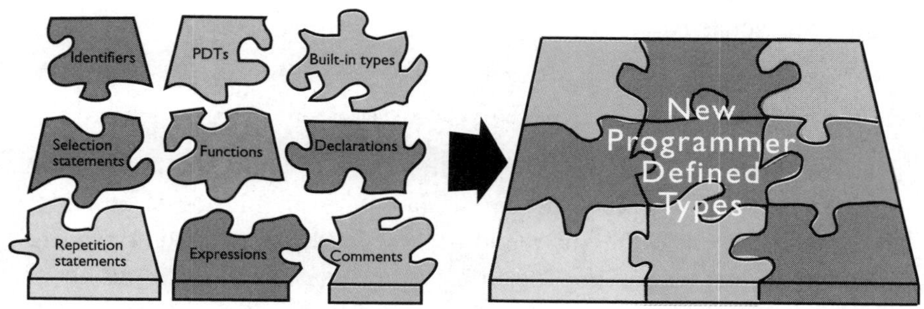

Bringing it all together

12.0 WHY DO YOU WANT NEW TYPES?

You've now covered all of the basic programming constructs of C++. Constructs like declarations, expressions, functions, selection and repetition statements are the basic building blocks from which larger software components can be built. However, consider the following. If you were given the task of constructing a car, which would you prefer to be given: a set of components such as an engine, a chassis, a body, wheels, etc., or a set of basic building blocks such as sheets of steel, nuts and bolts, etc.? Neither probably, which is why you're studying software engineering! But wouldn't one set of components make the job easier than the other? (You can guess which.) You can make the same overall decision when building a software system, and your hands stay much cleaner! The lessons you should appreciate are:

Lesson: A major element of software engineering is identifying software components that you can put together to simplify the construction of larger software systems.

Lesson: Being able to design, implement and test software components in isolation from other components is a key strategy in keeping the implementation of a large software system manageable.

In the previous chapter you saw how to build one form of software component: a function. Functions provide abstractions over sets of statements. A function call is an abstraction hiding all of the detail contained within the function's body. It's almost as if a new executable statement has been added to your programming language. But what else do you need to build programs? The answer is *types.*

PDTs in the software engineering process

Programs manipulate data in the form of objects that are instances of types. The built-in types provided by the language are the basic building blocks that have to be used. If the abstractions provided by these basic types are a long way from the abstractions needed in a system you're trying to design, then you'll have a lot of design work to do. However, if types can be identified at the design stage that are high-level and close to the needs of the problem you're trying to solve then the process of design can be very much simplified. If these types can be provided for a programmer to use (as what we've been calling PDTs) then the implementation stage will also be much simplified, even more so if suitable PDTs are already available.

Lesson: Providing PDTs is effectively extending the programming language to suit the problem at hand. The closer the programming language is to the problem domain, the easier the solution is going to be (that is, the less work you'll have to do :-).

EXAMPLE:

Recall the CD-playing program in Chapter 7. Did the availability of the `CDPlayer` PDT simplify the implementation task? Consider writing a program that draws squares and rectangles on your computer's screen; however, you're not allowed to use the `Canvas` PDT. Does the restriction make your job easier or more difficult?

Chapter 2 showed you how to identify types at the problem-solving stage. This is a skill that takes time to develop a proficiency in; it doesn't come overnight and it's difficult at first to identify types and their interfaces. Over time you'll gain experience and learn from your mistakes, and appreciate what should (and should not) constitute a type.

So far, you've not built any types, but you've used types a lot, without being concerned about how those types were implemented. We hope this has given you a firm appreciation of the benefits of types from a user's perspective. Here you're going to change hats, from being a type *user* to being the type *designer* and the type *implementer*, just as in the previous chapter you learned how to become a function definer to supplement your skills as a function user. In this chapter we concentrate on how PDTs can be implemented in C++, so you've yet more syntax to learn and understand. However, the ability to define PDTs provides you with another tool (a very important tool) in your toolbag and like all tools there's a learning hurdle to overcome. But there are enormous benefits to be gained from surmounting this initial hurdle. So, let's start surmounting!

12.1 C++ MECHANISMS FOR CONSTRUCTING NEW TYPES

There are three mechanisms for constructing new PDTs in C++:

1. `enum` – for simple enumerated abstract values.
2. `struct` – for aggregates of data values.
3. `class` – for PDTs with operations.

In general for a new PDT you have to know how to describe:

1. The **interface** supported by the PDT – that is, how the PDT appears to a user; we call this the **type definition**, as it defines what the type can do for a user.
2. The **implementation** of the PDT – that is, the additional C++ code you have to provide to implement the desired behavior.

It can be very helpful if these two aspects can be cleanly separated. If a user of a PDT has to be aware of implementation details, that user won't get all of the software engineering benefits they deserve.

As well as providing the interface for a user, a type definition also serves to introduce a new PDT to the compiler. As you'll see, there will be an identifier for this type, which must follow the syntax and style rules for type identifiers (Chapter 6). Once the compiler knows about a new PDT, you can use that PDT in subsequent program statements just like any other type. However, if you use a PDT before it has been defined then you'll get a compile-time error. As types often have a global significance it's most common for them to be defined with global scope, just like functions. In C++ this is normally achieved by placing the type definition in a separate file that's `#include`d into the program needing to use that type. Our normal rule for the placement of the include lines ensures such definitions have global scope. However, simple types, such as those defined using `enum`, often appear directly in the same file as the program using them, usually before the definition of `main()`, again giving these types global scope in that program. Thus, type definitions form part of the **compilation unit** syntactic element.

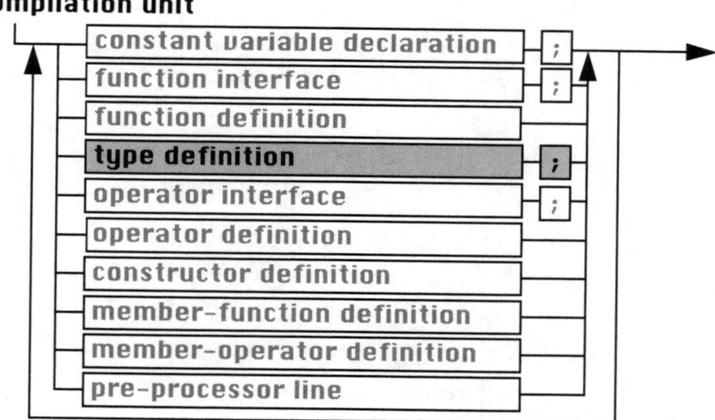

Here are the high-level syntax details of **type definition** that identify the three C++ mechanisms.

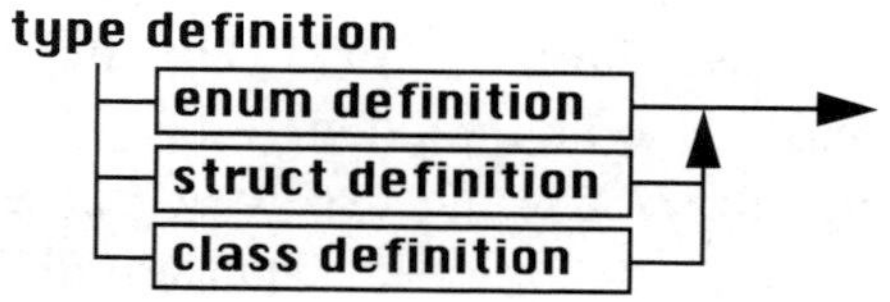

Of course, in order to run a program that uses a PDT, any code that forms part of the implementation of that PDT has to be available, usually in a compiled form to be picked up by the linker.

Let's see what the first and simplest type definition mechanism has to offer.

12.2 ENUMERATED VALUE TYPES

You're familiar with expressing particular values for the built-in types like `int`.

```
int answer = 42;
```

It's also useful to be able to express abstract values for some PDTs. You've seen how details of abstract values are captured in the PDT design notation.

EXAMPLE:

To remind you, here are the relevant fragments of a couple of PDTs from Chapter 5 and a new PDT to represent the main points on a compass.

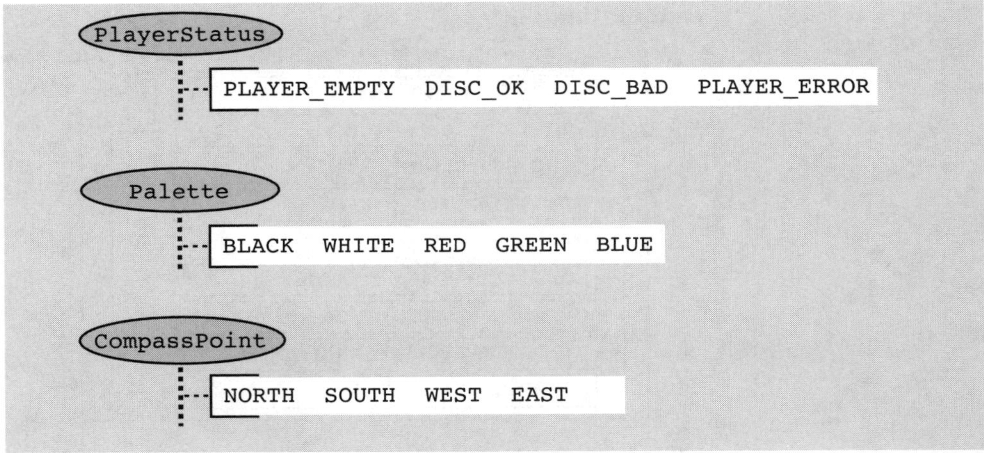

You know how to express abstract values for the built-in types in a program – you just follow the rules for the different literal types. The compiler is responsible for implementing these literals. For PDTs, however, you're the type provider and you have to define and implement the abstract values that a PDT provides. Implementing abstract values such as those for `PlayerStatus` requires use of the `enum` type definition mechanism in C++.

`enum` *definition and implementation*

The `enum` construct in C++ allows you to define simple PDTs consisting of enumerated abstract values with an identifier specified for each abstract value. These are called enumerated values because you have to enumerate, or list, the set of values. An `enum` definition introduces a simple type for which there are no further implementation details to be provided. The general form of an `enum` definition for a new PDT `TypeIdentifier` is:

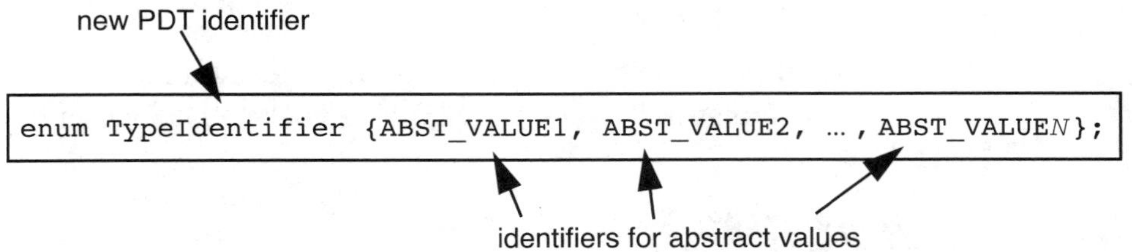

The keyword `enum` indicates to the compiler that a type definition is coming up. The next word is the new type identifier, and the comma-separated identifiers within the braces `{` and `}` define the literals that a programmer can use to represent the abstract values in a program. Note that the braces here aren't being used to surround a compound statement, and the `enum` definition must be terminated by a semicolon. Type definitions are one of the few places in C++ where a `}` is followed by a semicolon.

It's very important to give meaningful identifiers to the abstract values so that when these identifiers are used in a program, they will significantly aid the reading and comprehension of that program. In effect, such identifiers represent literal values for the PDT.

Lesson: Provide meaningful identifiers for the abstract values introduced in an `enum` definition.

Once the compiler has read an `enum` definition, the type identifier (and the literals) can be used in declarations and simple assignment statements in the same manner as any other type identifier or literal.

EXAMPLES:

```
enum PlayerStatus {PLAYER_EMPTY, DISC_OK, DISC_BAD,
                   PLAYER_ERROR};
enum Palette      {BLACK, WHITE, RED, GREEN, BLUE};
enum CompassPoint {NORTH, SOUTH, WEST, EAST};

PlayerStatus status;
Palette      background = WHITE;
CompassPoint direction;
```

You've probably been using the PDTs `Palette` and `PlayerStatus` already, by #including the appropriate header file in the "using" program. In fact, the header file basically just contains an `enum` definition exactly as shown above.

Note that the scope of the identifiers used for the abstract values is essentially the same as the scope of the type identifier that introduces them. So, you can't introduce two `enum` statements that, say, define an abstract value `RED` at the same scope level.

Lesson: The identifiers used to represent abstract values must be unique.

Don't confuse an `enum` definition with a variable declaration. In the `enum` type definition statements above, `Palette`, `PlayerStatus` and `CompassPoint` are not variables of type `enum`, they are the names of new types.

Let's fill in the syntax and style rules for `enum`s before we go any further.

`enum` *definition syntax diagram and style rules*

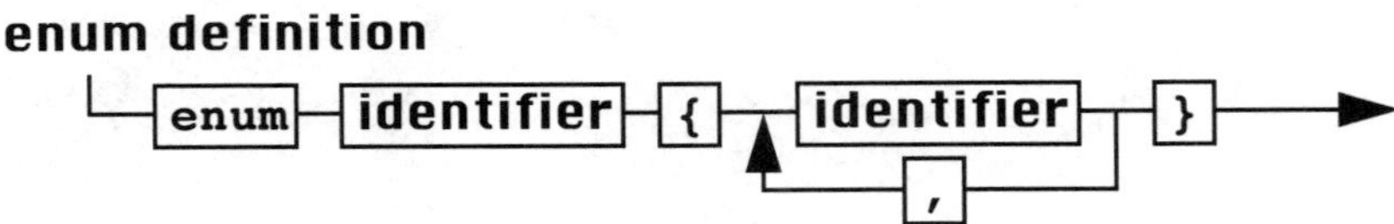

When you provide an **enum definition** as a **compilation unit**, don't forget to add a semicolon at the end.

The **identifier** following the keyword `enum` in the enum definition is the identifier that becomes the PDT identifier. The **identifiers** that occur within the braces are the identifiers that represent the abstract values.

As you've already seen, adopting style rules can help the reader of a program to distinguish between multiple uses of identifiers. The overall style rules for identifiers were given in Chapter 6, together with the additional style rules for PDT identifiers. Let's repeat the additional style rules for PDT identifiers to remind you.

✓ *Begin the type identifier with an UPPER-CASE letter.*
✓ *With identifiers that use multiple words, start the second and subsequent words with an UPPER-CASE letter; use lower-case letters elsewhere.*
✗ *Avoid using underscores (_) to separate words.*

What about style rules for the identifiers representing abstract values? Well, you might have noticed that the values are constant and never change, and it therefore follows that the identifiers should adopt the style rules provided in Chapter 6 for `const` values. In other words, these identifiers adopt the general style rules for identifiers, with the following additions:

✓ *Use UPPER-CASE only for a value identifier.*
✓ *Use underscores to separate multiple words.*

Let's examine a problem where `enum` can be used.

PROBLEM:

A software system is required to keep track of houses that are for sale. The details that need to be recorded include the type of material used in the construction of the house. Design and implement a type for this purpose.

DESIGN:

There is a set of different construction materials, such as:

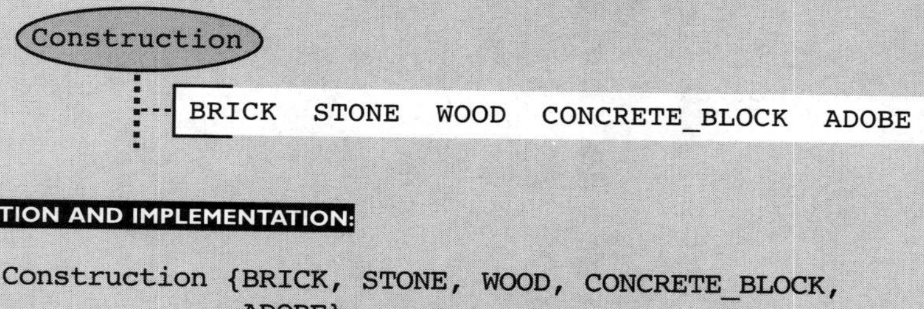

DEFINITION AND IMPLEMENTATION:

```
enum Construction {BRICK, STONE, WOOD, CONCRETE_BLOCK,
                   ADOBE};
```

Now that you know how to define and implement a PDT using `enum`, the next question is what operations can you apply to an instance of an `enum` type?

Operations supported by `enum` *PDTs*

For PDTs defined using `enum`, the compiler automatically provides an assignment operator (=) and the equality test operators (== and `!=`). These are the only operators you can apply to instances of `enum`s.

EXAMPLE:

Given the `enum` definitions you saw earlier, the following are some code fragments showing operations on instances of `enum` PDTs.

```
Palette      background = WHITE;
PlayerStatus status;
CompassPoint direction;
...
background = RED;
if (status == DISC_BAD) ...
```

```
if (direction != SOUTH)
{
  direction = WEST;
}
```

Here are some additional examples of the use of enum. These examples have been extracted from the implementation of the PDT CDPlayer that you've used.

```
enum OpenOrClosed   {OPEN, CLOSED};
enum LoadedUnloaded {LOADED, UNLOADED};

OpenOrClosed   drawerState;
LoadedUnloaded discState;

drawerState = CLOSED;
discState   = UNLOADED;

if (drawerState == OPEN)
{
  cout << "Warning: disc drawer is still open" << endl;
}
```

You may note that two of the enum examples above only define two abstract values. An alternative would be to use the bool type for the associated variables; after all, bool also defines two abstract values (true and false) so why bother introducing another type? The authors of the above code decided that it would be more readable if enums were defined. Were they right?

There isn't really an absolute "right" and "wrong" answer here. The code could be made to work using bools. The code could even be made to work using ints and int values (for example, 0 means OPEN and 1 means CLOSED). Sketch out the C++ code using both bools and ints and see what you think. Of course, we think the enum version is the best. We wouldn't give you second best, would we? :–)

Given the small set of operations automatically available for enum types you might think the following: "So, if I try to add 1 to a variable that's an instance of an enum type, or if I try to perform an ordering operation on such a variable, I'll get a compile-time error helping me not to make these mistakes, won't I?" Unfortunately, you won't. The compiler can coerce an enum abstract value into an int value, and it will apply this coercion implicitly if you try an addition or an ordering operation, both of which are defined for ints. Thus, you won't get a compile-time error. Try it and see. However, some clouds have a silver lining. The fact that the compiler can turn an `enum` into an `int` permits `enum` variables and abstract values to be used in `switch` statements, as was discussed in Chapter 10.

Providing an `enum` type definition gives you a new type, but I/O operations for that type won't be defined automatically. You, the type designer and implementer, have to provide these operations if they're needed, and they often are.

Overloading I/O operators

You could provide I/O operations for an `enum` type by defining functions to perform these operations: for example, functions called `input(...)` and `output(...)`. However, if you did, I/O concerning those `enum`s would be different from all of the other examples of I/O that you've seen and used so far involving `cin`, `cout`, and the operators >> and <<. Software engineering is complex enough without having to remember such differences, and wouldn't it be better if the normal I/O mechanism could be extended to work with `enum` values and variables?

EXAMPLE:

You would have a more uniform and consistent software environment if you could write:

```
CompassPoint direction;
cin  >> direction;
cout << direction;
```

In C++ you can define I/O operators for an `enum` to achieve this uniformity. Recall from Section 9.5 that operators such as >> are in fact "syntactic sugar" for calls to operator definitions.

EXAMPLE:

The two I/O statements from above are translated by the compiler into:

```
operator>>(cin,  direction);
operator<<(cout, direction);
```

Therefore if you provide appropriate operator interfaces and definitions, you can define I/O operators for new `enum` types. The generic interfaces you need for I/O operators for a PDT `TypeID` are as follows.

```
istream& operator>>(istream& inStream,  TypeID& forInput);
ostream& operator<<(ostream& outStream, TypeID  value);
```

Recall that the type of `cin` is `istream` and that of `cout` is `ostream`. Hence you can see the reason for the types of the first formal parameter in these operator interfaces. These formal parameters have to be reference parameters since the operators are going to change the state of the associated stream. Clearly, the input operator has to assign a value that was obtained as input, so its second parameter is a reference parameter (of the relevant type) to permit this. As the output operator simply needs a value, the second formal parameter for that function is a value parameter.

You might wonder why the first parameter is needed at all. Wouldn't the use of the global variables `cin` and `cout` remove the need to specify them in the interface?

The reason for parameterizing the I/O operators in this fashion is for generality. You'll see in Chapter 15 that a program can read from or write to files in exactly the same way that it reads from the keyboard using `cin` or writes to the screen using `cout`, and it's important that your I/O operators can be used in this way. Providing the first formal parameter as above permits this level of generality.

Why is the return type of each operator a reference to the appropriate stream type? To answer this question think about the following output statement. What does this statement translate to if you replace the output operator << with the corresponding function calls, assuming `d1` and `d2` are instances of an `enum` type?

```
cout << d1 << d2;
```

The statement translates to the following nested function calls:

```
operator<<(operator<<(cout, d1), d2);
```

In words, the first actual parameter of the call of the output operator function on `d2` is the result of the first call of the output operator function applied to `d1`, following the normal left-to-right evaluation rule for operators. Thus the result type of the function has to match the type of the first formal parameter; that is, `ostream&`. The return type of the I/O operators could be `void`, but if it was you'd be restricted to writing I/O statements that only involved a single use of the operators >> or <<.

Let's go through a problem to show you how to construct I/O operators for an `enum` PDT.

PROBLEM:

Define I/O operators for the `CompassPoint` PDT introduced earlier.

DESIGN:

The interfaces you require for the I/O operators are as follows.

```
// Operator interfaces for the I/O operators
istream& operator>>(istream& inStream,  CompassPoint& forInput);
ostream& operator<<(ostream& outStream, CompassPoint value);
```

Before you can define the code corresponding to these operator interfaces, you have to design the format of the input data and the form in which values will be output. You're the type designer and implementer so you have full control over this.

For the output of a `CompassPoint` value, it seems sensible to use the form in which it appears in the program; that is, as the words `NORTH`, `SOUTH`, `WEST`, or `EAST`. You might like to consider designing a function to achieve this behavior before you read the operator definition below that provides an implementation.

Now you need to design what the user has to provide as input from the keyboard. You could decide that the user has to supply the integer input value `0` to represent `NORTH`, the value `180` to represent `SOUTH`, the value `90` to represent `EAST` and the value `270` to represent `WEST`. However, again it might be desirable to require the input of text strings corresponding to the abstract value required. The input operator definition below takes the latter approach.

IMPLEMENTATION:

```
ostream& operator<<(ostream& outStream, CompassPoint value)
{
  switch (value)
  {
    case NORTH:
      {
        outStream << "NORTH";
      }
      break;
    case SOUTH:
      {
        outStream << "SOUTH";
      }
      break;
    case WEST:
      {
        outStream << "WEST";
      }
      break;
    case EAST:
      {
        outStream << "EAST";
      }
      break;
    default:
      {
        outStream << "Unexpected CompassPoint value";
      }
      break;
  } // end switch (value)

  return outStream;
} // end operator<<()
```

Yes, it's all that work to convert safely from abstract values in a program (such as `NORTH`) to text string values such as "`NORTH`". As these values are of different types you shouldn't be too surprised! Notice the defensive programming in the above code, providing the default arm to catch unexpected values.

```
istream& operator>>(istream& inStream,  CompassPoint& forInput)
{
  Text input;
  bool gotValue = false;

  while (!gotValue)          // While we've not got a value
  {
    gotValue = true;         // Reset to false if necessary
    inStream << input;
    if (input == "NORTH")
    {
      forInput = NORTH;
    }
    else if (input == "SOUTH")
    {
      forInput = SOUTH;
    }
    else if (input == "WEST")
    {
      forInput = WEST;
    }
    else if (input == "EAST")
    {
      forInput = EAST;
    }
    else
    {
      cout << "Error. Got '" << input << "'"
           << " try again"   << endl;
      gotValue = false;
    }
  } // end while (!gotValue)

  return inStream;
} // end operator>>()
```

Dealing with errors in input data is complex, and is covered in Chapter 15. If the user supplies an unexpected string to the code above, the approach is to print an error message and to loop continuously until an acceptable value has been input. This behavior isn't what normal C++ input operators do; they normally return an error status if illegal input is encountered. We'll cover the details of the features to add to an I/O operator definition to deal properly with errors in Chapter 15.

Header file

You recall that the mechanism for using a PDT is to `#include` the associated header file in the "using" program. So, should a header file be created for a PDT defined using the `enum` mechanism? The answer is usually "yes" and you need to provide a file, the name of which is the identifier for the PDT with a `.h` suffix. A user of your PDT can then `#include` the relevant header file in the same way as they would for other PDTs.

Can you figure out what should go in a header file for an `enum` PDT?

The header file has to contain the information necessary to support use of the PDT. It therefore has to contain the type definition together with the interfaces of any I/O operators that are provided. Should it also contain the definitions of those I/O operators? The answer is usually "no" – the implementation code is normally placed in a separate file (with a `.c`, or similar, suffix) that can be separately compiled and tested, and linked into a using program as appropriate.

EXAMPLE:

Here are the contents of a header file `CompassPoint.h`:

```
enum CompassPoint {NORTH, SOUTH, WEST, EAST};

// Operator interfaces for the I/O operators
istream& operator>>(istream& inStream,  CompassPoint& forInput);
ostream& operator<<(ostream& outStream, CompassPoint  value);
```

So, `enum` is a straightforward type mechanism for you to master. Try these exercises, and then you'll be ready to learn about the `struct` type mechanism.

EXERCISES FOR SECTION 12.2

1 Identify the syntax errors in the following `enum` definition:

```
enum PROG_LANGUAGES = {C, C++, MODULA-2, ADA, Fortran, };
```

2 A program contains the following type definitions. Identify the definitions that will cause compile-time errors, and the reason for those errors.

```
enum TeamGames     {FOOTBALL, CRICKET, ICE_HOCKEY, BASKETBALL};
enum Transport     {CAR, BUS, TRAIN, HORSE}
enum Accommodation {5STAR, 4STAR, BED&BREAKFAST};
enum char          {Y, N};
enum Sports        {TENNIS, FOOTBALL, BADMINTON, SKIING};
enum Primes        {1, 2, 3, 5, 7, 11, 13};
```

3 In Section 2.8 of Chapter 2, you analyzed the Fiddler's bank problem and designed some types for use in solving that problem. Revisit that section and the types designed. Identify one possible use for the `enum` type mechanism and provide an implementation for an appropriate PDT, including a header file, and functions for the I/O operators.

4 Define some `enum`s to represent: whether something is on or off; whether a door is open or closed; the status of a student in a lecture; the quality of a lecture; the different media that are used for recording music.

12.3 AGGREGATE TYPES

Say you were required to write a program that processes details of houses that are for sale. Associated with each house will be a set of data items recording the information about that house, like its address, what kind of house it is, how many bedrooms and garages, the type of its construction, the depth of its swimming pool, and what its selling price is. In programming terms, each of these items will be a data item in its own right, and each will be an instance of a type. But what about the set of items together? Is that set an instance of a type? Would it be useful to have such a type?

Just as an agent selling a house would keep all of a house's details together on a single sheet of paper to give to prospective purchasers who wish to view the information, so in programming terms it is useful to have a single type that represents the aggregation of all of the information. The aggregate type could permit an instance encompassing all of the items to be declared in a single declaration (rather than having to declare each of the individual items separately), yet it would have to permit access to the individual data items as required (for example, to answer the query "What's the price of this house?"). What's needed is provided by C++'s `struct` type mechanism.

`struct` *definition and implementation*

The `struct` mechanism in C++ permits you to define an aggregate type, the components of which are in effect variables, each with their own type and identifier. The general form of a `struct` type definition is:

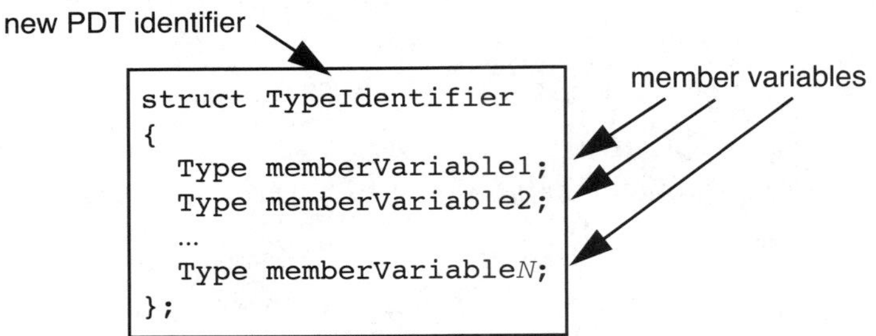

The keyword `struct` tells the compiler that a type definition is coming up, with the next word specifying the identifier for this PDT. There then follows a set of what look like variable declarations, each terminated by a semicolon, enclosed in braces with a final semicolon to indicate the end of the type definition. We term the variables the **member variables** of the `struct` as a parallel to the term "member functions" that you've seen with some PDTs. As with the `enum` type, there are no further implementation details to be provided; the definition provides all that's needed.

EXAMPLE:

Here's a `struct` type definition statement appropriate for some of the house details identified before.

```
struct HouseDetails
{
  Text         address;
  HouseType    houseType;
  int          bedrooms;
  int          garages;
  Construction builtFrom;
  int          sellingPrice;
};
```

Although the member variables look like variable declarations, and syntactically they are declarations, a `struct` definition in itself doesn't result in any variables being declared: the previous example is just defining the type `HouseDetails`. Declarations only occur when this type identifier is used in a variable declaration, as you'll see in a moment.

Having read the example `struct` definition above, did you understand it? You know about some of the types (for example, `Text` and `int`) and, given the other type identifiers used, you probably understand the general idea behind other member variables. To understand the definition completely you might legitimately ask the question: "What are the types `HouseType` and `Construction`?". Of course, the compiler will, metaphorically, ask the same question and will give a compile-time error if, on reading the above type definition, the types `HouseType` and `Construction` haven't been defined. We'll assume that they have been defined; indeed we defined `Construction` in the previous section.

Now that you know how to define a `struct` PDT, what can you do with it and with the member variables?

Declaring `struct` *variables and accessing member variables*

Having defined a type using the `struct` construct, you can declare variables that are instances of this type in the normal manner. Each use of the type effectively declares a set of variables corresponding to the member variables present in the `struct` definition.

EXAMPLE:

```
HouseDetails houseToBeSold;
HouseDetails buckinghamPalace;
HouseDetails whiteHouse;
```

For each of these variables you'll get something like the following in the computer's memory at run-time when the declaration is executed.

	houseToBeSold	buckinghamPalace	whiteHouse
address			
houseType			
bedrooms			
garages			
builtFrom			
sellingPrice			

Don't read anything into the fact that the member variables above have all been drawn the same size. In practice, the amount of memory used by each member variable will be dictated by its type.

The set of member variables that make up the definition of a `struct` *are visible to the user* of the PDT. Note this emphasis on the visibility of the member variables. This is an issue that we'll return to with the `class` mechanism, which takes a very different view.

How do you access the individual member variables of a `struct`? Could you just use the member-variable name?

```
address = "Buckingham Palace Road, London, UK";
```

It may be apparent to a reader of this book which variable the assignment is meant to be applied to. The compiler cannot apply such intelligence. Thus, to fully specify the member variable you wish to access, you have to qualify the member-variable's identifier with that of the identifier of the variable of which it's a part. This qualification of names is achieved using the dot operator that you've used previously for calling member functions:

```
structVariableID.memberVariableID
```

The dot operator permits selection of a member variable, and from that point on you write C++ code in the manner you would have written it if the variable in question wasn't embedded in a `struct`.

Lesson: Use the dot operator to specify a member variable in a `struct`.

EXAMPLE:

Here are some examples of the use of the dot operator.

```
buckinghamPalace.address    = "Buckingham Palace Road, " +
                              "London, UK";
whiteHouse.address          = "1600 Pennsylvania Ave, " +
                              "Washington DC, USA";
houseToBeSold.sellingPrice = 22000;
houseToBeSold.garages       = 2;
...
if (whiteHouse.bedrooms > buckinghamPalace.garages)
...
whiteHouse.builtFrom = ADOBE;  //  :-)
```

As an example of using a member variable that's an instance of a PDT, say a `Canvas` variable was added to the PDT `HouseDetails`:

```
struct HouseDetails
{
  Text          address;
  Canvas        floorPlan;
  // rest as before
};
```

This new member variable could be used in the following manner.

```
HouseDetails aHouse;
...
aHouse.floorPlan.penUp();
```

In this last statement, the identifier `aHouse.floorplan` identifies the member variable named `floorPlan` which is of type `Canvas`. From this point you write the C++ code just as you would for a non-member `Canvas` variable – so that the second dot operator is part of a member-function call.

`struct` *definition syntax diagrams and style rules*

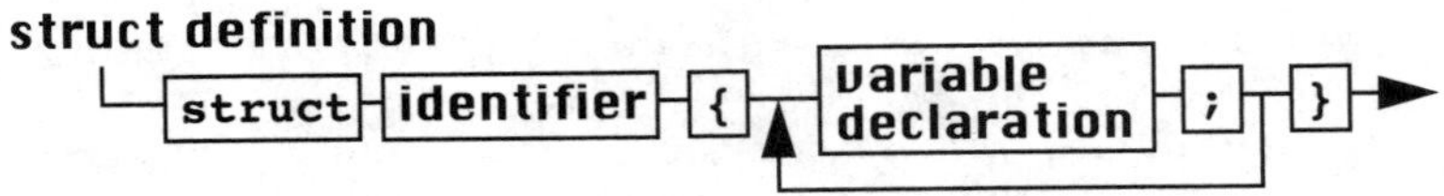

The syntactic elements **identifier** and **variable declaration** are those you saw in Chapter 6. Don't forget that a **struct definition** is followed by a semicolon when used in a **compilation unit**.

As far as accessing member variables is concerned, you can use a member variable wherever you can use a variable, and we can extend the syntactic element **variable** to show this.

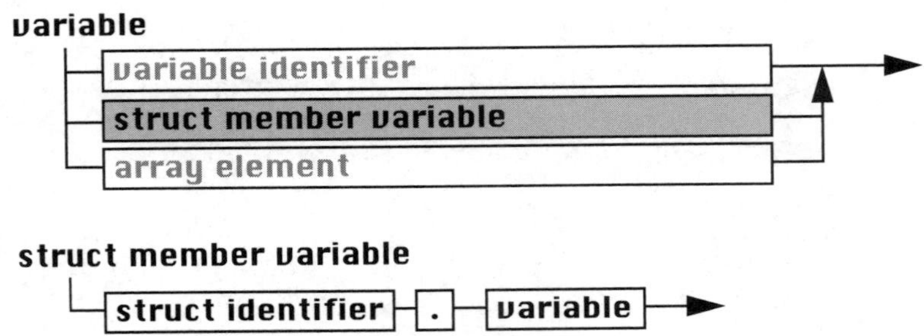

Here are the style rules for the layout of `struct` type definitions.

- ✓ *Follow the style rules for type identifiers.*
- ✓ *Place the opening brace on the line below the keyword* `struct` *and in the same column as the* `s`.
- ✓ *Place the closing brace and semicolon on a separate line, starting in the same column as the opening brace.*
- ✓ *Indent each member variable declaration by two spaces from the column in which the braces appear.*

Let's now see what operations you can apply to a `struct` and its member variables.

Operations supported by `struct` *types*

There are two questions to ask about operations and `struct` types.

1. What operations can be applied to a member variable of a `struct` variable?
2. What operations can be applied to the "whole" `struct` variable?

The answer to the first question is of course "Any operation that's defined by the type of that member variable." You guessed that, didn't you?

For the second question, namely what operations can you apply to the "whole" `struct` variable (for example, to the variable `buckinghamPalace`), instances of `structs` can be:

- declared, as you've seen above;
- assigned to each other.

That's it! The compiler only provides an assignment operator. Assignment of the value of one `struct` variable to another variable (of the same type) results in the value of each of the member variables of the variable on the right-hand side of the assignment operator being copied to the corresponding member variables of the variable on the left-hand side.

The equality operators aren't provided by the compiler, and of course I/O operators on the whole `struct` aren't defined. As discussed in the previous section on `enums`, you can usefully define overloaded functions for the I/O operators >> and <<, in this case to operate on a `struct` instance.

EXAMPLE:

Here are some fragments showing the use of `struct` variables, assuming that an output operator has been defined that outputs the values of all of the member variables within the `struct` variable in a suitable format.

```
HouseDetails houseForSale;
HouseDetails buckinghamPalace;
HouseDetails possibleHouse;
...
houseForSale = buckinghamPalace;
...
if (possibleHouse.garages == 2)
{
  cout << possibleHouse;
}
```

Passing a `struct` variable as a value parameter to a function follows the normal value-parameter behavior; a copy is made, which means a copy of all of the member variables of the actual parameter. Using a `struct` type as the return type in a function permits a function to return an instance of a `struct`, again copying all of the member variables but achieving the effect of returning multiple data items as a single item. This is sometimes useful to avoid having multiple reference parameters in the function signature, which is another way of obtaining multiple return values. Of course, a `struct` variable itself can be used as a reference parameter in a function call. Let's take a look at a problem that demonstrates some of these features.

PROBLEM:

Students love taking exams and professors love marking and grading exams :-). The result of an exam gives a grade that can be one of the following three values: PASSED (corresponding to a mark of 50 or more), FAILED (a mark of 49 or less) or ABSENT. Design and implement a program that constructs an exam record for each student who takes an exam.

An exam record consists of the student's identification number (an integer), first name, last name, and the grade on their exam. The program will permit the input of a student's identification number, first name and last name, together with the student's mark in the exam. A mark of 0 is entered if the student was absent (students present at the exam get a mark of 1 for at least writing their name and identification number on the test paper!). A record of the student and the exam grade is then output to a file. OK, you don't know about files yet, so simulate this part by outputting the student's name and exam grade on the screen. The program continues this input cycle until a zero identification number is entered to signify the end of the data. At this point the program will calculate and print out the statistics for the exam (that is, the number of passes, fails, and absences).

DESIGN:

Analyzing the above problem statement using the method suggested in Section 2.8 allows you to identify the common nouns *a grade* and *a student exam record*. Furthermore, the description suggests that a student record consists of a number of component parts (identification number, two names and exam grade). The only operations required seem to be to access the various components of a student exam record, and to be able to set the grade component. For the grade, the description identifies three abstract values for a grade. This analysis leads to the following designs for two types you could use to solve the problem.

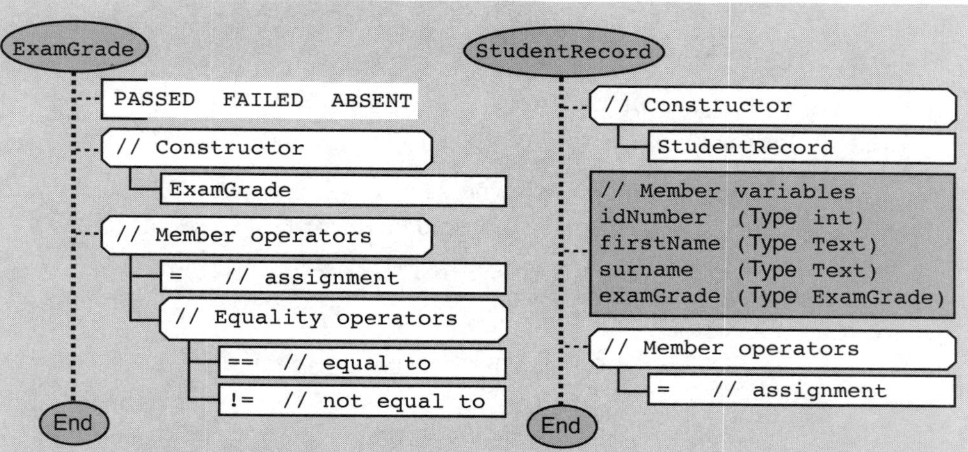

Using these two types, the next stage is to design the program that solves the problem. Here are the main parts of a design.

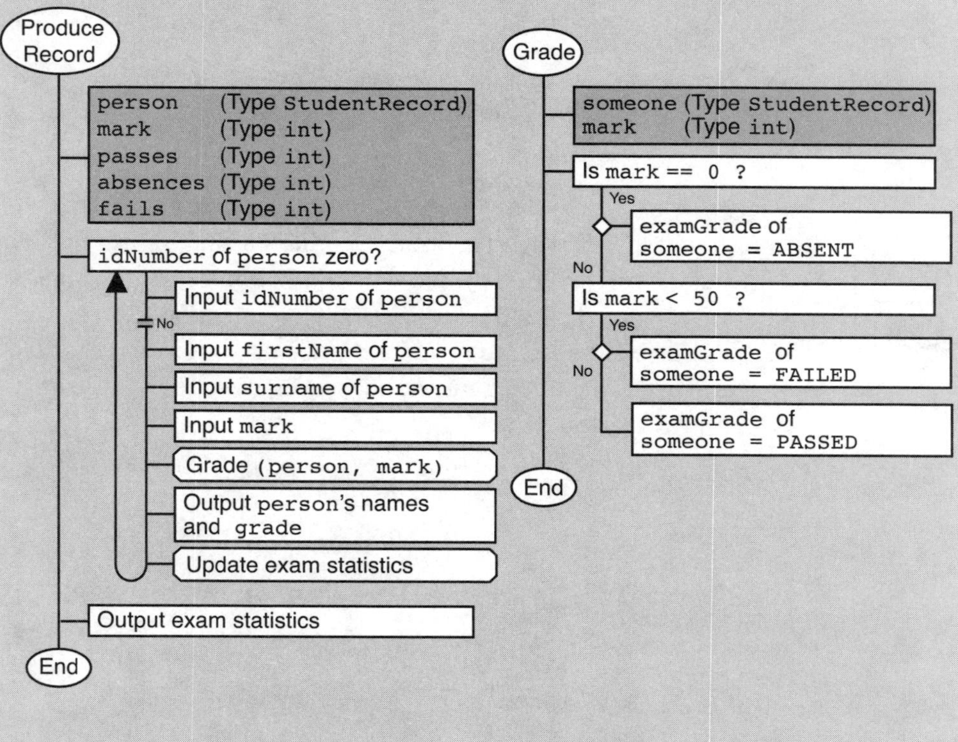

IMPLEMENTATION:

First, consider the two types identified in the design. Which type mechanisms do you think are appropriate for these types?

The "ExamGrade" type seems an ideal candidate for implementation using an enum, while the "StudentRecord" type seems to have a set of data components (member variables) and thus suggests the use of struct.

```
// Type definitions

enum ExamGrade {PASSED, FAILED, ABSENT};

struct StudentRecord
{
  int       idNumber;
  Text      firstName;
  Text      surname;
  ExamGrade examGrade;
};
```

The functional abstraction "Grade" identified in the design can be implemented as a function, and the following interface seems appropriate:

```
void grade(int examMark, StudentRecord& someone);
```

This function takes a first value parameter that represents a mark, and a second reference parameter that represents an instance of a StudentRecord, the examGrade member variable of which is going to be filled in by the "Grade" function. Using some of the other C++ skills you've learned in this chapter and earlier chapters, you can translate the design into the following C++ code.

```
// Type definitions as above

int main()
{
  StudentRecord aPerson;
  int           mark;
  int           absences = 0;
  int           fails    = 0;
  int           passes   = 0;
```

```
while(true)                    // Infinite loop, exit by break
{
  cout << "Enter student details:" << endl
       << "ID number (0 to terminate the program): ";
  cin  >> aPerson.idNumber;              // Input ID number
  if (aPerson.idNumber == 0)
  {                                      // Exit if idNumber is
    break                                //   given as zero
  }
  cout << "First name: ";                // Input first name
  cin  >> aPerson.firstName;             //   of person
  cout << "Surname: ";                   // Input surname
  cin  >> aPerson.surname;               //   of person

  mark = -1;
  while ((mark < 0) || (mark > 100))
  {
    cout << "Mark achieved in exam (0 - 100): ";
    cin  >> mark;                        // Input mark
  }

  grade(mark, aPerson);                  // Grade mark
                                         // Output details
  cout << endl << aPerson.firstName
       << ' '  << aPerson.surname ;
                                         // Update exam
                                         //   statistics and
                                         //   output grade
  if (aPerson.examGrade == PASSED)
  {
    cout << " has passed";
    passes += 1;
  }
  else if (aPerson.examGrade == FAILED)
  {
    cout << " has failed";
    fails += 1;
  }
  else if (aPerson.examGrade == ABSENT)
  {
    cout << " was absent from";
    absences += 1;
  }
  else
```

```
    {                                             // Defensive check
      cout << "ERROR: Unexpected value in examGrade?"
    }
    cout << " the exam" << endl << endl;
  } // end while

  cout << endl                                  // Output exam stats
       << "The number of absentees:      " << absences << endl
       << "The number of fails was       " << fails    << endl
       << "The number of passes was      " << passes   << endl;

  return 0;
} // end main()

void grade(int examMark, StudentRecord& someone)
{
  if (examMark == 0)
  {
    someone.examGrade = ABSENT;
  }
  else if (examMark < 50)
  {
    someone.examGrade = FAILED;
  }
  else
  {
    someone.examGrade = PASSED;
  }
  return;
} // end grade()
```

Limitations of the `struct` *type mechanism*

The `struct` mechanism is useful for forming aggregate data types, where you wish to treat a group of separate but related data items as a single entity. However, as you've seen, `struct` is somewhat restricted as a mechanism for PDTs in that the operations provided are quite limited and not extensible. The `struct` mechanism is concerned with representing data, but not with defining the behavior of instances of the new type.

Moreover, several software engineering problems can result from the use of the `struct` mechanism. First, the data representation is not hidden from the user of the type. The interface to the type *is* the data defined in the member variables; there's no separation between the abstract interface provided by the type and the implementation of that abstract interface.

Second, the data representation is not *encapsulated* and there's nothing the type definer can do to ensure that users of the type use it in the manner intended. For example, there's nothing to prevent a programmer from writing:

```
houseForSale.bedrooms *= 6;
```

even though this wouldn't be a sensible thing to do.

It may be difficult for you to appreciate the true significance of these engineering problems, and things may be somewhat clearer after you've seen what the final type mechanism in C++ can do for you. However, as an example of these two software engineering issues, when you used instances of the PDT `CDPlayer`, were you aware of any data representation it used? No you weren't. The representation was hidden from you, and encapsulated to prevent your program from manipulating things it shouldn't. You might infer from this example that `CDPlayer` isn't defined using the `struct` mechanism, and you'd be right. There's a better mechanism for defining PDTs. We've left this, the best C++ type mechanism, until last.

EXERCISES FOR SECTION 12.3

1 How many variables does this C++ fragment declare?

```
struct foo {int a; int b; int c; };
```

2 Identify which of the following lines would cause a compile-time error, and why.

```
#include "Text.h"

enum Fuel {GAS, DIESEL, STEAM, ELECTRICITY, NUCLEAR};
```

```
struct Vehicle
{
  Text make;
  int  fuelConsumption;
  Fuel fuel;
};

int main()
{
  Vehicle veteran;
  Vehicle greenVehicle;
  Vehicle forSale;

  veteran.make          = "Jowett";
  Jowett.fuel           = GAS;
  green.Vehicle.fuel = ELECTRICITY;
  if (veteran == greenVehicle)
  {
    forSale =                    veteran;
    forSale.fuelConsumption = 100mpg;
  }
  return 0;
} // end main()
```

3 The `Canvas` type uses two `int` values to specify the coordinates of a point on the `Canvas`. Write a C++ `struct` definition that could be used in place of these two values, and show the `moveTo(...)` interface as it would be if it were changed to use your new type.

12.4 CLASSES

In the previous section we implied that C++'s `class` mechanism is the "best" PDT type mechanism provided by the language. Why this accolade? After all there are the other two type definition mechanisms to consider.

Chapter 2 noted the importance of types in designing software systems. In particular, types allow real-world objects in the domain of the problem you are trying to solve to be easily modeled in the software domain. Clearly, it's important that types identified during the design phase can be carried forward and used (as PDTs) during the implementation phase. However, there are some important characteristics that the PDT mechanism in the programming language should exhibit so that the full software engineering benefits of types are obtained. These characteristics are given below, where a ***phrase in bold italics*** is the software engineering term used to describe the issue. We won't try to justify the importance of these issues now, but we'll return to each issue when there are detailed examples that can be referred to for exemplification of the important points.

A PDT mechanism should:

- clearly separate the interface of the PDT (needed by the user of that PDT) from its implementation (***separation of concerns*** and ***information hiding***);
- prevent "misuse" of implementation details by the PDT user (***encapsulation***);
- allow behavior to be defined as well as abstract values;
- permit compile-time checking of programs using a PDT;
- enable PDTs to be developed and tested separately from any "using program" and support reuse.

The reason for awarding the "Oscar for best PDT mechanism in C++" to the `class` candidate is the support it provides for all of the above issues. Given the list, you can perhaps identify the weaknesses with the `enum` and `struct` mechanisms, even though you don't know about classes yet.

Classes are the basis of implementing object-oriented techniques. You've already been *using* object-oriented techniques. You've been invoking type-defined operations on objects (through the use of member-function calls of the form `variableName.memberFunction()`), which is part of the "using" side of the object-oriented world. You've already used several PDTs implemented by classes, such as `Canvas`, `CDPlayer`, `CDisc`, `CSDiscSet`, and `Text`. So you're already an object-oriented software engineer. Take a bow! In this section you'll be introduced to the way you can use the class mechanism to define your own PDTs.

As the class mechanism permits the interface provided by a PDT to be clearly separated from the implementation of that interface, we can address these issues separately. The next two sub-sections do this, introducing the basic C++ syntax features for classes and how you normally use them. We'll further reinforce these ideas, as well as introduce some additional class features, in the next chapter where we'll go through the design, definition and implementation of more example classes.

`class` *definition*

So far you've already used and seen parts of several `class` interfaces. However, the full C++ details haven't been shown to you. We've used abstraction in the form of the design notation, as in Chapter 5, to describe a PDT's interface without exposing you to all of the C++ syntax for the definition of a `class`. But now you're just dying to learn some more C++ syntax, aren't you!

First, what do you think the purpose of a class definition is?

A class definition has two roles to play. First, it has a compile-time role, since it defines what the `class` consists of. This permits the compiler to compile source code that uses the type defined by that `class`, as well as to apply compile-time checks for illegal uses of the type in the source code. Second, as the definition is the true specification of all of the syntactic details of the interface provided by that `class`, it forms vital documentation for a (human) user of the `class` to look at. You'll need to start reading class definitions as a means of understanding the interface you need to use, especially for classes that aren't expressed using the design notation. So what's in a class definition?

C++ class definitions have the following overall structure:

```
class TypeIdentifier
{
  public:                     // Public part of the class definition
                              // Interfaces available to a user
    TypeIdentifier();                   // Constructors

    ResultType memberFunction(...); // Member functions

    ResultType operator+(Type rhs); // Member operators

  private:                    // Private part of class defn.
    ...                       // Declarations, type defn. and
                              //   function interfaces that are
                              //   NOT available to a user
};
```

A class definition has much the same overall structure as the `struct` construct you saw in the previous section: a keyword (`class`) followed by a *TypeIdentifier* followed by a pair of braces enclosing some items and terminated by a semicolon.

Within the class definition there are two clear sections: that labeled `public`, and that labeled `private`.

The `public` section defines the *publicly-available part* of the class definition; essentially, the C++ description of the PDT interface consisting of the constructors, member functions and member operators. We'll leave the details of member operators until the next chapter.

The `private` section contains declarations and interfaces relating to the *implementation* of the `class`. Any of the features that appear in the `private` section cannot be accessed directly by a program using the `class`, as you'll see. So the information there is effectively invisible to a user's program, even though it's visible to the user's eye. (It's there essentially to assist the compiler in compiling a program that's declaring variables using the `class`.) So, a C++ class definition doesn't really provide complete ***information hiding*** for the reader of the definition, although it does hide the information in that a program using the class can't get at that information.

Following, and separate from, the class definition there may be interfaces for I/O operators associated with the `class` just like you saw earlier for `enum`s and `struct`s. Since users may require I/O operators for variables that are instances of a class, the I/O operator interfaces are part of the interface provided for the PDT even though they aren't syntactically part of the class definition.

```
class TypeIdentifier
{
  // As above ...
};

// Interfaces of I/O operators
istream& operator>>(istream& inStream,  TypeIdentifier& forInput);
ostream& operator<<(ostream& outStream, TypeIdentifier  value);
```

The C++ convention is to place a class definition and its I/O operator interfaces in a header file called *`TypeIdentifier`*`.h` where *`TypeIdentifier`* is the name of the `class`. A user program can then

```
#include "TypeIdentifier.h"
```

to use this `class`, just like you've been doing for other PDTs in your programs. You might like to take a look inside some of the PDT `.h` files that you've been using in order to identify the information discussed above.

The C++ descriptions of the member functions within the public section of a class definition are simply the interfaces of those member functions. They're not the definitions (or implementations) of the member functions themselves; those are separate, as we'll discuss later. Do you have a feeling that you've seen something like this before? That's because you have. This is very similar to what's been discussed for (non-member) functions in Chapter 11. So, expect to place the member-function definitions in an implementation (`.c`) file. All the compiler needs to be able to compile programs using member functions of the `class` is their interfaces in the header file.

To provide a concrete example of these ideas, let's develop a class for a type you designed a long time ago, way back in the mists of time in Chapter 2.

PROBLEM:

Remember the English description of the Fiddler's Bank problem that you analyzed to identify some types? One of the types identified was a bank account with an associated set of operations. Let's develop that as a class.

DESIGN:

The design derived for the Bank Account in Chapter 2 was as follows.

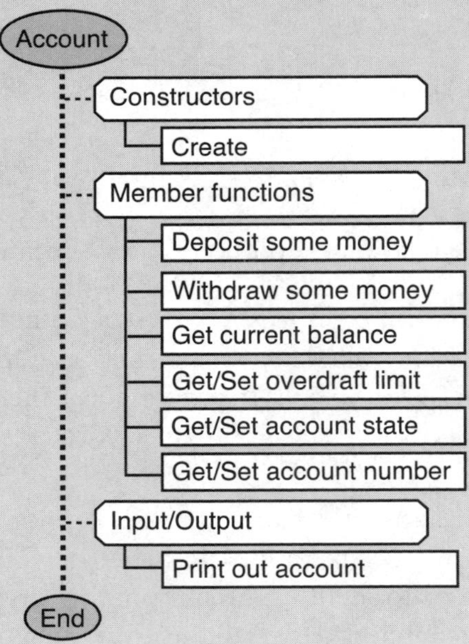

DEFINITION:

You're going to approach the definition and implementation of the `Account` PDT in easy stages. First you're going to provide a skeleton for the class definition that will eventually go into a file called `Account.h`. The following fragment shows the C++ outline you can start with.

```
class Account
{
  public:

    // Constructors

    // Member functions

  private:
    ... // To be completed later
};
```

Now, what are those things called "Constructors"?

Constructors

The constructors in a class interface are concerned with the declaration of variables that are instances of the `class`. You probably haven't been aware of the fact that a constructor in C++ is implemented as a function. Of course, there hasn't been any need for you to be aware of this implementation detail (the power of abstraction again), until now. If you need to define classes then you need to know what to put in the class definition for the constructors. Can you now guess what's required? Yes, a function interface.

However, the interface for a constructor is a little different from that of other member functions in two respects. First, the name of the function must be identical to the `TypeIdentifier` of the `class`. Thus constructor functions can't follow our normal style rule requiring function identifiers to start with a lowercase letter. Second, you must not specify a return type for the constructor, not even `void`.

The interface for the normal, or **default constructor** in a class definition specifies a parameterless function.

```
TypeIdentifier();     // Interface of default constructor
```

A declaration of the form:

```
TypeIdentifier variableID;
```

results in the compiler arranging for the default constructor to be called at run-time, when the variable is created. Since you don't use the parentheses when you're writing a normal declaration, we didn't show the constructors with parentheses `()` in the diagrams in Chapter 5.

Given that the constructor is a function that will be called, the definition of the function can provide some behavior such as initializing the variable that's being declared. However, for some classes you may find that there's nothing for the constructor to do. In these cases you can leave the constructor interface out of the class definition altogether. If you do, the compiler will generate a default constructor for you. So, if you see class definitions without a constructor, this doesn't mean that you can't declare variables of that type!

Let's provide a constructor for the Fiddler's Bank example and show you later what a constructor's implementation can do.

DEFINITION:

Add a constructor interface to the skeleton class definition:

```
class Account
{
    public:

    // Constructor
    Account();
    ...
```

Given that a constructor is just implemented as a function, you might wonder whether it's possible to specify a non-empty formal parameter list for a constructor, as you've seen for other functions. Not only is it possible, but the ability to pass parameters to constructors turns out to be a very useful feature. In fact, it's common for a `class` to define multiple constructors, and these constructors can serve very useful roles. However, let's walk before we try to run, so we'll postpone discussion of this additional feature until the next chapter. For the moment, note the following lessons about constructors.

Lesson: The identifier for a constructor function must be identical to the `TypeIdentifier` of the `class`.
Lesson: You must not specify a return type for the constructor.
Lesson: A constructor interface may be omitted from a class definition.

That's covered the constructor part of a class definition. Do you remember what member functions are all about? You should; you've used member functions quite a bit so far!

Member functions

The member functions define the operations that a class provides and are represented as function interfaces in the class definition. The standard rules for function interfaces apply, as discussed in Chapters 9 and 11. There's not much else to say about them at this point, except perhaps to mention the importance of choosing sensible, meaningful names for the member functions and their parameters. After all, a user is going to be reading those interfaces to figure out how to use your type.

DEFINITION:

For the next stage in the development of your `Account` class definition, you can provide member-function interfaces for all of the member functions identified in the design. You have to decide upon identifiers for the member functions, what their return type is, and what their formal parameter lists consist of. These interfaces are all going to be part of the public section of the class definition.

```
class Account
{
  public:

    // Constructor
    Account();

    // Member functions
    void  deposit(int amountMoney);
    bool  withdraw(int howMuch);
```

```
    int   balance();
    int   overdraftLimit();
    int   accountNumber();
    State accountState();
    void  setOverdraftLimit(int newLimit);
    void  setAccountNumber(int newNumber);
    void  setAccountState(State newState);
  private:
    ... // To be completed later
};
```

"What's that type `State` used above?" you might ask, and rightly so. It's the type used to represent the state of an account. If you completed Exercise 3 at the end of Section 12.2 you'll already have an appropriate PDT in your toolbag to reuse, with a type definition such as:

```
enum State {OPEN, CLOSED, OVERDRAWN, STOPPED, SPECIAL};
```

You know of course that this type definition has to precede any use of the type, otherwise you'll get a compile-time error. So, the header file for `Account` will need to `#include "State.h"` assuming that the PDT `State` has been engineered in the manner described in Section 12.2. We'll show this header file inclusion later.

Onward to the member operators. Fortunately, they won't take long to cover.

Member operators

We mentioned member operators earlier, only to say that we were going to postpone their discussion until the next chapter. Fortunately, the design for the `Account` class didn't identify the need for any member operators.

Hang on though. Are there any operators that you might need `Account` to provide?

If you're not going to provide any member operators for `Account`, does that mean you can't write an assignment statement that assigns the value of one `Account` variable to another?

Since assignment is a fundamental paradigm of C++, the compiler can automatically provide an implementation for the assignment operator for a new PDT.

While in Chapter 5 we've shown the assignment operator as part of the interface for PDTs, you often won't find an interface for an assignment operator in a C++ class definition.

Lesson: The compiler can automatically provide an assignment operator.

DEFINITION:

So, let's do no work in this respect for the `Account` type, and allow the compiler to provide an assignment operator.

What about I/O operators? Good question.

I/O operators

You can provide operator interfaces for the I/O operators for a class, just as you can for an `enum` or `struct`. These interfaces will be part of the class interface, but *not* part of the class definition, so they'll be a part of the header file and normally appear after the class definition.

DEFINITION:

For `Account`, the design indicates that you just need an output operator.

```
class Account
{
  ... // as before
};

ostream& operator<<(ostream& outStream, Account value);
```

Note that the definition of PDT `ostream` will be needed at compile-time, via a pre-processor line `#include <iostream.h>` that's not shown in the above fragment.

The `private` *section*

The final piece of the class definition jigsaw is concerned with the private section. Even though we're discussing class definition (the view of the class as seen by a user of that class) we're now beginning to think about how the class is going to work, and switching from being the class interface designer to being the class implementer. As some of the implementation details have to appear in the class definition (in the private section), this is a good place to start. But what are you going to use this section for? To begin to explain this, let's recap the notion of a variable's value.

You know that variables have a retained value. A variable's value may be changed by assignment and the value may be recalled as required; for example, for use in an expression. For some PDTs, the abstract value can also be changed indirectly as a result of member-function calls.

EXAMPLE:

A variable of type `Text` has a value that represents the string of characters assigned to that variable. This value can be recalled for use in an output statement.

Part of the state associated with the `CDPlayer` PDT is the status of the player, which is changed by member functions such as `nextTrack()`.

The value of an instance of the `Canvas` PDT includes the current color that's used for drawing. Once this color has been set for a particular `Canvas` instance, using the member function `setPenColor(...)`, that color is remembered and used for every subsequent drawing operation (unless changed again).

A class implementer has to implement retained values for variables that are instances of the `class`, to implement the abstract values that the `class` defines. In other words the implementer has to provide the **concrete representation** for the `class`. This is the main purpose of the `private` section of the class definition. In this section, the implementer can indicate the set of variables used to implement the abstract representation for each instance of the `class`, together with any other variables needed to implement the desired behavior.

DEFINITION:

What variables do you think you'll need to represent an instance of `Account`? What things have to be "remembered" for each bank account?

Looking back at the earlier work you've done on the class design and definition, you can identify that an account has a number, a current balance, a maximum overdraft and a current state. So you'll need variables to hold all of these quantities, and the variables are "declared" in the private section of the class definition:

```
class Account
{
  public:
    ... // as before

  private:
    // Member variables
    int   number;
    int   currentBalance;
    int   maxOverdraft;
    State state;
};
```

The member variables aren't declared when the class definition is read by the compiler. However, when an instance of the class is declared, the set of variables described in the private section is declared (and created). You get a complete set of the variables for each instance of the class that you declare.

Are you thinking "I've seen this behavior before somewhere . . ."?

You'd be correct in thinking this. The behavior is similar to that which occurs for `struct`. And now you might be thinking "So a program that's using a class can access the private member variables, just like it can access a `struct`'s member variables." Here, though, you'd be wrong in thinking this.

Identifiers that occur in the `private` section of a class cannot be accessed by a program that's using that class. In other words, **information hiding** is enforced so that a program using the class cannot accidentally (or maliciously) use any of the private variables. The private variables simply aren't in the scope of the "using" program, nor can they be brought into scope using the dot operator.

EXAMPLE:

The following fragment generates a compile-time error.

```
#include "Account.h"
...
  Account myAccount;
  ...
  myAccount.balance *= 10;    // Compile-time error
```

You might be thinking that maybe there should be some variables in the public section to get around this "feature." You might be thinking that this restriction on access to the items in the private section is a bit of an unnecessary nuisance. However, there are very important software engineering reasons why variables don't appear in the public section, and several advantages that accrue from the apparent restriction, even if you don't see the merit of the restriction. You wouldn't want to multiply your bank balance by 10, would you? :-) We discuss these advantages in more detail in the next chapter. For the moment, just note:

Lesson: There should be no variable declarations in the public section of a class definition.

The private section isn't limited to holding just variable declarations. If there are member functions that you (the class implementer) wish to be private, then the interfaces for those functions can also appear in the private section.

Do you think a "using" program can call a member function whose interface occurs in the private section of a class definition?

You answered "no" didn't you?

At an early stage in the development of a class it's unlikely that you will identify any private member functions. Their need will occur as you get further into implementation details, and as the need arises you add the interfaces to the private section of the class definition.

DEFINITION:

It turns out from later development that there are two private member functions that are useful for implementing `class Account`. Their purpose will become apparent in the following sub-sections. We're including them now so that we can show you the complete class definition. Here are the contents of the file `Account.h`.

```
#include <iostream.h>
#include "bool.h"
#include "State.h"

class Account
{
  public:
    // Constructor
    Account();

    // Member functions
    void  deposit(int amountMoney);         // Deposit  money
    bool  withdraw(int howMuch);            // Withdraw; true
                                            //   return if OK.
    int   balance();                        // Return current
                                            //   balance
    int   overdraftLimit();                 // Return over-
                                            //   draft limit
    int   accountNumber();                  // Return number
    State accountState();                   // Return state
    void  setOverdraftLimit(int newLimit);  // Set overdraft
                                            //   limit
    void  setAccountNumber(int newNumber);  // Set number
    void  setAccountState(State newState);  // Set state

  private:
    // Member variables
    int   number;
    int   currentBalance;
    int   maxOverdraft;
    State state;

    // Private member functions
    bool isInitialized();
    void accountOK();
};

ostream& operator<<(ostream& outStream, Account value);
```

Let's continue with the implementation aspects of classes, since you're dying to know the answer to the following question: "If a using program can't access the private member variables, who can?" "The implementations (or definitions) of the member functions" is the answer.

`class` *implementation*

The implementation of a `class` has to provide the C++ code that defines the constructors, member functions and I/O operators, the interfaces of which appear in the header file. Normally this implementation code is placed in a file named *`TypeIdentifier`*`.c` that can be compiled separately, and then linked with any program using the PDT. Thus the implementation code for a `class` can be kept separate from the interface, and from any program that wishes to use that `class`.

Is there anything special about writing definitions for `class` constructors and member functions? Well, apart from two main caveats, the answer is "No." Constructors and member functions are defined (that is, implemented) just like ordinary (non-member) functions, and can use the full range of C++ statements. The two caveats relate first to some additional syntax that's required to define the functions, and second to the scope of the private member variables.

The syntax that's required permits the compiler to associate a member-function definition with the associated class member-function interface, by using a new C++ operator that you haven't seen before: the **scope resolution operator `::`** This operator is used to prefix an identifier with the name of the class the identifier is associated with; that is, to specify the *scope* that the identifier has to be resolved with respect to. This is best seen in the context of an example of how you relate (member) function definitions to the class member-function interfaces.

EXAMPLE:

Given the class definition skeleton:

```
class TypeIdentifier
{
  public:                            // Interfaces
    TypeIdentifier();                        // Constructor interface
    ResultType memberFunction(...);  // Member-function interface
  private:
    ...
};
```

the definitions of the corresponding member functions are of the following form.

```
TypeIdentifier::TypeIdentifier()
{ // Constructor code
   ...
}

ResultType TypeIdentifier::memberFunction(...)
{ // Member-function code
   ...
}
```

The scope resolution operator is used to qualify the member-function identifier with the identifier of the `class` for which it's a member. This permits the compiler and linker to figure out which bodies go with which interfaces (for example, there could legitimately be two member functions in different classes with the same name).

Lesson: In the definitions of constructors and member functions, the identifier for the function is prefixed by the identifier of the class of which it's a part.

When the identifier of a function is prefixed by a class identifier and the scope resolution operator, the compiler can recognize that the function is part of the implementation of the associated class. Of course, this implementation may need to manipulate the private member variables in order to provide the (abstract) behavior required. Constructor and member-function definitions are therefore permitted direct access to private member variables in the associated class, unlike any program that's "using" that class. As far as the using program is concerned, the variable that's an instance of the class is a black box, the private internals of which can't be seen or accessed. Inside a constructor or member-function definition, the black box is opened up to make the private member variables visible (that is, to bring them into scope).

EXAMPLE:

The implementation of the member function `withdraw(...)` of `class Account` will need to subtract the amount being withdrawn from the current balance, as represented by the private member variable `currentBalance`.

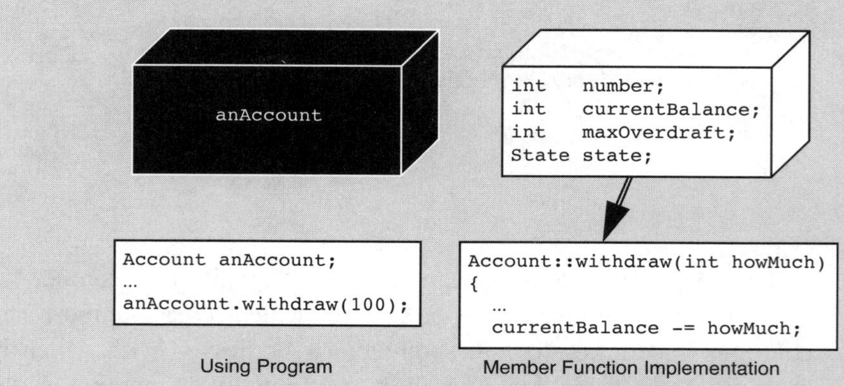

In effect, the private member variables are in scope inside the definitions of constructors and member functions. Using these variables doesn't require any further syntactic notation such as use of the scope resolution operator. You can simply use the variable's identifier without further fuss and bother.

Lesson: A constructor or member-function definition can access private member variables directly.

The upcoming examples will help clarify this. In the following sub-sections we concentrate primarily on implementation aspects and leave further discussions of some of the software engineering issues to the next chapter.

Constructor implementation

You recall that a constructor is a function that's called when a variable that's an instance of the class is declared. Suppose there's a class `Type` and the following declaration is made.

```
Type var;
```

At run-time this declaration results in the creation of the set of private member variables of the class `Type`. It's the compiler's responsibility to create (declare) all of the private variables and then to call the default constructor `Type()`.

If any of the private member variables are themselves instances of PDTs then the appropriate constructors of those classes are automatically called by the compiler as part of their declaration, before `var`'s constructor is invoked. Any private member variables that are instances of a built-in type are created just as in a non-member variable declaration (and you remember what such variables are (not) initialized to, don't you?).

EXAMPLE:

Consider the following fragments of code. What messages do you think are output when the program is executed?

```
class Class0
{
  public:
    Class0();
  private:
    int class0Private;
};

class Class1
{
  public;
    Class1();
  private:
    Class0 class1Private;
};

Class0::Class0()
{
  cout << "Class 0 constructor" << endl;
  return;
} // end Class0()

Class1::Class1()
{
  cout << "Class 1 constructor" << endl;
  return;
} // end Class1()
```

```
int main()
{
  Class1 instance;

  return 0;
} // end main()
```

Figure 12.1 Constructor invocation

OUTPUT:

Execution of the program in Figure 12.1 will result in the following output messages.

```
Class 0 constructor
Class 1 constructor
```

In processing the declaration of `instance`, the compiler has to create an instance of `Class0` for the private member variable `class1Private`. To do this, the compiler has to create the private member variable `class0Private` and then call the default constructor of `Class0`. Hence the first message. The declaration of `class1Private` is then complete and so `Class1`'s constructor is called, resulting in the second message. On termination of `Class1`'s constructor, the declaration of `instance` is complete.

One of the roles a constructor can play is to initialize the private member variables to something sensible. This is particularly important when private member variables are instances of the built-in types. To prevent a "using" program from using an uninitialized instance of your class, you might wish to use the constructor to record the fact that the instance hasn't been initialized. Let's do this for `Account`.

IMPLEMENTATION:

The constructor for `Account` can be defined as follows: use a sentinel value for the account number to indicate that an account hasn't been initialized (an account's number has to be set to initialize an account).

```
const int NOT_INITIALIZED = 0;

Account::Account()
{
  number         = NOT_INITIALIZED;
  currentBalance = 0;
  maxOverdraft   = 0;
  state          = OPEN;
  return;
} // end Account()
```

If you don't provide a constructor, it may be difficult to define clear semantics for the state of a variable that's declared as an instance of the class. The state of the private member variables will be whatever their default constructors provide (or will be random values if they're instances of the built-in types). Instead, it's much better if you provide a constructor that initializes each member variable (and hence the abstract state) to some sensible value, or to some value that permits the use of uninitialized variables to be detected in the implementations of the member functions and operators.

Lesson: Always explicitly provide a (default) constructor that initializes the state to a sensible abstract value, or to something that can be detected as representing an uninitialized value.

The next stage of development of a `class` is to provide definitions for the member functions.

Member function implementation

You have to write code for the member functions (both the public and private ones) that implement the behavior required. There's not a lot more to say than this! Let's see what's required for `Account`.

IMPLEMENTATION:

Following are some examples of definitions of the member functions of `Account`. The full set can be found in the indicated files. Note the role of the private member functions `isInitialized()` and `accountOK()` in the examples.

```
void Account::setAccountNumber(int newNumber)
{
  if (isInitialized())
  {
    error("Account::setAccountNumber()"
          " - the account already has a number");
  }
  else
  {
    number = newNumber;
  }
  return;
} // end setAccountNumber()

bool Account::withdraw(int howMuch)
{
  accountOK();
  if (howMuch > (currentBalance + maxOverdraft))
  { // If we get here, the amount requested is too much for
    //   the current balance and overdraft limit. Check
    //   state of account
    if (state != SPECIAL)
    {                             // Not in SPECIAL state-
      return false;               //   don't permit
    }
  }
  currentBalance -= howMuch;      // Decrease the amount in acc.
  if (currentBalance < 0)         // Become overdrawn?
  {
    if (state != SPECIAL)
    {                             // Set OVERDRAWN if it's
      state = OVERDRAWN;          //   not SPECIAL
    }
  }
  return true;
} // end withdraw()

int Account::balance()
{
  accountOK();
  return currentBalance;
} // end balance()
```

```
        /////////////////////////////////////////
        // Private member-function definitions//
        /////////////////////////////////////////

// isInitialized() - return true if initialized,
//                           false otherwise

bool Account::isInitialized()
{
  return (number != NOT_INITIALIZED);
} // end isInitialized()

// accountOK() - check the account, giving an error and halt
//               if the account shouldn't be manipulated

void Account::accountOK()
{
  if (!isInitialized())
  {
    error("Uninitialized Account variable");
  }
  switch(state)
  {
    case OPEN: case OVERDRAWN: case SPECIAL:
      break;  // Nothing to do for these cases
    case CLOSED:
      {
        error("Account:: This account has been closed");
      }
      break;
    case STOPPED:
      {
        error("Account:: This account has been stopped. "
              "Please call the manager");
      }
      break;
    default:
      {
        error("Account::accountOK() - unexpected account state");
      }
      break;
  } // end switch
  return;
} // end accountOK()
```

What's left in your staged development of a class? Just the I/O operators.

I/O operator implementation

The I/O operators are implemented just as you saw in the earlier sections for `enum` and `struct`, and there's only one new point to make here.

Do you need to qualify the definitions for the I/O operators with the class identifier and the scope resolution operator?

No, you don't need to use the scope resolution operator in the definitions of the I/O operators, since these operators are stand-alone operators and not part of the class definition. But remember that since the operators are not a part of the class implementation, they therefore can't access private member variables. An I/O operator definition is simply a "user" of a class with access through the normal public interface.

IMPLEMENTATION:

The output operator for `Account` can use member functions to obtain the information it needs. The code below assumes the existence of an output operator for the PDT `State`; you should already have one in your toolbag from Exercise 3 in Section 12.2.

```
ostream& operator<<(ostream& outStream, Account value)
{
  outStream << "Account Number:  "
            << value.accountNumber()  << endl
            << "Balance:          "
            << value.balance()        << endl
            << "Overdraft Limit: "
            << value.overdraftLimit() << endl
            << "Account State:    "
            << value.accountState()   << endl;
  return outStream;
} // end operator<<()
```

That covers all of the basics of implementing a class. Let's take a look at the syntax diagrams for the features we've examined.

`class` *definition syntax diagrams and style rules*

The syntax for a class definition is given by the following diagrams, highlighting the points covered in this chapter.

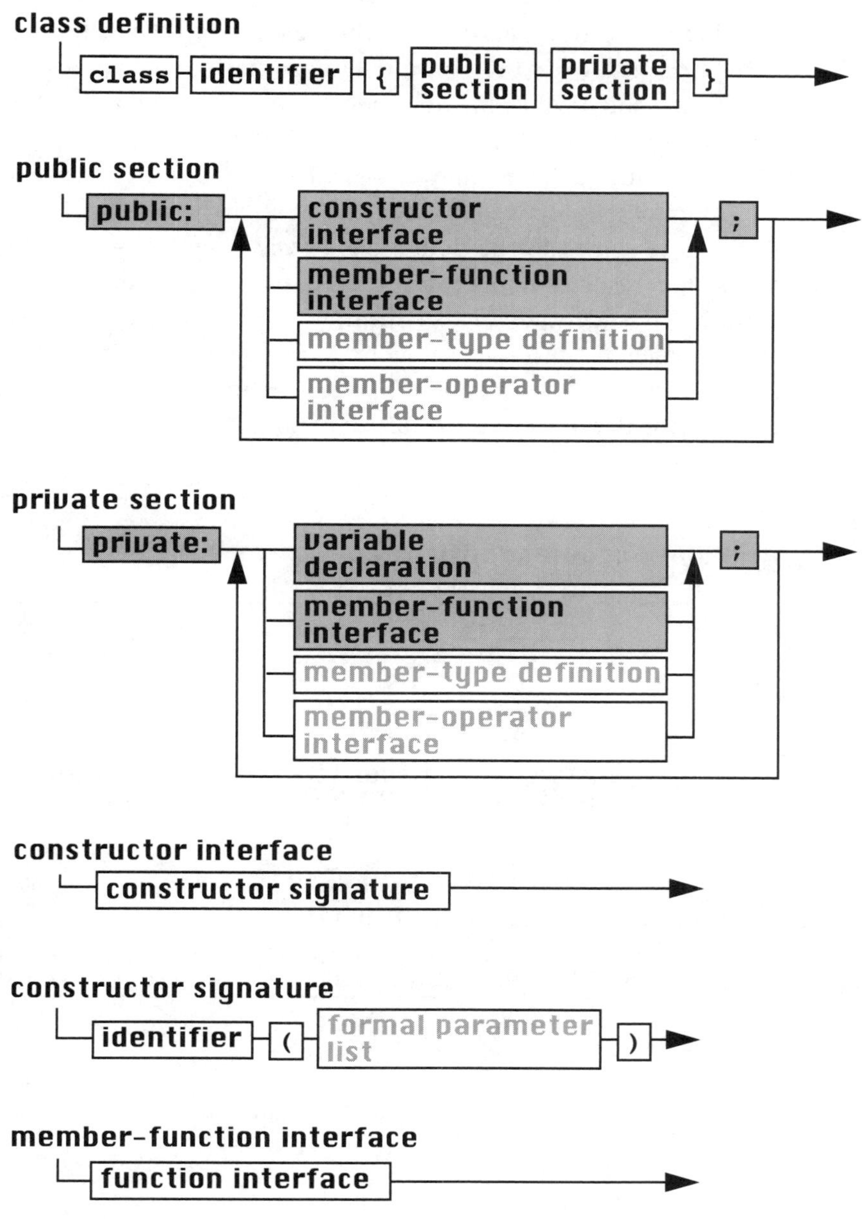

Don't forget that you turn a **class definition** into a statement by adding a semicolon to the end. This rule is captured in the syntax diagram for a **compilation unit**, given that a **class definition** is a **type definition**.

Note that you can't use a **declaration with initialization** in the private section, only a **variable declaration**. Any explicit initialization of a member variable has to be undertaken within the constructor definition.

You can see from the above diagrams that the syntax for a member-function interface is identical to the non-member function syntax you've seen before. The constructor interface is different in that it doesn't have a return type, and its identifier must be the same as the identifier used for the class. (Constructors with parameters are described in the next chapter.)

When it comes to the definitions of the constructors and member functions, the scope resolution operator has to be used to qualify the function name with the class identifier. This indicates to the compiler that the definition belongs to a particular class. Apart from this qualification, the syntax diagrams are the same as those you've already seen for functions, with the exception that the constructor doesn't have a return type and its identifier is the same as the class identifier.

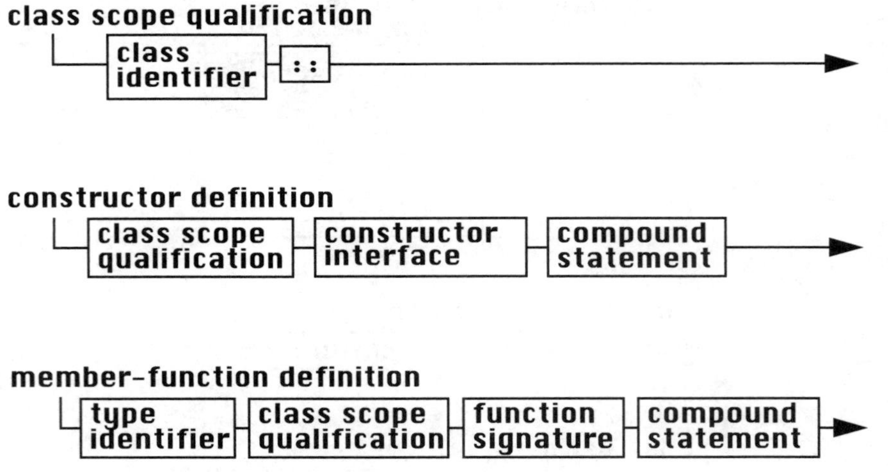

Both **definitions** are examples of a **compilation unit**.

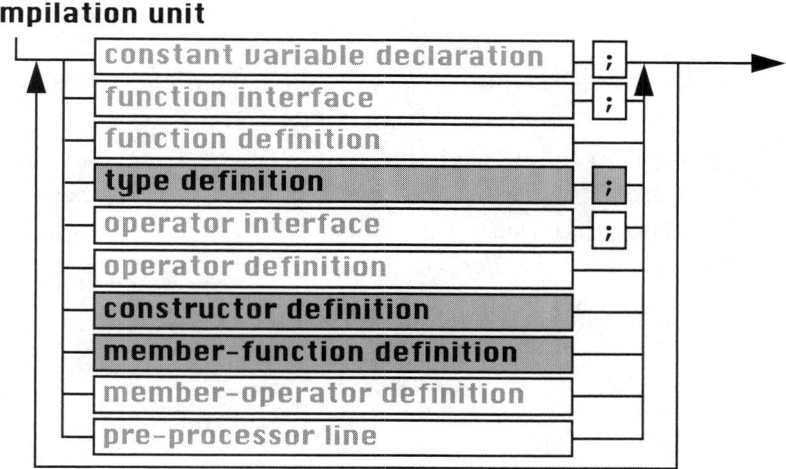

EXERCISES FOR SECTION 12.4

1 Consider the code fragments showing constructors in Figure 12.1. Try executing the program to confirm the answer given earlier concerning the sequence of output messages.

(i) Predict what will happen if you remove the constructor definition `Class1::Class1() {...}` but not the constructor interface in the class definition, and then try to compile and link the code. Confirm your prediction by trying this out. Can you explain the results you get?

(ii) Remove the constructor definition `Class1::Class1(){...}` *and* the corresponding constructor interface in the class definition. Will the resulting program compile and link?

(iii) Taking the program from (ii), predict the sequence of events that will occur if you execute the program. Try executing the program also.

2 The implementation of `Account` above uses a sentinel account number value to indicate that a variable is uninitialized. How else could you implement the behavior that uninitialized variables are detected?

12.5 SOFTWARE ENGINEERING ISSUES: TESTING

So, you've finished your first class implementation. Congratulations! Now all you have to do is send it off to the Fiddlers Bank for them to use, and wait for your payment to roll in. Well, not quite . . .

There's one part of the software engineering cycle that you haven't applied yet. You haven't tested the software you've constructed. Getting it to compile is the first test, but then you'll need to write some test programs to see whether other bugs are lurking.

IMPLEMENTATION:

Here's a simple test program for `class Account`.

```
#include <iostream.h>
#include "Account.h"

int main()
{
  Account anAccount;

  anAccount.setAccountNumber(12345);
  anAccount.deposit(100);
  cout << anAccount << endl;

  return 0;
} // end main()
```

OUTPUT:

The output produced by the test program is:

```
Account Number:  12345
Balance:         100
Overdraft Limit: 0
Account State:   Open
```

Is this output as expected? Yes, it looks like it.

Testing the software you've written is a key part of the software engineering development process. It can be one of the most satisfying parts of the process (when your software works as expected) and also one of the most depressing (when your program crashes in an apparently unfathomable manner).

There are two overall approaches that you can adopt for testing, which we'll term the big-bang approach and the incremental approach. In the **big-bang approach**, you leave any thoughts of testing until all of the software has been completed, and then start testing. With the **incremental approach**, you test as you go along, testing each incremental change you make when developing the software.

Which is best?

EXAMPLE:

If you're building a car and you're not sure about the reliability of the components you're using, would you first assemble the car and then try it out, or would you check each component as it becomes available? Why won't this car go? Because the engine isn't working. Why isn't the engine working? Because of . . . Why isn't . . . all caused by the omission of a little part in one of the components. Clearly, the accurate identification of any faults is best done before the components are assembled. The analogy with software is apt.

It's best to assemble a software system from tested components. It's also best to test components in isolation from the software system they'll eventually be a part of. This way you can concentrate on the component directly, rather than having it "obscured" by being embedded in the system. In other words, the incremental approach is the testing approach to adopt.

However, testing your software components individually doesn't mean that you won't need to test the system when the components are assembled together. System testing is still needed. But system testing will be simplified if most of the bugs in the components have already been eliminated. (Note we don't say that all of the bugs will have been eliminated!)

Functions provide one method for dividing a software system into components. PDTs are another form of component you can identify. In constructing these components, you should adopt the approach of testing each thoroughly by writing special test programs to try out the component. Even during the construction of the component you can apply incremental testing; you don't have to wait until the component is complete before commencing testing, as you'll see in the next chapter. The earlier you test, the easier it will be to find and fix bugs (but not all of them will show up).

So, a good test program is one that executes without showing up any problems, isn't it? No! Quite the opposite.

Lesson: A good test program is one that shows up bugs.

Remember that the likelihood that a software component has residual bugs is high even for so-called well-tested components, like ours :-).

EXERCISES FOR SECTION 12.5

1 Construct some additional test programs for `class Account`. Predict what you expect each test program to show before you try that program. (Hint: there's one bug we've left in on purpose. Can your testing uncover it? :-)

2 Assuming that your testing has uncovered a problem (or you've looked at the answer to Exercise 1 :-), can you predict what you think might be the bug that's caused this error without looking at the code in `Account.c`? Add statements to your test program to see if you can pinpoint where things appear to go wrong.

3 Examine the implementation code in `Account.c` to see if you can identify the bug. Then fix the code to remove this bug, and retest.

12.6 I/O OPERATORS REVISITED

You've seen that for classes the I/O operators are stand-alone operators (not part of the class definition) and thus have to access the abstract state of a class using the normal member-function interface. What if the input or output operator that you're implementing requires access to parts of a class that are not available via the public interface? Say there's a private member variable to which access is required just for I/O. What can you do in this situation?

You may have noticed that a class can have member operators, although we've postponed discussion of these until the next chapter. Could the I/O operators be member operators to solve the problem? It turns out that the I/O operators can't be member operators and we'll show you why in Chapter 13. So what else can you do in the above situation?

You have two choices. The first is to add member functions to make the desired features available. The second choice is to provide member functions that perform the I/O and have the stand-alone I/O operators call these member functions. Let's examine an example of the latter approach.

PROBLEM:

The output operator for `class Account` is effectively providing a brief printed statement about an account. The bank wants these statements to be numbered by a sequence number that's increased by one every time a statement is printed out.

IMPLEMENTATION:

To solve this problem you need to add a private member variable (say `int sequenceNo`) to the private section (the constructor will have to be altered to initialize this variable to zero). But how can the (stand-alone) output operator get at this variable to read or increment its value? One answer is to provide a new member function (let's call it, `print`) that can provide the appropriate output actions as well as access the private variable. Of course, you'll still need the definition of the output operator << since that's what the user is going to use. You don't want to force the user to use the member function instead of the normal mechanism. But the output operator definition will now simply call the new member function.

```
ostream& operator<<(ostream& outStream, Account value)
{
  value.print(outStream);
  return outStream;
} // end operator<<(Account)
```

The definition of `print(...)` is similar to the earlier output operator, except now the member-function calls such as `accountNumber()` don't need the qualification of the variable name and the dot operator. This qualification isn't needed since the member-function calls are occurring inside a member function, so the `Account` variable is implicitly "the one you're currently operating on."

```
void Account::print(ostream& outStream)
{
  sequenceNo += 1;
  outStream << "Account Number:  " << accountNumber()  << endl
            << "Balance:         " << balance()        << endl
            << "Overdraft Limit: " << overdraftLimit() << endl
            << "Account State:   " << accountState()   << endl
            << "Sequence Number: " << sequenceNo       << endl;
  return;
} // end print()
```

The definition of `print(...)` could access the relevant private member variables directly, but in general it's best to use the member functions since they provide the required values, regardless of the concrete representation of the quantities.

Let's see if this new implementation works.

OUTPUT:

Here's the result of a test program setting up an instance of `Account` and then invoking the output operator `<<` on that account twice in succession.

```
Account Number:  123321
Balance:         999
Overdraft Limit: 0
Account State:   Open
Sequence Number: 1
```

```
Account Number:  123321
Balance:         999
Overdraft Limit: 0
Account State:   Open
Sequence Number: 1
```

Hmmm. There's a problem with the sequence numbers. Can you see the error, and can you see what's causing it?

The error is that the sequence number isn't increasing as required. But why not? The `print(...)` member function adds one to it each time it's called doesn't it?

Take a look at the parameter list for the output operator <<. Looks like the typical set of parameters for an output operator but ... has the light dawned yet?

The problem is that the parameter representing an account is a value parameter. But now output has to have the effect of changing the account object, so this parameter must be changed to a reference parameter. Otherwise the increase in sequence number is applied to a copy of the account object, and the real account object's sequence number is never updated. We'll leave you to fix this fault and to retest the resulting code.

Let's note the lesson about member functions calling one another before we move on to compare the three type definition mechanisms.

Lesson: One member function can call another member function of the same class without the "`variableName.`" qualification.

EXERCISE FOR SECTION 12.6

1 Add the `print(...)` member function to the `Account` class and test its behavior.

12.7 WHICH TYPE DEFINITION MECHANISM TO USE

You now know the basic details of three type definition mechanisms:

1. The `enum` mechanism allows you to define a set of abstract values.
2. The `struct` mechanism permits you to group a set of variables together, and to treat the grouping as a single variable.
3. The `class` mechanism is the most powerful PDT mechanism, allowing you to define a new type together with a set of operations that can be applied to instances of that type.

Each of these mechanisms has its uses, and it's important to understand what each provides and hence where each should and should not be used.

When to use `enum`

The `enum` mechanism is useful when you need to represent a small number of related abstract values in a manner that helps the reader of source code to understand that code. If you need to represent a large set of abstract values such that you can't easily name them all, or if there's a need for operations other than I/O, assignment or equality comparisons on instances of the type (for example, operations to give you the next or previous abstract value in the sequence) then the `class` mechanism is a much better type vehicle than `enum`. Nevertheless, the `enum` mechanism does provide simple but useful abstractions, albeit in these limited situations.

If you look back at the description of the PDT `PlayerStatus` in Chapter 5 you'll see that its interface reflects the restricted set of operations available on instances of `enum` types. This is one of those "chicken-and-egg" situations; where did the restrictions come from first? The design of that type or the implementation of that type in C++? The answer is "a bit of both." In practice, when you're designing the interfaces for new types you'll have in mind the possible C++ type definition mechanisms. During the first design steps, when the types you identify are high-level and very abstract, limitations such as those imposed by the `enum` mechanism shouldn't come into your consideration. Later, when you are refining the designs with more of an eye on their eventual C++ implementation, the C++ mechanisms can and should have more of an influence.

However, this doesn't mean you should try to "shoe-horn" a type's design just to fit into an eventual `enum` definition. If the type you've identified needs more operations than can be provided by an `enum`, then you should be considering the class mechanism for its implementation. However, if your type has a simple set of abstract values, with assignment and equality tests as the only operations required, then `enum` will be an ideal mechanism.

When to use `struct`

The `struct` type definition mechanism is useful for grouping a set of data variables together, but the only operations you can apply to the grouping as a whole are assignment and I/O (if I/O operators have been defined). If you uncover the need for such groupings in your designs then the `struct` mechanism is useful. If, however, you determine that there are other operations that seem appropriate for the grouping, and indeed that you can separate out abstract behavior of your type from any concrete representation as member variables, then you should be using `class`es rather than `struct`s.

When to use `class`

You can only define classes Mondays through Fridays, otherwise you'll get compile-time errors. Only kidding :-)

Classes let you define new PDTs that have abstract behavior that's separate from any concrete representation of that behavior. If you need to implement a new type, and that type has the requirement for operations, then the `class` mechanism is the most appropriate type definition mechanism to use. Alternatively, if you need a new PDT and the `enum` and `struct` mechanisms aren't appropriate for the reasons discussed above, then the `class` mechanism beckons.

It should be clear to you that classes are the fundamental language feature that support the implementation of object-oriented software systems. You can now design new types and implement those types using the basic class features you've seen in this chapter, although there are additional features that will be identified in the next chapter. That chapter will also highlight some of the software engineering advantages that you can obtain by using classes.

EXERCISE FOR SECTION 12.7

1 Look back at the PDTs described in Chapter 5. Predict which type mechanism has been used for each PDT. How can you confirm your predictions?

SUMMARY

In this chapter you've taken some very important steps on your object-oriented apprenticeship. You've begun to switch from being a user of PDTs to being the implementer. In this chapter you've learned:

- **the `enum` mechanism** is used for defining simple sets of abstract values, with no additional operations other than I/O;
- **the `struct` mechanism** is used for defining aggregate data types, with no additional operations other than I/O; it just provides member variables;
- **the `class` mechanism** is the best mechanism for defining new PDTs and permits you to define member functions and member operators;
- **providing a new PDT** involves defining the PDT's interface (the type definition) and implementation;
- **a `class` definition** contains public interfaces for constructors, member functions and member operators, and private interfaces for member variables and other member functions;
- **a private section** is encapsulated; only the definitions of constructors, member functions and member operators can access the features defined in a private section;
- **constructors** are concerned with variable declarations;
- **the scope resolution operator** is used to qualify the identifiers of constructor, member-function and member-operator definitions;
- **I/O operators** can be defined so that I/O involving instances of new PDTs can be written using normal I/O infix operators.

Some important software engineering issues have also been covered:

- **separation of concerns** – the clear separation between a class' public interface and its private interface and implementation code;
- **testing** – the importance of testing software components to uncover bugs;
- **a successful test** – a test that causes a software component to generate errors;
- **header files** – how to provide header files containing the user's interface to a PDT.

You've been introduced to a few more C++ keywords and syntax details, but more importantly to the three type definition mechanisms in C++. "Do there have to be three?" you might ask. "Wouldn't one do?" In C++ all three have a useful role to play. Although there's no doubting the overall importance and power of the `class` mechanism, you should now know when to define `enum`s and `struct`s, but perhaps more importantly when to use a `class`. Anyway, it sounds better to say "My program has class" rather than "My program uses dumb enums" or "My program sucks with structs." :-)

More on classes is coming up in the next chapter. However, you may first like to attempt some of the exercises below, which concentrate on `enum`s and `struct`s only, to get a good feel for their use.

END-OF-CHAPTER EXERCISES

1 Explain the circumstances in which you'd use (or not use) `enum`, `struct`, `class`.

2 Construct an `enum` representing the set of colors that a traffic light can display. Define an output operator for this `enum`. Write a C++ program that sequences through the complete set of colors in the correct order, finishing at the color you started with. Does the construction of this program suggest any deficiencies with C++'s `enum` construct? Outline which type definition mechanism might be better and why.

3 Section 12.3 introduced the following `struct` example.

```
struct HouseDetails
{
  Text         address;
  HouseType    houseType;
  int          bedrooms;
  int          garages;
  Construction builtFrom;
  int          sellingPrice;
};
```

Use enums to define PDTs for HouseType (to represent the various categories of houses commonly identified) and Construction (to represent the overall kind of construction, such as brick, stone, wood, adobe, etc.). Write I/O operators for the two types. The input operator functions should print a prompt indicating the values available.

4 Define a PDT Address using the struct type definition mechanism. (Hint: identify the individual data components that you think comprise an address.) Write I/O operators for this PDT. The input operator function should print a prompt for each member variable in turn, and only a single word should be input for any Text member variable.

5 Rewrite struct HouseDetails given in Exercise 3 to use the Address PDT you wrote in Exercise 4. Write C++ code to implement the following two I/O operator functions. The input operator function should print a prompt for each member variable in turn. (Hint: reuse the I/O operators you wrote in Exercises 3 and 4.)

```
// Interfaces of I/O operators
istream& operator>>(istream& inStream,  HouseDetails& forInput);
ostream& operator<<(ostream& outStream, HouseDetails  value);
```

6 Predict what output the following code fragment will produce:

```
class Class0
{
  public:
    Class0();
  private:
    int private1;
};

class Class1
{
  public:
    Class1();
  private:
    Class0 private1;
};

class Class2
{
  public:
    Class2();
  private:
    Class1 private1;
    Class1 private2;
};
```

```
Class0::Class0()
{
  cout << "Class 0 constructor" << endl;
  return;
} // end Class0()

Class1::Class1()
{
  cout << "Class 1 constructor" << endl;
  return;
} // end Class1()

Class2::Class2()
{
  cout << "Class 2 constructor" << endl;
  return;
} // end Class2()

int main()
{
  Class2 instance;

  return 0;
} // end main()
```

13 Some example classes

Objective

To exemplify the use of the `class` type definition mechanism through the design and definition of some example classes, covering:

- the introduction of member operators;
- the software-engineering benefits of classes;
- the software-engineering issue of incremental testing;
- debugging;
- how to protect header files from multiple inclusions.

Another class

13.0 CLASSES AGAIN?

The previous chapter introduced you to the fundamentals of class definition and implementation, showing you how to assemble constructors, member functions and member variables into the public and private sections of a class. Since classes are such an important feature of object-oriented programming in C++ it's important that you understand how to use them. The purpose of this chapter is to provide further examples of class definitions and implementations, and to explore some of the issues you've already come across in more depth.

You know from Chapter 12 how to define member functions. But what if you've decided that you need a new type to represent dates and you want to write expressions involving instances of dates just like you write expressions involving the built-in numeric types. After all, a date is a form of number and you might want to write expressions to subtract two date instances to determine the number of days they are apart, or to compare two dates to see which one is the earliest. You could construct member functions and use member-function calls to invoke these operations, but it would be more preferable to be able to write expressions involving the usual set of binary and unary infix operators.

EXAMPLE:

```
Date startOfFirstSemester;
Date christmasDay;
Date myBirthday;
...                                    // Initialize these variables
int numberOfDays;

numberOfDays = christmasDay - startOfFirstSemester;
if (myBirthday > startOfFirstSemester)
{
...
```

The class mechanism in C++ allows you to define *member operators* for a class so that a user of your class can write expressions involving instances of that class; you may recall discussion of the interfaces of such operators in Chapter 9. You now need to know how to implement member operators, and this is one of the issues to be covered here.

In this chapter you'll go through the design and implementation of a new `class Duration`. This is a numeric type and requires you to design and implement member operators, in addition to constructors, member functions and I/O operators. In developing `Duration` you'll use the incremental-testing strategy to show how it can be applied during a software component's development.

Types such as `Duration` that require member operators aren't entirely typical of the use of the class mechanism, so in Section 13.3 we address the design and implementation of `class Square`, the instances of which behave more like typical objects in that they have a rich set of member functions but no member operators.

Finally, in Section 13.4 we take a brief look at a class that you should be familiar with from early chapters, `CDPlayer`. You've used this class extensively, and you should now be able to recognize most of the C++ features it uses. Examining the header file `CDPlayer.h` allows us to introduce a further feature of classes in C++, namely member types.

Before we commence with `class Duration` let's reexamine the issue of operators and member operators and how they are represented in C++.

13.1 MEMBERS, OPERATORS AND FUNCTIONS

You know there's an important distinction between calling a member function and calling a function, in that the former requires the use of a variable name and the dot operator preceding the function identifier, whereas the latter does not. It's important therefore to distinguish member functions from functions, as we do by using these terms, to permit a user to know which call syntax is required for a particular function.

What about operators? Are there differences between operators and member operators? The answer is "yes," but here the differences in the way that you use them are a touch more subtle. You saw in Chapter 9 how the infix operators (for example, + and <=) can be treated by the compiler as a shorthand for what is effectively a function call or member-function call. In Chapter 12 this feature was used to provide implementations of the I/O operators. Just as functions can be distinguished from member functions, so a similar distinction can be applied to operators. There can be operators (which essentially are stand-alone, like the I/O operators) and member operators which are closely associated with a type definition (you haven't seen many of these yet). The subtlety comes about because, from the user's point of view, you don't have to distinguish between the two types of operator when using the infix notation. You've actually been using both types of operator so far and you haven't noticed have you? However, from the operator definer's view there are differences, and since you're wearing the operator definer's hat in this chapter, the differences now have to become apparent.

Let's look at an example of how the compiler treats an expression such as `a + b` using the binary infix operator + with the assumption that `a` is an instance of some PDT. The compiler can treat the expression as having two possible translations:

```
a.operator+(b)
operator+(a, b)
```

The first translation would involve a member-operator call, while the second would require a stand-alone operator call. So the operator's definition could be a member-operator definition or an operator definition. The writer of the expression doesn't care which version is used, but if you're the PDT implementer who has to provide the definition for the operator, then you need to understand the implications of the two different possible signatures for `operator+(...)`.

"So, I can provide either a stand-alone operator definition or a member-operator definition for a particular infix operator applied to instances of a class? How do I decide between the two?" you ask. The answer to the first question is "yes," and the answer to the second follows.

Applying your knowledge of what functions and member functions are, what do you think the differences are between a member operator and an operator?

A member operator is an operator that's part of a class definition. As such, it will appear in the public section of a class definition and its implementation will be able to access the private member variables of the class. A stand-alone operator won't be part of the class definition and its implementation won't be able to access the private member variables. It's a stand-alone piece of code with no special privileges.

So, a first obvious rule for choosing between an operator and a member-operator implementation would seem to be: if the implementation for an infix operator requires access to the private member variables then you should provide a member-operator definition. However, if the implementation doesn't require such access should you use a stand-alone operator definition? Well, you could, but this wouldn't be our recommendation. We suggest that all infix operators that manipulate instances of a class you're defining should be member operators.

Lesson: A class should support infix operators by defining member operators.

Now you're dying to know why you were told in Chapter 12 that the I/O operator definitions for a new class can't be member operators, aren't you? The phrase "that manipulate instances of a class" is the key to understanding why.

I/O operators

In Chapter 12 we discussed the mapping of the I/O operators >> and << to (stand-alone) operator interfaces with the following form.

```
istream& operator>>(istream& inStream,  TypeIdentifier& forInput);
ostream& operator<<(ostream& outStream, TypeIdentifier  value);
```

In stand-alone form, these interfaces occur outside the class definition (and therefore they represent stand-alone operators). But could these interfaces appear inside the class definition and thus be member-operators for the I/O operators?

The answer is "no." They could appear as member operators, but they wouldn't work for I/O statements involving >> and <<. The reason is that these two operators are not operations on instances of `TypeIdentifier`. If they were, they could be member operators of `TypeIdentifier`. However, they're operations on `istream` and `ostream` variables. So, given the following declaration and output statement:

```
TypeIdentifier var = ...; // Initialized to a value
cout << var;
```

the output statement is an operation on the variable `cout`, *not* an operation on `var`. In the first instance, the compiler will attempt to translate the output statement as:

```
cout.operator<<(var);
```

If the class definition for `ostream` (that is, the type of `cout`) contains a matching operator interface, this translation will be permitted. But does `class ostream` contain such an interface? Bear in mind that `ostream` is an existing `class` whereas *`TypeIdentifier`* is a new `class`. Can you expect `ostream` to contain I/O operator interfaces for all possible new PDTs that might be introduced? Of course not.

When the `class ostream` was defined, it was able to include interfaces of I/O operators for the built-in types, since those types were known at that time, but clearly not for any PDTs invented subsequently. So, do you have to change the definition of `class ostream` to add any I/O operators for new PDTs? This is possible, but it would be a very bad thing to do from a software engineering point of view. Virtually all C++ programs share the `iostreams` library, and chaos would ensue if every software engineer defining a `class` had to add code to that common library, especially if those engineers were apprentices :-).

Instead, C++ permits you to use the mechanism you've already seen to get around this problem. To reiterate, the above translation of the output statement requires the compiler to look for a matching member-operator signature of the following form within the `public` section of `class ostream` (ignoring the result returned):

```
operator<<(TypeIdentifier value)
```

The compiler won't find this interface for the reasons just discussed. In this situation, the compiler then tries the following translation of the output statement:

```
operator<<(cout, var)
```

that requires an operator signature of the form:

```
operator<<(ostream& outStream, TypeIdentifier value)
```

This is a non-member operator signature. The key thing to note is that this last signature is something a class implementer can provide an implementation of without having to change `class ostream`, while still permitting the programmer to use the I/O operators >> and << in the normal manner.

So, each new `class` provides the abstraction of I/O operators by providing operator interfaces outside the class definition rather than member-operator interfaces inside. The abstraction is that the I/O classes have been extended with operations for the new `class`; the implementation is different from this, in the manner just described. Remember that the user of the I/O operators doesn't see this difference.

Lesson: The I/O operators for new PDTs are not member-operators.

In a given software system there are likely to be lots of operator definitions for the I/O operators. Won't the compiler complain about the multiple uses of the operator identifier?

The compiler won't complain as long as the interfaces for each operator are unique. Since a difference in parameters occurs naturally when you're defining I/O operators for different types, the overloading mechanism will be able to sort things out correctly.

Now that you know a little more about I/O operators, let's examine the definition of operators in general.

Which operators can be defined?

If you look through some of the type definitions given in Chapter 5, you'll see that several categories of operator have been identified:

- assignment, including update;
- arithmetic, both unary and binary;
- comparison;
- I/O.

Definitions for any and all of these operators can be provided, although not every `class` will need all operators. There weren't many arithmetic operators defined for PDTs `CDPlayer` and `Canvas`, for example. If a `class` represents some new form of numeric value then it makes sense to provide definitions for the arithmetic and comparison operators, as we've already discussed at the beginning of this chapter. The `class Duration` developed in the next section is an example of a new numeric type that provides the arithmetic and comparison operators. Many classes don't need these operators.

The fact that you can define member operators for a new `class` means you could provide nonstandard ways of using, say the arithmetic operators. For example, the designer of `CDPlayer` could have chosen to define "+" to mean load a CD into the player and "-" to take the CD out of the player. This would be a rather confusing thing to do. It's very bad practice to "misuse" the standard infix operators and give them meanings for a new `class` that are counterintuitive and not what a user of that `class` would expect. As the implementer of a new numeric PDT you might think it was neat to define a "+" operator that subtracted two values, but heaven help any other user of that PDT! Don't do it!

Lesson: Don't define operators that provide unusual or unexpected behavior.

The syntax diagrams coming up give you the list of operators that can be defined.

Syntax diagrams for member operators and operators

Member operators are another part of the public section of a class.

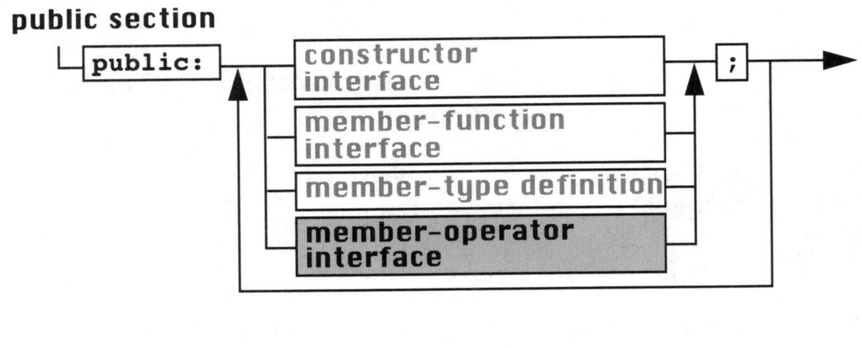

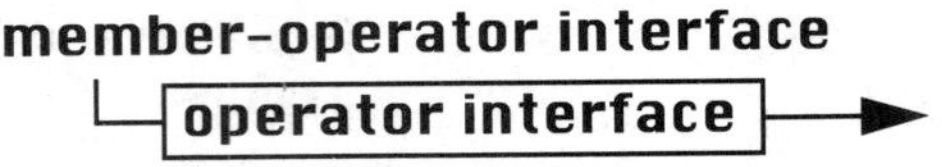

The following syntax diagrams give the syntax for an operator's interface.

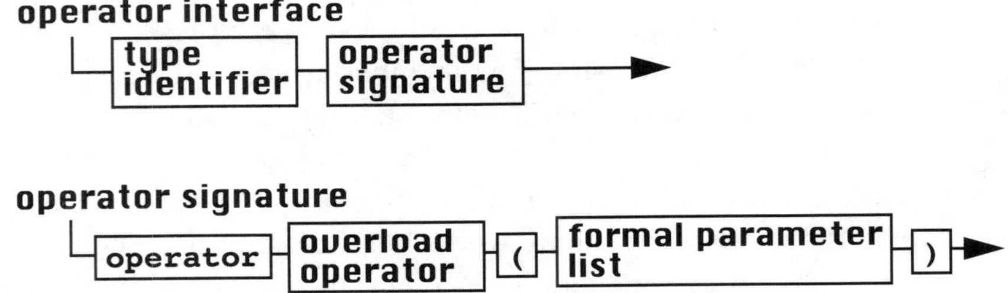

You can only define operators that correspond to the operator symbols that already exist in C++ for the built-in types, and in doing so you'll be overloading these operators (recall the discussion on overloading functions in Chapter 11). Thus the operators you can define are given in the syntactic element **overload operator**. Since assignment is a fundamental paradigm of C++, the compiler can automatically provide an implementation of the assignment operator for a new PDT, as you saw in Chapter 12. In the majority of cases, the default behavior provided by the compiler is sufficient, so we'll leave the implementation of assignment to a more advanced apprenticeship. The increment operators also involve additional complexity as they can be used in prefix and postfix forms, and since their behavior can be achieved using the more general update operators, we'll leave increment operators out in this chapter as well.

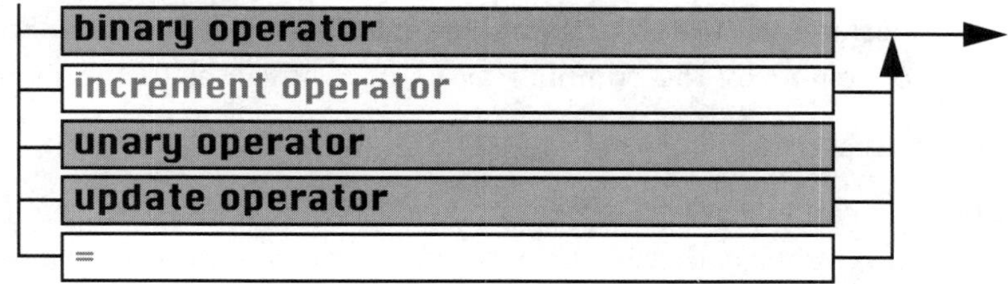

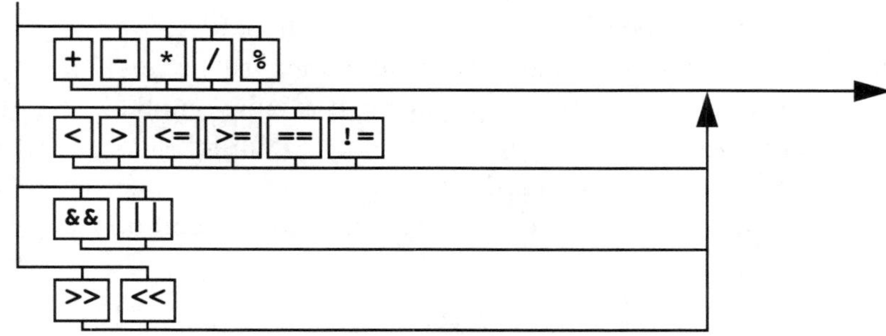

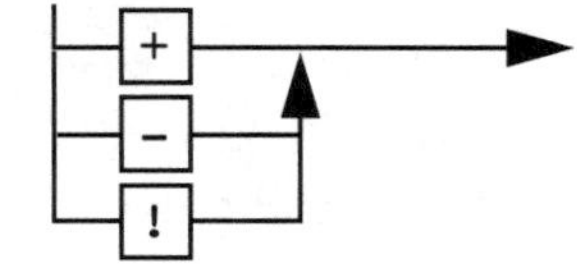

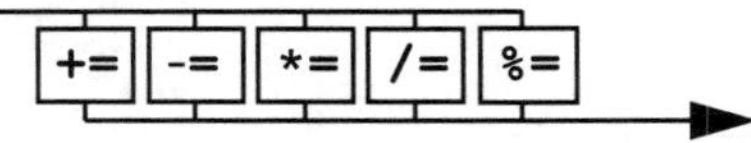

We need to examine further the interfaces of member operators that appear within a class definition, as there are some subtleties that require further examination.

Member operator interfaces

You recall that some operators are binary operators that take two operands, as in:

```
lhs + rhs
```

assuming that `lhs` and `rhs` are variable identifiers, chosen here to represent the operands on the left-hand side and the right-hand side. Such an expression can be treated by the compiler as being equivalent to the member-operator call:

```
lhs.operator+(rhs)
```

The call here has a single parameter representing the right-hand operand of the expression. It therefore follows that the signature of the operator has to have a similar structure for its parameter list, such as:

```
operator+(Type rhs)
```

What's happened to the operand for the left-hand size? As mentioned in Section 9.5, it doesn't appear in the parameter list because this operand is the variable to which the member-operator call is being applied. How does the implementation of this operator function "get at" the left-hand operand? A valid question, and one best answered with respect to a more specific example coming up in the next section. Rest assured, the implementation can "get at" the left-hand operand.

How many parameters do you think appear in the interface for a unary member operator?

The answer is none.

Turning to the return type in the interface of a member operator, there are some general observations that can be made. When you have an expression such as `a + b` where `a` and `b` are `int` variables, is the result of this addition an `int` value or an `int` destination? The result is an `int` value. You can't write `a + b = 3` which would be possible if the result was a destination. So, when you're defining member operators for the arithmetic operators the interface has the following form.

```
ResultType operator+(Type rhs);
```

The `ResultType` may or may not be the same as the type of the left-hand operand (you'll see examples of this with the up-coming `class Duration`). But you can probably recognize that the result type for the comparison operations is going to be `bool`.

What about the return type for the update operators? If you just want to use these operators in a simple statement such as:

```
a += b;  // Translates to  a.operator+=(b);
```

you can see that the translation is just like a member-function call used as a statement, for which the return type can be `void`. In C++ you can, however, use the result of an update operator either as a value in an expression or as a destination. We'd never do this, because the style rule from Chapter 8 suggested:

✓ *Don't use the result of an assignment, an update or an increment as an operand for some other operation.*

If you want to support the full C++ generality in your update operators the result type has to be something that can be used either as a value or as a destination. The result has to be a reference to a type, analogous to a reference parameter in a formal parameter list. A generic form of, say, the += update operator is then:

```
Type& operator+=(Type rhs);
```

where `Type` is the class you're defining the update operator for.

Having got these preliminary explanations out of the way, how are your powers of duration? Can you endure another class?

EXERCISES FOR SECTION 13.1

1 Identify the operations you think it would be appropriate for a `class Date` to provide, indicating informally what the type of the result of each operator would be.

2 Can you think of any other "numeric" types that require member operators?

13.2 CLASS DURATION

Because of your expertise in writing software involved with CDs (you did do all of the exercises in the previous chapters, didn't you?), you've been hired to provide a software system to assist a radio station's DJ in some tasks.

PROBLEM:

A DJ has to plan the use of tracks from a collection of CDs such that the time interval between commercials and/or news bulletins is occupied, but not overrun. The DJ needs to know the duration of a show and the individual CD tracks in the form H:MM:SS, so that during a show the length of sequences of tracks can be calculated by adding the individual track durations together. The DJ is also faced with the tricky task of filling the last slot before a break in the show. This slot needs a track that's as close as possible to the time interval left to fill, but certainly no longer otherwise the break will be late. This requires the DJ to search through the whole CD collection to find a track of the appropriate duration.

Design and implement two programs:

1. To allow the DJ to keep track of the total duration of the tracks played so far, using the format H:MM:SS.
2. To request the DJ to input a duration and then find the CD track that's closest to, but not greater than, that duration. The program will then print out the title of the disc, the track index, and the track's duration in the format given above.

You're not going to solve these problems entirely in this chapter. Instead you're going to identify a PDT as a component that would be very useful in solving both problems. If you want to write one of these programs subsequently, direct your attention to Exercise 1 at the end of the chapter.

Given the specification above, what are your first thoughts? Not to start programming immediately we hope! A first thought should be: "Have I got any PDTs in my toolbag that will help me solve this problem?"

Lesson: Apply software reuse wherever you can.

You've used the `CDisc` PDT and you know you can use that PDT together with the `CDPlayer` PDT to determine the length of a track in seconds. And there's the PDT `CSDiscSet` that could form the basis for the DJ's CD collection. That's a start. So, with this information at hand, you could start the design for the above programs. However, before you do, you should be considering the following question: "Can I identify any new PDTs that will help the design and implementation of this software system?"

Way back in Chapter 2 (Section 2.8) you saw a method for analyzing an English specification with the aim of identifying possible types and their operations. Apply this technique to the above specification to see if you can identify a possible type.

Did you identify the noun *duration* being used in essentially a possessive form (a track's duration). Posing the questions suggested in Section 2.8: "Can you say *a duration*?" and ask "What is *a duration*?" suggest this noun is a common noun and would form a useful type. Let's take this a little further.

The specification gives the general form of the abstract values for a duration (H:MM:SS). Can you identify any possible operations needed for this type?

The specification mentions two predicates: **closest to** and **not greater than** (sounds like a comparison operation using the operator <=). It also mentions that durations need to be **input** and **printed** (need the I/O operators >> and <<). You're already forming a picture of what this new type might provide in terms of operations. It's beginning to sound like a new PDT, `Duration`, is going to be useful.

To take this further, think about the design of the main part of one program, the part that determines whether a particular track's length is the closest found so far to a desired duration. Perhaps you'd like to sketch an outline design for this piece of code. Alternatively, here's a skeleton piece of C++ code expressing roughly the actions required.

```
Duration lookingFor;
Duration trackLength;
Duration howClose;      // Difference between required and
                        //   found-so-far
                        // Put values into these variables
                        // Repeat the following for all tracks
if ((trackLength <= lookingFor) &&
    ((lookingFor - trackLength) < howClose))
{
  // Identified a new candidate for the closest track
  howClose = lookingFor - trackLength;
  ...
}
```

This fragment isn't meant to be complete; it's just sketching out roughly what would be a natural way of expressing this part of the algorithm. You can see that additional arithmetic operators like binary "`-`" on `Duration` values are likely to be useful. Similarly, adding up the track durations to give a show's length is going to require a binary "+" operator. If `Duration` provides such arithmetic operations then you can write straightforward code.

So, it looks as if `Duration` will make a useful PDT for this software system.

Lesson: Make the features of the PDT match the problem's requirements.

But before you take this further, is it worth it? Why bother designing (and implementing) a `Duration` PDT? There are four main reasons why.

1. It's an abstraction that matches the problem domain. Hence it's availability will make the problems easier to solve; it will also simplify the task of reading that solution.
2. It can be designed, implemented and tested as a separate component, independent of the programs that are going to be designed to meet the original specification. This will minimize the complexity of the final software system and its testing process.
3. You're going to have to do most of the work anyway in order to meet the specification: for example, for inputting and outputting durations in the required form.
4. Once completed, `Duration` can go into your toolbag for potential reuse in the future. If someone comes along and wants you to construct a plane-journey planning program, you'll have a useful component ready for use.

So, where do you start? With the implementation of `Duration`? No, you start with completing the design of the interface to `Duration`. No second thoughts. Minute your actions. The hour has come.

Designing the interface to `Duration`

You've already analyzed the problem specification to identify the abstract values and operations that `Duration` should provide. You could just take this set of operations as being the required interface. However, it's worth spending a little more time to see if you can identify further operations that would be worth providing and thereby increase the generality, and hence the potential reusability, of this PDT.

Recall from Chapter 2 that a PDT interface generally contains the following features:

abstract values – the range and form of abstract values that the type supports;
constructors – for creating objects that are instances of the type;
member functions – the functions provided by the type, that is, the operations that can be applied to instances of the type;
member operators – for writing arithmetic expressions using the standard mathematical symbols (`+ - * /`), as well as the update and comparison operators;
input/output – the I/O operators.

Let's go though each of these features for `Duration`.

Abstract values

The problem specification states that durations are to be in the form H:MM:SS. You know that the seconds and minutes fields will be in the range $0 \rightarrow 59$. What about the hours? The specification hints that a single digit number of hours is required, and the need for a CD track greater than or equal to 10 hours doesn't make sense. However, to add generality to your new PDT, having a range for hours $0 \rightarrow N$ where N is greater than 9 may make sense.

Should N be limited to 23? Probably not. You're not implementing a clock type; having N as a large positive integer will probably be sufficient. Do you need negative durations? Probably not.

Should you add days, weeks, months or years fields to the abstract values? Again, the answer is "no." That would be moving more into the realms of a date type: perhaps useful in its own right, but not what's needed for this problem (but if you care to look at end-of-chapter Exercise 4 ...).

Notice the importance of considering such issues at the design stage, and eventually recording those decisions in the interface description. If someone wants durations to encompass weeks and days, they need to be able to see that PDT `Duration` may not exactly meet their needs.

DESIGN:

Using the design notation to express the interface to `Duration`, you've just designed the following part.

```
H:MM:SS where
  H  0 → 32767
  MM 0 → 59
  SS 0 → 59
```

Constructors

You know from Chapter 12 that constructors in a PDT's interface are primarily concerned with declarations of variables using that PDT, and that you don't necessarily need to define a constructor. However, you also remember the following lesson, don't you?

Lesson: Always explicitly provide a default constructor that initializes the state to a sensible abstract value, or to something that can be detected as representing an uninitialized value.

You therefore need a constructor of the form `Duration()` in the interface to permit `Duration` variables to be declared. Should a declaration of a `Duration` variable result in that variable being initialized or uninitialized? As the type designer you've got to decide about such things.

The worst decision would be to ignore the above lesson and say that a declaration doesn't initialize the variable and that this uninitialized state isn't detected by the type. This decision isn't conducive to defensive programming. It means that if a user forgets to initialize a `Duration` variable they're likely to get random values and the error will not show up directly, if it's noticed at all. So, the choices are:

1. To leave the variable uninitialized (but check for uninitialized states appropriately).
2. To initialize the variable to something useful.

Let's adopt the latter approach and say that a declaration will initialize a `Duration` variable to the abstract duration value 0:00:00. You'll have to remember this decision when you come to document the interface and implement the constructor function.

You recall from Chapter 6 that C++ supports the syntactic element **declaration with initialization** to permit the programmer to specify an initial value at variable declaration time. Would it be useful to have such a feature for PDT `Duration`? Thinking ahead, the `CDPlayer` PDT returns a track's duration as an integer number of seconds, and it's likely that you'll want to convert this into a `Duration` value. So, the ability to initialize a `Duration` variable to an integer number of seconds looks like it's going to be a useful feature.

Generalizing from this, wouldn't it be useful to be able to initialize a `Duration` variable with seconds, minutes:seconds, and hours:minutes:seconds? That flexibility should satisfy most users. Now, how do you do this?

In designing the interface, you can choose a suitable textual notation to permit the expression of abstract values, such as 0:10:23, for initializing a `Duration` variable. How can this be implemented in C++ though?

Unfortunately, you can't add additional forms of literal value to C++ to permit:

```
Duration trackLength = 0:10:23; // Won't work :-(
```

Instead, the answer involves the use of some additional features of constructors.

Constructors with parameters

You recall from the previous chapter that constructors are implemented as functions. The constructors you've seen so far have been parameterless, but can a constructor have parameters? If "yes," what can a constructor use parameters for?

Constructors can indeed have non-null parameter lists, and can be used:

1. To provide *declarations with initialization* for variables that are instances of a `class`.
2. To provide a mechanism for writing *literal values* for the new PDT.
3. To provide a *type conversion* mechanism.

Let's examine each of these important uses of constructors with parameters in turn.

Constructor for declaration with initialization

Consider the following constructor signature.

```
TypeIdentifier(Type1 formalParam1)
```

A call of this constructor can be used to pass a value of type `Type1` to the constructor definition. This value can then be used in the constructor to initialize the object being declared, and hence to support **declaration with initialization**, in the following fashion:

```
TypeIdentifier varId = TypeIdentifier(actualParam1);
```

assuming `actualParam1` is of type `Type1`.

A constructor, like any function, isn't limited to only one parameter.

EXAMPLE:

```
Duration noTime = Duration(0);     // Init to 0 seconds
Duration mile   = Duration(4, 0); // Init to 4 mins, 0 secs
```

Constructor as a PDT literal

Think again about the first declaration with initialization above. What does it consist of? A variable declaration as the destination for an assignment of a value that's of the same type as the variable. So,

```
TypeIdentifier(actualParam1)
```

produces a value of type `TypeIdentifier`; in other words you can regard it as being the expression of a *literal value* for the type. In C++ this is the only way you can write what are in effect literals for classes.

EXAMPLE:

The language doesn't permit you to express that you want to be able to write `0:9:17` as a literal for a `class Duration`. Instead you have to provide a constructor to permit you to write `Duration(0,9,17)`.

Constructor as a type coercion mechanism

Given a constructor:

```
TypeIdentifier(Type1 formalParam1)
```

you now know that this gives you a value of type `TypeIdentifier`. So, the constructor is given a value of type `Type1` and it produces a value of type `TypeIdentifier`. Doesn't this sound a bit like type coercion to you?

Constructors with a single parameter behave like type coercions, in a manner similar to those you've already seen for some of the built-in numeric types.

EXAMPLE:

`int(37.4)` converts a `double` value to an `int`
`Duration(53)` converts an `int` value into a `Duration`

Thus, in a class you can provide several flavors of constructor, both with and without parameters. As long as the signatures of those constructors are unique, the compiler won't complain.

Lesson: A class can contain multiple constructors, as long as their signatures are unique.

But note that if you've provided an interface for any constructor with parameters in a `class` definition, you also have to provide the interface for the default (parameterless) constructor. The compiler will not automatically assume the existence of a default constructor if other constructors have been defined.

Lesson: If constructors are explicitly defined in a class, the default constructor must be explicitly defined.

Now you've learned some additional ways of using constructors, you can return to the problem of designing the set of constructors for `class Duration`.

Constructors continued

To support declarations with initializations you must provide a number of constructors, each of which takes a set of parameters to represent the different parts of the initialization values.

EXAMPLE:

For PDT `Duration` you need constructors with the following interfaces.

```
Duration()
Duration(int secs)
Duration(int mins,  int secs)
Duration(int hours, int mins, int secs)
```

You'll eventually be able to use these constructors in the following fashion, where the function overloading mechanism is used by the compiler to select the correct constructor to call.

```
Duration d1 = Duration(45);        // Initialize to 45 secs
Duration d2 = Duration(1, 45);     // Initialize to 1 min 45 secs
Duration d3 = Duration(2, 34, 6);  // Initialize to 2 hours
                                   //   34 mins and 6 secs
```

DESIGN:

Now you've defined a second part of the interface of PDT `Duration`.

```
// Constructors

                                           // Initialization value
Duration()                                     // 0:00:00
Duration(int secs)                             // 0:00:secs
Duration(int mins,  int secs)                  // 0:min:secs
Duration(int hours, int mins, int secs) // hours:min:secs
```

Member functions

Do you need to provide any member functions for `Duration`? The initial analysis of the specification didn't identify any member functions at all. However, think a little more generally and see if you can identify any useful member functions. What might you wish to do with a `Duration` variable?

It will probably be useful to provide the ability to obtain the value of the individual time components of a `Duration` variable; that is, the hours component, the seconds component and the minutes component. Three member functions returning `int`s will do the job.

DESIGN:

Here's a third part of the interface.

```
// Member functions

int hours()  // Return hours component
int mins()   // Return minutes component
int secs()   // Return seconds component
```

Why use member functions to provide access to these components? Why don't we just show there being three `int` variables available as part of the (public) interface? Conceptually, this is what the interface is providing, but you'll see when we get to implementing `Duration` that putting variables into the public part of a class definition is a bad idea. It's therefore useful to make the interface reflect the member-function approach so you're not tempted to use public variables later on!

Member operators

First, will a user need to perform assignments involving variables of type `Duration`? Of course they will. However, as you already know, the compiler automatically provides the assignment operator so you don't need to consider that further.

Let's consider the arithmetic operators that are normally provided for numeric values, starting with the infix binary operators. Do you need any or all of these operators for `Duration`? Earlier you identified that the subtraction and addition operators are likely to be needed. Generalizing from this, if you think of durations as being a form of numeric value, then it makes sense to provide the normal set of binary arithmetic operators so that a user of this PDT can write expressions involving durations, just like they would write expressions involving any other numeric type.

However, you do need to think carefully about the types of the two operands required for each binary operator and the type of the result. One operand type will always be `Duration`, but what about the other? For example, does it make sense to multiply one `Duration` by another? Think about the interface for each of the binary operators, and list the operators and their operands.

Did you come up with a list something like the following?

```
+    // Duration + Duration,  Duration value as a result
-    // Duration - Duration,  Duration value as a result
*    // Duration * int,       Duration value as a result
/    // Duration / Duration,       int value as a result
/    // Duration / int,       Duration value as a result
%    // Duration % Duration,  Duration value as a result
```

This informal specification of the infix operators has to be translated into member-operator interfaces.

DESIGN:

Using member-operator interface syntax you can specify the next part of the interface.

```
// Arithmetic Operators

    Duration operator+(Duration rhs)
    Duration operator-(Duration rhs)
    Duration operator*(int rhs)
    int      operator/(Duration rhs)
    Duration operator/(int rhs)
    Duration operator%(Duration rhs)
```

Why only one parameter for these binary operators? Have you forgotten what we told you in the previous section already? :-)

Given this set of arithmetic operators, what would happen if you wrote some code that added an `int` value to a `Duration` value? For example:

```
int      timeInSecs = ...;
Duration usedUp     = ...;
...
usedUp = usedUp + timeInSecs;
```

In theory the addition would appear to require a member-operator interface of the form:

```
Duration operator+(int rhs)
```

However, if the compiler could convert the `int` value to a `Duration` then the existing addition operator interface would be appropriate. In fact, you've already defined something that will achieve this type coercion. The constructor:

```
Duration(int secs)
```

takes an `int` value and converts it into a `Duration`. The compiler will arrange an implicit call to this constructor in order to compile the expression `usedUp + timeInSecs`. In other words, the compiler will treat the earlier statement as:

```
usedUp = usedUp + Duration(timeInSecs);
```

However, we suggest that you don't rely on such implicit coercions, and our style rule first shown in Chapter 8 is:

✓ *Use explicit coercion wherever an implicit coercion would otherwise be performed.*

You'll then get the type coercions you intend, rather than those the compiler picks for you!

What about the following statement?

```
usedUp = timeInSecs + usedUp;
```

Now the first operand of + is an `int`, so the compiler would attempt to find the following interfaces:

```
operator+(Duration rhs);       // As a member-operator of int, or
operator+(int lhs, Duration rhs);
```

The compiler won't find either of these (can you see why?) and hence you'd get a compile-time error. In this situation the compiler won't try to convert the first parameter (the `int`) to match the earlier operator interface. You'd have to write the statement as:

```
usedUp = Duration(timeInSecs) + usedUp;
```

Having completed specifying the interfaces of the arithmetic operators, the next set of operators you should consider are the comparison operators.

DESIGN:

The comparison operators are all straightforward binary operators returning `bool` results of course.

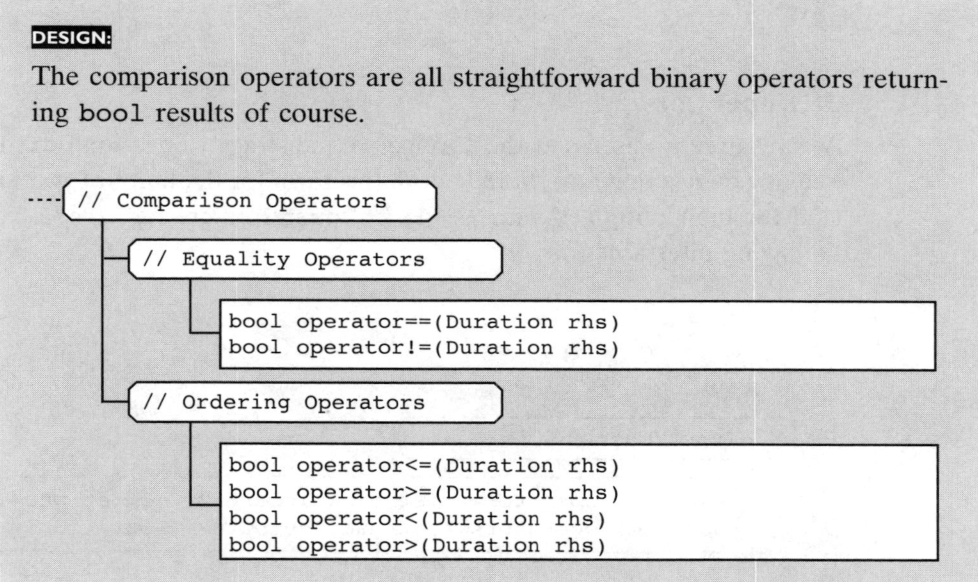

The final member operators to consider are the update operators. As discussed in Section 13.1, if you're going to support the full generality of C++ in the way it permits these operators to be used, these operators have a return type that's a reference to a `Duration`. You can therefore derive the following design for the interfaces of these operators.

DESIGN:

```
// Update Operators
    Duration& operator+=(Duration rhs)
    Duration& operator-=(Duration rhs)
    Duration& operator*=(int rhs)
    Duration& operator/=(int rhs)
    Duration& operator%=(Duration rhs)
```

I/O operators

We've already discussed the form of the abstract values for `Duration` and it seems obvious that you should adopt this form for the input of `Duration` values and for their output. As far as the I/O operators are concerned, you need the following interfaces.

DESIGN:

```
// Input/Output
    istream& operator>>(istream& inStream,  Duration& duration)
    ostream& operator<<(ostream& outStream, Duration  value)
```

`Duration` *header file*

You've now designed all of the constituent parts of `Duration`'s interface, so the next task is to write the C++ `class` definition. All of the features you've identified so far are available to a user of `Duration`, so all of the member interfaces must be placed in the `public` section of the definition for `class Duration`. The class definition itself will be placed in a header (`.h`) file that users of `Duration` will `#include` in order to use this type. Thus you have to create a file called `Duration.h` that contains the following code.

DEFINITION:

```
#include <iostream.h>
#include "bool.h"

class Duration
{
  public:

    // Constructors
                                                // Initialization values
    Duration();                                 // 0:00:00
    Duration(int secs);                         // 0:00:   secs
    Duration(int mins,  int secs);              // 0:mins: secs
    Duration(int hours, int mins, int secs); // hr:mins:secs

    // Member Functions

    int   hours();
    int   minutes();
    int   seconds();

    // Member operators

         // Assignment operator provided by the compiler

         // Arithmetic operators

    Duration  operator+(Duration rhs);
    Duration  operator-(Duration rhs);
    Duration  operator*(int rhs);
    int       operator/(Duration rhs);
    Duration  operator/(int rhs);
    Duration  operator%(Duration rhs);

         // Update Operators

    Duration& operator+=(Duration rhs);
    Duration& operator-=(Duration rhs);
    Duration& operator*=(int  rhs);
    Duration& operator/=(int  rhs);
    Duration& operator%=(Duration rhs);

         // Comparison operators

    bool      operator==(Duration rhs);
    bool      operator!=(Duration rhs);
    bool      operator<=(Duration rhs);
    bool      operator>=(Duration rhs);
    bool      operator<(Duration rhs);
    bool      operator>(Duration rhs);
```

```
    private:

        // To be completed later

};

istream& operator>>(istream&  inStream, Duration& duration);
ostream& operator<<(ostream& outStream, Duration  value);
```

There are a couple of things to note about this header file. First, it isn't complete yet. You have to add some further details to the `private` section. This is discussed below. Second, note that this header file itself `#includes` two other header files. These files are included because `Duration.h` uses the PDTs `ostream`, `istream` and `bool`. Remember, you can't use types before they are defined.

But now you're ready to switch hats from that of class interface designer to that of class implementer, to implement of all of the wonderful features you've designed in the interface.

Implementing `Duration`

So far, you've defined the behavior of the new abstraction `Duration` with little concern for its implementation. You've defined the abstract values that a `Duration` variable may take, and decided upon the constructors, member functions and operators that the type provides to permit `Duration` variables to be declared and manipulated. You know that the operations will be defined (that is, implemented) as C++ functions and operators. So far, so good. Now you need to consider implementation details, and the concrete representation of `Duration` instances is a good place to start.

Concrete representation

If you declare and use a variable of type `Duration` in a program, you'll expect this variable to be able to "remember" its state, just like an instance of the `int` type does. Assignments to the `Duration` variable will change its abstract state, and the arithmetic, update and comparison operators will require access to the (abstract) value that has been retained. Again, all just like you've come to expect. But how are you going to implement the abstract values, and storage of abstract values, that the type demands? To provide this implementation you have to decide on the **concrete representation** of the abstract state: the member variables that appear in the private section of the class definition.

Think for a moment how you might represent a `Duration` variable. In other words, what member variable, or variables, would you need to provide equivalent behavior?

You know that abstract durations have three components: hours, minutes and seconds. Thus one representation you could use is an `int` member variable for each of these components:

```
int hours;
int minutes;
int seconds;
```

An alternative representation is to use a single `int` member variable that represents the duration as a number of seconds:

```
int totalSecs;
```

Yet another representation might be to hold the duration in a textual form:

```
Text duration;
```

Any one of these representations could be satisfactory as a means of representing a duration, although each will have different trade-offs in terms of the C++ member function and operator definitions that you write (for example, to add two durations together).

How do you choose between these possible representations? There isn't an easy answer here, as experience plays a key part. One thing you could do is to try out each; sketch out some of the member-function implementations to see whether one representation turns out "better" than the others.

EXAMPLE:

If you outline the C++ needed to implement `operator+(...)` you'll find that the `Text` representation is difficult to deal with in terms of the ease with which the abstract duration components can be extracted and manipulated.

Let's choose the second representation, namely the single integer value holding the duration as a total number of seconds, for reasons that come up later. But note that it isn't necessary for the concrete representation to be a close match to the abstract representation. All that's required is that the abstract representation can be implemented using the concrete representation. This is the power of abstraction at work again; you're going to provide the abstract behavior of `Duration` from this concrete representation using one `int` member variable.

This is an illustration of one of the key features of object-oriented programming, so we make no excuse for continuing to emphasize the point! The issue is *separating the concerns* of the user from those of the implementer.

Note that to keep the concrete representation separate from the abstract interface, you must not place member variable declarations in the `public` section of the class definition. Were you to do so, you'd lose the flexibility to separate the user's view from that of the PDT implementer. A program using `Duration` with the interface you've designed isn't dependent upon the concrete representation, and this gives you the flexibility to change the implementation without requiring the source code of the using program to change. We'll return to this point with the next example class, but note the following lesson.

Lesson: Placing member variables in the private section permits you to separate the concerns of a user from those of the implementer.

IMPLEMENTATION:

Given the representation chosen, you have to add an `int` declaration to the class definition:

```
class Duration
{
  public:
    ... // As shown earlier
  private:

    int totalSecs;     // To hold the representation of
                       //   Duration values

};
...
```

Remember that compilation of the class definition itself doesn't result in any declarations occurring at run-time. The member variables are only declared when variables of type `Duration` are declared. The class definition simply provides information to the compiler about what is required when a variable of type `Duration` is declared, as you'll soon see.

Accessing private member variables

Whenever a variable of type `Duration` is declared, the compiler translates the declaration into two actions:

1. A declaration of all of the variables declared in the private section of the class definition (one `int` for `Duration`).
2. A call to the appropriate constructor.

Every `Duration` variable declared therefore has its own copy of the private variable. Don't forget that encapsulation is enforced by the C++ compiler to ensure that any private variables cannot be manipulated by the user, even though visible to the human eye when reading the class definition. If you're a user of a class and you try to manipulate the private variables directly, you'll get a compile-time error.

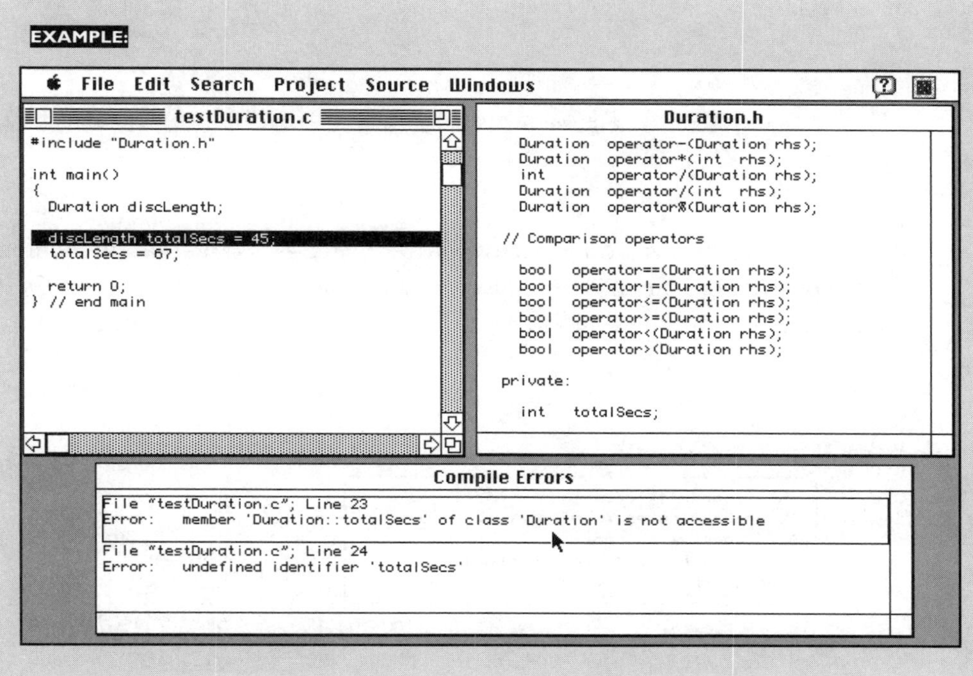

This encapsulation of the private data so that the class user can't manipulate it directly is a very important feature of object-oriented programming and not just another irritating source of compile-time errors. We'll come back to the significance of this feature later.

To the user, `Duration` variable declarations simply create "black boxes" somewhere in the memory of the computer. The user can't see inside the black boxes, but they don't need to; they simply use the variables as the abstractions that the class supports (Figure 13.1).

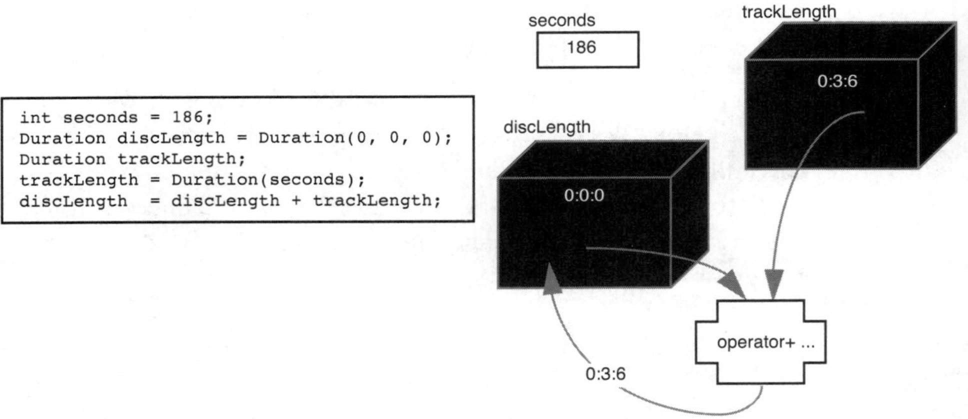

Figure 13.1 User's view of private member variables

However, as you already know, the C++ code that implements the class constructors, member functions and member operators is permitted to access the member variables in order to manipulate that representation to provide the

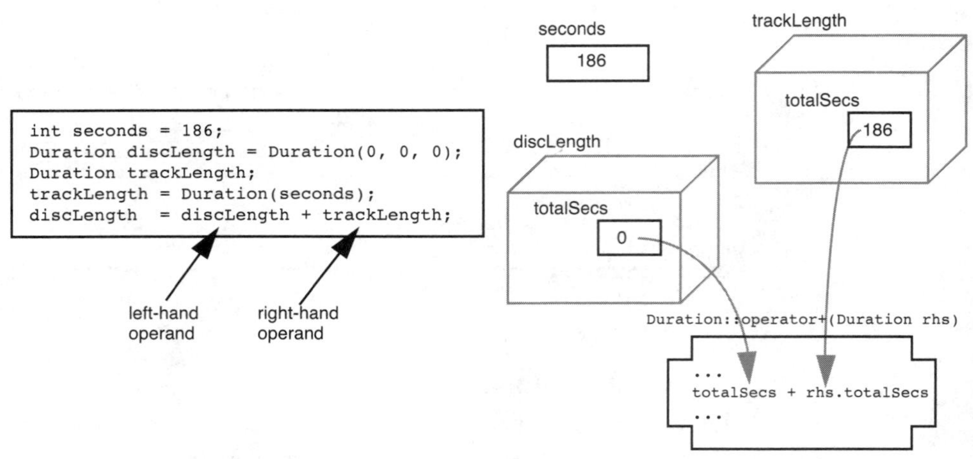

Figure 13.2 Implementer's view of private member variables

abstract behavior. The variable is in effect "opened up" when a member function is called so that the member function can access the private data of that variable (Figure 13.2).

Now it's time to implement `Duration`'s operations.

General features of `Duration` implementation

In implementing `Duration`, you have to provide C++ code to define all of the constructors, member functions, member operators and I/O operators that you provided the interfaces for in the header file. This code will be placed in the source file `Duration.c`. So, let's start placing, and construct a first skeleton file.

IMPLEMENTATION 1:

```
#include "Duration.h"
// Constructors
// Member Functions
// Member Operators
// I/O Operators
```

Why is `Duration.h` included? It is included to define the type `Duration` and to permit the compiler to determine the names and types of the private member variables in the class.

Well, that's a start on the code, but you now have to start defining functions. Let's begin with the constructors.

Constructor definitions

In `Duration`'s definition, there are four constructor interfaces:

```
Duration();
Duration(int secs);
Duration(int mins,  int secs);
Duration(int hours, int mins, int secs);
```

and you remember that in the design it was decided that the constructor with no parameters will initialize the variable to 0:0:0. The other three constructors will have to convert the values from the various integer parameters into the private representation. The following is the C++ code required in `Duration.c`.

IMPLEMENTATION: CONSTRUCTORS

```
#include "Duration.h"

const int  SECS_MIN     = 60;
const int  MINS_HOUR    = 60;
const int  SECS_HOUR    = SECS_MIN * MINS_HOUR;

// Constructors

Duration::Duration()
{
  totalSecs = 0;
  return;
} // end Duration()

Duration::Duration(int secs)
{
  totalSecs = secs;
  return;
} // end Duration(int secs)

Duration::Duration(int mins, int secs)
{
  totalSecs = (mins * SECS_MIN) + secs;
  return;
} // end Duration(int mins, int secs)

Duration::Duration(int hours, int mins, int secs)
{
  totalSecs = (hours * SECS_HOUR) + (mins * SECS_MIN) + secs;
  return;
} // end Duration(int hours, int mins, int secs)
```

Some useful constants are declared after the header file inclusion. Should the `const` declarations be here in `Duration.c` or in the `Duration.h` header file?

The `const` declarations should be in the `.c` file; they're needed only for the compilation of `Duration.c` and are not needed by any user of `Duration` (who will only need to `#include` the header file).

The definition of each constructor follows these constant declarations. Remember these three lessons introduced in Chapter 12.

1. A constructor doesn't have a return type.
2. The identifier of each constructor must be the same as the identifier of the class.

3. In the definition, the identifier of each constructor must be prefixed with the class identifier and the scope resolution operator `::` – by doing this, you're indicating to the compiler that the function is a part of the class `Duration`, and hence is permitted to access the private variables.

The code within each constructor definition is straightforward, setting the private `int` variable `totalSecs` to zero in the default constructor (that is, the one with no parameters), and setting it to the correct number of seconds in the others.

Note that within the constructor body the variable `totalSecs` can be directly accessed without using the dot operator. The `Duration` variable that's being declared is "opened" up, as discussed before, and hence can be accessed directly in the code.

Anything missing from the above constructors?

There should be some defensive programming checks; for instance, to prevent a user from specifying illegal values for some of the parameters – not illegal types such as `CDPlayer`, as those errors will be detected by the compiler, but out-of-range values such as:

```
Duration(1, 123, 456)
```

Does a call `Duration(1234)` contain an illegal value (number of seconds > `59`)? No, this isn't illegal, as that constructor turns any number of seconds into a `Duration`. We'll leave you to work out which constructor calls should have which defensive checks added.

Testing

Before moving on with any further implementation of `Duration`, let's consider the software engineering issue of testing. We've mentioned before that one of the advantages of defining a new type is that it gives you a software component that can be implemented and tested independently from any program that uses that type, thus reducing the overall complexity of the testing task. But which approach are you going to use to test the code that you're writing for this new class? Incremental or big-bang?

Of course, you're going to use the incremental approach, testing implemented features as you go along. Later we'll consider the design and implementation of an extensive test program for `Duration`, but it's worth checking the behavior a small part at a time since an error that shows up is likely to be in the part just written and therefore fresh in the mind.

A first test can check if the code just written compiles without errors. A second test requires the construction of a small C++ test program to check some features of the class. Note that you don't have to define all of the class features before an executable test program is constructed. As long as the test program only uses features for which there are definitions then a test program can be built. What happens if your test program uses a member function for which there's an interface in the header file but which you haven't provided a definition for? The answer is that you'll get a link-time error.

Lesson: You only need to have definitions for the operations of a class that a (test) program uses.

Here's a first simple test program to check out the constructors.

IMPLEMENTATION: TEST 1

```
#include <iostream.h>
#include "Duration.h"

void test1();       // First test written for class Duration

int main()
{
  test1();
  return 0;
} // end main()

void test1()
{
  // First test function - test constructors only

  Duration unInit;
  Duration initSecs            = Duration(35);
  Duration initMinsSecs        = Duration(15, 40);
  Duration initHoursMinsSecs = Duration(23, 59, 58);

  cout << "End of Duration test 1" << endl;
  return;
} // end test1()
```

The first test has been written as a function `test1()` called from the main test program. All this function does is to create four `Duration` variables, each making use of a different constructor. You can try the above test program and check that it compiles and executes. Note that the testing code doesn't go in the `Duration.c` file. We've created a separate file for the test program (`testDuration.c`) that's compiled and linked with the separately-compiled `Duration.c` file.

Since this test program doesn't produce any output of `Duration` values, it's a little difficult to check whether the constructors have worked correctly. You can only see if there are any run-time errors. To extend the test you'd like to print out the values of the declared `Duration` variables. To do that, you need the output operator for `Duration`. So that's the next operation we'll look at implementing.

Output operator definition

You decided earlier that output of `Duration` values is to be of the form:

```
1:15:45
```

So, this form is what you must design the output operator function to produce: each of the abstract components of a `Duration` value separated by a ":".

For `Duration` you've defined the following interface:

```
ostream& operator<<(ostream& outStream, Duration value)
```

This isn't a member operator so its definition can't access the private member variables of the `Duration` class. As a consequence, it can only use features present in the interface of `Duration` using the normal "dot" operator to call the relevant member functions or member operators. Fortunately, you provided relevant member functions so the definition of the output operator is straightforward.

IMPLEMENTATION: OUTPUT OPERATOR

```
const char IO_SEPARATOR = ':';

ostream& operator<<(ostream& outStream, Duration value)
{
  outStream << value.hours()   << IO_SEPARATOR
            << value.minutes() << IO_SEPARATOR
            << value.seconds();
  return outStream;
} // end operator<<()
```

This is a rather simplistic implementation of the output operator, but it will do for now. This definition also goes in the file `Duration.c` as it provides part of the interface you've designed for `Duration`. Note that as it's not a member operator, you don't use the scope resolution operator to qualify the operator's name.

Can you now construct a second test program? Not yet, since you need to implement the three member functions used in the definition of the output operator.

Member function definitions

You're back to implementing functions that are part of the class definition so, as with the constructors, the identifiers for the function definitions have to be qualified with `Duration::` and the private member variable can then be accessed directly. For `Duration` each member function returns an `int` value representing one of the components of the abstract state, and we assume that you can understand the arithmetic necessary to turn a number of seconds into the relevant component.

IMPLEMENTATION: MEMBER FUNCTIONS

```
int Duration::hours()
{
  return totalSecs / SECS_HOUR;
} // end hours()

int Duration::minutes()
{
   return (totalSecs - (hours() * SECS_HOUR)) / SECS_MIN;
} // end minutes()
```

```
int Duration::seconds()
{
  return totalSecs % SECS_MIN;
} // end seconds()
```

Note that the definition of the `minutes()` member function contains a call to the `hours()` member function. As this call is already inside a member function, it isn't necessary to use the full member-function call syntax (applying the lesson you saw in Section 12.6).

These functions are one of the implementation areas where you can appreciate the effect of the choice of concrete representation for `Duration`. Had the representation consisting of three `int` variables been chosen then the implementation of these member functions would have been trivial. With your chosen representation you've had to do a bit more work. You'll see that what you lose here you'll gain later in some of the operator implementations. This is an example of a typical trade-off when designing and implementing software.

Back to testing. You're now in a position to compile the new member-function and output-operator definitions added to `Duration.c`. Then you can generate a second test function to provide a more comprehensive test of whether the constructors work properly, whether the output operator works and thus whether the member functions work.

The following test function is additionally trying out an assignment operation. This is to emphasize the point made earlier that the compiler will automatically provide an assignment operator definition for you. How does the compiler implement this operator? Simply by copying the value in the member variable of the `Duration` variable on the right-hand side (that is, `int totalSecs`) into the member variable of the `Duration` variable on the left-hand side.

IMPLEMENTATION: TEST 2

```
void test2()
{
  // Second test function - testing assignment, output operation

  Duration unInit;
  Duration initSecs          = Duration(35);
  Duration initMinsSecs      = Duration(15, 40);
  Duration initHoursMinsSecs = Duration(23, 59, 58);
  Duration aTime;
```

```
  cout << "Uninitialized variable:          "
       << unInit              << endl
       << "35 Seconds:                      "
       << initSecs            << endl
       << "15 mins, 40 secs:                "
       << initMinsSecs        << endl
       << "23 hours, 59 mins, 58 secs:      "
       << initHoursMinsSecs << endl;

  aTime = initHoursMinsSecs;      // See if assignment works
  cout << "Assignment should give 23:59:58 "
       << aTime               << endl;

  cout << "End of Duration test 2" << endl;
  return;
} // end test2()
```

OUTPUT:

Running the test program produces the following (satisfactory) output on some C++ systems.

```
Uninitialized variable:         0:0:0
35 Seconds:                     0:0:35
15 mins, 40 secs:               0:15:40
23 hours, 59 mins, 58 secs:     23:59:58
Assignment should give 23:59:58 23:59:58
End of Duration test 2
```

This second test function demonstrates an important testing point.

Lesson: You should indicate what the expected output is, as well as providing the actual output. This makes it easier to check that the test program has functioned correctly.

If this test function had produced an error in the values printed, you'd have to locate the bug that caused it. The problem could be in the output operator, in the member functions or even in the constructors. You'd have to check out each possibility carefully to find the bug. This is often one of the key issues in testing software, in that an error can often be caused by many different bugs. One of the advantages of the incremental approach to testing is that you can build up confidence slowly, testing items one at a time (if you can) and building on previously tested code. This way a new error is likely have been caused by the new code, rather than by existing tested code. However, this isn't always the case, and it may be that the new code is showing up an error in the old code that your previous testing didn't uncover.

Lesson: Incremental testing helps you to pinpoint bugs.

Lesson: A tested component can still contain residual bugs.

Although the above test output was satisfactory, when the implementation of `Duration` was tried with the same test function on another C++ system, the following output was produced.

OUTPUT:

```
Uninitialized variable:          0:0:0
35 Seconds:                      0:0:35
15 mins, 40 secs:                0:15:40
23 hours, 59 mins, 58 secs:      5:47:42
Assignment should give 23:59:58 5:47:42
End of Duration test 2
```

So there's a bug that shows up on one system but not another. This immediately suggests a system-dependency problem, but have you any idea what it is?

The symptoms are that things appear to go wrong for a large `Duration` value. Do you remember what was said about the `int` type in Chapter 5? Recall that on some systems `int`s have a maximum positive value of 32,767, so if `Duration` is implemented on such a system, the total number of seconds must be less than this value, a `Duration` value representing just over nine hours. This is the problem that caused the above effect, and since integer overflow doesn't generate a run-time error, the program simply gives a wrong answer.

What should you do about this problem if your system has this range of `int`s? One approach is to change the specification for `Duration` so that the maximum value that can be represented is nine hours. A second approach is to abandon the concrete representation of a single `int` variable and adopt the representation of three `int` variables holding the hours, minutes and seconds components separately. A third approach is to use a "bigger" integer type if there is one. In fact, C++ supports two main sizes of integers, represented by two built-in types named `short` and `long`. Of course there's `int` as well, and `int` is equivalent to either `short` or `long`, depending on which is most convenient for a particular computer and compiler. For the system on which the test didn't fail, `int` is equivalent to `long`, while on the system that it did fail `int` is equivalent to `short`.

The built-in type `long` generally provides a maximum positive value of over two billion which is more than sufficient for the abstract values for `Duration` specified earlier. So, one fix for the problem identified is to change the declaration of the private member variable of `Duration` to

```
long totalSecs;   // To hold the representation of Duration values
```

(To see the problem demonstrated on all systems, use the type `short` in this declaration instead.) For simplicity we'll assume this approach is taken to fix the problem, but we'll continue to use the `int` version of the declaration in this chapter and assume you'll change your copy of the program to use `long` as necessary (Exercise 7 at the end of this section addresses this problem). Don't forget the following lesson.

Lesson: Integer overflow occurs without a run-time error being reported.

What's next? It's time to implement the member operators.

Member operator definitions

The definitions for the member operators are relatively straightforward, given the concrete representation chosen. Rather than waste trees, we'll just show the definition of the addition and test-for-equality operators, as well as the update-with-addition operator. The others are similar.

IMPLEMENTATION: MEMBER OPERATORS

```
Duration Duration::operator+(Duration rhs)
{
  return Duration(totalSecs + rhs.totalSecs);
} // end operator+()
```

```
bool Duration::operator==(Duration rhs)
{
  return (totalSecs == rhs.totalSecs);
} // end operator==()

Duration& Duration::operator+=(Duration rhs)
{
  totalSecs += rhs.totalSecs;
  return *this;
} // end operator+=()
```

All of these operators are binary operators, and we explained at the beginning of this chapter why only the right-hand operand appears in the parameter list. The left-hand operand is of course the `Duration` variable to which the operator is being applied and hence has been "opened" so that the use of the unqualified identifier `totalSecs` refers to the `int` variable of this left-hand operand.

However, the operators also need access to the value of the `int` concrete representation variable of the right-hand operand. Since the type of the parameter that represents the right-hand operand is the same as the class that you're writing the operator definitions for, the compiler permits this right-hand operand to be treated as if the member variables were public. Hence, you can use the dot operator to access the `totalSecs` part of the right-hand operand using the expression `rhs.totalSecs`. Again, note that a "normal" user of the class `Duration` can't perform this access. Since you're implementing the class it's assumed that you can be "trusted" to access private variables, a level of trust that must not be extended to other users.

As the addition operator has to return a value of type `Duration`, it adds together the two `int` values, giving a result as an `int` number of seconds. The result value is then turned into a `Duration` value using the constructor that takes an `int` as its initializing value. This result type then matches the interface for this operator that indicates that the value returned from the operator is of type `Duration`. Note that the addition operator doesn't change the value of either of its operands. That's not part of its behavior. You wouldn't expect the addition of two integer variables to change either variable, would you?

The equality member operator simply returns the result of the `bool` expression comparing the values of the two private member variables.

For the update-with-addition operator, the implementation has to add the value of totalSecs from the right-hand operand to that of the left-hand operand, updating the concrete representation of the left-hand operand in the process. You'll recall from Section 13.1 that the definition must have a reference to a Duration as the result type (not a value as in the addition operator). To achieve this you have to write the statement:

```
return *this;
```

To explain fully what this does would require explanation of some C++ language features that you've not needed to cover in this apprenticeship. Suffice it to say that this statement does the job of returning a reference to an instance of a type, as the interface requires. In fact, it returns a reference to the variable that's just been updated – the left-hand operand. You'd write this statement in the definitions of an update operator in any class you were defining; it's not specific to Duration.

In the above operator definitions, you can see an example of the trade-off mentioned earlier. Think about an implementation of these member operators if the concrete representation of three int variables had been chosen. You'll then see why we chose the other concrete representation, even though the implementations of the member functions hours(), minutes() and seconds() were made slightly more complex.

Time for another test function? You bet. Here's a third test function that assumes the remaining member operators have been implemented. Again the strategy is a simple test of the operators with Duration values for which you can work out what the results should be. Now that some comparison operators are available, checks against expected values can be built into the test program itself and errors reported, rather than relying on you scanning the output that the program produces to detect errors.

IMPLEMENTATION: TEST 3

```
void test3()
{
  // Third test - testing assignment, output operation as in
  // test 2, extended with some simple tests of operators

  Duration unInit;
  Duration initSecs            = Duration(35);
  Duration initMinsSecs        = Duration(15, 40);
  Duration initHoursMinsSecs = Duration(23, 59, 58);
  Duration aTime;
```

```
  cout << "Uninitialized variable:          "
       << unInit               << endl
       << "35 Seconds:                      "
       << initSecs             << endl
       << "15 mins, 40 secs:                "
       << initMinsSecs         << endl
       << "23 hours, 59 mins, 58 secs:      "
       << initHoursMinsSecs << endl;

  aTime = initHoursMinsSecs;       // See if assignment works
  cout << "Assignment should give 23:59:58 "
       << aTime                << endl;

  aTime = aTime + Duration(2);     // Should get to 24 hours
  cout << "Add 2 secs should give 24:0:0   "
       << aTime                << endl;

  initSecs = initSecs + Duration(3);
  cout << "After add, should be 38 secs:   "
       << initSecs             << endl;
  if (initSecs != Duration(38))
  {
    cout << "InEquality comparison failed: << endl;
  }
  aTime = initMinsSecs * 2;
  if ((aTime/2) != initMinsSecs)
  {
    cout << "Multiply/divide error?" << endl;
  }
  if ((aTime/initMinsSecs) != 2)
  {
    cout << "Error in divide by Duration? Expecting 2 got "
         << aTime/initMinsSecs << endl;
  }
  aTime  = initHoursMinsSecs;          // Some tests of
  aTime += initSecs;                   //   update operators
  if (aTime != (initHoursMinsSecs + initSecs))
  {
    cout << "Update-by-add failed. The variable has the value: "
         << aTime                              << " but expected: "
         << (initHoursMinsSecs + initSecs) << endl;
  }
  ... // Other tests on update operators in here ...

  cout << "End of Duration test 3 "   << endl;
  return;
} // end test3()
```

We won't bore you with the output from executing this test. The code works, honest.

Input operator definition

The only part of the class interface left to implement is the input operator. As with the output operator, this isn't a member operator and hence doesn't have direct access to the private variables. The implementation below is rather simple, and doesn't perform any checking that the input is provided in the correct format (it allows the input of a number of minutes or seconds greater than 59, for example). The implementation simply gets three integer values, reading and ignoring a separation character between these values. The values are then turned into a `Duration` value and assigned to the reference parameter. Finally the `istream` reference parameter is returned so that cascaded input can be supported.

IMPLEMENTATION: INPUT OPERATOR

```
istream& operator>>(istream& inStream, Duration& duration)
{
  int  hours;
  int  minutes;
  int  seconds;
  char separator;

  inStream >> hours   >> separator
           >> minutes >> separator
           >> seconds;
  duration = Duration(hours, minutes, seconds);
  return inStream;
} // end operator>>()
```

Another test function is called for (and this time it really is called 4). Here we've chosen a particular sentinel `Duration` value to terminate the `while` loop.

IMPLEMENTATION: TEST 4

```
void test4()                    // Simple test of input operator
{
  Duration inputTime = Duration(0);

  cout << "Testing the input operator. "
       << "Type 99:0:0 to terminate." << endl;
  while (inputTime != Duration(99,0,0))
  {
    cout << "Duration (h:m:s): ";
    cin  >> inputTime;
    cout << " Got value: " << inputTime << endl;
  }
  cout << "End of Duration 4 program" << endl;
  return;
} // end test4();
```

A comprehensive test program

The implementation of `class Duration` is now complete, and the test functions used so far have provided some confidence that the code written is correct. But now a more comprehensive test program is needed, one that will exercise `Duration` much more thoroughly with many more of the possible values. The full test program is provided, but here is its outline.

IMPLEMENTATION: FULL TEST

```
Duration oldDuration = Duration(-1);
int totSecs = 0;

for (int hours = 0 ; hours < 25; hours += 1)
{
  for (int mins = 0; mins < 60; mins += 1)
  {
    for (int secs = 0; secs < 60; secs += 1)
    {
      Duration duration = Duration(hours, mins, secs);

      checkDuration(duration, oldDuration,
                    hours, mins, secs, totSecs);
      oldDuration = duration;
      totSecs += 1;
    } // end for (int secs = 0; ...)
  } // end for (int mins = 0; ...)
} // end for (int hours = 0; ...)
```

The test program is basically trying all `Duration` values from `0:0:0` up to `24:59:59` using three nested `for` loops. It maintains one `Duration` variable (`oldDuration`) which should be 1 second behind the new value being tested. The check function `checkDuration(...)` applies a set of tests of the `Duration` values against what their constituent components should be, as well as testing the arithmetic operators.

Note that although we originally said "probably no negative `Duration` values" in fact they will work satisfactorily for everything except output, and a duration of -1 seconds has been used in the test program. To support negative values fully you'd have to reconsider the implementation of the output operator as well as provide a unary minus operator.

If this test program runs without errors (which it does, incidentally) then you're done with the class implementation. That's all there is to it :-). You now have an implemented and tested software component to go into your toolbag. It was some work to get to this stage, but going back to the original problem of providing a program for the DJ should show the benefit of having this type available for use in solving the original problem.

EXERCISES FOR SECTION 13.2

1 A definition for a `class SomeErrors` contains the following constructor interfaces. If the complete definition is compiled, what compile-time errors will be reported concerning the constructors, and why?

```
SomeErrors(int count);
SomeErrors(int count, char severity);
SomeErrors(bool stop);
SomeErrors(int systemErrorNo);
```

2 Assuming you fixed the compile-time errors from Exercise 1 by removing any offending constructor interfaces, would the following declaration cause any additional compile-time errors?

```
SomeErrors aVariable;
```

3 The `class Duration` always initializes a variable to `0:0:0` if it isn't initialized explicitly. How could you change this behavior so that an uninitialized `Duration` variable is remembered as being uninitialized and this is detected when an attempt is made to use the value of the uninitialized variable?

4 Identify some defensive programming checks that could be included in `class Duration`, and change the code to implement these checks. Do all of the test programs still work?

5 Given `class Duration` and the following declarations, what's wrong with the expression used in the `cout` statement? How can you get around the problem?

```
Duration dur1 = Duration(1, 20);
int      time = 37;

cout << time + dur1 << endl;
```

6 Write a test program whose output will show whether `int` on your computer is equivalent to `long` or `short`.

7 Which interfaces in the class definition of `Duration` would need to be changed if you needed to make explicit use of `long`?

13.3 CLASS SQUARE

In Chapter 11 you defined some functions for drawing shapes on a `Canvas`. Think back to the function to draw a square starting at a particular coordinate on a `Canvas`. What was that function's interface? What would you have to tell someone who wanted to use your function in a graphics system they were building? You'd have to tell them something like the following.

"Well, the function interface is:

```
bool drawSquare(Canvas& picture, int sideLength,
                int xPos, int yPos);
```

Therefore you'll probably need to declare three `int` variables to represent each instance of a square, set the values of those variables appropriately and call the above function."

They then might say "OK, but I want to be able to change a square's size and then rotate the square."

You'll remember another function you constructed that took an additional parameter to indicate the degree of rotation.

```
bool drawSquare(Canvas& picture, int sideLength,
                int xPos, int yPos,
                double rotationAngle);
```

No problem. Isn't software reuse wonderful!

But the potential user notices that there's no update of the variables recording the square's actual position (the function only uses value parameters), and you can point out that, yes, they'll have to maintain the variables that record the position and rotation angle that the square should be at, and they'll have to be sure that they're kept up-to-date. You're telling the user that it's their responsibility to maintain the variables that form the representation of a square.

"Have you also got a function that will move a square's origin so that the square moves on the screen?" might be another question.

> "Well, no I don't have a function for that, but all you need to do is to update the *x* and *y* coordinates you're maintaining for each square and then you can call one of the above functions to redisplay the result."

They might say "OK, I'll take your code" to which you can reply hopefully "That'll be $50 please." Well, you've got to start making your fortune somewhere.

However, the user might also think: "Hmmm. This isn't an especially good set of components. I've got to keep these variables representing each square, and make sure I don't mess them up accidentally (no information hiding, nor separation of concerns). I've got to do much of the work involving operations on squares ..." and reply politely "Thanks, but I'll think about it." Ah well, you didn't need $50, did you?

Think through this scenario again, but now think about the replies you could give if you had a PDT `Square` in your toolbag. Using this PDT the user could declare instances of `Square` without any concern for how they are represented. An instance of `Square` could "remember" all of the information required to represent it, describing its location, its angle of rotation, and so on, without requiring the user to do this. There would be member functions available to move the square's origin, to rotate it, and the like. In short, a `class` that gives the user objects that are appropriate to the problem domain, and that have the appropriate set of member functions, is a much better solution for this user. So, let's design and implement `class Square`.

Designing the interface

The first step is to design the interface of `Square`. The abstraction you're trying to provide is that of a square shape that exists in two-dimensional coordinate space. An instance of `Square` is going to be a completely self-contained object. All of the information concerning the instance, such as its coordinates and its angle of rotation, will be contained in the private member variables of the instance.

You could decide that a `Square` instance was also associated with, and drawn on, a particular instance of a `Canvas`. (This would imply that a `Canvas` variable was one of the private variables.) However, a more general abstraction is to separate these two concepts and permit a `Square` instance to be separate from any graphical representation of that instance.

With these considerations in mind, the following set of constructors and member functions seem appropriate.

DESIGN:

```
class Square
{
  public:
    Square();
    Square(int xBottomLeft, int yBottomLeft, int size);
```

```
    void drawYourself(Canvas& picture);
    void rotate(double angleDegrees);
    void setSize(int newSize);
    void move(int xIncrement, int yIncrement);

  private:
    // to be completed later
};
```

There could be other member functions (for example, to return the *x* and *y* coordinates of a square), but let's concentrate on the above set. Notice that there aren't any operators explicitly defined for `Square`, unlike `Duration` which was numerical and therefore required operators. When designing classes, it's quite common to find that operators aren't required. Recall, however, that an assignment operator is provided automatically by the compiler.

Concrete representation and header file

Your next task is to decide on the concrete representation for a square. As always, there are several alternatives. You could choose to record the coordinates of the four corners of the square (8 `int` private variables). However, as it's straightforward to calculate the coordinates of three corners given the square's size and the coordinates of the fourth corner, recording the coordinates of the bottom left-hand corner of the square together with the size of the square will be sufficient, although we'll revisit this decision later.

With this decision you can come up with the following header file `Square.h`.

DEFINITION:

```
                        // Version 1 of Square.h
#ifndef SQUARE_H
#define SQUARE_H

#include "Canvas.h"

class Square
{
  public:
    Square();
    Square(int xBottomLeft, int yBottomLeft, int size);

    void drawYourself(Canvas& picture);
```

```
    void rotate(double angleDegrees);
    void setSize(int newSize);
    void move(int xIncrement, int yIncrement);

  private:
    int xCoord;
    int yCoord;
    int sideLength;
};

#endif
```

We've introduced a new feature here: the use of the `#ifndef` ... `#define` ... `#endif` lines. These are **pre-processor line**s and are instructions to the compilation system rather than being part of the C++ code. What are they for? Well, consider what happens if you try to declare two variables with the same name at the same scope level. You'll get a compile-time error. You run into the same problem with type definitions. If you try to define a type twice, the compiler will complain. Therefore if you `#include` the same header file twice in a program you are compiling, you'll get a compile-time error. OK so far?

As one include file might include other files, as happens with `Canvas.h` in the above file, it can be difficult for a programmer to keep track of which files have been included and which have not. Therefore C++ provides a mechanism that permits you to set up each header file so that it's protected against multiple inclusions. The line:

```
#ifndef SQUARE_H
```

says to the compilation system "**if** SQUARE_H has **n**ot been **def**ined then read and process all of the information down to the matching `#endif` line." In other words, the line is an instruction to conditionally compile the file's contents. You'll note that the next line:

```
#define SQUARE_H
```

defines `SQUARE_H`. The first time this file is included `SQUARE_H` hasn't been defined and the rest of the file is read, thus defining `SQUARE_H`. If the file was then included a second time in the same program, the contents would not be reread and the type identifier `Square` would not be redefined.

It's normal in C++ header files to provide protection against multiple inclusions in this way. For some C++ compilation systems there's an option to process header files once only, but that's not part of the C++ standard. The safe and portable option is that shown above.

Lesson: Protect header files from multiple inclusion by use of the `#ifndef` … `#define`… `#endif` pre-processor lines.

Syntactically, the identifier used in the `#ifndef` … `#define` … pre-processor lines must be an **identifier**. It's useful to define a style rule for such identifiers:

✓ *Use an UPPER-CASE version of the name of the header file, with the "." replaced by a "_".*

Implementing `Square`

You can now start defining the member functions for `Square`. Following the incremental testing approach adopted in the previous section for `Duration` is again sensible, even though you have a lot less implementation work to do with `Square` as it doesn't have lots of operators. The implementation of the constructors and the first few member functions is straightforward. You might like to contrast the implementation code below with that for the square-drawing functions developed in Chapter 11.

IMPLEMENTATION:

```
#include "Canvas.h"
#include "Square.h"

Square::Square()
{
  xCoord = 0;
  yCoord = 0;
  setSize(0);
  return;
} // end Square()

Square::Square(int xBottomLeft, int yBottomLeft, int size)
{
  xCoord = xBottomLeft;
```

```
    yCoord = yBottomLeft;
    setSize(size);
    return;
} // end Square(...)

void Square::setSize(int size)
{
    sideLength = size;
    return;
} // end setSize()

void Square::drawYourself(Canvas& picture)
{
    picture.penUp();
    picture.moveTo(xCoord, yCoord);
    picture.penDown();
    picture.moveRelative(sideLength, 0);
    picture.moveRelative(0, sideLength);
    picture.moveRelative(-sideLength, 0);
    picture.moveRelative(0, -sideLength);
    picture.penUp();
    return;
} // end drawYourself()
```

Note that both constructors call the `setSize(...)` member function rather than just initialize the appropriate private member variable. Since `setSize(...)` is the function that has to deal with whatever needs to be done with the size of the square, it's best to call this function from the constructors rather than for each constructor to deal with the size itself. While in this simple example nothing much needs to be done with the size, later you'll see an advantage of using the member function.

IMPLEMENTATION: TEST I

Here's a first test program to check out these features, and its expected output.

```
int main()
{
  Canvas drawing;

  drawing.setSize(120, 120);
  for (int size = 100; size >= 10; size -=5)
  {
    Square square = Square(10, 10, size);

    square.drawYourself(drawing);
  }
  return 0;
} // end main()
```

So far, so good. Now on to the member function `rotate(...)`. First you need to clarify the specification for this member function. What's the rotation point? Does the square have to be rotated by an angle about one corner as was chosen for the functions in Chapter 11, or about the center of the square? Let's choose the latter, so a square is going to spin around its center in response to `rotate(...)` member-function calls. Is the rotation clockwise or counterclockwise? Let's assume it's the former. These are all things that matter to the user, and it's important that they're specified. In fact, changing the name of the member function to reflect the rotation direction is probably a good idea. So it is `rotateClockwise(...)` from here on, and the header file needs to be changed appropriately. We should have thought about this earlier, rather than rushing into the implementation. There's a lesson developing here, but let's continue for a moment.

The implementation of `rotateClockwise(...)` requires some elementary trigonometry, as shown in Figure 13.3. Don't worry if you can't understand this; you can trust our code, honest.

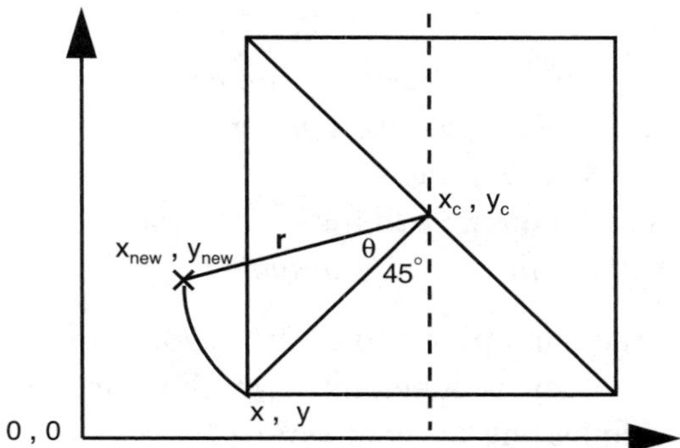

Figure 13.3 Rotating a square around its center

The corners of a rotating square will describe a circle of course, the radius of which is the length of the line from the center of the square to a corner. To work out the new coordinates x_{new}, y_{new} from the current coordinates x, y is most easily performed by using the coordinates of the square's center x_c, y_c. If you can remember some high-school mathematics (see Figure 13.3):

$x_{new} = x_c - r\cos(\theta + 45)$ and $y_{new} = y_c - r\sin(\theta + 45)$

These calculations can be expressed in terms of the coordinates x, y of the bottom left-hand corner of the square, which are the values currently stored in the private member variables. However, the calculation would clearly be much easier if you had the quantities r and x_c, y_c directly available. You could add private member variables to store these quantities as well. But do you then need to store the coordinates of the bottom left-hand corner? In fact you don't, as the coordinates can always be calculated given r and x_c, y_c. Indeed, you don't need to store the size either.

So, why not change the private member variables of `Square`. This means you've also got to change the code already written for the member functions, but fortunately you hadn't written much! You might legitimately argue that you jumped into implementation too early with this class. A bit of forward thought to include the design and implementation of the rotate member function would have avoided the need to change code already written. Yes, yes and yes again! We wanted to demonstrate exactly this point; it's an important lesson to learn:

Lesson: Complete the design before you start to implement. It will save you time in the long run.

When designing a class for a square
You didn't take quite enough care
To complete the design
You would have saved time
And avoided this state of despair.

Here's the main part of the new header file. Note the switch to using `doubles` so that accuracy is maintained in the concrete representation. While you're changing things the original `move(...)` member function can be replaced by a more useful pair of member functions.

DEFINITION:

```
class Square
{
  public:
    Square();
    Square(int xBottomLeft, int yBottomLeft, int size);

    void drawYourself(Canvas& picture);
    void rotateClockwise(double angleDegrees);
    void setSize(int newSize);
    void moveRelative(int xIncrement, int yIncrement);
    void moveCenter(int xCoord, int yCoord);

  private:
    double xCenter;
    double yCenter;
    double angle;
    double radius;
    void   giveCoordinates(int& x, int& y, double angleDegrees);
};
```

There are now private member variables for the origin's coordinates as well as for the length of the radius and the angle of the square (the r and θ in the mathematics earlier). Did you notice that there is a new function interface `giveCoordinates(...)` that's been added to the private section of the class definition? We'll explain its purpose in a moment.

Recoding of the member functions gives the following C++ code.

IMPLEMENTATION:

```
#include <math.h>
#include "Canvas.h"
#include "Square.h"

Square::Square()
{
  xCenter = 0;
  yCenter = 0;
  angle   = 45.0;
  setSize(0);
  return;
} // end Square();

Square::Square(int xBottomLeft, int yBottomLeft, int size)
{
  xCenter  = double(xBottomLeft) + double(size)/2.0;
  yCenter  = double(yBottomLeft) + double(size)/2.0;
  setSize(size);
  angle    = 45.0;
  return;
} // end Square(...)

void Square::drawYourself(Canvas& picture)
{
  int xCoord;
  int yCoord;

  picture.penUp();

  // Convert from concrete representation to x,y coordinates
  // of the bottom left-hand corner of the square
```

```
   giveCoordinates(xCoord, yCoord, angle);
   picture.moveTo(xCoord, yCoord);
   picture.penDown();

   // Draw four sides, each 90 degrees around from start corner
   for (double addAngle = 90.0;
        addAngle < 361.0;
        addAngle += 90.0)
   {
     giveCoordinates(xCoord, yCoord, angle + addAngle);
     picture.moveTo(xCoord, yCoord);
   }
   picture.penUp();
   return;
} // end drawYourself()

void Square::setSize(int size)
{
   radius = double(size) / sqrt(2.0);
   return;
} // end setSize()

// Private functions and private member functions

// atan(1.0) = PI/4
// 2 * PI * radians = 360 degrees

const double DEG_TO_RAD_FACTOR = atan(1.0) / 45.0;

double degreesToRadians(double angle)
{
   return angle * DEG_TO_RAD_FACTOR;
} // end degreesToRadians()

void Square::giveCoordinates(int& x, int& y, double angleDegrees)
{
   double angleRads = degreesToRadians(angleDegrees);

   x = int(xCenter - (radius * sin(angleRads)));
   y = int(yCenter - (radius * cos(angleRads)));
   return;
} // end giveCoordinates()
```

The header file `math.h` has been included since the member functions use various mathematical functions. The constructors have to set the initial value for the `angle` private member variable to 45 (the initial square's corner is at an angle of 45° from the square's center), and set the coordinates of the center.

The member function `setSize(...)` has to change the variable `radius`, making use of that algorithm from the ancient programmer Pythagoras[1]. Recall the earlier discussion of this member function and its use in the constructors. You can see that the calculation of the `radius`'s length is now concentrated in a single place, so it's only that one place that has to be changed following the change to the member variables.

The implementation of the member function `drawYourself(...)` is now a little more complex as it needs to calculate the coordinates of the corners of the square. To perform this calculation, a new member function `giveCoordinates(...)` has been introduced, which you may remember was the function that was introduced in the private section of the class definition.

If you look at the implementation of `drawYourself(...)` you can see that it performs the trigonometry calculations discussed earlier. Because the functions `sin(...)` and `cos(...)` in the C++ library take an actual parameter representing an angle in radians, there's an additional function `degreesToRadians(...)` that performs the transformation from an angle in degrees to an angle in radians using the fact that 2π radians = 360°.

Note that `degreesToRadians(...)` isn't a private member function. It doesn't need access to the private member variables, hence it doesn't need to appear in the class definition, and is just a normal stand-alone function. Indeed, if statements in this function tried to access the member variables, a compile-time error would result.

There are two other style points to think about with the above code. First, should the numbers in the code such as 45.0 and 90.0 be replaced by `const double` declarations? Second, note the test in the `for` statement: `addAngle < 361.0`. Why isn't this test written as `addangle <= 360`?

The literals could of course be replaced by constant declarations, but using literal values makes the code clearer. The answer to the second question is that the `double` arithmetic on the loop control variable might just give a value `360.000000000001` instead of `360.0`, and the test as coded doesn't go wrong if this value is produced.

Now you've made all these changes to the code in `Square.c` it's time for another test to see if they all work. Can you use the test program generated earlier? After all, a lot of code has changed.

Has any part of the interface to `Square` changed as a result of all of these changes to its concrete representation? No, the interface is still the same, and

[1] Pythagoras was a Greek philosopher and mathematician around 500BC. His philosophy included obedience and silence, abstinence from food, and simplicity in dress. Sounds like a typical software engineer!

OUTPUT:

Well, the new implementation almost produces squares! Clearly, there's a bug somewhere in the implementation. The output is close to what was expected, but it looks like some inaccuracy is creeping in, causing some of the coordinates to be generated inaccurately.

therefore any program that's using this interface should be the same. So, let's give that very same test program another try.

Before you start examining the code, think about the error symptoms to see if you can eliminate some possibilities. First, you can see that two sides of the square (the right-hand vertical and the bottom) look OK, so the overall algorithms being used must be sound; any gross errors in them wouldn't have produced these results. Perhaps it's the calculations of `radius` or the center's coordinates that are wrong? Unlikely, given the two correct looking sides? Could `sin(...)` and `cos(...)` be giving inaccurate answers? That's also unlikely as these functions have usually been extensively debugged.

The finger is pointing at the function `giveCoordinates(...)` giving inaccurate coordinates, although the bug isn't clear yet. Can you see anything wrong with that code? You have to do some additional debugging here.

Debugging

Debugging is the process of taking a set of error symptoms and identifying the bug that caused those errors. Sometimes this is a very easy process (when it's obvious what the bug is), but most times debugging can require some good detective work.

One of the big problems with debugging is the error symptoms (or lack thereof). With the above test program's output you can see that there's an error in the squares drawn, but there isn't much information to work from. Nevertheless, you've already performed some analysis of the error symptoms obtained and identified one area that you need to look at in more detail. This is the first lesson in debugging.

Lesson: Start the debugging process by thinking about the error symptoms and the code you're debugging, identifying areas for further investigation and eliminating other areas.

This may seem an obvious lesson, but all too often software engineers start with some of the next techniques we're going to discuss, rather than spending a few moments thinking, eliminating some possibilities and highlighting others.

The next stage is to determine what additional information you'll need to help you figure out what's going on. Your C++ system may support a **debugger** that permits you to run a program, stop it at preselected points and examine the values in the variables at those points. If your system has a debugger, you might like to think about how you'd use it to help identify the bug. In fact you can use a debugger to achieve the same effect as the approach we're going to explain below.

The function `giveCoordinates(...)` has been identified as a suspicious character requiring further investigation. To obtain further information you'll have to add some output statements temporarily to the existing code, to print out some values from which you may be able to see where the errors are creeping in.

EXAMPLE:

```
void Square::giveCoordinates(int& x, int& y,
                             double angleDegrees)
{
  double angleRads = degreesToRadians(angleDegrees);

  cout << "x coord: " << xCenter - (radius * sin(angleRads))
       << ", int: "   << int(xCenter - (radius * sin(angleRads)))
       << endl
       << "y coord: " << yCenter - (radius * cos(angleRads))
       << ", int: "   << int(yCenter - (radius * cos(angleRads)))
       << endl;
  x = int(xCenter - (radius * sin(angleRads)));
  y = int(yCenter - (radius * cos(angleRads)));
```

```
    return;
  } // end giveCoordinates()
```

The output statements have been added to print out the calculated coordinates, both in their original (double) form and in the int form returned by the function. (As these statements are only temporary, the inefficiency of having to do the calculation several times over is not a matter for concern.)

OUTPUT:

Running the test program with this extended version of giveCoordinates(...) produces the following output for the first square to be drawn (your system may give slightly different results).

```
x coord: 10, int: 9
y coord: 10, int: 10
x coord: 10, int: 10
y coord: 110, int: 110
x coord: 110, int: 110
y coord: 110, int: 109
x coord: 110, int: 110
y coord: 10, int: 10
x coord: 10, int: 9
y coord: 10, int: 10
```

You know that the first square drawn should be of size 100 with (10, 10) as the coordinates of the bottom left-hand corner. The additional output statements have shown up a clear problem, in that the value of three of the coordinates after conversion to an int (the second of the two printed values on a line) is one less than its real value (the first value on the line). That explains the jagged line produced – the coordinates are one pixel off.

The problem is clearly being caused by the conversion of the double value to an int. If you recall, the type conversion int(...) always rounds towards zero. So, the values going wrong must be just below an integral value such that the int conversion rounds them down, even though their output as a double suggests they are close to the integer value above. (The factors controlling the output of double values are explained in Chapter 15; basically, for the accuracy of printing that has been used by default in the additional output statements, the `double` values have been rounded to the nearest integer value, which in these error cases is up and not down towards zero.)

Now we have the hypothesis that the rounding down by the `int(...)` type conversion is the bug. A fix for this problem is to add 0.5 to the `double` value before it's converted to an `int`. This causes rounding up or rounding down depending on whether a positive `double` value has a fractional part above or below 0.5. Let's try this.

IMPLEMENTATION:

```
cout << "x coord: "
     << xCenter - (radius * sin(angleRads))
     << ", int: "
     << int(xCenter - (radius * sin(angleRads)) + 0.5)
     << endl
     << "y coord: "
     << yCenter - (radius * cos(angleRads))
     << ", int: "
     << int(yCenter - (radius * cos(angleRads)) + 0.5)
     << endl;
x = int(xCenter - (radius * sin(angleRads)) + 0.5);
y = int(yCenter - (radius * cos(angleRads)) + 0.5);
```

Trying this code produces the expected output on the `Canvas` as well as on the output stream `cout`. It looks like you were successful at identifying and fixing the bug.

Now what do you have to do? Remove those temporary output statements, of course.

While additional output statements can provide useful debugging information, too many can provide so much information that the errors are swamped by the mass of information provided.

Lesson: Add some output statements, but not too many. Initial analysis of a problem should help you decide where to put these statements.

A very important lesson

You've just been through the following sequence of events.

1. Design `Square` interface.
2. Decide on the concrete representation.
3. Implement some member functions.
4. Write and execute a test program.
5. Completely change the concrete representation.
6. Rewrite the member functions.
7. Reexecute the same test program from step 4 and get the same results.

We've skipped the debugging steps in Step 7, because it isn't relevant to the point we want to examine.

Think about the sequence of events that you would go through if you continued to develop the square functions from Chapter 11, and then you decided to change the representation for a square. Just as above, you'd have to rewrite all the square functions, but wouldn't their interfaces also have to change because of the representation change? Yes, they would. Therefore, wouldn't the test program also then require changing? Yes, it would.

So, with the functional approach, changing the representation has a follow-on effect requiring changes to any programs using those functions. However, with the approach of making `Square` a proper type, changes to the concrete representation are isolated to just the member functions. Any user program does *not* have to change. Doesn't this strike you as being beneficial? It should do!

You shouldn't be surprised by the above discussion. After all, it's just a concrete example of the software engineering issues of *separation of concerns*, *information hiding*, and *encapsulation* introduced in Section 12.4. The clear and useful distinction between the interface of a type and the implementation of that interface, as provided by the `class` mechanism, permits the interface to remain constant even though the implementation changes.

It may be difficult for you to appreciate the true benefits of being able to change some code without those changes having any effects elsewhere. But it's a key issue in software engineering in the real world, often such that changes to existing code have to be proposed and reviewed in depth before being allowed to proceed (because of the potential of unknown related effects). Object-oriented techniques are clearly beneficial in this area, for the reasons discussed. They don't eliminate the problem completely – a change to an interface is clearly going to have an effect elsewhere – but they're a significant step forward.

Lesson: Classes are good for you.

In the previous section on `class Duration`, the issue of placing variable declarations in the public section of a class definition was discussed; you remember that we said this is a bad thing to do. The above discussion illustrates further why this is bad. If public variables are part of the concrete representation then you no longer have isolated representation changes to the member functions. As those variables are part of the interface, user programs will also have to be changed. Here's that lesson again.

Lesson: There should be no variable declarations in the public section of a class definition.

Implementing `Square` *continued*

We digressed from the implementation of `Square` before finishing the implementation of the member functions. There are just the three remaining member functions to implement. In fact, all are very straightforward. In particular, the member function `rotateClockwise(...)` is now trivial given the amended concrete representation.

IMPLEMENTATION:

```
void Square::rotateClockwise(double angleDegrees)
{
  angle += angleDegrees;
  return;
} // end rotateClockwise()

void Square::moveRelative(int xIncrement, int yIncrement)
{
  xCenter += xIncrement;
  yCenter += yIncrement;
  return;
} // end moveRelative()

void Square::moveCenter(int xCoord, int yCoord)
{
  xCenter = xCoord;
  yCenter = yCoord;
```

```
   return;
} // end moveCenter()
```

That's it? Well, you should test these final member functions to ensure that they behave as expected. But following those tests, the class is complete and ready for use. That doesn't mean to say it's bug-free or that it couldn't be improved upon. No doubt there are additional member functions you can think of, and there are no defensive programming checks built into the definition of the member functions and operators. But we've got to leave something for you to do at the end of the chapter, haven't we?

EXERCISES FOR SECTION 13.3

1 Using the header file `Duration.h` developed in the previous section, consider the following program.

```
#include "Duration.h"
#include "Duration.h"                    // A second time

int main()
{
  Duration dur1;

  return 0;
} // end main()
```

Predict the compile-time error messages that this program will generate. Fix the header file so that the above program will compile without errors.

2 Add `getX()` and `getY()` member functions to `Square` to return the *x*, *y* coordinates of the bottom left-hand corner of the square.

13.4 CLASS CDPlayer

By now you will have recognized that `CDPlayer` is defined using the class type mechanism; when you were studying Chapter 5 you may even have taken a peek at the header file `CDPlayer.h` although if you did at that time you probably didn't recognize all of the C++ features in the file. Will most of those features still look foreign to you? We hope not, and to show you just how far you've come in your apprenticeship, let's take a look at `CDPlayer.h`. In doing this you'll discover another feature of classes, namely the definition and use of member types.

Here's the header file `CDPlayer.h` (we've deleted some lines to save space):

```
#ifndef CDPLAYER_H
#define CDPLAYER_H

#include "bool.h"
#include "CDisc.h"
#include "DisplayMode.h"
#include "PlayerStatus.h"
#include "Text.h"

class CDPlayer
{
  public:

    // Constructor
    CDPlayer();

    // Member Functions (some of)
    void         on();                       // Switch player on
    void         open();                     // Open CD Drawer
    void         load(CDisc disc);           // Load a disc
    CDisc        unload();                   // Unload a disc
    void         play();                     // Start playing
    PlayerStatus status();                   // Status of player

    // Member operators  -  none defined

  private:

    // Private member types
    enum  OnOff          {ON,      OFF};
    enum  OpenClosed     {OPEN,    CLOSED};
    enum  LoadedUnloaded {LOADED, UNLOADED};

    // Private member functions
    void            doDisplay(Text prefix);
    void            stopIfOff(Text memberName);

    // Private member variables
    OnOff           powerState;
    OnOff           showGraphics;
    OpenClosed      drawerState;
    LoadedUnloaded discState;
    bool            stopped;
    CDisc           loadedDisc;
    int             currentTrack;    // Numbered 0, 1, 2, ...
    ...
};

#endif
```

This header file demonstrates the use of most of the features covered in this and the previous chapter. You can see that the file is protected from multiple inclusions using the preprocessor line mechanism discussed in the previous section. Within the file, the `#include` files include all of the PDTs that `CDPlayer` uses, including `PlayerStatus` which is defined using the `enum` mechanism as you saw in Chapter 12. In the `public` section of the class you recognize the member function interfaces, and you now realize why of course there are no member operators for this class. (Why would you want to add two `CDPlayers` together?)

When you look at the private section, you can see that there are three new PDTs defined using `enum`, namely `OnOff`, `OpenClosed` and `LoadedUnloaded`. This is the first example you've seen of the use of **member types**, here in the private section although they could also occur in the public section of a class, as the following syntax diagrams show:

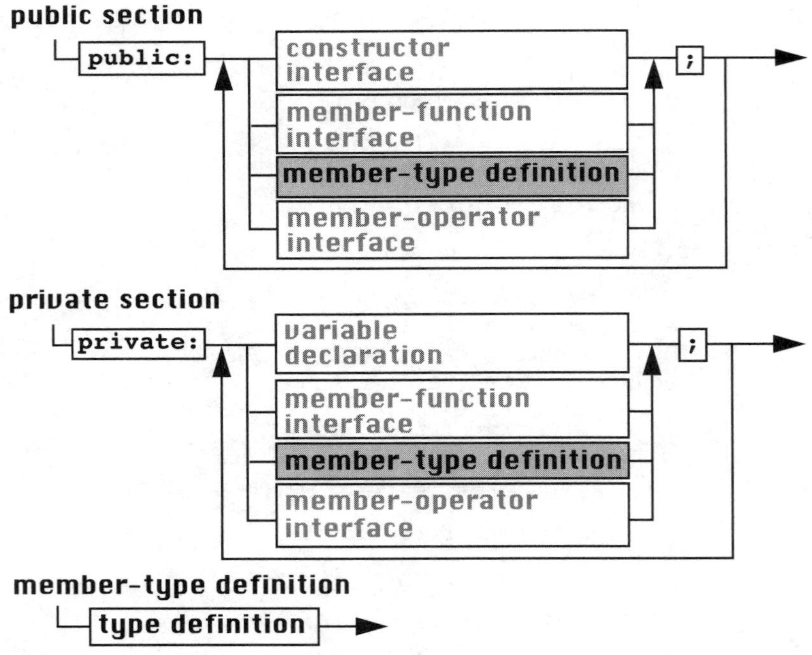

What do you think it means to have a type defined in the public section of a class, or in the private section as in `CDPlayer.h`? You know enough C++ now to answer this question.

A type defined in the public section of a class is available to users of that class, while a type defined in the private section is not available to the class users but is available to the class implementer. Indeed, you can see uses of the private member type identifiers in `CDPlayer.h` in declaring some of the private member variables (for example, `powerState` and `drawerState`). Clearly, those types must be defined before the compiler reads the associated variable declaration, but why place the definitions in the private section? The answer is to reduce the scope of those type identifiers. The identifiers for member types such as `OnOff` are not global and are visible only in the scope of their enclosing class. This is good from a software engineering point of view in that it reduces the potential for name clashes, that is, an attempted reuse of an identifier elsewhere. While this is not likely to be a problem in small software systems constructed by a single person, it can be a major problem in multi-person software implementations.

You might now be wondering why the type `PlayerStatus` isn't defined as a member type in the public section of `CDPlayer`. After all, it is a type intimately associated with `CDPlayer`, yet has to be available to users of `CDPlayer` – this latter point is currently solved by `PlayerStatus` being a global type. The answer is that, from a software engineering point of view, `PlayerStatus` should have been defined as a public member type. OK, so why didn't we define it that way?

Think about what a user would have to write in order to use `PlayerStatus` were it to be defined as a public member type. Since the scope of its identifier would then be restricted to the scope of the class in which it was defined, the scope resolution operator would have to be used for both the type identifier and the literal abstract values that it defines.

EXAMPLE:

```
CDPlayer::PlayerStatus  myStatus;        // Declare a variable
...
if (myStatus == CDPlayer::EMPTY)
{
  ...
```

From a software engineering point of view this is better than having `PlayerStatus` and its abstract value identifiers globally visible (after all, someone else might wish to use the identifier `EMPTY`). We chose not to do this for the simple pragmatic reason that we didn't want to have to explain all of this scope resolution operator complexity to you for the programs you were writing at the start of your apprenticeship. In the next chapter you'll see some examples of public member types and their use, and the following syntax diagram shows how the scope resolution operator has to be used when member type identifiers are being used.

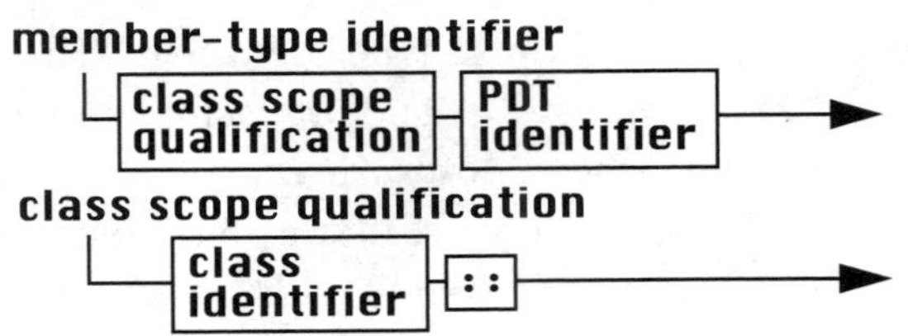

Why doesn't the scope resolution operator have to be used in the private member variable declarations in `CDPlayer` that use the private member types? Would the scope resolution operator be used in the definition of a member function that makes use of a private member type?

Since all items in the private section are in scope in the private section itself, and in a member function's definition, use of the scope resolution operator is not required in these situations.

If you look at the private member variables in `CDPlayer.h` you can see that there quite a few of them. The concrete representation of a `CDPlayer` needs these variables to record various things that should be obvious given the identifiers chosen for these variables (a good example of the utility of our style rule of choosing meaningful identifiers for variables). There are other member variables that we've not shown above, that are associated with the graphics displayed when an instance of `CDPlayer` is manipulated by a program – take a look at the header file, and the source file containing the definitions of the member functions if you would like to see more. But again, to emphasize the power of information hiding and the class mechanism, you didn't need to know about all of these member variables and private member types in order to use `CDPlayer`, did you. Back in the early days of your apprenticeship (in Chapter 7) could you have used `CDPlayer` if you had needed to know all of this detail? Are you convinced about the power of classes yet?

EXERCISES FOR SECTION 13.4

1 Take a copy of the header file `CDPlayer.h` and change it to make the type `PlayerStatus` a member type of `CDPlayer` instead of being a global type. (You don't need to change `CDPlayer.c` for this exercise.) Make use of your new header file and PlayerStatus in a program (for example, a version of `IfPlayCD` from Chapter 10).

2 The following C++ code demonstrates the attempted use of public member types. For all of the places in the code identified by `****` identify what (if anything) needs to be written in place of the `****` in order for this code to compile. Then type in this program with your alterations and see if it compiles and executes correctly.

```
#include <iostream.h>

class NewPDT1
{
  public:

    // Member Types
    enum   NewPDT2 {LITERAL_1, LITERAL_2};
    struct NewPDT3
    {
      ****NewPDT2 anEnum;
      int     anInt;
    };

    void aMemberFunction();

  private:
    ****NewPDT3 aMemberVar;
};

int main()
{
  NewPDT1     instancePDT1;
  ****NewPDT2 instancePDT2;
  ****NewPDT3 instancePDT3;

  instancePDT1.****aMemberFunction();
  instancePDT2         = ****LITERAL_1;
  instancePDT3.anInt  = 37;
  instancePDT3.anEnum = ****LITERAL_2;
```

```
  return 0;

}// end main()

void NewPDT1::aMemberFunction()
{
  cout << "aMemberFunction() in class NewPDT1 called"
       << endl;
  aMemberVar.anInt  = 99;
  aMemberVar.anEnum = ****LITERAL_1;
  return;
}
```

SUMMARY

Even though some people are trying to make the world into a classless society, we're promoting quite the reverse for the software population. This chapter has shown you some examples of how to design and construct classes. It may look a long-winded and hard process, and there's more syntax for you to master, but we hope we've amply demonstrated the advantages of mastering the class construct in C++.

In this chapter you've learned some additional C++ skills. You've covered:

- **member operators** – how to define and implement operators so a user can employ a PDT with numerical characteristics in expressions using the normal infix operator syntax;
- **member types** – how to define types within the scope of a class, and why you'd want to do this.
- **I/O operators** – why they're not member operators in a new PDT;
- **constructors with parameters** – can be used to support:
  1. Declarations with initializations.
  2. Writing literal values for the new PDT.
  3. A type conversion mechanism;
- **header files** should be protected from multiple inclusion using preprocessor lines such as `#ifndef`.

You've also seen more software engineering issues in action:

- **designing types** involves analyzing a problem specification to identify PDTs;

- **design before implementation** – jumping into implementation before all aspects of design have been thought through will waste time and effort;
- **separation of concerns** – the user's (abstract) interface should be kept completely separate from any issues concerning the concrete representation (or, public member variables are bad news);
- **the class mechanism** allows you to separate the user completely from a class' implementation – the concrete representation can be changed without affecting any user programs;
- **encapsulation** prevents misuse of implementation details by allowing only the implementations of a class' operations to access private member variables;
- **testing** is the process of exercising a software component with the aim of highlighting errors;
- **incremental testing** permits you to test your code in small pieces, and concentrate just on the (small) set of features added since the last test;
- **debugging** is the process of analyzing error symptoms in order to identify the fault (bug) that caused the errors;
- **adding output statements** can help you track down errors;
- **residual bugs** may be present even in a well-tested software component.

You haven't yet seen all of the features of the `class` mechanism in C++. Some features are beyond the scope of this book, and form part of a more advanced apprenticeship. But you've covered all of the basic features necessary to construct new PDTs to help your construction of software systems. Start putting a touch of class into your programs!

END-OF-CHAPTER EXERCISES

1 Write a program that requests the user to input a duration in the format H:MM:SS and then finds the CD track that is closest to, but never greater than, that duration. The program should then print out the title of the disc, the track index, and the track's duration in the format given above.

You are expected to use `class Duration`. Consider also the "result" that this program is expected to produce. Design a PDT suitable for this result (Hint: it's going to be a `struct`).

2 Add defensive checks to the implementation of `class Duration`. Implement a test program that shows these checks in action.

3 Design and implement a class that can be used to represent money, along with an extensive test program.

4 Design and implement a `Date` class together with an extensive test program.

5 Design, implement and test a `Rectangle` class.

6 Use `class Square` to generate the following picture.

14 Arrays

OBJECTIVE

To familiarize you with the use of arrays by:

- introducing the concept of an array data structure by;
- describing the `Array` PDT;
- differentiating between array elements and array variables;
- highlighting the pitfalls of C++'s built-in arrays.

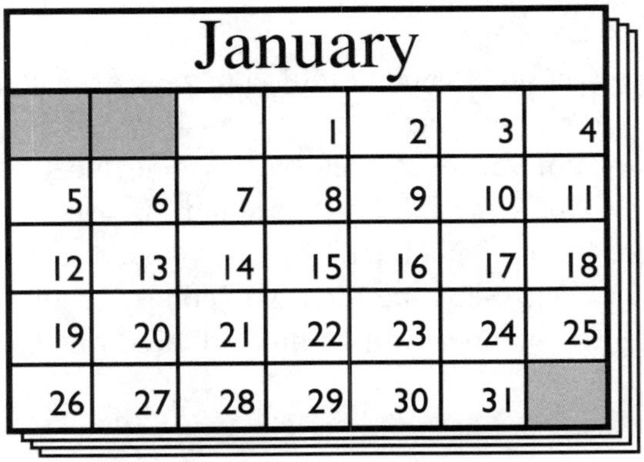

January						
			1	2	3	4
5	6	7	8	9	10	11
12	13	14	15	16	17	18
19	20	21	22	23	24	25
26	27	28	29	30	31	

An array of dates

14.0 ARRAYS: IN GENERAL AND PROGRAMMING TERMS

Declaring variables of different types should now be second nature to you. You need to count something in a program? Declare an `int`. You need to calculate something involving fractional numbers? Use `doubles`. You want a simulated CD? Declare an instance of PDT `CDisc`. You want a collection of variables of different types? Define and use a `struct` PDT. No problem. Or is there?

PROBLEM:

What if you need a program to calculate the average score obtained by a class of students on each of 100 questions in an exam? You'll need a variable to form a total for each question, so will you declare and use 100 `doubles`, one for each question's total, with different names (`total1`, `total2`, . . ., `total100`)?

What about a program that is used to reserve seats on a plane that has 60 rows of seats with six seats in each row. Declare 360 variables with unique names?

Think about a program for reserving seats on a train that has 12 cars each containing 24 rows of four seats. It's getting harder to calculate just how many variables that represents, let alone think of that many unique (but meaningful) identifiers!

Perhaps you need some additional ways of declaring and naming variables.

What the above problems demonstrate is that you need the ability to declare collections of variables each of the same type. "Gimme: 100 `double` or 60 × 6 `Seat` variables please, C++ compiler" is what you want to say.

In programming language terms, a data structuring mechanism called an **array** is used to represent the idea of a collection of variables of the same type. An array can have one, two, or more dimensions.

EXAMPLE:

The list of exam question totals is a one-dimensional (or 1-D) array – a row of 100 numbers. The plane seats require a two-dimensional (2-D) array (60 rows and 6 columns). The train seats require a three-dimensional (3-D) array (12 x 24 rows x 4 columns). We can picture these structures as shown in Figure 14.1.

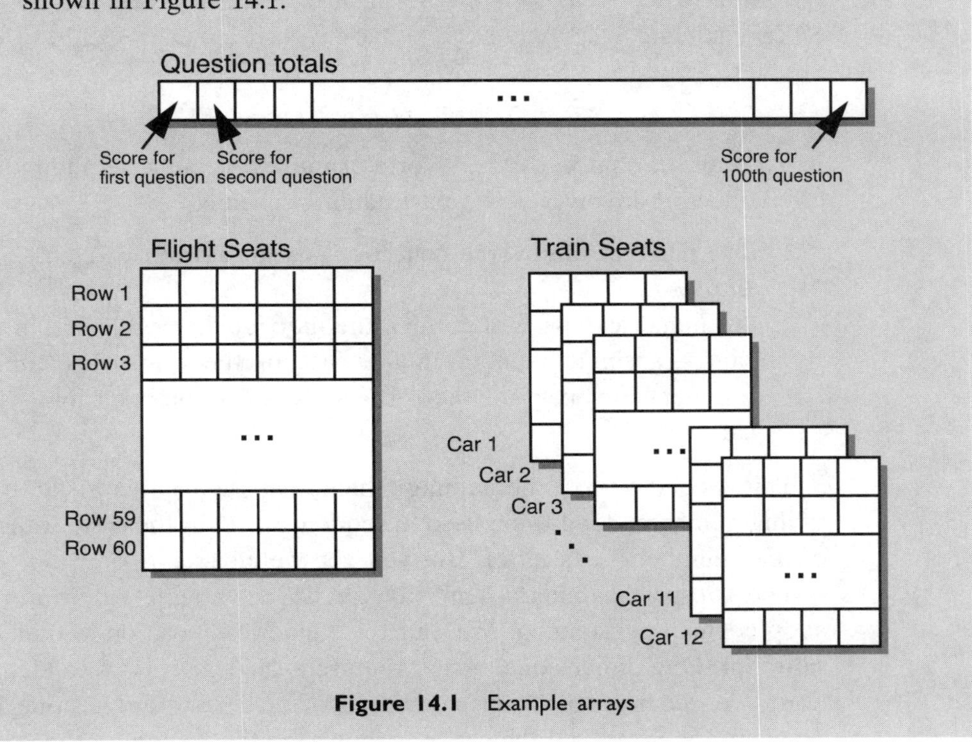

Figure 14.1 Example arrays

An array is a mechanism for representing a collection of component variables (with each component variable being of the same type) as a single variable. In a program, you'll declare an array variable and give that array an identifier in the usual manner. You'll need some way to set the size and "shape" of the array and the type of the variables within the array. We'll come to the C++ syntax for doing this in a moment.

However, getting the set of variables is only part of the solution. How do you refer to each of the variables individually, without the rigmarole of having *N* different identifiers? How's this naming problem solved in the real world?

Let's have a look at some examples.

EXAMPLE:

If you had to calculate the averages of the 100 exam questions using pencil and paper, you'd keep an array (with an identifier `questionTotals`) of 100 doubles. When there was a mark for question 42, you'd add that mark to the 42nd number of `questionTotals`. How do airlines and railroads "name" their seats? "Row 13 Seat A on `flightBC267` for you, Mr. Eratosthenes." "Mr and Ms Fibonacci, your train is `BR0930` to London and you're seated in Car 1, Row 1, Seats 3 and 5."

You can see that in the real-world examples, naming the individual items out of a collection involves a two part naming scheme:

1. The name of the overall collection – `questionTotals`, `flightBC267`, `BR0930`.
2. A "numerical" way of naming the individual variable within the collection – a single number in the case of the `questionTotals`, or a number-letter pair for the plane seats, or a number triple for the train cars.

This second part of the naming scheme has the characteristic that the "identifying numbers" tend to be used in sequence, and in the case of the airlines one of the "numbers" is a letter. But you get the idea.

The two-part naming scheme to "get at" a variable within an array is also adopted in programming. We call the numerical position within an array the **subscript**. One-dimensional arrays require a single subscript to identify the position; two-dimensional arrays require two integer subscripts: one identifying a "row" in the array and the second identifying the "column." Accessing a particular variable in the array requires you to specify an array variable (one part) and apply a subscripting operation to that variable with the subscript(s) representing the second part of the naming scheme.

To help distinguish between the variable that is the whole array, and each of variables that's within the array, we use the term **element** to talk about a variable within an array. Sometimes you'll want to do things to the whole array (for example, assign it to another array variable, or pass it as a parameter to a function), but most times your programs will be operating on the array elements themselves. What can you do to those elements? You know the answer to this: anything that is defined by the type of the element. They're just variables after all.

Time for further C++ details of arrays. Yippee! Three cheers:

```
for (int cheers = 0; cheers < 3; cheers += 1)
{
  cout << "Hip, hip, array!" << endl;
}
```

EXERCISE FOR SECTION 14.0

1 Visit your local football stadium to find out what seat numbering system is used. Do likewise for your local theater.

14.1 ARRAYS: IN C++ TERMS

Arrays are a fundamental part of C++, built into the language definition. However, there are many pitfalls for the unwary apprentice in using built-in arrays. You don't need any more pits to fall down, do you? We don't think so either, so we're going to introduce arrays using a PDT Array that overcomes many of the disadvantages that follow from using the built-in arrays. However, as you're likely to come across built-in arrays at some stage (for example, in other people's code) we'll cover built-in arrays briefly at the end of the chapter.

We've used the class mechanism to implement PDT Array. The first thing we can show you is the interface provided by this PDT, using the usual design notation (Figure 14.2).

We've shown the assignment operator in Figure 14.2, even though it's an operation that's usually provided but not normally shown in our diagrams. It's included here to emphasize the fact that this is an operation on the whole array, not just on one of the elements.

There are a couple of new things you'll notice in Array's interface. The first is the additional syntax in the constructor (<Type>), and the second is the interfaces for the member operator () hinting that you're going to be using the parentheses (and) in subscripting operations. You can see that these member operators return a reference to something as their result. In fact, they return a reference to an array element and this permits you to use an array element as the source or destination of a value, just like a simple variable.

Let's start examining arrays in more detail by using the simplest form of array: the one-dimensional array.

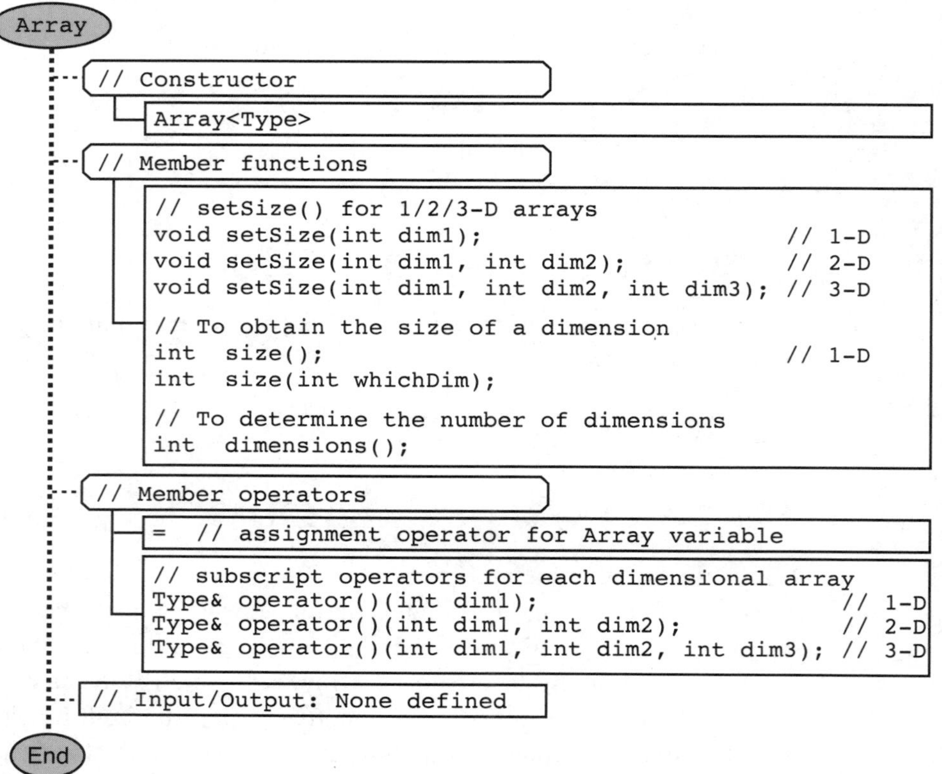

Figure 14.2 `Array` PDT interface

Declaring one-dimensional arrays

An array variable declaration is just like any other variable declaration, except you have to provide an additional piece of information at declaration time: the type of the elements within the array. An array declaration takes the form

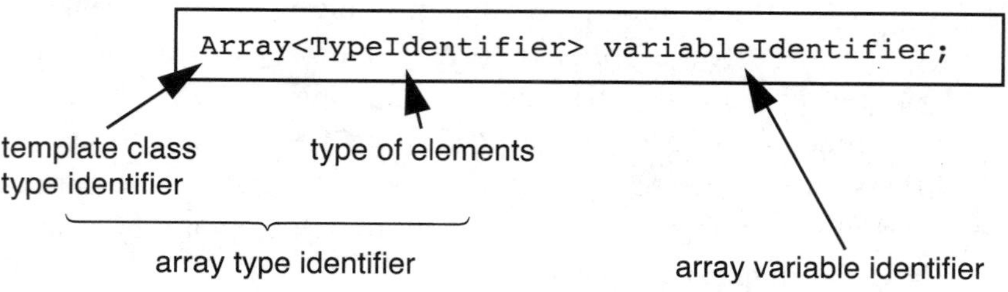

You can see that the type of variable `variableIdentifier` has two parts:

1. `Array` – indicates that `variableIdentifier` is an `Array` variable;
2. `<TypeIdentifier>` – indicates that each element within `variableIdentifier` is of type `TypeIdentifier`.

We say "the type of `variableIdentifier` is `Array` of `TypeIdentifiers`."

Note that the type used inside the < > brackets can be any type that has been defined at the time the compiler reads the array variable declaration. For example, you can declare arrays of `ints` or `doubles`, or any defined PDT, such as `Palette`, or `Duration`.

EXAMPLE:

Assuming that the PDTs `PlaneSeat` and `TrainSeat` have been defined, here are some declarations of array variables for the problem introduced in the previous section.

```
Array<int>        examMarks;
Array<PlaneSeat> flight;
Array<TrainSeat> hexhamExpress;
```

If you're thinking that `<int>`, `<PlaneSeat>` and `<TrainSeat>` look a bit like parameters, as if `Array` were a parameterized type, you'd be close to the mark. In fact `class Array` is an example of a **template class** in C++. It's a class parameterized so that a type can be provided as a parameter at compile-time. In this way, you can use one class to declare `Arrays` of `Things`, where `Thing` can be any type. Without this ability to parameterize the class' type, you'd need separate classes for an `ArrayOfInts`, an `ArrayOfTexts`, and so on.

Template classes are an important part of the object-oriented mechanisms provided in C++. We'll concentrate on using a template class (`Array`), and leave issues of how you define your own template class to a more advanced apprenticeship. Just note that the type identifier comprises both the class identifier `Array` and the `<Type>` and the normal syntax for variable declarations then applies to array variable declarations.

Just declaring an `Array` variable gives you an uninitialized variable; if you try to use the array in this state you'll get a run-time error. Part of your responsibility for initializing an `Array` variable is to set its size, that is, the number of elements it contains. There's a member function:

```
void setSize(int number)
```

you can use to set the size of a one-dimensional array. Note that you can only set the size of an array once; if you try a second time, you'll get a run-time error.

EXAMPLE:

Let's declare an array of `CDiscs` called `cdRack` and set its size.

```
Array<CDisc> cdRack;
cdRack.setSize(18);
```

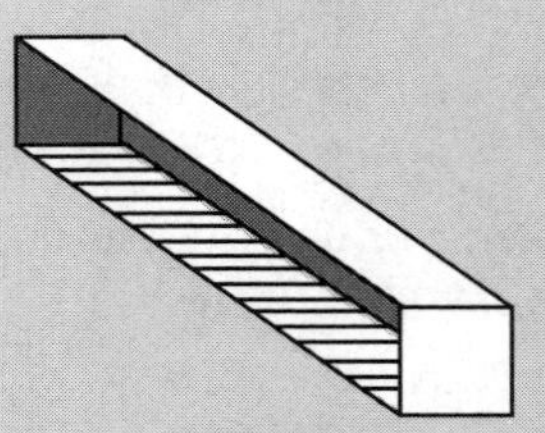

When these statements are executed, you'll get the computer-equivalent of this figure: an 18-element array where each element is a `CDisc` variable. Effectively, 18 `CDisc` variables will be created. Since declaring a `CDisc` variable gives you an uninitialized variable (you may remember this from Chapter 7) the array `cdRack` will contain 18 uninitialized `CDisc` elements, and you'll have to do something explicitly in your program to initialize those elements.

Lesson: The type of the elements determines whether an array of that type contains initialized or uninitialized elements.

EXAMPLE:

An `Array` of any of the built-in types will not be initialized, and will just contain random values.

An `Array` of `Text` strings will be uninitialized.

An `Array` of `CDPlayers` will contain initialized elements.

Now you know what an array declaration looks like and how to set the size of a one-dimensional array, let's put the two things together.

EXAMPLE:

Here is a code fragment illustrating the use of `Array`. Note the inclusion of the header file `Array.h` along with other header files, in the normal fashion.

```
#include <iostream.h>
#include "Array.h"
#include "CDisc.h"
#include "Text.h"

const int FREQ_SIZE    = 100;
const int ROCK_CDS     =   8;
const int CLASSICS_CDS =   4;
const int DOUBLE_CDS   =   3;

struct ClassInfo
{
  Text   firstName;
  Text   lastName;
  double averageMark;
};

int main()
{
  int               numInClass;
  Array<CDisc>      cdRack;
  Array<int>        numberFreq;
  Array<double>     classAverages;
  Array<ClassInfo> classOf95;

  cin >> numInClass;
  cdRack.setSize(ROCK_CDS + CLASSICS_CDS + (2 * DOUBLE_CDS));
  numberFreq.setSize(FREQ_SIZE);
  classAverages.setSize(numInClass);
  classOf95.setSize(numInClass);
  ...
```

How do you initialize an element in an array? Assign a value to an element. But, how do you get at each element in a program? The answer is to use a **subscripting operation** to access the array elements.

Accessing array elements

Each element in an array is identified by its subscript (or position) within the overall array; a convenient abstraction is to think about each element occurring in order of increasing subscript values. In a one-dimensional array, there'll be the first element, and then the second, and so on until the last element.

> **Lesson:** An individual array element is identified by an array subscript.

Sequentially increasing integer numbers are used as subscripts for array elements. However, C++ starts counting from 0, not from 1, so the first element in a one-dimensional array has subscript 0, the second element has subscript 1, and the last element has subscript $N - 1$, where N is the number of elements in the array, counting from 1.

> **Lesson:** The first element of an array has subscript 0, and the last element has subscript $N - 1$, where N is the number of elements in the array.

All you need to know now is how to specify in C++ the two-part naming scheme for array elements. As hinted at in the interface diagram, the subscripting operator in C++ is the character pair `()` which follows the identifier for the array variable and encloses the subscript value:

```
arrayVariableIdentifier(subscript)
```

where `subscript` is an expression producing an integer value such that

$0 \leq$ `subscript` $< N$

> **Lesson:** To access an individual array element, place a subscript in parentheses after the array identifier.

Since the subscript of the element that you wish to access is an `int` value, any expression that produces an `int` value can be used as a subscript. Use of a subscript looks a lot like a function call, where the subscript is the parameter. However, it's actually a call of the unary member-operator `()` applied to the array variable.

EXAMPLE:

In the previous example, the size of the `Array` of `CDiscs` `cdRack` was set to be equal to 18. The individual elements of `cdRack` may therefore be accessed as `cdRack(0)`, `cdRack(1)`, ..., `cdRack(17)`.

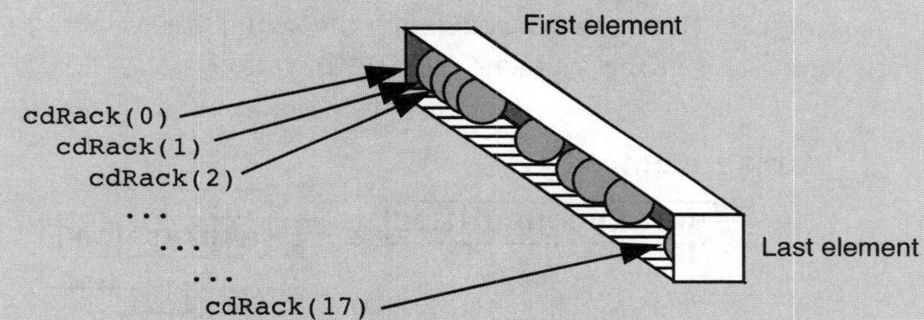

Accessing the array element `cdRack(10)` is equivalent to the member-operator call `cdRack.operator()(10)`.

There's something interesting about using subscripting as the means of naming variables that a program is going to use. All of the variables you've used in programs so far have been *statically* named in the sense that an identifier written in a program is associated with a single variable. Subscripting gives you the ability to *dynamically* name variables within an array, in the sense that your program can be written in terms of manipulating, say, the ith element of an array, where the value of i is provided at run-time.

EXAMPLE:

Assuming that `myPlayer` is of type `CDPlayer`, and `cdRack` is the array declared earlier, suitably initialized, the following code fragment prompts the user for the index of an element of `cdRack` and then loads the corresponding disc in the drawer of `myPlayer`.

```
int i;

cout << "Which CD do you want?: ";
cin  >> i;
myPlayer.load(cdRack(i));
```

In all other respects, array elements act as normal variables in a program. They can produce values to be used in an expression, they can form the destination for an assignment statement, and they can be used as reference parameters. Thus, as well as defining the syntax for an **array element**, we need to look again at the syntactic element **variable**.

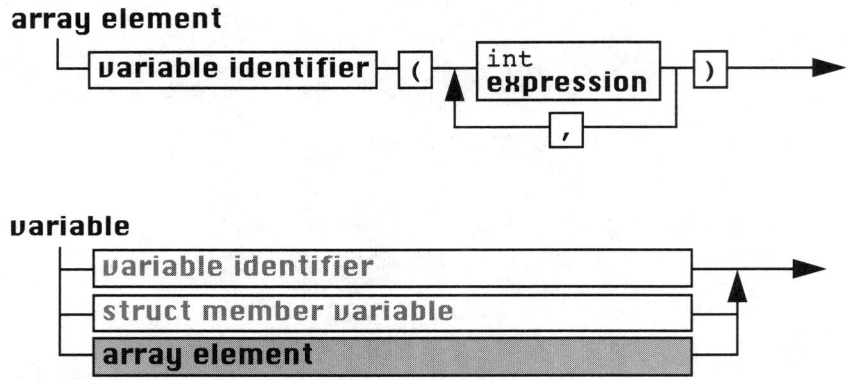

For a one-dimensional array you're only allowed one `int` **expression** inside the parentheses when accessing an **array element**.

Given the notion that your program can dynamically generate subscripts for array elements, can you see how to loop through an array initializing all of the elements?

You can use a repetition control abstraction, but which one? Since the number of repetitions is known (it's the number of elements in the array) a `for` repetition is the normal choice. You'll find that this idea of looping through all of the elements in an array is a very common programming idiom, and takes the general form:

```
for (int subscript = 0;
     subscript < array.size();
     subscript += 1)
{
  // Statements involving element array(subscript)
}
```

where `array` is assumed to be a one-dimensional `Array` variable. Here we're using the member function `int size()` to obtain the number of elements in the array. Some specific examples of the use of this idiom follow shortly.

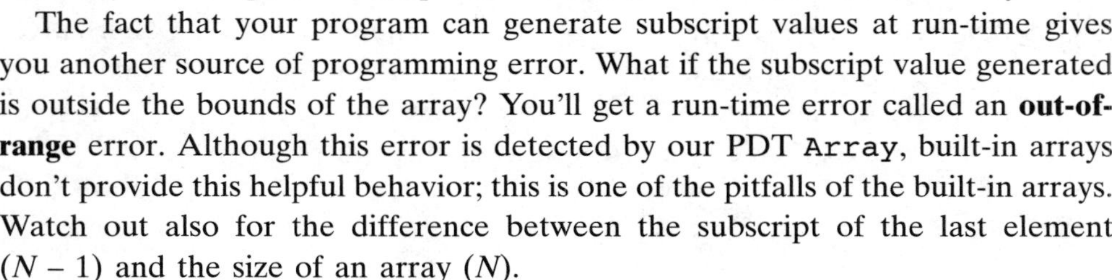

The fact that your program can generate subscript values at run-time gives you another source of programming error. What if the subscript value generated is outside the bounds of the array? You'll get a run-time error called an **out-of-range** error. Although this error is detected by our PDT `Array`, built-in arrays don't provide this helpful behavior; this is one of the pitfalls of the built-in arrays. Watch out also for the difference between the subscript of the last element ($N - 1$) and the size of an array (N).

Lesson: It's very easy to make an off-by-one error when subscripting arrays.

EXAMPLE:

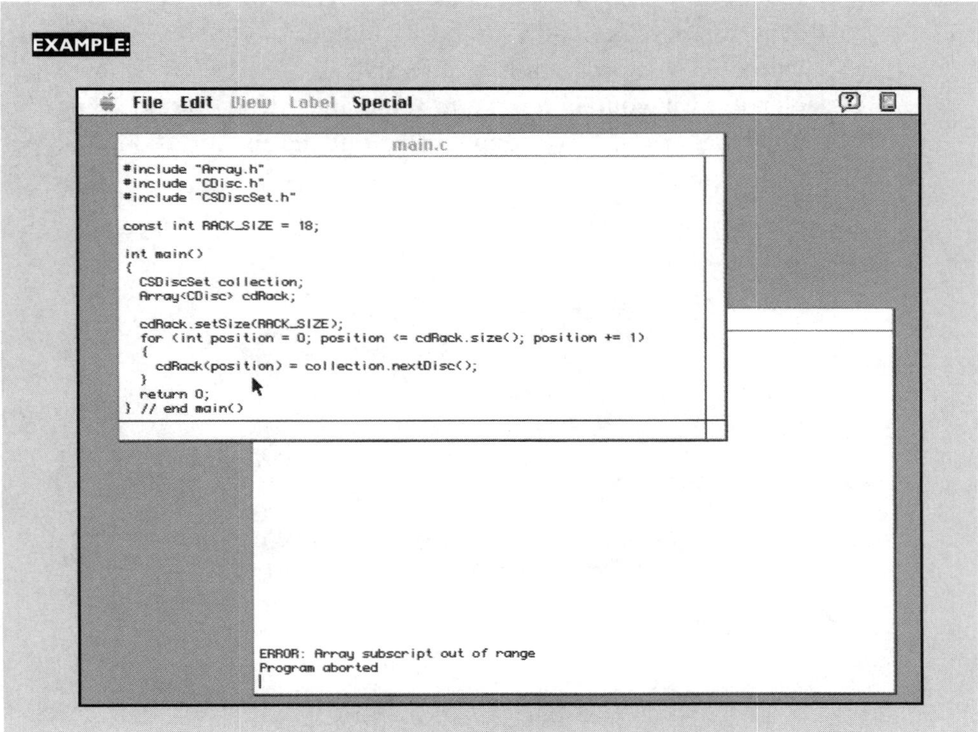

Can you see the bug that caused the out-of-range error?

The Boolean expression controlling the repetition permits one subscript too many, and the statement inside the body of the `for` statement tries to access `cdRack(18)`, which is out-of-range.

Note the use of the `for` repetition in this example to initialize the `Array<CDisc>` variable `cdRack`. Using the `const int RACK_SIZE` in the `for` repetition's Boolean expression would be an alternative to calling the `size()` member function in this example. Do you think that using `RACK_SIZE` would be better or worse than using the member function `size()`? We'll return to answer this shortly.

Are you ready for another example of array subscripting?

EXAMPLE:

Here's a fragment of code for keeping a count of the frequency of occurrences of integer numbers that a user types at the keyboard. Note that the array's size is set and then each element of the array is initialized with a value. As this program is using an array of `int`s, remember that each `int` element will contain a random value unless you do something about it. You don't believe us? Try commenting out the initialization code and running the program.

```
const int  RANGE = 10;     // 1 more than the upper limit
int        inputValue;
int        i;
bool       notFinished = true;
Array<int> freqCount;

freqCount.setSize(RANGE);
for (i = 0; i < freqCount.size(); i += 1)   // Initialize
{                                           //   the array
  freqCount(i) = 0;
}
cout << "Type an out-of-range value to "
     << "terminate the program" << endl;
```

```
while (notFinished)                              // Input values
{
  cout << "Value (0 - 9): ";
  cin  >> inputValue;
  if ((inputValue < 0) || (inputValue >= RANGE))
  {
    notFinished = false;
  }
  else
  {
    freqCount(inputValue) += 1;
  }
} // end while ()

for (i = 0; i < freqCount.size(); i += 1)      // Output results
{
  cout << i << ": " << freqCount(i) << endl;
}
```

An array element is just a variable of a specified type and hence you can apply any member functions or member operators of the type to that array element. What about the array itself? What member functions and member operators are supported by the `Array` type?

Operations on `Array` *variables*

You've seen from the `Array` interface that assignment is supported for array variables. Assignment of one array variable to another requires that both arrays have the same size and contain the same type of element, but otherwise an array assignment behaves just like any other assignment. In other words, copies of the values of the elements from the array variable on the right-hand side of the assignment operator are assigned to the equivalent elements of the array variable on the left-hand side of the assignment operator. The original contents of the array on the left-hand side are lost.

Other member functions you can apply to an array variable are to determine the number of dimensions, and the size of each dimension (as you've already seen). The relevant member function interfaces are as follows.

```
// To obtain the size of a dimension
int  size();                                  // 1-D
int  size(int whichDim);

// To determine the number of dimensions
int  dimensions();
```

"Why would I ever want to use these?" you might be thinking. After all, once you've declared an array you know all of these quantities, don't you? You may, but what if an array is passed to a function as an actual parameter? How can that function determine the size of the array? The size could be passed as a value parameter to the function, but using the `size()` member function permits the size to be determined. You can therefore write general-purpose functions that aren't tied to a single-sized array.

Let's think further about using arrays with functions. What's going to happen when you use an array variable in the following three situations?

1. As a value parameter.
2. As a reference parameter.
3. As the result `returned` by a function.

The answers to these three questions are no different from the answers for other types. If you use an array variable as a value parameter then a copy of the whole array is made and passed to the function. This may be inefficient in terms of time and space, especially if the array is large, so reference parameters are most commonly used when arrays are parameters, to avoid the need for that copying. Similarly, returning an array as a result of a function also results in the copying of the whole array from the function to the destination.

If you wanted to declare an array of `int`s as a formal reference parameter for a function, which of the following would you use?

```
1. Array& <int>    formalParam
2. Array  <int>&   formalParam
3. Array  <int&>   formalParam
4. Array& <int>&   formalParam
5. Array  <int&>&  formalParam
```

The answer is that 2 is the correct version to use. The type identifier of an array variable comprises the class identifier `Array` and `<Type>`, and the `&` indicating a reference parameter follows the type identifier in the normal fashion.

EXAMPLE:

Here's an example of the use of arrays with functions, showing how you can implement a function that manipulates a one-dimensional array of any size, and showing the use of array value and reference parameters.

```
#include <iostream.h>
#include "Array.h"
#include "Text.h"

void zeroArray(Array<int>& clearArray);
Text checkZeroArray(Array<int> checkArray);

int main()
{
  Array<int> examTotals;

  examTotals.setSize(100);
  examTotals(0) = 12345;
  cout << "Array examTotals should contain "
       << "non-zero elements: "
       << checkZeroArray(examTotals) << endl;
  zeroArray(examTotals);
  cout << "Array examTotals should contain "
       << "all-zero elements: "
       << checkZeroArray(examTotals) << endl;
  return 0
} // end main()

void zeroArray(Array<int>& clearArray)
{
  for (int i = 0; i < clearArray.size(); i += 1)
  {
    clearArray(i) = 0;
  }
} // end zeroArray()

Text checkZeroArray(Array<int> checkArray)
{
  for (int i = 0; i < checkArray.size(); i += 1)
  {
```

```
      if (checkArray(i) != 0)
      {
        return "Contains non-zero elements";
      }
    }
    return "All elements are zero";
  } // end checkZeroArray()
```

As you saw in Chapter 11, there's a potential drawback with reference parameters in that, while the intention might be that a function call doesn't change the contents of an array parameter, you could mistakenly write a function definition that assigns a value to one or more array elements. Is there some way that you can avoid copying and yet retain security?

Yes, there is. As you saw in Chapter 11, you can use a constant reference parameter.

EXAMPLE:

Changing the interface of the function `checkArray(...)` in the previous example from

```
Text checkZeroArray(Array<int> checkArray)
```

to

```
Text checkZeroArray(const Array<int>& checkArray)
```

ensures that no array copying takes place when a call is made to this function and that the function can't attempt any changes to the formal (and therefore actual) parameter.

Assignment is the only operation defined for an array variable (that is, on the whole array). If you want to input values to all of an array, or output all of the values contained in an array, you have to provide the necessary code. How would you do that? You would define I/O operators using an array as one of the parameters.

Do you feel comfortable with one-dimensional arrays now? Yes? Good. Time to move into the fourth dimension. Only joking. Two-dimensional arrays are next.

Two-dimensional arrays

A one-dimensional array can be thought of as a single row of elements. A first generalization from this to multiple rows of elements gives rise to two-dimensional arrays. It's convenient to think of a two-dimensional array as a regular grid of rows and columns.

EXAMPLE:

An array with 7 rows of 11 elements each may be pictorially represented as shown in Figure 14.3. There's a natural alignment of rows (across the grid) that gives rise to the notions of columns (down the grid).

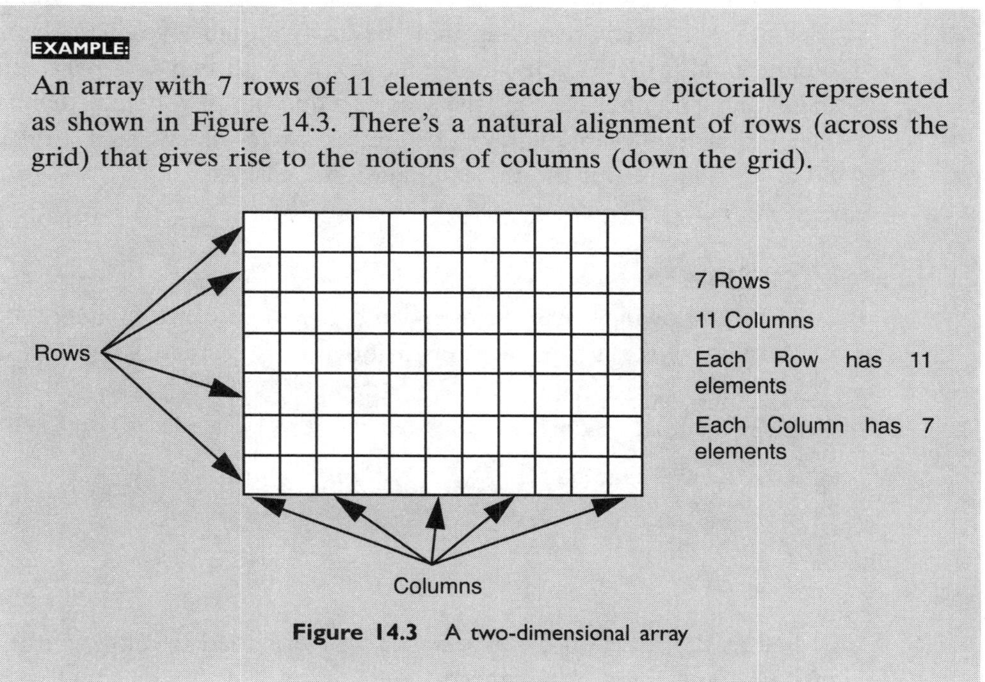

Figure 14.3 A two-dimensional array

So far you've seen how the PDT `Array` can be used to represent a one-dimensional array. In fact, PDT `Array` is more versatile than this; you can use the same PDT to represent two- (and three-) dimensional arrays. The declaration of a two-dimensional array follows the same rules as the declaration of a one-dimensional array, so a declaration takes the form:

```
Array<TypeIdentifier> variableIdentifier;
```

So how do you distinguish between one- and two-dimensional arrays in your programs if they are declared in exactly the same way?

There are two situations where the way you treat a two-dimensional array is different to the way you treat a one-dimensional array:

1. When you set the size of the array.
2. When you access an array element.

We'll deal with setting the size of a two-dimensional array first.

If you glance back to the interface for PDT `Array` you'll note that C++'s ability to support overloading of function names is exploited to provide three functions with the name `setSize`. If you call `setSize(...)` with a single `int` parameter then you're saying that the array variable you've declared is a one-dimensional array. If you call `setSize(...)` with two `int` parameters, the first indicating a number of rows, the second a number of columns, then you're saying that the array variable you've declared is a two-dimensional array. You should be able to figure out the three-dimensional case.

EXAMPLE:

In the following code fragment an array of `double` elements is declared and its size is set as a two-dimensional array to match that in Figure 14.3.

```
#include "Array.h"
Array<double> matrix;

matrix.setSize(7,11); // 7 rows and 11 columns
```

Just as the function `setSize(...)` is overloaded to allow you to set the size of one- and two- (and three-, but no more) dimensional arrays, so the subscripting operator `()` is overloaded to allow you to access individual elements of one- and two- (and three-) dimensional arrays. A combination of a row position and a column position are used to uniquely identify each element within a two-dimensional array.

EXAMPLE:

Assume that the two-dimensional array matrix has been declared as in the previous example. Then `matrix(i, j)` accesses the array element in row `i` and column `j`.

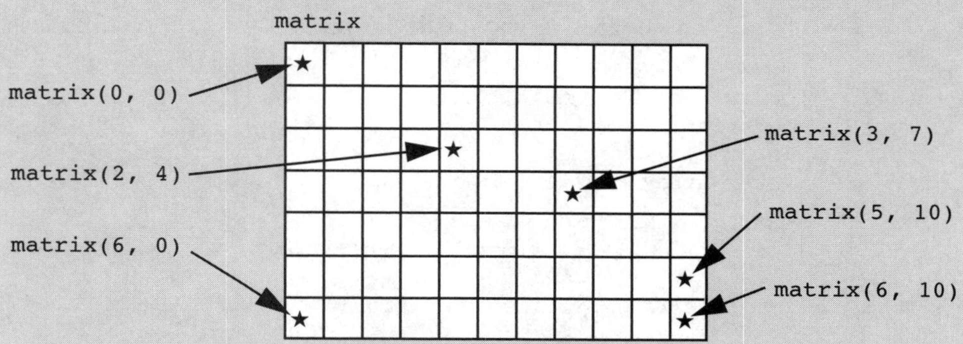

Here's a code fragment to initialize all of the elements in `matrix`. Note the use of the `size(...)` member function (overloading again) with an `int` parameter to determine the size of each dimension.

```
const int NUM_ROWS =  7;
const int NUM_COLS = 11;
int row;
int col;
Array<double> matrix;

matrix.setSize(NUM_ROWS, NUM_COLS);
for (row = 0; row < matrix.size(1); row += 1)
{
  for (col = 0; col < matrix.size(2); col += 1)
  {
    matrix(row, col) = 0.0;
  }
}
```

The subscripting operation for two-dimensional arrays simply involves specifying the row and column positions as parameters to the subscript operator. As you can see, two-dimensional arrays are a straightforward generalization of one-dimensional arrays, so we won't bore you with the obvious details of what you do with three-dimensional arrays. If you want four-dimensional arrays, then sorry, because our `Array` PDT doesn't support them. We reckon three dimensions should be enough for most of your needs. However, you can always declare an array of arrays.

EXAMPLE:

Here's an alternative way of declaring and using a two-dimensional array.

```
const int NUM_ROWS =  7;
const int NUM_COLS = 11;
int row;
int col;
Array<Array<double> > matrix;

matrix.setSize(NUM_ROWS);
for (row = 0; row < matrix.size(); row += 1)
{
  matrix(row).setSize(NUM_COLS);
}

for (row = 0; row < matrix.size(); row += 1)
{
  for (col = 0; col < matrix(row).size(); col += 1)
  {
    matrix(row)(col) = 0.0;
  }
}
```

Contrast the indexing operation `matrix(row)(col)` used here with the indexing operation `matrix(row,  col)` of the previous example.

Note the possibility of having exotic, non-regular two-dimensional arrays since it's not necessary that each element of `matrix` (which is a one-dimensional array of one-dimensional arrays) has the same length. Here's an example of a "triangular" array in which the "rows" are of increasing length.

```
const int NUM_ROWS = 7;
int row;
Array<Array<double> > matrix;

matrix.setSize(NUM_ROWS);
for (row = 0; row < matrix.size(); row += 1)
{
  matrix(row).setSize(row + 1);
}
```

Let's now look at some more detailed problem-solving examples that require the use of arrays.

EXERCISES FOR SECTION 14.1

1 Change the function `zeroArray(...)` in program `cleararray.c` so that the function has the following interface.

```
Array<int> zeroArray(Array<int> clearArray);
```

How would you then use this function in the program to set array `examTotals` to zero?

2 Write I/O operators for one-dimensional `Arrays` of `ints`.

3 Write I/O operators for two-dimensional `Arrays` of `ints`.

4 Indicate the structures you would use to represent a checkers (draughts) board in which each square is identified by the color of the piece occupying that square (black, red or none). Write a code fragment that initializes the board for the start of a game.

14.2 EXAMPLES USING ARRAYS

The Sieve of Eratosthenes

PROBLEM:

Use the Sieve of Eratosthenes to find the prime numbers in the range 1 to N.

DESIGN:

A long time ago in Chapter 2 (Section 2.6) we developed a design for finding prime numbers using the Sieve of Eratosthenes. As part of that design, we identified the need for the container type shown below. An array forms an ideal PDT for implementing this container type. Rather than waste space in reproducing the earlier design, now might be a good time to zip back to Section 2.6 for a quick refresher on the algorithm and the design.

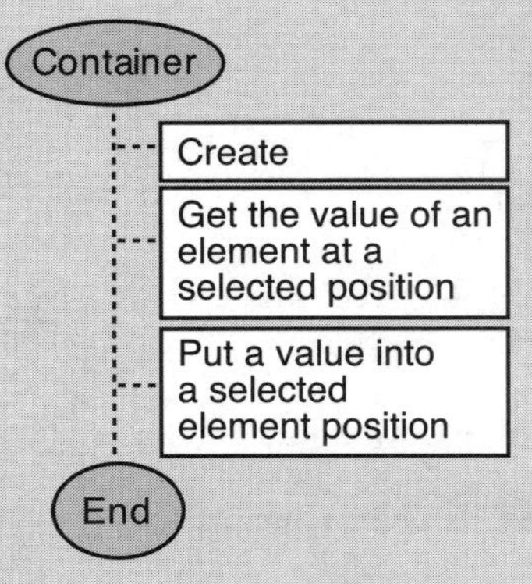

The Sieve design centered around the use of a container called `possibles`. You've already guessed that an array can be used to implement this container, but what should the type of the elements be? Since all prime numbers are integers, `int` might be your first guess. You could create an array of `int`s, put the value 1 in the first element, 2 in the second and so on. You could use the value 0 to represent a canceled value in the array (that is, to indicate that the integer corresponding to that position in the array is not a prime number). Yes, that would all work OK.

However, think about the element type a little more. Do you actually need to store the integer value in the array? Doesn't the subscript also provide information about the integer value? In fact it does: you know that the first element represents the number 1, the second the number 2, and so on. The only piece of information that needs to be stored in the array is whether a particular element represents a possible prime number or not. Sounds like a `bool` will suffice for this job.

IMPLEMENTATION:

Let's start translating the design into C++. Following our lesson of starting by translating the design into C++ comments we can obtain the first version.

```
int main()
{
  // Create container object "possibles"
  Array<bool> possibles;

  // Fill possibles

  // Cancel non-primes in possibles

  // Print out uncanceled elements

  return 0;
} // end main()
```

The two principal steps in `main()` can be represented by the following:

```
// Cancel non-primes in possibles
  // For each element in possibles
      // Has this one been canceled?
            // No: Cancel in rest of possibles
               // Hop down the array in nextCheck
               //   steps canceling elements

// Print out uncanceled elements
  // Print out uncanceled numbers in possibles
      // For each element in possibles
            // Has element been canceled?
                  // No - print value
```

Let's choose to implement "fill," "cancel" and "print" as functions to demonstrate the use of array parameters. We need to know how many integers to test for primality, so we should add some I/O statements to ask the user to specify what integer value to use as the final value to be tested. The translation of the other steps in the above skeleton is straightforward. One thing to decide is the correspondence between subscript and integer value – do we use array element 0 to represent the value 1, element 1 to represent the value 2, and so on? We could do that (and there are other optimizations that can also be applied), but for the next version let's keep a straightforward mapping and get that working first. We'll use subscript *i* for integer value *i*. Once we get that working, and we're happy that the overall algorithm is working we can add these additional optimizations (optimizations == complications). Here's the next version.

IMPLEMENTATION:

The following program was presented to you in Chapter 3 (we've left out the part of the code that draws a frequency histogram).

```
#include <iostream.h>
#include "Array.h"
#include "bool.h"
```

```
void fillPossibles(Array<bool>& possibles);
void cancelPossibles(Array<bool>& possibles);
void printPossibles(Array<bool> possibles);

int main()
{
  int          n;
  Array<bool> possibles;          // Create possibles

  cout << "Type the number to stop at: ";
  cin  >> n;
  if (n <= 1)
  {
    cout << "Error: number must be greater than 1" << endl;
    return -1;                    // Terminate the program
                                  // with error flag
  }
  possibles.setSize(n);
  fillPossibles(possibles);       // Fill possibles
  cancelPossibles(possibles);     // Cancel non-primes in
                                  //   possibles
  printPossibles(possibles);      // Print out uncanceled
                                  //   elements

  return 0;                       // Terminate the program
} // end main()

void fillPossibles(Array<bool>& possibles)
{
  for (int initial = 0;
           initial < possibles.size();
           initial += 1)
  {
    possibles(initial) = true;
  }
  return;
} // end fillPossibles()

void cancelPossibles(Array<bool>& possibles)
{                              // For each element in possibles
  for (int nextCheck = 2;
       nextCheck < possibles.size();
       nextCheck += 1)
  {
    if (possibles(nextCheck))    // Has it been canceled?
    {                                  // No: cancel in rest
                                       //   of possibles
      for (int cancel = nextCheck + nextCheck;
```

```
            cancel < possibles.size();
            cancel += nextCheck)
        {
          possibles(cancel) = false;     // Set to CANCEL
        } // end for cancel
      } // end if possibles
    } // end for nextCheck
    return;
  } // end cancelPossibles()

  void printPossibles(Array<bool> possibles)
  {
    int count = 0;
    cout << "The primes are:" << endl;
    for (int prime = 1; prime < possibles.size(); prime += 1)
    {
      if (possibles(prime))        // Has element been canceled?
      {
        cout << prime << ' ';          // No - print value
        count += 1;
      }
    }
    cout << endl << endl << "The total number was "
         << count << endl;
    return;
  } // end printPossibles()
```

We'll now return to a problem that was briefly mentioned in Section 14.0 : use an array to represent the seats on a plane.

Airline seat reservations

PROBLEM:

SOTP (Seat Of The Pants) Airlines is about to start a daily flight service between Hexham and Ovington (both in Northumberland, England – you'll need a good atlas to find them :-). You've been contracted to provide a very simple computerized seat reservation system. You've discussed the system with SOTP officials, and as a result you've drawn up the following outline description of what the company requires of the software.

- Create a seat plan for a flight.
- Set the size of a flight, in terms of the number of rows of seats on a plane and the size of a row. For all of SOTP's current planes, the rows contain an equal number of seats. After the size has been set, all seats are marked as being unoccupied.
- Reserve a seat, specifying row and seat number and some passenger information:
  - the rows in a plane are numbered from the front starting at 1;
  - the seats are numbered by consecutive letters from the left-hand side, starting with "A";
  - the passenger information consists of a surname and initials.
- Release a seat, specifying a row and seat number.
- Find the first available seat. If a customer doesn't want the seat found, the next available seat needs to be found.
- Indicate the number of seats occupied on a flight.
- Indicate the number of free seats left on a flight.
- Provide the information concerning a specified seat – whether it's occupied or unoccupied, and if occupied, the passenger information.

SOTP has other requirements for the software, such as the need to retain reservation information for a particular flight, but for the moment let's concentrate on the above feature list. What are your initial thoughts about design and implementation?

Did you think "arrays"? Anything else? While a 2-D array might form a useful part of an implementation, the first thing that should have popped into your mind is PDT (class would be an acceptable alternative!). Wouldn't it be useful to provide a PDT that captures the above behavior? You can then imagine the complete software system declaring an instance of this PDT for each flight (perhaps declaring an array of seven of them for a week's flights), and manipulating each flight's seating plan as customer reservations arrive. Sure, an array is also likely to be useful for implementing the concrete representation of the PDT, but the first thing to design is the PDT's interface. The starting point is the above English description of SOTP's needs. By applying the approach of identifying nouns, verbs and attributes (see Section 2.8) you can begin to derive the PDTs needed and the features each PDT needs to provide.

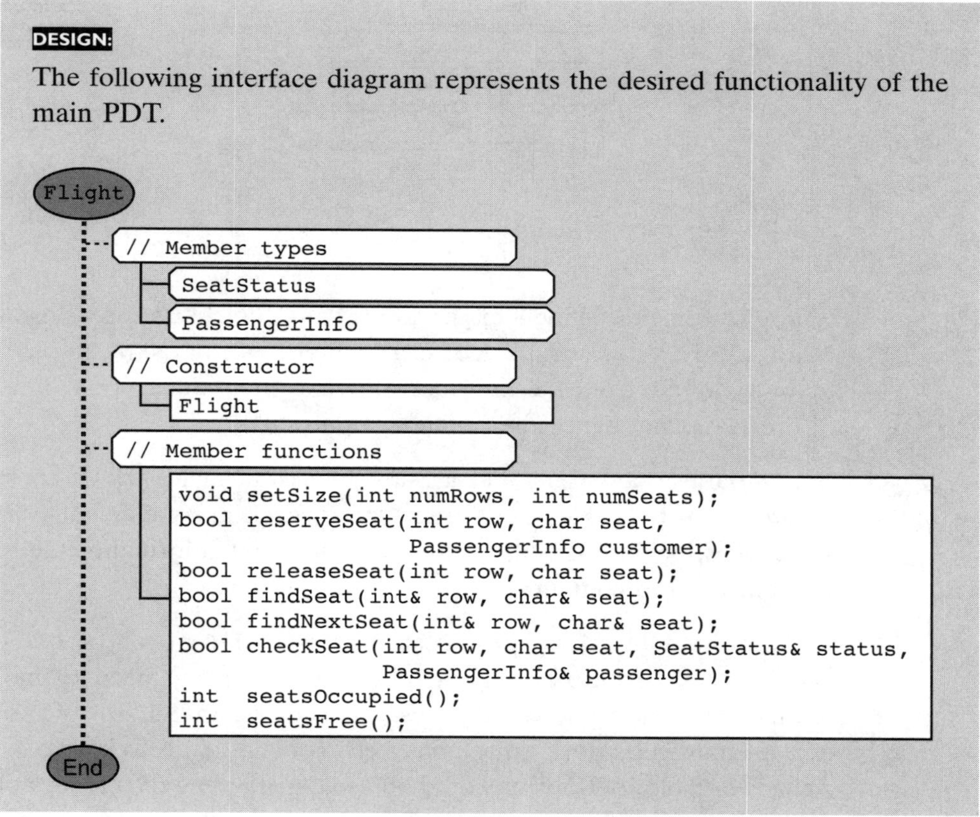

In the above figure we've identified two member types of the `Flight` PDT; that is, types `SeatStatus` and `PassengerInfo` that are associated with `Flight` and defined within its scope. These member types represent the abstract states for a seat on a plane and the aggregate of the information needed to represent a passenger, and are depicted in the interface diagrams following.

What type mechanisms do you think are appropriate for all of these types?

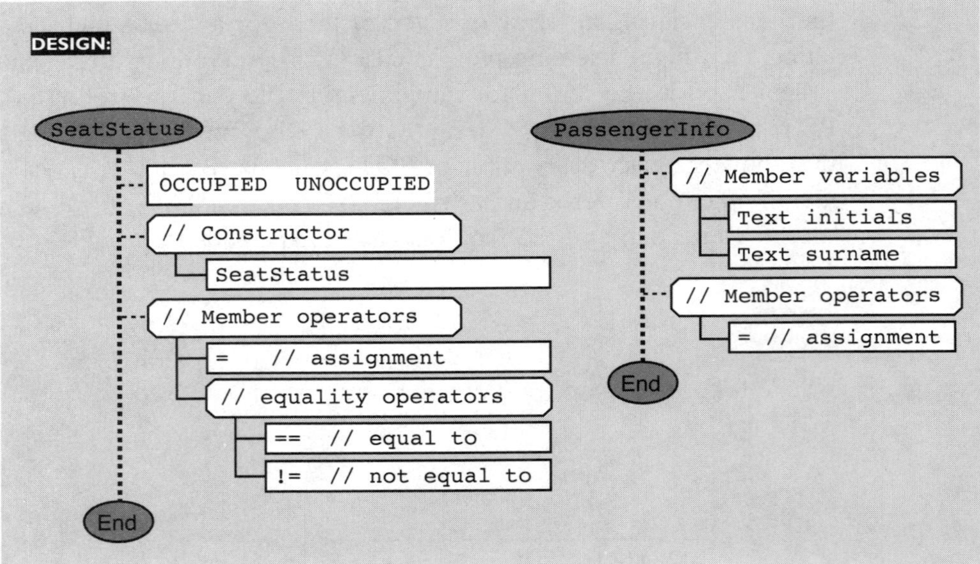

You're going to define `Flight` as a `class`, `SeatStatus` using an `enum`, and `PassengerInfo` using a `struct`. The public part of the header file for `Flight` follows directly from the interface diagram. Let's think about the private part of this class, and hence the concrete representation.

It should be apparent that a 2-D array is an ideal way of representing the seating plan, but what should the type of each array element be? Asking the same question in a slightly different way, what information does each array element need to contain?

From the above description it seems that each seat can be free or occupied, and if occupied the passenger's initials and surname need to be retained. A sentinel surname value could be used to indicate that a seat is unoccupied (for example, an empty text string), but a cleaner solution is to have a separate "seat status" variable. A Boolean could be used as the type of this variable, but using `SeatStatus` will permit easier enhancement in the future; for instance, if SOTP purchase some planes which have some rows with fewer seats, an additional status `UNAVAILABLE` could be easily introduced.

The `struct` mechanism can be used to define a (private) type to group together all of the data variables needed for each array element and hence to define the element type to be used in the array declaration.

Lesson: If an array element needs to consist of an aggregate of variables, use the `struct` mechanism to define a type for the aggregate.

DEFINITION:

Putting all of this together, you come up with the following header file.

```
#include "Array.h"
#include "bool.h"
#include "Text.h"

#ifndef FLIGHT_H
#define FLIGHT_H

class Flight
{
  public:

    // Member Types
    enum   SeatStatus {OCCUPIED, UNOCCUPIED};
    struct PassengerInfo
    {
      Text surname;
      Text initials;
    };

    // Constructor
    // Flight();    Provided by default by the compiler

    // Member functions - some return false if an error occurs
    void setSize(int numRows, int seatsInRow);
    bool reserveSeat(int row, char seat, PassengerInfo customer);
    bool releaseSeat(int row, char seat);
    bool findSeat(int& row, char& seat);
    bool findNextSeat(int& row, char& seat);
    bool checkSeat(int row, char seat, SeatStatus& status,
                   PassengerInfo& passenger);
    int seatsOccupied();
    int seatsFree();
```

```
  private:
    // Private member types
    struct SeatInfo
    {
      PassengerInfo passenger;
      SeatStatus    seatStatus;
    };

    Array<SeatInfo> plane;
    int lastRow;                      // Last row searched for seat
    int lastCol;                      // Last col searched for seat

    // Private member functions

    bool mapValidateSeat(int  userRow, char userCol,
                         int& realRow, int& realCol);
    void realToUserCoords(int  realRow, int realCol,
                          int& userRow, char& userCol);
    char realColToUserCol(int col);
    int  realRowToUserRow(int row);
    int  countSeats(SeatStatus state);
}; // end class Flight

#endif
```

Notice that the types `PassengerInfo` and `SeatStatus` have been defined as member types inside the class, part of the `public` section. Why there, and not as global type definitions?

The reason is to limit the scope of the type's identifiers by making them part of type `Flight`. In large software systems it is sometimes a problem to avoid name clashes, and limiting the scope of an identifier can help minimize such problems. A disadvantage is that the use of types `PassengerInfo` or `SeatStatus` in code other than the member function definitions will require the use of the scope resolution operator, as in:

```
Flight::PassengerInfo customer;
```

The type `SeatInfo` is also defined within the class but in the `private` section, which means that only the member variable declarations and member function definitions may use it. PDT `SeatInfo` is used in the array declaration in the `private` section.

There are other private member variables and member functions in the header file. These reflect implementation aspects of defining the member functions; they were added as needed as the implementation proceeded and you're seeing the final result in the header file.

Did you notice that the header file doesn't contain a constructor interface? (There is one but it's commented out.) Does this mean that there isn't a constructor for this type? It doesn't. It turns out, as you'll see later, that there isn't anything for the constructor to do and so we can omit the constructor interface. This is the first time you've seen this. All of the classes we've defined up to this point have had constructors explicitly defined.

Now all you have to do is define the member functions (in a file `Flight.c`). As usual it's worth concentrating on the design of the member functions first, so you can get their logic right before plunging into C++ code. The member function implementation can then follow in an incremental fashion, with incremental testing of the code as you go along. We've already gone through the design process so let's examine some of the implementation aspects of the member functions, paying particular attention to the examples of the two-dimensional array manipulation.

IMPLEMENTATION:

First, let's look at the member function that sets the size of the flight. (The code shown below has had some of its comments removed to save space.)

```
void Flight::setSize(int numRows, int seatsInRow)
{
  plane.setSize(numRows, seatsInRow);
  for (int row = 0; row < plane.size(1); row += 1)
  {
    for (int col = 0; col < plane.size(2); col += 1)
    {
      plane(row, col).seatStatus = UNOCCUPIED;
    }
  }
  lastRow =  0;
  lastCol = -1;
  return;
} // end setSize()
```

The `Flight` PDT member function `setSize(...)` defines the size of the two-dimensional array used in the concrete representation (using the `Array` `setSize(...)` member function) and then initializes the array so that all seats are marked as unoccupied. Note the two nested `for` repetition statements that achieve this initialization. Note also the joint use of subscripting and the dot operator in the assignment statement. The `plane(row, col)` part of the statement gives an element of the array that is an instance of the `struct SeatInfo`. The dot operator is then applied to this element to select the `seatStatus` part of this `struct`. As you saw in the syntax diagrams earlier, an array element is just a **variable** to which anything appropriate for the type of that **variable** can be applied. The final action in this member function is to initialize a couple of private member variables whose purpose is explained shortly.

IMPLEMENTATION:

Now, look at the code for the member function that reserves a seat.

```
bool Flight::reserveSeat(int row, char seat,
                         PassengerInfo customer)
{
  int realRow;
  int realCol;

  // Defensive checks
  if ( !mapValidateSeat(row, seat, realRow, realCol) ||
       (plane(realRow, realCol).seatStatus == OCCUPIED))
  {
    return false;
  }
  plane(realRow, realCol).passenger  = customer;
  plane(realRow, realCol).seatStatus = OCCUPIED;
  return true;
} // end reserveSeat()
```

Recall that the SOTP airline wishes to name seats with row numbers starting at 1 and seat numbers starting at "A." Within the implementation of the member functions it's necessary to map these "user coordinates" to array subscripts; this is one purpose of the private member function `mapValidateSeat(...)`. The first two parameters of this function are value parameters representing the row and seat numbers in user coordinates, while the last two parameters are reference parameters through which the array subscript values corresponding to the user coordinates are returned.

The function `mapValidateSeat(...)` has a second purpose, which is to check that the given seat coordinates are valid with respect to the size of the flight. If the seat coordinates are invalid, a `false` value is returned, so the situation depicted above should not happen! Note that the Boolean expression in the `if` selection statement has two parts, and generates a `true` result if the seat coordinates are invalid or if the seat is already occupied. What's going to be executed if the seat coordinates are invalid? Does this mean that an attempt is going to be made to access the `plane` array with invalid subscripts, and hence result in an out-of-range error?

This error does not occur. If you recall, Section 8.5 discussed how Boolean expressions are evaluated and explained that once the result of a Boolean expression can be determined unambiguously, then any remaining parts of that expression are not evaluated. In the above example, if the first part of the Boolean expression evaluates to `true`, the result of the whole Boolean expression must be `true`, and so the second expression (accessing the array) is not evaluated. So no illegal array access is attempted.

IMPLEMENTATION:

Here's the implementation of the private member function `mapValidateSeat(...)`. There's a corresponding private member function to map from array subscript values back to user seat coordinates which is also shown.

```
bool Flight::mapValidateSeat(int  userRow, char userCol,
                              int& realRow, int& realCol)
```

```
{
  realRow = userRow - 1;
  realCol = int(userCol) - int('A'); // convert 'A' to 0,
                                     //    'B' to 1, ...
  return !((realRow < 0) || (realRow >= plane.size(1)) ||
          (realCol < 0) || (realCol >= plane.size(2))    );
} // end mapValidateSeat()

void Flight::realToUserCoords(int  realRow, int realCol,
                              int& userRow, char& userCol)
{
  userRow = realRowToUserRow(realRow);
  userCol = realColToUserCol(realCol);
  return;
} // end realToUserCoords()

char Flight::realColToUserCol(int realCol)
{
  return char(realCol + int('A'));
} // end realColToUserCol()

int Flight::realRowToUserRow(int realRow)
{
  return realRow + 1;
} // end realRowToUserRow()
```

The implementations of the member functions `findSeat(...)` and `findNextSeat(...)` demonstrate an interesting use of `for` repetition statements. Take a look at the following code and note anything suspicious.

IMPLEMENTATION:

```
bool Flight::findSeat(int& row, char& seat)
{
  for (lastRow = 0; lastRow < plane.size(1); lastRow += 1)
  {
    for (lastCol = 0; lastCol < plane.size(2); lastCol += 1)
    {
      if (plane(lastRow, lastCol).seatStatus == UNOCCUPIED)
      {
        // Found a possible seat. Assign values to ref parameters
        realToUserCoords(lastRow, lastCol, row, seat);
        return true;
      }
```

```
    } // end for lastCol
  } // end for lastRow
  return false;        // No free seat found. Plane must be full.
} // end findSeat()

bool Flight::findNextSeat(int& row, char& seat)
{
  for (; lastRow < plane.size(1); lastRow += 1)
  {
    for (lastCol += 1; lastCol < plane.size(2); lastCol += 1)
    {
      if (plane(lastRow, lastCol).seatStatus == UNOCCUPIED)
      {
        // Found a possible seat. Assign values to ref parameters
        realToUserCoords(lastRow, lastCol, row, seat);
        return true;
      }
    } // end for lastCol
    lastCol = -1;
  } // end for lastRow
  lastRow = 0;
  return false;
} // end findNextSeat()
```

The implementation of `findSeat(...)` is a straightforward application of two nested `for` statements, unusual only in that the loop control variables don't seem to be declared. In fact, the declarations of these variables are in the `private` section of the class. They are there because we need to retain the subscripts of the last seat found, since the semantics required from the member function `findNextSeat(...)` are that it starts searching from the last seat position found to return the coordinates of the next available seat (if any). Hence, by declaring the loop control variables in the `private` section, the values they contain when the nested `for` statements are returned from will be the values of the last seat found. Thus you see in the implementation of `findNextSeat(...)` that there are two nested `for` statements but there is no initializing statement for the outer loop control variable (so this `for` statement continues searching on the same row as was being searched last time), while the inner `for` statement's initializing statement is to move onto the seat following the one that was returned previously. What if the seat returned previously was the last seat in the row? You'll find that the code above works correctly for this situation. Go through it by hand to convince yourself of this.

Since the initializing statements in the `for` statements in `findNextSeat(...)` are unusual in that they depend on the loop control variables having valid values, care has to be taken to reset these values explicitly if either `for` statement completes; for example, the inner `for` statement terminates when it reaches the end of a row of seats. Hence the assignment statements involving `lastCol` and `lastRow` in the above code. Why does one assignment use the value -1 while the other uses the value 0? It turns out these are the right values to use; again, work through the code by hand to convince yourself that we haven't made a mistake.

The other member function definitions are straightforward and not reproduced here. You'll find them on the accompanying disk, together with the incremental test functions that were written to test these member functions, so take a look at those source files as well.

Following the style introduced in Chapter 11, the approach taken for reporting errors back to the caller of the member function is to use a `bool` return value, and the complete set of reasons for a `false` value being returned should be documented somewhere. Adopting a `bool` return value, however, is not so informative for the caller when an error can be caused by one of several reasons, since the return value cannot then distinguish those error cases. An example is in the member function `reserveSeat(...)` which can return an error either because the specified seat number is illegal, or because the seat is already occupied. A program using this member function would probably wish to distinguish between these two cases.

The error cases could be distinguished by having the member function print an error message as well as returning a `false` value; you might remember that the member functions of `CDPlayer` took this approach. However, this is a strategy we do not, in general, recommend. It's better to leave any error printing to the user program, rather than embedding that printing into the class. The calling program can decide what error reporting to provide to a user. A case in point is the test functions for `Flight`. The test programs wish to exercise the error-detection facilities of member functions as well as the normal functions. If the class produces error messages, the user of the test program might think that errors were occurring, whereas if the member functions simply return a `false` value, the test function can determine when this value was expected and only produce an error message for the user when the unexpected occurs.

Lesson: Member functions should report errors through return values, not by printing messages.

Changing the error indications to permit the different cases to be distinguished by a caller requires the design of the interface of some of the member functions to be reconsidered and changed. How might you change them?

One approach would be to define a PDT enumerating the different possible return values, and use an instance of that type as the return value.

We started off this sub-section as an example of using a two-dimensional array yet have finished up using many of the C++ features you've learned about so far. In doing so, we've derived another useful PDT. You're not convinced of its utility? Well, certainly the real airlines won't be beating a path to your (or our) door in a rush to use `Flight`. Nevertheless, try some of the exercises associated with `Flight` and hopefully the ease with which you complete them will convince you of the utility of building software components such as `Flight`, as well as giving you some practice with arrays.

Of course, a real flight reservation system has some features that the use of `Flight` currently doesn't support. For example, the fact that all of the seat reservation information is lost once a program using instances of `Flight` terminates could be a bit of a handicap for SOTP airlines. To overcome this difficulty, the ability to store a flight's state into a file and to be able to read that state from the file is needed. File I/O is covered in Chapter 15, but first let's take a brief look at C++ built-in arrays.

EXERCISES FOR SECTION 14.2

1 The Sieve program can be optimized in a number of ways, to reduce both its execution time and its storage requirements. Identify some optimizations, and change the program to incorporate those optimizations.

2 The member functions `reserveSeat(...)` and `releaseSeat(...)` in class `Flight` return a `bool` value that doesn't permit the caller to distinguish between the different error cases that can occur. Define an `enum` PDT that can be used to represent the various error cases and then change the member functions' interfaces accordingly.

14.3 C++ BUILT-IN ARRAYS

You're likely to come across descriptions or uses of C++'s built-in arrays in other books and other people's code. It's important that you are able to recognize and identify their use, even though we've introduced you to a superior array PDT and we normally expect you to use this PDT.

You'll recall that with the `Array` PDT you need one statement to declare an array and another statement to set the size of an array. With built-in arrays a single statement suffices for both actions; that is, a built-in array declaration introduces a name for the array variable and indicates the number of dimensions and number of elements in each dimension. Here's the format for the declaration of a one-dimensional array.

```
ArrayType arrayIdentifier[numberOfElements];
```

EXAMPLE:

Given the declarations:

```
const int FREQ_SIZE = 100;
const int NUM_CLASS = 125;

struct ClassInfo
{
  Text   firstName;
  Text   lastName;
  double averageMark;
};
```

here are some `Array` declarations and sizings you are familiar with, along with their built-in array equivalents.

C++ Built-in Array Declaration	`Array` PDT Declaration
`CDisc cdRack[18];`	`Array<CDisc> cdRack;` `cdRack.setSize(18);`
`int numFreq[FREQ_SIZE];`	`Array<int> numFreq;` `numFreq.setSize(FREQ_SIZE);`
`ClassInfo class95[NUM_CLASS];`	`Array<ClassInfo> class95;` `class95.setSize(NUM_CLASS);`

What the above table doesn't illustrate, however, is that the size of a built-in array must be a constant known at compile-time. Thus, you can't input an integer value and then use that value to declare a built-in array of that size.

To declare a built-in two-dimensional array, you need to specify the number of elements in each direction, so you need a declaration of the form:

```
ArrayType arrayIdentifier[numberOfRows][numberOfColumns];
```

EXAMPLE:

Here are two ways to represent a chessboard. One uses the `Array` PDT, the other a built-in array.

C++ Built-in Array Declaration	**`Array` PDT Declaration**
`bool chessboard[8][8];`	`Array<bool> chessboard;` `chessboard.setSize(8, 8);`

Accessing individual elements of one-dimensional built-in arrays is similar to accessing individual elements of the `Array` PDT, except that you use square, rather than round, brackets. To access an element of a two-dimensional array, you need square brackets around each index.

EXAMPLE:

Assume that `cdRack` is declared as above. Then the following code mirrors a fragment you saw in Section 14.1.

```
int i;

cout << "Which CD do you want?: ";
cin  >> i;
myPlayer.load(cdRack[i]);
```

Here's how you would set up the "occupied" status of a chessboard at the start of a game of chess.

```
const int BOARD_SIZE = 8;
int row;
int col;

// Set Black's positions
for (row = 0; row < 2; row += 1)
{
```

```
  for (col = 0; col < BOARD_SIZE; col += 1)
  {
    chessboard[row][col] = true;
  }
}

// Set White's positions
for (row = BOARD_SIZE - 2; row < BOARD_SIZE; row += 1)
{
  for (col = 0; col < BOARD_SIZE; col += 1)
  {
    chessboard[row][col] = true;
  }
}
```

Table 14.1 shows you the negative and positive points concerning built-in arrays and the `Array` PDT.

Table 14.1 Comparing built-in arrays with the `Array` PDT

C++ Built-in Array	**`Array` PDT**
● Subscript using `[i]` for 1-D array	● Subscript using `(i)` for 1-D array
● Subscript using `[i][j]` for 2-D array	● Subscript using `(i, j)` for 2-D array
✗ Number of elements must be defined by compile-time constant	✓ Number of elements can be defined by compile-time or run-time value
✗ Array size not a property of the array variable and can't be determined dynamically	✓ Array size is a property of the array variable and can be deter mined dynamically
✗ No subscript range checking	✓ Subscript range checking
✗ No assignment between array variables	✓ Assignment between array variables
✗ Comparison of array variables does not give compile-time error, nor do what you might expect	✓ Comparison of array variables gives a compile-time error
✓ Any number of dimensions	● Up to 3 dimensions, although an array element can itself be an array

An array is just a collection of variables. But so is a `struct`. Let's end this chapter with a brief comparison of the two.

EXERCISE FOR SECTION 14.3

1 Repeat Exercise 4 of Section 14.1 using a built-in array.

14.4 ARRAYS VERSUS STRUCTS

`Arrays` (and built-in arrays) and `structs` are both type mechanisms that permit you to declare "collections" of variables. However, there are some important differences to recognize.

First, all of the elements in an `Array` must be the same type, while the elements (member variables) in a `struct` can be of different types. Second, the elements in an array are selected by subscripting, while a `struct`'s member variables are selected using the dot operator.

Finally, `Arrays` let your program dynamically generate element "names" (that is, via subscript values) while `struct` member variables can only be named statically in your program; there's no way to read in an integer value and then use that value to access the *i*th member variable in a `struct`.

Confused? Work through some of the `Array` exercises, and as you are doing so ask yourself the question "How could I solve this problem using a `struct`?" The answer usually is "You can't" but hopefully this thought process will help you clarify the differences between arrays and `structs`.

EXERCISE FOR SECTION 14.4

1 Suppose you want a type to represent a point on a two-dimensional canvas. Indicate the `Array` and `struct` types you could use. What are the advantages and disadvantages of each representation?

SUMMARY

This chapter has introduced you to arrays, another useful addition to your toolbag. The array is the most pervasive data structure in programming. You now know that:

- **built-in arrays** are fraught with danger;
- **the `Array` PDT** protects you from many of these dangers;
- **an array** is a collection of items of the same type;
- **an instance of a PDT `Array`** can be one-, two- or three-dimesional;
- **an array element** is just a variable;
- **subscripting** is used to identify an individual array element using an `int` value for each dimension;
- **the subscripting operator** for the `Array` PDT is `()`, but for built-in arrays is `[]`;
- **the initial subscript** in any dimension is zero;
- **the final subscript** in any dimension is *N*—1, where *N* is the length of that dimension;
- **a subscripting error** occurs if the subscript used is out of range;
- **a C++ Apprentice** will make lots of subscripting errors :-(
- **SOTP Airlines** offer an excellent service linking Ovington and Hexham :-)

Declaring arrays permits your program to deal with potentially vast numbers of variables. Providing the input values for an array from the keyboard would tax your typing skills, as well as your patience. What you need is to be able to perform input from a file of values, and generate output to a file. Chapter 15 beckons.

END-OF-CHAPTER EXERCISES

1 Think of some real-world examples of the use of arrays, and identify the subscripting operations that are used to access the elements of the array.

2 A random-number generator should produce values that are evenly distributed across the range of possible values. Write a program to test the `rand()` function you saw in Chapter 9 by generating a large number of random values between the values 0 and 999 and keep track of the number of occurrences of each value. (Hint: the expression `(rand() % 1000)` produces values in the range 0 → 999.) Then for each value print the difference between the expected number of occurrences and the actual number. If differences occur, can you explain why?

3 Write a function that takes an array of `int`s as one parameter and an initializing value as a second parameter, and sets all of the elements of that array to the initializing value. The function must be able to deal with both one-dimensional and two-dimensional arrays of `int`s.

4 A variation of the Sieve algorithm is described in Exercise 3 in Section 2.6. Implement this variation in C++.

5 SOTP Airlines is going to initiate a daily flight service between Hexham and Ovington. Use the `Flight` class to construct a simple reservation system for a week's flights. When started, the program should create seat plans for seven days, and then permit the user to request reservations, search for seats, etc. for a specified day of the week. The program must also allow the user to print a seat plan for a particular day's flight, indicating only which seats are free and which are occupied. Also, the program must allow the user to print out a passenger list for a specified flight, showing each passenger's name and which seat they are in. (Hint: you'll find a rudimentary user-interface for reserving seats etc. in one of the test functions created to test `Flight` and provided on the disk.)

6 Design and implement a `class Matrix` that provides the standard mathematical matrix operations such as addition and multiplication of two matrices. Assume that the type of each element in a matrix is `double`.

7 Exercise 8 at the end of Chapter 10 was concerned with drawing rosettes, and involved calculating the coordinates of each point on the rosette many times. Modify your solution to calculate the coordinates of each point on the rosette once only, to store the coordinates in an array, and to use the array elements to draw a rosette.

8 Using your solution to Exercise 4 of Section 14.1, write a program to implement a "move" in a game of checkers.

15 Input and Output

Objective

To gather together and expand on the features of I/O that have been covered in earlier chapters. In particular, to cover:

- I/O to and from files;
- formatting of output;
- dealing with errors in input and output.

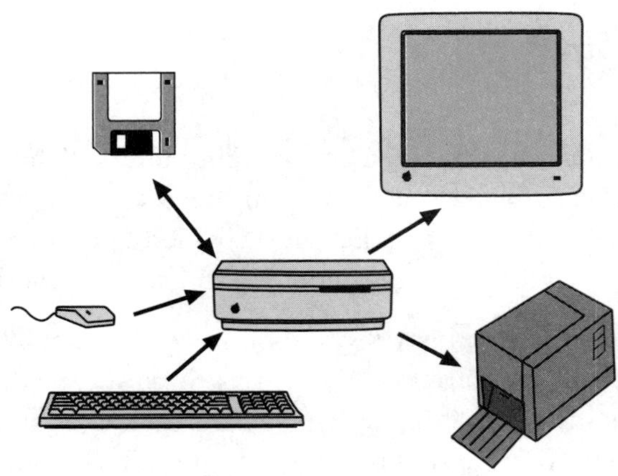

I/O, I/O, it's off to work we go

15.0 I/O: IN GENERAL TERMS

It's a rare program that doesn't involve some input and/or output. The very first program you wrote, way back in Chapter 4, printed your name. Other programs you've worked on have produced images of a CD player, have drawn pictures on a canvas, and so on. Depending on the application, the exact format of the output will vary.

EXAMPLE:

Output may consist of:

- text – a prompt to the user to type their name;
- numerical values – the results of some computation to determine the average rainfall in Guatemala;
- pictures – a histogram showing sales figures for this book.

The output may be sent to a device other than the screen; for example, it may be sent to a file. Similarly, the form of the input is likely to vary, as well as the device used to communicate the input. The input device could be a keyboard, a mouse, a bar code reader, or a floppy disk drive used to access the results saved in a file produced by some other program.

Many of the software systems you are familiar with in everyday life work in **interactive** mode. There are programs executing that are always awaiting prompts from you. However, there are some operations that are dealt with "off-line" in **background**, or **batch** mode, typically at the end of the day.

EXAMPLE:

You operate a bank automatic teller interactively in that after you've placed your card in the machine, you are asked for your ID and the amount of money you want to take out. Provided that your responses are correct, you remove your card and money and head for the burger bar.

This part of a bank's operation acts in interactive mode. The automatic teller produces output data (a list of cash withdrawals for that day) that it has stored in a data file. This data is then used as input for another program. The output from this other program will be a complete set of updated accounts, and there may be messages to the bank manager to send out threatening letters to some customers informing them that their account has become overdrawn.

From an overall perspective the distinction between interactive and batch modes, and the devices used for input and output, are unimportant. A program runs, receives data from somewhere and sends output somewhere. As long as the program "knows" where to read data from and where to send results to, input can be taken from the keyboard or from a file interchangeably, and output can be printed to the screen or to a file. As an abstraction, the source/destination of input/output should not matter; these are details only.

Lesson: Write your programs in such a way that they are flexible with respect to the source/destination of I/O. Then when you need to switch input from a keyboard to input from a file, the changes you have to make to the code are minimal.

Another important aspect of output is the **formatting** of data: the way results appear on the screen or on paper. Again, these are details only, but correctly formatted output (such as in aligned columns with headings) is preferable to a mass of numbers and characters printed out in a disorderly fashion. Good formatting of output can give a professional feel to your software. If your output is well-engineered then the expectation is that your program is well-engineered too.

Lesson: Engineering your software includes engineering the output statements so that results are presented neatly.

Just as important is the correct formatting of data for input. The user of your programs needs to be aware of the format in which to present data (for example, from the keyboard or a file). With keyboard input, the use of prompts will help to identify:

1. What information the program user is expected to supply.
2. The format the information should appear in.

Should the format of the input not be correct, your program should be able to react by outputting user-friendly messages and allowing a further opportunity for correct input.

EXAMPLE:

A message such as

```
Please type Y to continue or N to terminate:
```

makes it clear that the computer is waiting for the user to type something, and the something should be either `Y` or `N`, as appropriate.

If the user provides an incorrect response then a message such as

```
You typed an integer when I really wanted a letter;
please try again:
```

makes it clear that the response has not been accepted.

Lesson: If input from the keyboard is expected, print helpful messages indicating what the user should type next.

It's time to look at C++ I/O in detail, including:

- I/O from/to files;
- formatting of output;
- dealing with errors.

But first let's have a brief summary of the I/O facilities that you've been using now for some time.

EXERCISES FOR SECTION 15.0

1 A compiler is a program. What input does it expect? What output does it produce?

2 What input does a linker expect and what output does it produce?

3 What I/O sources and destinations would you associate with the software packages that you've been using, such as a word processor, graphics system, or e-mail facility?

15.1 I/O: IN C++ TERMS

The use of I/O is fundamental to practically any useful program, yet I/O can be complicated, messy, hard to understand, and a real pain in any programming language. C++ ducks the issue, providing no support for I/O whatsoever, so I/O in C++ is easy – you can't do it! Of course, that's not the entire story. Your C++ system has a useful library of PDTs for dealing with I/O that you've been using for some time. You're probably even used to inserting `#include <iostream.h>` at the top of every program you write on the grounds that it's highly likely you're going to want to make use of the I/O operators >> and << and the standard I/O streams `cin` and `cout`. So are `cin` and `cout` instances of the PDT `iostream`? No, there's no such PDT as `iostream`. `cin` is an instance of the `istream` PDT and `cout` is an instance of the `ostream` PDT.[1]

But what is an I/O stream? An I/O stream object is the means by which a C++ program can communicate with the outside world. It's an abstraction of the way I/O is dealt with by both the operating system of your computer and the software that controls the I/O devices. Fortunately when you output a value to a screen, you don't have to deal directly with the individual pixels that are going to represent that value. Aren't you glad that abstractions distance you from all the messy bits of I/O!

Since I/O is achieved using stream PDTs we can't guarantee consistency across various systems. However, you can be confident that for the most part the discussion in this chapter will apply to your system. Only in a very small number of places

1 A slight terminological inexactitude. `cin` is an instance of the PDT `istream_withassign` and `cout` is an instance of the PDT `ostream_withassign`. These subleties need not concern you here.

is there likely to be any variation, and even then that variation will be pretty small. Fortunately, implementers of the I/O stream PDTs were working to roughly the same designs, even if the details of the designs have some subtle differences.

Like any other PDT, the I/O stream PDTs support member functions and member operators. In addition you've seen that many of the PDTs introduced in Chapter 5 have I/O (non-member) operators. So far all I/O statements you've written have made use of the operators >> and <<.

EXAMPLE:

```
int i;
cin  >> i;
cout << "Value read is " << i << endl;
```

Let's have a detailed look at how the input operator works with some of the built-in types. Like the assignment operator, the `istream` input operator >> requires a destination, the name of a variable to which the value to be input is assigned. This variable appears as the right-hand operand. The input operator needs to know details of the source of the input, and this source appears as the left-hand operand. For the moment we assume that the source is the standard instance of `istream` called `cin` (representing the keyboard).

Just as with literals, a set of one or more characters typed at a keyboard may represent:

- an integer – a sequence of digits, possibly preceded by a sign;
- a floating-point number – for example, integer whole and fractional parts separated by a decimal point;
- a single character – but (unlike a character literal) single quotes are not required.

When you type in characters representing integers, floating-point numbers, or whatever, those characters have to be converted into an appropriate value for assignment to a **destination** (usually, a variable).

Before the characters-to-value conversion takes place (and therefore before any assignment of the final result to the destination takes place), the characters are buffered (held in some temporary store). The action of pressing the <Return> key acts as a signal that the characters in the buffer are now available for consumption. Thus it's possible to make changes to any characters typed in between presses of the <Return> key by using the <Del> key.

In summary, input takes place according to the following design.

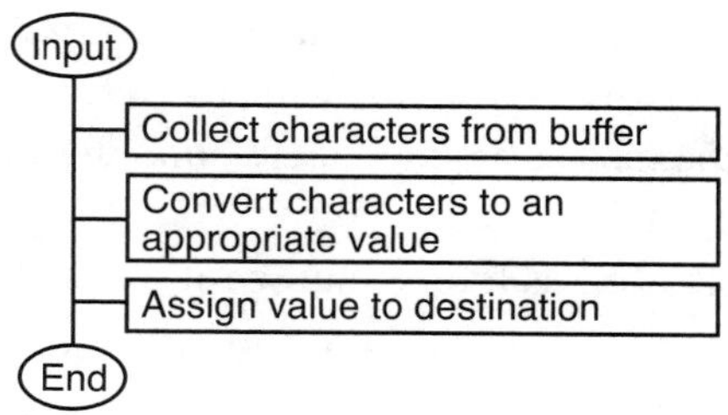

But how is a set of one or more characters recognized as an integer, or as a floating-point number? How does the **Collect characters from buffer** operation know when to stop?

You've seen how the ability to overload the input operator >> allows you to use the same operator symbol for input of an `int`, `char`, etc. The compiler therefore knows which operator you're calling from the type of the right-hand operand. It follows that the implementation of that operator "knows" what type of value to expect. Characters are processed one by one until a terminating character (often white space, used to separate one "value" from another) is encountered and the characters are interpreted as integers, character strings, and so on, as appropriate. If a character is encountered in the buffer that is invalid with respect to the type (say, you're reading to an `int` variable and the first character encountered is a letter) then an error flag is set. This mode of operation is summarized by the following design.

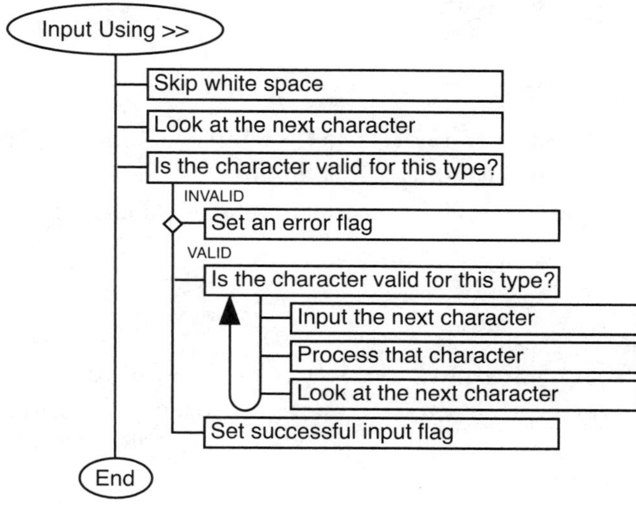

Note that **Look at the next character** doesn't mean consume that character from the buffer, but just have a sneak peek and see what's coming up. If the first character to be input is valid, then read it in; otherwise, leave it alone and set an error flag. You'll see what to do with this error flag in Section 15.5. For subsequent **Look at the next character** operations the error flag is not set, as you'll see in the next section.

White space is used as a terminator for all of the built-in types. For `int` input, any non-digit character acts as a terminator.

EXAMPLE:

Valid input for an integer (123), followed by a floating-point number (26.56) and a character (?) is:

```
123   26.56   ?
```

Note that the design for **Input using >>** indicates that

```
123      26.56?
```

is also valid input in this context. Reading of the floating-point number ceases as soon as the "`?`" is encountered. Hence the "`?`" is acting as a terminating character for the floating-point number but is left in the buffer and is therefore available to be read by a subsequent input statement. Typing

```
123   ?   26.56
```

will cause an error flag to be set when an attempt is made to read the question mark as a floating-point number.

Input to a `char` variable using the input operator is like input to an `int` or a `double` in that white space is ignored. However, it's not necessary to terminate characters by white space as only a single character is read.

EXAMPLE:

The code below will produce `OrangUtan` regardless of whether the input is typed as `OrangUtan` or `Orang Utan` or even `O r a n g U t a n`.

```
char nextChar;

cin >> nextChar;
while (nextChar != ';')
{
  cout << nextChar;
  cin  >> nextChar;
}
```

What about output? Values that you output are also held in a buffer, this time an output buffer. This buffer will contain sequences of characters too: character sequences that have been produced by performing an inverse operation to that used for input; that is, a value is converted into a sequence of characters. So output occurs according to the following diagram.

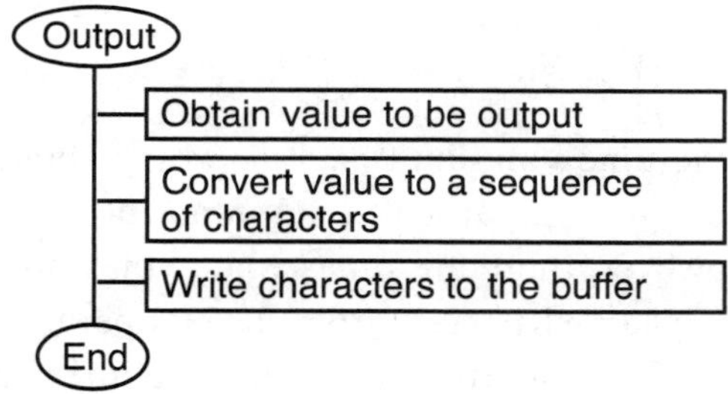

How are the contents of the buffer turned into visible output? See Section 15.3 for the answer.

We've looked at the issue of valid input: getting the format of the input right so that it can be recognized by the computer. Formatting is an important issue for output too, but this time it's a human reader that has to recognize the output. One of the aspects of formatting is the use of the output member functions, and we'll look at this in Section 15.3, but let's look at the input member functions first.

EXERCISES FOR SECTION 15.1

1 For each of the following pairs of types explain what happens when a variable that's used as the destination of the input operator is of the first type but the value that's supplied as input is of the second type.

(a)	`int`	`double`	(b)	`double`	`int`
(c)	`int`	`char`	(d)	`char`	`int`
(e)	`char`	`double`	(f)	`double`	`char`

2 Run a program that executes the following output statement.

```
cout << 2.0 << "   " << 2.1 << "   " << 0.5 << "   "
     << 0.000005 << endl;
```

In what way does the form of the output vary for each number?

15.2 INPUT STREAM

Most of the time you don't have to worry about how the input operator works; you just use the operator to read in an integer value, or a character string, and so on. However, there are times when you want to exercise a little more control over the Collect characters from buffer operation shown earlier, and to do this you need to know a little more about the interface for the `istream` PDT. Figure 15.1 shows a simplified version of this interface which will do for now.

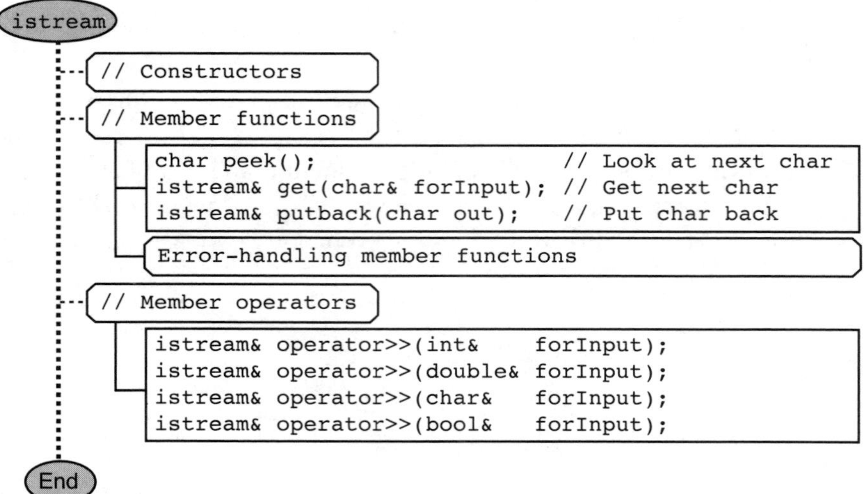

Figure 15.1 `istream` interface

Details of the constructors have deliberately been omitted, since you are not likely to want to use them. The member operators for input have been dealt with extensively in previous chapters, particularly in Chapters 12 and 13 where you saw how to define operators for PDTs. We'll deal with the error-handling functions in Section 15.5, so here we'll concentrate on the input member functions `peek()`, `get(...)` and `putback(...)` which deal with input of single characters. We'll use an example of input of someone's name to illustrate their use.

PROBLEM:

It's sometimes the case that you explicitly wish to recognize white space characters as characters, rather than as just something to be implicitly skipped before the next value is read. For example, you may want to read in and output a person's full name and wish to ensure that your program can deal with a wide variety of name formats, such as: Franklin D. Roosevelt, Margaret Hilda Thatcher, Sammy Davis Junior, Davis Love III, kd lang, Madonna, Sting, The Artist Formerly Known as Prince.

Input of a name is to be terminated by pressing the <Return> key.

DESIGN:

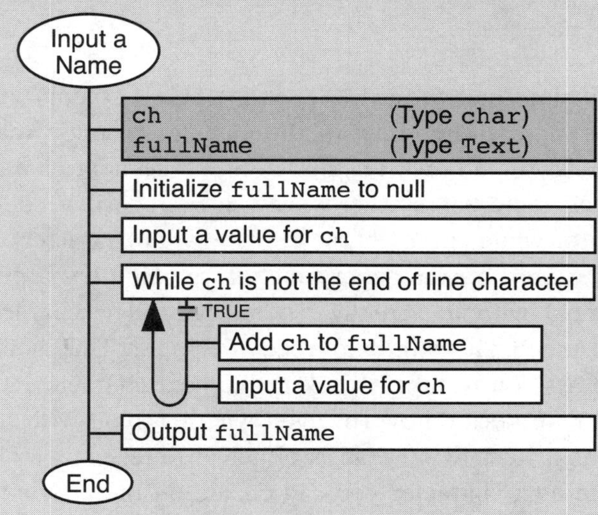

You need some mechanism for your program to obtain and recognize white space characters on input to be able to write the design as above:

IMPLEMENTATION:

Input of the next character, regardless of whether it's a white space character or not, is achieved using the member function `get(...)` of the class `istream`, whose use is illustrated in the following code fragment:

```
char nextChar;
Text fullName = "";

cout << "Input a name, terminated by pressing "
    << "the return key." << endl << endl;

cin.get(nextChar);
while (nextChar != '\n')
{
  fullName += Text(nextChar);
  cin.get(nextChar);
}
```

The `while` repetition terminates when the end-of-line character is encountered (that is, the repetition continues until the <Return> key is hit) and any characters typed are assembled in the `Text` variable `fullName`.

The interface for `get(...)` shows that it accepts a reference parameter of type `char`, and so the effect of the member-function call `cin.get(nextChar)` is to assign to `nextChar` the value of the next character to be input, whatever that character is. In other words, `get(...)` will read any character, including any form of white space character, as a valid character.

The `istream` member function `peek()` has a peek at the next character to be input without actually reading it in. The character is looked at but is not "consumed"; it's still there ready for input. This member function is useful since it allows you to take a peek at the next character, without consuming from the buffer, to decide how (or even whether) you wish to read it in. It may be that the next item to be read is either an integer or a character string. By peeking at the next character you can decide on the appropriate action to take.

EXAMPLE:

```
Text string;
int  i;
char nextChar;

nextChar = cin.peek();
while (isspace(nextChar))     // Skip over white space
{
  cin.get(nextChar);
  nextChar = cin.peek();
}
if (isletter(nextChar))       // Test for letter
{
  cin >> string;
}
else if (isdigit(nextChar))
{
  cin >> i;
}
else
{
  cout << "I was expecting a letter or digit" << endl;
}
```

This code explicitly skips over any leading white space and then tests the category of the first non-space character.

Note that `peek()` acts like `get(...)` in that it recognizes any white space character as a valid character.

There's an important syntactic difference between `get(...)` and `peek()` concerning their parameter lists and return types. The return type of `get(...)` is `istream&` and `get(...)` assigns the value of the next character read to its formal reference parameter. In contrast, `peek()` has an empty parameter list but a return type of `char`, so `peek()` uses the `return` mechanism to return the value of the next character in the input buffer. This can be a little confusing and we guarantee that at some stage you'll attempt an incorrect call to `get(...)` or `peek()`.

An alternative way of making sure that your program reacts correctly to the format of the input data is to use `putback(...)`. As its name suggests, `putback(...)` puts a character back to the input buffer.

EXAMPLE:

We can rewrite the previous code fragment as:

```
// Declarations as before
do                               // Skip over white space
{
  cin.get(nextChar);
} while (isspace(nextChar));
cin.putback(nextChar);           // Put the first non-space
                                 //   character back

// Test for letter as before
```

Since `get(...)` and `putback(...)` both return an item of type `istream&` (the value of the stream being used for input), a call to either of these functions can appear on the left-hand side of the >> operator. Clearly, `peek()` can't be used in this way; it can only be used in the context of a member-function call statement.

Now you know a little more about `istream`, let's have a look at `ostream`.

EXERCISES FOR SECTION 15.2

1 Can you use `putback(...)` to put back into the buffer a character other than the last character read?

2 Write a program that reads a line of text input from a keyboard and outputs the number of words typed in and the total number of spaces.

3 PDT `istream` supports a member function `istream& ignore(int n)`. Work out by experimentation what this function does. Similarly, work out by experimentation what the member function `istream& ignore(int n, char delimiter)` does.

4 Write a definition for a function that returns the next non-white space character in the input stream without consuming that character.

15.3 OUTPUT STREAM

Let's have a look at the class interface for ostream using the design notation:

```
ostream
  // Constructors
  // Member functions
      ostream& put(char out); // Output a char
      ostream& flush();       // Flush the buffer
    Formatting member functions
      long setf(long bits, long mask);   // Set format flags
      int  width(int newWidth);          // Set width
      int  precision(int newPrecision); // Set precision
      char fill(char newFillChar);       // Set fill char
    Error-handling member functions
  // Member operators
      ostream& operator<<(int    value);
      ostream& operator<<(double value);
      ostream& operator<<(char   value);
      ostream& operator<<(bool   value);
End
```

Figure 15.2 ostream interface

As with istream, we've deliberately left out the constructors since to do otherwise would introduce unnecessary complications. We've also omitted the error-handling member functions, which will be dealt with in Section 15.5. We'll restrict our attention here to the output member functions and the formatting member functions.

Output stream member functions

The member function put(...) is the ostream equivalent of the istream member function get(...). A call to put(...) results in output of the single character specified by the actual parameter. You recall from Section 15.1 that output is buffered, so how can you ensure that the contents of the buffer appear on the screen or are written to a file? One way of flushing the buffer is to make a call to the member function flush().

EXAMPLE:

```
// Output a character and then flush the output buffer
cout.put('Z');
cout.flush();
```

A further way to flush the buffer is to output `endl`, although this also outputs a newline character. Additionally, `cout` is tied to `cin` in that the output buffer is automatically flushed when output through `cout` is followed by input using `cin`.

EXAMPLE:

```
cout << "Please supply a number in the range 1 to 50";
cin  >> nextNumber;                    // Output buffer
                                       //   flushed by use of
                                       //   the input operator
cout << "The value you supplied is "
     << nextNumber << endl;            // Output buffer
                                       //   flushed by endl
cout << "Have a nice day!";
cout.flush();                          // Output buffer
                                       //   flushed by call
                                       //   of flush()
```

OK, so now you know a new way to output a character and a new way to flush the output buffer. "Big deal" you might say, and then continue by asking "but are there any functions that give me some control over the way my results are presented?" The answer is "yes," since that's what the formatting member functions are for.

Formatting member functions

Often you want to have some control over the precise way values are output to the screen or to a file.

EXAMPLE:

You might wish to print a `double` value using:

- floating-point notation;
- fixed-point notation.

(The difference between floating- and fixed-point formats for literals was covered in Chapter 8, so go back and refresh your memory if you've forgotten.) Furthermore, in floating-point notation you may wish to control the number of digits printed after the decimal point.

The term used to describe the form in which a value is printed is **format**. The `ostream` formatting member functions can be used to control the format of output. Unless you make calls to the formatting member functions, a default output style is assumed for printing a value. "OK, what's the default," you ask, quickly followed by "and how do I indicate that I want to use a style other than the default?" We'll answer the second question first, and in so doing answer the first question.

Output of `double`

Fixed- and floating-point format

Some control over the output format of floating-point numbers is achieved using the function `setf(...)` shown in Figure 15.2, with the interface:

```
long setf(long bits, long mask)
```

You'll recall from Section 13.2 that the `long` type is just a "big" `int` type.

For the second actual parameter (known as the **mask** or **field flag**) you use `ios::floatfield` to indicate that you're setting the output format for floating-point numbers. Note the use of the scope resolution operator `::` linking `floatfield` with `ios`. The PDT `ios` is known as the **base class** for I/O. Exactly what the relationship is between `ios` and `istream` and `ostream` needn't concern you here. However, the fact that there can be such a strong association between PDTs is an important feature of object-oriented programming that we'll have to leave to a more advanced apprenticeship.

Depending on the first actual parameter of `setf(...)`, a `double` value is printed out in:

- **scientific mode** (floating-point format with an exponent) if the value is `ios::scientific`;
- **fixed-point mode** if the value is `ios::fixed`;
- **default mode** if the value is `0`.

There's always a non-zero digit before the decimal point in scientific (floating-point) mode. If no call to `setf(...)` is made, a `double` value is normally output in fixed-point format. However, for output of "small" values, scientific format is used.

EXAMPLE:

```
cout << 1234.56789 << '\t' << "default"           << endl;
cout.setf(ios::scientific, ios::floatfield);
cout << 1234.56789 << '\t' << "scientific"        << endl;
cout << 1234.56789 << '\t' << "still scientific" << endl;
cout.setf(ios::fixed, ios::floatfield);
cout << 1234.56789 << '\t' << "fixed"             << endl;
```

OUTPUT:

```
1234.56789       default
1.234568e+03     scientific
1.234568e+03     still scientific
1234.56789       fixed
```

This assumes that other default settings are in force that control, for example, the number of digits printed after the decimal point. We'll have more to say about this very soon.

EXAMPLE:

Try running the following program to get some idea of what "small" means for your system, in the context of the default format for output of `double` values.

```
char response = 'y';
double value  = 1.0;

while (response != 'n')
{
  value /= 10.0;
  cout << "Current value is " << value    << endl
       << "Reduce still further? (y/n): " << endl;
  cin  >> response;
}
```

Once the output mode for `doubles` has been set by a call to `setf(...)`, that mode applies to the subsequent output of all `double` values until a further call of `setf(...)` is made that changes the mode.

The value returned by `setf(...)` is the value of the format flag prior to the call of `setf(...)`, so by retaining this value you can reset the format flag to a previous value.

EXAMPLE:

```
long previousFlag = setf(ios::scientific, ios::floatfield);
...
// Now go back to the previous setting
setf(previousFlag, ios::floatfield);
```

Precision

The member function `precision(...)` sets the number of digits to be output for a floating-point number after the decimal point (with a default of 6). The exact meaning of a call of `precision(...)` depends on the mode as set by a call to `setf(...)`:

- with fixed or scientific mode, the parameter of `precision(...)` refers to the number of digits after the decimal point;
- with the default mode, the parameter of `precision(...)` refers to the number of digits occupied by the complete number.

EXAMPLE:

```
cout.precision(5);
cout << "\t\tprecision 5"                      << endl;
cout << 1234.56789 << '\t' << "default"    << endl;
cout.setf(ios::scientific, ios::floatfield);
cout << 1234.56789 << '\t' << "scientific" << endl;
cout.setf(ios::fixed, ios::floatfield);
cout << 1234.56789 << '\t' << "fixed"      << endl;
```

OUTPUT:

```
                precision 5
1234.6          default
1.23457e+03     scientific
1234.56789      fixed
```

Once the precision has been set by a call to `precision(...)`, any subsequent output of a `double` conforms to that precision until the next call of `precision(...)`. The value returned by `precision(...)` is the value of the previous setting.

Output of `double` *and* `int`

Width

The member function `width(...)` sets the number of character positions that an item to be output will occupy. By default, the width will be just enough to contain the value. If the width setting is too small for a particular value (say you try to output the integer value 100 but specify a width of only one) the width used is the minimum required to output the value. Setting the width to zero provides the default behavior (which explains why there are no spaces between items on output unless you explicitly put them there). If the specified width is greater than that needed by the value to be output then the value is right-justified in the number of character positions available, with padding spaces occupying the leading unused positions.

Unlike the previous member functions we've considered here, the width setting applies *to the next value output only.* When that has been output, the default setting is used for any subsequent output unless there's a further call to `width(...)`.

EXAMPLE:

The following calls to `width(...)` illustrate that you can use this member function when formatting both `double`s and `int`s.

```
cout.width(10);
cout << 12345    << '\t'
     << "width set to 10"                  << endl;
cout << 12345    << "\t\t"
     << "now back to the default"          << endl;
cout.precision(2);
cout.width(10);
cout << 3.14159 << 't'
     << "precision set to 2, width to 10" << endl;
```

OUTPUT:

```
     12345     width set to 10
12345          now back to the default
       3.1     precision set to 2, width to 10
```

The value returned by `width(...)` is the setting that prevailed before the call. This value can also be determined by calling the member function `int width()`.

Left- and right-justification

By default, when you print a `double` or `int` value, that value will appear right-justified within the number of character spaces defined by a call to `width()`, with leading spaces for character positions unoccupied by the value itself. This default right-justification can be changed using a further call to the function `setf(...)`, this time using a second actual parameter of `ios::adjustfield`. For the first parameter to `setf(...)` you can choose:

- `ios::left` for left-justification;
- `ios::right` for right-justification.

The following code illustrates that once the justification has been set it applies to subsequent output of all the built-in types.

EXAMPLE:

```
cout.width(10);
cout.setf(ios::left, ios::adjustfield);
cout << 12345   << '\t' << "width 10, left justified"  << endl;
cout.width(10);
cout.setf(ios::right, ios::adjustfield);
cout << 12345   << '\t' << "width 10, right justified" << endl;
cout.precision(2);
cout.width(10);
cout << 3.14159 << '\t'
     << "precision 2, width 10, still right justified" << endl;
cout.width(10);
```

OUTPUT:

```
12345          width 10, left justified
     12345     width 10, right justified
       3.1     precision 2, width 10, still right justified
```

The fill character

Inherent in the concept of width is that there is a character (by default, a space) that pads the output field when it exceeds the minimum required for a value's output. This character can be changed using the member function `fill(...)`.

EXAMPLE:

Insert the following before the code fragment in the previous example.

```
cout.fill('*');
```

OUTPUT:

```
12345*****     width 10, left justified
*****12345     width 10, right justified
*******3.1     precision 2, width 10, still right justified
```

Once the fill character has been set it remains unchanged until the next call of `fill(...)`. The value returned by `fill(...)` is the previous fill character. In the above example we've chosen simply to ignore the return value.

So now you have a little more control over I/O. What's that you say? You've a contract to process examination results and they fill a 1.44MB floppy disk! You don't fancy printing the results out and typing them as input to your program? Sounds like you need to find out about file input (and output, while you're at it).

EXERCISES FOR SECTION 15.3

1 Design and implement functions for I/O of integer values formatted such that a comma is used as a separator between the thousands and hundreds digits (for example, 21,900). Will your implementation work for a non-zero hundreds digit?

2 What is the effect of the calls to `width()` in the following code fragment?

```
cout.width(10);
cout << 10    << endl;
cout.width(10);
cout << endl << 10 << endl;
cout.width(10);
cout << '\n' << 10 << endl;
```

15.4 FILE I/O

Simple programs usually involve only small amounts of input and output data. When testing such programs, it's no big deal to retype the input data for each test run and to look at the output produced on the screen. However, more complex problems often require vast amounts of data to be read:

- in a "production run" when the program is used to solve a real, rather than test, problem;
- in an exhaustive test that makes sure that a significant number of eventualities have been covered by processing a wide variety of input data.

Clearly, it would be extremely tedious to have to retype the data each time you want to run the program. Similarly, it would be inconvenient to retype C++ code every time you wished to run it, but you're used to the idea of saving the source in a file. You can do the same with data input by creating a file that contains all the input data. Furthermore, it may well be useful to save the output from a program into another file so that you can analyze the results of your program at leisure.

A data file is just like a program file. The file will consist of a sequence of characters representing whatever data the program reading the file requires. The data file may have been produced by a previous program or it could be data that you've prepared using your favorite editor. To produce a valid data file you'll need to know the order the program expects data to be presented. You should be able to work this out by reading your program or studying the excellent documentation you've provided :-).

Having put the data into a file, the question is now how you "connect" the data file to the program in such a way that data is read from the file instead of (or, possibly, in addition to) from the keyboard. Fortunately, in C++ the answer is simple. To use file input you need to declare a variable of type `ifstream` that represents a (file) input stream corresponding to the data file and then use that identifier where you would otherwise have used `cin`. (You'll need to `#include <fstream.h>` to have access to the PDT `ifstream`.)

EXAMPLE:

```
Text name;
int number;
ifstream dataFile;

// Additional code required here
dataFile >> name >> number; // Attempt to read from a file
```

The differences between `istream` and `ifstream` are minimal and unimportant here, except that in the following interface diagram for the PDT `ifstream`, there are two additional member functions, the file-handling member functions `open(...)` and `close(...)`. The input functions and input operators are the same as for `istream`, so you really can use `dataFile` in exactly the same way that you've been using `cin`. You can use an input operator to input integers, floating-point numbers, characters, or values of any PDT for which you've provided an input operator. You can use the member functions `get(...)`, `peek()` and `putback(...)`, as well as the error-handling functions that we'll be describing in the next section. In Figure 15.3, we've given you the form of one of the constructors since, as you've already seen, you're going to need a declaration to use file I/O.

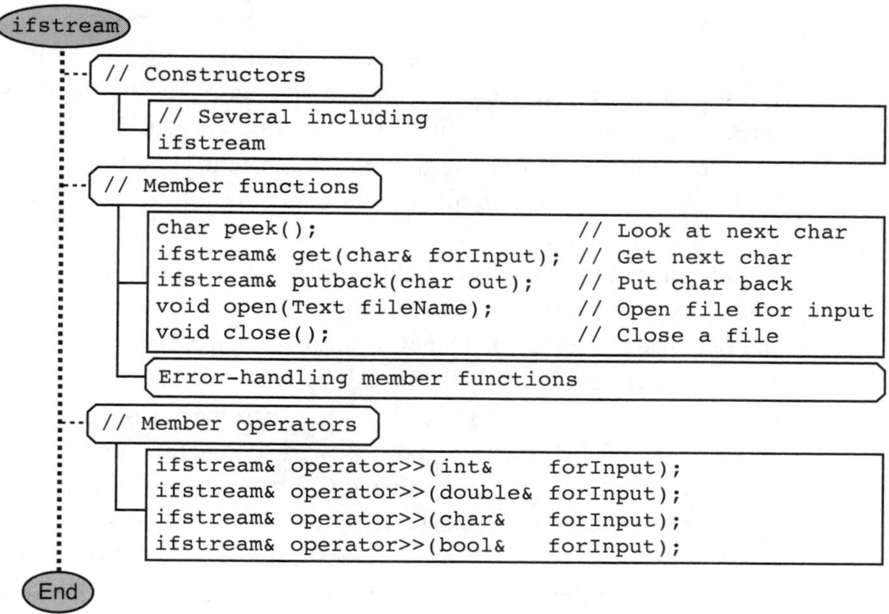

Figure 15.3 `ifstream` interface

But how does a variable of type `ifstream` become associated with an actual data file?

You need an initialization to associate the variable identifier with a particular file. There's more than one way to do this, but we suggest you use the member function `open(...)` of the class `ifstream`. The single parameter of `open(...)` is a `Text` string that specifies the name of the data file. There's another member function `close()` that can be used to close the file when you've finished input of data from it; program termination closes an input file automatically since the stream declaration goes out of scope.

EXAMPLE:

```
ifstream dataFile;

dataFile.open("MyData");      // Open the file for input
// Now input values using the input operator
...
dataFile.close()              // Finished with the file so close it
```

You can declare as many instances of type `ifstream` as you like and therefore read from several different files within the same program. For example, as a financial whiz kid you may wish to put current share prices in one file and money exchange rates in another. Further, you can still instruct your program to take some data from the keyboard. All you have to do is to make sure that each time you use the input operator >>, the left-hand operand corresponds to the actual stream you wish to read from.

Output to a file follows in a similar fashion. You just need to introduce an identifier (such as `resultsFile`) of type `ofstream` (again, `fstream.h` contains the necessary interface). The class interface for `ofstream` is very similar to that for the `ostream` PDT, with the addition of the file-handling member functions `open(...)` and `close()`. Rather than produce a separate diagram for PDT `ofstream`, we'll leave it to you to work it out for yourself; just adapt the diagram for `ifstream`. To output values to a file you use the `open(...)` member function to associate the variable with an actual file (such as `MyResults`), use `resultsFile` as the left-hand operand of the output operator <<, and use the formatting member functions with `resultsFile`, just as you would with `cout`.

EXAMPLE:

To output a table of results you might write something like the following.

```
const int WIDTH  = 20;
Text      name;
int       marksObtained;
ofstream  resultsFile;

resultsFile.open("MyResults");
resultsFile << "Name";
resultsFile.width(WIDTH - Text("Mark").length());
resultsFile << "Mark"    << endl;

name          = "Mike";
marksObtained = 10;
resultsFile << name;
resultsFile.width(WIDTH - name.length());
resultsFile << marksObtained << endl;

name          = "Samantha";
marksObtained = 65;
resultsFile << name;
resultsFile.width(WIDTH - name.length());
resultsFile << marksObtained << endl;
```

I/O to more than one file within a program is permitted; all you have to do is to declare several instances of type `ifstream/ofstream` and use the appropriate identifier when performing I/O. As mentioned before, you can continue to input from the keyboard using `cin` and direct output to the screen using `cout`.

EXAMPLE:

The following program fragment sorts some random integers into even and odd numbers.

```
ofstream evenNumbers;
ofstream oddNumbers;
int      n;
int      nextNumber

// Open the output files
evenNumbers.open("Even");
oddNumbers.open("Odd");

evenNumbers << "A list of random even numbers"
            << endl << endl;
oddNumbers  << "A list of random odd numbers"
            << endl << endl;

cout << "How many numbers do you want to process? ";
cin  >> n;
for (int i = 0; i < n; i += 1)
{
  nextNumber = rand();
  if (nextNumber % 2 == 0)
  {
    evenNumbers << nextNumber << endl;
  }
  else
  {
    oddNumbers  << nextNumber << endl
  }
}
cout << "Finished. Check the Contents of files "
     << "\"Even\" and \"Odd\"." << endl;
```

Let's now look at a problem that involves use of file I/O.

PROBLEM:

In the previous chapter you developed a `Flight` class for use by SOTP Airlines. We mentioned that there are times when output of all details associated with a flight might be appropriate; for example, to provide a file back-up in case the computer system fails.

DESIGN:

In Chapters 12 and 13 you saw how to design and implement PDT I/O operators, and your first reaction here should be that you need to provide an output operator for PDT `Flight`. However, it's not quite as straightforward as that since the output operator needs to have access to all the private data of the class. How can you provide that access?

One way of providing (read) access to the private data of PDT `Flight` would be to make available additional member functions that return the values of the private data members. Alternatively, as you saw in Section 12.6, the output operator could simply call a public member function `print()` of PDT `Flight` that performs all the detailed output. Since the private data of the PDT is in scope for all member functions, it's not necessary to provide any member functions other than `print()`.

IMPLEMENTATION:

```
ostream& operator<<(ostream& outStream, Flight value)
{
  value.print(outStream);
  return outStream;
}
```

Even though we intend to use the output operator mainly for output to a file, its first parameter is of type `ostream&` rather than `ofstream&`. This actually allows you to use the operator for output to a file or output to a screen, since a variable of type `ofstream&` can be treated by the compiler as if it were a variable of type `ostream&`. Hence you can use the same operator for output to the screen for testing purposes in the early stages of program development as you can during a later "production run."

Lesson: The first parameter of your I/O operators should be of type `istream&/ostream&`, even if you intend to use instances of type `ifstream&/ofstream&` as the first operand.

Moreover, when changing your program so that it outputs to a file, you don't even have to make changes to all those places where you've used `cout`. You can switch the destination of output by assigning a new value to `cout`.

EXAMPLE:

```
ofstream results;
results.open("MyResults");
cout = results;
```

Wherever `cout` is subsequently used in this program as an actual left-hand operand for an output operator, the output will be directed to the results file `MyResults`, rather than to the screen.

Although the compiler is able to regard an instance of type `ofstream` as being of type `ostream`, the converse doesn't hold. Can you figure out why this is the case?

Recall that PDT `ofstream` has all the member functions of `ostream`, along with two additional member functions for file-handling, namely `open(...)` and `close()`. The compiler won't let you apply the `open(...)` operation to an `ostream` variable, since this operation is not supported by the `ostream` PDT. Further, the compiler won't even let you use an `ostream` variable where an `ofstream` variable is required.

If the first parameter of your output operator were to be of type `ofstream&`, then you couldn't use the operator for output using `cout` as the actual left-hand operand. So if you want to make sure that output can only go to a file, then define the operator in terms of `ofstream&`. We suggest you go for flexibility here and use `ostream&` as the first parameter type for an output operator. The same arguments apply to `istream` and `ifstream`.

Remember all our scriptures about reuse. Do you think that `ostream` and `ofstream` have their own separate functions called `peek()`, etc., or do you think that `ostream` and `ofstream` in some sense share a common set of functions?

The "natural" answer should be that `ostream` and `ofstream` share a set of member functions, but that there are some functions that PDT `ofstream`

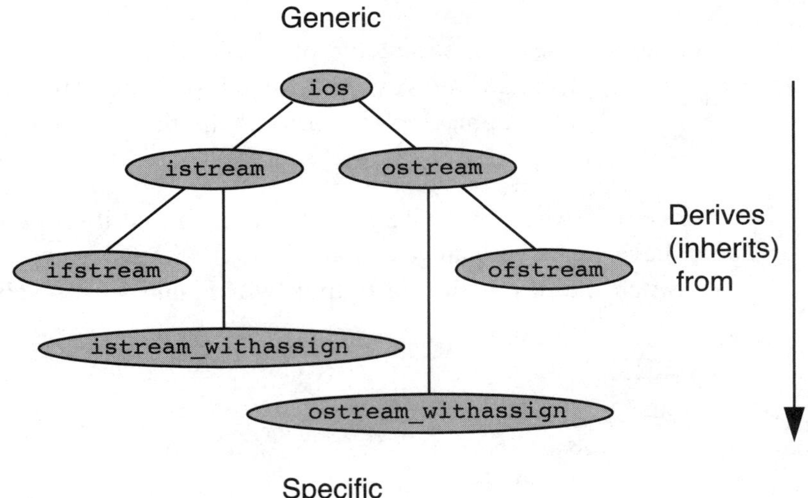

Figure 15.4 Relationships between the stream PDTs

doesn't share with `ostream`. We say that PDT `ofstream` **inherits** the behavior of `ostream`. You'll not be surprised to learn that PDT `ifstream` inherits the behavior of `istream`. But where does PDT `ios` fit into the picture? PDT `ios` is termed the **base class** for I/O, and just as `ofstream` and `ifstream` inherit from `ostream` and `istream`, respectively, so `ostream` and `istream` both inherit from PDT `ios`. Figure 15.4 represents these relationships diagrammatically.

The figure shows that wherever a variable of type `ostream` is specified (for example, as a function's formal parameter) you can use an instance of type `ofstream` or `ofstream_withassign` (for example, as a function call's actual parameter); that is, `ostream` is type-compatible with `ofstream` and `ofstream_withassign` (but not vice versa). Hence you can write output operators in terms of `ostream` yet still use `ofstream` variables as actual parameters.

"What are `istream_withassign` and `ostream_withassign`?" you ask. They're PDTs that inherit from `istream` and `ostream` that include assignment. You saw an assignment to `cout` (which is an instance of `ostream_withassign`) in the example on the previous page, and you'll see an example of the use of these PDTs in Chapter 16.

Inheritance is an important feature of object-oriented programming that you can only hope to touch upon in an apprenticeship. When your apprenticeship is complete, we strongly recommend that you pursue the advantages of inheritance, where reuse is clearly an important feature.

Let's return now to the problem of SOTP's output requirements.

DESIGN:

The member function `print (...)` has to handle the discrepancy between the user's view of the seat numbering and the internal numbering that's used to index into the `plane` array. In the output, a grid can be used to indicate the seating plan, with an asterisk used to indicate an occupied seat and a space used to indicate a free seat. There has to be a mapping from the `enum SeatStatus` to an asterisk or space. You could define the output operator for PDT `SeatStatus` to exhibit this behavior, but more typically you'd define an output operator for an `enum` to produce a clearer interpretation of its abstract value. So we suggest you design and implement a function `seatStatusToText(...)`.

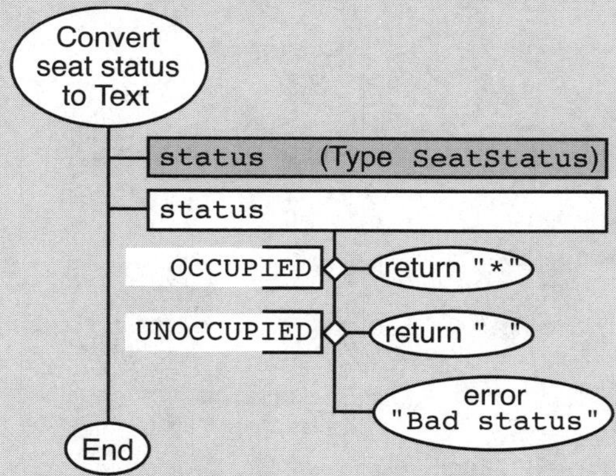

IMPLEMENTATION:

Now that you've got a seat-status-to-text conversion routine, you can complete the function to print the full flight details. The member-function `print(...)` prints a header, a table indicating seat occupancy, and a list of passengers. Having reached this far in the book you should be able to go straight to the implementation.

```
Text Flight::seatStatusToText(SeatStatus status)
{
  Text answer = "?";

  switch(status)
  {
```

```
    case OCCUPIED:
      {
         answer = "*";
      }
      break;
    case UNOCCUPIED:
      {
        answer " ";
      }
      break;
    default:
      {
        error("Attempt to output invalid seat status");
      }
      break;
  }
  return answer;
} // end seatStatusToText()

void Flight::print(ostream& outStream)
{
  int realCol;
  int realRow;

  outStream << "The following grid indicates the status of seats"
            << endl << endl;
  if (!bool(outStream.good()))
  {
    error("Output stream not good");
    return;
  }
  for (realCol = 0; realCol < plane.size(2); realCol += 1)
  {
    outStream << '\t' << realColToUserCol(realCol);
  }
  outStream << endl;
  for (realRow = 0; realRow < plane.size(1); realRow += 1)
  {
    outStream.width(3);
    outStream << realRowToUserRow(realRow);
    for (realCol = 0; realCol < plane.size(2); realCol += 1)
    {
      outStream << '\t'
                << seatStatusToText(
                     plane(realRow, realCol).seatStatus);
    }
    outStream << endl;
```

```
  }
  outStream << endl << endl
            << "Total number of seats occupied\t\t";
  outStream.width(4);
  outStream << seatsOccupied()   << endl
            << "Total number of seats unoccupied\t";
  outStream.width(4);
  outStream << seatsFree() << endl << endl << endl;
  outStream << "Passenger Information" << endl << endl;
  for (realRow = 0; realRow < plane.size(1); realRow += 1)
  {
    for (realCol = 0; realCol < plane.size(2); realCol += 1)
    {
      if (plane(realRow, realCol).seatStatus == OCCUPIED)
      {
        int  userRow;
        char userCol;

        realToUserCoords(realRow, realCol, userRow, userCol);
        outStream << "Row\t";
        outStream.width(4);
        outStream << userRow << "\tSeat\t" << userCol << endl
                  << "Name\t"
                  << plane(realRow, realCol).passenger.initials
                  << ' '
                  << plane(realRow, realCol).passenger.surname
                  << endl << endl;
      }
    }
  }
  return;
} // end print()
```

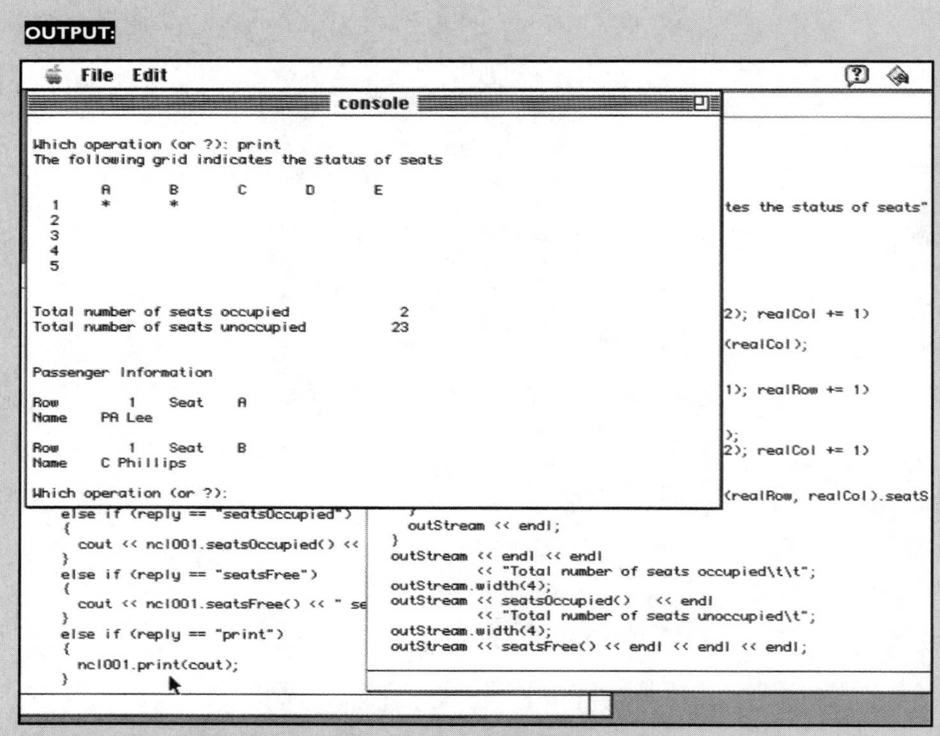

OK, the output reproduced here is for a pretty small plane, but output to the screen is being used for performing simple tests only.

To perform file output using the output operator for PDT `Flight` you'll have to declare a variable of type `ofstream`. What if you then try to use that variable on the right-hand side of an output operator without calling the `open(...)` `ofstream` member function first. Will you get a compile-time error? Or will you get a run-time error?

You'll get a compile-time error only if you make a syntax error; failure to call the `open(...)` function before attempting output is a semantic error. You'll get a run-time error, but only because the definition of `print(...)` checks the status of the file stream right at the start (can you see how?) and calls the `error(...)` function if something is wrong. Invalid I/O operations cause an error flag to be set, but you won't know about this unless you write some code that tests the status of the error flag. And for this you're going to need to use an error-handling function. Guess what the next section is about!

EXERCISES FOR SECTION 15.4

1 What happens if you try to `open(...)` a file that doesn't exist? The answer depends on the default behavior of your system; for output, a new file may be created (and the operation is successful) or not (and the operation fails). You can override this default behavior using an appropriate call to the I/O `ifstream/ofstream` member function `void open(Text fileName, int ioMode)`. If the actual value used for `ioMode` is `ios::nocreate` then no new `ofstream` file will be created if the file doesn't exist. If `ioMode` is `ios::in` or `ios::out` then input or output is allowed, as appropriate. If `ioMode` is `ios::noreplace` then the `open()` operation will fail if an `ofstream` file exists. Run some simple test programs to verify this behavior.

2 Write a program that prompts the user for the name of a file and then sums a sequence of integers to be found in that file. The sequence should be terminated by a 0.

15.5 ERROR HANDLING

You know that to input a value typed at the keyboard or from a file, the type of the value supplied must match the type of the variable that appears on the right-hand side of the input operator. What happens if the types don't match? You get a **format error** and input fails without assigning a value to the variable being input to.

> **Lesson:** Don't assume that input (or output) always succeeds. Make sure your programs are able to detect errors and take appropriate action should they arise.

EXAMPLE:

The following fragment of code sums a sequence of integers read in, terminated by a zero.

```
int sum = 0;
int nextNumber;

cin >> nextNumber;
while (nextNumber != 0)
{
  sum += nextNumber;
  cin >> nextNumber;
}
```

What happens if one of the "numbers" starts with a non-digit character?

Unfortunately, you then get an infinite loop, since every subsequent input operation will fail to assign a new value to `nextNumber`, which will retain the last value successfully input.

The I/O stream classes support a number of error-handling member functions that are of help in classifying and recovering from I/O errors. The following diagram indicates some of the error-handling member functions supported by PDT `istream`. The corresponding `ostream`, `ifstream` and `ofstream` member functions are similar.

Error-handling member functions

```
int good();                     // Test for good state
int eof();                      // Test for end of file state
int fail();                     // Test for fail state
int bad();                      // Test for bad state
istream& clear();               // Clear failure
istream& clear(int newState);   // Set failure
```

End

An I/O stream can be in one of four possible states:

- good – an I/O operation may be attempted on the stream;
- end-of-file – the end-of-file has been encountered;
- fail – the last I/O operation failed due to a format error;
- bad – the last input operation failed for some reason and the stream has become corrupted.

The status of the stream can be determined using the member functions `good()`, `eof()`, `fail()` and `bad()`. These functions return a 0/1 (`false`/`true`) answer as appropriate. Once an error has occurred on an I/O stream, any subsequent operation on that stream will also fail. Note that `good()`, `eof()`, `fail()` and `bad()` indicate the state of the stream after an I/O operation has taken place, not what the state of the stream will be following the next I/O operation.

Lesson: The error-handling functions classify the success of the previous operation, not the next.

You can reset the stream to the good state by making a call to the member function `clear()`. We'll show you how to use the member function `clear(...)` with an `int` parameter in the next section.

EXAMPLE:

Here's an alternative way of summing numbers that uses the error-handling functions to detect and act on input errors.

```
int sum = 0;
int nextNumber;
char ch;

cin >> nextNumber;
while (true)
{
   if (bool(cin.eof()))
   {
      break;
```

```
  }
  else if (bool(cin.bad()))
  {
    error("Stream has become corrupted");
  }
  else if (bool(cin.fail()))
  {
    cin.clear();
    cin  >> ch;
    cout << "Illegal int character read: " << ch << endl;
  }
  else
  {
    sum += nextNumber;
  }
  cin >> nextNumber;
}
```

If, on input, this program fragment encounters an illegal character as the first character of an assumed integer, the error is cleared and the offending character is read in and ignored.

The member function `eof()` returns `1` if an attempt is made to read data but there's no more data left in the file. For example, suppose the data file contains the following values.

```
1  3  5  7  11  13  17  23
```

The state of the input stream is tested each time around the repetition statement. Assuming no failure, the last value read is added to the sum and the next value read is assigned to `nextNumber`. Eventually the value 23 will be read. The member function `eof()` will still return the value 0 (since the 23 was read successfully). The value 23 is added to the sum and then an attempt is made to read another integer. There are no more values left, so the next call of `eof()` returns 1 and the repetition terminates. The way you indicate end-of-file when typing data at a keyboard is system dependent, but the combination of keystrokes <Ctrl>+D usually works.

The above example shows how you can deal with, among other things, format errors in your data file. But what if you try to open a file for input that doesn't exist?

If you try to open a file that doesn't exist then the operation may, or may not fail (see Exercise 1 at the end of the previous section). One way of detecting success or failure of an `open(...)` operation on a stream is to test the stream using the member function `good()`.

EXAMPLE:

```
ifstream dataFile;

dataFile.open("Raw Data");
if (bool(dataFile.good()))
{
  // Input stream datafile OK
}
else
{
  // Input stream dataFile not OK
  error("Problem with opening data file");
}
```

A simple mechanism for detecting the existence of an I/O error that you may see employed is to test the "value" of the appropriate I/O stream. An implicit type coercion allows you to use an `istream` or `ostream` variable where a Boolean value is expected.

EXAMPLE:

```
ifstream dataFile;

dataFile.open("Raw Data");
if (dataFile)
{
  // Input stream datafile OK
}
else
```

```
{
  // Input stream dataFile not OK
  error("Problem with opening data file");
}
```

You can use this simple paradigm to test the value of an instance of any stream type to determine whether an I/O operation has been successful. But what if there is an error? What type of error is it? The error-handling member functions give you more information than you get by simply testing the value of an I/O stream, and so our style rule is:

✓ *Use the I/O stream member functions to test for I/O errors.*

However, you should always check for errors one way or another.

Lesson: Adopt the defensive programming approach of always testing for I/O errors.

The correct handling of I/O errors is something that should always be built into your programs. Let's address this matter further, along with some other software engineering issues.

EXERCISES FOR SECTION 15.5

1 What happens when you try to run the second example of this section with the call to `clear()` commented out?

2 Write a program that sums a sequence of integers read from the keyboard. If an invalid character is encountered then the rest of the current line should be ignored before a further attempt is made to read a number.

3 Verify the default action of `open(...)` for your system (see Exercise 1 of Section 15.4) by testing the return value of `good()`, and the value of the I/O stream.

15.6 SOFTWARE ENGINEERING ISSUES

I/O is a very important aspect of your software; to the user of that software it could be the key aspect. The user will want to have confidence that your programs are well-written, that you have adopted good programming principles, that you have used an object-oriented approach, that you have read this book and followed all the style rules we've proposed. But there are a number of questions a user may ask about your software before they're willing to invest in your product.

EXAMPLE:

"How easy is the software to use?"

"If the program is to be run in interactive mode, are useful prompts displayed that tell me what to type?"

"Is the program able to deal sensibly with invalid responses to those prompts?"

"Will the program display helpful error messages?"

"Or does it just print the message `Aaaaargh; something wrong` and then fall over every third time I run the program?"

"Are the results produced presented in a readily digestible manner, with graphs, summary tables, and so on?"

"Are the results labeled with text that indicate their significance?"

"Are the numbers neatly formatted and aligned in columns?"

"Or will the program produce a mass of numbers in what appears to a totally random order?"

"Is it easy to redirect I/O so that data can be taken from a file and results can be written to a file?"

For much of this book we've concentrated on interfaces: type interfaces (type definitions) and function interfaces. Get the interfaces right and using those types and functions becomes straightforward. It's the same with the program's user interface; make this user-friendly and you'll be rewarded with further contracts to develop software. Get it wrong and, metaphorically speaking, your software will gather dust and you may need to consider a change of direction in your chosen career.

So how much time should you spend working on the user interface? A difficult question for which there's no simple answer. Getting the user interface right is important, but, ultimately, a good interface can't completely disguise a badly-written program. It's no good producing a fancy user interface for a program that produces the wrong results. You've got to strike a balance and apportion your efforts accordingly.

But just as you shouldn't leave documentation to the last minute, you shouldn't leave the user interface as the last task to be completed. The initial design for your software must involve user-interface considerations as these will influence the overall design. Start a new project with "I/O, I/O, it's off to work we go" in mind.

A key part of the user-interface is the ability to deal with errors. A program that fails to deal with I/O errors properly can be a nightmare for the user, and for you when you're trying to fix run-time errors. In the previous sections you saw what sort of errors can be detected by I/O streams and how to deal with them. New PDTs that you design may involve overloading of the I/O operators, and the operator definitions you provide should be capable of dealing with errors in a controlled way.

PROBLEM:

In Chapter 13 we introduced I/O operators for the `enum CompassPoint`. In particular, the input operator >> employed a variable `gotValue` that was used to indicate whether the value read was valid. You now know that this is not the way that the input operator works for the built-in types; if an input error occurs then an internal error flag is set. From a software engineering point of view, it's desirable for the mode of operation of the input operator to be consistent across types, so let's do this for the `CompassPoint` PDT input operator.

DESIGN:

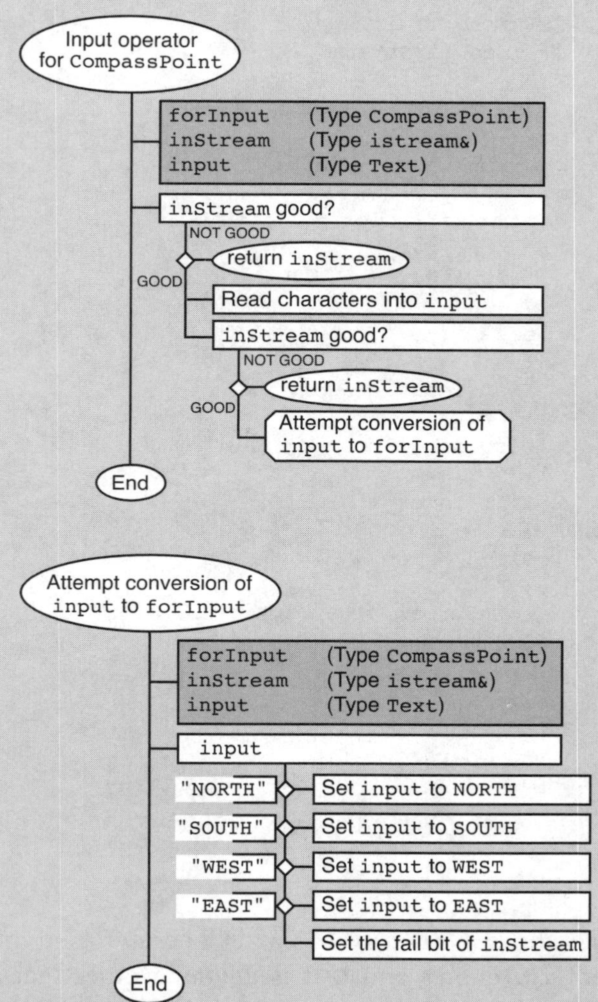

IMPLEMENTATION:

The second design diagram suggests the use of a `switch` statement. Unfortunately there's no constructor to convert a `Text` value to an `int` and so a multiway selection has to be implemented using `if` statements.

```
istream& operator>>(istream& inStream, CompassPoint& forInput)
{
  Text input;
```

```
  if (bool(inStream.good()))
  {
    inStream >> input;
    if (bool(inStream.good()))
    {
      if (input == "NORTH")
      {
        forInput = NORTH;
      }
      else if (input == "SOUTH")
      {
        forInput = SOUTH;
      }
      else if (input == "WEST")
      {
        forInput = WEST;
      }
      else if (input == "EAST")
      {
        forInput = EAST;
      }
      else
      {
        inStream.clear(ios::failbit);
      }
    }
  }
  return inStream;
} // end operator>>()
```

The above version of the input operator first checks the state of the input stream `inStream` and if it is anything other than **good** the operator returns `inStream` immediately. If `inStream` is in the **good** state then an attempt is made to read a character string. If, as a result, the stream is no longer in the **good** state (say end-of-file is encountered) then the operator again returns `inStream` immediately. Otherwise a character string has been successfully read. If this character string is valid (that is, one of `NORTH`, `SOUTH`, `WEST` or `EAST`) then `inStream` is left in the **good** state. If the character string is not valid then a format error has been detected and so `inStream` is set to the **fail** state using the function `clear(...)` with an actual parameter of `ios::failbit`. Arguably the choice of the name `clear` is a little unfortunate since the function can be used to clear the stream for subsequent I/O using an actual parameter of `ios::goodbit`, or to "block" further input using an actual parameter of `ios::failbit`. Note that if any error occurs, no value is assigned to the formal parameter `forInput`.

EXERCISES FOR SECTION 15.6

1 Write an input operator for PDT `Palette` that successfully deals with input errors.

2 What circumstances might cause file input using `get(...)` to fail?

SUMMARY

In this chapter, we've put together some of the ideas of I/O that were introduced only informally in earlier chapters, as well as some new material. You now know that:

- **I/O buffers** act as intermediary storage between the program and the user;
- **flushing a buffer** results in the contents of the buffer being available for input or output to/from the final destination;
- **I/O streams are PDTs** and so have a number of member functions such as `peek()` and `get(...)`, and the I/O operators >> and <<;
- **format member functions** such as `width(...)` and `precision (...)` can be used to control the format of your results;
- **file I/O** is just like keyboard/screen I/O except that you use instances of types `ifstream` and `ofstream`;
- **error-handling member functions** such as `fail()` and `clear()` can be used to deal with I/O errors.
- **inheritance** allows you to specify `istream` and `ostream` as formal function parameter types even if you intend to use actual parameters of types `ifstream` and `ofstream`.

You've covered some additional software engineering issues:

- **formatting** is concerned with the neat presentation of your results;

- **checking for errors** is required so that appropriate action can be taken if I/O fails;

The second stage of your apprenticeship is complete. You're now in a position to tackle some quite complicated problems, and we suggest that you turn to Part 3 to look at the worked projects described there. Go out and celebrate the fact that you have made it this far. Then come back and prepare yourself for Part 3.

END-OF-CHAPTER EXERCISES

1 Produce the multiplication table, neatly formatted, for your kid sister.

2 According to Mr. Micawber "Annual income twenty pounds, annual expenditure nineteen nineteen six, result happiness. Annual income twenty pounds, annual expenditure twenty pounds ought and six, result misery." (For non-scholars of Charles Dickens the moral is that you'll be happy if income exceeds expenditure, and miserable otherwise.) Create a data file containing a sequence of transactions, one per line, of the form:

```
<transaction description>     <credit/debit>     <amount>
```

where each transaction description is terminated by a colon, credit or debit is indicated by the words `CREDIT` or `DEBIT`, as appropriate, and the amount of money is indicated by two integers, denoting dollars and cents, separated by a period. Write a program that reads the transactions and produces a summary balance sheet indicating the total income and the total expenditure, along with a message that indicates happiness or misery, as appropriate.

3 Modify your solution to Exercise 2 by catering for errors in the format of the data. Invalid lines should be reported and then ignored as far as the final calculation is concerned.

4 In Chapter 13 you developed a `Duration` class. Can you spot any limitations with the definition of the output operator? What if the number of minutes and/or seconds is less than ten? Remove these limitations.

5 Write functions for I/O of floating-point numbers formatted as in, for example, 1,012,234.56 that is, with a comma separator after the thousands, millions, etc. digits.

6 Write a program that inputs amounts of money expressed in several currencies and expresses the amount in $. For example, the input for amounts in Australian Dollars, German Marks, and French Francs might appear as:

```
A$15.31     DM18.24   FF100.95
```

(Use exchange rates of 0.85 A$, 0.76 DM and 5.38 FF to the US dollar.)

7 Design and implement a PDT `Binary` for integer numbers that uses I/O operators that read and write values in binary format.

PART 3

Practicing your trade

16 Example problems and solutions

OBJECTIVE

- To show the application of all of the features introduced in the book to solve some example problems.

Using your toolbag

16.0 BRINGING IT ALL TOGETHER

You now know all there is to know about C++? Well, not quite, even if you've diligently learned all of the material presented. However, you've covered a significant amount of ground, and you now know enough C++ to tackle complex problems and to produce quite sophisticated solutions to those problems. OK, make that "should know enough C++"; you just need a bit more practice :-)

The purpose of this chapter is to work through the design and implementation of solutions to two problems: the eight queens problem briefly introduced in Chapter 2, and a supermarket cash register control problem. Both problems require designing some new PDTs to assist with the solution. As we work through these solution designs and implementations, you'll see the various software engineering lessons introduced in earlier chapters put into practice.

The solution to the queens problem shows how the "brute-force" approach to problem solving can be applied, getting the computer to check each of a very large set of possible solutions to find the answer. The solution also involves the use of recursion to provide an elegant design and solution. The supermarket problem is a more straightforward data processing application, whose design and implementation is much simplified by the PDTs that will be designed.

EXERCISE FOR SECTION 16.0

1 Remind yourself of all those good things you've learned from the first 15 chapters.

16.1 THE EIGHT QUEENS PROBLEM

A queen is one of the pieces used in the game of chess. When a queen is placed on a chess board it can attack any other piece that lies on a horizontal, vertical, or diagonal line of squares centered on the placed queen. This is illustrated in Figure 16.1.

PROBLEM:

Design a program that determines whether eight queens can be placed on a chessboard such that, following the usual chess rules, no queen can capture any other queen. Print out the solution if one is found.

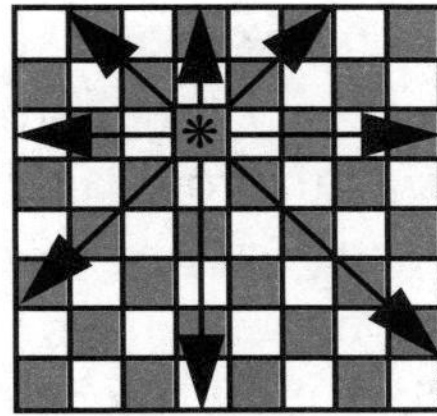

Figure 16.1 Queen coverage on a chess board

Let's think about how you can attack this problem.

DESIGN:

A first brute-force strategy suggests the following high-level design.

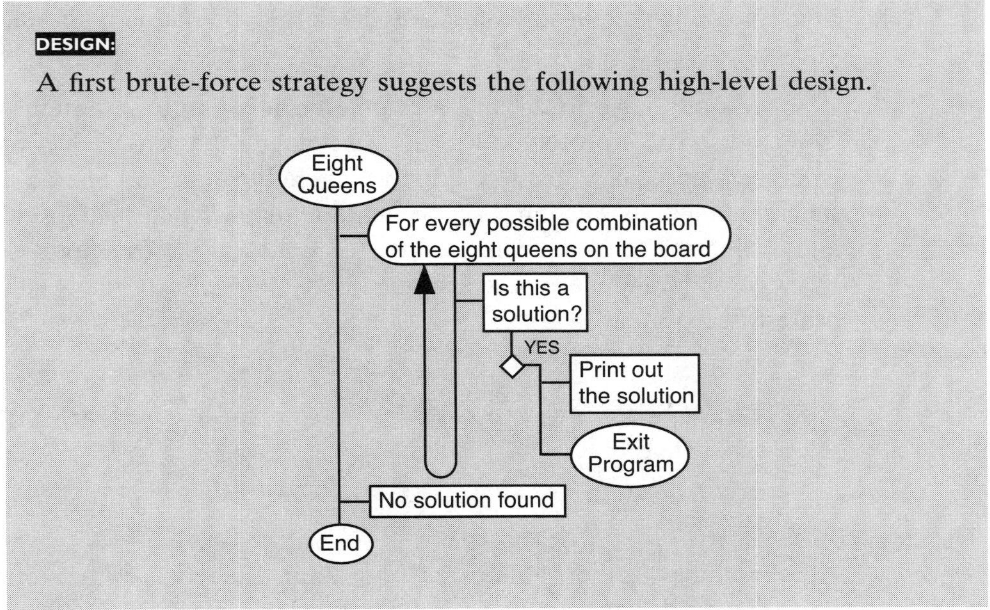

This is a relatively simple design, but is it feasible? In particular, does it satisfy the design property we identified in Chapter 2, namely that the algorithm must terminate in a finite time? Applying some engineering thought to this design, you'll notice that there are a rather large number of possibilities to be evaluated – approximately 178 billion (see Section 2.5, Chapter 2 for the derivation of this number) – so it's unlikely that this program will terminate soon enough! You need to refine this design, to eliminate the need to consider all possible combinations of all eight queens.

Looking back at the capture rules, you'll notice that once a queen has been placed in a row (or in a column), no other queen can be placed in that row (or column). You can make use of this fact to cut down the maximum possible combinations to less than 17 million. Furthermore, every time you're about to place a queen in a square, you can check whether that position is available. If it's not, there's no point in trying to place that queen, or the remaining queens, on the board. As you might imagine, this will cut down the number of combinations to be checked even further. Experiment with pencil and paper, or a real chess board, trying to place eight queens. You'll see that in following this strategy many potential solutions are quickly eliminated before there are many queens on the board. Maybe there aren't any solutions at all…

If you were still concerned that, even with the reduced number of combinations, the design might still not satisfy the finite termination criterion, what would you do?

What you'd have to do is apply some engineering to determine the answer. You could write a prototype function to simulate the actions necessary to check whether a particular board position is covered or not, and embed a call to that function in a loop repeating, say, one million times. Timing the resulting program and scaling the result up will give you some idea of the execution time required by a program that checks each combination, and hence of the feasibility of your brute-force strategy.

Lesson: When using brute-force strategies, make sure that your design is feasible.

Let's think further about the algorithm needed for the refined design. Basically, what you need to do is the following.

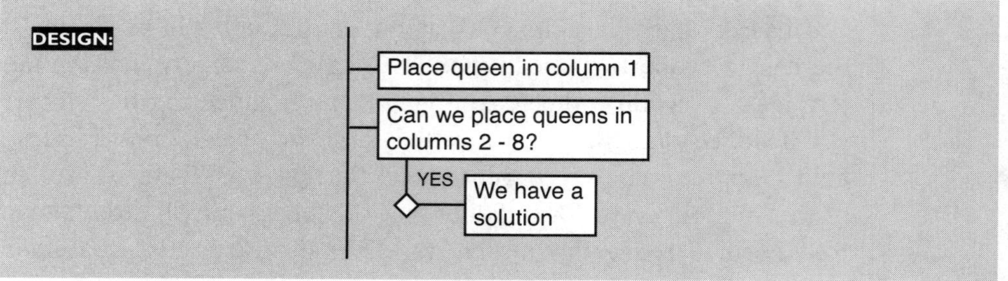

In words, you want to place a queen in column 1; if it's then possible to place queens in columns 2 to 8 you've found a solution. Here, "placing a queen" means placing a queen in a square that isn't covered by any already-placed queen; the details of how you do this can come later.

Do you notice anything recursive about the above design fragment?

The solution to placing queens in the eight columns has been broken down into the sub-problem of placing a queen in column 1 followed by the sub-problem of placing queens in the remaining seven columns. And how do you solve the latter sub-problem? Well, you need to place a queen in column 2 and then solve the sub-subproblem of placing queens in columns 3–8, and so on until you get to column 8.

Let's explore this further. You're heading for the following design for the main program (Figure 16.2).

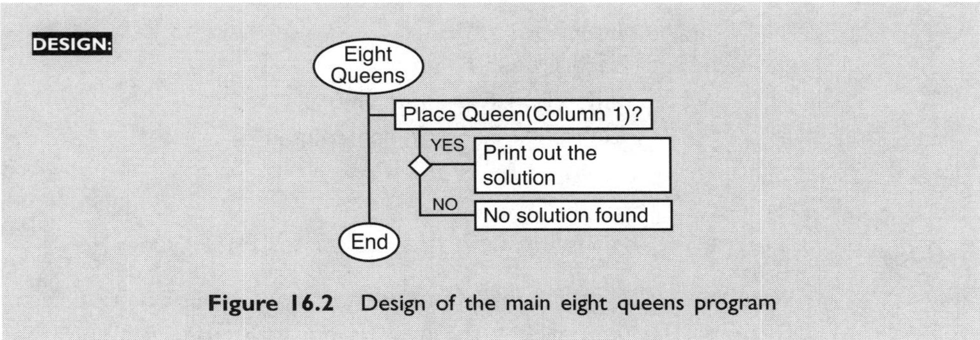

Figure 16.2 Design of the main eight queens program

The function **Place Queen** takes a parameter that's the starting column, and has to place a queen in the starting column and all subsequent columns, returning `true` if this is possible. An initial design for this function is shown below.

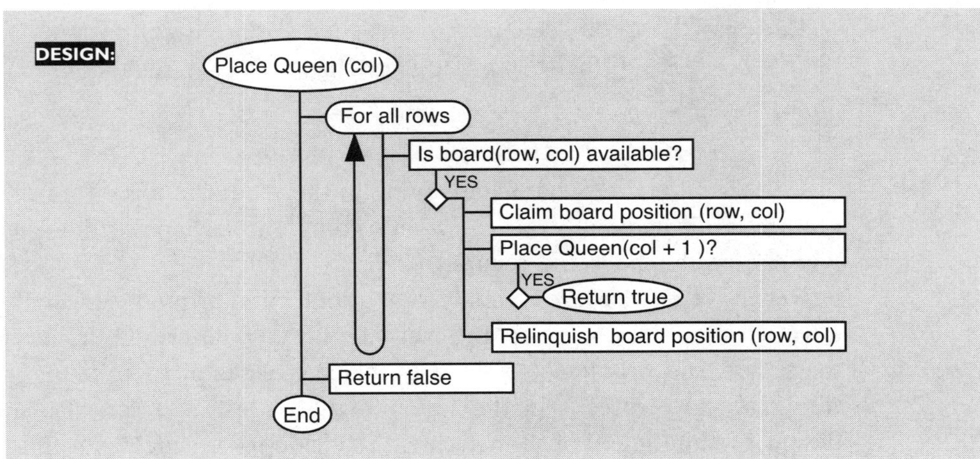

For a given starting column number, Place Queen tries all of the row positions in that column. If none are available `false` is returned. However, if a position is available (meaning that it's not covered by any of the other queens so far placed on the board) then that position is claimed, and a recursive call to Place Queen determines whether or not this newly-claimed position permits queens to be placed in all of the remaining columns. If the recursive call returns `false` then this newly-claimed board position is no good and must be relinquished, and the next position in the column tried. If the recursive call returns `true`, then `true` can be returned as the result of the original call of Place Queen.

Thus, the sequence of function calls would be as follows. The main program calls:

Place Queen(column 1)
  which calls Place Queen(column 2)
    which calls Place Queen(column 3)
      which calls Place Queen(column 4)
      ... and so on.

Can you see a problem with this design for Place Queen?

What stops the recursion? Finding an unavailable position is one condition for stopping the recursion, but what's going to happen if a solution is found? If the program tries to place a queen in column 8 and finds an available square, it's then going to try to place a queen in column 9! So, the design for Place Queen needs a further refinement as shown in Figure 16.3.

> **Lesson:** If you're developing a recursive design (or program) carefully check the terminating conditions for the recursion.

If you're not sure what's happening in the recursive algorithm of Figure 16.3, go through it by hand, tracking what's going on, perhaps with a 4 by 4 board so you can easily check the recursive calls.

Recursive designs are difficult to get your mind around, especially for designs developed by someone else. In Figure 16.3, we've described the design "outside-to-inside"; the problem is solved by placing a queen in column 1 followed by trying to place queens in the remaining columns. You can also approach the design by thinking about the recursion "inside-to-outside" as trying to solve the

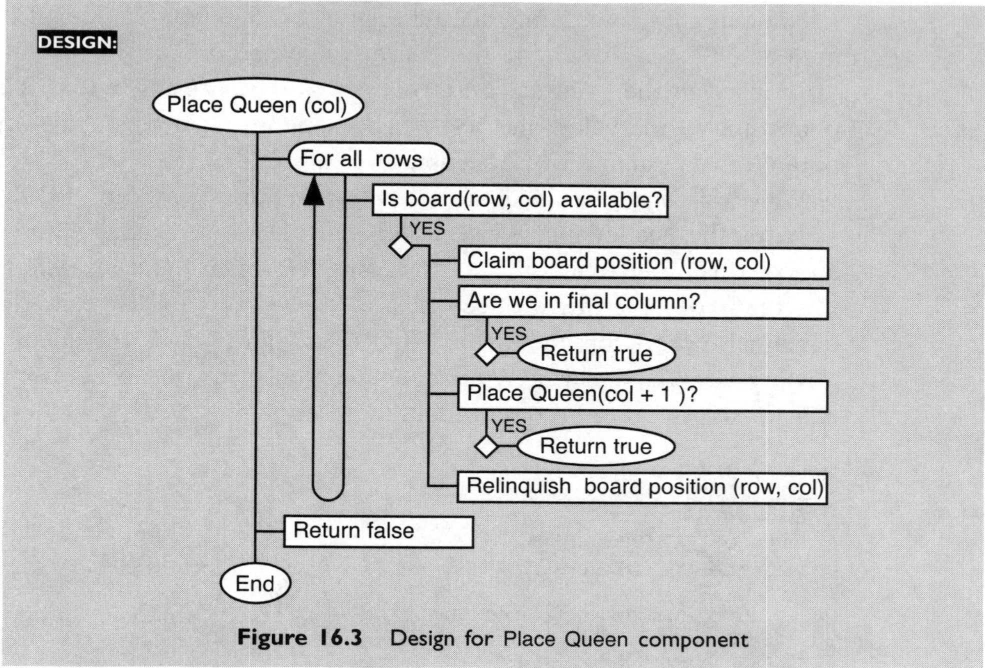

Figure 16.3 Design for Place Queen component

problem of placing a queen in a one-column board (easy!), generalized to solving the problem of a two-column board, and so on.

You can see that the recursive solution to this problem is rather elegant and straightforward. The power of recursion! Time to start writing C++ code? No, not yet.

What else can you design to help you write the C++ code? Are there any PDTs that would be useful? Study the designs (and English descriptions of the actions), and see if you can identify any useful PDTs.

Did you notice that something representing the chess board is central to the designs? Think about the board's implementation for a moment. Did you think "2-D array"? Well, that seems an obvious thing to use to represent the board, but should you just use an array directly? Did you notice that there are several operations that you performed on the board?

1. Check that a particular square is available.
2. Claim a particular square (that is, placing a queen).
3. Relinquish a claim to a square.
4. Print out the board and its contents if a solution is found.

Noticing these operations should suggest PDT to you. Sure, a 2-D array would do, but a PDT representing the board would provide a more useful abstraction to be used in the eventual C++ code. In addition, using a PDT gives you the opportunity to develop and test it as a separate component, before it's incorporated in the main eight queens problem.

We've already identified the operations required for this PDT, so here's a start for the header file. We've called the PDT `QueenBoard` and have added an extra member function `isOccupied(...)` which indicates whether a square is actually occupied by a queen or not (as opposed to just being covered by a queen elsewhere on the board; that's the purpose of the member function `isCovered(...)`). This new member function turns out to be useful for testing and for use in an output operation.

DEFINITION:

```
#ifndef QUEENBOARD_H
#define QUEENBOARD_H

// Rows and columns are numbered 0 .. 7

class QueenBoard
{
  public:
    // Constructor
    QueenBoard();

    // Member Functions
    void claim(int row, int col);
    void relinquish(int row, int col);
    bool isCovered(int row, int col);  // Return true if covered
    bool isOccupied(int row, int col); // Return true if occupied
    void print(ostream& outStream);

   // Member operators: none defined

  private:
   // To be defined

};

ostream& operator<<(ostream& outStream, QueenBoard value);

#endif
```

Note that there isn't a member function `placeQueen(...)` in this PDT. It seems more appropriate to have this as a function separate from the PDT and to use the PDT simply to represent the board. You're then free to use the PDT in different algorithms for solving the problem.

Note also that the numbering scheme has been documented for the rows and columns as expected by this PDT; you're moving into the implementation phase.

Producing the implementation

Let's start the implementation of the eight queens program by considering the implementation of `QueenBoard`. As we've already discussed, a 2-D array seems directly appropriate for representing the board. What should the type of its elements be? A square is either occupied by a queen or unoccupied, so `bool` could be appropriate for the element type. You might also notice that a square can be covered, so an alternative for the element type would be to define another PDT (say `SquareState`) representing the states of a square (and what C++ mechanism would you use for that?[1]). What are the consequences of these decisions?

If the element type is `bool`, the member functions that check whether a square is covered or not will have to perform this checking computationally; that is, by checking the appropriate rows, columns and diagonals in the array. However, placing and removing a queen on a particular square simply involves assigning `true` or `false` to the relevant square. Using `SquareState` requires the placement (and removal) of a queen to set (clear) the covered state of all effected squares, while simplifying the check whether a square is covered to being a simple check of the state of that square. This is a typical trade-off that you come across in software designs: trading off the potential increase in element sizes against the extra computation required. But how do you decide which option to choose?

For this problem the element size isn't a major issue; with the 2-D array representation there are only going to be 64 elements. As you're more concerned about the execution time of the program (due to the potentially large number of possibilities to be considered) the overall efficiency of the main program should be considered. Thus, a deciding factor in evaluating the trade-off for this problem is the relative frequencies of execution of the various member functions. You might be able to decide between the two options by thinking about the problem and the design you've come up with. If not, you'll have to apply

[1] The `enum` construct could be used to declare the type as part of the `public:` part of `QueenBoard`.

some engineering to your implementation to help you decide. Let's do the latter: let's choose the `bool` element type and once you've got a working prototype program you can apply some engineering (take some measurements) to try to decide which trade-off to select. If you do decide to change later, you will of course be delighted that you used a PDT to represent the board since the changes will be to this PDT only and should not alter the main eight queens program.

There are other potential representations that you could use to represent the board but we'll return to this topic later. For the moment, let's stick with the straightforward 2-D array, but emphasize (yet again:-) that the advantage of using a PDT is that the representation is hidden from the program using the PDT. You can develop your eight queens program to use the PDT, and changing the internal representation in the PDT will have no effect on this program. In fact, changing the internal representation will make an interesting exercise for you to try later.

DEFINITION:

Here's the private part of `QueenBoard`. There are some private member functions that you'll see later are used in the implementation, although you can probably guess their purpose.

```
private:

   // Private member variable
   Array<bool> board;

   // Private member functions
   bool queenOnRow(int row);
   bool queenOnCol(int col);
   bool queenOnDiagonal(int actualRow, int actualCol);
```

IMPLEMENTATION:

The implementation of the constructor for `QueenBoard` is straightforward. (The following code shows some constants that are used elsewhere.)

```
#include "QueenBoard.h"

const int SIZE          = 8;    // Length of side of the board
const int ROW_DIMENSION = 1;    // Parameter for Array
                                //   size() member fn
const int COL_DIMENSION = 2;    // Parameter for Array
                                //   size() member fn

QueenBoard::QueenBoard()
{
  board.setSize(SIZE, SIZE);
  for (int row = 0; row < SIZE; row += 1)
  {
    for (int col = 0; col < SIZE; col += 1)
    {
      board(row, col) = false;
    }
  }
  return;
} // end Queenboard()
```

The member functions are also straightforward to write, given the private member functions that you saw earlier.

```
void QueenBoard::claim(int row, int col)
{
  board(row, col) = true;
  return;
} // end claim()

void QueenBoard::relinquish(int row, int col)
{
  board(row, col) = false;
  return;
} // end relinquish()

bool QueenBoard::isCovered(int row, int col)
{
  return (queenOnRow(row) || queenOnCol(col)
                          || queenOnDiagonal(row, col));
} // end isCovered()
```

```
bool QueenBoard::isOccupied(int row, int col)
{
  return board(row, col);
} // end isOccupied()
```

The private member functions that check whether queens elsewhere on the board are covering any rows or columns of interest are a straightforward application of `for` statements.

```
bool QueenBoard::queenOnRow(int row)
{
  for (int col = 0; col < board.size(COL_DIMENSION); col += 1)
  {
    if (board(row, col))
    {
      return true;
    }
  }
  return false;
} // end queenOnRow()

bool QueenBoard::queenOnCol(int col)
{
  for (int row = 0; row < board.size(ROW_DIMENSION); row += 1)
  {
    if (board(row, col))
    {
      return true;
    }
  }
  return false;
} // end queenOnCol()
```

The private member function that checks if there's a queen on any diagonal emanating from the square of interest has a more complex control-flow. You may wish to develop a design for this private member function, as the loop conditions are a little tricky.

```
bool QueenBoard::queenOnDiagonal(int actualRow, int actualCol)
{
  int row;
  int col;
  // Need to check four diagonals from current position:

  // Check up-to-left diagonal
  row = actualRow - 1;
  col = actualCol - 1;
  while ((row >= 0) && (col >= 0))
  {
    if (board(row, col))
    {
      return true;
    }
    row -= 1;
    col -= 1;
  }
  // Check up-to-right diagonal
  row = actualRow - 1;
  col = actualCol + 1;
  while ((row >= 0) && (col < board.size(COL_DIMENSION)))
  {
    if (board(row, col))
    {
      return true;
    }
    row -= 1;
    col += 1;
  }
  // Check down-to-left diagonal
  row = actualRow + 1;
  col = actualCol - 1;
  while ((row < board.size(ROW_DIMENSION)) && (col >= 0))
  {
    if (board(row, col))
    {
      return true;
    }
    row += 1;
    col -= 1;
```

```
  }
  // Check down-to-right diagonal
  row = actualRow + 1;
  col = actualCol + 1;
  while ((row < board.size(ROW_DIMENSION)) &&
        (col < board.size(COL_DIMENSION))     )
  {
    if (board(row, col))
    {
      return true;
    }
    row += 1;
    col += 1;
  }
  return false;
} // end queenOnDiagonal()
```

To complete `QueenBoard`, there's the implementation of the output operator. Recall that in Chapters 13 and 14 it was found useful to implement an output operator as a call to a member function `print(...)` that has access to the private data of a PDT.

```
void QueenBoard::print(ostream& outStream)
{
  int row;
  int col;

  outStream << "+-+-+-+-+-+-+-+-+" << endl;
  for (row = 0; row < board.size(ROW_DIMENSION); row += 1)
  {
    cout << '|';
    for (col = 0; col < board.size(COL_DIMENSION); col += 1)
    {
      if (isOccupied(row, col))
      {
        outStream << "Q|";
      }
      else
      {
        outStream << " |";
      }
    } // end for col
    outStream << endl;
  } // end for row
  outStream << "+-+-+-+-+-+-+-+-+" << endl;
```

```
  return;
} // end print()

// Output operator

ostream& operator<<(ostream& outStream, QueenBoard board)
{
  board.print(outStream);
  return outStream;
} // end operator<<()
```

That completes the initial implementation of PDT `QueenBoard`. Now on to the code for the eight queens problem? Not yet. The next thing to do is to write a test program for `QueenBoard` so you can determine if what's been written so far seems to work correctly. In the programs that accompany the book you'll find a file containing a function for testing `QueenBoard`. This function is interactive, permitting the user to enter commands (and square coordinates) in order to exercise all of the member functions.

OK, so the code wasn't quite right the first time. The code shown above is the code after testing had been completed and some bugs had been eliminated. Most people, even experienced software engineers, make mistakes. Hence the test program and the demonstration of the advantages of testing components separately. The bugs in `QueenBoard` would have been difficult to find if you'd tried to test it using the eight queens program, since you wouldn't know whether it was that program or the PDT that was at fault.

Lesson: Testing software components in isolation makes it much easier to identify their residual bugs.

Finally, you can develop the code for the main program and for the recursive function `placeQueen(...)`. Given the designs in Figures 16.2 and 16.3, together with the PDT `QueenBoard`, these C++ components are straightforward. The instance of `QueenBoard` is passed as a reference parameter to `placeQueen(...)` so that all of the recursive calls update the same instance.

IMPLEMENTATION:

```
int main()
{
  QueenBoard board;

  if (placeQueen(board, 0))
  {
    cout << board << endl;
  }
  else
  {
    cout << "Couldn't find solution" << endl;
  }
  return 0; // Terminate the program
} // end main()

bool placeQueen(QueenBoard& board, int col)
{
  for (int row = 0; row < 8; row += 1) // For all rows
  {
    if (!board.isCovered(row, col))     // Square available?
    {
      board.claim(row, col);              // Yes - claim it
      if (col == 7)                       // Final column?
      {
        return true;                        // Return true
      }
      if (placeQueen(board, col + 1))     // Place queens in
      {                                   //   rest of cols?
        return true;                        // Return true
      }
      board.relinquish(row, col);         // Relinquish
                                          //    position
    } // end if !isCovered
  } // end for row
  return false;                         // Return false
} // end placeQueen()
```

Now for the moment of truth. Does this program produce a solution to the eight queens problem? Here's the output.

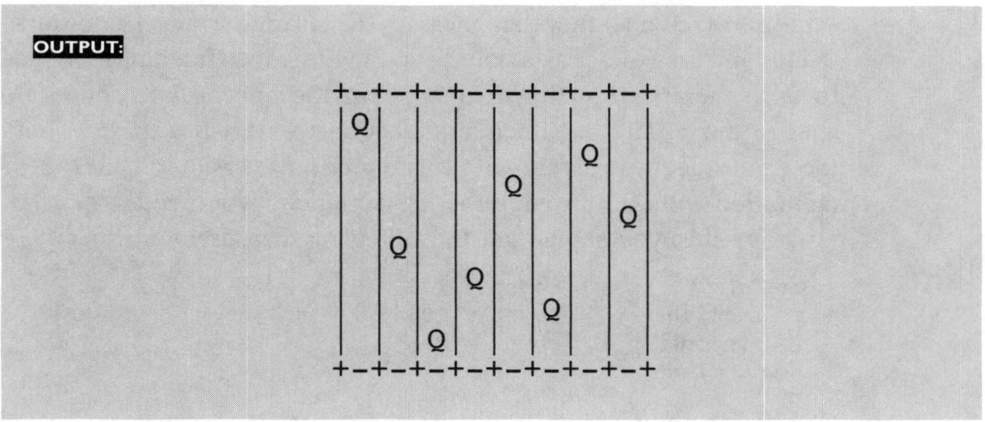

Checking by hand, this looks like a valid solution. So there's at least one solution to the eight queens problem.

So we're done? Not quite. Let's go back to the efficiency considerations raised during the early part of the implementation.

Refining the implementation

Earlier we discussed the trade-off between array element size and the computation time of the various member functions. If you've executed the above programs, you'll have seen that the first solution is generated almost instantaneously, so is efficiency a problem? If you only had to run the program once simply to get an answer (and you weren't going to be graded on how good your program is!) then this would be a good place to stop. However, what if this program had to be changed to work for a board that was 16 by 16 squares? What if the program was going to be used thousands of times an hour in some larger software system? What if you want to improve your grade for your submission? In all of these cases you'll want to consider the program and its efficiency.

The trade-off discussed earlier primarily covered the execution time differences caused by different implementations of the member functions, and the relative frequencies of execution of those functions. Clearly, it's important to have the most frequently-executed member functions being the most efficient. How can you determine these relative frequencies?

To perform this determination, you need to measure how many times each member function is called. Let's do this by temporarily changing the implementation code of `QueenBoard` to do some counting. Take a copy of `QueenBoard.c` (rather than mess up the current version), add some `int` private data members (to act as a count for each member function) and add statements to each member function to increment the appropriate counts. You can also change the `print(...)` member function to print out these counts. Rerunning the eight queens program with this temporary version of `QueenBoard`'s implementation will then provide the measurements you need.

Doing this, you should get the following measurements.

```
claim(...)          count = 113
relinquish(...)     count = 105
isCovered(...)      count = 876
isOccupied(...)     count = 0
```

Clearly, it's not worth spending time on optimizing `isOccupied(...)`![2] However, you can see that `isCovered(...)` has the heaviest usage and it may be worth optimizing its efficiency at the expense of that of the `claim(...)` and `relinquish(...)` member functions. As long as the average execution time of `claim(...)` and `relinquish(...)` is less than four times the average execution time of `isCovered(...)` (200 calls versus 800) you'll finish up with a gain in efficiency.

So it's probably worth investigating the implementation of `QueenBoard` that records in each element whether it's occupied, unoccupied, or covered by a queen elsewhere on the board. Sounds like a good end-of-chapter exercise.

You could perform additional detailed timing experiments to determine the actual execution times of the various implementations of the member functions. Some compilation systems allow you to perform **profiling** to show where execution time is spent. You'll have to look at your system manuals to find out how to do this, and we'll not go further here.

Similarly, there are other representations that you can use to represent the board and the covered rows, columns and diagonals. You'll have to apply experience and engineering to choose between the alternatives. But you can see how, in applying some engineering to improve your programs, you're beginning to move from being an apprentice to becoming a software engineer! Let's see how you get on with another problem.

[2] You may get a non-zero count for `isOccupied(...)` depending on where in `print(...)` you output its value; the `print(...)` member function uses `isOccupied(...)`.

EXERCISES FOR SECTION 16.1

1 Design and implement a recursive function `countQueens(...)` that counts the total number of solutions (without printing them out).

2 Design a representation for `QueenBoard` that makes use of only 1-D arrays (perhaps more than one such array). Hint: see if you can determine an algorithm for numbering the diagonals based on row, column coordinate pairs.

16.2 A SUPERMARKET CHECKOUT CASH REGISTER

Basic requirements analysis

The aim of this project is to simulate the workings of a supermarket checkout cash register. The approach to solving the problem is going to be very much top-down. You'll start with a brief description of the problem to be solved and gradually add detail. This is going to be far less daunting than starting with a full detailed description of the problem and taking a "big-bang" approach to a solution. Initially you'll be concerned with the types required to solve the problem. Having sorted the type requirements out, you'll start to concern yourself more with algorithmic aspects.

Let's begin with that brief description of the problem in hand.

PROBLEM:

You've been approached by the Save-A-Lot Supermarkets chain to write software for a checkout cash register. A checkout cash register processes the bar code that appears on the label of each of a customer's goods, and produces a receipt for that customer. The software is to run on the single register at the company's Main Street branch.

To solve the problem according to Save-A-Lot's requirements, you're going to need more detail than given here, but you've already got enough information to start thinking about the problem without worrying about all that detail, and this is a good place to start. When you have a clearer view of what the problem is and how you can solve it, that is the time to consider further details for the design and implementation of your program.

Lesson: When faced with a lengthy problem description, try to extract the essential high-level features of what's required, ignoring all the low-level details initially.

Given the above brief description of the problem, try to identify the types and objects that are likely to be required to solve this problem. To do this you need to recognize the nouns employed. In principle, all nouns suggest a type or object, with the use of the indefinite article ("a") suggesting a type and the definite article ("the") suggesting an object.

You should have identified:

- *the Save-A-Lot Supermarkets chain* and *the company's Main Street branch*;
  It definitely sounds like there are two objects here: one for the supermarket chain, and one for the Main Street branch. If you were being asked to computerize more than one of the operations of the Save-A-Lot company, you should seriously be thinking about designing types for these objects. However, you can safely ignore these objects since you're only supposed to be dealing with cash registers. If you get the cash register software right, then Save-A-Lot may well come back to you with more work.

- *a checkout cash register* and *the single register*;
  There's the suggestion here that you're going to need a type to represent a checkout register, and that the register at the Main Street branch is going to be an instance of that type. But what type of type should the checkout register type be? An `enum`, or a `struct` or a `class`? For the moment, the C++ type mechanism to use should be of no concern to you. You're still designing a solution to the problem. Further into the design phase, when you're closer to implementation, start thinking about the type mechanism to use. By then it should be obvious.

- *the bar code*;
  A bar code[3] is to be read by a bar code reader, so you're going to have to understand how to translate the information produced by the reader

[3] See End-of-chapter Exercise 6 for a description of a bar code. For the moment we're ignoring the check digit mentioned in that exercise.

(an optical input device) into something that can be recognized by your program. Maybe further details supplied with the problem specification will reveal that processing bar codes isn't quite as bad as it appears at first sight. But bar codes are clearly going to be an integral part of the program, so perhaps you're going to need a bar code type. But again, now isn't the time to think about precisely what C++ type mechanism you should use here.

- *a receipt*;
  On a supermarket receipt you expect to find lots on information that you probably don't care too much about; the name of the supermarket chain, the name of the store where the receipt was issued, the date of the purchases, the instruction to "Have a nice day" when the last thing you want to be doing on a Saturday morning is waiting at a checkout, and even the name of the checkout assistant. More importantly, you expect to find an itemized list of the goods purchased. It looks like you're going to need more information about what Save-A-Lot requires to appear on the receipt, and therefore further clarification of the problem specification. At first sight, it looks like you're going to need a type to represent a customer's receipt (but then again, maybe not, as you'll soon see).
- *the label* and *the goods*.
  While clearly of relevance to the physical situation in which a customer arrives at a checkout register to pay for goods, the operations of a can of baked beans and/or its packaging are not important here. You can safely ignore these nouns, other than recognize that there's some representation of each item purchased that needs to appear on the receipt. Again, maybe some further clarification will help here.

In summary, the main type requirements at the moment appear to be a checkout cash register, a bar code and a receipt.

Let's look at the checkout cash register type further and analyze the operations that are required. You've recognized that you'll need to declare an instance of this type, process bar codes and print a receipt. On the face of it, there's nothing else. So you can now think about producing an initial design diagram for the type `CashRegister`.

Before you produce a design for `CashRegister` you may care to think a little more about the problem. Take a trip to your local supermarket to see how the checkout works there. What happens when the register processes a bar code? Is there really a separate operation for printing the whole of a receipt? You'll probably discover that the receipt is printed as bar codes are read; a swipe of a bar code across the bar code reader results in output being sent to the receipt printer. The receipt is completed when the checkout assistant presses the "Total" button. There's also likely to be a button to signal that a new customer's goods are to be processed, resulting in some header message being printed on the receipt. Hence at no time is a receipt object required, so there doesn't appear to be a need for a receipt PDT. But maybe there's the need for a PDT to represent entries on the receipt? Further clarification is required.

Lesson: Inevitably problem specifications will be incomplete, and you'll be expected to use your intuition and experience to complete the missing details. Where possible, it's a good idea to go back to the client to check that you've made the correct assumptions. Involving the client in this way at an early stage is better than making (possibly false) assumptions and delivering software that doesn't match the client's expectations. Modifications to your software following delivery are likely to require extensive effort, particularly if a complete redesign is involved.

Proceeding under the assumption that Save-A-Lot accepts your interpretation of the specification, you come up with the following initial design for the PDT `CashRegister`.

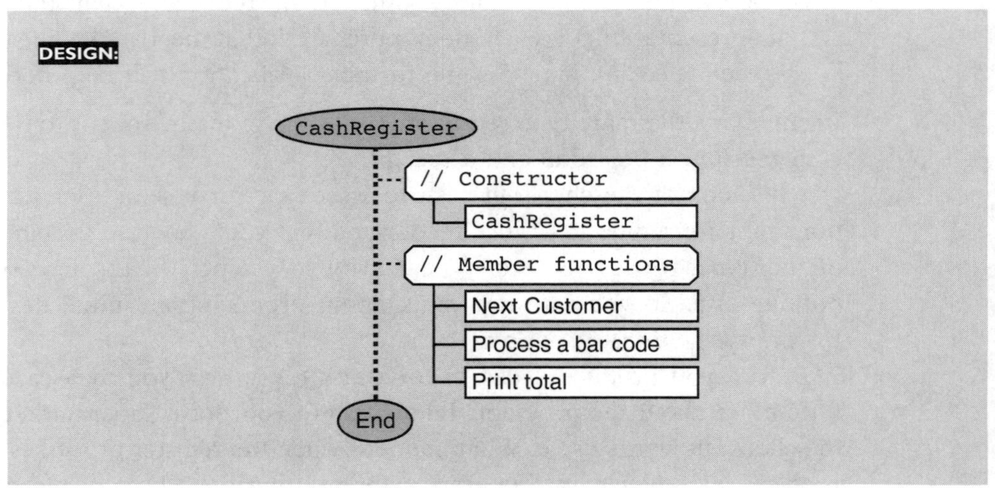

Since `CashRegister` isn't a numeric type (even if it's almost certainly going to have to deal with money in some way), we haven't included any member operators. We're not suggesting any I/O operators either, in the same way as we didn't feel it appropriate for `CDPlayer` to have I/O operators.

As yet there's no clear indication about the abstract values of a `CashRegister` instance, but they are likely to involve customer purchases in some way. Arguably the abstract values should also involve the total amount of money in the cash drawer, but this is not part of the requirements. To proceed further it's necessary to find out a little more about those requirements, particularly with respect to I/O.

You can also start to think about the basic structure of your program. It's important to make a clear distinction between the two different hardware systems involved here: the checkout assistant and the cash register.

The checkout assistant's view

DESIGN:

The checkout assistant's view is represented by Figure 16.4.

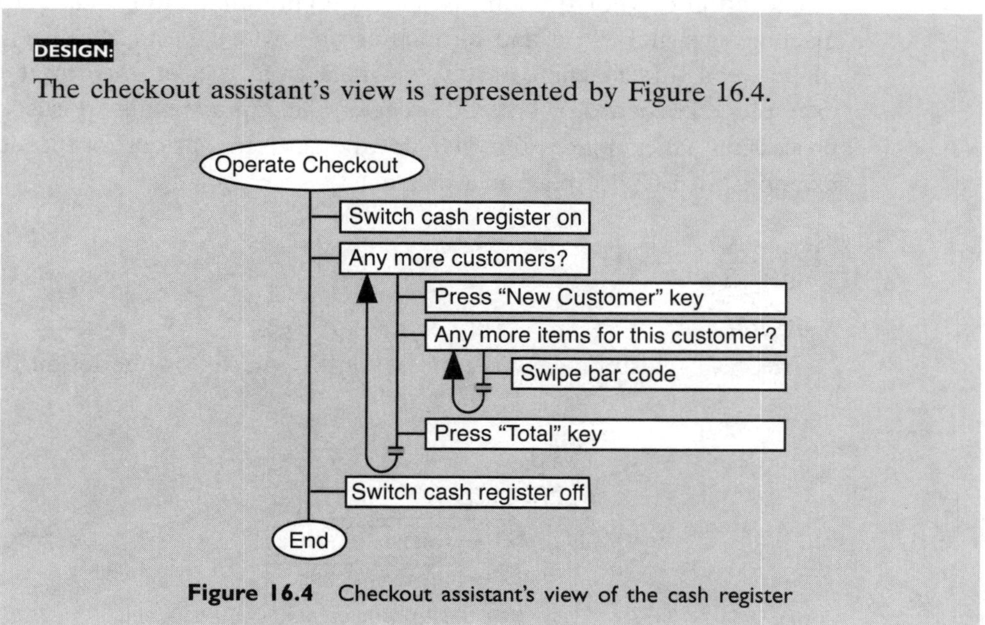

Figure 16.4 Checkout assistant's view of the cash register

The checkout assistant arrives at the register at the start of the day and switches the register on. At the end of the day, the assistant switches it off. In between, customers arrive at the checkout and for each customer the checkout assistant:

- presses a "Next Customer" key on the register keyboard to signal the arrival of a new customer;

- repeatedly swipes bar codes across the bar code reader until all the customer's goods have been processed;
- presses a "Total" key indicating that all the customer's goods have now been processed and the receipt may be completed.

(This is a simplified version of what might actually happen, but we don't want to get into swiping credit cards, dealing with money-back coupons, etc.)

If you were being asked to simulate the checkout assistant's view of a checkout register then this design would need to be converted into a definition of `main()`. However, the task here is to design software that will execute on the register itself; you need to look at the cash register's "view." However, the above design will help you to understand the order in which data is to be processed by the cash register software, and hence help you to prepare appropriate test data later on.

The cash register's view

A cash register is just a machine to be controlled by your program, so the model of execution of your program is that of a continuous loop that starts when the machine is switched on and terminates only when the machine is switched off. In between, the machine receives signals from the various input devices (for example, a keyboard or bar code reader). As input signals are recognized some processing takes place and signals are sent to various output devices (for example, an LCD display or a printer).

DESIGN:

The cash register's view is represented by the following design diagram.

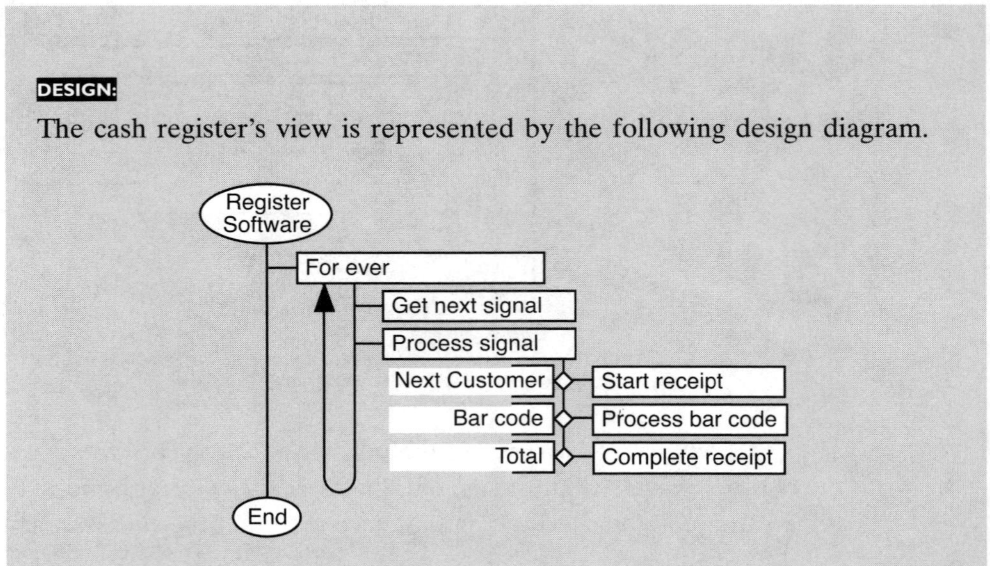

You should be able to make a connection between the checkout assistant's view and the cash register's view; if you don't, there may be a lot of angry customers at the checkout waiting for the assistant to come to terms with your software. The cash register software recognizes input of bar codes and use of the "Next Customer" and "Total" keys. You'll note that there's nothing in the cash register software that corresponds to the on/off operations identified in the checkout assistant's view. Switching the cash register on simply starts the software on the register running. Switching the cash register off terminates execution.

There's the question of how the receipt can be constructed by the "Process bar code" operation, but this requires more information about how Save-A-Lot expects the checkout register to operate. Again, you need to find out more about the I/O requirements of the overall software system.

I/O requirements

One of the main I/O requirements of the register software is the need to input bar codes. Save-A-Lot Supermarkets haven't yet purchased bar code readers, so bar codes have to be keyed in by the checkout assistant.

PROBLEM (CONTINUED):

For each item purchased by a customer, the corresponding bar code is to be input as a sequence of 11 digits.

But what does the software for a checkout register need to do with a bar code? Somehow there's a translation from a bar code to an item on the receipt that involves an update of the total cost of purchases to date. Before you can decide how to make that translation, you need to know what an item on the receipt looks like.

PROBLEM (CONTINUED):

For each customer, the receipt must consist of an itemized list of purchases, suitably annotated. A purchase must appear as the description of the item followed by the cost of the item. Some items are on special offer, according to Save-A-Lot's current pricing strategy:

1. Three-for-the-price-of-two;
   If a customer purchases three items of the same product that are subject to this offer then they pay for two only. The three items purchased must appear on the receipt in the normal manner. An additional entry on the receipt should indicate a refund of the cost of one item. The price should be preceded by a minus sign and the characters `CR` should follow immediately after the price.

2. Reduced-price.
   Reduced-price items are subject to a 25% reduction in price. The receipt entry for such an item should show the normal price and should then be followed by an appropriate refund entry along the lines of that for the three-for-the-price-of-two offer.

The receipt should clearly distinguish between the two types of refund. The list is to be terminated by the total amount to be paid by the customer.

EXAMPLE:

Thus a receipt might look like the following.

```
Save-A-Lot Superstores Inc.
***************************

Baked Beans                    0.95
Tomato Ketchup                 0.84
Baked Beans                    0.95
Tomato Ketchup                 0.84
Tomato Ketchup                 0.84
Refund (3 for 2)           -   0.84CR
Save-A-Lot Bran                2.75
Refund (reduced price)     -   0.68CR
Apprentice C++ Programmer      0.99
***********************************
Total                          6.64

Have a nice day!
```

Now that you're getting further into the details of the specification you're finding out that there are even more nouns involved:

- *a purchase*;
  It seems that you're going to need a type `Product` to represent a purchased product, with two components which correspond to the description of a product and its cost.

- *the cost*, *the price* and *the total amount payable*;
  Looks like you're going to need a type here to represent money. Since you're going to have to work out the total amount payable, some operation that permits the addition and subtractions of amounts of money will be necessary.

- *the description*;
  For the description of a product, all you need is a type to represent a character string. Maybe you'll be able to make use of an existing type here.

- *an itemized list*;
  A list is a collection of items, in this case a collection of instances of type `Product`. However, you've already made the design decision that the receipt is printed as bar codes are read. Hence there's no need internally for a type to represent an itemized list; the full receipt is going to exist on paper only.

- *Save-A-Lot's current pricing strategy*;
  You're going to need to be able to recognize the different pricing strategies employed by the store. There are two specifically mentioned above, corresponding to the three-for-two and reduced-price offers. If the "normal" price is also included as a possibility, that makes three options.

Now you know that a bar code has to be translated to a purchase item on the receipt, and that some items on the receipt correspond to refunds. But how can you make such a transformation? How can you associate a bar code with a product description and its cost? How do you determine which items are on special offer? You need to go back to Save-A-Lot for more details.

Initialization

The final information you require from Save-A-Lot concerns the stock information: details about the products on sale in Save-A-Lot's supermarkets.

PROBLEM (CONTINUED):

Details of the products stocked by Save-A-Lot supermarkets are stored in a text data file. The first line of the file consists of four column headings, followed on separate lines by a list of the information about each stock item. For each stock item there are four pieces of information:

1. The bar code for the item (for example, `01649921551`).
2. A description for the item (for example, `Baked_Beans`). An underscore is always used as a word separator.
3. The normal unit cost of an item (for example, 0.65).
4. An offer status indicating any special offer that may apply. Possibilities are:
   a) *normal* the normal price applies;
   b) *three-for-two* buy any two items and get a third free;
   c) *reduced* a 25% reduction.

So, for example, the first few lines of the stock data file might look like:

```
Bar Code       Stock Description    Price Per Unit    Offer
01649921551    Baked_Beans          0.95              NORMAL
06780284967    Tomato_Ketchup       0.84              THREE_FOR_TWO
05472122113    Save-A-Lot_Bran      2.75              REDUCED_PRICE
```

There's at least one space separator between each component of the data for a particular stock item. An underscore is used as a word separator in the product description and in the price status, simply to make the input of product descriptions more straightforward than might otherwise be the case.

There are yet more nouns introduced by this further clarification of Save-A-Lot's requirements, the most important being:

- *the information about each stock item*;
  You're going to need to use this information since it provides the key for a transformation from a bar code to a product item. Given a bar code you need to look up the product description, price per unit and price offer status in order to produce the appropriate receipt item.

- *a list.*
  You've decided that a list of purchases is unnecessary, so is a list of stock items necessary? In principle, no, since you can always perform a search on the data file. However, I/O operations tend to be very time-

consuming compared with non-I/O operations and hence there are good reasons for introducing an object that represents the whole stock.

Does that complete the types you require to solve the problem? Possibly, but as you develop the design you may discover that there are other types that you need. You've identified all the types initially suggested by the problem specification, so it's time to move on to some of the implementation aspects.

Type definitions

Your approach to the identification of types was very much top-down; you identified the need for a PDT to represent a cash register and realized that for its implementation you required PDTs for a bar code, a product, a stock item, money, a product description and the offer status. Because of the dependencies of one PDT on another, it makes sense to implement the PDTs bottom-up. Get the money and description PDTs working and you can implement the PDT for the product. Get the bar code and offer status PDTs working and you can implement the stock item PDT; get all these working and you can implement the PDT for the cash register. It may be that you don't get things right first time. For example, when developing the cash register PDT you may find that there's a money PDT operation that you need but haven't provided for. Refinements like this are inevitable, but if you've given plenty of thought to the design of your PDTs, there shouldn't be too many afterthoughts to deal with. And using PDTs should make subsequent additions easier to cope with.

As you implement your PDTs, so you should thoroughly test them. Hence whenever you introduce a new PDT that makes use of existing PDTs, you'll have confidence that any bugs detected are likely to be in the recently-added code for your new PDTs, rather than in tried-and-tested implementations of your earlier PDTs.

Let's start with the `OfferStatus` PDT. A simple `enum` is sufficient here. Anything else associated with this PDT? Well, it's likely that you're going to want to perform some I/O involving instances of this PDT, so why not produce definitions for the I/O operators. It's clear from the problem specification that you're going to need an input operator to read in the stock information, part of which involves the offer status. At present there doesn't appear to be any need for an output operator, but a later refinement of the problem (see Exercise 1 at the end of this section) may require this operator, so you may as well implement it now. In any case, you're probably going to want to use an output operator for testing your implementation of the `OfferStatus` PDT, and PDTs that use `OfferStatus`. So let's complete the definition of the `OfferStatus` PDT and leave you to provide the implementation of the I/O operators.

DEFINITION:

```
enum OfferStatus {NORMAL, THREE_FOR_TWO, REDUCED_PRICE};

istream& operator>>(istream& inStream,  OfferStatus& forInput);
ostream& operator<<(ostream& outStream, OfferStatus  value);
```

In many ways, a PDT `Money` to represent money will be similar to the `Duration` PDT developed in Chapter 13, with arithmetic and Boolean operators, I/O operators, public member functions to yield whole numbers of dollars or cents, etc. Since the `Money` PDT is so similar to the `Duration` PDT, we'll leave it to you to develop a detailed design. (If you've completed Exercise 4 at the end of Chapter 13 you'll already have a design, and an implementation too.) We're confident that your design will match the interface assumed later. To solve the Save-A-Lot problem you're probably not going to require a full set of operations. So should you restrict yourself to just the ones you need? No, you should provide a reasonably full set of operations so that your PDT can be used in a wide variety of situations. It's just possible that you'll be able to reuse your `Money` PDT elsewhere, so the time invested now is likely to pay off in the future.

You've recognized that all you need for the product description is a type to represent a character string. Fortunately there's one already available: `Text`. That'll do nicely.

Now that you've got the description and a `Money` PDT sorted out you can implement a PDT for a product – `Product`. You're going to need an output operator for this PDT for the purposes of printing the receipt. It's difficult to envisage any operations on instances of type `Product`, so here a simple `struct` will suffice. You may as well provide an input operator while you're at it.

DEFINITION:

```
struct Product
{
  Text description;
  Money price;
};

istream& operator>>(istream& inStream,  Product& forInput);
ostream& operator<<(ostream& outStream, Product  value);
```

Next the bar code. You know that a bar code can be represented as a sequence of digits. An `enum` doesn't appear appropriate here, unless you want to have one that covers all possible bar codes! A `struct` might be appropriate if you wanted to break the bar code down into its constituent parts, but this doesn't seem necessary here. What about a `class`? Well, it's not clear that there are any operations you might want to implement. Add two bar codes together? Hardly. Or multiply a bar code by a `double`? Not really. So a new PDT is probably not required here. Can you make use of any existing types? An `int`? Possibly, but you could have problems with a bar code being greater than the largest integer representable. A `Text` object looks more sensible, and as you'll see later, this proves to be a wise choice.

Having sorted out PDTs for the offer status, a product and a bar code, you can define the PDT for a stock item. As with the PDT `Product`, it's difficult to think of any operations on this PDT,[4] so a simple `struct` will again do. You're going to need an input operator for this PDT so that you can use it when reading the stock data file. You may as well provide an output operator since you may need it for testing purposes, if nothing else.

DEFINITION:

```
struct StockItem
{
  Text        barCode;
  Product     product;
  OfferStatus currentStatus;
};

istream& operator>>(istream& inStream,  StockItem& forInput);
ostream& operator<<(ostream& outStream, StockItem  value);
```

Now that you've got all the basic PDTs sorted out, you can start thinking about the main PDT – `CashRegister`.

PDT CashRegister

Earlier in this section we looked at the design for the interface of the `CashRegister` PDT. Now's the time to answer the question "What type of

[4] At least, as far as the Save-A-Lot specification is concerned. However, there's plenty of scope for developing a more comprehensive `StockItem` PDT.

type should the checkout register type be?" A simple enum looks inappropriate since there are more than simple values involved here. A struct looks inappropriate too, since your design suggests you plan to support operations on instances of the PDT. So class appears to be the correct C++ mechanism to use.

Recall that apart from a constructor, the design provides for three public member functions: a function to process a bar code (let's call it processBarCode(...)), a function to print the final total (printTotal()), and a function to prepare the receipt for the next customer (nextCustomer()). Do you need I/O operators? Probably not.

You now have a first draft of your PDT definition.

DEFINITION I:

```
class CashRegister
{
  public:

    // Constructor
    CashRegister();

    // Public member functions
    void nextCustomer();
    bool processBarCode(Text barCode);
    void printTotal();

  private:

    // To be completed
};
```

Rightly, you haven't yet given too much thought to the private data of the class, but since the member functions (and constructor) are going to manipulate the private data, now's a good time to start thinking about the internal representation.

It's not clear that a checkout register has any "value" as such. However, you know that processBarCode(...) needs to have access to details of the stock list. Since the stock list is a collection of items of the same type, you can use the Array PDT here. Making this array part of the private member variables of the

CashRegister PDT means that only instances of this PDT can manipulate the list. So include in the private data the declaration:

```
Array<StockItem> stockList;
```

Associated with this array there will be a size, but you don't know in advance how big the stock list is. This implies two things. Somewhere you're going to need to set the array to be of a sufficiently large size that your program will be able to deal with Save-A-Lot's requirements, but this is an implementation issue so put it to one side for the moment. Second, you're going to need to keep track of the number of items in the array, so you'll need a private member variable numberOfStockItems for this purpose. Hence include the declaration:

```
int numberOfStockItems;
```

The member function printTotal(...) needs to have available the total cost of the goods purchased. Hence introduce the private member variable:

```
Money totalPurchaseCost;
```

There's one further item whose need for inclusion in the private data may not be immediately obvious. Think about how you're going to deal with the three-for-two offer. When the bar code of a product subject to this offer is read, you're going to have to check whether this is the third item of that product to be purchased. To do this implies the need to keep a count. You're going to need a collection of counts, and although this can be restricted to items subject to the three-for-two offer, it's computationally easier to have a potential count for all stock items (another example of a time/space trade-off). It's possible that you could make use of this count in other circumstances. So add to the private section the declaration:

```
Array<int> purchaseCount;
```

The public member function nextCustomer(...) will need to reset the entries in this array. It will also need to print out the header for the next customer's receipt, and consequently need to know where to output this message. Because of this, and the requirement to read the initial stock data in, add two further items to the private section:

```
istream_withassign server;
ostream_withassign printer;
```

Note that server (the source stream for the stock data) is declared to be of type istream_withassign, rather than istream. The reasons for this need not concern you, since you can regard the types `istream_withassign` and `istream` as being compatible. Similar arguments apply to the type of `printer` (the stream source for the output of items to appear on the receipt). You could set the value of `server` and `printer` using a constructor that takes two parameters, or provide a member function for this purpose. Let's take the latter approach and add a public member function `setStreams(...)` and a private member variable `streamsSet`, whose value can be tested to ensure that a call to `setStreams(...)` has been made before any other operation is allowed.

Time for a second draft of your PDT definition.

DEFINITION 2:

```
class CashRegister
{
  public:

    // Constructor
    CashRegister();

    // Public member functions
    void nextCustomer();
    bool processBarCode(Text barCode);
    void printTotal();
    void setStreams(istream& inStream, ostream& outStream);

  private:

    // Private member variables
    Array<StockItem>    stockList;
    Array<int>          purchaseCount;
    int                 numberOfStockItems;
    Money               totalPurchaseCost;
    istream_withassign server;
    ostream_withassign printer;
    bool                streamsSet;
};
```

Note that the parameters to `setStreams(...)` are of type `istream&` and `ostream&` respectively. When you're testing the code you can use `cin` and `cout` as actual parameters, but when it comes to a "production run" the actual parameters can be file I/O streams, emphasizing further the inheritance relationship between the various I/O streams PDTs mentioned in Chapter 15.

Now that the private data has been decided upon, let's start thinking about the member functions in the public section of the class.

First the constructor. Recall that any declaration of a `CashRegister` variable results in a call to an appropriate constructor, and it's often the case that a constructor performs some form of initialization. In the context of the problem in hand, you need to:

- set the size of the arrays `stockList` and `purchaseCount`;
- initialize `streamsSet` to `false`.

Here's an implementation for the constructor that achieves these two tasks.

IMPLEMENTATION:

```
CashRegister::CashRegister()
{
  stockList.setSize(MAX_STOCK);
  purchaseCount.setSize(MAX_STOCK);
  streamsSet = false;
  return;
} // end CashRegister()
```

What is `MAX_STOCK`? It's a constant whose principal purpose is to set the size of the arrays. Further discussions with Save-A-Lot indicate that the number of different stock items is limited to 100, so you need the declaration

```
const int MAX_STOCK = 100;
```

In line with adopted style rules, this declaration should be global in the class implementation file.

The implementation of `setStreams(...)` is straightforward.

IMPLEMENTATION:

```
void CashRegister::setStreams(istream& inStream,
                              ostream& outStream)
{
  server      = inStream;
  printer     = outStream;
  streamsSet = true;
  readStockDetails();
  return;
} // end setStreams()
```

"Wait a minute. You told me in Chapter 15 that while I can use a value of type `istream_withassign` wherever one of type `istream` is required, the converse isn't true. So how come the following assignment is allowed?"

```
server = inStream
```

An excellent question. You're beginning to understand inheritance. It so happens that there's an assignment operator for PDT `istream_withassign` that takes an `istream` as its right-hand operand.

What's this function `readStockDetails()`? It's a private member function of `CashRegister`. We're going to leave you to fill in the details, but since you already have an input operator for the `StockItem` PDT, and a declaration for the array containing the list of stock details, this should be reasonably straightforward. Produce a design based on a repetition statement and then implement the function using a `while` statement that terminates when end-of-file is encountered. We suggest that you make use of a private member function `void addToStockList(StockItem nextItem)` (which again we've left you to write a definition for) that puts a stock item read into the array `stockList`.

What about initialization of the array `purchaseCount`? Or of the two variables `totalPurchaseCost` and `numberOfStockItems`? By reading the stock details in, you can find out how many items of stock there are, so the variable `numberOfStockItems` should have been set by the execution of `readStockDetails()` in the body of `setStreams(...)` The variables `purchaseCount` and `totalPurchaseCount` will need to be reset for each new customer receipt, so let's take a look at the functions that control the printing of the receipt.

As already indicated, `nextCustomer()` needs to initialize the array of counts of products sold. Additionally it should print a header for the receipt.

IMPLEMENTATION:

```
void CashRegister::nextCustomer()
{
  streamsOK();
  for (int nextStockItem = 0;
       nextStockItem < numberOfStockItems;
       nextStockItem += 1 )
  {
    purchaseCount(nextStockItem) = 0;     // Reset  counts
  }

  // Print receipt header
  printer << "Save-A-Lot Superstores Inc." << endl
          << "***************************" << endl << endl;

  totalPurchaseCost = Money(0, 0);
  return;
} // end nextCustomer()
```

The call to `streamsOK()` – a private member function – checks the value of the `streamsSet` flag and terminates execution if the value is `false`.

IMPLEMENTATION:

```
void CashRegister::streamsOK()
{
  if (!streamsSet)
  {
    error("Server and printer streams not set");
  }
  return;
} // end streamsOK()
```

The member function `printTotal()` needs to print the total purchase cost and a friendly farewell message. Since the format of the entry on the receipt corresponding to the total is identical to that for a purchase item, you can treat the "Total" entry as a product and make use of the output operator for the `Product` PDT, ensuring consistency of alignment on the receipt.

IMPLEMENTATION:

```
void CashRegister::printTotal()
{
  streamsOK();

  Product total;

  total.description   = "Total";
  total.price         = totalPurchaseCost;

  printer << "**********************************" << endl
          << total              << endl  << endl
          << "Have a nice day!" << endl;
  return;
} // end printTotal()
```

All you're left with now is a definition for the member function `processBarCode(...)`. Compared with the other member functions, it's less clear what this function should do, and so it's back to the design drawing board before you start to think about implementation aspects.

First, there's the need to associate a bar code read with a particular stock item as represented in the array `stockList`. In addition, you have to take into account any price offers that may be associated with the product. Let's produce a design that recognizes these complications.

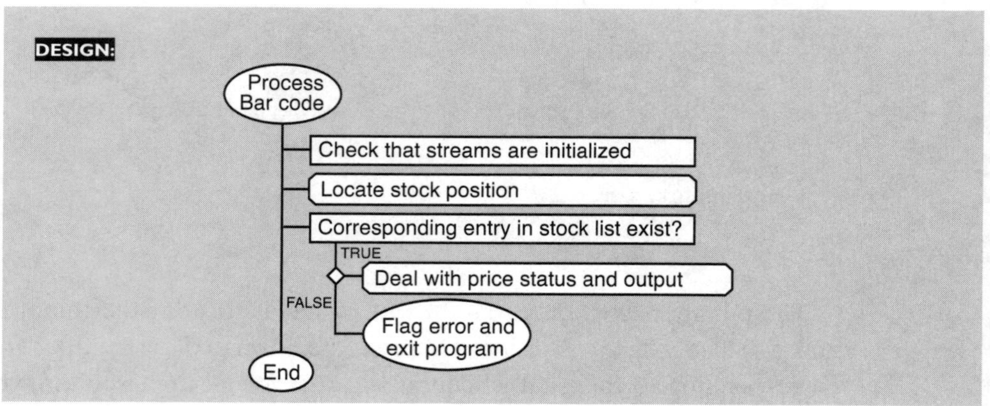

The most direct way of locating the item in the stock list corresponding to the bar code read uses a technique known as a **linear search**. Starting with the first item in the array `stockList`, you compare the bar code read with the bar code of the array item. If the bar codes agree, you've found the item you're searching for, otherwise move on to the next array item and perform another comparison. Repeat this process until you locate the bar code you're looking for. You're interested in the location (array subscript) of the sought bar code in the array, so use a `for` statement with an exit when you've located the required item – a successful search. The value of the loop counter at the point of exit is the required array index.

It's a good idea to employ some defensive programming techniques here. It's just possible that the bar code read doesn't match the bar code of an item in the stock data; maybe the checkout operator typed in the wrong bar code; or maybe Save-A-Lot's stock data file is incomplete. In the event of an unsuccessful search, you need to report an error. You will know that the search is unsuccessful when you test the last item in the stock list array and you still haven't located the bar code you're looking for. The following diagram encapsulates these ideas.

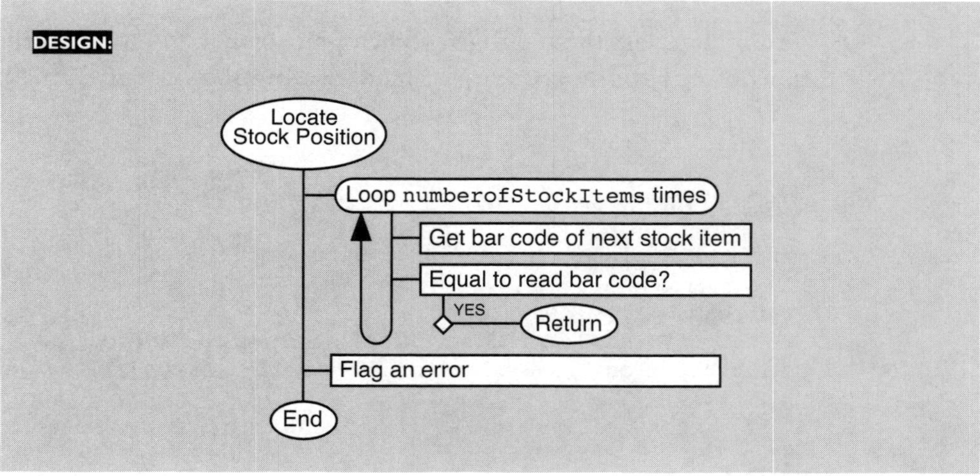

Now for an expansion of the Deal with price status and output box shown in an earlier diagram. This is reasonably straightforward. You need to print on the receipt an entry for the item purchased, plus a further entry if the product is subject to any special price offer.

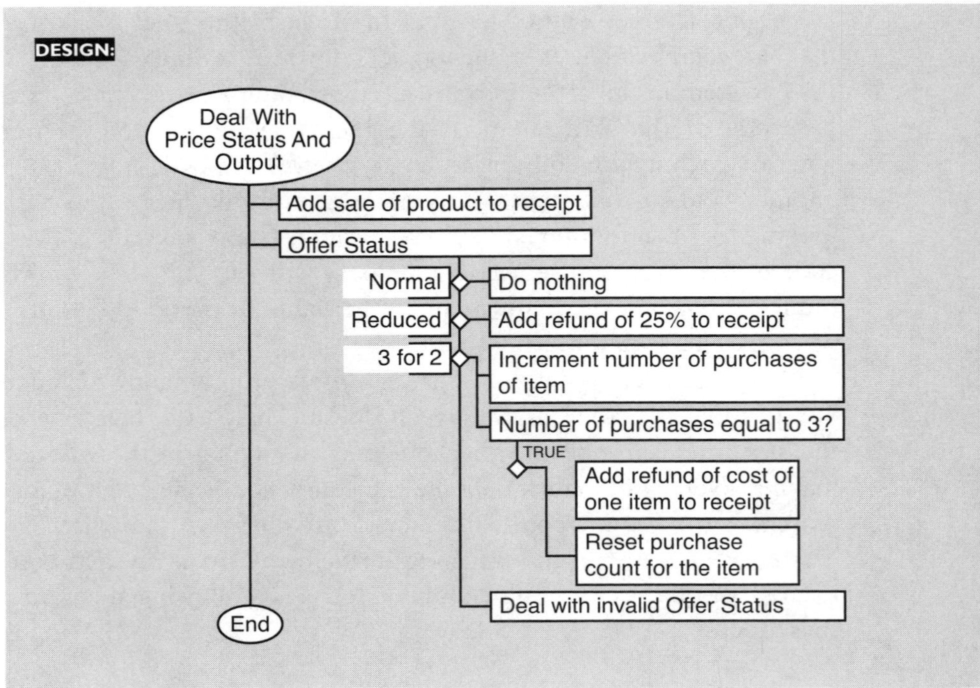

From these last three designs you can now generate the following implementations of `processBarCode(...)` and `locateStockPosition()`.

IMPLEMENTATION:

```
bool CashRegister::processBarCode(Text barCode)
{
  streamsOK();
  // Locate stock position corresponding to bar-code
  int stockPosition = locateStockPosition(barCode);

  if (stockPosition >= 0)  // Corresponding entry in stock
                           //   list exists?
  {
    // Deal with price status and output
    // Add sale of product to receipt
    Product nextPurchase;

    nextPurchase       = stockList(stockPosition).product;
```

```
totalPurchaseCost += nextPurchase.price;

// Output the purchase details
printer << nextPurchase << endl;

// Check for special price offer status
switch (stockList(stockPosition).currentStatus)
{
  case NORMAL:
    break;
  case THREE_FOR_TWO:
    {
      // Increment number of purchases of the item
      purchaseCount(stockPosition) += 1;
      // Number of purchases equals 3?
      if (purchaseCount(stockPosition) == 3)
      {
        // Add refund of cost of one item to receipt
        Product refund;

        refund.description = "Refund (3 for 2)        -";
        refund.price       = nextPurchase.price;
        totalPurchaseCost -= refund.price;
        printer << refund << "CR" << endl;
        purchaseCount(stockPosition) = 0; // Reset count
      }
    }
    break;
  case REDUCED_PRICE:
    {
      // Add refund of 25% to receipt
      Product refund;

      refund.description  = "Refund (reduced price)  -";
      refund.price        = nextPurchase.price * DISCOUNT;
      totalPurchaseCost  -=  refund.price;
      printer << refund << "CR" << endl;
    }
    break;
  default:
    {
      // Defensive check
      error("Unrecognized price status");
    }
    break;
}
return true;
```

```
  }
  else
  {
    // Flag error and exit program
    error("Barcode does not correspond to any item in stock");
    return false;
  }
} // end processBarCode()

int CashRegister::locateStockPosition(Text barCode)
{
  streamsOK();
  for (int stockPosition = 0;
           stockPosition < numberOfStockItems;
           stockPosition += 1)
  {
    if (barCode == stockList(stockPosition).barCode)
    {
      return stockPosition;
    }
  }
  return -1;
} // end locateStockPosition()
```

The definition of the member function `processBarCode(...)` makes use of the update operators += and -= for the `Money` PDT. When you implemented the `Money` PDT, you did provide an implementation of these operators, didn't you? If not, you'd better go back and do it now. What is `DISCOUNT`? It's a constant `double` declared global to the PDT implementation whose value is set to 0.25.

The Flag an error operation of Locate Stock Position has been implemented by returning sentinel subscript (–1) from `locateStockPosition(...)`. It's then left to the function `processBarCode(...)` to decide how to deal with this error. Terminating execution when the checkout assistant types in an invalid bar code, as the code above shows, may seem a little harsh. Maybe in a later version you'll be a little more tolerant and allow the assistant to reenter the bar code.

In the process of implementing the PDT `CashRegister`, we found it useful to introduce a number of private member functions. These functions represent well-defined operations, and the use of these functions has made it easier to write (and read) the definitions of the public member functions. Now that all definitions are complete, let's have a final look at the PDT `CashRegister` interface, to be placed in the header file `CashRegister.h`, with the interfaces of the private member functions included.

DEFINITION:

```
#ifndef CASHREGISTER_H
#define CASHREGISTER_H

#include <iostream.h>
#include "Array.h"
#include "bool.h"
#include "Money.h"
#include "StockItem.h"
#include "Product.h"

class CashRegister
{
  public:

    // Constructor
    CashRegister();

    // Public member functions
    void nextCustomer();
    bool processBarCode(Text barCode);
    void printTotal();
    void setStreams(istream& inStream, ostream& outStream);

  private:

    // Private member functions
    void addToStockList(StockItem nextItem);
    int  locateStockPosition(Text barCode);
    void readStockDetails();
    void streamsOK();

    // Private member variables
    Array<StockItem>            stockList;
    Array<int>                  purchaseCount;
    int                         numberOfStockItems;
    Money                       totalPurchaseCost;
    istream_withassign          server;
    ostream_withassign          printer;
    bool                        streamsSet;
};

#endif
```

Almost finished. To complete the task in hand you need to write a main program for a complete system test using the checkout assistant's view as expressed by the design in Figure 16.4. You can use the supplied files for examples of test data, but you should also generate some test data of your own. You also need to write some documentation for your code, or, rather, you need to complete the documentation that you started to write when you produced your initial designs :-).

EXERCISES FOR SECTION 16.2

1 Provide implementations of the I/O operators for PDT `OfferStatus`.

2 Design and implement a PDT `Money`.

3 Provide implementations of the I/O operators for PDT `Product`.

4 Provide implementations of the I/O operators for PDT `StockItem`.

5 Complete the definitions of the member functions of PDT `CashRegister`.

6 Write a test program for your implementation of PDT `CashRegister`.

SUMMARY

That's it! Just take some time to reflect on the elements of C++ that you've employed in the solutions to the two problems: new PDTs – `class`, `struct` and `enum`; control abstractions – selection statements (`switch` and `if`), repetition statements (`while` and `for`), and built-in control statements (`break` and `return`); functions; expressions, declarations and I/O; and comments. In fact, the solutions to these apparently simple problems involves practically the entire range of C++ that you've covered in this book. And, of course, there are lots of software engineering aspects that have gone into the solutions too.

Time to celebrate. Off to the supermarket to buy a chessboard and few bottles of "milk." While you're there, see if you can interest the management in some software for the checkout cash registers.

END-OF-CHAPTER EXERCISES

1 Change the implementation of `QueenBoard` so that each element records whether it's occupied, unoccupied, or covered by a queen elsewhere on the board. Compare the execution time of the program from Section 16.1, Exercise 1 using the old and new implementations of `QueenBoard`. Some systems have library functions that permit you to read the system's clock (see Section 9.2), so your program can measure its own execution time; alternatively, use your wrist watch. Do the different implementations result in any appreciable timing differences?

2 Change `QueenBoard` so that it works for different-sized (square) boards. Add a member function `setSize(int size)` to initialize the board's size. Change your `main()` program to solve the *N* queens problem. Determine the total number of solutions for values of *N* from 2 to 10. What do you notice about the execution time of this program for the larger values of *N*?

3 Many of the solutions generated for the eight queens problem turn out to be rotations or reflections of each other. Design and implement a version of the *N* queens problem that eliminates any solutions that are rotations or reflections of an already obtained solution, and prints out only the unique solutions.

4 The managing director of Save-A-Lot supermarkets is so impressed with your work that she has asked you to extend your software. For each stock item there's an additional entry that indicates the number of items of stock available at the beginning of the working day. Make modifications to your PDTs `StockItem` and `CashRegister` to take this enhancement into account. In particular, define an output function for the PDT `CashRegister` that writes out the stock information, taking into account the purchases that have been made. Additionally, make further modifications that ensure that in `printTotal()` you print out the total amount of money saved on special offers.

5 Save-A-Lot Supermarkets plan to invest in a new model of the checkout cash register. This new model has an additional key "Subtotal." Pressing this key prints out the total cost of items on the receipt so far. Modify your PDTs accordingly.

6 Various formats are used for bar codes, of which the most popular is the Universal Product Code (UPC). A UPC is represented on a product as lines of various thicknesses to be read by a bar code reader, accompanied by all but the

last of the digits that correspond to those lines. In a UPC there are 12 digits. The first digit is a generic product type code (for example, 0 for groceries), the next five digits correspond to a particular product, the next five digits after that correspond to a manufacturer, and the final digit (which isn't printed, only the bar line representation for that digit) is a check digit that can be used to assess the validity of the UPC. To check a UPC you need to take the digits one by one. Counting the first digit as being in position zero, add the digits in the even positions and multiply by 3. Add to this the sum of the digits in the odd positions, including the check digit. The total sum should be a multiple of 10, otherwise the UPC is invalid.

For example, given the UPC `016499215514` form the sum

```
3 (0 + 6 + 9 + 2 + 5 + 1) + 1 + 4 + 9 + 1 + 5 + 4 = 90
```

so this UPC is valid.

Modify the supplied data files so that the bar codes used correspond to the UPC format. Make modifications to the member functions of `CashRegister` so that whenever a bar code is read its validity is checked.

7 Save-A-Lot stores have introduced a new promotion gimmick; buy an item of one product and get an item of another product at a 50% discount. This pairing of goods is to be indicated in the stock data file by the offer status `PAIRED`, which is followed (after a space) by the bar code of the corresponding other product. The discount is given on the cost of the lower-priced item. Make changes to `OfferStatus`, `StockItem` and `CashRegister` to accommodate these modifications.

8 A simple modification of the search technique used in `locateStockItem (...)` employs a sentinel. (The idea is similar to the use of sentinels introduced in Chapter 10.) Each time you search for a bar code, insert that bar code into the next free array position (with index `numberOfStockItems`). All searches are then "successful," except that if the index located has the same value as `numberOfStockItems`, then the search is in reality unsuccessful. Using this technique, replace the `for` statement in `locateStockItem (...)` with a `while` repetition statement. What do you perceive to be the advantages of this approach?

9 Your local library is offering a contract for the purchase of computer software, written in C++, that will store details of the books in its small collection. For each book the following information is to be recorded.

```
Title
Name of author(s)
ISBN
Status
```

The first three items are to be stored as character strings, the fourth as an enumerated type representing the values `In stock` and `Out on loan`.

Data for the software will consist of a number of commands, one per line. Each command, specified in terms of a keyword in upper-case letters, is followed (on zero or more separate lines) by information relating to that command, which may include the book title, the name of the author(s) and the ISBN (International Standard Book Number). Each of these quantities (title, names, ISBN) appears on a separate line. Hence the full details of a book may be given as:

```
The Apprentice C++ Programmer: A Touch of Class
Lee, P.A. and Phillips, C.
1850321604
```

Note that the ISBN does not include any separating hyphens or spaces.

Your program should recognize the following commands.

`ADD`
Add a book to the collection. The information provided consists of the book title, name of author(s), and ISBN.

`TAKE`
Take out a book from the collection. The information provided consists of the book title only.

`RETURN`
Return a book to the collection. The information provided consists of the book title only.

`FINDTITLE`
Look for a book title in the collection. The information provided consists of the book title only.

`FINDAUTHOR`
Look for all books written by an author in the collection. The information provided consists of the author's name.

`LIST`
Print a full list of all books in the collection, ordered according to alphabetical order of book titles. No further information is provided.

Whenever a new book is added to the collection, the ISBN should be checked for validity. To do this you need to form an integer from the ten characters of the ISBN. These are always digits, except that the final character may be an `X`, representing 10. For each digit, multiply by the position in the ISBN and accumulate the sum. If the ISBN is correct then the sum is a multiple of 11. For example, the sum for *The Apprentice C++ Programmer: A Touch of Class*, with ISBN 1850321604, is 1*1+2*8+3*5+4*0+5*3+6*2+7*1+8*6+9*0+10*4 = 154 = 14*11. If the ISBN is incorrect then this should be reported and the book details should not be recorded. [*Publisher's note:* the ISBN for the American edition of this book is 0534 953395.]

10 The leader of your local children's playgroup wishes to recruit your services to electronically process the financial records that they have kept on behalf of the playgroup for the calendar year 1996 with the aim of producing a final balance sheet. The records consist of opening balances kept in cash and in a bank account, followed by a sequence of transactions. For each transaction, there is a date in the form `dd/mm/yy` where each of `dd`, `mm` and `yy` is a two-digit integer, a character string giving a description of the transaction, followed by two amounts of money indicating the change made to the cash and bank account balances. Money, in dollars and cents, is indicated by a decimal number with two digits after the decimal point. Amounts to be added to the balances are indicated by a positive sign; those to be deducted are indicated by a negative sign. All amounts of money are separated from each other, and from the string description, by a vertical bar. So, for example, the few first lines of the records might look like

```
                                     Cash          Bank
Opening Balances:               |   +20.23  |   +1024.96  |
                                |           |             |
01/01/95    Room rental         |           |    -250.00  |
02/01/95    Christmas Fayre     |   +33.21  |    +323.25  |
04/01/95    Santa's presents    |           |     -58.27  |
```

The absence of a figure in either the Cash or Bank column indicates that there is no change to the appropriate balance for that transaction. For some transactions, the description is given as `Transfer`, indicating a transfer of funds from cash to the bank account, or vice versa. Thus, for example, the entry:

```
04/01/96 Transfer               |   +58.20  |     -58.20  |
```

indicates a transfer of $58.20 from the bank account to cash. The final balance sheet should list all transactions resulting in income (without dates), followed by all transactions which resulted in expenditure (again, without dates). For each transaction there should be a single (unsigned) figure giving the total amount credited or debited; for example, given the above data, the list of transactions showing income should include:

```
Christmas Fayre                                    356.46
```

Income should include annual interest credited by the bank at the rate of 1.5% of the lowest balance held at any time in the year. The income and expenditure listings should be followed by a summary giving the opening and closing balances and the net changes.

Define and test a class to represent the playgroup's accounts. Provide operations to:

(a) initialize the balances;
(b) store the details of an income or expenditure transaction, without the date but with the total amount of the transaction, and update the balances;
(c) update the balances in response to a transfer transaction;
(d) add interest at the current rate;
(e) produce the final balance sheet.

Appendix A
Alphabetic syntax diagrams

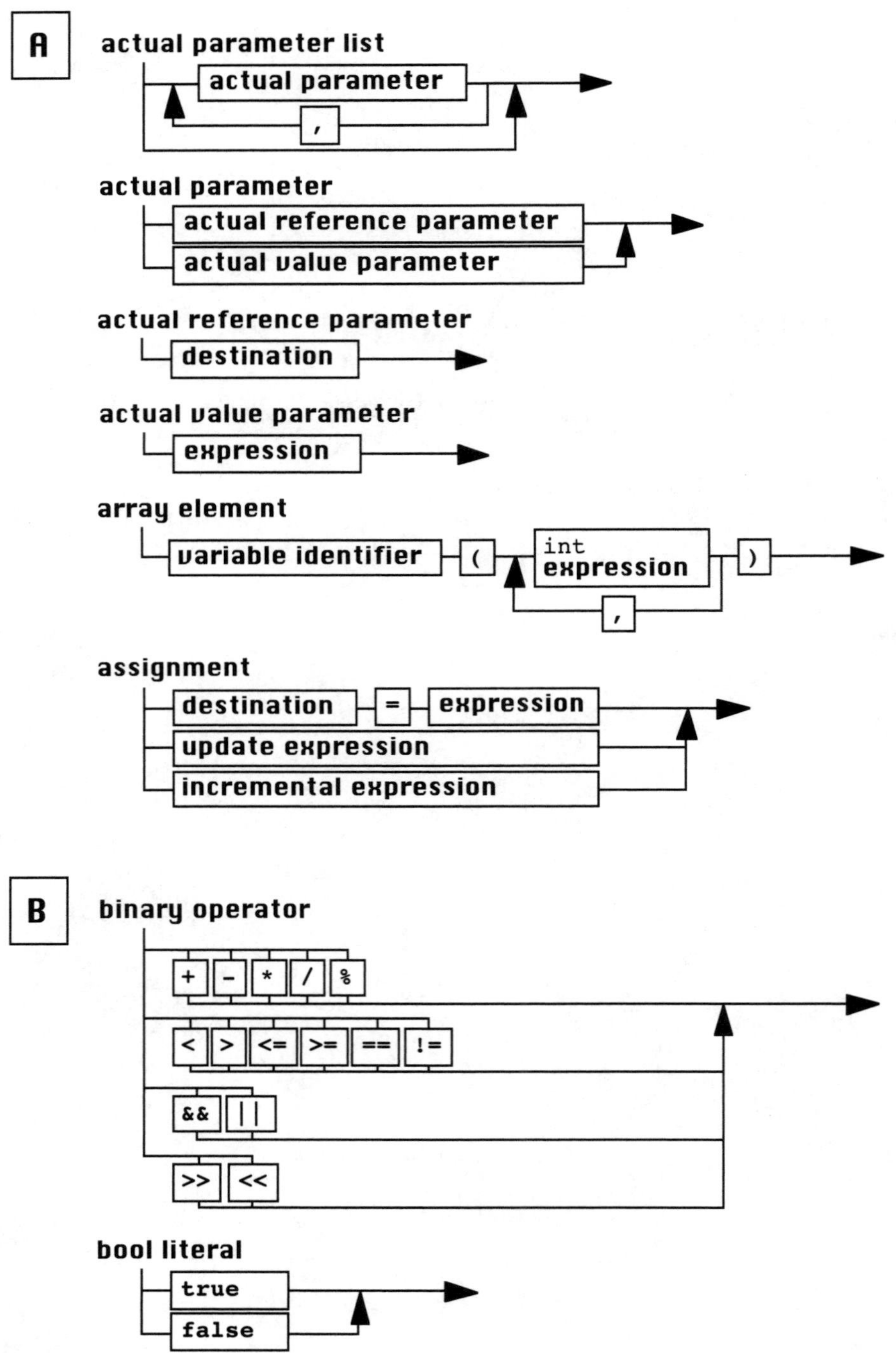
A
actual parameter list
actual parameter
,
actual parameter
actual reference parameter
actual value parameter
actual reference parameter
destination
actual value parameter
expression
array element
variable identifier
(
int expression
,
)
assignment
destination
=
expression
update expression
incremental expression
B
binary operator
+
-
*
/
%
<
>
<=
>=
==
!=
&&
||
>>
<<
bool literal
true
false

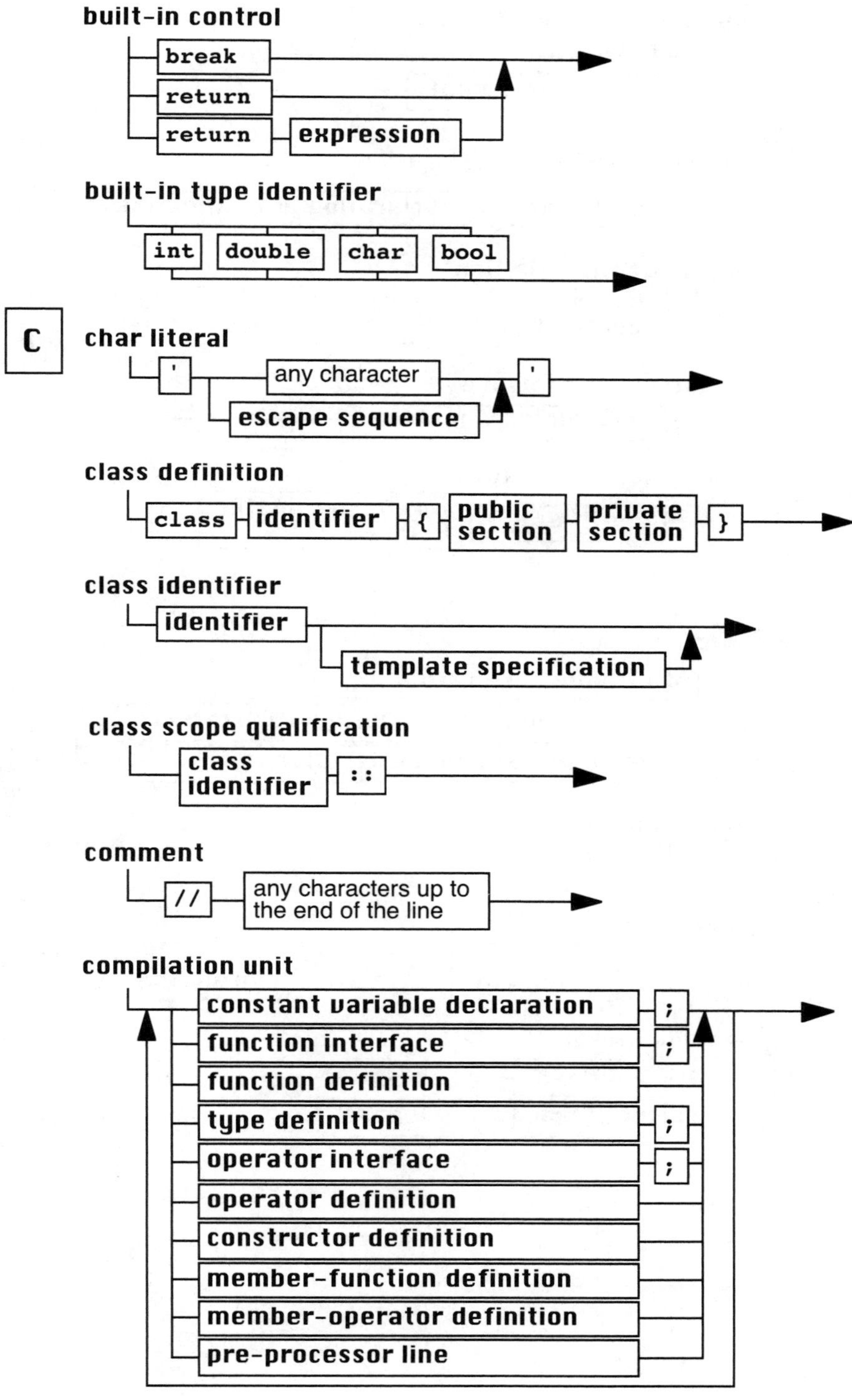
built-in control
break
return
return
expression
built-in type identifier
int
double
char
bool
C
char literal
'
any character
escape sequence
'
class definition
class
identifier
{
public section
private section
}
class identifier
identifier
template specification
class scope qualification
class identifier
::
comment
//
any characters up to the end of the line
compilation unit
constant variable declaration
;
function interface
;
function definition
type definition
;
operator interface
;
operator definition
constructor definition
member-function definition
member-operator definition
pre-processor line

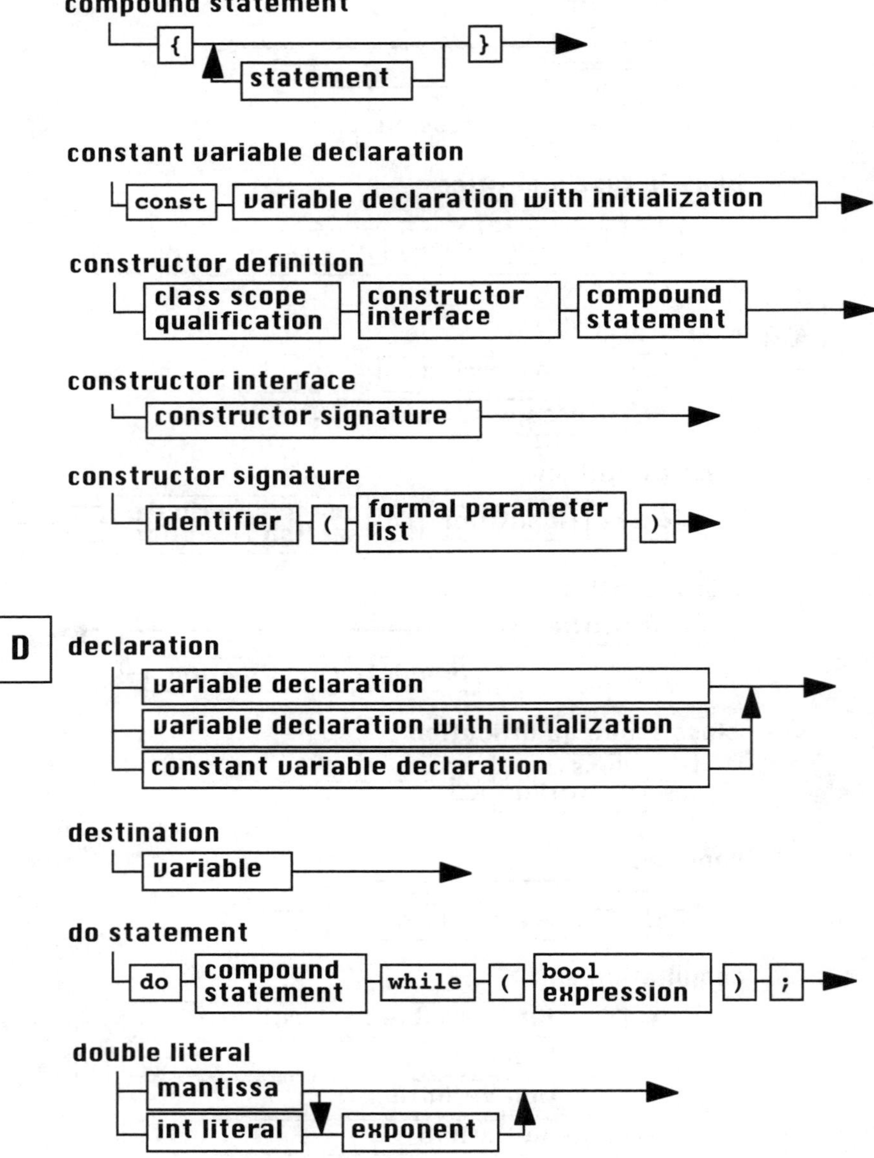
compound statement
{
statement
}
constant variable declaration
const
variable declaration with initialization
constructor definition
class scope qualification
constructor interface
compound statement
constructor interface
constructor signature
constructor signature
identifier
(
formal parameter list
)
D
declaration
variable declaration
variable declaration with initialization
constant variable declaration
destination
variable
do statement
do
compound statement
while
(
bool expression
)
;
double literal
mantissa
int literal
exponent

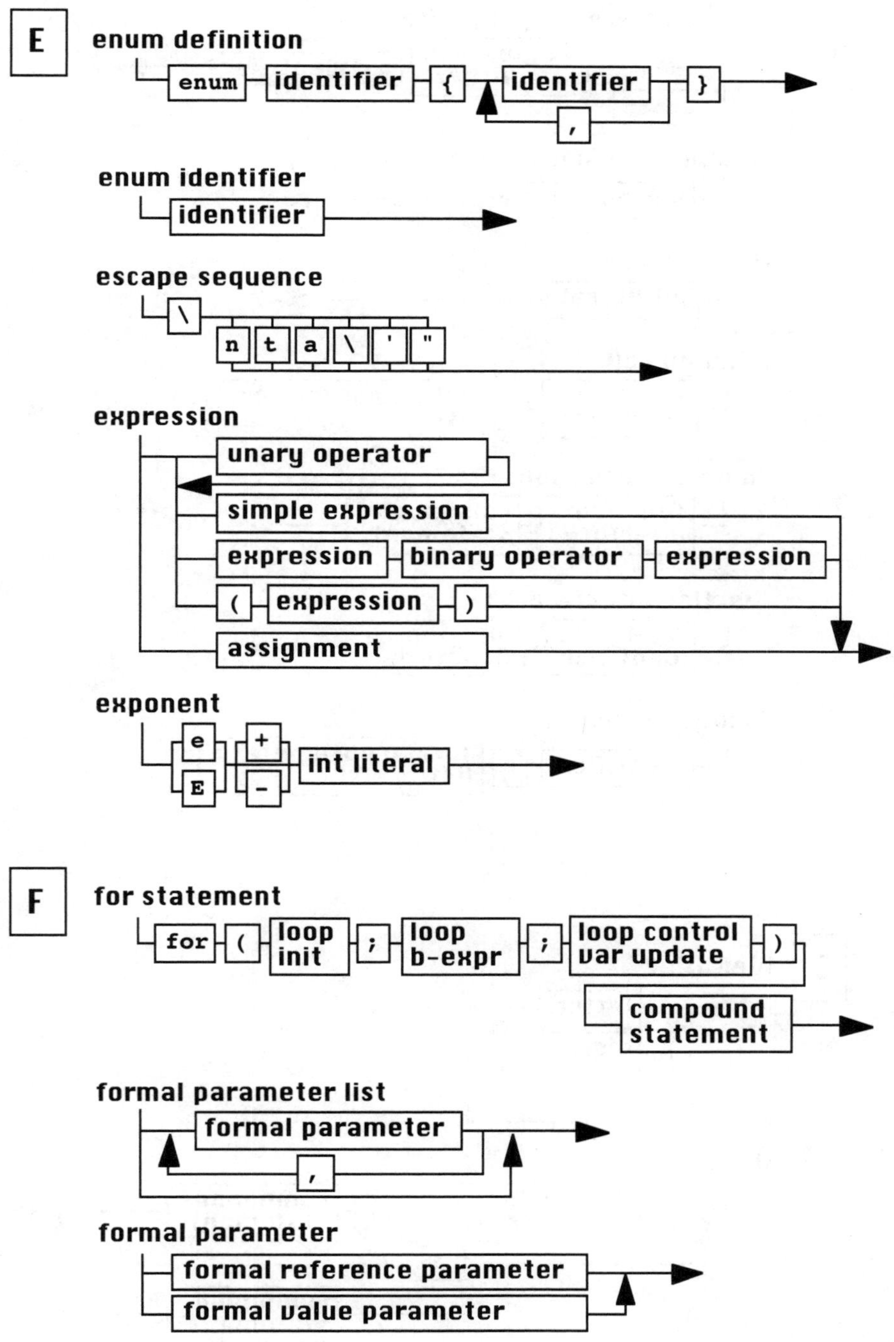
E
enum definition
enum
identifier
{
identifier
,
}
enum identifier
identifier
escape sequence
\
n
t
a
\
'
"
expression
unary operator
simple expression
expression
binary operator
expression
(
expression
)
assignment
exponent
e
E
+
-
int literal
F
for statement
for
(
loop init
;
loop b-expr
;
loop control var update
)
compound statement
formal parameter list
formal parameter
,
formal parameter
formal reference parameter
formal value parameter

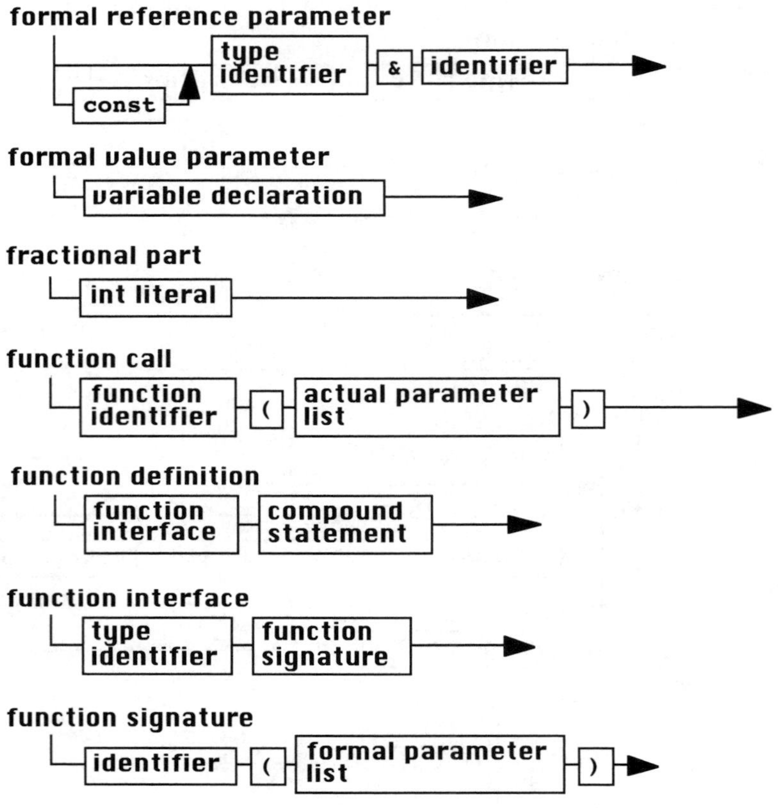
formal reference parameter
const
type identifier
&
identifier
formal value parameter
variable declaration
fractional part
int literal
function call
function identifier
(
actual parameter list
)
function definition
function interface
compound statement
function interface
type identifier
function signature
function signature
identifier
(
formal parameter list
)

I

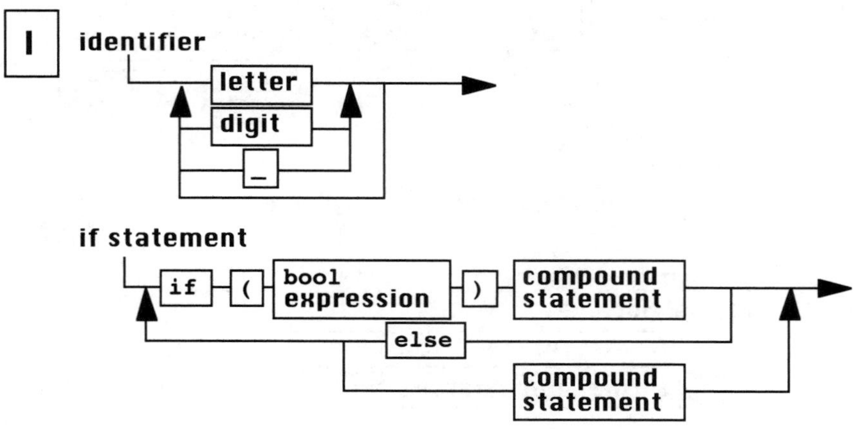
identifier
letter
digit
_
if statement
if
(
bool expression
)
compound statement
else
compound statement

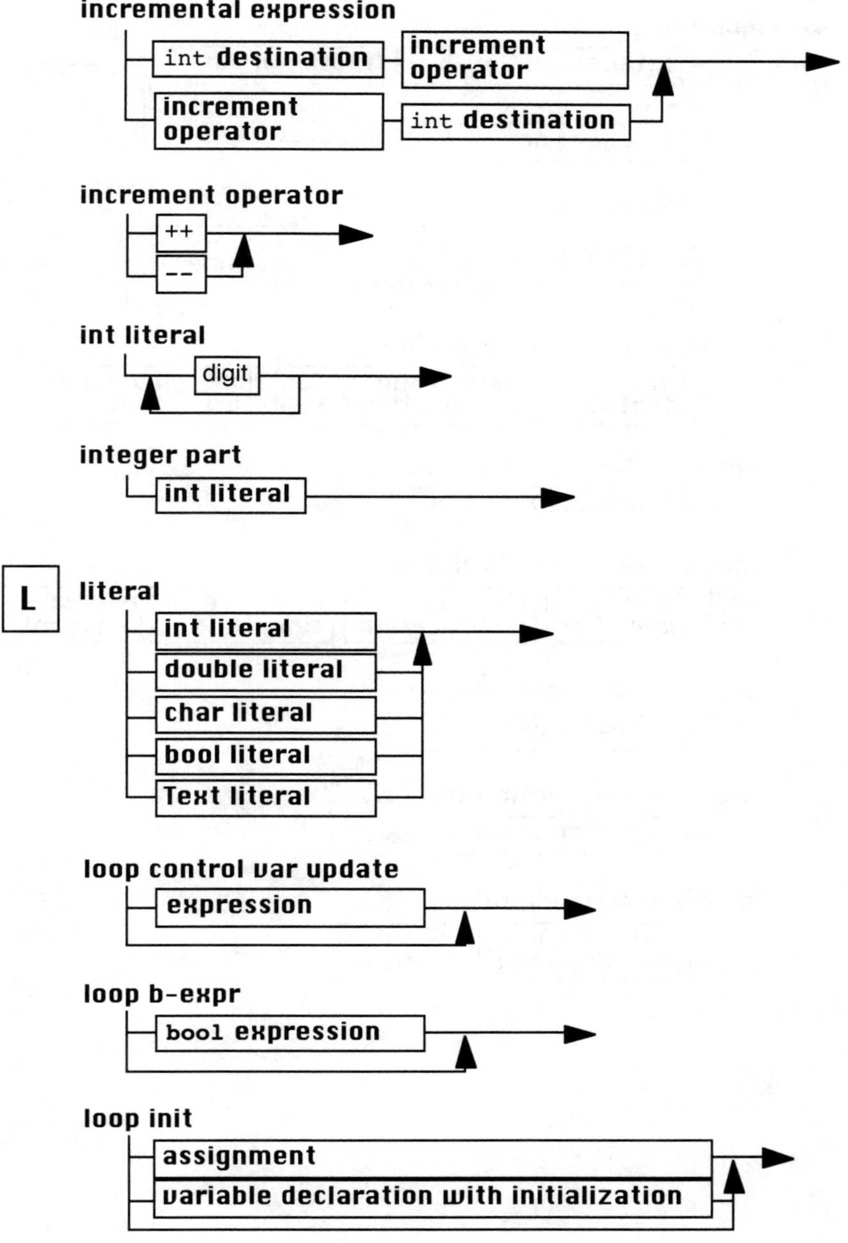
incremental expression
int destination
increment operator
increment operator
int destination
increment operator
++
--
int literal
digit
integer part
int literal
L
literal
int literal
double literal
char literal
bool literal
Text literal
loop control var update
expression
loop b-expr
bool expression
loop init
assignment
variable declaration with initialization

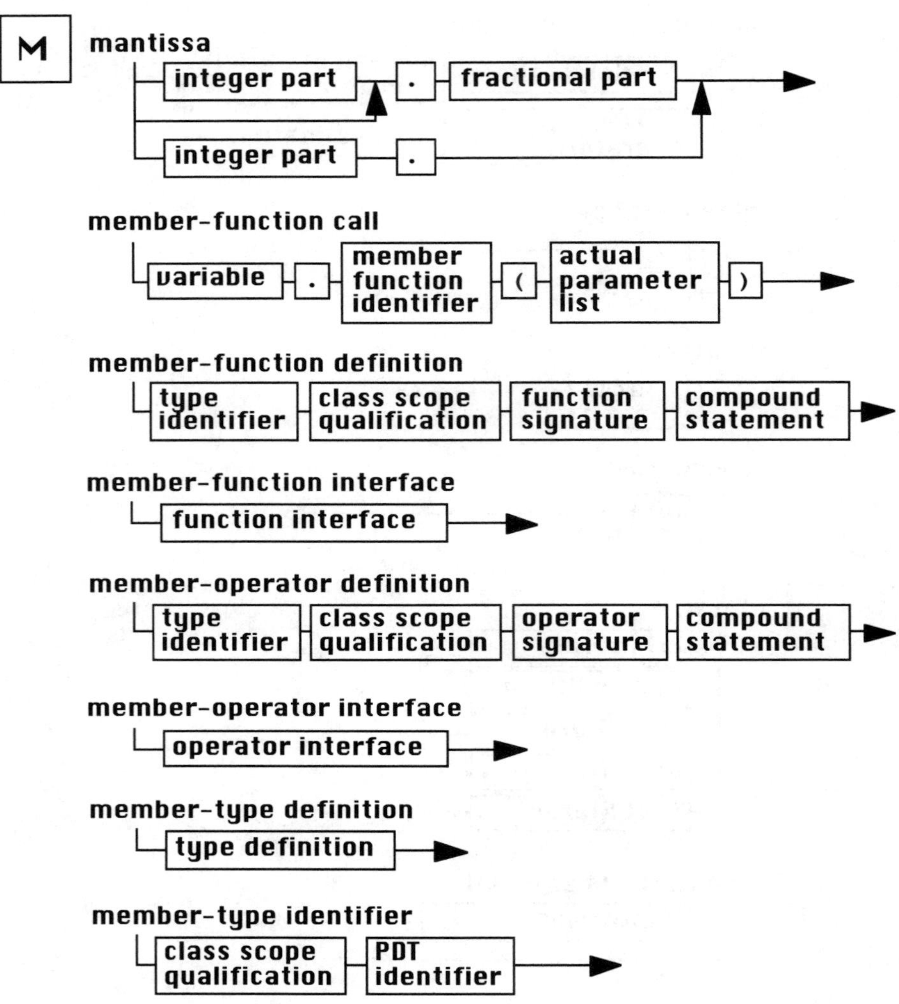
M
mantissa
integer part
.
fractional part
integer part
.
member-function call
variable
.
member function identifier
(
actual parameter list
)
member-function definition
type identifier
class scope qualification
function signature
compound statement
member-function interface
function interface
member-operator definition
type identifier
class scope qualification
operator signature
compound statement
member-operator interface
operator interface
member-type definition
type definition
member-type identifier
class scope qualification
PDT identifier

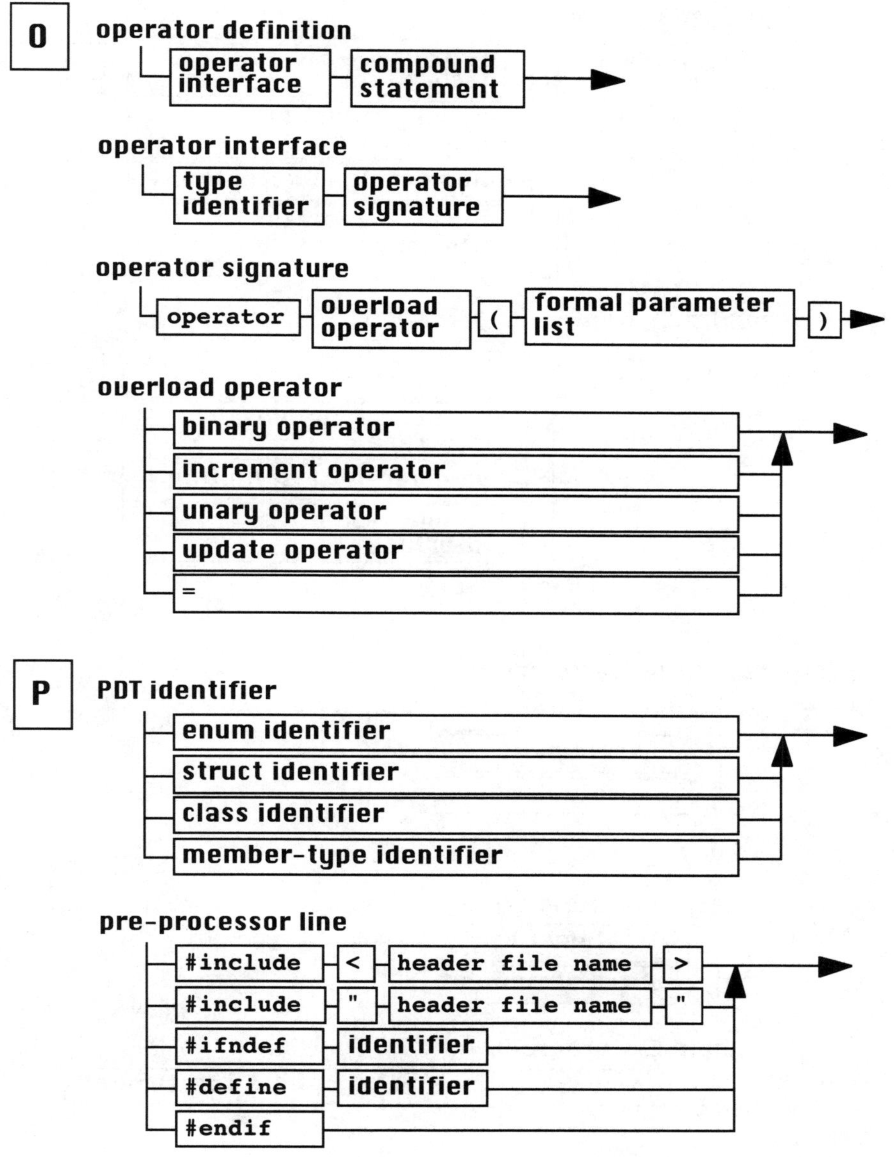
O
operator definition
operator interface
compound statement
operator interface
type identifier
operator signature
operator signature
operator
overload operator
(
formal parameter list
)
overload operator
binary operator
increment operator
unary operator
update operator
=
P
PDT identifier
enum identifier
struct identifier
class identifier
member-type identifier
pre-processor line
#include
<
header file name
>
#include
"
header file name
"
#ifndef
identifier
#define
identifier
#endif

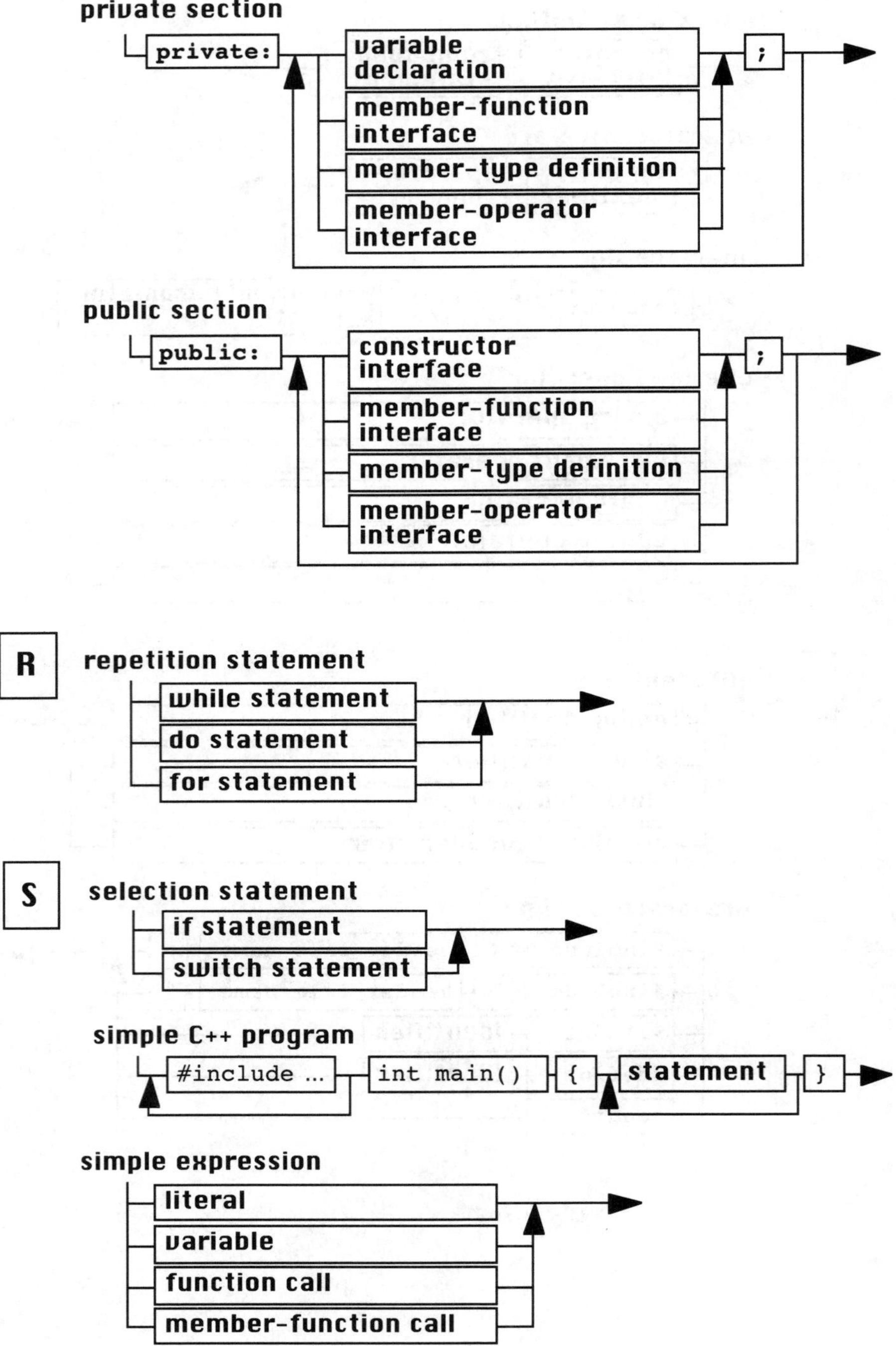
private section
private:
variable declaration
member-function interface
member-type definition
member-operator interface
;
public section
public:
constructor interface
member-function interface
member-type definition
member-operator interface
;
R
repetition statement
while statement
do statement
for statement
S
selection statement
if statement
switch statement
simple C++ program
#include ...
int main()
{
statement
}
simple expression
literal
variable
function call
member-function call

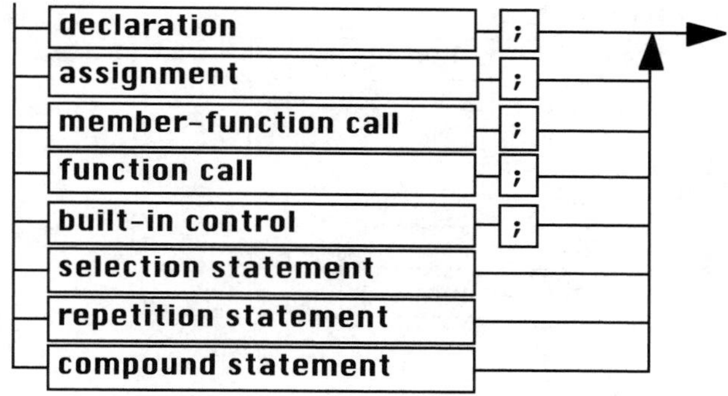

struct identifier

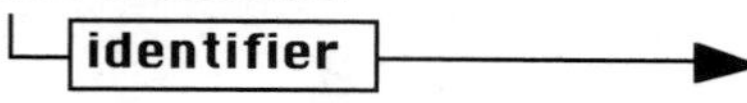

struct definition

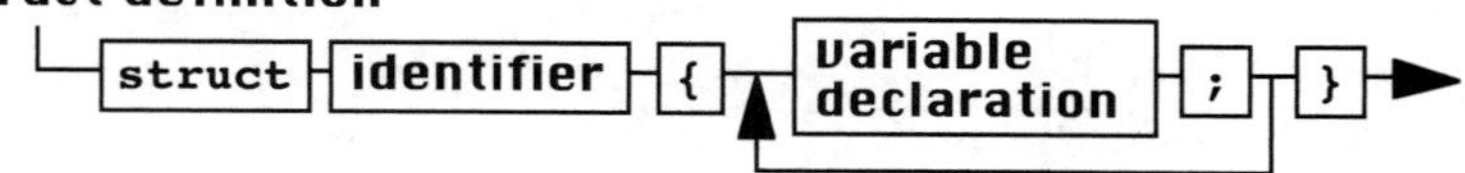

struct member variable

switch statement

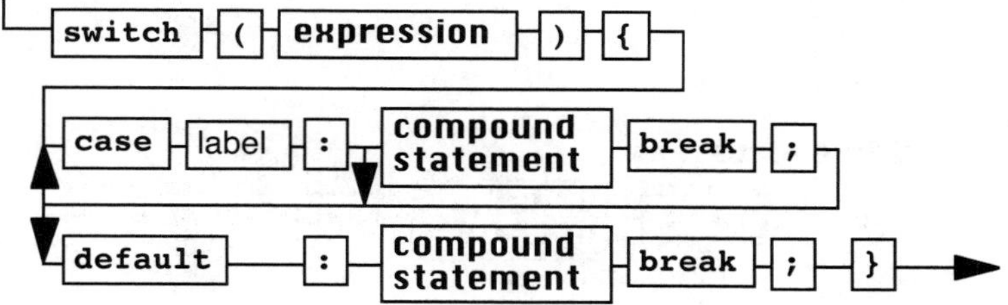

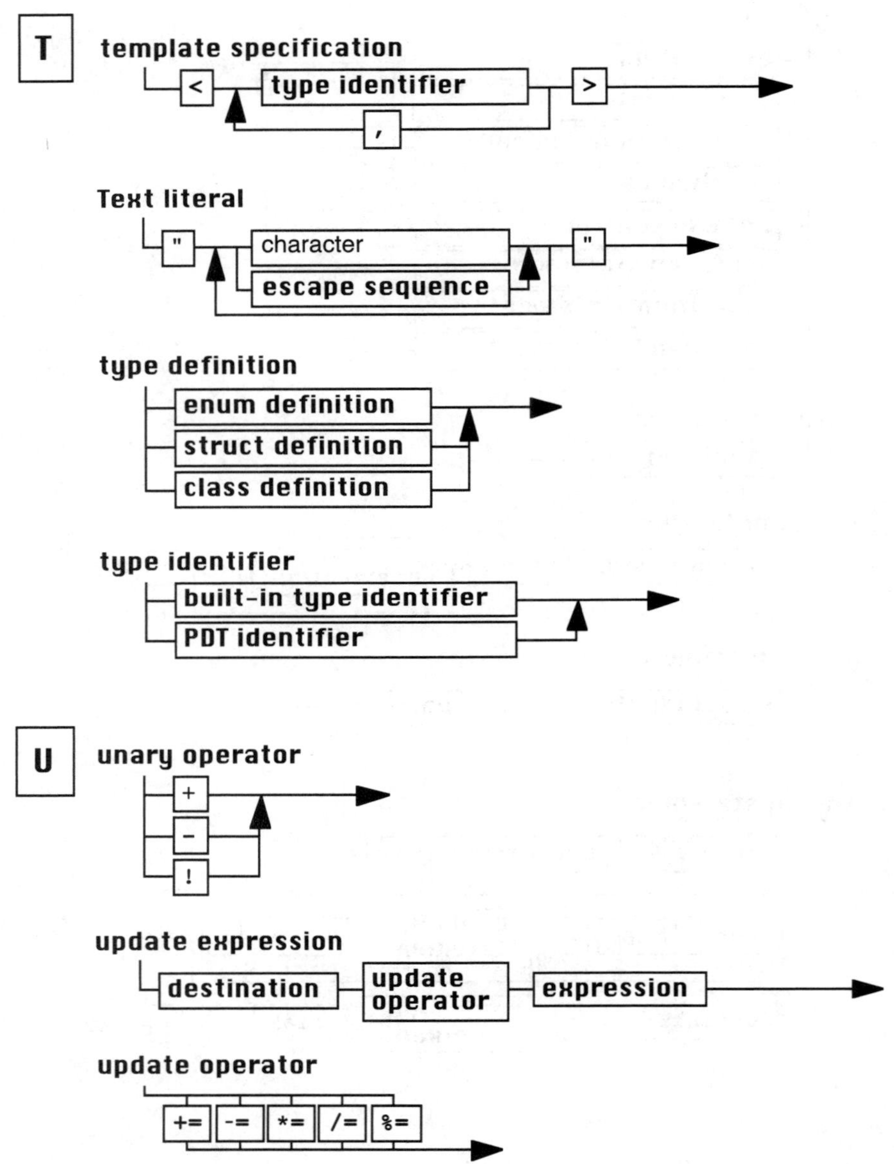
T
template specification
<
type identifier
,
>
Text literal
"
character
escape sequence
"
type definition
enum definition
struct definition
class definition
type identifier
built-in type identifier
PDT identifier
U
unary operator
+
-
!
update expression
destination
update operator
expression
update operator
+=
-=
*=
/=
%=

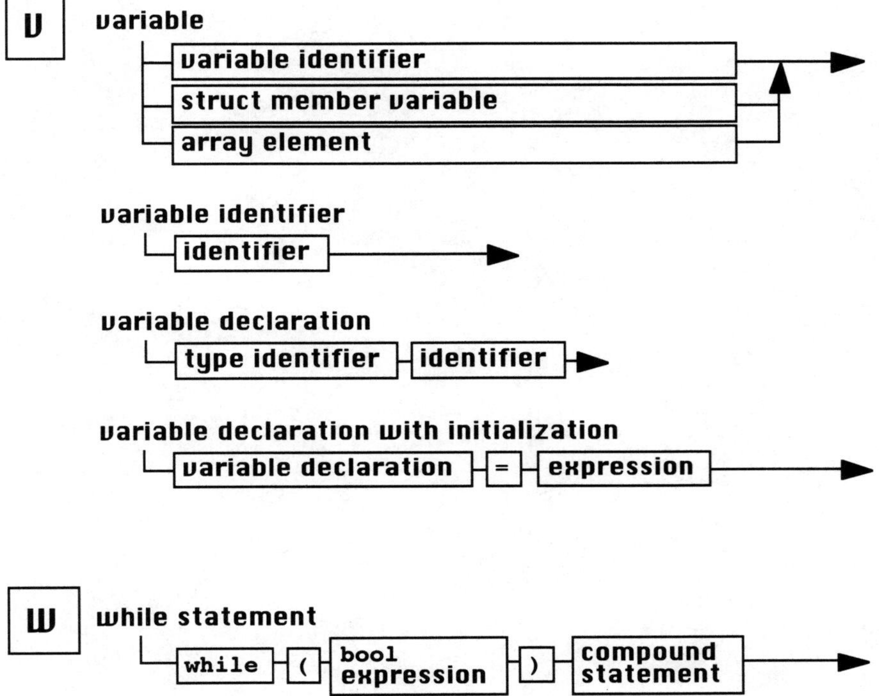
V
variable
variable identifier
struct member variable
array element
variable identifier
identifier
variable declaration
type identifier
identifier
variable declaration with initialization
variable declaration
=
expression
W
while statement
while
(
bool expression
)
compound statement

Appendix B
Answers to in-chapter exercises

CHAPTER 1

Section 1.1

1 A library contains components that can be *reused*. If the library contains software components ready for use, those components don't need to be designed and implemented, and they should have been tested. Reusing such components rather than re-inventing them will save time (and therefore money).

2 You'd want to know what components the library contains (e.g. their name), what are the characteristics of those components (e.g. their shape and how they fit together), and possibly some information on how the component should be used. Some components would be useful for the design stage (e.g. a plan for a model house); some components would be useful for the implementation stage (e.g. an already-constructed roof). You might also want to know the name of the person who created the component and placed it in the library in case you have some further questions to ask.

3 If errors in the design aren't uncovered before implementation starts then those errors are very likely to be copied into the implementation. Re-doing parts of the design subsequently to remove the errors is likely to mean that some of the implementation has to be thrown away or reworked. Moreover, uncovering the design errors by examining the implementation can be difficult. To take a real-world analogy, say there's a design error that omits a fuel tank in a new automobile that is being developed. There might be a lot of implementation work that has to be scrapped to rectify this omission. The error might show up because the engine won't start, but linking this problem eventually to the missing fuel tank may take some time (there could be lots of reasons why the engine doesn't work; there could be several reasons why the fuel isn't reaching the engine; and so on).

Section 1.3

1 Example of non-computer programs might include:

- Instructions in a model aircraft kit: objects would include the parts in the kit, the cement and paint; the statements in the algorithm would specify the steps (glue the left-hand half of the body to the right-hand half), and the sequencing of those steps (first build the left-hand half, then the right-hand half, then . . .).
- Details of how to get to a particular place: objects include particular buildings or landmarks, forms of transport (take the number 27 bus); the statements would say things like: "Take the second on the right, go for 100 meters, . . ."
- Some first-aid procedures: objects might include parts of the person requiring attention, bandages, thermometers; the algorithm would indicate the order in which the procedures should be applied.
- Instructions for taking an examination: objects include the questions; the rubric (or heading) on the exam paper may give some details of what constitutes a legal set of answers (e.g. you must only answer a maximum of four questions), but isn't an algorithm – certainly not an algorithm for passing the exam! An algorithm for taking the exam might identify steps such as: 1. Read the paper; 2. Panic; 3. Answer *n* questions; . . .

2 A recipe program might say "beat the eggs" – so challenge them to a game of something, or threaten them with violence! The recipe almost certainly won't give you precise instruction for getting the contents of the egg out of the shell and only using the contents. "Place the thermometer in the person's mouth" – what, the whole thermometer? "Take the exam" – where do you want it taken to? Instruction books that have been translated from another language often contain interesting mis-translations!

3 (b) Program for: Operate TV, with specified `channel number` and `volume level`.

1. If TV isn't plugged in to the electricity supply then plug it in.
2. Execute the sub-program "Switch TV on".
3. Execute the sub-program "Select channel(`channel number`)".
4. Execute the sub-program "Select the volume(`volume level`)".
5. Open the bag of pretzels and watch the program.
6. Execute the sub-program "Switch TV off".

The sequence is defined by the ordering of the instructions and the assumption that they will be executed in turn. Note the use of sub-programs in the above. The details of, say, how you switch the TV on need to be specified in a separate program. Whether this is then achieved by a remote control or by buttons on the TV itself won't alter the program. Notice also that the sub-programs require some input data in the form of which channel is to be selected, or what level the volume should be at. The program isn't for watching a specific channel at a specific volume: it's more general than that. Note that there are some assumptions that have been made: that the TV is already connected to the aerial for receiving the signal; that the TV has been tuned to the correct channels; and that you actually have a TV! Finally, note the level of precision that you have to go to in the program to describe accurately the actions required. Computer programs require a similar level of precision.

4 Program for "Calculate Body Mass index for a given `weight` and `height`."

1. Get a calculator.
2. Execute sub-program "Switch calculator on".
3. Execute sub-program "Enter number (`weight`)".
4. Press button for divide operation.
5. Execute sub-program "Enter number (`height`)".
6. Press button for divide operation.
7. Execute sub-program "Enter number (`height`)".
8. Press button for equals operation.
9. Read the answer from the display.
10. Execute sub-program "Switch calculator off".

The sub-programs are straightforward so we've not provided them here, but they really require spelling out in detail to complete the exercise. There are assumptions about the type of calculator and the features it provides: would your program work for a different type of calculator? Did you have step 1 in your solution?

Section 1.4

2 Both the ATM and the checkout register have a similar form of instruction execution to that in Figure 1.6. That is, they're switched on, and then obey instructions until they're switched off. The ATM has instructions relating to banking that it gets from the user via a touch-screen or small keyboard ("Press 1 if you want to withdraw cash, . . ."). The register gets instructions from the operator pressing keys (e.g. the "total" key) or from a barcode reader.

Section 1.6

1 How many programming languages did you find? Were you surprised by the number and variety? They're an indication of how the field has developed. You should have found languages that started a long time ago and are still being covered in recent books, perhaps for different versions of the language (e.g. Fortran, Basic, Cobol, Lisp), languages that have been and gone (e.g. Algol), current languages (Pascal, C, C++, Ada, Modula, Miranda). You may have come across assembly language books – were they old or new books? (Not many people need or want to program in those languages these days.)

2 Wirth invented the programming language Pascal to provide a better vehicle for the teaching of programming. The language found widespread use, not only for teaching but in industry as well. Subsequently, he has worked on languages following on from Pascal called Modula-1 and Modula-2 (and there's also a Modula-3 language developed by others).

CHAPTER 2

Section 2.0

1 (a) From the top, a three-course meal consists of an appetizer component, a main dish component, and a dessert component. The appetizer component consists of the sub-components shrimp, butter and garlic. The main dish consists of sub-components meat, potatoes, and two other vegetables. And so on. Don't forget the champagne, the soft lights and the music.

(b) Music requires an orchestra component. The orchestra consists of sub-components: wind-section, string-section, brass-section and percussion.

More likely for (b) you identified a hi-fi system as the top-level component required, and that consists of an amplifier, a CD-player, two speakers and some CDs. An amplifier consists of . . . lots of electronic bits.

Note that either of these answers for (b) is a solution to the original problem of providing music. The problem specification didn't rule out the orchestra solution, although the size of your college room may!

Section 2.1

1 The dictionary definition for abstraction may refer to the process of getting a liquid out of the ground – not relevant to this book; that for type may refer you to fonts or to the actions you undertake at a keyboard.

2 Types: chair, TV, table, desk, bed, bar – wow, there's a lot in this college room :-). The room may contain various instances of these types – there may be two chairs. The interface of a chair type is rather simple: you can sit on an instance and you can move it! The TV has a more interesting interface: on/off switch; volume and picture controls; channel selection mechanism.

3 Data abstractions: *a retrieval component* that when given a name returns the phone number. (Could be a phone book or directory inquiries.) *A telephone component* with the obvious interface.

Control-flow abstractions: *dial a number:* dial the individual digits in sequence; *wait-while-busy*: while the telephone line is in use wait 10 seconds; *wait-while-ringing*: while the called number is ringing, if you've not waited long-enough, wait until it is answered; *ringing-long-enough*: if you've waited long enough disconnect the call.

Program: 1. Get a telephone and a retrieval component. 2. Look up the "name" using the retrieval component and get the number. 3. Wait-while-busy. 4. Dial the number using the telephone. 5. Wait-while-ringing.

Section 2.2

1 Mouse operations: move left; move right; move up; move down (all of these could indicate how far the mouse has moved); mouse button *N* down; mouse button *N* up. Mouse abstract states: mouse moving; button *N* is Up or Down.

2 A diagram for a simple telephone type is given below. (There may be some different features on different types of telephone.) The type captures attributes common to all telephones (e.g. they all have a phone number associated with them). The type describes the behavior of instances, but doesn't exhibit this behavior itself. The instance of this type in your home can be regarded as having a particular value for the phone number that identifies it (although it could be argued that the number is a property of the phone line and not the phone itself). There could be other attributes of the telephone type (e.g. its color) that your phone would have a specific value of.

3 The calculator type interface diagram is given below. Again, this diagram captures features that are common to all calculators. Your calculator has some identity such as a specific serial number, or your name on the identity tag. As in the answer to 2, the type describes the behavior of instances whereas the instances can exhibit the behavior.

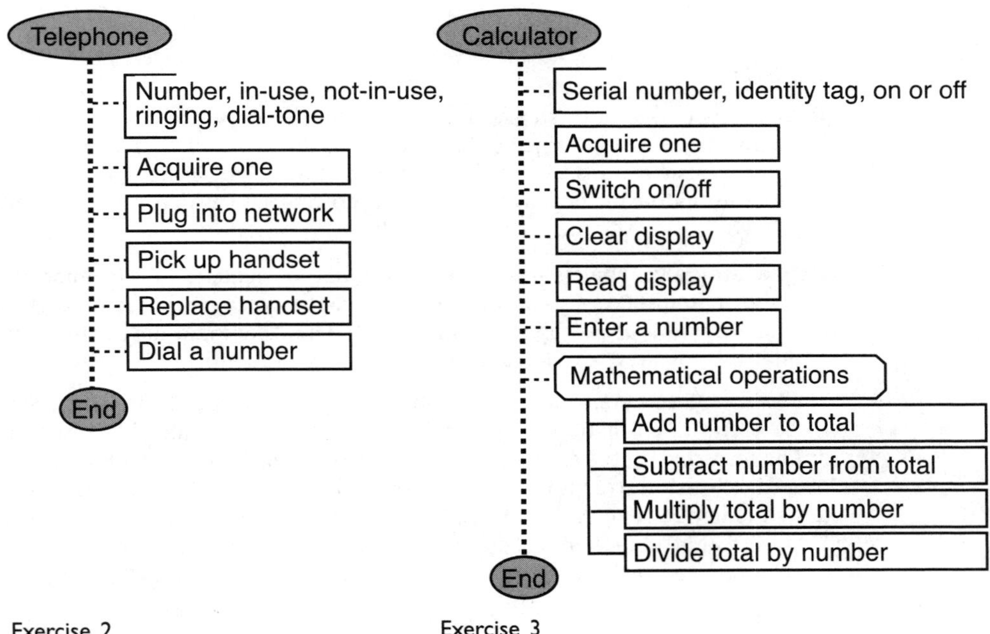

Exercise 2

Exercise 3

4 The operations identified in Exercise 4 in Section 1.3 should all be available as features provided by the Calculator type. The sub-programs identified in the answer to this earlier exercise (such as "Switch calculator on") have a straightforward translation given the operations identified above, but if you had identified that the calculator had ON/OFF buttons then that sub-program would have translated into the instruction "Press the ON button".

5 Types: a number type is the only type required, assuming numbers can have a fractional part. Objects that are instances of this type would include one for the weight, one for the height, and one for the index. The type has to permit a value to be assigned to each object, and the only operations required are multiply (or square) and divide. And an output operator would be useful too.

6

Directory

Acquire one

Lookup a name returning either a list of names and numbers or a "not-found" message

End

You could have expressed a much more complicated directory type, involving alphabetic sections containing information. Here we've taken a much higher-level approach, identifying just the salient "lookup" operation that really captures what this type should provide.

Section 2.3

1 **Recipe.** Types – sirloin steaks, butter, oil, mushrooms, cream, wire rack, roasting pan, bowl, oven. There are objects that are instances of all of these types. There aren't any functional abstractions clearly identified in the recipe, although there are steps that a dumb automaton would have difficulty following and which require additional steps to be inferred, for example, "grill the steaks."

Repair program. Objects – the bonnet, the battery lead, the air cleaner, the radiator, the clip, the engine. The types in this program are the types that these objects are all instances of – an engine type, a clip type, and so on. The functional abstractions are: remove the bonnet; remove the air cleaner; and remove the radiator.

2 Types are: `CDPlayer` and `CDisc`; objects are `myPlayer` and `aDisc`. Strictly speaking, there aren't any functional abstractions in Figure 2.14 as all of the operations are operations provided by the `CDPlayer` type. However, each operation has many characteristics of a functional abstraction. The functional abstractions are those identified in the earlier design (Figure 2.13), such as `Put disc into player` (the designator boxes in that design). However, those functional abstractions aren't present in the C++ implementation, having been translated into sequences of operations on the object `myPlayer`.

3

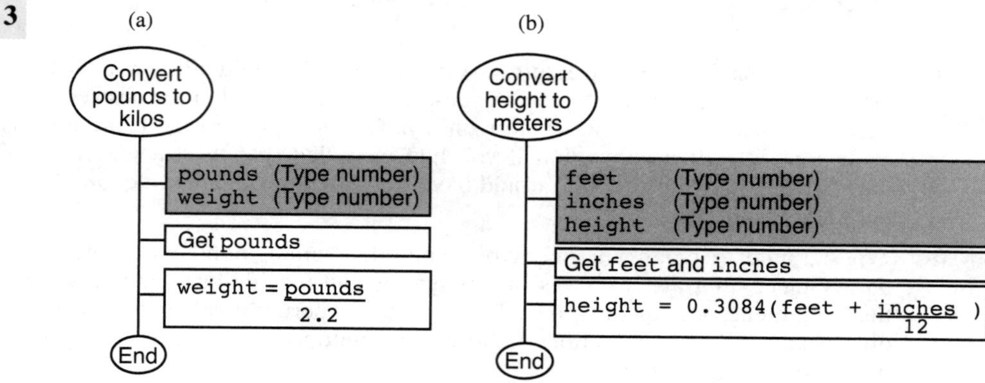

(c)

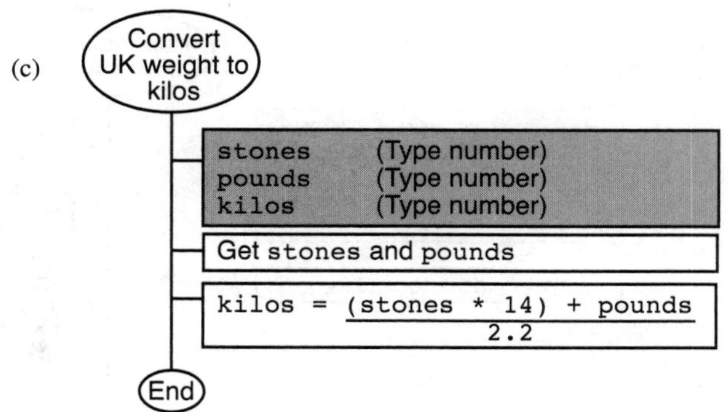

4 The following design captures what you'd have to do if the phone wasn't already installed.

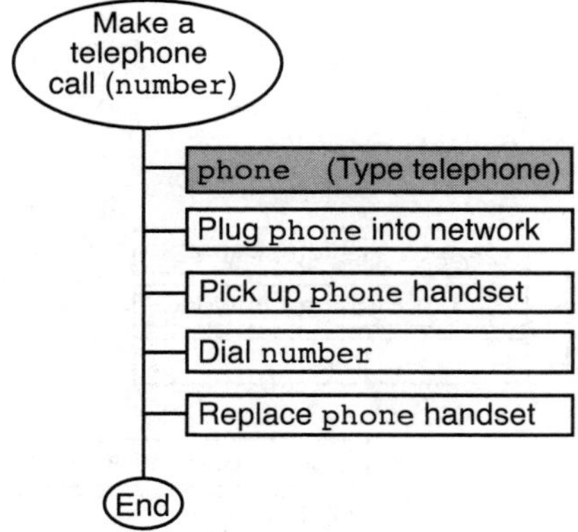

Section 2.4

1 When number has the value 4 the sequence is:

> A; Does number have the value 3? (answer NO); C; Does number have the value 4? (answer YES); E; D; B.

When number has the value 1 the sequence is:

> A; Does number have the value 3? (answer NO); C; Does number have the value 4? (answer NO); F; D; B.

2 Multiply number by 3 to give 45. Add 1 to give 46. Now Change number. Subtract 5 to give 41. Now Sub Calculation. Multiply by 2 to give 82. Add 1 to give 83 as the final result.

The letter sequence is SZYIYANMHPKXAYIYANMHPKX.

3

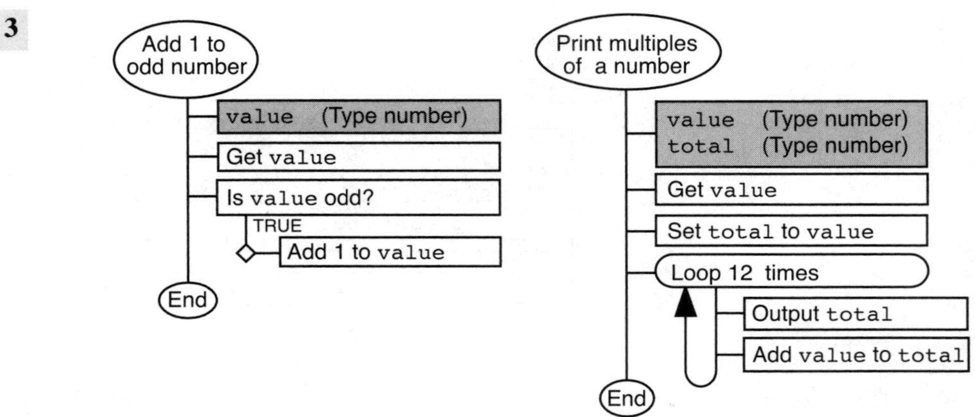

4

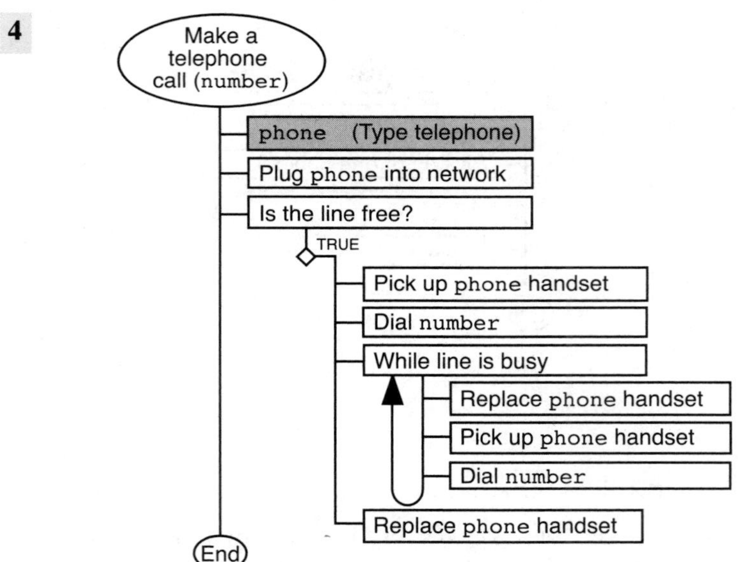

5 The Select dial from list operation in the design below needs refining. This is likely to require a person's address, and you need to deal with the possibility that the person whose number you're trying to find doesn't have a telephone number.

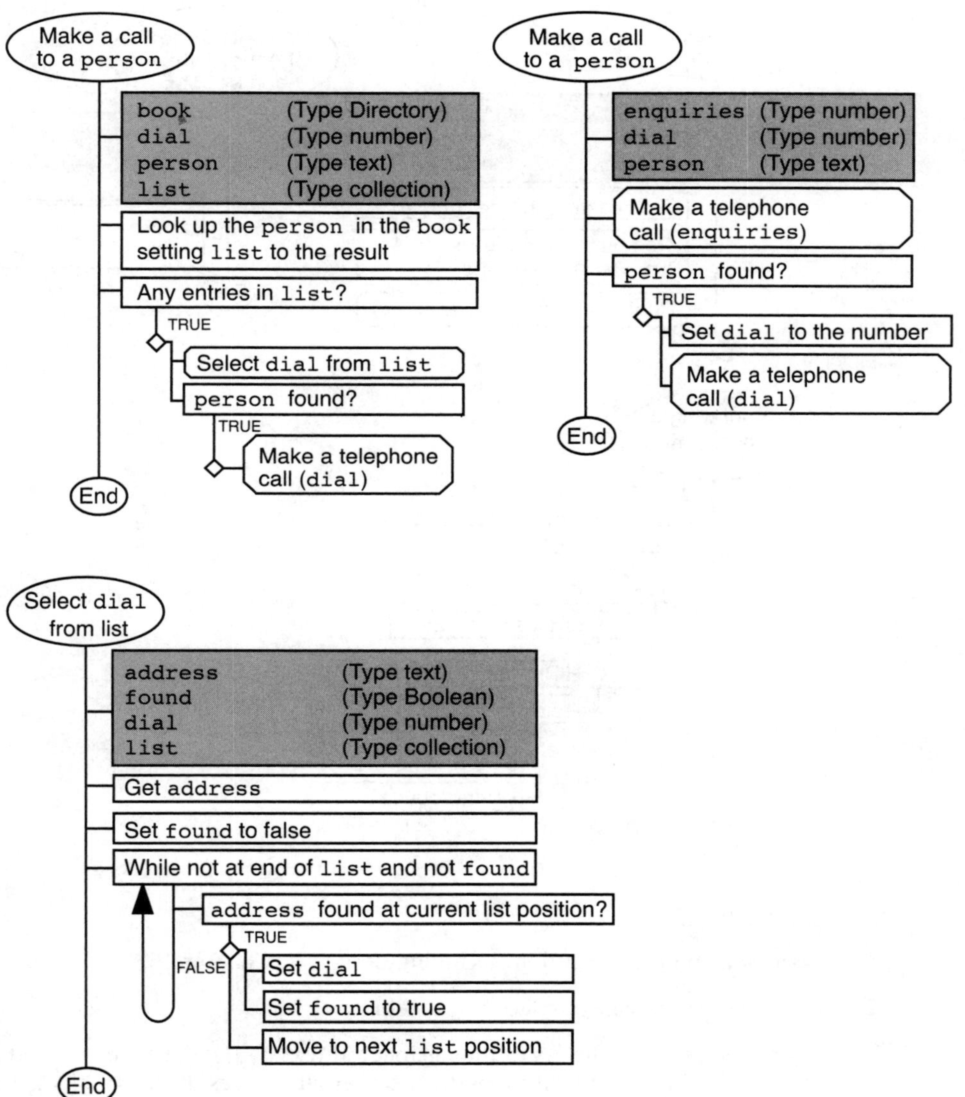
Make a call
to a person
book (Type Directory)
dial (Type number)
person (Type text)
list (Type collection)
Look up the person in the book
setting list to the result
Any entries in list?
TRUE
Select dial from list
person found?
TRUE
Make a telephone
call (dial)
End
Make a call
to a person
enquiries (Type number)
dial (Type number)
person (Type text)
Make a telephone
call (enquiries)
person found?
TRUE
Set dial to the number
Make a telephone
call (dial)
End
Select dial
from list
address (Type text)
found (Type Boolean)
dial (Type number)
list (Type collection)
Get address
Set found to false
While not at end of list and not found
address found at current list position?
TRUE
FALSE
Set dial
Set found to true
Move to next list position
End

6

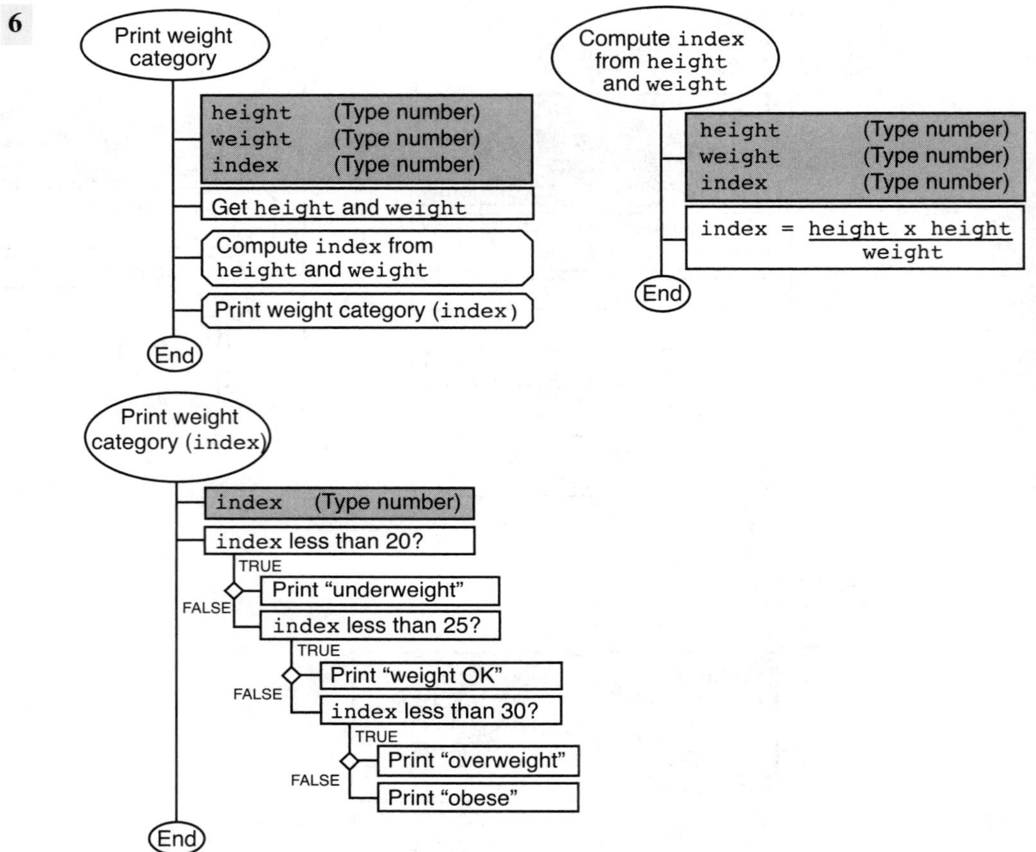

Section 2.5

1 There's a complete solution, including design, in Chapter 16.

2 Only one queen can be placed in a column or row.

3 Try replacing all of the As in the enciphered text by Bs, the Bs by Cs and so on. Display the result of these substitutions to the user. If the result doesn't look like English try again but this time replace the As in the enciphered text by Cs, the Bs by Ds, and so on. The brute-force technique is to try all possible single-letter substitutions until the clear text emerges from a try. There are only 23 combinations to try, so the approach is feasible.

4 After an attempted decipher, count the total number of letters and the total number of each letter. If the number of Es is the greatest, display the text to the user to see if it's English. An alternative strategy would be to analyze the enciphered text, to find the letter that occurs most frequently. That (enciphered) letter ought to represent the (deciphered) letter E, so perform a deciphering based on that encoding, and display the results.

Section 2.6

1

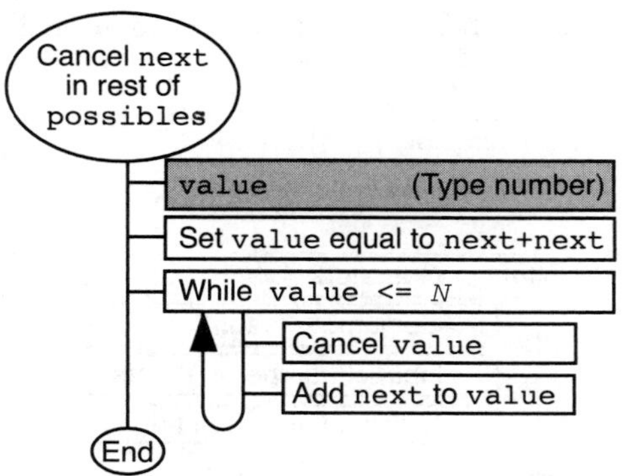

2 Don't bother with the even numbers.

3

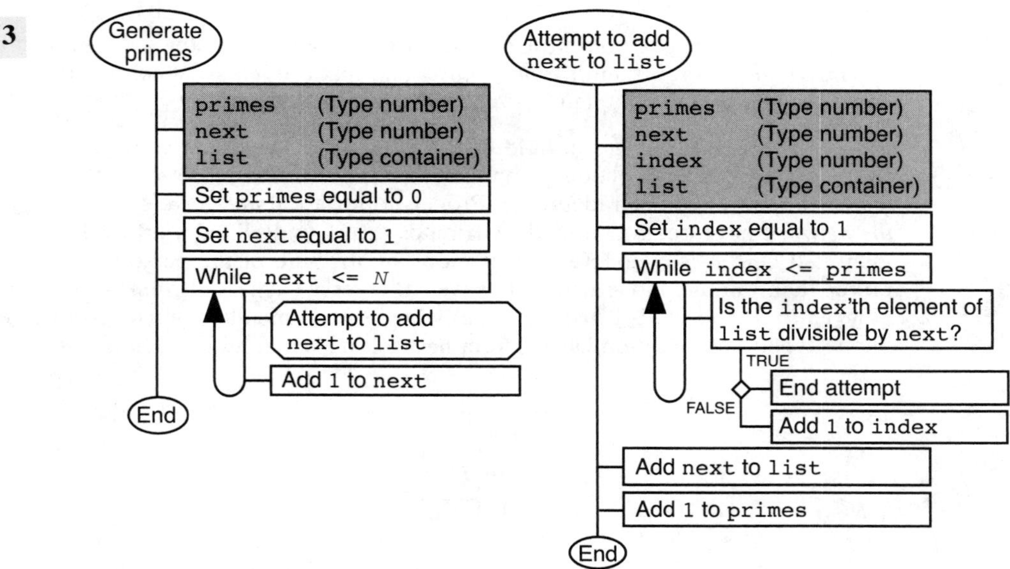

You need to store the prime numbers explicitly, but the collection need only be as big as the number of prime numbers, rather than containing all numbers up to the largest. The above version involves a divide operation, which may be more expensive than the add operations of the original version.

Section 2.7

1 The main parts are below. There may be additional member operators (e.g. square root).

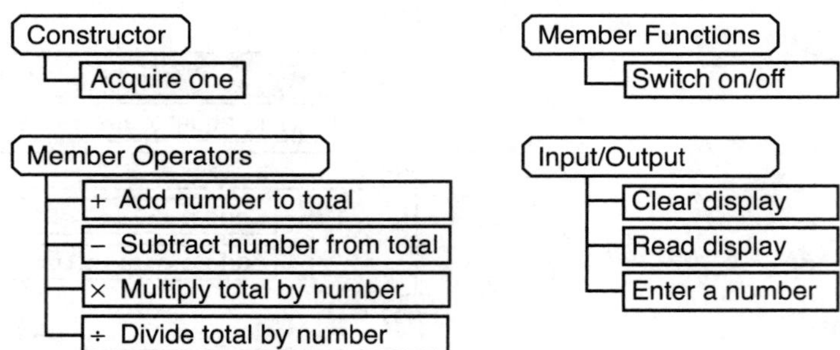

Section 2.8

1 To operate *a telephone* you must first **acquire** one, and then **plug** it into *a network*. Having done this you then **lift** <u>*the handset*</u> and **dial** *a number*. When your call <u>**is complete**</u> you **replace** the handset and then **unplug** from <u>*the network*</u>.

The verbs (operations) are in **bold**, of which **acquire** suggests a constructor and the rest suggest member functions. Common nouns are in *italics*, so *a telephone*, *a network* and *a number* have been identified. Proper nouns are <u>*underlined*</u>, so <u>*the handset*</u> and <u>*the network*</u> have been identified. Attributes are in <u>**underlined bold**</u>, and the only one identified here is <u>**is complete**</u>. This is more an attribute of the person making the call, rather than the telephone itself. However, the verbs suggest attributes, such as is <u>**plugged in**</u>, (handset) <u>**is lifted**</u>, etc. See below for the member functions for a telephone type. An operation Unplug from network has been added. Just testing you!

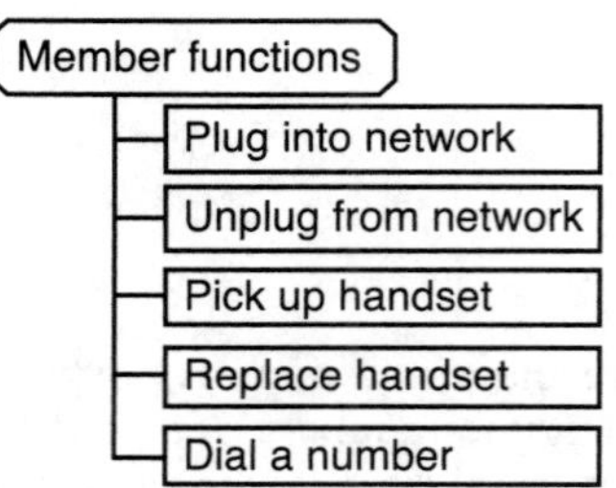

2 For a possible description see the solution to Exercise 1 of Section 2.2. There aren't any member operators or I/O operators, so here's the PDT definition in our notation.

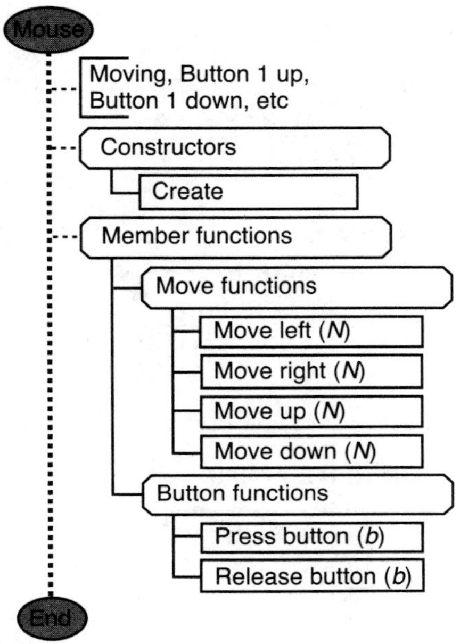

3 To borrow a book, first you have to determine the author and title of the book you want to borrow. Next find a library. Go to the library of your choice and search the shelves for the book you want to borrow. Remove the book from the shelves and take it to the checkout desk. A record of the fact that you're borrowing the book will be made and a date stamped to indicate the day you have to return the book. Take the book home and enjoy a good read.

Useful types: library, book, author, title, record, date, comfy chair :-).

CHAPTER 3

Section 3.0

1 In Chapter 2 you met data abstraction and control-flow abstraction. Data abstraction involves types with operations and state, and there's the idea of introducing an object of a given type. Control-flow abstraction is concerned with the sequencing of program steps, the idea of a designator box as an abstraction, selection and repetition. You'd rightly expect a decent programming language like C++ to support all of these concepts.

Section 3.1

1

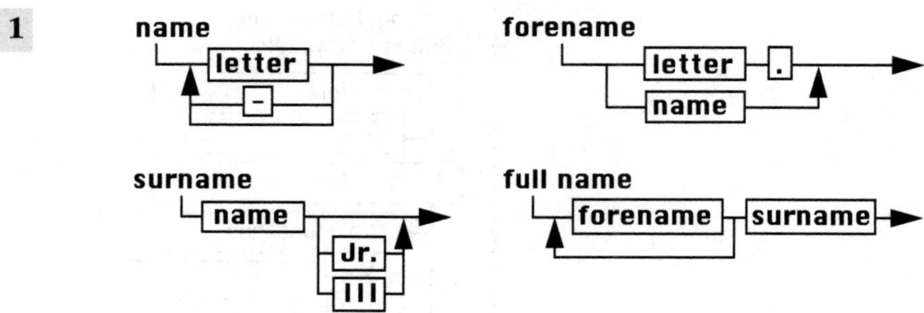

Add other surname prefixes as appropriate.

2

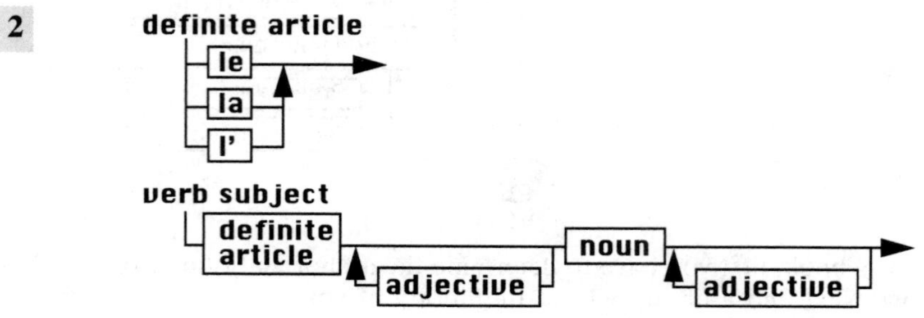

3 *I've just been to buy a PC*
So that I'll be able to see
If my problem designs
Are on the right lines
How's that for an answer to 3?

4 Get up; wash; make a cup of coffee; drink the coffee; eat some breakfast; leave the house. There's grouping in all of these instructions since each can be described using more detail. For example, to make a cup of (instant) coffee you've got to boil some water, put coffee, milk, sugar into a cup, then pour water into the cup. Parameters for this operation are the amounts of water, coffee powder, milk and sugar. Note that "make a cup of coffee" is a valid description regardless of the way you make the coffee (you may use a percolator or cafétière). Abstraction allows you to hide the details.

Section 3.2

1 The box in Figure 2.25 containing Create possibles appears in Figure 3.2 as `Array<bool> possibles;`. The designator box Fill possibles appears as `fillPossibles(possibles)`. Similarly, the designator boxes Cancel from possibles and Print out uncanceled numbers in possibles appear as `cancel(possibles)` and `printPossibles(possibles)`. The loop repetition is contained within `cancelPossibles (possibles)`.

2 The **terminating character** for several **statement**s in C++ is a semicolon, although not all statements end with this character (e.g. **compound statement**).

3 Comments can occupy a whole line and can be placed on the same line as, but after, C++ statements.

Section 3.3

1 In soaps look out for the spoiled brat, the scatterbrained kid, the self-made man, the sports fanatic, etc. Often in soaps you can identify family traits. Many "classic" books are based around a tragic hero/heroine. Of course, all your Professors are really intelligent, helpful, super people :-).

2 You should be able to recognize the syntactic elements **declaration** (e.g. `int freq;`) and **assignment** (e.g. `freq = 0`) that are included in the **statement** syntax diagram.

Section 3.4

1 For many board games a "turn" is a variation on the following:

(a) Initial actions
(b) Throw the die or dice
(c) Act on that throw
(d) Final actions

In Risk the initial action is to work out how many armies you're entitled to. There's a selection statement involved here; if you have all the countries in South America, or you have an appropriate set of cards, take extra armies. Then there's a loop repetition: for each army add it to one of your countries. Steps (b) and (c) are part of a while repetition; repeat the steps while you still have at least enough armies to challenge your opponent and you're still willing to take the risk of a challenge. The final action involves another selection statement; if you've captured a country take a card.

2 Most children's songs are loop repetitions counting down. Here are two that we know:

(a) *There were 10 in the bed and the little one said*
"Roll over, Roll Over"
So they all rolled over and one fell out
Repeat, decreasing the number in the bed until
There was one in the bed and the little one said
"Good Night"

(b) *Five currant buns in a baker's shop*
Round and fat with sugar on top
Along came Mike with a penny one day
Bought a currant bun and took it right way

Repeat, decreasing the number of currant buns by one each time until there are none left. Change the name as appropriate.

3 For a **for statement** you need to recognize the keyword `for`, the open and close parentheses enclosing three syntactic elements separated by two semicolons, and a compound statement. For an **if statement** you need to recognize the keyword `if`, a Boolean expression enclosed by parentheses, and a compound statement.

Section 3.5

1 The functions `fillPossibles(...)` and `cancelPossibles(...)` are implementations of the abstractions expanded in Figure 2.26, while `printPossibles(...)` is an implementation of Figure 2.27.

2
```
// fillPossibles(...)    initializes the container possibles
// cancelPossibles(...) cancels the non-primes in possibles
// printPossibles(...)  prints out the prime numbers
// drawFrequencies(...) draws a histogram distribution of
//                      the prime numbers
```

CHAPTER 4

Section 4.0

1 Two lines should be changed to something like the following:

```
cout << "Bert Eratosthenes" << endl;
cout << "Welcome to CS101 at Newcastle" << endl;
```

2 The `cout ...` lines should be changed to something like the following:

```
cout << "Hello"        << endl;
cout << "Bert"         << endl;
cout << "Eratosthenes" << endl;
cout << "Welcome"      << endl;
cout << "to"           << endl;
```

. . . and so on.

3 (a)
```
---------------

---------------
```

(b)
```
  * ********   |-----
```

As there isn't an `<< endl` anywhere, the program won't draw the expected tree. Each `cout` statement needs `<< endl` before the semicolon.

4 (a) Terminating semicolon missing; (b) Closing double quotation character missing before the semicolon; (c) The space between the two << characters is illegal.

6 All of the semicolons *except* for the final one need to be removed. The single-statement version that draws the tree is:

```
cout << "  *" << endl << " *** " << endl << "*****" << endl
     << "  |" << endl << "-----" << endl;
```

Clearly, it's not so easy to see from this version that the statements are drawing a tree, and therefore the multiple-line version is preferred. You'll be seeing another version in the exercises in Section 4.2 that overcomes this problem.

Section 4.1

1 (a) You'll get a set of error messages. As the start of the program cannot be identified, expect the compiler to flag most of the following lines as being illegal.

(b) There should be a message about "incrude" not being recognized, and some follow-on effects giving errors on subsequent statements, particularly those involving `cout` (which is most of them!).

(c) Deleting a semicolon tends to give lots of error messages; deleting a double quote should give at least one message about an unterminated string.

(d) As long as you only changed the word inside the double quotes, there shouldn't be any compile-time errors. This is not a syntax error.

2 The errors are highlighted in **underlined bold**.

```
#include <iostream.h"
int main[]
{
  return 0;
)
```

```
#Include <iostream.h>
imt main()
{
  return 0;
};
```

Section 4.2

1 The first program will not compile since the compiler won't recognize `intmain` or `return0`. The second program will compile and produce the same output as the program in Figure 4.1. But which program is easier to read?

2 The output statement should be of the following form:

```
cout << "Department of Computing Science" << endl
     << "The University of Newcastle"     << endl
     << "Claremont Road"                  << endl
     << "Newcastle upon Tyne"             << endl << endl
     << "NE1 7RU"                         << endl
     << "ENGLAND"                         << endl;
```

You can see above where white space has been added to make the statement's appearance more pleasing to the eye. Adding spaces between the letters in words such as `main` or `cout` or `endl` will cause compile-time errors. Adding spaces inside the pairs of double quotes will affect the output, although if these spaces are at the end of some printed characters, you won't see them on the screen.

3
```
cout << "  *  "    << endl
     << " *** "    << endl
     << "*****"    << endl
     << "  |  "    << endl
     << "-----" << endl;
```

4 You'll get a compile-time error since it will appear to the compiler that the first line doesn't have a closing " character.

Section 4.3

1 The constant declaration needs to be changed – both its name (otherwise the program would be very confusing to read) and its value. The expression that converts the number of years using this constant also needs to be changed to match the new name of the constant. The output statement that printed out the fact that the person is "hours young" also needs to be changed. Here's part of the answer:

```
const double MINUTES_YEAR = 365.0 * 24.0 * 60.0;
```

2 `Their 150 is 150.`

Propose a change to the code fragment so that the message printed is

`Their iq is 150.`

3 Check the program's output by using a calculator for some value of the age in years and comparing the answers with those of the program (e.g. for ages 1, 10, 100).

4 You'll get a compile-time error concerning the lines on which the wrong operators were used.

5 Different systems have different keyboard sequences for interrupting an executing program. On UNIX and PC systems, typing a letter C while holding down the <Ctrl> key usually works. On Macintosh systems, try typing a period while holding down the or ⌘ key.

Section 4.4

1 *Valid:* (a); (b); (e) and we hope you agree with the sentiment in (e) as well. *Invalid:* (c) wrong characters for commencing a comment; (d) space between / characters is not permitted; (f) this line doesn't contain a comment, since the // are within the double quotes and are therefore part of the message that would be output. However, our syntax rule doesn't identify this possibility as being illegal.

2 Placing those characters turns the statement into a comment, which will be ignored by the compiler. The resulting program therefore won't print out that message.

CHAPTER 5

Section 5.2

1 Generally, C++ systems on PCs have the `int` range –32768 → 32767 while most other systems have the range –2147483648 → 2147483648. The range for `doubles` is normally that shown in Figure 5.3. However, note that some compilers have settable options that permit different ranges to be selected.

2 The different ranges of `ints` correspond to different numbers of bits used to represent them in the computer – 16 bits give the smaller range, while 32 bits give the larger range. Read up about two's complement representation to discover how numbers are represented. Double numbers use 64 bits; read about floating-point number representation if you want to know more.

Section 5.3

1 The last two `cout` statements produce the same output. In the statement containing the + operators, the sets of characters are concatenated before being output.

2 The various components of someone's address; messages to be printed by a program; entries in a diary program; source lines in your C++ program.

Section 5.4

1 For the PDTs you should be able to find the member functions fairly easily in the header files, although you'll find there's a lot of additional C++ detail. After you've dealt with Chapters 12 and 13, the purpose of all of this detail will become clear. (You won't find any header files for the built-in types of course.)

2 Moving the `include` to the end of the program means that the compiler won't have any of the information about the I/O PDTs the program uses, and thus any I/O statement will result in a compile-time error message.

CHAPTER 6

Section 6.0

1 The mechanic following the repair program is going to need some tools to effect the repair. It would be useful to have a list of these tools at the beginning so the mechanic can ensure the tools are available before starting (a screwdriver, a 35mm wrench, a hammer, a six-pack of beer, . . .). Similarly for the instructions for assembling a piece of furniture, so you know not to start if you haven't, say, got any glue for the joints.

Section 6.1

1
```
#include "Canvas.h"

int main()
{
  Canvas anInstance;   // Declaration statement

  return 0;
} // end main()
```

Executing the declaration statement for the `Canvas` variable results in a canvas object being created in the computer's memory. However, there's no visual representation of this on your computer's screen yet since the size of the `Canvas` variable needs to be set before it can be made visible.

2 The **type identifiers** and *variable identifiers* in the following C++ declaration statements are:

int	*count*;	**bool**	*isPlaying*;
PlayerStatus	*status*;	**Palette**	*forText*;
double	*salary*;	**Text**	*address*;
Duration	*cdLength*;	**Product**	*packetOfSoap*;

The style rules are coming up in following sections, but did you note any particular uses of capital letters?

3 `#include "CDPlayer.h"`

```
int main()
{
  CDPlayer myPlayer;
  CDPlayer myOldPlayer;
  CDPlayer myNewPlayer;
  double   theFirstDouble;
  double   theSecondDouble;

  return 0;
} // end main()
```

When executed, you will see three instances of the CD player graphics appear briefly on the screen.

4 The program will give compile-time errors. The following line is required to include the header file associated with the `Canvas` PDT (strictly, the `iostream` include isn't needed):

```
#include "Canvas.h"
```

Section 6.2

1 The syntactically legal type identifiers are those that are *not* crossed out:

`RecordPlayer`	~~`Floppy-DiskType`~~	~~`switch`~~
`integer`	~~`double`~~	`Vinyl_Record_Player`
`ReCoRdPlAyEr`	`Boolean`	`Aaaaaaaaaaaaa`
~~`Floating.Point`~~	~~`2ndTrack`~~	`C_D_P_l_a_y_e_r`
`RecordPlayerWithSpeedControlFor78RPMVinylDisks`		

The following are not legal type identifiers:

`Floppy-DiskType`	(minus sign not permitted)
`switch`	(keyword)
`double`	(keyword)
`Floating.Point`	(dot character not permitted)
`2ndTrack`	(identifier must commence with a letter)

2 The following type identifiers should be rejected on style grounds:

```
integer  Vinyl_Record_Player  ReCoRdPlAyEr  Aaaaaaaaaaaaa
C_D_P_l_a_y_e_r  RecordPlayerWithSpeedControlFor78RPMVinylDisks
```

3 The identifiers that are *not* suitable for use as variable identifiers are crossed out:

~~`RecordPlayer`~~	`x`	`count`
`complex`	~~`3rdWindow`~~	`sideLength`
`weightKG`	`try`	~~`repeat`~~
~~`speed-RPM`~~	`window`	`name`

Section 6.3

1 The following are the invalid compound statements.

(b)	`{ cout << "Hello"; )`	wrong closing bracket.
(c)	`cout << "Hello";`	no enclosing braces.
(e)	`{{{ cout << "Hello"; }}`	one missing closing brace.

Having looked at these exercises that didn't follow our style rule for the layout of braces, are you persuaded that the rule helps you avoid making brace-matching mistakes in the first place?

2 The following styles may be found in other books

1.
```
int main() {
  ...
  return 0;
}
```

2.
```
int main()
  {
    return 0;
  }
```

3.
```
int main
{ ... return 0; }
```

Style 1 makes it less obvious where the matching pairs of braces are, although the statement indenting gives you a hint. Style 2 is close to ours, although runs into difficulties with the length of lines since the statements inside a compound statement are indented by four spaces each time. Style 3 is rarely feasible due to the statements inside the braces. Finally, you'll probably come across compound statements where the braces are placed without any consistent style – the worst kind of style usage!

Section 6.4

2 Use of the built-in types `double` and `char` results in the declared variables being uninitialized, but having a random value. A `bool` variable is given the value `false` when it is declared. A `CDisc` variable is uninitialized, and this is detected at run-time if you try to use the variable in this state. If you got compile-time errors when using `bool` or `CDisc`, did you remember to change the program to `#include` the relevant files?

Section 6.5

1 The statements that will give rise to a compile-time error are crossed out:

(a) `double minusPi = -3.14159;`
(b) ~~`char letters = "C++";`~~
(c) ~~`Text digits = 1234567890;`~~
(d) ~~`bool end = FALSE;`~~
(e) `int fourHundred = 4 * 10;`
(f) `char letterP = 'P';`
(g) `Text name = "Debbie";`
(h) `int nine = 9;`

(b) has the wrong type for the initialization value. The double quote characters are missing in (c). The `bool` value should be `false` in (d). Note that (e) will not give rise to a compile-time error, although it's a rather suspicious statement given the variable's name and its initialization value!

Section 6.6

1 The statements that will give rise to a compile-time error are crossed out:

(a) `const double MINUS_PI = -3.14159;`
(b) ~~`const Text COPYRIGHT "Copyright (c) 1996";`~~
(c) ~~`const int ANSWER = "Forty two";`~~
(d) ~~`const bool = true;`~~
(e) `const char OPEN_BRACE = '{';`
(f) ~~`const 2PI = 6.28318;`~~

The equals sign is missing in (b). The value is the wrong type in (c). The variable identifier is missing in (d). The identifier is illegal in (f).

CHAPTER 7

Section 7.0

1 Generally sequential execution is represented in the design notation by rectangular boxes representing the steps being directly below each other. For example, see diagram on right.

Start
A
B
C
End

2 If you're following the reading plan, you won't be reading sequentially. You should have jumped to this chapter while part way through Chapter 6.

Section 7.1

1
```
#include "CDPlayer.h"

int main()
{
  CDPlayer player1;
  CDPlayer player2;

  player1.on();
  player2.on();
  player1.off();
  player2.off();

  return 0;
} // end main()
```

2 The design is along the following lines:

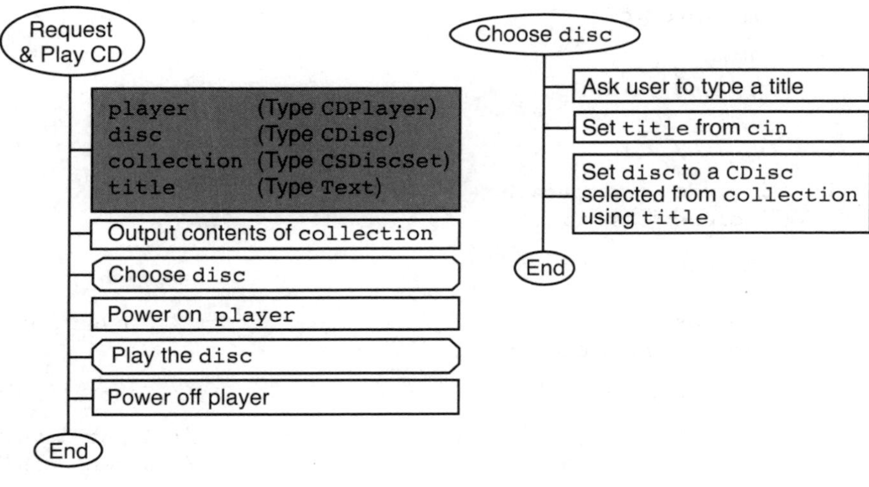


```
#include <iostream.h>
#include "CDPlayer.h"
#include "CDisc.h"
#include "CSDiscSet.h"
#include "Text.h"

int main()
{
  CDPlayer  myPlayer;      // Declare the objects
  CDisc     aDisc;
  CSDiscSet someDiscs;
  Text      title;
                           // Output collection contents
  cout << "The following discs are available:" << endl;
  cout << someDiscs;
                           // Choose disc
  cout << "Type the title you want: ";
  getline(cin, title);           // Get the title
  aDisc = someDiscs.selectDisc(title);   // Select the disc

  myPlayer.on();           // Power on player
                           // Play the disc
                               // Put disc into player
  myPlayer.open();                   // Open drawer
  myPlayer.load(aDisc);              // Load disc
  myPlayer.close();                  // Close drawer
                               // Instruct player to play
  myPlayer.play();                   // Press "Play" button
                               // Remove disc from player
  myPlayer.open();                   // Open drawer
  aDisc = myPlayer.unload();         // Unload disc
```

```
  myPlayer.close();                        // Close drawer

  myPlayer.off();          // Power off player

  return 0;
} // end main()
```

Section 7.2

1

```
#include <iostream.h>
#include "Canvas.h"

int main()
{
  Canvas window;                              // Create objects
  int    sideLength;

  window.setSize(200, 200);                   // Initialize window

  cout << "Length of square side: ";          // Input a value for
  cin  >> sideLength;                         // sideLength

  window.moveTo(10, 10);                      // Move to start pos.

  window.penDown();                           // Put the pen down

  window.moveRelative(sideLength, 0);         // Horiz. line forward
  window.moveRelative(0, sideLength);         // Vertical line up
  window.moveRelative(-sideLength, 0);        // Horiz. line back
  window.moveRelative(0, -sideLength);        // Vertical line down

  return 0;
} // end main()
```

2 The above program could be changed to use the following constant variable declarations (with changes to the member-function calls to remove the explicit numbers and to use the appropriate variable identifier in their place):

```
const int WIN_SIZE_X = 200;
const int WIN_SIZE_Y = WIN_SIZE_X;
const int START_X    = 10;
const int START_Y    = START_X;
```

These changes permit all of the "magic" numbers controlling the program's behavior to be in one place. It's then easy for the reader to identify these values. It's also easier to change one constant, say, if the starting position needed to be changed, than it would be to change all of the instances of the value in the program.

3 You'll get a run-time error, since a disc with that title doesn't exist. Read the next section to find out about run-time errors.

Section 7.3

1 The compile-time error messages will be system-dependent, so can't be reproduced here. However, did you try the following faults: misspelling a member function name; missing out the "dot" in a member-function call; missing out the variable name in a member-function call; missing out one of the parentheses (or) in a member-function call; calling

the load(...) member function with a different variable type as a parameter (e.g. myPlayer.load(27);).

2 You'll get a link-time error. The program is in fact a syntactically legal C++ **compilation unit**, although it doesn't match the syntax element **simple C++ program** that you've used so far. Thus it will compile without errors, but the linker will detect an error when it comes to construct the executable program as the `main()` function won't be found.

3 Illegal side lengths result in a run-time error being reported by the `Canvas` PDT. The values 0 and –5 are OK, but –20 will give a run-time error. If you think all of these peculiar side length values should give a run-time error, a thought for which there is some justification, see Chapter 11.

CHAPTER 8

Section 8.0

1 Suit (Clubs, Diamonds, Hearts, Spades) and face value (Ace, King, Queen, Jack, 10 down to 2).

2 For a computer, component values could include make and model, serial number, processor type, whether the machine is switched on or off, whether or not there's a floppy disk in the disk drive, and the size of the hard disk or RAM. For a washing machine, there could also be component values of model and serial number, and the load capacity. Additionally you could include the selected wash program (often numerical, but could be expressed as MEDIUM WASH, DELICATES, WOOL, etc.) and what stage an executing program is at. Component values for a car could include the engine capacity, what extras the car is fitted with, the gear selected, current speed, and amount of gasoline in the tank.

Section 8.1

1 See the answer to Exercise 1 of Section 5.2.

2 `NORTH SOUTH WEST EAST`

3

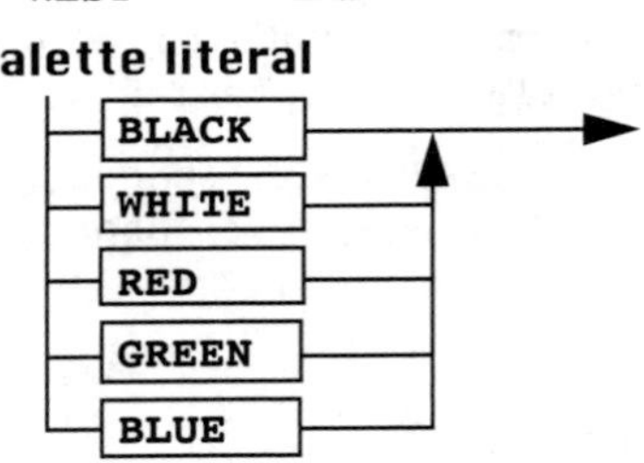

Section 8.2

1 (a) `int`; (b) illegal (it's an expression); (c) `double`; (d) `double`; (e) `double`; (f) `double`; (g) `int` (but may not be representable); (h) illegal; (i) `double`; (j) illegal; (k) illegal (exponent must be an `int` literal); (l) illegal (an expression); (m) `int` (octal); (n) illegal (an expression); (o) `double`.

2 (a) `int`; (b) `bool`; (c) `char`; (d) `PlayerStatus`; (e) unknown; (f) `Text`; (g) unknown; (h) `double`; (i) unknown; (j) `Text`; (k) `char`; (l) `Text`; (m) `Palette`.

3 The following are examples of legal declarations-with-initialization.

```
int          pageNumber    = 33;
double       weight        = 155.12;
bool         test          = false;
char         terminator    = ';';
Text         message       = "Isn't this great?";
Palette      brushColor    = BLUE;
PlayerStatus currentStatus = ON;
```

4 The assignments to `weight` and `message` are the only valid assignments.

Section 8.3

1 (a) `r+(s-t)/(v*v)` (b) `(a+b)/(c+d/(e+f))`
(c) `n*(n+1)*(2*n+1)/6` (d) `4*PI*r*r*r*h/3`

2 In the following, brackets have been added to indicate the order.

(a) `(((a * b) / c) + (d * e)) - f`
(b) `(((a * b) / (c + d)) * e) - f`
(c) `(a * b) / (c + (d * (e - f)))`
(d) `(a * b) / ((c + (d * e)) - f)`

3 When n is equal to 7 the values of the expressions are (a) 28; (b) 24; (c) 28; (d) 0. When n is equal to 8 the values of the expressions are (a) 36; (b) 36; (c) 32; (d) 0.

4 (a) `double(1000) / double(8) + double(9) * 6.0`
(b) `int('A') + int('a')`
(c) `double(5) * (98.4 - double(32)) / double(9)`
(d) `"Hi" + Text(' ') + "Ho"`

5 Assume all quantities are of type `double`.

(a) `taxablePay = income - 10000.0`
(b) `taxPercentage = (taxablePay / income) * 100.0`
(c) `superTax = (income - 50000.0) * 0.2`
(d) `taxBill = superTax + higherTax + basicTax`,

where `higherTax = (50000.0 - 20000.0) * 0.1`
and `basicTax = (20000.0 - 10000.0) * 0.05`

Section 8.4

1 (a) 7; (b) 8; (c) 8; (d) 8; (e) 3.

2 Change `product *= nextTerm` to `product += nextTerm`.

Section 8.5

1 (a) `false`; (b) `true`; (c) `false`; (d) `true`; (e) `true`.

2 `(test1 || test2) && (!(test1 && test2))`.

3 (a) `income > 50000.0`
(b) `(20000.0 < income) && (income <= 50000.0)`
(c) `income <= 10000.0`

4 (a) `('a' <= ch) && (ch <= 'z')`
(b) `(('a' <= ch) && (ch <= 'z')) || (('A' <= ch) && (ch <= 'Z'))`
(c) `(ch == 'a') || (ch == 'e') || (ch == 'i') || (ch == 'o') || (ch == 'u')` (unfortunately there's no short-hand version).

CHAPTER 9

Section 9.0

1 (a) Function name – howManyPages; parameter – the number of a chapter (an integer); result – a number of pages (an integer); (b) Function name – whichPage; parameters – the word or phrase being searched for (a text string); result – a page number (an integer);

2 Parameters could involve the length of a side and the coordinates of one corner, or the coordinates of all four corners. Other variations will be discussed in Chapter 11.

Section 9.1

1 The body of `main()` can be as follows:

```
int time1 = clock();
int time2 = clock();
cout << "Time difference " << time2 - time1 << endl;
```

A call to the `clock()` function involves a time overhead (a slight delay) which may, or may not, be negligible. If you get strange answers, try replacing `int` by `long`. We'll explain the difference between `int` and `long` in Chapter 13.

The loop has to be large enough that the time spent in the loop is large compared to the first and last `clock()` call overheads.

Section 9.2

1 An implicit type coercion will take place; –6.7 will get truncated to –6 and the absolute value of this is 6 (as an `int`). Of course, you'll avoid implicit type coercions, won't you?

2 `atan(...)` returns a value in the range $-\pi/2$ to $\pi/2$. Since `atan2(...)` requires x and $y$coordinates, a value in the range $-\pi$ to π can be determined.

3 Yes, if the unary operator is defined for the return type of the function. Otherwise, no.

4 Don't expect a run-time error to be flagged, unfortunately. See if any system documentation describes this situation. And if it doesn't, what do you learn from this about the importance of documentation?

5 Any printable character other than a space or an alphanumeric character. The full set is
`# $ % * ( ) " ' \ ' ~ : ; . < > / ? \ | [ ] { } - _ = +`

6 The characters whose literals are `' '` `'\f'` `'\n'` `'\r'` `'\t'` `'\v'`

7 `bool(isalpha(ch)) && (!bool(islower(ch)))`

8 The value of the actual parameter.

9 The answer to the first question is that you should get a compile-time error. The answer to the second question is that you may get a compile-time warning only. In writing a statement, you can choose to "throw away" or ignore any result returned from a function call if you want to.

10 If the parameter is a value parameter the assumption is that the function is going to make use of the value passed. If the variable was uninitialized the actual value used is not predictable. So, this is likely to lead to an error.

Section 9.3

1 Reposition the pen on the first call to `moveRelative(...)` as follows:

```
myPicture.moveRelative(xCenter - HOUSE_WIDTH / 2,
                       yCenter - HOUSE_HEIGHT / 2);
```

where `xCenter` and `yCenter` are the required coordinates. This example is assuming that the pen is at position (0,0) when the `Canvas` is created. An alternative would be to replace the `moveRelative(...)` member-function call by `moveTo(...)`.

2 Add the following code to the end.

```
const int DOOR_WIDTH  = 10;
const int DOOR_HEIGHT = 20;

myPicture.moveTo(START_X_POSITION +
                 (HOUSE_WIDTH + DOOR_WIDTH) / 2, 0);
myPicture.moveRelative(0, DOOR_HEIGHT);
myPicture.moveRelative(-DOOR_WIDTH, 0);
myPicture.moveRelative(0, -DOOR_HEIGHT);
```

Section 9.4

1 No!

2 No! Not even type coercion can come to your rescue here.

3 No! The types must be identical.

4 If the parameter is a reference parameter then it's possible that the function doesn't attempt to make use of any value passed into the function, so this would be OK. If it does use the value then this would be an error, as you saw earlier for a value parameter (Exercise 10, Section 9.2).

5 When the parameter is a reference parameter, expect `3      cheers` to be output. When the parameter is a value parameter, expect `1      cheers` to be output :-(.

Section 9.5

1 `cin.operator>>(i)   // It's a member operator`

2 Recall that you can write, for example, `cin >> i >> j`. The first "call" of the operator >> returns a variable rather than a value, and this variable is then used for the second call. If you write the code as `(cin.operator>>(i)).operator>>(j)` you can see that a variable is required for the second dot operator.

3
```
Text&  operator+=(Text& lhs, Text rhs); // Stand-alone operator
Text& operator+=(Text rhs);             // Member operator
```

Note that the first parameter for the stand-alone operator is a reference parameter, and therefore the corresponding actual parameter must be a variable. When you write `name += "Jr."` the value of the actual parameter is changed.

CHAPTER 10

Section 10.0

1/2 Possible designs for these two exercises are given below. Note that to use the design for Which Chapter in the Find Chapter design would require the declaration of variable `found` in Which Chapter to be removed.

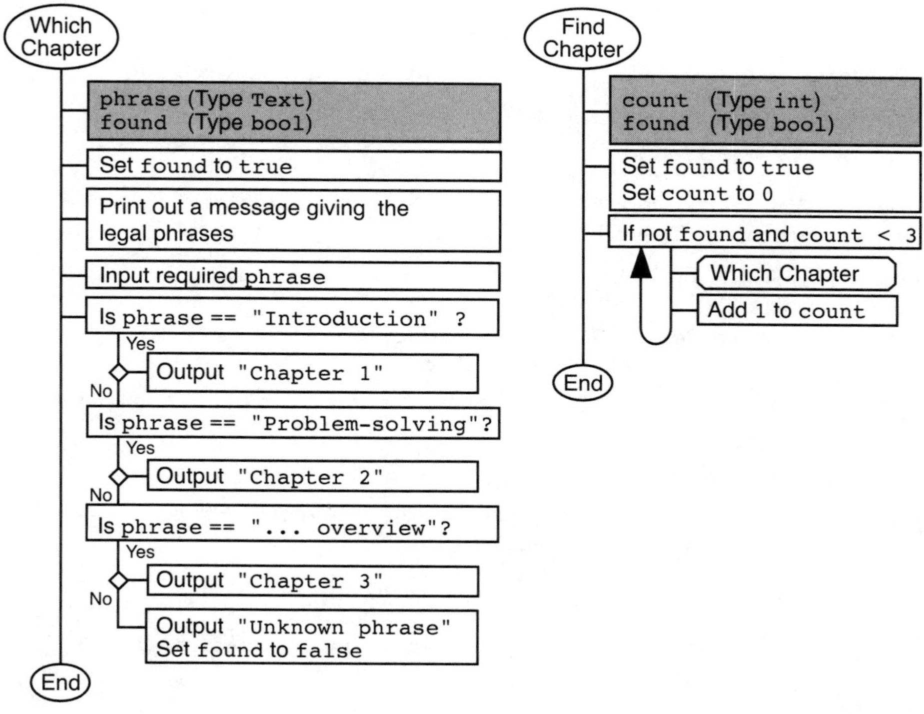

Exercise 1 Exercise 2

3 Designs for the designator boxes **Output trunk** and **Output base** are similar to the Output rows chart given, and therefore are not provided here. C++ code for the complete design will be found in the solution to Exercise 5 in Section 10.2.

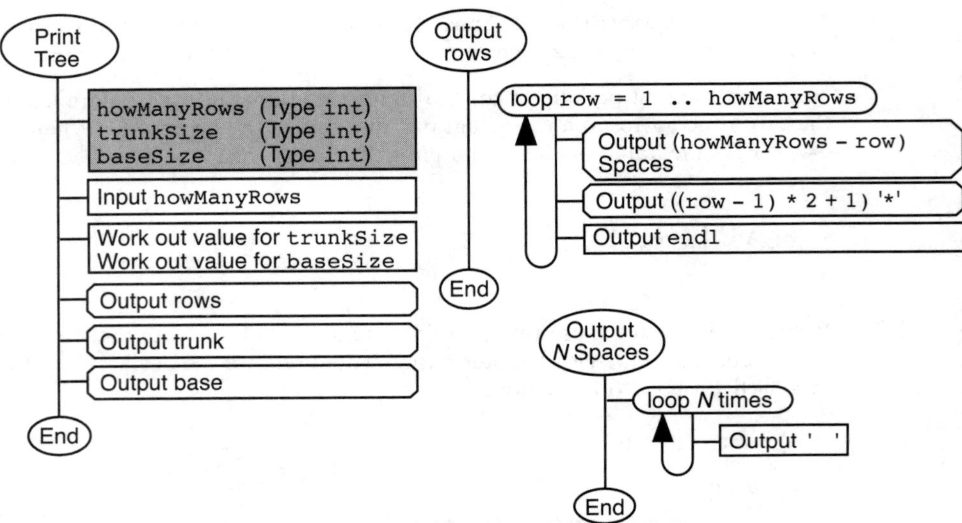

Section 10.1

1
```
#include <iostream.h>
#include "bool.h"
#include "Text.h"

int main()
{
  const Text CHAP1 = "Introduction";
  const Text CHAP2 = "Problem-solving";
  const Text CHAP3 = "Programming language overview";

  bool found = true;
  Text phrase;

  cout << "These are the phrases known: " << endl << endl
       << CHAP1 << endl
       << CHAP2 << endl
       << CHAP3 << endl << endl;

  cout << "Which phrase do you want to read up about: ";
  getline(cin, phrase);

  if (phrase == CHAP1)
  {
    cout << "Read Chapter 1" << endl;
  }
```

```
  else if (phrase == CHAP2)
  {
    cout << "Read Chapter 2" << endl;
  }
  else if (phrase == CHAP3)
  {
    cout << "Read Chapter 3" << endl;
  }
  else
  {
    cout << "Sorry, unknown phrase" << endl;
    found = false;
  }

  return 0;
} // end main()
```

2 Test the `PLAYER_EMPTY` arm by not loading a CD into the player (e.g. comment out the `load(...)` member-function call). Test the `PLAYER_ERROR` arm by commenting out the `close()` member-function call.

3

(i) Fragment 1: `Msg2 Msg4`	Fragment 2: `Msg2`
(ii) Fragment 1: `Msg1 Msg2 Msg4`	Fragment 2: `Msg1`
(iii) Fragment 1: `Msg3`	Fragment 2: `Msg3`

4 The following case labels are illegal since they don't represent a constant value known at compile-time:

```
case count:        case count + 1:    case LABEL_FOUR + count:
```

The following case label is illegal since it is an incomplete expression:

```
case LABEL_FOUR +:
```

The following case labels are illegal since they don't represent an integral value:

```
case today:        case "Monday":         case "3":
```

The following case label is illegal since `case` can't be a label:

```
case case:
```

The following case label is illegal since the label is missing:

```
case :
```

5 The illegal case labels are crossed out:

`case int(3.3):`	`case 75:`	`case 3.14159:`
`case -53:`	~~`case yes:`~~	~~`case theAnswer:`~~
`case ALABEL:`	~~`case "Quit":`~~	`case 'N':`
~~`case color:`~~	`case RED:`	`case 3 + 4:`

Note that floating-point numbers will be accepted by the compiler, which will apply an implicit type coercion to convert the values into `int` values.

6 Testing the following fragment with values such as 3, 2, and 99 will ensure that each arm has been executed.

```
int number;

cout << "Please enter an integer in the range 1 to 10: ";
cin  >> number;

switch (number)
{
  case 1: case 3: case 5: case 7: case 9:
    {
      cout << "It's an odd number" << endl;
    }
    break;
  case 2: case 4: case 6: case 8: case 10:
    {
      cout << "It's an even number" << endl;
    }
    break;
  default:
    {
      cout << "It's outside the requested range" << endl;
    }
  break;
} // end switch (number)
```

Section 10.2

1 The key difference is the position of the evaluation of the controlling Boolean expression, which is *before* the statements have been executed in the `while` statement, and *after* for the `do` statement. As a consequence, a `while` statement's body may be executed *zero* or more times; a `do` statement's body may be executed *one* or more times.

2 `Repetition statement 1:` (i) 1, (ii) 3, (iii) 0, (iv) a potentially infinite number of times, although the number representation of the computer normally "wraps around" and will eventually come back to zero.

`Repetition statement 2:` (i) 1, (ii) 3, (iii) potentially infinite, (iv) potentially infinite. Note the differences with the counts for `Repetition statement 1`.

3 `For statement 1:` (i) 1, (ii) 2, (iii) 0, (iv) 0.

`For statement 2:` (i) 1, (ii) 1, (iii) 1, (iv) 0.

4
```
#include <iostream.h>

int main()
{
  const int FACTOR  = 293;
  const int STOP_AT = 32000;
  int       count   = 0;
```

```
  for (int i = FACTOR; i <= STOP_AT; i += FACTOR)
  {
    cout << i << " ";
    count += 1;
  }
  cout << endl << endl
       << "There were " << count << " factors of "
       << FACTOR << " between 1 and " << STOP_AT << endl;

  return 0;
} // end main()
```

5

```
#include <iostream.h>

int main()
{
  int howManyRows = 0;
  int trunkSize   = 0;
  int baseSize    = 0;

  cout << "How many rows: "; // Input howManyRows
  cin  >> howManyRows;
                           // Work out trunkSize & baseSize
  trunkSize = (howManyRows/3) + 1;
  baseSize = trunkSize + ((trunkSize + 1) % 2);

                           // Output rows
  for (int row = 1; row <= howManyRows; row += 1)
  {
    for (int spaces  = 1;
             spaces <= (howManyRows - row);
             spaces += 1)
    {
      cout << ' ';
    }
    for (int stars = 1; stars <= ((row - 1) * 2 + 1); stars += 1)
    {
      cout << '*';
    }
    cout << endl;
  } // end for row
                           // Output trunk
  for (int trunk = 1; trunk <= trunkSize; trunk += 1)
  {
    for (int spaces = 1; spaces <= (howManyRows - 1); spaces += 1)
    {
      cout << ' ';
    }
    cout << '|' << endl;
  } // end for trunk
                               // Output base
```

```
  for (int base = 1; base <= trunkSize; base += 1)
  {
    for (int spaces  = 1;
             spaces <= ((howManyRows * 2) - baseSize)/2;
             spaces += 1)
    {
      cout << ' ';
    }
    for (int hashes = 1; hashes <= baseSize; hashes += 1)
    {
      cout << '#';
    }
    cout << endl;
  } // end for base

  return 0;
} // end main()
```

Section 10.3

1 The repetition can be terminated by testing for a newline character as the sentinel value. The design is straightforward, and captured in the comments in the code.

```
const int FACTOR = 7;
char ch;
int  checkSum;

checkSum = 0;
cout << "Enter the number for which the check digit is required."
     << endl << " Number: ";

do                            // Is the character a newline character?
{
  cin.get(ch);                            // Get the next character
  if (isdigit(ch))                        // Is it a digit
  {
    checkSum += (int(ch) - int('0'));    // Add to checksum
  }
} while (ch != '\n');
                              // Calculate check digit
cout << "Check digit is "
     << FACTOR - (checkSum % FACTOR)  << endl;
```

2 Test values should include various length unencoded account numbers, with values that you've already checked by hand to see what the check digit should be, for example, (encoded result in parentheses): 0 (07), 1 (16), 2 (25), 3 (34), 4 (43), 5 (52), 6 (61), 7 (70 – or is it 77: see Exercise 4 below), 11 (115), 111 (1114), 7777 (77777).

3 The following changes and additions need to be made to the answer given for Exercise 1.

```
bool badInput;

checkSum = 0;
badInput = false;
...
do                          // Is the character a newline character?
{
  cin.get(ch);                          // Get the next character
  if (isdigit(ch))                      // Is it a digit
  {
    checkSum += (int(ch) - int('0'));   // Add to checksum
  }
  else if (ch != '\n')                  // Bad input?
  {
    badInput = true;                       // Set flag
  }
} while (ch != '\n' && !badInput);

if (!badInput)
{
  cout << "Check digit is "
       << FACTOR - (checkSum % FACTOR)  << endl;
}
else
{
  cout << "Illegal input was detected" << endl;
}
```

4 The principal part of a decode program is as follows:

```
int  checkSum;
bool blankLine;
char ch;

while (true)
{
  cout << "Number to decode: ";

  checkSum = 0;
  blankLine = true;
  do                                // Is the next char a newline?
  {
    cin.get(ch);                        // Get the next character
    if (isdigit(ch))                    // Is it a digit?
    {
      blankLine = false;
      checkSum += (int(ch) - int('0'));  // Add to checksum
    }
  } while (ch != '\n');
```

```
  if (blankLine)            // Was there a blank line?
  {
    break;                          // Terminate repetition
  }
  else if ((checkSum % FACTOR) == 0) // Is checksum correct?
  {
    cout << "A valid account number" << endl;
  }
  else
  {
    cout << "An  invalid account number" << endl;
  }
} // end while (true)
```

Both of the values 7777 and 7770 produce a message indicating that they are legal. This is a problem not detected in the code above. Only one of the check digits 0 and 7 should be legal, and the encoding and decoding programs need to be designed appropriately.

5 Typical sequences are:

```
Type in a number between 4 and 20: 4
Step 2: 0 2 0

Type in a number between 4 and 20: 5
Step 2: 0 2 4 1 3 0

Type in a number between 4 and 20: 6
Step 2: 0 2 4 0
Step 3: 0 3 0

Type in a number between 4 and 20: 7
Step 2: 0 2 4 6 1 3 5 0
Step 3: 0 3 6 2 5 1 4 0

Type in a number between 4 and 20: 8
Step 2: 0 2 4 6 0
Step 3: 0 3 6 1 4 7 2 5 0
Step 4: 0 4 0

Type in a number between 4 and 20: 11
Step 2: 0 2 4 6 8 10 1 3 5 7 9 0
Step 3: 0 3 6 9 1 4 7 10 2 5 8 0
Step 4: 0 4 8 1 5 9 2 6 10 3 7 0
Step 5: 0 5 10 4 9 3 8 2 7 1 6 0

Type in a number between 4 and 20: 13
Step 2: 0 2 4 6 8 10 12 1 3 5 7 9 11 0
Step 3: 0 3 6 9 12 2 5 8 11 1 4 7 10 0
Step 4: 0 4 8 12 3 7 11 2 6 10 1 5 9 0
Step 5: 0 5 10 2 7 12 4 9 1 6 11 3 8 0
Step 6: 0 6 12 5 11 4 10 3 9 2 8 1 7 0
```

The sequences produced contain values in the range `0` to (`number - 1`), they always terminate with the value `0`, and no value apart from the terminating `0` is produced more than once for every `step` value. In addition, (a) If the `step` value is not a factor of the input `number`, the sequence generated contains all of the values between `0` and (`number - 1`); (b) if `number` is a prime number, all of the sequences are of equal length and they all contain each value between `0` and (`number - 1`).

CHAPTER 11

Section 11.0

1 (a) Determine the start page number of the chapter; determine the end page number; subtract the start page number from the end page number; add 1 to the result; (b) Go to the first page of the book; while the word/phrase is not found read the page to determine if the word/phrase appears on that page; repeat for each phrase until the word/phrase is found.

2 Name – drawHouse. Information exchange – the object on which the house is to be drawn, side lengths for the house "body" and the height of the roof. Return type – none. The design is covered in Section 9.3.

Section 11.1

1
```
void drawHouse(Canvas& picture, int houseWidth, int houseHeight,
               int roofHeight);
```

2
```
bool isOdd(int n);
bool isVowel(char ch);
```

Section 11.2

1 As far as the semantics of the language are concerned, the effect is that a local copy of the parameter is made on each call of `drawSquare(...)` and any calls to member functions of the `Canvas` PDT are applied to that local copy. The actual parameter thus remains unchanged. The issue of how this is interpreted visually in terms of the image that appears on the screen is a separate matter that has to be dealt with by the implementer of PDT `Canvas`. Run a test program to find out how the implementer of PDT `Canvas` dealt with this.

2
```
void drawRectangle(Canvas& picture, int longSide, int shortSide,
                   bool& successfulCall)
{ // Code to draw a rectangle
  if ((shortSide <= 0) || (longSide <= 0))
  {
    successfulCall = false;
  }
  else
  { // Draw the rectangle
    ...     // Similar to drawSquare(...) function in the Chapter
    successfulCall = true;
```

```
  }
  return;
} // end drawRectangle()
```

3 (i) There's a compile-time error; in the function body `aNumber` is an undeclared variable; (ii) `aNumber contains the value : 456`; (iii) `aNumber contains the value : 123`; (iv) Compile-time error since the function definition attempts to change the value of the (constant) parameter.

4 There's a clear need for a function that outputs a given character a specified number of times:

```
void output(char ch, int howMany)
{
  for (int count = 0; count < howMany; count += 1)
  {
    cout << ch;
  }
  return;
} // end output()
```

You could also have identified a function for drawing the rows, one for drawing the trunk, and another for drawing the base, each of which takes as a parameter the "size" of the tree.

5
```
void drawSquare(Canvas& picture, int sideLength,
                bool& successfulCall)
{
  // Code to draw a square
  int currentX;
  int currentY;
  int pictureWidth;
  int pictureHeight;

  picture.getPosition(currentX, currentY);
  pictureWidth  = picture.sizeX();
  pictureHeight = picture.sizeY();
  if(sideLength <= 0 ||
     (currentX + sideLength > pictureWidth) ||
     (currentY + sideLength > pictureHeight))
  {
    successfulCall = false;
  }
  // etc.
} // end drawSquare()
```

Section 11.3

1

```
bool isOdd(int n)
{
  return ((n % 2) != 0);
} // end isOdd()

bool isVowel(char ch)
{
  return ((ch == 'a') || (ch == 'e') || (ch == 'i')
                     || (ch == 'o') || (ch == 'u'));
} // end isVowel()
```

2

```
int lotteryNumber()
{
  return rand() % 50 + 1;
} // end lotteryNumber()
```

3

```
Text paletteToText(Palette color)
{
  Text textColor;

  switch(color)
  {
    case BLACK:
      {
        textColor = "Black";
      }
      break;
    case WHITE:
      {
        textColor = "White";
      }
      break;
    case RED:
      {
        textColor = "Red";
      }
      break;
    case GREEN:
      {
        textColor = "Green";
      }
      break;
    case BLUE:
      {
        textColor = "Blue";
      }
      break;
    default:
      {
```

```
        textColor = "Unknown color";
      }
      break;
  }
  return textColor;
} // end paletteToText()
```

Section 11.4

1

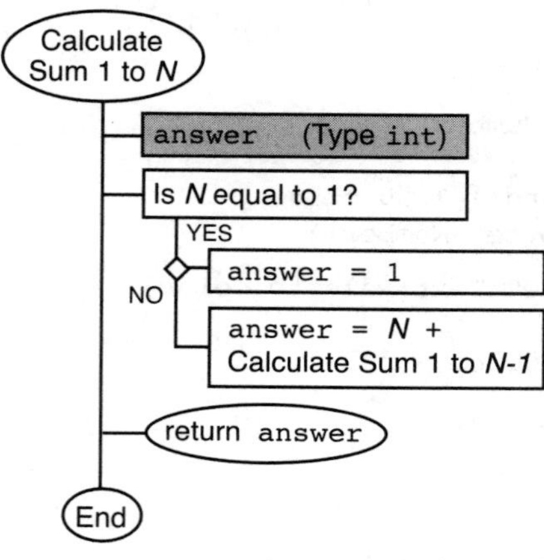


```
int sumIntegers(int n)
{
  int answer;

  if (n == 1)
  {
    answer = 1;
  }
  else
  {
    answer = n + sumIntegers(n - 1);
  }
  return answer;
} // end sumIntegers()
```

2

```
void printIntegers(int start, int finish)
{
  if (start <= finish)
  {
    int mid = (start + finish) / 2;

    printIntegers(start, mid - 1);
    cout << mid << " ";
    printIntegers(mid + 1, finish);
```

```
  }
  return;
} // end printIntegers()
```

3 When the actual parameter is 5, there are 5 calls with an actual parameter of 1 and 3 with an actual parameter of 0. When the actual parameter increases to 6, the numbers of calls increase to 8 and 5 respectively. These are, of course, just numbers in the Fibonacci sequence.

4
```
void towersOfHanoi(int numberOfDiscs, char towerA, char towerB,
                   char towerC) // Move From towerA to towerB
{
  if (numberOfDiscs > 1)
  {
    towersOfHanoi(numberOfDiscs - 1, towerA, towerC, towerB);
  }
  moveADisc(towerA, towerB);
  if (numberOfDiscs > 1)
  {
    towersOfHanoi(numberOfDiscs - 1, towerC, towerB, towerA);
  }
  return;
} // end towersOfHanoi()
```

Section 11.5

1 Output is

```
5        times 3        is equal to  15
7.5      times 2.5      is equal to  18.75
```

The first call corresponds to the `int` version; the second call corresponds to the `double` version.

Output is

```
5        times 2.5      is equal to  12.5
7.5      times 3        is equal to  22.5
```

In both cases it's the `double` version that gets called as a result of implicit coercions. Don't forget the recommendation not to rely on implicit coercions!

3 Use the square-drawing functions as a basis.

CHAPTER 12

Section 12.2

1 Contrast the following error-free version of the definition with the original to identify the syntax errors. The final identifier doesn't follow our style rules (it should be `FORTRAN` for that), but this doesn't contravene C++'s syntax rules:

```
enum PROG_LANGUAGES {C, C_PLUS_PLUS, MODULA_2, ADA, Fortran};
```

2 The illegal definitions are the following:

```
enum Transport     {CAR, BUS, TRAIN, HORSE}
enum Accommodation {5STAR, 4STAR, BED&BREAKFAST};
enum char          {Y, N};
enum Sports        {TENNIS, FOOTBALL, BADMINTON, SKIING};
enum Primes        {1, 2, 3, 5, 7, 11, 13};
```

The first is missing a terminating semicolon. The second and fifth contain illegal identifiers – you can't start an identifier with a digit, nor use the `&` character. You can't use the keyword `char` in the third. In the fourth, the identifier `FOOTBALL` has already been used at this scope level.

3 The analysis that led to Figure 2.31 suggests the use of `enum` to define a PDT representing the `State` of an account. The header file would contain:

```
// Header file    State.h

enum State {OPEN, CLOSED, OVERDRAWN, STOPPED, SPECIAL};

// I/O operator interfaces

istream& operator>>(istream& inStream,  State&  forInput);
ostream& operator<<(ostream& outStream, State   value);
```

The definitions of the I/O operators in file `State.c` could be:

```
#include <iostream.h>
#include "bool.h"
#include "State.h"
#include "Text.h"

// Definition for output operator << for State PDT

ostream& operator<<(ostream& outStream, State value)
{
  switch (value)
  {
    case OPEN:
      {
        outStream << "Open";
      }
      break;
    case CLOSED:
      {
        outStream << "Closed";
      }
      break;
    case OVERDRAWN:
      {
        outStream << "Overdrawn";
      }
```

```
      break;
    case STOPPED:
      {
        outStream << "Stopped";
      }
      break;
    case SPECIAL:
      {
        outStream << "Special";
      }
      break;
    default:
      {
        outStream << "Unexpected State value";
      }
      break;
  } // end switch (value)
  return outStream;
} // end operator<<()

istream& operator>>(istream& inStream, State& forInput)
{
  Text input;
  bool gotValue = false;

  while (!gotValue)   // while we've not got a value
  {
    inStream >> input;
    gotValue = true;  // Set false below if this isn't the case
    if (input == "OPEN")
    {
      forInput = OPEN;
    }
    else if (input == "CLOSED")
    {
      forInput = CLOSED;
    }
    else if (input == "OVERDRAWN")
    {
      forInput = OVERDRAWN;
    }
    else if (input == "STOPPED")
    {
      forInput = STOPPED;
    }
    else if (input == "SPECIAL")
    {
      forInput = SPECIAL;
    }
    else
    {
```

```
      cout << "Error. Got '" << input << "'"
           << " try again" << endl;
      gotValue = false;  // Go around while loop again
    }
  } // end while (!gotValue)
  return inStream;
} // end operator>>();
```

4
```
enum OnOrOFF          {ON, OFF};
enum OpenOrClosed     {OPEN, CLOSED};
enum StudentStatus    {LISTENING, READING, SLEEPING, TALKING};
enum LectureQuality   {EXCELLENT, SATISFACTORY, BORING,
                       AVERAGE,   POOR};
enum MusicMedium      {CD, VINYL, CASSETTE_TAPE, REEL_TAPE};
```

Did you apply the style rules to your enums? Any of the enum type's you've identified should have the characteristic that the only operations expected are assignment, equality, and possibly I/O.

Section 12.3

1 That fragment declares *no* variables. It's just a type definition.

2 There are compile-time errors on the following lines:

```
Jowett.fuel = GAS;                      No variable with identifier Jowett
green.Vehicle.fuel = ELECTRICITY;       "greenVehicle.fuel  = ..."
if (veteran == greenVehicle)            Equals operator not defined
{
  forSale.fuelConsumption = 100mpg;     Illegal int literal
}
```

3
```
struct Coordinates
{
  int xCoordinate;
  int yCoordinate;
};

void moveTo(Coordinates newPosition); // Member function of Canvas
```

Section 12.4

1 (i) You'll get a link-time error. A constructor definition is required if a constructor interface appears in the class definition. If the interface is in the class definition, the linker won't be able to find the equivalent function at link-time.

(ii) Yes, the program will compile and link.

(iii) The following sequence of events occurs. Processing the declaration in `main()`, the private member variable of `Class1` needs to be created. To do this the memory for the `int` private member variable is allocated and then the constructor of `Class0` is called, which generates the following output:

```
Class 0 constructor
```

Now `Class1`'s private member variable exists, and since there's no explicit constructor code in `Class 1`, the processing of the variable declaration is complete.

2 Add a `bool` private member variable that the constructor can set to indicate that the `Account` variable is uninitialized. Change the `accountOK()` private member function to test the value of this `bool`.

Section 12.5

1 Does the following sequence of operations and output indicate a problem?

```
anAccount.setAccountNumber(12345);
anAccount.setOverdraftLimit(10);
anAccount.withdraw(8);
anAccount.deposit(10);
cout << anAccount << endl;
```

```
Account Number:  12345
Balance:         2
Overdraft Limit: 10
Account State:   Overdrawn
```

2 Add output statements to the above sequence to try to identify the point at which errors occur. You should be able to identify that after the deposit operation the account's state hasn't been reset correctly. Maybe the bug is in that operation.

3 Looking at the implementation of `Account::deposit(...)` you should notice that the state of the account isn't reset at all, whereas if the state is `OVERDRAWN` and the balance is now greater than or equal to zero, then the state should be reset to `OPEN`. Make this change and retest.

Section 12.6

1 The code is given in the section. Did you remember to initialize `sequenceNo` in the constructor and change the second parameter of the output operator to be a reference parameter?

Section 12.7

1 Given that `Text`, `CDPlayer`, `CDisc`, `CSDiscSet` and `Canvas` all provide member functions, it should be obvious that they are implemented as `class`es. `PlayerStatus`, `DisplayMode` and `Palette` only provide abstract values, assignment and equality operators, so are implemented using `enum`s.

Confirm your predictions by looking at the header file associated with each PDT. You should be able to recognize much (but not necessarily all) of the C++ in those files.

CHAPTER 13

Section 13.1

1
```
+   // Date + int,  giving a Date
-   // Date - Date, giving an int (number of days)
```

Types representing money, weight, height, complex numbers, rational numbers.

Section 13.2

1 The following constructor interface would cause a compile-time error since its signature isn't unique:

```
SomeErrors(int systemErrorNo);
```

2 The compiler will generate an error since the default (parameter-less) constructor hasn't been specified. Remember that if you provide a constructor interface, you must provide the default constructor explicitly.

3 Add a `bool` private member variable and set its value in the default constructor to indicate that the variable is uninitialized. Then every member function and operator should check the value of this `bool` and report an error if the variable is uninitialized (a good use for a private member function). Alternatively you could use a negative value for the private member variable `totalSecs` as a sentinel value to indicate the uninitialized state.

4 Use defensive checks for the values of parameters in the constructors – for example the constructor that takes two parameters representing initial values for minutes and seconds should check that the seconds parameter is in the range 0 to 59. Use checks in the input operator for illegalities such as an incorrect separator character. The test program should work, but maybe these defensive checks will show up some problems with the implementation.

5 The expression `time + dur1` requires an operator interface either `int::operator+(Duration rhs)` or `operator+(int lhs, Duration rhs)`, neither of which are provided. The expression should have been written as `Duration(time) + dur1` or `dur1 + time`.

6
```
int main()
{
  int   intVariable   = 32767;
  short shortVariable = 32767;
  long  longVariable  = 32767;

  cout << "Initial values of     int:short:long are "
       << intVariable   << ':'
       << shortVariable << ':'
       << longVariable  << endl;

  intVariable   += 1;
  shortVariable += 1;
  longVariable  += 1;
  cout << "After addition of 1   int:short:long are "
```

```
      << intVariable   << ':'
      << shortVariable << ':'
      << longVariable  << endl;
  if (intVariable == shortVariable)
  {
    cout << "Looks like int is the same as short." << endl;
  }
  else if (intVariable == longVariable)
  {
    cout << "Looks like int is the same as long." << endl;
  }
  else
  {
    cout << "Should never get here :-(" << endl;
  }
  return 0;
} // end main()
```

7 Any constructor, member function or member operator that might take a value that needs the "big" integer should be changed to `long`. The constructor that takes a single `int` parameter is one candidate. Note that the compiler will coerce `int` values to `long` when actual/formal parameters are `int`/`long`.

Section 13.3

1 The compile-time error message will indicate that the type `Duration` has been defined twice. Add pre-processor lines to the header file:

```
#ifndef DURATION_H
#define DURATION_H
. . . // The current header file in here
#endif
```

2 The class definition should include

```
int getX();
int getY();
```

A definition for `getX()` follows; `getY()` is very similar:

```
int getX()
{
  int xCoord;
  int yCoord;

  giveCoordinates(xCoord, yCoord, angle);
  return xCoord;
} // end getX()
```

Section 13.4

1 The main items that should (and should not) have changed are:

```
// #include "PlayerStatus.h" //Must NOT be included

class CDPlayer
{
  public:

    // Member Types
    enum PlayerStatus {PLAYER_EMPTY, DISC_OK,
                       DISC_BAD, PLAYER_ERROR};
    ...
    // The following interface does NOT need changing!
    PlayerStatus status();                    // Status of player
    ...

};

int main()
{
  CDPlayer  myPlayer;
  ...
  if (myPlayer.status() == CDPlayer::PLAYER_EMPTY}
  {
..
```

2 The starred lines should have changed to:

```
NewPDT2 anEnum;
NewPDT3 aMemberVar;
aMemberVar.anEnum = LITERAL_1;
NewPDT1::NewPDT2 instancePDT2;
NewPDT1::NewPDT3 instancePDT3;
instancePDT1.aMemberFunction();
instancePDT2        = NewPDT1::LITERAL_1;
instancePDT3.anEnum = NewPDT1::LITERAL_2;
```

CHAPTER 14

Section 14.0

1 Stadia seats are often arranged into blocks. Theater seats are often divided into stalls and circles. After that, a row number/letter and seat number within a row are often used.

Section 14.1

1 The `return` statement in the body of `zeroArray(...)` needs to be changed to `return clearArray;` and the function call to `examTotals = clearArray(examTotals)`.

2 Here's the input operator. The output operator is similar.

```
istream& operator>>(istream& inStream, Array<int>& forInput)
{
  for (int i = 0; i < forInput.size(); i += 1)
  {
    inStream >> forInput(i);
  }
  return inStream;
}
```

3 Expecting the array to be input by rows, change the loop in the solution to Exercise 2 to:

```
  for (int row = 0; row < forInput.size(1); row += 1)
  {
    for (int col = 0; col < forInput.size(2); col += 1)
    {
      inStream >> forInput(row, col);
    }
  }
```

For the output operator you'll probably want to output a new line at the end of each row.

4

```
const int BOARD_SIZE = 8;
enum SquareOccupancy {BLACK, RED, UNOCCUPIED};
Array<SquareOccupancy> checkersBoard;
checkersBoard.setSize(BOARD_SIZE, BOARD_SIZE);
```

All pieces occupy the same color square. Red pieces occupy the first three rows; black pieces occupy the last three rows.

```
for (row = 0; row < BOARD_SIZE; row += 1) // Set all UNOCCUPIED
{
  for (col = 0; col < BOARD_SIZE; col += 1)
  {
    checkersBoard(row, col) = UNOCCUPIED;
  }
}
for (row = 0; row < 3; row += 1)
{
  assignRow(checkersBoard, row, BLACK);
}
for (row = BOARD_SIZE - 3; row < BOARD_SIZE; row += 1)
{
  assignRow(checkersBoard, row, RED);
}
```

where

```
void assignRow(Array<SquareOccupancy>& board, int row,
               SquareOccupancy color)
```

```
{
  for (int col = (row + 1) % 2; col < BOARD_SIZE; col += 2)
  {
    board(row, col) = color;
  }
  return;
} // end assignRow()
```

Section 14.2

1 See Section 2.6 for some ideas.

2 `enum SeatEnquiryStatus {OK, OCCUPIED, NO_SUCH_SEAT};`

Section 14.3

1 We've not told you about using built-in arrays as parameters to a function, and their use illustrates another pitfall with the built-in arrays in that the reference parameter mechanism can't be used. The reasons why are an advanced topic not covered in this book. The code below works, or you could simply write in-line code in place of the function calls.

```
void assignRow(SquareOccupancy board[][BOARD_SIZE], int row,
               SquareOccupancy color)
{
  for (int col = (row + 1) % 2; col < BOARD_SIZE; col += 2)
  {
    board[row][col] = color;
  }
  return;
} // end assignRow()

SquareOccupancy checkersBoard[BOARD_SIZE][BOARD_SIZE];

for (row = 0; row < BOARD_SIZE; row += 1)
{
  for (col = 0; col < BOARD_SIZE; col += 1)
  {
    checkersBoard[row][col] = UNOCCUPIED;
  }
}
for (row = 0; row < 3; row += 1)
{
  assignRow(checkersBoard, row, BLACK);
}
for (row = BOARD_SIZE - 3; row < BOARD_SIZE; row += 1)
{
  assignRow(checkersBoard, row, RED);
}
```

Section 14.4

1 For an `Array` use

```
Array<int> point;
point.setSize(2);
```

For a `struct` use

```
struct Point
{
  int xCoordinate;
  int yCoordinate;
};
```

Look through the pros and cons listed in Section 14.4 and apply them to these two representations. Note that the use of `struct` gives you a new type which the use of the array doesn't.

CHAPTER 15

Section 15.0

1 A compiler expects as input source code in the form of a sequence of characters. The output it produces depends on the success or otherwise of the compilation process. If compilation fails, error messages are produced but object code is not. If you get a compilation warning, you'll still get object code. If compilation succeeds, your system may indicate this to you in some way, and object code will be produced.

2 The linker requires object code as input and produces a binary program as output if linkage is successful. An error message is output if linkage is unsuccessful.

3 A word processor or graphics package expects input from a keyboard or mouse, and from a file. Output is to the screen, to a printer, and to a file. E-mail systems take input from the keyboard or mouse and from the network, and output messages to a network, the screen, a printer or to a file.

Section 15.1

1 (a) The digits before the decimal point will be input as an `int`; (b) this works OK since, in effect, a type coercion will be applied by the compiler; (c) if the character isn't a digit then no value will be read in so the variable will be uninitialized. If the character is a digit, that digit will be read as an `int`; (d) the first digit will be read as a `char`; (e) as for (d); (f) as for (c) but also applying (b) if the character is a digit.

2 Since `ostream` is a PDT that often varies between systems, we can't guarantee an answer that will hold for all systems. Even though it's a `double` value, `2.0` may be output without the decimal point and trailing zero. `2.1` and `0.5` are output in fixed-point format, while `0.000005` may be output in floating-point format.

Section 15.2

1 A yes-and-no answer. You can try it but the effect is undefined. Try this out on your system.

2
```
char nextChar;
int countSpaces = 0;
int countWords  = 0;

cin.get(nextChar);
while (nextChar != '\n')
{
  while (isspace(nextchar))
  {
    countSpaces += 1;
    cin.get(nextChar);
  }
  while (!isspace(nextChar))
  {
    cin.get(nextChar);
  }
  countWords += 1;
}
```

3 It consumes, but ignores, the next n characters. If the delimiter is included then the recognition of the delimiter in the input stream will terminate the skipping of characters. The delimiter itself is consumed.

4
```
char nextChar(istream& inStream)
{
  char c;

  cin.get(c);
  while (isspace(c))
  {
    cin.get(c);
  }
  cin.putback(c);
  return c;
}
```

Section 15.3

1
```
int inputInt(istream& inStream)
{
  const char COMMA = ',';
  char separator;
  int  firstInt;
  int  secondInt;

  inStream >> firstInt;
```

```
  if (inStream.peek() == COMMA)
  {
    inStream >> separator >> secondInt;
    firstInt = firstInt * 1000 + secondInt;
  }
  return firstInt;
} // end inputInt()

void outputInt(ostream& outStream, int value)
{
  Text convertedValue = "";
  int  count          = 0;

  while (value > 0)
  {
    if ((count != 0) && (count % 3 == 0))
    {
      convertedValue = Text(',') + convertedValue;
    }
    convertedValue = Text(char((value % 10) + int('0')))
                     + convertedValue;
    value /= 10;
    count += 1;
  }
  outStream << convertedValue;
  return;
} // end outputInt()
```

Unfortunately, if the hundreds digit is non-zero then the second number will be read in octal format :-(. Use `peek()` to check for this and `get(...)` to consume the zero if present. Do likewise for the tens digit, if necessary.

2 In the first and second output statements the width setting applies to the output of the `int` literal `10`. In the third output statement the width setting is applied to character output (\n), not the output of 10.

Section 15.4

1 Try, for example, `myResults.open("Results", ios::noreplace)` with `Results` an existing file that already has data in it. Then output to it and see if the contents of `Results` change. Systems seem to vary with respect to the default value they assume if the (second) formal parameter `ioMode` is not used in a call.

2 Set the input stream using:

```
Text     inputFileName;
ifstream input;

cout << "What's the name of the file that the numbers are in: ";
cin  >> inputFileName;
input.open(inputFileName);
```

Section 15.5

1 If all the data is of the correct format there will be no difference in execution. If, however, there is an invalid character in the data then all subsequent input operations will fail and the `while` repetition will be in an infinite cycle unless you intervene.

2 Here's the main fragment.

```
int sum = 0;
int nextNumber;
char ch;

cin >> nextNumber;        // Get the first value
while(true)
{
  if (bool(cin.eof()))
  {
    break;                // Exit from infinite loop on end of file
  }
  else if (bool(cin.bad()))
  {
    error("Stream has become corrupted");
  }
  else if (bool(cin.fail()))
  {
    Text restOfLine;

    cin.clear();          // Clear the error state
    getline(cin, restOfLine);
  }
  else
  {
    sum += nextNumber;
  }
  cin >> nextNumber;      // Get the next value
}
```

3 Given the suggestion in the solution to Exercise 1 of Section 15.4, test the value of `bool(!myresults)`, and of `bool(myResults.good())` after opening a file that doesn't exist.

Section 15.6

1

```
istream& operator>>(istream& inStream, Palette& forInput)
{
  Text input;

  if (bool(inStream.good()))
  {
    inStream >> input;
```

```
        if (bool(inStream.good()))
        {
          if (input == "BLACK")
          {
            forInput = BLACK;
          }
          else if (input == "WHITE")
          {
            forInput = WHITE;
          }
          else if (input == "RED")
          {
            forInput = RED;
          }
          else if (input == "GREEN")
          {
            forInput = GREEN;
          }
          else if (input == "BLUE")
          {
            forInput = BLUE;
          }
          else
          {
            inStream.clear(ios::failbit);
          }
        }
      }
      return inStream;
    } // end operator>>()
```

2 The file has not been opened, or the stream is already in the fail state, or the end of the file has been reached.

CHAPTER 16

Section 16.0

1
```
for (int chapterNo = 1; chapterNo < 16; chapterNo += 1)
{
  chapter(chapterNo).reRead();
}
```

Section 16.1

1

```
int countQueens(QueenBoard& board, int col, int size)
{
  int count = 0;

  for (int row = 0; row < size; row += 1) // For all rows
  {
    if (!board.isCovered(row, col))       // Square available?
    {
      board.claim(row, col);               // Yes - claim it
      if (col != (size - 1))               // In final column?
      {
        count += countQueens(board, col + 1, size);
                                // Add in number of solutions
                                // for this position
      }
      else
      {
        count += 1;                        // In last column
                                           // Add 1 to total
      }
      board.relinquish(row, col);         // Relinquish this
                                          // position
    } // end if !isCovered
  } // end for row
  return count;                         // Return count
} // end countQueens()
```

There are 92 possible solutions.

2 Use four arrays of `bool`; one of length 8 for the rows; one of length 8 for the columns; one of length 15 for the top-left-to-bottom-right diagonals; one of length 15 for the bottom-left-to-top-right diagonals. For an element at position (`row`, `col`) the corresponding top-left-to-bottom-right diagonal element is position `(7 - row + col)`, and the corresponding top-right-to-bottom-left diagonal element is position `(row + col)`.

Section 16.2

1–6 All solutions are on the accompanying disk. Here are some samples.

1

```
istream& operator>>(istream& inStream, OfferStatus& forInput)
{
  Text input;

  if (bool(inStream.good()))
  {
    inStream >> input;
    if (bool(inStream.good()))
    {
      if (input == "NORMAL")
```

```
      {
        forInput = NORMAL;
      }
      else if (input == "THREE_FOR_TWO")
      {
        forInput = THREE_FOR_TWO;
      }
      else if (input == "REDUCED_PRICE")
      {
        forInput = REDUCED_PRICE;
      }
      else
      {
        inStream.clear(ios::failbit);
      }
    }
  }
  return inStream;
} // end operator>>()

ostream& operator<<(ostream& outStream, OfferStatus value)
{
  switch(value)
  {
    case NORMAL:
      {
        outStream << "NORMAL";
      }
      break;
    case THREE_FOR_TWO:
      {
        outStream << "THREE_FOR_TWO";
      }
      break;
    case REDUCED_PRICE:
      {
        outStream << "REDUCED_PRICE";
      }
      break;
    default:
      {
        error("Invalid status");
      }
      break;
  };
  return outStream;
} // end operator<<()
```

2 The header file Money.h.

```
#ifndef MONEY_H
#define  MONEY_H

#include <fstream.h>
#include "bool.h"

class Money
{
  public:
    // Constructors
    Money();
    Money(int cents);
    Money(int dollars, int cents);

    // Member functions
    int amountInDollars();
    int amountInCents();
    int totalCents();

    // Member operators

    // Arithmetic operators
    Money operator+(Money rhs);
    Money operator-(Money rhs);
    Money operator*(double rhs);
    Money operator-();

    // Update operators
    Money& operator+=(Money rhs);
    Money& operator-=(Money rhs);
    Money& operator*=(double rhs);

    // Comparison operators
    bool operator==(Money rhs);
    bool operator!=(Money rhs);
    bool operator>(Money rhs);
    bool operator<(Money rhs);
    bool operator>=(Money rhs);
    bool operator<=(Money rhs);

  private:

    // Private member variable
    int cents;

};

// Input/output operators
istream& operator>>(istream& inStream,  Money& forInput);
ostream& operator<<(ostream& outStream, Money  value);

#endif
```

5

```
void CashRegister::addToStockList(StockItem nextItem)
{
  streamsOK();
  stockList(numberOfStockItems) = nextItem;
  numberOfStockItems += 1;
  return;
} // end addToStockList()
```

6

```
#include <iostream.h>
#include <fstream.h>
#include "CashRegister.h"

int main()
{
  ifstream stockData;                      // Declare and open input
  ifstream customerData;                   // streams for stock and
                                           // customer data
  stockData.open("Stock Data");
  customerData.open("Customer Data");

  CashRegister cashRegister;
  cashRegister.setStreams(stockData, cout);
  Text nextCommand;
  customerData >> nextCommand;

  while (customerData)
  {
    if (nextCommand == "NEXT_CUSTOMER")
    {
      cashRegister.nextCustomer();
    }
    else if (nextCommand == "TOTAL")
    {
      cashRegister.printTotal();
    }
    else
    {
      cashRegister.processBarCode(nextCommand);
    }
    customerData >> nextCommand;
  }
  return 0;
} // end main()
```

Index

B

C

D

G

H

I

N

O

Q

R

S

T

U

V

W

Although every care has been taken in the production of this publication to ensure that any projects, designs, modifications and/or programs, etc., contained or referred to operate in a correct and safe manner, and that any components specified are normally available in the United Kingdom or the United States of America, the Publishers and the Authors do not accept any responsibility:

i) for the failure (whether due to fault in design or otherwise) of any project, design, modification and/or program to work correctly;
ii) damage caused to any equipment that the project, design, modification and/or program may be connected to or used in conjunction with;
iii) any other damage or injury resulting from use of any project, design, modification and/or program; or
iv) the failure to obtain specific components.

The publishers advise users of the publication to satisfy themselves that any project design, modification and/or program used is appropriate for the purpose for which it is required, and to follow any instructions supplied by the manufacturer.